CYCLING
2004-05

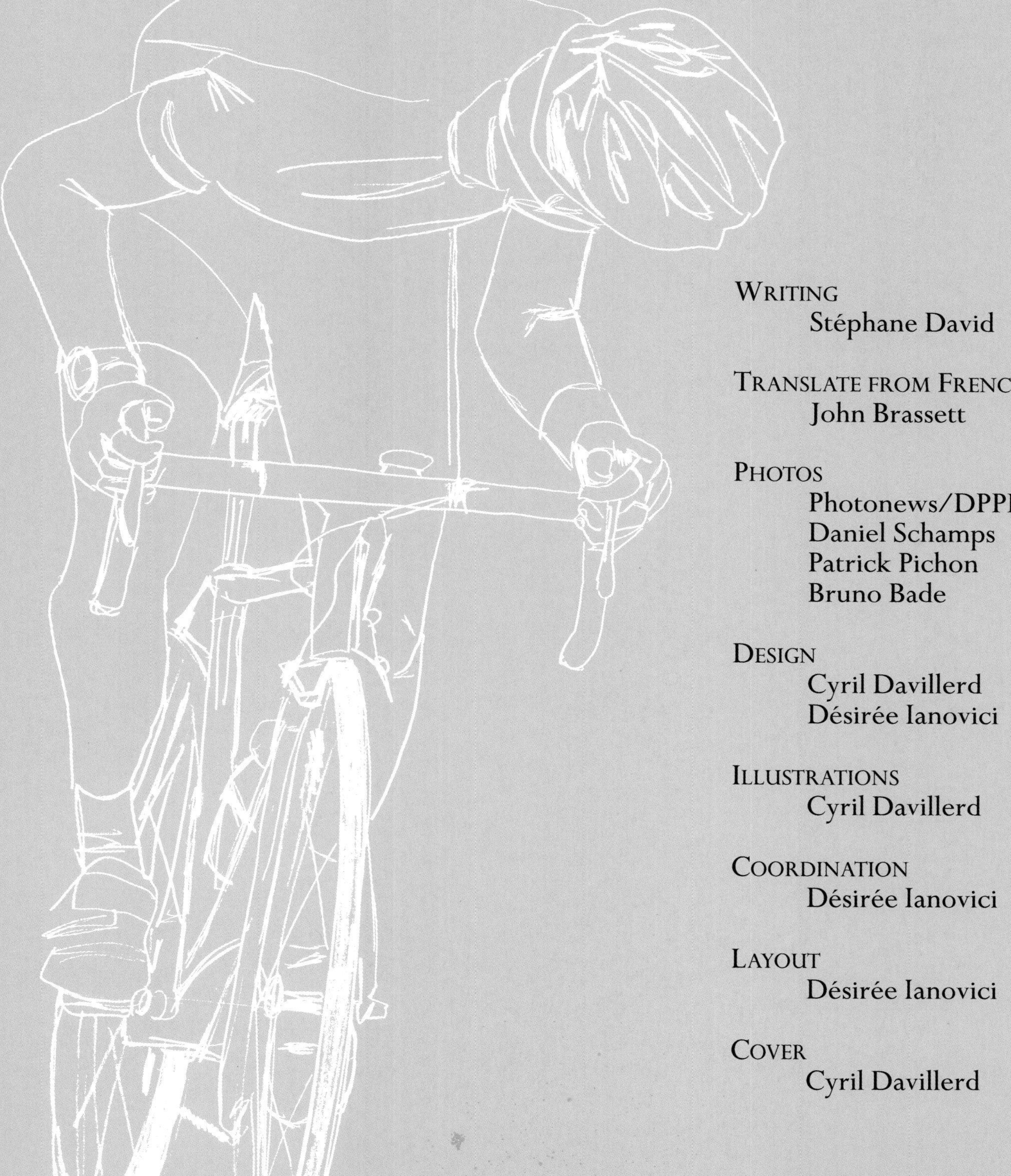

WRITING
Stéphane David

TRANSLATE FROM FRENCH
John Brassett

PHOTOS
Photonews/DPPI
Daniel Schamps
Patrick Pichon
Bruno Bade

DESIGN
Cyril Davillerd
Désirée Ianovici

ILLUSTRATIONS
Cyril Davillerd

COORDINATION
Désirée Ianovici

LAYOUT
Désirée Ianovici

COVER
Cyril Davillerd

For French Edition:
ISBN 2-84707-079-6

For English Edition:
ISBN 2-84707-066-4

Jordils Park, Chemin des Jordils 40, CH-1025 St-Sulpice, Switzerland.
Tél: (+41 21) 694 24 44.
Fax: (+41 21) 694 24 46.
E-mail: info@chronosports.com
www.chronosports.com

Printed in France by Imprimerie Clerc.
Bound in France by S.I.R.C.

prodi
LAZER
davitamon
Davitamon
QUICK ST
deda
TIME
SIDI

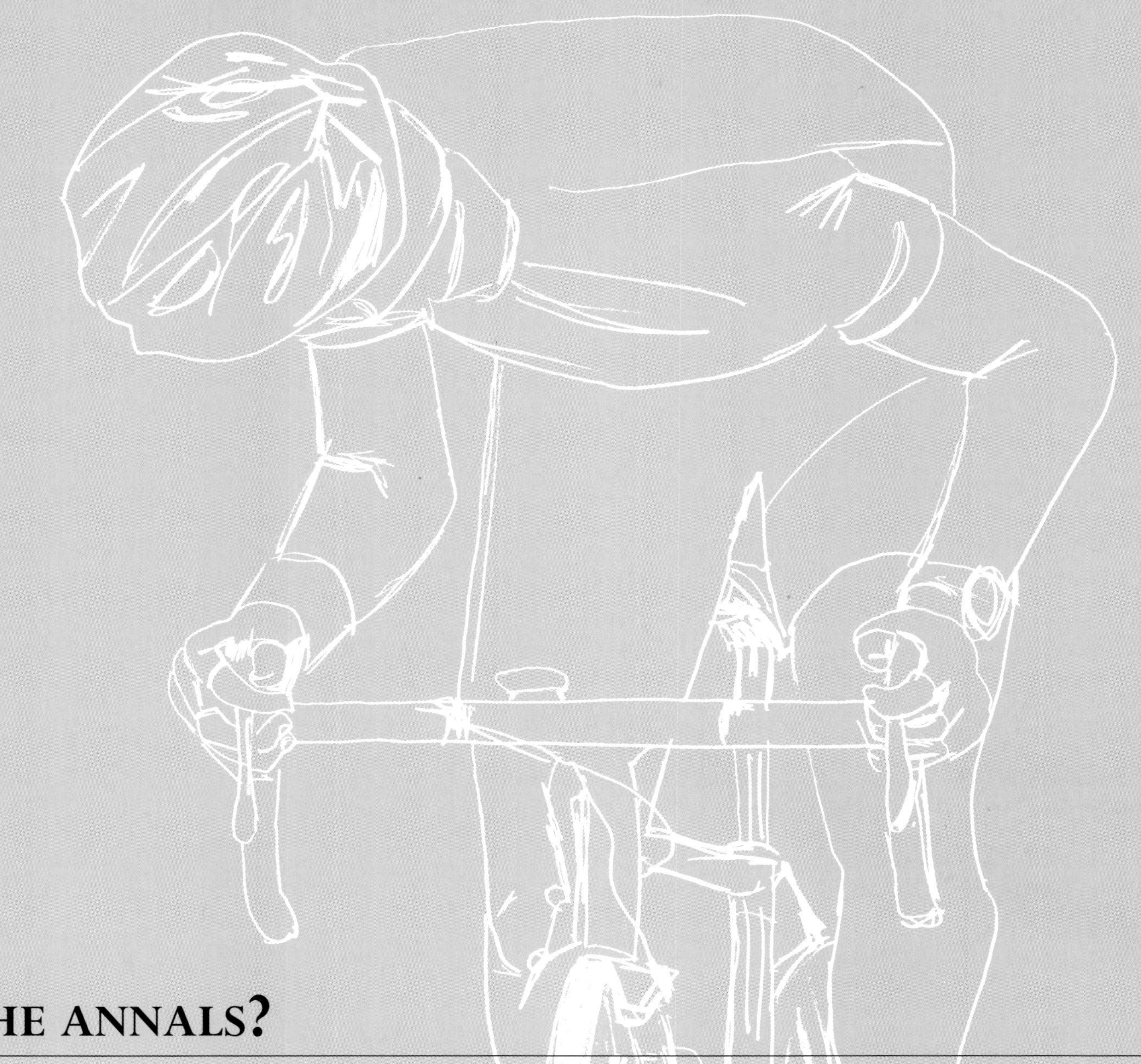

IN THE ANNALS?

Since the days when the young, rich and bored, affronted each other in the gardens of the Palais Royal in the Paris of the end of the 18th century, the competition between men riding on what were the ancestors of what we now know as bicycles, perpetuate from year to year. With some moments more famous than others. Will the year 2004 rest in the annals? It's certainly too soon to know. It was a year marked by several new entries in the record books. For example, in the greatest of classics, the Tour de France. 2004 will forever be the year when the already legendary record of five straight wins was broken. A Texan was the man responsible. Making history with six consecutive wins. On another level, the trophy which for the last few years has significantly raised its profile, that of the red spotted jersey for the king of the mountains, went for the seventh time to Richard Virenque. This also was an unprecedented record. Virenque will not attempt to break his new record, his retirement being announced at the end of the season.

Not so Lance Armstrong. Some might say the race was a boring foregone conclusion, but Armstrong could never be blamed for the apparent weakness of his rivals.

This year also saw the third victory for Oscar Freire in the World Championships. A rare performance putting him up there with the greats, even if the Spaniard has yet to justify his winner's jersey for the rest of the season.

But 2004 will perhaps go down in cycling history as the year when a bright new champion really made his mark. The Italian Damiano Cunego himself set a record as the youngest ever rider to be ranked number one by the UCI at just 23. A ranking which will disappear at the end of this year to be replaced that of the UCI Pro Tour. Will 2005 herald the start of a new era in cycling? Perhaps, and that may well put 2004 with its various high and low points in the shade.

Stéphane David

WINNERS TABLE

COUPE DU MONDE

FINAL INDIVIDUAL RATINGS

1.	Paolo Bettini (Ita)	340 points
2.	Davide Rebellin (Ita)	327 points
3.	Oscar Freire (Esp)	252 points
4.	Erik Dekker (Ned)	251 points
5.	Juan Antonio Flecha (Esp)	140 points
6.	Steffen Wesemann (Ger)	131 points
7.	Peter van Petegem (Bel)	105 points
8.	Igor Astarloa (Esp)	96 points
9.	Mirko Celestino (Ita)	72 points
10.	Leon van Bon (Ned)	68 points

FINAL TEAM RATINGS

1.	T.MOBILE (Ger)	69 points
2.	RABOBANK (Ned)	68 points
3.	GEROLSTEINER (Ger)	47 points
4.	FASSA BORTOLO (Ita)	47 points
5.	LOTTO- DOMO (Bel)	45 points

PODIUMS OF CLASSICS 2004

MILAN-SAN REMO (ITA)
1. Oscar Freire (Esp)
2. E. Zabel (Ger)
3. S. O'Grady (Aus)

TOUR OF FLANDRES (BEL)
1. Steffen Wesemann (Ger)
2. L. Hoste (Bel)
3. D. Bruylandts (Bel)

GAND -WEVELGEM (BEL)*
1. Tom Boonen (Bel)
2. M. Bäckstedt (Swe)
3. J. Kirsipuu (Est)

PARIS - ROUBAIX (FRA)
1. Magnus Bäckstedt (Swe)
2. T. Hoffman (Ned)
3. R. Hammond (Gbr)

AMSTEL GOLD RACE (NED)
1. Davide Rebellin (Ita)
2. M. Boogerd (Ned)
3. P. Bettini (Ita)

FLÈCHE WALLONNE (BEL)*
1. Davide Rebellin (Ita)
2. D. Di Luca (Ita)
3. M. Kessler (Ger)

LIÈGE - BASTOGNE - LIÈGE (BEL)
1. Davide Rebellin (Ita)
2. M. Boogerd (Ned)
3. A. Vinokourov (Kaz)

HEW CYCLASSICS (GER)
1. Stuart O'Grady (Aus)
2. P. Bettini (Ita)
3. I. Astarloa (Esp)

CLASICA SAN SEBASTIAN (ESP)
1. M.A Martin Perdiguero (Esp)
2. P. Bettini (Ita)
3. D. Rebellin (Ita)

CHAMPIONSHIP OF ZURICH (SUI)
1. Juan Antonio Flecha (Esp)
2. P. Bettini (Ita)
3. J. Pineau (Fra)

PARIS - TOURS (FRA)
1. Erik Dekker (Ned)
2. D. Hondo (Ger)
3. O. Freire (Esp)

TOUR OF LOMBARDIE (ITA)
1. Damiano Cunego (Ita)
2. M. Boogerd (Ned)
3. I. Basso (Ita)

* Non world Cup event.

The German T. Mobile team (top left) pips the Rabobank team at the post to win the final edition of the World Cup. Individually it's Paolo Bettini who takes the honours for the third year in a row, even though he was unable to win any event.

T··Mobile·
ARD
adidas

FREIRE WIPES OUT ZABEL!

At 33, Erik Zabel commits a beginners error. Just as he prepares to celebrate victory, Oscar Freire passes him on the line. Alessandro Petacchi, right, finally fourth having once again buckled under the pressure of a Classic finish...

Four times winner of the Primavera,Erik Zabel thought he had a fifth success in sight when he pulled out from behind Alessandro Petacchi 100 metres from the finishing line. The Teutonic Hitman, as he's sometimes called,was already celebrating his victory on the Via Roma when the impish Oscar Freire came into the frame. In the next instant, we were treated to the following scene: the German champion, hands held high in celebration of his immanent victory, realised- too late ! his mistake. His face, contorted with disbelief told the sorry story. Oscar Freire had just won the first classic of the season!

The crowd scenes following the end of the Milan San Remo are always unreal. However Oscar Freire is visibly unaware of the frenzy. He waits for the confirmation of his victory. It's the reporter from the RAI who gives him the good news seconds later. The rider from Torrelavega con now express his joy. Some weeks earlier he had suffered the same fate: on the final stage of the Tour of Andalousia, Erik Zabel had ambushed him on the line depriving him of what seemed like certain victory. Of course, the stakes were not the same. There's no comparison betw een a stage event, even a well rated one, and a World Cup Classic! Some seven hours earlier, the volunteers to take part in the inevitable morning breakaway (always doomed to failure since the exploit of Marc Gomez and Alain Bondue in 1982) were numerous. Jacky Durand, of course, but also Roberto Petito, Patrick Calcagni, Matthew White or the young pros Alexandre Naulleau and Guilio Tomi. We need to await, however, the 62 km mark for this breakaway to take shape.It is composed of the almost veteran (see statistics on page 179) Ludo Dierckxsens (Landbouwkrediet), Antonio Tauler (Illes Ballears), Nicolas Portal (AG2R) and Carlos Barredo (Liberty Seguros) followed at some distance by Guilio Tomi who had decided to try his luck once again. While Carlos Da Cruz,victim of a crash, causing a fractured vertebrae, is transported to hospital in Pavia, the leading group construct a useful lead of 17 mins at 100 kms before being pulled back to 10mins 30sec at Turchino (157 kms). Estimating that the rhythm was slowing dangerously, "Sterke" Ludo Dierckxsens attacks at 55 kms from the line. Barredo, then Portal follow in his wake. The Belgian pushes

Yes! Oscar Freire has just learnt from the reporter of the RAI that he's the winner. He raises a fist in triumph.

again some kilometers later showing himself to be no pushover: he will be caught by the peloton just before attacking la Cipressa. A difficulty which, as usual, is made worse by a rapid tempo, particularly for the returning Erik Dekker (Rabobank) – he fractured a knee cap just two years ago on this stage- and Steffen Wesemann (T- Mobile) who lead by a few seconds a peloton still imposing but deprived of Mario Cipollini who fails at the first climb. On the decent, the two men are caught by the peloton. Marko Celestino (who lives nearby) takes the initiative. Just the same, he doesn't manage to distance himself from the chasing peloton. It's a tightly packed but determined peloton which attacks le Poggio. Matteo Carrara (Lampre) breaks out after just a few metres. Erik Dekker (decidedly) and Angel Vicioso (Liberty Seguros) join him. They are themselves caught by an impressive Oscar Pereiro (Phonak) but what can be said of the following offensive of Paolo Bettini catching Philippe Gilbert (Fdjeux.com) before catching and passing the leaders. Only Vicioso manages to follow. But the two men pass the famous telephone box marking the summit of this celebrated climb closely followed by a group of sixty riders. The decent changes nothing! The Fassa Bortolo, sure of the strength of their leader Alessandro Petecchi, take things in hand. They are six in this group. Things seem to be well under control for the new king of the sprinters who fires up at 300 metres. A little too sure of himself. Erik Zabel passes with ease and Oscar Freire follows him home. His second of glory approaches... ■

Decending la Cipressa, Michele Bartoli is unable to avoid a crash between Davide Rebellin and Leon Van Bon. The Tuscan remounts having lost any chance of a win.

The breakaway group of five arrive at the coast. Their adventure will soon be over.

194 Competitors

QUICK STEP - DAVITAMON			
1.	BETTINI Paolo (Ita)	**8th**	s.t
2.	BOONEN Tom (Bel)	75th	+ 27"
3.	BRAMATI Davide (Ita)	151st	+ 8'01"
4.	NUYENS Nick (Bel)	176th	+ 11'03"
5.	PAOLINI Luca (Ita)	83rd	+ 27"
6.	ROGERS Michael (Aus)	94th	+ 2'23"
7.	HORRILLO Pedro (Esp)	44th	s.t
8.	ZANINI Stefano (Ita)	108th	+ 5'40"

AG2R Prévoyance			
11.	BROCHARD Laurent (Fra)	43rd	s.t
12.	NAZON Jean-Patrick (Fra)	162nd	+ 11'03"
13.	DUMOULIN Samuel (Fra)	81st	+ 27"
14.	FLICKINGER Andy (Fra)	136th	+ 5'40"
16.	KRIVTSOV Yuriy (Ukr)	37th	s.t
17.	SCANLON Mark (Irl)	78th	+ 27"
18.	PORTAL Nicolas (Fra)	178th	+ 12'57"

ALESSIO - BIANCHI			
21.	BALDATO Fabio (Ita)	16th	s.t
22.	SUNDERLAND Scott (Aus)	67th	+ 27"
23.	BÄCKSTEDT Magnus (Swe)	141st	+ 7'14"
24.	IVANOV Ruslan (Mda)	98th	+ 3'08"
26.	PELLIZOTTI Franco (Ita)	46th	s.t
27.	MORENI Cristian (Ita)	19th	s.t
28.	TAFI Andrea (Ita)	159th	+ 11'03"

Brioches LA BOULANGÈRE			
31.	CHAVANEL Sylvain (Fra)	52nd	s.t
32.	GESLIN Anthony (Fra)	42nd	s.t
33.	PICHON Mickaël (Fra)	31st	s.t
34.	LEFÈVRE Laurent (Fra)	154th	+ 8'01"
35.	MARTIAS Rony (Fra)	182nd	+ 13'53"
36.	PINEAU Jérôme (Fra)	60th	s.t
37.	NAULLEAU Alexandre (Fra)		*Abandon*
38.	RENIER Franck (Fra)	40th	s.t

Ceramiche PANARIA - MARGRES			
41.	FIGUERAS Giuliano (Ita)	49th	s.t
42.	TIRALONGO Paolo (Ita)	71st	+ 27"
43.	MAZZANTI Luca (Ita)	84th	+ 27"
44.	MATVEYEV Serhiy (Ukr)	134th	+ 5'40"
46.	BORRAJO Alejandro (Arg)	183rd	+ 13'53"
47.	BROWN Graeme (Aus)	184th	+ 20'21"
48.	DAVIS Scott (Aus)	103rd	+ 4'47"

COFIDIS			
51.	ASTARLOA Igor (Esp)	**6th**	s.t
52.	FARAZIJN Peter (Bel)	87th	+ 27"
53.	FERNANDEZ BUSTINZA Bingen (Esp)	53rd	s.t
54.	MILLAR David (Gbr)	129th	+ 5'40"
55.	O'GRADY Stuart (Aus)	**3rd**	s.t
56.	TOMBAK Janek (Est)	76th	+ 27"
57.	TRENTIN Guido (Ita)	47th	s.t
58.	WHITE Matthew (Aus)	69th	+ 27"

DE NARDI			
61.	HONCHAR Serhiy (Ukr)	29th	s.t
62.	BORGHI Ruggero (Ita)	132nd	+ 5'40"
63.	GASPARRE Graziano (Ita)	88th	+ 27"
64.	CADAMURO Simone (Ita)	167th	+ 11'03"
65.	GOBBI Michele (Ita)	22nd	s.t
66.	LORENZETTO Mirko (Ita)	70th	+ 27"
67.	MIORIN Devis (Ita)	131st	+ 5'40"
68.	PUGACI Igor (Mda)	177th	+ 11'03"

DOMINA VACANZE			
71.	CIPOLLINI Mario (Ita)	109th	+ 5'40"
72.	AUG Andrus (Est)	169th	+ 11'03"
73.	COLOMBO Gabriele (Ita)	64th	+ 9"
74.	DERGANC Martin (Slo)	114th	+ 5'40"
75.	FAGNINI GianMatteo (Ita)	139th	+ 5'40"
76.	GALLETTI Alessio (Ita)	118th	+ 5'40"
77.	LOMBARDI Giovanni (Ita)	119th	+ 5'40"
78.	SCIREA Mario (Ita)	138th	+ 5'40"

EUSKALTEL - EUSKADI			
81.	VERDUGO Gorka (Esp)	127th	+ 5'40"
82.	GONZALEZ LARRANAGA Gorka (Esp)	128th	+ 5'40"
83.	LANDALUZE Iñigo (Esp)	23rd	s.t
84.	SANCHEZ Samuel (Esp)	20th	s.t
85.	SILLONIZ Josu (Esp)	15th	s.t
86.	GALPARSORO Dionisio (Esp)	156th	+ 8'01"
87.	ISASI Iñaki (Esp)	68th	+ 27"
88.	ZUBELDIA Joseba (Esp)		*Abandon*

FASSA BORTOLO			
91.	PETITO Roberto (Ita)	101st	+ 4'47"
92.	TOSATTO Matteo (Ita)	91st	+ 1'38"
93.	SACCHI Fabio (Ita)	35th	s.t
94.	PETACCHI Alessandro (Ita)	**4th**	s.t
95.	POZZATO Filippo (Ita)	63rd	+ 9"
96.	TRENTI Guido (Usa)	17th	s.t
97.	VANDENBROUCKE Frank (Bel)	66th	+ 20"
98.	VELO Marco (Ita)	62nd	s.t

FDJEUX.COM			
101.	COOKE Baden (Aus)		*Abandon*
102.	DA CRUZ Carlos (Fra)		*Abandon*
103.	EISEL Bernhard (Aut)		*Abandon*
104.	GILBERT Philippe (Bel)	14th	s.t
105.	McGEE Bradley (Aus)	93rd	+ 2'23"
106.	RENSHAW Mark (Aus)	166th	+ 11'03"
107.	FRITSCH Nicolas (Fra)	171st	+ 11'03"
108.	WILSON Matthew (Aus)	73rd	+ 27"

GEROLSTEINER			
111.	HONDO Danilo (Ger)	32nd	s.t
112.	LANG Sebastian (Ger)	158th	+ 10'38"
113.	REBELLIN Davide (Ita)	168th	+ 11'03"
114.	SERPELLINI Marco (Ita)	110th	+ 5'40"
115.	WEGMANN Fabian (Ger)	28th	s.t
116.	WROLICH Peter (Aut)	33rd	s.t
117.	ZBERG Marcus (Sui)	18th	s.t
118.	ZIEGLER Thomas (Ger)	179th	+ 13'29"

ILLES BALEARS - BANESTO			
121.	BECKE Daniel (Ger)		*Abandon*
122.	RADOCHLA Steffen (Ger)	148th	+ 7'14"
123.	GUTIERREZ PALACIOS J. Ivan (Esp)	72nd	+ 27"
125.	LASTRAS Pablo (Esp)	38th	s.t
126.	TAULER Antonio (Esp)		*Abandon*
127.	REYNES Vicente (Esp)		*Abandon*

LAMPRE			
131.	PICCOLI Mariano (Ita)	153rd	+ 8'01"
132.	BARBERO Sergio (Ita)	45th	s.t
133.	BOSSONI Paolo (Ita)	123rd	+ 5'40"
134.	CARRARA Matteo (Ita)	79th	+ 27"
135.	CORTINOVIS Alessandro (Ita)	80th	+ 27"
136.	SVORADA Jan (Cze)	142nd	+ 7'14"
137.	PAGLIARINI Luciano (Bra)	149th	+ 8'00"
138.	VAINSTEINS Romans (Lat)	**7th**	s.t

LANDBOUWKREDIET - COLNAGO			
141.	BERNUCCI Lorenzo (Ita)	51st	s.t
142.	DUMA Vladimir (Ukr)	137th	+ 5'40"
143.	BILEKA Volodymir (Ukr)	146th	+ 7'14"
144.	DIERCKXSENS Ludo (Bel)	164th	+ 11'03"
145.	POPOVYCH Yaroslav (Ukr)	24th	s.t
146.	DURAND Jacky (Fra)	181st	+ 13'53"
148.	LAGUTIN Serguey (Uzb)	105th	+ 5'40"

LIBERTY Seguros			
151.	ANDRLE René (Cze)	173rd	+ 11'03"
152.	BARREDO Carlos (Esp)	174th	+ 11'03"
153.	CARUSO Gianpaolo (Ita)	130th	+ 5'40"
154.	DAVIS Allan (Aus)	25th	s.t
155.	HERAS Roberto (Esp)	126th	+ 5'40"
156.	GONZALEZ de GALDEANO Igor (Esp)	116th	+ 5'40"
157.	VICIOSO Angel (Esp)	61st	s.t
158.	HRUSKA Jan (Cze)	143rd	+ 7'14"

LOTTO - DOMO			
161.	VAN PETEGEM Peter (Bel)	**10th**	s.t
162.	McEWEN Robbie (Aus)	106th	+ 5'40"
163.	MERCKX Axel (Bel)	30th	s.t
164.	VIERHOUTEN Aart (Ned)	113rd	+ 5'40"
165.	VANSEVENANT Wim (Bel)	175th	+ 11'03"
166.	VAN BON Leon (Ned)	121st	+ 5'40"
167.	MARICHAL Thierry (Bel)	180th	+ 13'53"
168.	HOSTE Leif (Bel)	100th	+ 3'26"

PHONAK			
171.	AEBERSOLD Niki (Sui)	170th	+ 11'03"
172.	CAMENZIND Oscar (Sui)	26th	s.t
173.	FERTONANI Marco (Ita)	150th	+ 8'00"
174.	ELMIGER Martin (Sui)	27th	s.t
175.	GRABSCH Bert (Ger)	57th	s.t
176.	MURN Uros (Slo)		*Abandon*
177.	PEREIRO Oscar (Esp)	39th	s.t
178.	RAST Gregory (Sui)	124th	+ 5'40"

RABOBANK			
181.	DEKKER Erik (Ned)	11st	s.t
182.	DEN BAKKER Maarten (Ned)	90th	+ 1'38"
183.	DE GROOT Bram (Ned)	163rd	+ 11'03"
184.	FREIRE Oscar (Esp)	**1st**	**7h11'23"**
185.	HUNTER Robert (Rsa)	50th	s.t
186.	HAYMAN Mathew (Aus)	155th	+ 8'01"

187.	BOVEN Jan (Ned)	135th	+ 5'40"
188.	WAUTERS Marc (Bel)	99th	+ 3'08"

SAECO

191.	CELESTINO Mirko (Ita)	12nd	s.t
192.	DI LUCA Danilo (Ita)	54th	s.t
193.	BALDUCCI Gabriele (Ita)	55th	s.t
194.	BERTAGNOLLI Leonardo (Ita)	85th	+ 27"
195.	FORNACIARI Paolo (Ita)	145th	+ 7'14"
196.	PETROV Evgueni (Rus)	86th	+ 27"
197.	PIERI Dario (Ita)	144th	+ 7'14"
198.	SPEZIALETTI Alessandro (Ita)	82nd	+ 27"

SAUNIER DUVAL - PRODIR

201.	BERTOGLIATI Rubens (Sui)	125th	+ 5'40"
202.	LOBATO Ruben (Esp)	95th	+ 2'57"
203.	CASERO Rafael (Esp)	48th	s.t
204.	MARTIN PERDIGUERO M.Angel (Esp)	**9th**	s.t
205.	MORI Manuele (Ita)	77th	+ 27"
206.	RODRIGUEZ OLIVER Joaquin (Esp)	112nd	+ 5'40"
207.	VENTOSO Francisco (Esp)	147th	+ 7'14"
208.	STRAZZER Massimo (Ita)	165th	+ 11'03"

CSC

211.	BLAUDZUN Michael (Den)	161st	+ 11'03"
212.	GUIDI Fabrizio (Ita)	102nd	+ 4'47"
213.	HØJ Frank (Den)	122nd	+ 5'40"
214.	MICHAELSEN Lars (Den)	160th	+ 11'03"
215.	VOIGT Jens (Ger)	36th	s.t
216.	JULICH Bobby (Usa)	65th	+ 15"
217.	BARTOLI Michele (Ita)	120th	+ 5'40"
218.	SCIANDRI Maximilian (Gbr)	107th	+ 5'40"

T-MOBILE

221.	ALDAG Rolf (Ger)	34th	s.t
222.	IVANOV Serguei (Rus)	133rd	+ 5'40"
223.	KESSLER Matthias (Ger)	97th	+ 3'08"
224.	KLIER Andreas (Ger)	21st	s.t
225.	NARDELLO Daniele (Ita)	172nd	+ 11'03"
226.	VINOKOUROV Alexandre (Kaz)	59th	s.t
227.	WESEMANN Steffen (Ger)	58th	s.t
228.	ZABEL Erik (Ger)	**2nd**	s.t

US POSTAL - BERRY FLOOR

231.	CRUZ Antonio (Usa)	89th	+ 52"
232.	NOVAL Benjamin (Esp)	41st	s.t
233.	EKIMOV Viatcheslav (Rus)	74th	+ 27"
234.	HINCAPIE George (Usa)	13rd	s.t
235.	JOACHIM Benoît (Lux)	140th	+ 5'40"
236.	PADRNOS Pavel (Cze)		*Abandon*
237.	PEÑA Victor Hugo (Col)	92nd	+ 2'07"
238.	VAN HEESWIJK Max (Ned)	**5e**	s.t

Vini CALDIROLA - NOBILI Rubinetterie

241.	ZANOTTI Marco (Ita)	111st	+ 5'40"
242.	SIRONI Gianluca (Ita)	96th	+ 3'08"
243.	MILESI Marco (Ita)	104th	+ 5'40"
244.	CALCAGNI Patrick (Sui)	115th	+ 5'40"
245.	MASCIARELLI Simone (Ita)	56th	s.t
246.	TOMI Giulio (Ita)	157th	+ 10'18"
247.	GEROSA Mauro (Ita)	117th	+ 5'40"
248.	ZINETTI Mauro (Ita)	152nd	+ 8'01"

TOTAL OF POINTS UCI OBTAINED IN THE RACE

RABOBANK	313 points
COFIDIS	234 points
T.MOBILE	195 points
FASSA BORTOLO	161 points
US POSTAL	156 points
LAMPRE	107 points
QUICK STEP - DAVITAMON	95 points
SAUNIER DUVAL - PRODIR	88 points
LOTTO - DOMO	83 points
EUSKALTEL - EUSKADI	77 points
SAECO	74 points
ALESSIO - BIANCHI	69 points
GEROLSTEINER	58 points
FDJEUX.COM	51 points
DE NARDI	49 points
LIBERTY Seguros	45 points
PHONAK	42 points
LANDBOUWKREDIET - COLNAGO	41 points
CSC	40 points
DOMINA VACANZE	40 points
Vini CALDIROLA - NOBILI	40 points
AG2R Prévoyance	35 points
Brioches LA BOULANGÈRE	35 points
PANARIA - MARGRES	35 points
ILLES BALEARS - BANESTO	15 points

PAST WINNERS AT THE START **4**

ZABEL Erik	1997, 1998, 2000 & 2001
COLOMBO Gabriele	1996
CIPOLLINI Mario	2002
BETTINI Paolo	2003

ROOKIES AT THE START (LESS THAN ONE YEAR AS A PROFESSIONAL): **10**

3 YOUNGEST

RENSHAW Mark (Aus)	22/10/1982
GILBERT Philippe (Bel)	05/07/1982
VENTOSO Francisco (Esp)	06/05/1982

3 OLDEST

SCIREA Mario (Ita)	07/08/1964
DIERCKXSENS Ludo (Bel)	14/10/1964
EKIMOV Viatcheslav (Rus)	04/02/1966

Oscar Freire,
first leader of the
2004 World Cup.

THE DAY OF THE OUTSIDERS

Considered until now as an authentic specialist of the "Course de la Paix" (he has won five and taken seventeen stage wins) Steffen Wesemann has come close to the top in the Classics – in 2002, he was beaten only by Johan Museeuw on the Paris Roubaix – but he was definitely not among the favourites for the 88th edition. Peter Van Petegem, the previous winner;Johan Museeuw who was taking part in his last Tour of Flanders and Frank Vandenbroucke were the clear favourites of the experts. But the race itself was never to be in their favour...

When, at the "Flamme rouge" in the streets of Meerbeke, Dave Bruylandts - knowing a sprint would be a bad option for him- pushed for the finish, all looked to be decided. But Steffen Wesemann was playing a waiting game with Leif Hoste. The Latter decides to go for Bruylandts who had not yet got a sufficient lead. From that moment the result of this Tour of Flanders was not in doubt. The German, reputedly the fastest, only had to show his speed and to get himself into the ideal third place. Effectively, a few instants later, he made his point with Leif Hoste, six years his junior, when Dave Bruylandts proved once again that sprinting was not his strong point. Forty years after Rudi Altig, Steffen Wesemann took a second victory for the Germans. The rider, sometimes considered as a dilettante, obtained here the greatest success of a career begun eleven years earlier. And once again it was at the summit of the famous Muur de Grammont that the race was decided.

THE FAVOURITES HIDDEN IN THE PELOTON

Well before this penultimate difficulty, some riders had settled into a lead. In successive waves, a group of 27 riders was established. A sort of mini peloton! Several teams had sent out riders as scouts. This was these with Lotto-Domo with Hoste and Marichal, Chocolat Jaques with Hiemstra and Van Velzen, Landbouwkrediet with Durand and Streel, Mr Bookmaker.com with Coenen Wuyts, Vlaanderen with Spiegelaere and Schoonacker, Librty Seguros with Barredo and Diaz Justo, Gerolsteiner with Lang and Rich, Saeco with Commesso and Ludewig, Rabobank with de Jongh and Sentjens and also US Postal with Cruz and Joachim. Seven other riders (Ongarato, Putsep, Elmiger, Zanini, Bruun, Eriksen, Schaffrath and Pagliarini) being the only representatives of their teams. With seventeen teams out of twenty five in the race now installed at the front this large breakaway group quickly opened a gap (1 min 30 sec at 40 kms and 4 mins 15 after 95 kms) on a still in touch peloton. In effect, if it seems relatively easy to claw back fifteen minutes on a group of 4 or 5 riders, its another kettle of fish when the group is composed of 27 riders as in the early stages of this stage. The reaction from behind was to come at the 143rd km when a group of 12 riders mounted a counter attack. Those involved included Sacchi and Petito, Moreni, Knaven, Arvesen, Dierckxsens, Hervé, Hondo, Bazhenov, Wauters,de Vocht and Mattan. At kilometre 150 the impressive leading group (less - Pagliarini, Rich and Barredo - victims of the cobble stones) lead the counter attack by 2 mins 50 sec, the peloton being at the reasonable distance of 3 mins 40 sec. The passage of the first climbs (Rekelberg, Molenberg, Vieux Kwaremont) splits the leading group which finally numbers only 7 riders (Zanini, Ludewig, de Jongh, Elmiger, Schaffrath and the two Lotto riders, Hoste and Marichal) after the difficult passage of Taaieenberg (km200). The group of counter attacking riders (who had recuperated several riders left by the leaders) is at 1 min 20 sec when the veteran (39) Ludo Dierckxsens decides to go it alone. In the paved section at Haaghoek (38 kms from the line) "Sterke

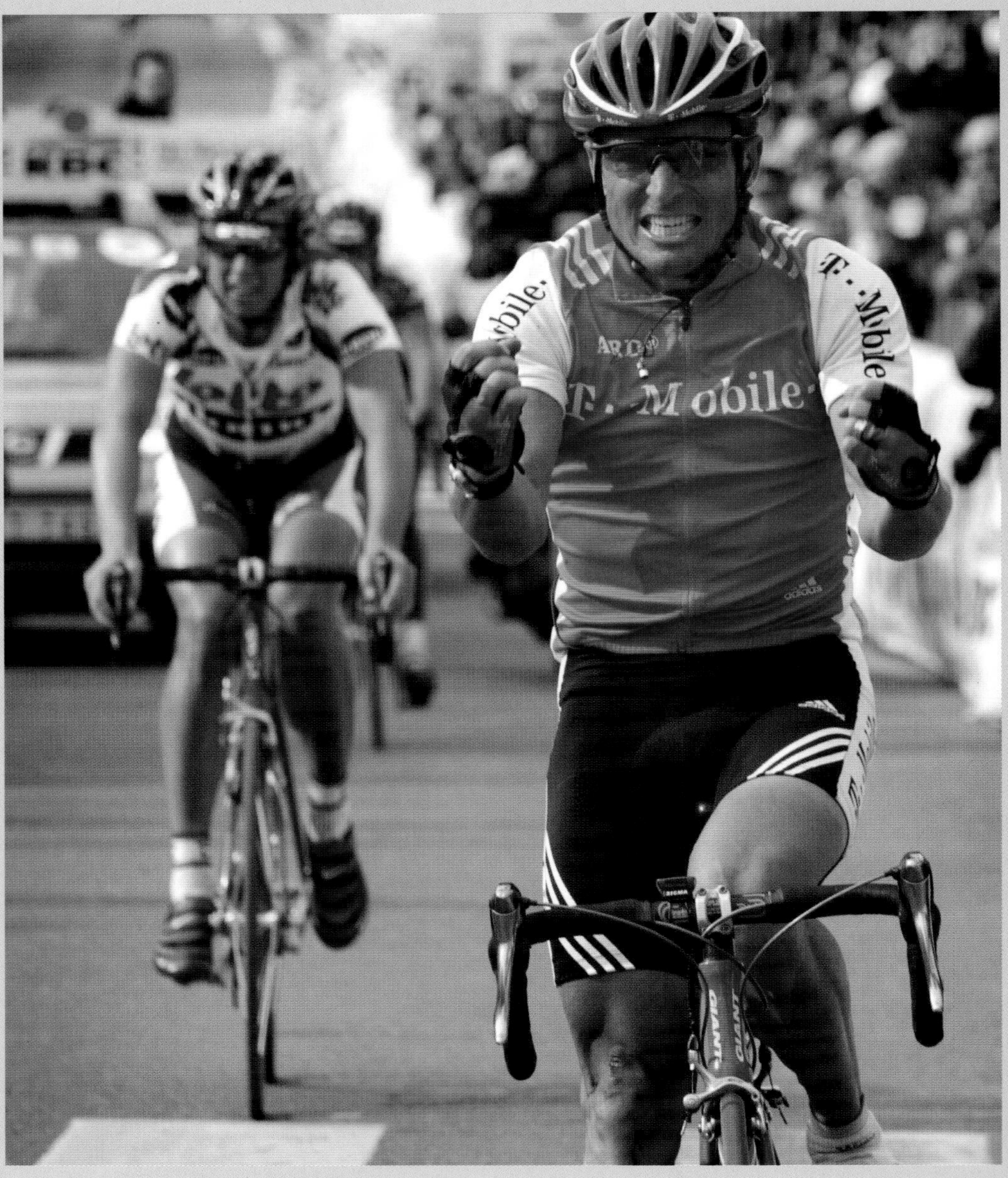

Day of glory for Steffen Wesemann. The German rider muscles in on one of the monuments of cycling, the Tour of Flanders.

A still numerous peloton (fifty riders) takes on the penultimate challenge of the day, the famous Muur de Grammont.

Ludo" consolidates his position: he joins the seven leaders, momentarily minus Thierry Marichal victim of a puncture luckily without serious consequences. Behind, the main peloton (at last) reacts, and at the approach to the Muur de Grammont (km 243), Seguei Ivanov 5T Mobile) then George Hincapie and Leon Van Bon (a third Lotto!) take the lead. An extraordinary vision passing through Geraardsbergen (Grammont): the peloton reformed. Only Frank Vandenbroucke, victim of a puncture some kilometers beforehand was missing. VDB joined the rest of the stars as soon as the climb of the terrifying, recently resurfaced, muur began.We await the final blow from Peter van Petegem or Johan Museeuw or perhaps Paolo Bettini. But, nothing of the sort comes about.

THE MUUR DE GRAMMONT AS JUDGE AND JURY

It's Steffen Wesemann followed by Dave Bruylandts that passes the chapel at the summit of the Muur in first place, watched by the usual enthusiastic crowd. The incredible Leif Hoste (alone purser for most of the day, let's not forget) manages to get into contact with the two leaders. At the moment the leading trio begin their descent towards Bosberg, the final climb of the race, they have a lead of 10 seconds over a quartet composed of Erik Dekker (Rabobank), Juan Antonio Flecha (Fassa Bortolo) as well as Leon Van Bon (Lotto) and Andreas Klier (T Mobile), two teams already present in the leading group. Things don't look easy for the following group, particularly as the locally based Spaniard Juan Antonio Flecha, seems unable to keep up with the pace in le Bosberg.Can Erik Dekker reduce the gap now standing at 15 seconds? The answer comes rapidly: it's in the negative. In the lead, Hoste, worn by a day spent in a lonely combat, refuses to take any relays. Such is life, as they say. Steffan Wesemann shows a remarkable ease at this point. He has the perfect build for a "Flandrienne" rider, low centre of gravity, muscular legs, he gives the impression of being calm as opposed to the likes of Dave Bruylandts. Bruylandts had words with Leif Hoste who seemed intent on slipstreaming him. Bruylandts plays his last card as they come to the final kilometre, but... Leif Hoste brings him back to reality. From this point Steffan Wesemann has it all his own way. The sprint, logically, is in his favour...

"LE LION DES FLANDRES", PVP AND VDB SIDELINED!

No forth success then for Johan Museeuw (which would have made him the record holder for wins in this race), nor a third win for Peter Van Petegem, even less glory for Frank Vandenbroucke,finishing respectively, 15th, 16th and 44th in this second leg of the World Cup. These logical favourites failed for various reasons: Van Petegem was not in form, Johan Museeuw lacked the punch to sail up these climbs he knows by heart and Frank Vandenbroucke, handicapped by the previously mentioned mechanical incident, was unable to attack at the crucial moment from a favourable position.

As opposed to the T Mobile team,finishing with a surprising three riders in the first seven, the hot favourite Quick Step- Davitamon formation, conceived for this sort of race, often came out loosers, Bettini- "reserve" leader, being exposed too soon, sometimes taking the role of team member,which should be the domain of riders such as Cretskens or Hulsmans, being passed too quickly.
The same could be said for Tom Boonen, half protected,half devoted to thankless tasks. Others cited as outside chances remained invisible throughout the day: van Heeswijk, Pieri, Guesdon (plagued by bad luck), Bortolami or Baldato (as with Museeuw, age got the better these two). Finally, a word on the positive performance of Laurent Brochard, thirteenth home and first Frenchman, along with the young Cedric Hervé being the only representatives from the "Hexagon" to put up a good show on this very peculiar day... ■

This last Tour of Flanders for Johan Museeuw didn't go as he would have liked. The three times winner was never able to influence the result this time.

193 Competitors

LOTTO - DOMO

1.	VAN PETEGEM Peter (Bel)	16th	+ 1'38"
2.	VANSEVENANT Wim (Bel)	119th	+ 17'53"
3.	VIERHOUTEN Aart (Ned)	36th	+ 2'10"
4.	EECKHOUT Nico (Bel)		*Abandon*
5.	HOSTE Leif (Bel)	**2nd**	s.t
6.	VAN BON Leon (Ned)	**4th**	+ 28"
7.	MARICHAL Thierry (Bel)	11st	+ 1'16"
8.	BAGUET Serge (Bel)	88th	+ 7'38"

Chocolade JACQUES - WINCOR NIXDORF

11.	KOERTS Jans (Ned)		*Abandon*
12.	BRUYLANDTS Dave (Bel)	**3rd**	s.t
14.	LÖWIK Gerben (Ned)		*Abandon*
15.	PEERS Chris (Bel)	42nd	+ 2'10"
16.	VERHEYEN Geert (Bel)	52nd	+ 4'56"
17.	VAN VELZEN Jan (Ned)	99th	+ 11'20"
18.	VOSKAMP Bart (Ned)	86th	+ 7'38"
19.	HIEMSTRA Bert (Ned)	56th	+ 5'07"

LANDBOUWKREDIET - COLNAGO

21.	DURAND Jacky (Fra)		*Abandon*
22.	DIERCKXSENS Ludo (Bel)	27th	+ 2'10"
23.	CAPELLE Ludovic (Bel)		*Abandon*
24.	VAN BONDT Geert (Bel)	90th	+ 7'38"
25.	BERNUCCI Lorenzo (Ita)	81st	+ 7'38"
26.	STREEL Marc (Bel)		*Abandon*
27.	VERSTREPEN Johan (Bel)	117th	+ 17'53"
28.	DE WAELE Bert (Bel)	91st	+ 7'38"

Mr BOOKMAKER.COM - PALMANS

31.	DE SMET Andy (Bel)		*Abandon*
32.	HAMMOND Roger (Gbr)	30th	+ 2'10"
33.	COENEN Johan (Bel)	71st	+ 7'38"
34.	OMLOOP Geert (Bel)	98th	+ 11'20"
35.	PLANCKAERT Jo (Bel)	78th	+ 7'38"
36.	THIJS Erwin (Bel)	67th	+ 7'38"
37.	WUYTS Peter (Bel)	79th	+ 7'38"
38.	VAN HAECKE Michel (Bel)	48th	+ 2'10"

QUICK STEP - DAVITAMON

41.	BETTINI Paolo (Ita)	**9th**	+ 1'16"
42.	BOONEN Tom (Bel)	25th	+ 2'10"
43.	CRETSKENS Wilfried (Bel)	74eth	+ 7'38"
44.	HULSMANS Kevin (Bel)	110th	+ 17'53"
45.	KNAVEN Servais (Ned)	51st	+ 4'56"
46.	MUSEEUW Johan (Bel)	15th	+ 1'38"
47.	PAOLINI Luca (Ita)	26th	+ 2'10"
48.	ZANINI Stefano (Ita)	49th	+ 2'22"

VLAANDEREN - T INTERIM

51.	CAETHOVEN Steven (Bel)		*Abandon*
52.	DEMEYERE Geoffrey (Bel)		*Abandon*
53.	KUYCKX Jan (Bel)	63rd	+ 7'38"
54.	SCHOONACKER Jehudi (Bel)		*Abandon*
55.	VAN HUFFEL Wim (Bel)	70th	+ 7'38"
56.	VAN SPEYBROECK Wesley (Bel)		*Abandon*
57.	WILLEMS Frederik (Bel)		*Abandon*
58.	DE SPIEGELAERE Bart (Bel)		*Abandon*

CSC

61.	MADSEN Jimmi (Den)	106th	+ 17'53"
62.	HØJ Frank (Den)	**8th**	+ 1'16"
63.	ARVESEN Kurt-Asle (Nor)	54th	+ 5'07"
64.	MICHAELSEN Lars (Den)	62nd	+ 7'38"
65.	BARTOLI Michele (Ita)	57th	+ 5'07"
66.	BRUUN ERIKSEN Thomas (Den)	122nd	+ 17'53"
67.	HOFFMAN Tristan (Ned)	40th	+ 2'10"
68.	SCIANDRI Maximilian (Gbr)	84th	+ 7'38"

EUSKALTEL - EUSKADI

71.	ARTETXE Mikel (Esp)	97th	+ 11'20"
72.	FERNANDEZ DE LARREA Koldo (Esp)		*Abandon*
73.	IRIZAR Markel (Esp)		*Abandon*
74.	LANDALUZE Iñigo (Esp)		*Abandon*
75.	MARTINEZ de ESTEBAN Egoi (Esp)		*Abandon*
76.	PEÑA IZA Aketza (Esp)		*Abandon*
77.	SILLONIZ Aitor (Esp)		*Abandon*
78.	SILLONIZ Josu (Esp)	101st	+ 11'20"

LIBERTY Seguros

81.	ANDRLE René (Cze)		*Abandon*
82.	BARANOWSKI Dariusz (Pol)		*Abandon*
83.	BARREDO Carlos (Esp)		*Abandon*
84.	DAVIS Allan (Aus)		*Abandon*
85.	DIAZ JUSTO Rafael (Esp)		*Abandon*
86.	RAMIREZ ABEJA Javier (Esp)		*Abandon*
87.	SANCHEZ GIL Luis Leon (Esp)		*Abandon*

RELAX - BODYSOL

91.	DOCKX Bart (Bel)		*Abandon*
92.	FLORENCIO Xavier (Esp)	18th	+ 1'38"
93.	MATTAN Nico (Bel)	39th	+ 2'10"
94.	ROESEMS Bert (Bel)	68th	+ 7'38"
95.	DE VOCHT Wim (Bel)	92nd	+ 7'38"
96.	VANLANDSCHOOT James (Bel)		*Abandon*
97.	VAN SUMMEREN Johan (Bel)	120th	+ 17'53"
98.	VAN HECKE Preben (Bel)		*Abandon*

AG2R Prévoyance

101.	BROCHARD Laurent (Fra)	13rd	+ 1'30"
102.	KIRSIPUU Jaan (Est)	22nd	+ 2'10"
103.	FLICKINGER Andy (Fra)	96th	+ 11'20"
104.	BERGÈS Stéphane (Fra)		*Abandon*
105.	KRIVTSOV Yuriy (Ukr)	109th	+ 17'53"
106.	NAZON Jean-Patrick (Fra)		*Abandon*
107.	PÜTSEP Erki (Est)	124th	+ 17'53"
108.	SCANLON Mark (Irl)		*Abandon*

COFIDIS

111.	ASTARLOA Igor (Esp)	35th	+ 2'10"
112.	CASPER Jimmy (Fra)		*Abandon*
113.	ENGOULVENT Jimmy (Fra)	95th	+ 9'49"
114.	FARAZIJN Peter (Bel)		*Abandon*
115.	O'GRADY Stuart (Aus)	123rd	+ 17'53"
116.	SCHEIRLINCKX Staf (Bel)	34th	+ 2'10"
118.	WHITE Matthew (Aus)		*Abandon*

As a strange turn of fate, Briek Schotte, nicknamed "the last of the Flandriens", seen here caricatured as are other past winners of the "Ronde", left a short while after the start...

As can be seen here with Tom Boonen and Paolo Bettini (ahead of Michael Boogerd), the Quickstep team employed disorganised tactics throughout the day...

FDJEUX.COM

No.	Rider	Place	Result
121.	COOKE Baden (Aus)		*Abandon*
122.	McGEE Bradley (Aus)		*Abandon*
123.	EISEL Bernhard (Aut)	103rd	+ 12'38"
124.	GUESDON Frédéric (Fra)	69th	+ 7'38"
125.	MENGIN Christophe (Fra)	75th	+ 7'38"
126.	MOUREY Francis (Fra)		*Abandon*
127.	SANCHEZ Fabien (Fra)		*Abandon*
128.	WILSON Matthew (Aus)		*Abandon*

GEROLSTEINER

No.	Rider	Place	Result
131.	FÖRSTER Robert (Ger)		*Abandon*
132.	HONDO Danilo (Ger)	24th	+ 2'10"
133.	LANG Sebastian (Ger)		*Abandon*
134.	POLLACK Olaf (Ger)		*Abandon*
135.	RICH Michael (Ger)		*Abandon*
136.	SERPELLINI Marco (Ita)	125th	+ 17'53"
137.	WROLICH Peter (Aut)	102nd	+ 12'38"
138.	ZBERG Marcus (Sui)		*Abandon*

T-MOBILE

No.	Rider	Place	Result
141.	AERTS Mario (Bel)	72nd	+ 7'38"
142.	ALDAG Rolf (Ger)	**7th**	+ 1'09"
143.	IVANOV Serguei (Rus)	17e	+ 1'38"
144.	KLIER Andreas (Ger)	**6th**	+ 28"
145.	SCHRECK Stephan (Ger)	43rd	+ 2'10"
146.	NARDELLO Daniele (Ita)	47e	+ 2'10"
147.	SCHAFFRATH Jan (Ger)	45e	+ 2'10"
148.	WESEMANN Steffen (Ger)	**1st**	**6h01'33"**

ALESSIO - BIANCHI

No.	Rider	Place	Result
151.	BÄCKSTEDT Magnus (Swe)	66th	+ 7'38"
152.	BALDATO Fabio (Ita)	60th	+ 7'38"
153.	LJUNGQVIST Marcus (Swe)		*Abandon*
154.	MORENI Cristian (Ita)	32nd	+ 2'10"
155.	HVASTIJA Martin (Slo)	113rd	+ 17'53"
157.	SUNDERLAND Scott (Aus)	76th	+ 7'38"

FASSA BORTOLO

No.	Rider	Place	Result
161.	CANCELLARA Fabian (Sui)	41st	+ 2'10"
162.	FLECHA Juan Antonio (Esp)	12nd	+ 1'17"
163.	KIRCHEN Kim (Lux)	87th	+ 7'38"
164.	ONGARATO Alberto (Ita)	93rd	+ 8'36"
165.	PETITO Roberto (Ita)	19th	+ 1'38"
166.	POZZATO Filippo (Ita)	108th	+ 17'53"
167.	SACCHI Fabio (Ita)	55th	+ 5'07"
168.	VANDENBROUCKE Frank (Bel)	44th	+ 2'10"

LAMPRE

No.	Rider	Place	Result
171.	BORTOLAMI Gianluca (Ita)	64th	+ 7'38"
172.	BOSSONI Paolo (Ita)	114th	+ 17'53"
173.	CARRARA Matteo (Ita)		*Abandon*
174.	CORTINOVIS Alessandro (Ita)	115th	+ 17'53"
175.	PAGLIARINI Luciano (Bra)		*Abandon*
176.	BALLAN Alessandro (Ita)	82nd	+ 7'38"
177.	VAINSTEINS Romans (Lat)	31st	+ 2'10"
178.	HAUPTMAN Andrej (Slo)		*Abandon*

SAECO

No.	Rider	Place	Result
181.	BALDUCCI Gabriele (Ita)	112nd	+ 17'53"
182.	BONOMI Giosue' (Ita)		*Abandon*
183.	CELESTINO Mirko (Ita)	28th	+ 2'10"
184.	CASAGRANDA Stefano (Ita)	111st	+ 17'53"
185.	COMMESSO Salvatore (Ita)	53rd	+ 5'07"
186.	FORNACIARI Paolo (Ita)	77th	+ 7'38"
187.	LUDEWIG Jörg (Ger)	14th	+ 1'38"
188.	PIERI Dario (Ita)		*Abandon*

DOMINA VACANZE

No.	Rider	Place	Result
191.	KOLOBNEV Alexandr (Rus)	94th	+ 9'49"
192.	MORI Massimiliano (Ita)	61st	+ 7'38"
193.	CLINGER David (Usa)	105th	+ 15'24"
194.	COLOMBO Gabriele (Ita)		*Abandon*
195.	NAUDUZS Andris (Lat)	107th	+ 17'53"
196.	FAGNINI GianMatteo (Ita)		*Abandon*
197.	BAZHENOV Alexandr (Rus)	73rd	+ 7'38"
198.	GIUNTI Massimo (Ita)		*Abandon*

RABOBANK

No.	Rider	Place	Result
201.	FREIRE Oscar (Esp)	23rd	+ 2'10"
202.	BOOGERD Michael (Ned)	20th	+ 1'38"
203.	DEKKER Erik (Ned)	**5th**	+ 28"
204.	DE JONGH Steven (Ned)	46th	+ 2'10"
205.	DEN BAKKER Maarten (Ned)	65th	+ 7'38"
206.	KROON Karsten (Ned)	89th	+ 7'38"
207.	SENTJENS Roy (Ned)	100th	+ 11'20"
208.	WAUTERS Marc (Bel)	50th	+ 2'34"

PHONAK

No.	Rider	Place	Result
211.	ALBASINI Michael (Sui)		*Abandon*
212.	CAMENZIND Oscar (Sui)	83rd	+ 7'38"
213.	ELMIGER Martin (Sui)	29th	+ 2'10"
214.	GRABSCH Bert (Ger)	37th	+ 2'10"
215.	MURN Uros (Slo)	59th	+ 7'38"
216.	RAST Gregory (Sui)	85th	+ 7'38"
217.	JALABERT Nicolas (Fra)	33rd	+ 2'10"
218.	USOV Alexandre (Blr)		*Abandon*

US POSTAL - BERRY FLOOR

No.	Rider	Place	Result
221.	CRUZ Antonio (Usa)	118e	+ 17'53"
222.	DEVOLDER Stijn (Bel)	21st	+ 1'38"
223.	EKIMOV Viatcheslav (Rus)		*Abandon*
224.	MIKHAILOV Guennadi (Rus)		*Abandon*
225.	HINCAPIE George (Usa)	**10th**	+ 1'16"
226.	JOACHIM Benoît (Lux)	58th	+ 5'07"
227.	PADRNOS Pavel (Cze)		*Abandon*
228.	VAN HEESWIJK Max (Ned)	80th	+ 7'38"

Illes BALEARS - BANESTO

No.	Rider	Place	Result
231.	BECKE Daniel (Ger)		*Abandon*
232.	GALVEZ Isaac (Esp)		*Abandon*
233.	COLOM Antonio (Esp)		*Abandon*
235.	LASTRAS Pablo (Esp)	121st	+ 17'53"
236.	LOPEZ GIL Antonio (Esp)		*Abandon*
237.	RADOCHLA Steffenl (Ger)		*Abandon*

CRÉDIT AGRICOLE

No.	Rider	Place	Result
241.	AUGÉ Stéphane (Fra)		*Abandon*
242.	DEAN Julian (Nzl)		*Abandon*
243.	HINAULT Sébastien (Fra)	116th	+ 17'53"
244.	HUSHOVD Thor (Nor)	38th	+ 2'10"
245.	JÉGOU Lilian (Fra)		*Abandon*
246.	KAGGESTAD Mads (Nor)		*Abandon*
247.	HERVÉ Cédric (Fra)	104th	+ 13'51"
248.	WIGGINS Bradley (Gbr)		*Abandon*

TOTAL OF POINTS UCI OBTAINED IN THE RACE

T.MOBILE	439 points
LOTTO - DOMO	341 points
RABOBANK	150 points
Chocolade JACQUES-WINCOR NIXDORF	145 points
QUICK STEP - DAVITAMON	120 points
CSC	95 points
FASSA BORTOLO	88 points
US POSTAL	78 points
AG2R Prévoyance	63 points
SAECO	58 points
RELAX-BODYSOL	41 points
Mr BOOKMAKER-PALMANS	35 points
PHONAK	31 points
LANDBOUWKREDIET - COLNAGO	28 points
ALESSIO - BIANCHI	25 points
DOMINA VACANZE	ditto
LAMPRE	ditto
GEROLSTEINER	21 points
COFIDIS	20 points
CRÉDIT AGRICOLE	15 points
FDJEUX.COM	ditto
EUSKALTEL - EUSKADI	10 points
VLAANDEREN - T INTERIM	ditto
ILLES BALEARS - BANESTO	5 points
LIBERTY Seguros	0 point

PAST WINNERS AT THE START — 5

MUSEEUW Johan	1993, 1995 &1998
VAN PETEGEM Peter	1999 & 2003
BORTOLAMI Gianluca	2001
BARTOLI Michele	1998
DURAND Jacky	1992

RIDERS IN TEH UCI TOP 100: 38

ROOKIES AT THE START (LESS THAN ONE YEAR AS A PROFESSIONAL): 10

3 YOUNGEST

SANCHEZ GIL Luis Leon (Esp)	23/11/1983
SANCHEZ Fabien (Fra)	30/03/1983
VAN HECKE Preben (Bel)	09/07/1982

3 OLDEST

DIERCKXSENS Ludo (Bel)	14/10/1964
MUSEEUW Johan (Bel)	13/10/1965
EKIMOV Viatcheslav (Rus)	04/02/1966

Tom Boonen at last

Ten days after winning in a sprint finish at Harelbeke (at the end of the well known GP E3), Tom Boonen reaped an even more prestigious success, winning in the same way at Wevelgem and this despite two punctures in the closing stages of the race.

Six! The Quick Step - Davitamon team could count on six riders in the group of 25 men who broke away on the first ascension of Mont Kemmel. An obstacle made even more difficult than usual by a slippery surface caused by the incessant rain which followed the riders for quite some time already. A week before his retirement (taken after the GP de l'Escaut, the 14th April), Johan Museeuw was of course well and truly present. As was the case with the majority of his team mates, Boonen, Bodrogi, Cretskens, Knaven and Nuyens all being able to join the group of strong men that made the difference on the cobbles of Kemmel. Shortly before this critical moment, Tom Boonen suffered a rear wheel puncture, but his devoted team mate Kevin Hulsmans went quickly to his aid. Had it not been for this selfless act, he too would have been in the leading group! A group led therefore by the men in blue and white but also containing some serious contenders such as, Jaan Kirsipuu, Magnus Backstedt, Frank Hoj (accompanied by Goussev and Hoffman), Roger Hammond or the Swiss Fabian Cancellara (with Flecha, decidedly at ease in these northern races).

AN INEVITABLE SPRINT

On the other hand, Nico Mattan had missed his chance. The Flamand,on his home ground,found it hard going to get out of a following group, trailing by half a minute, before recuperating Jimmy Casper (left behind on the second climb on Kemmelberg) and Nick Nuyens,who'd helped out Tom Boonen, once again victim of a puncture! It's the same Mattan helped by the competition with his young team mate Sebastien Rosseler) who was the only rider to trouble the strategy of the Quick Step team. There were just two kilometers to go. Johan Museeuw in person chased Mattan, but he was unable to keep to the plan worked out earlier. But luck was once again with Tom Boonen. The impressive Swede Magus Backstedt went for the sprint. Surely too early. Boonen pulled out from behind and

188 Competitors

T-MOBILE

1.	KLIER Andreas (Ger)	**10th**	s.t
2.	AERTS Mario (Bel)		*Abandon*
3.	IVANOV Serguei (Rus)	38th	+ 4'38"
4.	KORFF André (Ger)		*Abandon*
5.	NARDELLO Daniele (Ita)	47th	+ 4'38"
6.	SCHAFFRATH Jan (Ger)		*Abandon*
7.	SCHRECK Stephan (Ger)		*Abandon*
8.	BAUMANN Eric (Ger)		*Abandon*

GEROLSTEINER

11.	FÖRSTER Robert (Ger)	23rd	+ 14"
12.	FOTHEN Markus (Ger)		*Abandon*
13.	HASELBACHER René (Aut)	18th	s.t
14.	HONDO Danilo (Ger)		*Abandon*
15.	KRAUSS Sven (Ger)		*Abandon*
16.	LANG Sebastian (Ger)	55th	+ 10'04"
18.	WROLICH Peter (Aut)		*Abandon*

LOTTO - DOMO

21.	D'HOLLANDER Glen (Bel)		*Abandon*
22.	DE CLERCQ Hans (Bel)	42nd	+ 4'38"
23.	EECKHOUT Nico (Bel)	49th	+ 4'38"
24.	GARDEYN Gorik (Bel)		*Abandon*
25.	VAN BON Leon (Ned)		*Abandon*
26.	STEEGMANS Geert (Bel)	11st	s.t
27.	VAN DIJK Stefan (Ned)	30th	+ 4'38"
28.	VANSEVENANT Wim (Bel)	50th	+ 4'38"

QUICK STEP - DAVITAMON

31.	BRAMATI Davide (Ita)		*Abandon*
32.	BODROGI Laszlo (Hun)	25th	+ 26"
33.	BOONEN Tom (Bel)	**1st**	**4h34'51"**
34.	CRETSKENS Wilfried (Bel)	24th	+ 21"
35.	HULSMANS Kevin (Bel)		*Abandon*
36.	KNAVEN Servais (Ned)	21st	+ 9"
37.	MUSEEUW Johan (Bel)	20th	+ 9"
38.	NUYENS Nick (Bel)	22nd	+ 14"

Mr BOOKMAKER.COM - PALMANS

41.	DE SMET Andy (Bel)		*Abandon*
42.	HUNT Jeremy (Gbr)	45th	+ 4'38"
43.	HAMMOND Roger (Gbr)	**6th**	s.t
44.	OMLOOP Geert (Bel)	43rd	+ 4'38"
45.	PLANCKAERT Jo (Bel)	46th	+ 4'38"
46.	ROODHOOFT Christoph (Bel)		*Abandon*
47.	TROUVÉ Kristof (Bel)	54th	+ 10'04"
48.	VAN HAECKE Michel (Bel)		*Abandon*

LANDBOUWKREDIET - COLNAGO

51.	CAPELLE Ludovic (Bel)		*Abandon*
52.	VAN BONDT Geert (Bel)		*Abandon*
53.	MONFORT Maxime (Bel)	39th	+ 4'38"
54.	MITLUSHENKO Yuriy (Ukr)		*Abandon*
55.	VAITKUS Tomas (Ltu)	12nd	s.t
56.	BERNUCCI Lorenzo (Ita)	19th	s.t
57.	BRACKE Tony (Bel)		*Abandon*
58.	VERSTREPEN Johan (Bel)		*Abandon*

VLAANDEREN - T INTERIM

61.	CAETHOVEN Steven (Bel)		*Abandon*
62.	VAN MECHELEN Wouter (Bel)		*Abandon*
63.	DE SPIEGELAERE Bart (Bel)		*Abandon*
64.	VAN SPEYBROECK Wesley (Bel)		*Abandon*
65.	SCHOONACKER Jehudi (Bel)		*Abandon*
66.	KUYCKX Jan (Bel)		*Abandon*
67.	VAN DER SLAGMOLEN Kevin (Bel)		*Abandon*
68.	MEYS David (Bel)		*Abandon*

Chocolade JACQUES - WINCOR NIXDORF

71.	ABAKOUMOV Igor (Bel)		*Abandon*
72.	BLANCHY Michael (Bel)		*Abandon*
73.	KOERTS Jans (Ned)	52nd	+ 7'23"
74.	LÖWIK Gerben (Ned)		*Abandon*
75.	PEERS Chris (Bel)	29th	+ 4'38"
76.	PLANCKAERT Francesco(Bel)		*Abandon*
77.	HIEMSTRA Bert (Ned)		*Abandon*
78.	VERHEYEN Geert (Bel)		*Abandon*

FASSA BORTOLO

81.	CANCELLARA Fabian (Sui)	14th	s.t
82.	KIRCHEN Kim (Lux)	48th	+ 4'38"
83.	PETITO Roberto (Ita)		*Abandon*
84.	SACCHI Fabio (Ita)		*Abandon*
85.	FLECHA Juan Antonio (Esp)	**7th**	s.t
86.	ONGARATO Alberto (Ita)		*Abandon*
87.	POZZATO Filippo (Ita)		*Abandon*
88.	CHICCHI Francesco (Ita)		*Abandon*

DOMINA VACANZE

91.	BAZHENOV Alexandr (Rus)		*Abandon*
92.	GIUNTI Massimo (Ita)		*Abandon*
93.	COLOMBO Gabriele (Ita)		*Abandon*
94.	FAGNINI GianMatteo (Ita)		*Abandon*
95.	NAUDUZS Andris (Lat)		*Abandon*
96.	KOLOBNEV Alexandr (Rus)		*Abandon*
98.	CLINGER David (Usa)		*Abandon*

SAECO

101.	BALDUCCI Gabriele (Ita)	36th	+ 4'38"
102.	BONOMI Giosue' (Ita)		*Abandon*
103.	LUDEWIG Jörg (Ger)	27th	+ 4'38"
104.	CASAGRANDA Stefano (Ita)		*Abandon*
105.	COMMESSO Salvatore (Ita)		*Abandon*
106.	FORNACIARI Paolo (Ita)	41st	+ 4'38"
107.	GAVAZZI Nicola (Ita)		*Abandon*
108.	PIERI Dario (Ita)		*Abandon*

LAMPRE

111.	BORTOLAMI Gianluca (Ita)		*Abandon*
112.	CARRARA Matteo (Ita)		*Abandon*
113.	BALLAN Alessandro (Ita)		*Abandon*
114.	QUINZIATO Manuel (Ita)		*Abandon*
115.	BOSSONI Paolo (Ita)		*Abandon*
116.	CORTINOVIS Alessandro (Ita)		*Abandon*
117.	HAUPTMAN Andrej (Slo)		*Abandon*
118.	VAINSTEINS Romans (Lat)		*Abandon*

ALESSIO - BIANCHI

121.	BÄCKSTEDT Magnus (Swe)	**2nd**	s.t
122.	HVASTIJA Martin (Slo)	40th	+ 4'38"
123.	MORENI Cristian (Ita)		*Abandon*
124.	LJUNGQVIST Marcus (Swe)		*Abandon*
127.	SUNDERLAND Scott (Aus)		*Abandon*

RABOBANK

131.	FREIRE Oscar (Esp)		*Abandon*
132.	BOOGERD Michael (Ned)		*Abandon*
133.	DE JONGH Steven (Ned)		*Abandon*
134.	HAYMAN Mathew (Aus)		*Abandon*
135.	HUNTER Robert (Rsa)	44th	+ 4'38"
136.	KROON Karsten (Ned)		*Abandon*
137.	SENTJENS Roy (Ned)		*Abandon*
138.	WAUTERS Marc (Bel)	37th	+ 4'38"

BANKGIROLOTERIJ

141.	BAK Lars Ytting (Den)		*Abandon*
142.	BLIJLEVENS Jeroen (Ned)		*Abandon*
143.	TEN DAM Laurens (Ned)		*Abandon*
144.	ENGELS Addy (Ned)		*Abandon*
145.	JOHANSEN Allan (Den)		*Abandon*
146.	KEMNA Rudi (Ned)		*Abandon*
147.	SMINK Julien (Ned)		*Abandon*
148.	VAN DER VEN Remco (Ned)	32nd	+ 4'38"

CSC

151.	GOUSSEV Vladimir (Rus)	**8th**	s.t
152.	MICHAELSEN Lars (Den)		*Abandon*
153.	HØJ Frank (Den)	15th	s.t
154.	BRUUN ERIKSEN Thomas (Den)		*Abandon*
155.	CHRISTENSEN Bekim (Den)		*Abandon*
156.	HOFFMAN Tristan (Ned)	16th	s.t
157.	MADSEN Jimmi (Den)		*Abandon*

could raise his arms in victory without fear of disappointment. "I just wanted to be on my own in the photo" he joked afterwards. Alone, the unfortunate Dutchman Julien Smink (Bankgiroloterij) was just that for fifty kilometers. He was dreaming of victory when his lead over the peloton reached 6 mins only for that dream to be dashed when wind, rain and the cold took their toll and wiped it out. Inevitably the hard men did their work, leaving only about fifty men in the running. Le Kemmel further sorted out the men from the boys. This edition of the Gand -Wevelgem had now taken shape, and underlined the show of force by the Quick Step team, just a few days before the Paris - Roubaix and just afew days after their less successful showing in the Tour of Flanders. This intervening Classic put the book straight. ■

The great work of his Quick Step team mates, overpowering in the leading group, came up trumps for Tom Boonen, a new Classic contender we haven't heard the last of.

US POSTAL - BERRY FLOOR

161.	CRUZ Antonio (Usa)		*Abandon*
162.	MIKHAILOV Guennadi (Rus)		*Abandon*
163.	HINCAPIE George (Usa)	**4th**	s.t
164.	PADRNOS Pavel (Cze)		*Abandon*
166.	HESJEDAL Ryder (Can)		*Abandon*
167.	JOACHIM Benoît (Lux)		*Abandon*
168.	VAN HEESWIJK Max (Ned)		*Abandon*

NAVIGATORS

171.	ZAJICEK Phil (Usa)		*Abandon*
172.	LOUDER Jeff (Usa)		*Abandon*
173.	O'BEE Kirk (Usa)		*Abandon*
174.	WALTERS Mark (Can)		*Abandon*
175.	DAVIDENKO Vassili (Rus)		*Abandon*
176.	McKENZIE David (Aus)		*Abandon*
177.	POWER Ciaran (Irl)		*Abandon*
178.	VOGELS Henk (Aus)		*Abandon*

COFIDIS

181.	CASPER Jimmy (Fra)	**5th**	s.t
182.	COYOT Arnaud (Fra)		*Abandon*
183.	O'GRADY Stuart (Aus)		*Abandon*
184.	FARAZIJN Peter (Bel)	17th	s.t
185.	WHITE Matthew (Aus)		*Abandon*
186.	SCHEIRLINCKX Staf (Bel)		*Abandon*

FDJEUX.COM

191.	COOKE Baden (Aus)		*Abandon*
192.	DEREPAS David (Fra)		*Abandon*
193.	EISEL Bernhard (Aut)		*Abandon*
194.	GUESDON Frédéric (Fra)		*Abandon*
195.	MENGIN Christophe (Fra)		*Abandon*
196.	SANCHEZ Fabien (Fra)		*Abandon*
197.	VAUGRENARD Benoît (Fra)		*Abandon*
198.	WILSON Matthew (Aus)		*Abandon*

AG2R Prévoyance

201.	AGNOLUTTO Christophe (Fra)		*Abandon*
202.	BERGÈS Stéphane (Fra)		*Abandon*
203.	FLICKINGER Andy (Fra)		*Abandon*
204.	INAUDI Nicolas (Fra)		*Abandon*
205.	KIRSIPUU Jaan (Est)	**3rd**	s.t
206.	NAZON Jean-Patrick (Fra)		*Abandon*
207.	PÜTSEP Erki (Est)		*Abandon*
208.	SCANLON Mark (Irl)	33rd	+ 4'38"

CRÉDIT AGRICOLE

211.	KAGGESTAD Mads (Nor)		*Abandon*
212.	DEAN Julian (Nzl)	31st	+ 4'38"
213.	HERVÉ Cédric (Fra)		*Abandon*
214.	HINAULT Sébastien (Fra)	53rd	+ 7'23"
215.	HUSHOVD Thor (Nor)		*Abandon*
216.	JÉGOU Lilian (Fra)		*Abandon*
217.	LEQUATRE Geoffroy (Fra)		*Abandon*
218.	WIGGINS Bradley (Gbr)		*Abandon*

RELAX - BODYSOL

221.	DE VOCHT Wim (Bel)		*Abandon*
222.	DOCKX Bart (Bel)	56th	+ 10'04"
223.	FLORENCIO Xavier (Esp)		*Abandon*
224.	MATTAN Nico (Bel)	13rd	s.t
225.	ROESEMS Bert (Bel)		*Abandon*
226.	VAN HECKE Preben (Bel)	51st	+ 4'38"
227.	ROSSELER Sébastien (Bel)	**9th**	s.t
228.	VAN SUMMEREN Johan (Bel)		*Abandon*

Illes BALEARS - BANESTO

231.	BECKE Daniel (Ger)		*Abandon*
232.	GALVEZ Isaac (Esp)		*Abandon*
233.	COLOM Antonio (Esp)		*Abandon*
235.	LASTRAS Pablo (Esp)	35th	+ 4'38"
236.	LOPEZ GIL Antonio (Esp)		*Abandon*
238.	RADOCHLA Steffenl (Ger)	26th	+ 4'38"

PHONAK

241.	ALBASINI Michael (Sui)		*Abandon*
242.	ELMIGER Martin (Sui)	28th	+ 4'38"
243.	JALABERT Nicolas (Fra)		*Abandon*
245.	GRABSCH Bert (Ger)		*Abandon*
246.	MURN Uros (Slo)		*Abandon*
247.	RAST Gregory (Sui)	34th	+ 4'38"
248.	USOV Alexandre (Blr)		*Abandon*

TOTAL OF POINTS UCI OBTAINED IN THE RACE

QUICK STEP - DAVITAMON	213 points
ALESSIO - BIANCHI	115 points
AG2R Prévoyance	95 points
COFIDIS	84 points
CSC	79 points
FASSA BORTOLO	ditto
US POSTAL	78 points
Mr BOOKMAKER-PALMANS	76 points
RELAX-BODYSOL	63 points
LOTTO - DOMO	46 points
LANDBOUWKREDIET - COLNAGO	44 points
T.MOBILE	ditto
GEROLSTEINER	19 points
SAECO	15 points
ILLES BALEARS - BANESTO	10 points
PHONAK	ditto
RABOBANK	ditto
BANKGIROLOTERIJ	5 points
Chocolade JACQUES-WINCOR NIXDORF	ditto
CRÉDIT AGRICOLE	ditto
DOMINA VACANZE	0 point
LAMPRE	ditto
FDJEUX.COM	ditto
VLAANDEREN - T INTERIM	ditto
NAVIGATORS	ditto

PAST WINNERS AT THE START ***4***

KLIER Andreas	2003
HINCAPIE George	2001
VAN BONDT Geert	2000
MICHAELSEN Lars	19xx

RIDERS IN THE UCI TOP 100: ***23***

ROOKIES AT THE START (LESS THAN ONE YEAR AS A PROFESSIONAL): ***10***

3 YOUNGEST

SANCHEZ Fabien (Fra)	30/03/1983
MONFORT Maxime (Bel)	14/01/1983
KRAUSS Sven (Ger)	06/01/1983

3 OLDEST

MUSEEUW Johan (Bel)	13/10/1965
SUNDERLAND Scott (Aus)	28/11/1966
KEMNA Rudi (Ned)	05/10/1967

The huge form of Swedish giant Magnus Backstedt pulls ahead in the velodrome. Roger Hammond (left) Fabian Cancellara (hidden) and Tristan Hoffman fight for the podium.

Museeuw and Van Petegem, companions in misfortune

As in San Remo and Meerbeke, it's an outsider that carried off this third round of the World Cup. The giant Swede (1m 93) Magnus Backstedt allowed his country, for the first time, to take a Classic win, but at the same time deprived Johan Museeuw of a perfect swansong and Peter van Petegem of a double in the northern city. The two Belgian favourites shared bad luck in this 102nd Paris Roubaix, victims of punctures at the very moment the race was taking shape.

Tired and unhappy. Johan Museeuw would have liked another result in his last Paris Roubaix. But luck was not on his side.

sections proved hard work for the leaders, seeing their advantage slip away. With the exception of Salvatore Commesso who received help from Geert van Bondt, coming out in a counter attack, they are all absorbed during the first seven sectors. Commesso and van Bondt knew the same fate just before the first strategic point in the race, zone 15 also known as la tranché de Wallers – Arenberg. It's the German Rolf Aldag, with a slight lead who attacks this infamous obstacle in front. 2400 metres later it's not the German but the Swiss Fabian Cancellara (Fassa Bortolo) who's in the lead. Aldag like many others had problems mastering the moist and mossy cobbles. After this passage it's time to take account of the damage caused in the ranks. A group of twenty riders, soon to be joined by fifteen more, head the race. There are 90 kms remaining and the majority of the peloton are already out of contention...

AN UNEXPECTED QUARTET

Of the favourites only Andrea Tafi (Alessio Bianchi), Frank Vandenbroucke (Fassa Bortolo) and the Rabobank riders are missing. The Quick Step Davitamon team, particularly Tom Boonen control the peloton. This turns out to be hard work and the team

Magnus Backstedt (here preceding Fabian Cancellara) was confident of victory long before the finish. Here he relishes the winners trophy.

Reserved,even timid when he appears in public, Johan Museeuw is much more at ease at the Roubaix Velodrome. We still recall his painful knee injury when winning in 2000, then two years later, his mud spattered face and blood covered fingers at the end of his second victorious ride. This time it's the accolade with his "Best enemy" Peter van Petegem another great hunter of Classic wins which sticks in the memory. The two men arrived side by side on the concrete banking of Roubaix, but when the time came to sprint for the... fifth place they shook hands warmly (still managing to stay in the saddle)! Their eyes, even though they were dryed by several hours of dusty roads seemed close to tears. The symbol was a strong one, seeming to show a passing of the burden already evident on the road last year during the fabulous week of Peter van Petegem (double Flanders – Roubaix).

WIND... AND COBBLES

If the Tour of Flanders the previous week was marked by a morning breakaway of 27 riders,nothing of the sort was to happen during the long procession towards Troisvilles, which for the last fifteen years marks the beginning of the paved sections. Things were not helped by a facing wind which prevented any breakaways getting a real advantage. The attempts of Guillaume Auger (RAGT), Erki Putsep (AG2R), and Eelke van der Wal (Bankgiroloterij) then Erwin Thijs (Mr Bookmaker.com) never came to much. Guillaume Auger had another go at 72 kms. This time he was accompanied by the Italians Bonomi and Commesso(Saeco), the Swiss Albasini (Phonak) and the German Krauss (Gerolsteiner). The peloton lets go and the breakaway can do its stuff. At Troisvilles they have a lead of 5 mins 45 sec ahead of a peloton already weakened by falls (Gadret, Lowik, Bracke). The first paved mates of Johan Museeuw let Jaan Kirsipuu slip away on a tarmaced section between Tilloy and Orchies, 65 kms from the line. In the peloton, several attemts to counter attack come to nothing, like that of Johan Museeuw in the sector of Auchy-les-Orchies. Jaan Kirsipuu is, however, caught 48 kms from the finish, at Mons en Pevele. The peloton is once again bunched, but only for an instant. In effect, on the cobbles of Mons en Pevele, Frank Hoj (CSC) and Leon van Bon (Lotto Domo) escape. The adventure of the two outsiders goes no further than Moulin de Vertain. There are only 32 kms to go, and unusually, a large number of riders can still hope for a win. Going through Cysoing, Christophe Mengin opens up hostilities once again. He is accompanied by Fabio Baldato (Alessio Bianchi), Tom Boonen (Quick Step Davitamon), Juan Antonio Flecha (Fassa Bortolo) a spaniard who hates the mountains but loves the northern Classics, and Leif Hoste (Lotto Domo), one of the heros of the recent Tour of Flanders. The latter is dropped by the group following an incident with an unruly flag waving supporter. Leif Hoste avoids a fall, but loses contact with the leaders, as does Christophe Mengin. This offensive is also wiped out exiting Camphin-en -Pevele and a group of twenty riders are still there 15 kms from the line. However, Peter van Petegem is missing, victim of a puncture at the wrong moment. Things come into place at Gruson, 13 kms from the Roubaix Velodrome. Johan Museeuw accelerates. Those who were unable to follow were not necessarily those who we could imagine: Magnus Backstedt, Fabian Cancellara the young Swiss, the British champion Roger Hammond and the hard working Dutchman Tristan hoffman, already fourth on two occasions (2000 and 2002). The five men build a decisive lead and move into the paved sector at Hem, less treacherous than those preceding, having tarmac bands each side. Just the same, it's here that Johan Museeuw pulls over and raises an arm. His rear tyre is flat. While the wheel is being changed, Peter Van Petegem takes off, but his four ex companions are already in the distance! Fate is cruel. Johan Museeuw loses his last Paris Roubaix with a puncture at 6 kms from the line. Quickly realising that the favourite had disappeared from their group, Backstedt, Cancellara, Hammond and Hoffman lose no time in the streets of Roubaix. They arrive in the velodrome packed with Belgian supporters of Johan Museeuw, knocked back by the bad luck of their idol. In the final metres Magnus Backstedt surges through to take the greatest victory of his career. ■

For Rolf Aldag and Serguei Ivanov (below) it's time for a well earned shower. Will it manage to wash away the memories of those terrible cobble stones.

177 Competitors

LOTTO - DOMO			
1.	VAN PETEGEM Peter (Bel)	**6th**	+ 17"
2.	DE CLERCQ Hans (Bel)		*Abandon*
3.	HOSTE Leif (Bel)	12nd	+ 29"
4.	MARICHAL Thierry (Bel)	32nd	+ 12'18"
5.	STEEGMANS Geert (Bel)		*Abandon*
6.	VAN BON Leon (Ned)	**7th**	+ 29"
7.	VANSEVENANT Wim (Bel)	67th	+ 13'32"
8.	VIERHOUTEN Aart (Ned)	34th	+ 12'19"
SAECO			
11.	PIERI Dario (Ita)	70th	+ 13'33"
12.	BALDUCCI Gabriele (Ita)		*Abandon*
13.	BONOMI Giosue' (Ita)		*Abandon*
14.	CASAGRANDA Stefano (Ita)	37th	+ 13'19"
15.	COMMESSO Salvatore (Ita)	36th	+ 13'19"
16.	FORNACIARI Paolo (Ita)	60th	+ 13'19"
17.	GAVAZZI Nicola (Ita)	55th	+ 13'19"
18.	LUDEWIG Jörg (Ger)	46th	+ 13'19"
T-MOBILE			
21.	WESEMANN Steffen (Ger)	16th	+ 58"
22.	ALDAG Rolf (Ger)	26th	+ 3'54"
23.	BAUMANN Eric (Ger)	39th	+ 13'19"
24.	IVANOV Serguei (Rus)	19th	+ 2'52"
25.	KLIER Andreas (Ger)		*Abandon*
26.	NARDELLO Daniele (Ita)	15th	+ 36"
27.	SCHAFFRATH Jan (Ger)	27th	+ 3'54"
28.	SCHRECK Stephan (Ger)	65th	+ 13'19"
FASSA BORTOLO			
31.	VANDENBROUCKE Frank (Bel)		*Abandon*
32.	CANCELLARA Fabian (Sui)	**4th**	s.t
33.	CHICCHI Francesco (Ita)	89th	+ 31'09"
34.	FLECHA Juan Antonio (Esp)	13rd	+ 29"
35.	ONGARATO Alberto (Ita)		*Abandon*
38.	TOSATTO Matteo (Ita)		*Abandon*
RABOBANK			
41.	WAUTERS Marc (Bel)		*Abandon*
42.	BARTKO Robert (Ger)		*Abandon*
43.	BOVEN Jan (Ned)		*Abandon*
44.	DE JONGH Steven (Ned)	41st	+ 13'19"
45.	DEN BAKKER Maarten (Ned)	58th	+ 13'19"
46.	HUNTER Robert (Rsa)	31st	+ 7'59"
47.	SENTJENS Roy (Ned)	73rd	+ 14'58"
48.	TRAKSEL Bobbie (Ned)	92nd	+ 43'09"
US POSTAL - BERRY FLOOR			
61.	HINCAPIE George (Usa)	**8th**	+ 29"
62.	CRUZ Antonio (Usa)	49th	+ 13'19"
63.	DEVOLDER Stijn (Bel)	91st	+ 35'10"
64.	JOACHIM Benoît (Lux)	64th	+ 13'19"
65.	LANDIS Floyd (Usa)		*Abandon*
66.	PADRNOS Pavel (Cze)		*Abandon*
67.	PEÑA Victor Hugo (Col)		*Abandon*
68.	VAN HEESWIJK Max (Ned)	66th	+ 13'19"
QUICK STEP - DAVITAMON			
71.	MUSEEUW Johan (Bel)	**5th**	+ 17"
72.	BODROGI Laszlo (Hun)	52nd	+ 13'19"

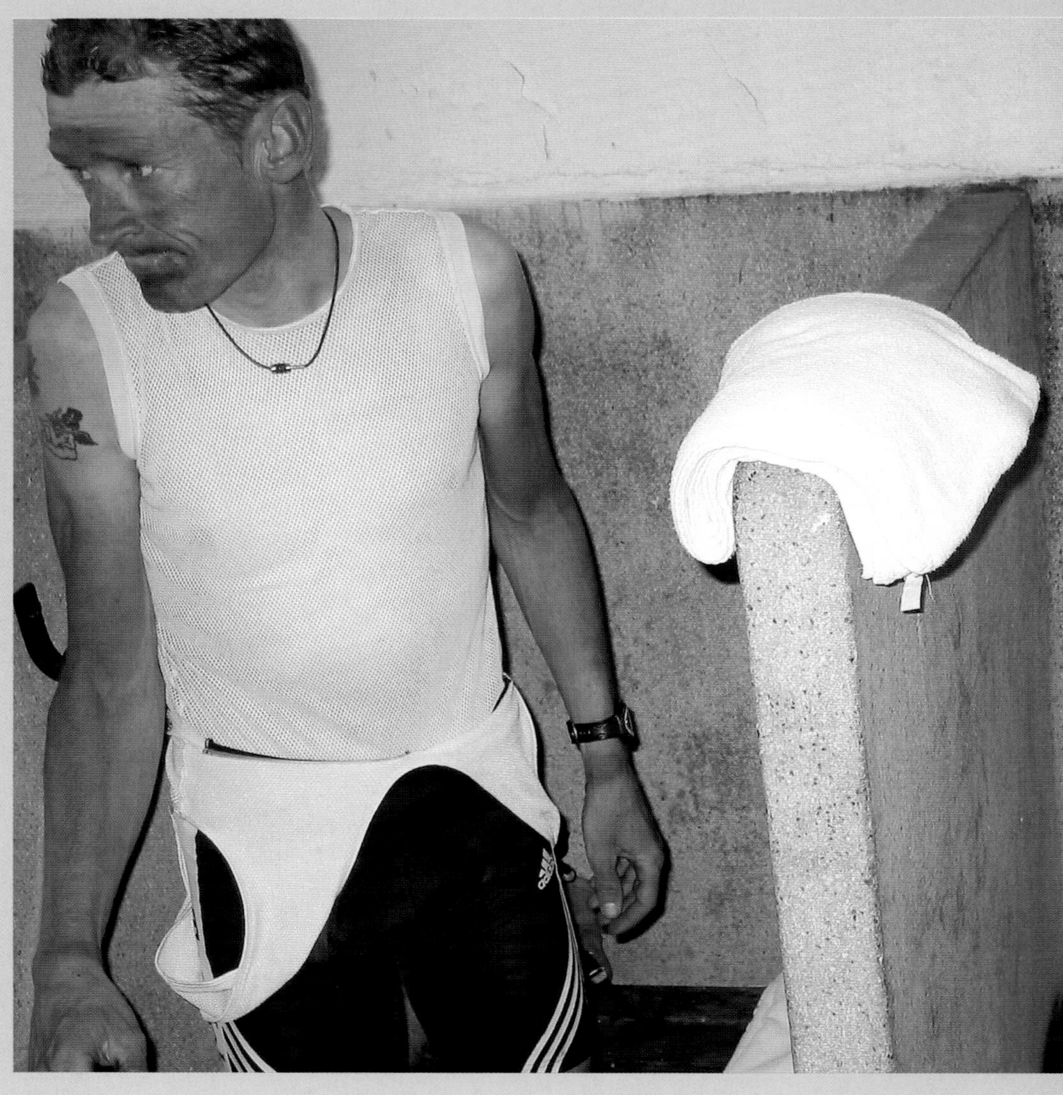

No.	Rider	Place	Time
73.	BOONEN Tom (Bel)	**9th**	+ 29"
74.	CRETSKENS Wilfried (Bel)	30th	+ 7'59"
75.	HORRILLO Pedro (Esp)	42nd	+ 13'19"
76.	HULSMANS Kevin (Bel)	29th	+ 6'36"
77.	KNAVEN Servais (Ned)	33rd	+ 12'19"
78.	ZANINI Stefano (Ita)	69th	+ 13'33"

PHONAK

No.	Rider	Place	Time
81.	USOV Alexandre (Blr)	80th	+ 31'03"
82.	ALBASINI Michael (Sui)		*Abandon*
83.	ELMIGER Martin (Sui)	51st	+ 13'19"
84.	GRABSCH Bert (Ger)		*Abandon*
86.	MURN Uros (Slo)		*Abandon*
87.	RAST Gregory (Sui)	57th	+ 13'19"

GEROLSTEINER

No.	Rider	Place	Time
92.	FÖRSTER Robert (Ger)		*Abandon*
94.	KRAUSS Sven (Ger)		*Abandon*
95.	LANG Sebastian (Ger)		*Abandon*
96.	POLLACK Olaf (Ger)		*Abandon*
97.	RICH Michael (Ger)	72nd	+ 14'58"
98.	STRAUSS Marcel (Sui)		*Abandon*

Chocolade JACQUES - WINCOR NIXDORF

No.	Rider	Place	Time
101.	PEERS Chris (Bel)	61st	+ 13'19"
102.	ABAKOUMOV Igor (Bel)		*Abandon*
103.	CAPPELLE Andy (Bel)	82nd	+ 31'09"
104.	GADRET John (Fra)		*Abandon*
105.	HIEMSTRA Bert (Ned)	53rd	+ 13'19"
106.	KOERTS Jans (Ned)		*Abandon*
107.	LÖWIK Gerben (Ned)		*Abandon*
108.	VOSKAMP Bart (Ned)	63rd	+ 13'19"

ALESSIO - BIANCHI

No.	Rider	Place	Time
111.	TAFI Andrea (Ita)	43rd	+ 13'19"
112.	BÄCKSTEDT Magnus (Swe)	**1st**	**6h40'26"**
113.	BALDATO Fabio (Ita)	24th	+ 3'50"
114.	HVASTIJA Martin (Slo)		*Abandon*
115.	LJUNGQVIST Marcus (Swe)		*Abandon*
116.	SUNDERLAND Scott (Aus)	44th	+ 13'19"

CSC

No.	Rider	Place	Time
121.	SCIANDRI Maximilian (Gbr)		*Abandon*
122.	BARTOLI Michele (Ita)	21st	+ 2'56"
123.	CHRISTENSEN Bekim (Den)	45th	+ 13'19"
124.	BRUUN ERIKSEN Thomas (Den)	47th	+ 13'19"
125.	GOUSSEV Vladimir (Rus)	20th	+ 2'52"
126.	HOFFMAN Tristan (Ned)	**2nd**	s.t
127.	HØJ Frank (Den)	**10th**	+ 29"
128.	MICHAELSEN Lars (Den)	23rd	+ 3'50"

The two favourites for this 102nd edition of "l'Enfer du Nord" race side by side in the velodrome... But only for the fifth place!

Brioches LA BOULANGÈRE

No.	Rider	Place	Time
131.	ROUS Didier (Fra)		*Abandon*
132.	BELOKI Gorka (Esp)		*Abandon*
133.	CHAVANEL Sébastien (Fra)		*Abandon*
134.	GESLIN Anthony (Fra)		*Abandon*
135.	MARTIAS Rony (Fra)		*Abandon*
136.	RENIER Franck (Fra)		*Abandon*
137.	VOECKLER Thomas (Fra)	77th	+ 20'37"
138.	YUS Unai (Esp)	78th	+ 20'37"

Illes BALEARS - BANESTO

No.	Rider	Place	Time
141.	BECKE Daniel (Ger)		*Abandon*
142.	COLOM Antonio (Esp)		*Abandon*
143.	GALVEZ Isaac (Esp)		*Abandon*
144.	LASTRAS Pablo (Esp)		*Abandon*
145.	LOPEZ GIL José Antonio (Esp)		*Abandon*
146.	RADOCHLA Steffen (Ger)	68th	+ 13'32"

LIBERTY Seguros

No.	Rider	Place	Time
151.	BARANOWSKI Dariusz (Pol)		*Abandon*
152.	ANDRLE René (Cze)		*Abandon*
153.	BARREDO Carlos (Esp)		*Abandon*
154.	DAVIS Allan (Aus)		*Abandon*
155.	DIAZ JUSTO Rafael (Esp)		*Abandon*
156.	SANCHEZ GIL Luis Leon (Esp)		*Abandon*

FDJEUX.COM

No.	Rider	Place	Time
161.	GUESDON Frédéric (Fra)	18th	+ 2'52"
162.	DEREPAS David (Fra)	87th	+ 31'09"
163.	EISEL Bernhard (Aut)	35th	+ 13'19"
164.	MENGIN Christophe (Fra)	25th	+ 3'50"
165.	MOUREY Francis (Fra)		*Abandon*
166.	ROY Jérémy (Fra)	93rd	+ 51'08"
167.	VAUGRENARD Benoît (Fra)		*Abandon*
168.	WILSON Matthew (Aus)		*Abandon*

Mr BOOKMAKER.COM - PALMANS

No.	Rider	Place	Time
171.	PLANCKAERT Jo (Bel)		*Abandon*
172.	DE SMET Andy (Bel)		*Abandon*
173.	HAMMOND Roger (Gbr)	**3rd**	s.t
174.	HUNT Jeremy (Gbr)	79th	+ 28'07"
175.	OMLOOP Geert (Bel)		*Abandon*
176.	THIJS Erwin (Bel)	71st	+ 14'58"
177.	TROUVÉ Kristof (Bel)	59th	+ 13'19"
178.	VAN HAECKE Michel (Bel)	74th	+ 14'58"

AG2R Prévoyance

No.	Rider	Place	Time
181.	KIRSIPUU Jaan (Est)	22nd	+ 3'50"
182.	AGNOLUTTO Christophe (Fra)		*Abandon*
183.	BERGÈS Stéphane (Fra)	83rd	+ 31'09"
184.	FLICKINGER Andy (Fra)	48th	+ 13'19"
185.	INAUDI Nicolas (Fra)		*Abandon*
186.	NAZON Jean-Patrick (Fra)	88th	+ 31'09"
187.	PORTAL Nicolas (Fra)	54th	+ 13'19"
188.	PÜTSEP Erki (Est)		*Abandon*

LANDBOUWKREDIET - COLNAGO

No.	Rider	Place	Time
191.	DIERCKXSENS Ludo (Bel)	14th	+ 29"
192.	BERNUCCI Lorenzo (Ita)	28th	+ 3'54"
193.	BRACKE Tony (Bel)		*Abandon*
194.	CAPELLE Ludovic (Bel)		*Abandon*
195.	DURAND Jacky (Fra)	76th	+ 14'58"
196.	STREEL Marc (Bel)		*Abandon*
197.	VAN BONDT Geert (Bel)		*Abandon*
198.	VERSTREPEN Johan (Bel)	86th	+ 31'09"

CRÉDIT AGRICOLE

No.	Rider	Place	Time
201.	HUSHOVD Thor	17th	+ 2'52"
202.	DEAN Julian		*Abandon*
203.	HERVÉ Cédric		*Abandon*
204.	HINAULT Sébastien	56th	+ 13'19"
205.	JÉGOU Lilian		*Abandon*
206.	KAGGESTAD Mads		*Abandon*
207.	LEQUATRE Geoffroy (Fra)		*Abandon*
208.	WIGGINS Bradley (Gbr)		*Abandon*

LAMPRE

No.	Rider	Place	Time
211.	BORTOLAMI Gianluca (Ita)	38th	+ 13'19"
212.	BALLAN Alessandro (Ita)		*Abandon*
213.	BOSSONI Paolo (Ita)		*Abandon*
214.	CARRARA Matteo (Ita)		*Abandon*
215.	CORTINOVIS Alessandro (Ita)	50th	+ 13'19"
216.	HAUPTMAN Andrej (Slo)		*Abandon*
217.	QUINZIATO Manuel (Ita)		*Abandon*
218.	VAINSTEINS Romans (Lat)	11st	+ 29"

BANKGIROLOTERIJ

No.	Rider	Place	Time
221.	ANDRESEN Allan Bo (Den)		*Abandon*
222.	BAK Lars Ytting (Den)	90th	+ 31'09"
223.	BLIJLEVENS Jeroen (Ned)		*Abandon*
224.	JOHANSEN Allan (Den)	62nd	+ 13'19"
226.	VAN DER VEN Remco (Ned)	81st	+ 31'09"
227.	VAN DER WAL Eelke (Ned)		*Abandon*
228.	VAN DULMEN Frank (Ned)		*Abandon*

RAGT Semences - MG ROVER

No.	Rider	Place	Time
231.	SEIGNEUR Eddy (Fra)		*Abandon*
232.	AUGER Guillaume (Fra)		*Abandon*
233.	BUFFAZ Mickaël (Fra)		*Abandon*
234.	DION Renaud (Fra)	85th	+ 31'09"
235.	LAURENT Christophe (Fra)	84th	+ 31'09"
236.	LUHOVYY Roman (Ukr)		*Abandon*
237.	MUTSCHLER Klaus (Ger)		*Abandon*
238.	THIBOUT Bruno (Fra)		*Abandon*

DOMINA VACANZE

No.	Rider	Place	Time
242.	BAZHENOV Alexandr (Rus)	75th	+ 14'58"
243.	CLINGER David (Usa)		*Abandon*
244.	DERGANC Martin (Slo)		*Abandon*
245.	FAILLI Francesco (Ita)		*Abandon*
246.	FISCHER Murillo (Bra)	40th	+ 13'19"
248.	NAUDUZS Andris (Lat)		*Abandon*

TOTAL OF POINTS UCI OBTAINED IN THE RACE

ALESSIO - BIANCHI	261 p.
CSC	252 p.
LOTTO - DOMO	210 p.
QUICK STEP - DAVITAMON	180 p.
FASSA BORTOLO	148 p.
Mr BOOKMAKER - PALMANS	140 p.
T.MOBILE	99 p.
US POSTAL	80 p.
LAMPRE	53 p.
LANDBOUWKREDIET - COLNAGO	48 p.
FDJEUX.COM	46 p.
AG2R Prévoyance	33 p.
SAECO	30 p.
CRÉDIT AGRICOLE	28 p.
RABOBANK	25 p.
Chocolade JACQUES-WINCOR NIXDORF	20 p.
BANKGIROLOTERIJ	15 p.
Brioches LA BOULANGÈRE	10 p.
DOMINA VACANZE	10 p.
PHONAK	10 p.
RAGT Semences - MG ROVER	10 p.
GEROLSTEINER	5 p.
ILLES BALEARS - BANESTO	5 p.
LIBERTY Seguros	0 p.

PAST WINNERS AT THE START — 6

Rider	Year(s)
MUSEEUW Johan	1996, 2000 &2002
BORTOLAMI Gianluca	1995 &1998
GUESDON Frédéric	1997
KNAVEN Servais	2001
TAFI Andrea	1999
VAN PETEGEM Peter	2003

RIDERS IN THE UCI TOP 100: 22

ROOKIES AT THE START (LESS THAN ONE YEAR AS A PROFESSIONAL): 14

3 YOUNGEST

Rider	Date of birth
FAILLI Francesco (Ita)	16/12/1983
SANCHEZ GIL Luis Leon (Esp)	23/11/1983
ROY Jérémy (Fra)	22/06/1983

3 OLDEST

Rider	Date of birth
DIERCKXSENS Ludo (Bel)	14/10/1964
MUSEEUW Johan (Bel)	13/10/1965
TAFI Andrea (Ita)	07/05/1966

Rebellin finds the key to success!

Often relegated to the minor places in one day races, Davide Rebellin has at last returned to winning form in a World Cup event, renewing a series of successes interrupted since almost seven years (he won the Clasica San sebastian and the Championnat de Zurich in 1997). Showing a good deal of cool headedness at the end of this 39th edition of the Amstel Gold Race, run in cool but dry conditions, Rebellin overtook the local favourite Michael Boogerd in the final run in. Boogerd recognising he could not trouble his on form rival settled for second place in his favourite race (the same went for the 2000 and 2003 races). Luckily he managed to win in 1999!

The young Belgian pros Johan van Summeren (Relax- Bodysol) and Jan Kuyckx (Vlaanderen - T Interim) know their only chance to shine in such a high profile race is to get up front early on. At the 15th kilometre there they are, in front, but in the company of the well established Erik Dekker. Seriously injured on the Milan – San Remo two years ago, the rider is only just getting back to his best form- he took the Tour de Drenthe a week earlier, following a difficult 2003 season. Just the same, the Rabobank rider soon understood that his presence in the leading group would bring about its demise. At the 40th kilometre he eases up and leaves the two youngsters to their adventure. This is also the moment chosen by two other outsiders, Peter Wuyts (Mr Bookmaker.com) and Alain van Katwijk (Bankgiroloterij) to go after the leading duo. These two needed a full 100 kms to realise their effort was in vain.

Up front, Kuyckx and van Summeren keep up the pace. Their lead at km 106 stretching to 10 mins 55 sec. Eighty kilometers later, Kuyckx is left behind on one of the 31 climbs of the day, but his rival is soon to suffer the same fate. In fact, at the 200 km mark, van Summeren is forced to a standstill by a mechanical incident and is overtaken by two men (Rolf Aldag and Karsten Kroon) just ahead of a greatly weakened peloton. Under the influence of the Fassa Bortolo team (perhaps working for Frank Vandenbroucke) and to a certain extent of Rabobank (Boogerd, Dekker, Freire) things soon take shape. Multiple attempts are made at a breakout. The most remarkable being Leon van Bon (Lotto Domo) but also Kolobnev (Domina Vacanze), Horrillo (quick step) and in particular his team mate Jurgen van Goolen (two attempts) and Marcus Zberg (Gerolsteiner), Sandy Casar (Fdjeux.com), the Danish champion Nicki Sorensen (CSC) and Verheyen (Chocolade Jacques).
The favourites, hungry for success, bide their time...

THE FAVOURITES GET GOING

One such is the German Matthias Kessler (T Mobile). He remembers that last year a group of strong men used the Eyserbosweg

Le Cauberg is invaded by an enthusiastic crowd from early in the morning. Just the same, on the first lap the battle has not yet commenced, it's a tightly packed peloton that begins the ascent of the mont du Limbourg.

(km 232) as the launch pad for an attack. Anticipating another such event he attacks himself at the 28th climb of the day with just a slight lead over his rivals. Things are hotting up behind. The Italian champion Paolo Bettini lights the fuse. Only a few manage to follow: Davide Rebellin, Michael Boogerd, Peter van Petegem, Danilo Di Luca... and Mathias Kessler caught half way up the climb. The next difficulty, le Fromberg comes only 4 kms later. The leaders attack this 800 metre hill with the throttle wide open. What a surprise! Paolo Bettini, the instigator of the attack is unable to follow the push of his compatriot Davide Rebellin. Only Michael Boogerd can stay with the leader. The two men have a lead of 37 sec as they plunge towards Valkenburg where the amstel Gold Race now ends. At the Red Flame the two men slow and the chasing group has them in its sights. Michael Boogerd, visibly the less confident of the two, fires up first. At 350 metres he begins the sprint on 53 x 17, not really ideal from such a slow speed on a steady climb! Rebellin draws level in the final metres and takes the win. Paolo Bettin gets the better of the following group and takes third place, whereas, a little further back, world Cup leader Steffen Wesemann reaches the line in a group including Erik Zabel and Oscar Freire. The latter, scoring one point less than Wesemann misses the chance to wear the Rainbow jersey in the Liege-Bastogne-Liege the following week.

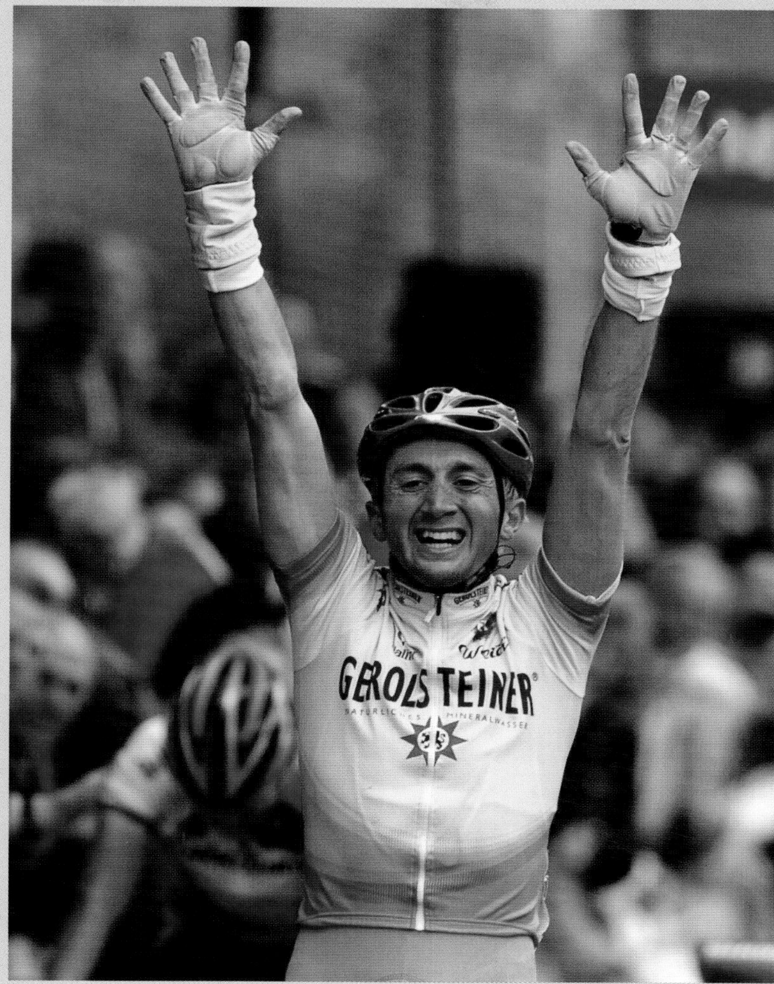

It's a confident Davide Rebellin who prepares his ascention of the Cauberg. Michael Boogerd sprints for the line too early and in the wrong gear and is soon overtaken by the Italian.

REBELLIN, MORE OF A WINNER THAN YOU MAY THINK!

The springtime Classics which had favoured the outsiders - with the exception of the Milan- San Remo, found a more typical outcome in this Amstel Gold Race. Is that to say that the only Dutch portion of the World Cup is too predictable? That at least was the impression given by Michael Boogert a few days before the race. Certainly, everyone expected the previously in form riders to take the honours. Vinokourov, Bartoli and Vandenbroucke stayed out of the limelight throughout the day, but a winner such as Davide Rebellin was no surprise. Taking a closer look at his record, he has clocked up more than thirty wins since turning pro in September 1992. Born in San Bonifacio in 1971, the rider, described by his first team manager, Giancarlo Ferretti, as an altar boy (the young David intended to take the cloth in his teenage years) exploded into the cycling elite in 1994, finishing 5th in the Amstel Gold Race, won that year by Johan Museeuw. He followed this with a top twenty finish in the Giro and already sensed that his future success would be in one day races or one week events rather than the big tours. Forth in the following year's Milan - San Remo and 5th in the 1996 Tour of Lombardie wearing the Polti jersey, he continued to build his reputation. That said, he still hadn't quite given up on the three week tours as was evident in his 6th and 7th places in the Giro and the Vuelta. To everybody's surprise he turned to a French team in 1997.The newly formed Francaise des Jeux. Despite his two World Cup successes in San Sebastian and Zurich, he left the Madiot brothers after a mediocre season. Back home with Polti, the victories began to roll in: the Tour of Venetie - three years running, the 3 Vallées Varésines,the Tour du Haut Var, the Tour Mediterranéen, the Tour du frioul, but all this was overshadowed by a prolific 2001 season, with 11 wins and near misses in Liege - Bastogne - Liege (2nd) and the Clasica San Sebastian (3rd). Another second place in the Tour of Lombardie confirmed his predisposition to narrowly miss the ultimate prize but not the podium. On the evening of this 18th april Davide Rebellin can boast a great record in World Cup events: 9 podiums and 28 top ten finishes! A little like Raymond Poulidor who, remember, clocked up more wins than second places at the end of his career, the Italian has a reputation as a well placed rider but rare winner. ■

184 Competitors

T-MOBILE

No.	Rider	Place	Time
1.	VINOKOUROV Alexandre (Kaz)	27th	+ 1'28"
2.	ALDAG Rolf (Ger)	43rd	+ 3'43"
3.	IVANOV Serguei (Rus)	**8th**	+ 52"
4.	KESSLER Matthias (Ger)	**6th**	+ 26"
5.	KLIER Andreas (Ger)		*Abandon*
6.	NARDELLO Daniele (Ita)	65th	+ 6'13"
7.	WESEMANN Steffen (Ger)	20th	+ 1'16"
8.	ZABEL Erik (Ger)	16th	+ 1'16"

AG2R Prévoyance

No.	Rider	Place	Time
11.	BROCHARD Laurent (Fra)	25th	+ 1'23"
12.	CHAURREAU Iñigo (Esp)		*Abandon*
13.	GOUBERT Stéphane (Fra)		*Abandon*
14.	KRIVTSOV Yuriy (Ukr)	79th	+ 11'31"
15.	LAIDOUN Julien (Fra)		*Abandon*
16.	SCANLON Mark (Irl)	86th	+ 11'44"

ALESSIO - BIANCHI

No.	Rider	Place	Time
21.	BERTOLINI Alessandro (Ita)	36th	+ 3'43"
22.	IVANOV Ruslan (Mda)	99th	+ 12'04"
23.	MIHOLJEVIC Vladimir (Cro)	28th	+ 1'28"
24.	MORENI Cristian (Ita)	50th	+ 3'55"
25.	PELLIZOTTI Franco (Ita)	30th	+ 1'28"
26.	NOE' Andrea (Ita)	47th	+ 3'55"
27.	RASTELLI Ellis (Ita)	68th	+ 6'13"
28.	TAFI Andrea (Ita)		*Abandon*

DOMINA VACANZE

No.	Rider	Place	Time
41.	BAZHENOV Alexandr (Rus)	78th	+ 11'23"
42.	GENTILI Massimiliano (Ita)	59th	+ 6'13"
43.	GIUNTI Massimo (Ita)	81st	+ 11'44"
44.	FAILLI Francesco (Ita)	80th	+ 11'44"
45.	KOLOBNEV Alexandr (Rus)	64th	+ 6'13"
46.	SCARPONI Michele (Ita)	22nd	+ 1'16"
47.	SIMEONI Filippo (Ita)	101st	+ 12'04"
48.	VALOTI Paolo (Ita)	37th	+ 3'43"

FDJEUX.COM

No.	Rider	Place	Time
51.	COOKE Baden (Aus)		*Abandon*
52.	CASAR Sandy (Fra)	74th	+ 8'37"
53.	EISEL Bernhard (Aut)		*Abandon*
54.	GILBERT Philippe (Bel)	34th	+ 3'43"
55.	McGEE Bradley (Aus)		*Abandon*
56.	MENGIN Christophe (Fra)		*Abandon*
57.	MOUREY Francis (Fra)		*Abandon*
58.	LÖVKVIST Thomas (Swe)		*Abandon*

FASSA BORTOLO

No.	Rider	Place	Time
61.	CANCELLARA Fabian (Sui)	53rd	+ 3'55"
62.	CODOL Massimo (Ita)		*Abandon*
63.	FLECHA Juan Antonio (Esp)	69th	+ 6'13"
64.	KIRCHEN Kim (Lux)	100th	+ 12'04"
65.	PETITO Roberto (Ita)	95th	+ 11'44"
66.	POZZATO Filippo (Ita)	75th	+ 9'15"
67.	SACCHI Fabio (Ita)		*Abandon*
68.	VANDENBROUCKE Frank (Bel)	18th	+ 1'16"

GEROLSTEINER

No.	Rider	Place	Time
71.	FARESIN Gianni (Ita)		*Abandon*
72.	REBELLIN Davide (Ita)	**1st**	**6h 23'44"**
73.	SCHOLZ Ronny (Ger)		*Abandon*
74.	SERPELLINI Marco (Ita)		*Abandon*
75.	WEGMANN Fabian (Ger)	57th	+ 6'13"
76.	WROLICH Peter (Aut)	82nd	+ 11'44"
77.	ZBERG Beat (Sui)		*Abandon*
78.	ZBERG Marcus (Sui)	40th	+ 3'43"

Illes BALEARS - BANESTO

No.	Rider	Place	Time
81.	COLOM Antonio (Esp)		*Abandon*
82.	GUTIERREZ PALACIOS J. Ivan (Esp)	76th	+ 9'55"
83.	HORRACH Joan (Esp)		*Abandon*
84.	LASTRAS Pablo (Esp)	45th	+ 3'43"
85.	OSA Unai (Esp)		*Abandon*
86.	REYNES Vicente (Esp)		*Abandon*

LAMPRE

No.	Rider	Place	Time
91.	BORTOLAMI Gianluca (Ita)	89th	+ 11'44"
92.	BARBERO Sergio (Ita)		*Abandon*
93.	BALLAN Alessandro (Ita)	90th	+ 11'44"
94.	CORTINOVIS Alessandro (Ita)		*Abandon*
95.	HAUPTMAN Andrej (Slo)	61st	+ 6'13"
96.	RIGHI Daniele (Ita)	96th	+ 11'44"
97.	BOSSONI Paolo (Ita)	88th	+ 11'44"
98.	VAINSTEINS Romans (Lat)	54th	+ 3'55"

LIBERTY Seguros

No.	Rider	Place	Time
101.	BARANOWSKI Dariusz (Pol)	84th	+ 11'44"
102.	CARUSO Gianpaolo (Ita)	**10th**	+ 55"
103.	RAMIREZ ABEJA Javier (Esp)	87th	+ 11'44"
104.	SANCHEZ GIL Luis Leon (Esp)	77th	+ 9'55"
105.	SERRANO Marcos (Esp)	19th	+ 1'16"
106.	VICIOSO Angel (Esp)	51st	+ 3'55"

PHONAK

No.	Rider	Place	Time
111.	CAMENZIND Oscar (Sui)	11st	+ 57"
112.	ELMIGER Martin (Sui)	23rd	+ 1'16"
113.	GRABSCH Bert (Ger)		*Abandon*
114.	MURN Uros (Slo)	91st	+ 11'44"
115.	PEREIRO Oscar (Esp)	26th	+ 1'23"
116.	RAST Gregory (Sui)	52nd	+ 3'55"
117.	USOV Alexandre (Blr)		*Abandon*

QUICK STEP - DAVITAMON

No.	Rider	Place	Time
121.	BETTINI Paolo (Ita)	**3rd**	+ 18"
122.	BRAMATI Davide (Ita)	93rd	+ 11'44"
123.	HORRILLO Pedro (Esp)	33rd	+ 3'43"
124.	PAOLINI Luca (Ita)	12nd	+ 1'00"
125.	ROGERS Michael (Aus)		*Abandon*
126.	TANKINK Bram (Ned)	48th	+ 3'55"
127.	VAN GOOLEN Jurgen (Bel)	42nd	+ 3'43"
128.	ZANINI Stefano (Ita)	62nd	+ 6'13"

RABOBANK

No.	Rider	Place	Time
131.	BOOGERD Michael (Ned)	**2nd**	+ 1"
132.	DEKKER Erik (Ned)	**7th**	+ 41"
133.	FREIRE Oscar (Esp)	14th	+ 1'16"
134.	WAUTERS Marc (Bel)		*Abandon*
135.	DEN BAKKER Maarten (Ned)		*Abandon*
136.	DE JONGH Steven (Ned)		*Abandon*
137.	KROON Karsten (Ned)	46th	+ 3'55"
138.	LOTZ Marc (Ned)	39th	+ 3'43"

SAECO

No.	Rider	Place	Time
141.	DI LUCA Danilo (Ita)	**4th**	+ 18"
142.	BALDUCCI Gabriele (Ita)		*Abandon*
143.	CASAGRANDA Stefano (Ita)		*Abandon*
144.	CELESTINO Mirko (Ita)	**9th**	+ 53"
145.	MAZZOLENI Eddy (Ita)	17th	+ 1'16"
146.	PETROV Evgueni (Rus)		*Abandon*
147.	SABALIAUSKAS Marius (Ltu)		*Abandon*
148.	SPEZIALETTI Alessandro (Ita)		*Abandon*

CSC

No.	Rider	Place	Time
151.	SCHLECK Frank (Lux)	66th	+ 6'13"
153.	ARVESEN Kurt-Asle (Nor)	63rd	+ 6'13"
154.	CALVENTE Manuel (Esp)		*Abandon*
155.	BLAUDZUN Michael (Den)	41st	+ 3'43"
156.	BARTOLI Michele (Ita)	15th	+ 1'16"
157.	SØRENSEN Nicki (Den)	21st	+ 1'16"
158.	GOUSSEV Vladimir (Rus)		*Abandon*

US POSTAL - BERRY FLOOR

No.	Rider	Place	Time
161.	AZEVEDO José (Por)	31st	+ 1'44"
162.	BARRY Michael (Can)	35th	+ 3'43"
163.	DEVOLDER Stijn (Bel)		*Abandon*
164.	HESJEDAL Ryder (Can)		*Abandon*
165.	LANDIS Floyd (Usa)	29th	+ 1'28"
166.	JOACHIM Benoît (Lux)	67th	+ 6'13"
167.	PEÑA Victor Hugo (Col)		*Abandon*
168.	RUBIERA José Luis (Esp)	32nd	+ 1'54"

LOTTO - DOMO

No.	Rider	Place	Time
171.	VAN PETEGEM Peter (Bel)	**5th**	+ 18"
172.	MERCKX Axel (Bel)	13rd	+ 1'12"
173.	VAN BON Leon (Ned)	72nd	+ 6'56"
174.	HOSTE Leif (Bel)		*Abandon*
175.	VANSEVENANT Wim (Bel)		*Abandon*
176.	MOERENHOUT Koos (Ned)	58th	+ 6'13"
177.	VIERHOUTEN Aart (Ned)	70th	+ 6'13"
178.	MARICHAL Thierry (Bel)		*Abandon*

BANKGIROLOTERIJ

No.	Rider	Place	Time
181.	BOS Marco (Ned)		*Abandon*
182.	TEN DAM Laurens (Ned)		*Abandon*
183.	VAN DULMEN Frank (Ned)		*Abandon*
184.	ENGELS Addy (Ned)		*Abandon*
185.	JOHANSEN Allan (Den)		*Abandon*
186.	VAN KATWIJK Alain (Ned)		*Abandon*
187.	PETERSEN Jørgen Bo (Den)		*Abandon*
188.	VAN DER VEN Remco (Ned)		*Abandon*

Chocolade JACQUES - WINCOR NIXDORF

No.	Rider	Place	Time
191.	VAN DE WALLE Jurgen (Bel)		*Abandon*
192.	VERHEYEN Geert (Bel)	38th	+ 3'43"
193.	HIEMSTRA Bert (Ned)	73rd	+ 7'50"
194.	KOERTS Jans (Ned)		*Abandon*
195.	ABAKOUMOV Igor (Bel)		*Abandon*
196.	PEERS Chris (Bel)	60th	+ 6'13"
197.	VAN VELZEN Jan (Ned)	92nd	+ 11'44"
198.	VOSKAMP Bart (Ned)		*Abandon*

DE NARDI

No.	Rider	Place	Time
201.	HONCHAR Serhiy (Ukr)	24th	+ 1'16"
202.	CADAMURO Simone (Ita)	83rd	+ 11'44"
203.	GASPARRE Graziano (Ita)		*Abandon*
204.	GOBBI Michele (Ita)		*Abandon*
205.	JURCO Matej (Svk)		*Abandon*
206.	MIORIN Devis (Ita)		*Abandon*
207.	NURITDINOV Rafael (Uzb)		*Abandon*
208.	VANOTTI Alessandro (Ita)		*Abandon*

Paolo Bettini, Peter van Petegem, Matthias Kessler and Danilo Di Luca (hidden) couldn't follow the acceleration of Rebellin and Boogerd in the Fromberg. Their efforts were to be in vain.

The duel between Boogerd, who did more than his share of the work, and Rebellin, who saves his energy.

LANDBOUWKREDIET - COLNAGO

211.	POPOVYCH Yaroslav (Ukr)	71st	+ 6'46"
212.	DUMA Vladimir (Ukr)		*Abandon*
213.	GASPERONI Cristian (Ita)		*Abandon*
214.	DIERCKXSENS Ludo (Bel)		*Abandon*
215.	SIJMENS Nico (Bel)	49th	+ 3'55"
216.	VERSTREPEN Johan (Bel)		*Abandon*
217.	VAN BONDT Geert (Bel)	97th	+ 12'04"
218.	STREEL Marc (Bel)		*Abandon*

Mr BOOKMAKER.COM - PALMANS

221.	COENEN Johan (Bel)	56th	+ 6'13"
222.	THIJS Erwin (Bel)	55th	+ 6'13"
223.	HAMMOND Roger (Gbr)	85th	+ 11'44"
224.	HUNT Jeremy (Gbr)		Abandon
225.	PLANCKAERT Jo (Bel)		*Abandon*
226.	VAN DE WOUWER Kurt (Bel)		*Abandon*
227.	VAN HAECKE Michel (Bel)		*Abandon*
228.	WUYTS Peter (Bel)		*Abandon*

RELAX - BODYSOL

231.	BURGOS Nacor (Esp)		*Abandon*
232.	FLORENCIO Xavier (Esp)		*Abandon*
233.	MATTAN Nico (Bel)	94th	+ 11'44"
234.	ROESEMS Bert (Bel)		*Abandon*
235.	MARTINEZ TRINIDAD Alberto (Esp)		*Abandon*
236.	SCHEUNEMAN Niels (Ned)		*Abandon*
237.	VAN SUMMEREN Johan (Bel)		*Abandon*
238.	VAN HECKE Preben (Bel)		*Abandon*

VLAANDEREN - T INTERIM

241.	DEMEYERE Geoffrey (Bel)		*Abandon*
242.	DE SCHROODER Benny (Bel)		*Abandon*
243.	MERTENS Pieter (Bel)	98th	+ 12'04"
244.	PEETERS Jef (Bel)		*Abandon*
245.	VAN HUFFEL Wim (Bel)	44th	+ 3'43"
246.	VEUCHELEN Frederik (Bel)		*Abandon*
247.	WILLEMS Frederik (Bel)		*Abandon*
248.	KUYCKX Jan (Bel)		*Abandon*

TOTAL OF POINTS UCI OBTAINED IN THE RACE

RABOBANK	263 points
GEROLSTEINER	255 points
T.MOBILE	204 points
QUICK STEP - DAVITAMON	184 points
SAECO	ditto
LOTTO-DOMO	146 points
LIBERTY Seguros	87 points
PHONAK	74 points
CSC	58 points
DOMINA VACANZE	48 points
FASSA BORTOLO	46 points
ALESSIO - BIANCHI	37 points
LAMPRE	30 points
US POSTAL	26 points
AG2R Prévoyance	20 points
Chocolade JACQUES-WINCOR NIXDORF	ditto
DE NARDI	16 points
LANDBOUWKREDIET - COLNAGO	15 points
Mr BOOKMAKER-PALMANS	ditto
FDJEUX.COM	10 points
ILLES BALEARS - BANESTO	ditto
VLAANDEREN - T INTERIM	ditto
RELAX-BODYSOL	5 points
BANKGIROLOTERIJ	0 point

PAST WINNERS AT THE START	*5*
MUSEEUW Johan	1993, 1995 &1998
VAN PETEGEM Peter	1999 & 2003
BORTOLAMI Gianluca	2001
BARTOLI Michele	1998
DURAND Jacky	1992

RIDERS IN THE UCI TOP 100: ***40***

ROOKIES AT THE START (LESS THAN ONE YEAR AS A PROFESSIONAL): ***12***

3 YOUNGEST

SANCHEZ GIL Luis Leon (Esp)	23/11/1983
SANCHEZ Fabien (Fra)	30/03/1983
VAN HECKE Preben (Bel)	09/07/1982

3 OLDEST

DIERCKXSENS Ludo (Bel)	14/10/1964
MUSEEUW Johan (Bel)	13/10/1965
EKIMOV Viatcheslav (Rus)	04/02/1966

CLASSIFICATION

1.	Davide Rebellin (Ita)	GST	6h23'44"
2.	Michael Boogerd (Ned)	RAB	+ 1"
3.	Paolo Bettini (Ita)	QSD	+ 18"
4.	Danilo Di Luca (Ita)	SAE	s.t
5.	Peter van Petegem (Bel)	LOT	s.t
6.	Matthias Kessler (Ger)	TMO	+ 26"
7.	Erik Dekker (Ned)	RAB	+ 41"
8.	Serguei Ivanov (Rus)	TMO	+ 52"
9.	Mirko Celestino (Ita)	SAE	+ 53"
10.	Giampaolo Caruso (Ita)	LST	+ 55"

REBELLIN AT SPEED

Fresh from his triumph in the Amstel Gold Race three days earlier, Davide Rebellin took control of the Flèche Wallonne in a record time. At an average speed of more than 44kph (exactly 44.08), the Gerolsteiner team, at the heart of which the veteran Gianni Faresin once again worked like a titan, placed the now unbeatable Rebellin in a perfect position at the foot of the Mur de Huy in the company of forty other riders. At the steepest part of the climb, the Italian pulled out from the slipstream of his last rival, Danilo Di Luca, to take a second major victory in his 2004 season. The work of a master.

No matter that the Flèche Wallonne doesn't count for the world Cup,many a rider at the start (Charleroi for the last few years) wanted to take the race. This always works wonders. Jan Ullrich, in preparation for the Tour de France was not seeking this goal. The race itself proved this point. The first ascention of the Mur de Huy, after 66 kms of the race, is already fatal for him. Relegated to a position a minute adrift of the peloton, the German doesn't fight for long and soon after announces he will pull out of the Liege - Bastogne - Liege he had intended to race. He has two months to get in to form... The extremely rapid pace from the start dashed the hopes of many riders hoping it would be their day. However, just before the second time around for the Mur de Huy, a group containing Oscar Pereiro, Sandy Casar, Juan Antonio Flecha and Unai Etxeb arria manage to open a small gap, only to see it disappear at the summit.
At 70 kms from the line the race is still wide open. The first serious breakaway is the work of Jerome Pineau (La Boulangere), soon to be joined by the young Jurgen van den Broeck (US postal) and Alessandro Bertolini (Alessio). Without extending their lead, the group stay ahead for around twenty kilometers before being joined by Kolobnev (Domina Vacanze), Elmiger (Phonak) Vicioso (Liberty seguros) and de Weert (Rabobank). But the long and difficult climb at Bohissau is too much for Constantino Zaballa (Saunier Duval) and Philippe Gilbert (Fdjeux.com), the chasing duo, as well as the leaders,reabsorbed soon after the summit.

ERIK DEKKER THE ILLUSIONIST

All that now remains to sort out the winners and losers is the Cote d'Ahin and the climb to Huy. Anticipating the difficulties to come, Erik Dekker makes his move 26 kms from the finish. The effort of the veteran Gianni Faresin, working for his leader Davide Rebellin deprives the Rabobank rider the possibility of tasting the fruits of his labours. He is caught on the first slopes of Cote de Ahin where a counter attack is led by Alexandre Vinokourov, Samuel Sanchez and Kim Kirchen. The trio receives the help of Mirko Celestino as they swoop towards Huy before a reaction from thirty riders as they enter the town. Kloden (T Mobile) raises the pace to discourage any attempt at attack before leaving his leader Matthias Kessler to wind things up in the final 500 metres. The German is soon passed though by a particularly incisive Danilo Di Luca who just the same cannot shake off Davide Rebellin. With 100 metres to go the Florentine rider races past his compatriot to mark a second major success in four days! ■

193 Competitors

SAECO

1.	DI LUCA Danilo (Ita)	**2nd**	+ 3"
2.	CELESTINO Mirko (Ita)	35th	+ 1'20"
3.	GLOMSER Gerit (Aut)	111st	+ 10'46"
4.	MAZZOLENI Eddy (Ita)	38th	+ 1'40"
5.	PETROV Evgueni (Rus)		*Abandon*
6.	SABALIAUSKAS Marius (Ltu)	117th	+ 11'21"
7.	SPEZIALETTI Alessandro (Ita)		*Abandon*
8.	STANGELJ Gorazd (Slo)		*Abandon*

CSC

11.	BARTOLI Michele (Ita)	73rd	+ 2'42"
12.	ARVESEN Kurt-Asle (Nor)	75th	+ 2'48"
13.	BASSO Ivan (Ita)	30th	+ 54"
14.	BLAUDZUN Michael (Den)		*Abandon*
15.	LUTTENBERGER Peter (Aut)	74th	+ 2'42"
16.	SASTRE Carlos (Esp)		*Abandon*
17.	SCHLECK Frank (Lux)	94th	+ 9'26"
18.	SØRENSEN Nicki (Den)	15th	+ 22"

RABOBANK

21.	FREIRE Oscar (Esp)	32nd	+ 1'00"
22.	DE WEERT Kevin (Bel)		*Abandon*
23.	DEKKER Erik (Ned)	26th	+ 47"
24.	DEN BAKKER Maarten (Ned)		*Abandon*
25.	LEIPHEIMER Levy (Usa)	80th	+ 5'15"
26.	LOTZ Marc (Ned)		*Abandon*
27.	MUTSAARS Ronald (Ned)		*Abandon*
28.	VENEBERG Thorwald (Ned)		*Abandon*

QUICK STEP - DAVITAMON

31.	BETTINI Paolo (Ita)		*Abandon*
32.	BRAMATI Davide (Ita)		*Abandon*
33.	NUYENS Nick (Bel)	54th	+ 1'53"
34.	PAOLINI Luca (Ita)		*Abandon*
35.	ROGERS Michael (Aus)		*Abandon*
36.	SINKEWITZ Patrik (Ger)	21st	+ 33"
37.	TANKINK Bram (Ned)	53rd	+ 1'53"
38.	VAN GOOLEN Jurgen (Bel)	50th	+ 1'53"

T-MOBILE

41.	ULLRICH Jan (Ger)		*Abandon*
42.	AERTS Mario (Bel)		*Abandon*
44.	GUERINI Giuseppe (Ita)	87th	+ 6'14"
45.	KESSLER Matthias (Ger)	**3rd**	+ 9"
46.	KLÖDEN Andreas (Ger)	**6th**	+ 18"
47.	VINOKOUROV Alexandre (Kaz)	**5th**	+ 16"
48.	WERNER Christian (Ger)	83rd	+ 6'03"
49.	IVANOV Serguei (Rus)	98th	+ 10'18"

GEROLSTEINER

51.	REBELLIN Davide (Ita)	**1st**	**4h 31'33"**
52.	FARESIN Gianni (Ita)	81st	+ 6'03"
53.	ORDOWSKI Volker (Ger)		*Abandon*
54.	SERPELLINI Marco (Ita)		*Abandon*
55.	STRAUSS Marcel (Sui)	118th	+ 11'22"
56.	TOTSCHNIG Georg (Aut)	46th	+ 1'43"
57.	WEGMANN Fabian (Ger)	13rd	+ 22"
58.	ZBERG Marcus (Sui)	**9th**	+ 20"

LOTTO - DOMO

61.	VERBRUGGHE Rik (Bel)	18th	+ 29"
62.	BAGUET Serge (Bel)	23rd	+ 40"
63.	BRANDT Christophe (Bel)	44th	+ 1'43"
64.	D'HOLLANDER Glen (Bel)		*Abandon*
65.	MARICHAL Thierry (Bel)	89th	+ 6'14"
66.	MERCKX Axel (Bel)	29th	+ 53"
67.	MOERENHOUT Koos (Ned)		*Abandon*
68.	WADECKI Piotr (Pol)	64th	+ 2'08"

US POSTAL - BERRY FLOOR

71.	AZEVEDO José (Por)	28th	+ 49"
72.	BARRY Michael (Can)	41st	+ 1'43"
73.	BELTRAN Manuel (Esp)	**10th**	+ 20"
74.	HESJEDAL Ryder (Can)		*Abandon*
75.	LANDIS Floyd (Usa)	25th	+ 43"
76.	NOVAL Benjamin (Esp)	57th	+ 1'58"
77.	RUBIERA José Luis (Esp)	56th	+ 1'58"
78.	VAN DEN BROECK Jurgen (Bel)	84th	+ 6'04"

FASSA BORTOLO

81.	VANDENBROUCKE Frank (Bel)	**7th**	+ 18"
82.	CIONI Dario (Ita)	100th	+ 10'22"
83.	CODOL Massimo (Ita)	51st	+ 1'53"
84.	FLECHA Juan Antonio (Esp)		*Abandon*
85.	KIRCHEN Kim (Lux)	34th	+ 1'20"
86.	PETITO Roberto (Ita)	112nd	+ 10'48"
87.	SACCHI Fabio (Ita)		*Abandon*

Having disposed of Michael Boogerd three days earlier at the end of the Amstel Gold Race, Davide Rebellin does the same to his compatriot Danilo Di Luca in the last struggling metres on the Mur de Huy, marking the finish of the Flèche Wallon these last ten years. For the leader of the Gerolsteiner team the victorious charge continues...

Illes BALEARS - BANESTO

92.	COLOM Antonio (Esp)		*Abandon*
93.	GUTIERREZ PALACIOS J. Ivan (Esp)	20th	+ 33″
94.	HORRACH Joan (Esp)	103rd	+ 10′27″
95.	LASTRAS Pablo (Esp)	58th	+ 1′58″
96.	REYNES Vicente (Esp)		*Abandon*

SAUNIER DUVAL - PRODIR

102.	BERTOGLIATI Rubens (Sui)	66th	+ 2′10″
103.	JEKER Fabian (Sui)	82nd	+ 6′03″
104.	MORI Manuele (Ita)	42nd	+ 1′43″
105.	RODRIGUEZ OLIVER Joaquin (Esp)	72nd	+ 2′36″
106.	VENTOSO Francisco (Esp)		*Abandon*
107.	ZABALLA Constantino (Esp)	17th	+ 27″
108.	ZAUGG Oliver (Sui)		*Abandon*
109.	GOMEZ Angel "Litu" (Esp)		*Abandon*

ALESSIO - BIANCHI

111.	NOE' Andrea (Ita)	19th	+ 33″
113.	BERTOLINI Alessandro (Ita)	61st	+ 2′04″
114.	IVANOV Ruslan (Mda)		*Abandon*
115.	MIHOLJEVIC Vladimir (Cro)	97th	+ 10′18″
116.	MORENI Cristian (Ita)	36th	+ 1′20″
117.	PELLIZOTTI Franco (Ita)	11st	+ 22″
118.	RASTELLI Ellis (Ita)	71st	+ 2′28″

EUSKALTEL - EUSKADI

121.	ETXEBARRIA David (Esp)	33rd	+ 1′05″
122.	ALBIZU Joseba (Esp)	96th	+ 9′43″
123.	ARTETXE Mikel (Esp)	115th	+ 11′09″
124.	CAMAÑO Iker (Esp)	105th	+ 10′32″
125.	ETXEBARRIA Unai (Ven)	39th	+ 1′42″
126.	ISASI Iñaki (Esp)	86th	+ 6′06″
127.	LANDALUZE Iñigo (Esp)	24th	+ 43″
128.	SANCHEZ Samuel (Esp)	12nd	+ 22″

LIBERTY Seguros

131.	SERRANO Marcos (Esp)	**8th**	+ 18″
132.	BARANOWSKI Dariusz (Pol)	106th	+ 10′32″
133.	CARUSO Gianpaolo (Ita)	27th	+ 49″
134.	GIL Koldo (Esp)		*Abandon*
135.	HRUSKA Jan (Cze)	52nd	+ 1′53″
136.	RAMIREZ ABEJA Javier (Esp)	90th	+ 6′14″
137.	SANCHEZ GIL Luis Leon (Esp)	88th	+ 6′14″
138.	VICIOSO Angel (Esp)	37th	+ 1′40″

Mr BOOKMAKER.COM - PALMANS

141.	COENEN Johan (Bel)	55th	+ 1′53″
142.	DAY Ben (Aus)		*Abandon*
143.	GABRIEL Frédéric (Fra)	109th	+ 10′34″
144.	LEUKEMANS Björn (Bel)	16th	+ 27″
145.	RENDERS Jens (Bel)		*Abandon*
146.	THIJS Erwin (Bel)	99th	+ 10′19″
147.	VAN DE WOUWER Kurt (Bel)	62nd	+ 2′04″
148.	WUYTS Peter (Bel)		*Abandon*

AG2R Prévoyance

151.	BROCHARD Laurent (Fra)	45th	+ 1′43″
152.	AGNOLUTTO Christophe (Fra)		*Abandon*
153.	ASTARLOZA Mikel (Esp)		*Abandon*
154.	CHAURREAU Iñigo (Esp)		*Abandon*
155.	GOUBERT Stéphane (Fra)		*Abandon*
156.	KRIVTSOV Yuriy (Ukr)	78th	+ 4′35″
157.	LAIDOUN Julien (Fra)		*Abandon*
158.	TURPIN Ludovic (Fra)	113rd	+ 10′48″

FDJEUX.COM

161.	GILBERT Philippe (Bel)	69th	+ 2′23″
162.	BICHOT Freddy (Fra)		*Abandon*
163.	CASAR Sandy (Fra)	40th	+ 1′43″
164.	FRITSCH Nicolas (Fra)	70th	+ 2′23″
165.	McGEE Bradley (Aus)	95th	+ 9′28″
166.	ROBIN Jean-Cyril (Fra)		*Abandon*
167.	VAUGRENARD Benoît (Fra)		*Abandon*
168.	VOGONDY Nicolas (Fra)	110th	+ 10′39″

PHONAK

171.	HAMILTON Tyler (Usa)	31st	+ 56″
173.	CAMENZIND Oscar (Sui)	92nd	+ 7′46″
174.	ELMIGER Martin (Sui)	93rd	+ 7′46″
175.	GRABSCH Bert (Ger)	101st	+ 10′22″
176.	GUTIERREZ CATALUÑA J. Enrique (Esp)		*Abandon*
177.	PEREIRO Oscar (Esp)	47th	+ 1′50″
178.	RAST Gregory (Sui)		*Abandon*
180.	GONZALEZ CAPILLA Santos (Esp)		*Abandon*

Brioches LA BOULANGÈRE

181.	ROUS Didier (Fra)	60th	+ 1′58″
182.	BENETEAU Walter (Fra)		*Abandon*
183.	BOUYER Franck (Fra)	107th	+ 10′32″
184.	CHARTEAU Anthony (Fra)		*Abandon*
185.	HARY Maryan (Fra)		*Abandon*
186.	LEFÈVRE Laurent (Fra)	108th	+ 10′34″
187.	PICHON Mickaël (Fra)		*Abandon*
188.	PINEAU Jérôme (Fra)	79th	+ 4′40″

LANDBOUWKREDIET - COLNAGO

191.	POPOVYCH Yaroslav (Ukr)	14th	+ 22″
192.	DE WAELE Bert (Bel)	43rd	+ 1′43″
193.	DUMA Vladimir (Ukr)		*Abandon*
194.	GASPERONI Cristian (Ita)		*Abandon*
195.	MONFORT Maxime (Bel)	116th	+ 11′19″
196.	SIJMENS Nico (Bel)		*Abandon*
198.	VERSTREPEN Johan (Bel)		*Abandon*

Chocolade JACQUES - WINCOR NIXDORF

201.	ARDILA Mauricio (Col)	102nd	+ 10′24″
202.	BRARD Florent (Fra)		*Abandon*
203.	PIATEK Zbigniew (Pol)		*Abandon*
204.	VAN DE WALLE Jurgen (Bel)	85th	+ 6′04″
205.	VAN VELZEN Jan (Ned)		*Abandon*
206.	VERHEYEN Geert (Bel)	49th	+ 1′51″
207.	VOSKAMP Bart (Ned)		*Abandon*
210.	BELOHVOSCIKS Raivis (Lat)		*Abandon*

CRÉDIT AGRICOLE

211.	MOREAU Christophe (Fra)		*Abandon*
212.	BOTCHAROV Alexandre (Rus)	48th	+ 1′51″
213.	FEDRIGO Pierrick (Fra)		*Abandon*
214.	HALGAND Patrice (Fra)		*Abandon*
215.	KASHECHKIN Andrey (Kaz)	65th	+ 2′08″
216.	LE MEVEL Christophe (Fra)		*Abandon*
217.	POILVET Benoît (Fra)	104th	+ 10′30″
218.	SALMON Benoît (Fra)	91st	+ 6′14″

LAMPRE

221.	VAINSTEINS Romans (Lat)		*Abandon*
222.	BALLAN Alessandro (Ita)		*Abandon*
223.	BARBERO Sergio (Ita)		*Abandon*
224.	BOSSONI Paolo (Ita)		*Abandon*
226.	PINOTTI Marco (Ita)		*Abandon*
227.	RIGHI Daniele (Ita)	22nd	+ 35″
228.	SCOTTO D'ABUSCO Michele (Ita)	63rd	+ 2′04″
230.	BORTOLAMI Gianluca (Ita)		*Abandon*

Vini CALDIROLA - NOBILI Rubinetterie

231.	BEUCHAT Roger (Sui)	77th	+ 3′24″
232.	CELLI Luca (Ita)		*Abandon*
233.	CHEULA Gianpaolo (Ita)		Abandon
234.	MASCIARELLI Simone (Ita)	114th	+ 10′55″
235.	MASON Oscar (Ita)	68th	+ 2′21″
236.	MILESI Marco (Ita)		*Abandon*
237.	ZAMPIERI Steve (Sui)	119th	+ 11′29″

DOMINA VACANZE

241.	SCARPONI Michele (Ita)	**4th**	+ 12″
242.	BAZHENOV Alexandr (Rus)		*Abandon*
243.	FAILLI Francesco (Ita)		*Abandon*
244.	GENTILI Massimiliano (Ita)	67th	+ 2′13″
245.	GIUNTI Massimo (Ita)	76th	+ 3′11″
246.	KOLOBNEV Alexandr (Rus)	59th	+ 1′58″
247.	SIMEONI Filippo (Ita)		*Abandon*
248.	VALOTI Paolo (Ita)		*Abandon*

TOTAL OF POINTS UCI OBTAINED IN THE RACE

GEROLSTEINER	243 points
T.MOBILE	221 points
SAECO	120 points
DOMINA VACANZE	78 points
FASSA BORTOLO	57 points
LIBERTY Seguros	54 points
US POSTAL	49 points
ALESSIO - BIANCHI	47 points
EUSKALTEL - EUSKADI	44 points
LOTTO - DOMO	29 points
LANDBOUWKREDIET - COLNAGO	27 points
CSC	24 points
SAUNIER DUVAL - PRODIR	19 points
Mr BOOKMAKER - PALMANS	16 points
QUICK STEP - DAVITAMON	14 points
ILLES BALEARS - BANESTO	10 points
PHONAK	ditto
RABOBANK	ditto
LAMPRE	8 points
AG2R Prévoyance	5 points
Chocolade JACQUES - WINCOR NIXDORF	ditto
CRÉDIT AGRICOLE	ditto
FDJEUX.COM	ditto
Brioches LA BOULANGÈRE	0 point
Vini CALDIROLA - NOBILI Rubinetterie	ditto

PAST WINNERS AT THE START ***3***

AERTS Mario	2002
VERBRUGGHE Rik	2001
BARTOLI Michele	1999

RIDERS IN THE UCI TOP 100: ***43***

ROOKIES AT THE START
(LESS THAN ONE YEAR AS A PROFESSIONAL): ***12***

3 YOUNGEST

FAILLI Francesco (Ita)	16/12/1983
SANCHEZ GIL Luis Leon (Esp)	23/11/1983
SCOTTO D'ABUSCO Michele (Ita)	05/03/1983

3 OLDEST

FARESIN Gianni (Ita)	16/07/1965
PIATEK Zbigniew (Pol)	01/05/1966
VERSTREPEN Johan (Bel)	21/10/1967

On a roll

Davide Rebellin has done it! Following the Amstel Gold Race a week earlier, the Flèche Wallonne four days earlier, the Florentine has also conquered the great Liege - Bastogne – Liege race, often considered the most difficult of the season. Disposing of the hot favourite on the way, the peroxide headed ridershowed the touch of a master in the final stages of the race. He managed to beat off challenges from his two greatest rivals, Alexandre Vinokourov and Michael Boogerd in the sprint for the line in the Liege suburb of Ans at the end of a disappointing fifth round of the World Cup.

Normally introverted, Davide Rebellin shows his joy to the very tips of his fingers. It's not easy to be thrown so abruptly into the limelight.

Beaten by Davide Rebellin in the final metres of the Mur de Huy, Danilo Di Luca in unable to take his revenge on this last Sunday of april. Victim of a urinary infection that had already spoilt his chances in the 2003 Tour de France, the Saeco leader is forced to pull out of the final spring Classic, hours before the start of the race. It is therefore a peloton of 193 riders that takes to the road for some 250 kilometers of racing across the Ardennes, already luxuriant with foliage. The weather seems unlikely to play a big part in the proceedings! The first hour of the race is marked by a fast average speed and several attacks. Among them being the effort from Jan van Velzen (Chocolade Jacques) and Peter Wuyts (Mr bookmaker.com) which comes to an end after a short distance. It's just before Bastogne (km 60) that the attack of the day takes place. The breakaway is formed by Jorg Strauss (Gerolsteiner), Bram Tankink (Quick step), Laurent Lefèvre (La Boulangere), Inaki Isasi (Euskaltel), and two representatives of the Chocolade Jacques team, Jurgen van de Walle and Raivis Belohvosciks. In fact, the latter came out of the peloton a little later, necessitating a wearing persuit for which he will pay at a later stage. The lead of the first group (almost 10 minutes) fritters away on the climb towards Liege. The lead over the peloton is reduced to 4 mins 30sec at the beginning of the ascention of the Cote St. Roch, just 90 kilometers from the finish. Belohvosciks having left his companions to lead the way for some time.

IS IT JAKSCHE... OR HAMILTON?

At the Cote du Rosier (64kms from ans) the fate of the breakaway seems settled: they now have a lead of only two minutes over the peloton. This is also the moment chosed by the CSC team to play its trump card. In the company of Alexandre Botcharov (Credit Agricole), Kurt - Asle Arvesen and Jorg Jaksche go after the leaders. Jacsche is surprising. With bandaged arms, following a crash during training for the Amstel Gold Race, the German rider, in his CSC jersey brings back memories of Tyler Hamilton in the centenary Tour. Like him, he's racing despite a fracture. Like him, he does well. The counter attacking trio arrive at their goal on the cote de la Vecquée (at 52 kms from the finish line). Strauss and Tankink, the last survivors of the breakaway, are caught.

THE GREAT HILL (ALMOST) CONQUERED

... And left behind on the first slopes of the impressive Cote de la Redoute, taken, in the lead by Botcharov followed by the two CSC riders and twenty others jockeying for position. Just before one of the final difficulties of the day, the Cote de Sprimont, there is even a partial regrouping of the pack. Fifty riders are still together at only 25 kilometers from the line! The cote de Sart - Tilman, situated 18 kilometers from the finish, is taken with

great force by the Basque Inigo Landaluze (Euskaltel) and the German Patrik Sinkewitz (Quick Step) at the same time that Michael Boogerd punctures (luckily time is not lost, due the help of his team mates). Landaluze and Sinkewitz cannot create a big enough lead to attack the often decisive Cote de St. Nicolas (1.1 kms at 10%) with any great confidence. The chasing group bunches at the foot of the climb, only to explode a little further up the road. Peter Van Petegem, then Michael Boogerd attack. There are only two danger men: Alexandre Vinokourov and... Davide Rebellin. The Gerolsteiner rider, invisible the whole day is now making it look easy.
It should be noted that Vino and Boogerd do most of the work to assure the success of this breakaway. The trio arrive at Ans, at the start of this long straight which has so often been the scene of dramatic finishes. From behind, three men - Ivan Basso, Samuel Sanchez and the surprising Bjorn Leukemans - go after the leaders. Erik Dekker, tem mate of Michael Boogerds joins them, but things seem to be sewn up. The victory is decided by the three top men in the Amstel Gold Race (this year Rebellin, last year Vinikourov and in 1999 Boogerd). Alexandre Vinokourov, knowing a sprint would not help hi cause, accelerates 1300 metres from the line, forcing Boogerd into an effort in order to keep the trio together. This is achieved as they enter the final kilometre.
The Dutchman himself attacks as they go into the last 700 metres. A desperate attack which none the less forces Rebellin to play his hand. The Italian, following some effort, manages to stay with Michael Boogerd, as opposed to Vino who seems out of contention. Some distance from the line Rebellin is once again in a comfortable position, forcing Boogerd to go for the final sprint, then passing him. Three prestigious victories in eight days! The unfortunate Michael Boogerd is beaten for the second time in a week by the same man. ■

The attack from the two men of the CSC team, Jorg Jaksche (front) and Kurt – Asle Arvesen, followed by Alexandre Botcharov just before the climb at the Col de la Redoute, will not suffice to turn the race in their favour.

Never afraid to have a go, Michael Boogerd climbs the Cote de St-Nicolas in the Liege - Bastogne - Liege.

193 Competitors

PHONAK

No.	Rider	Place	Time
1.	HAMILTON Tyler (Usa)	**9th**	+ 12"
2.	AEBERSOLD Niki (Sui)		*Abandon*
3.	CAMENZIND Oscar (Sui)	54th	+ 1'32"
4.	ELMIGER Martin (Sui)	95th	+ 11'38"
5.	GRABSCH Bert (Ger)	107th	+ 11'38"
6.	GUTIERREZ CATALUÑA J. Enrique (Esp)		*Abandon*
7.	PEREIRO Oscar (Esp)	43rd	+ 1'05"
8.	RAST Gregory (Sui)		*Abandon*

T-MOBILE

No.	Rider	Place	Time
11.	WESEMANN Steffen (Ger)	11st	+ 12"
12.	AERTS Mario (Bel)		*Abandon*
13.	GUERINI Giuseppe (Ita)	116th	+ 11'38"
14.	KESSLER Matthias (Ger)	**6th**	+ 12"
15.	KLÖDEN Andreas (Ger)	87th	+ 6'52"
16.	NARDELLO Daniele (Ita)	122nd	+ 11'38"
17.	VINOKOUROV Alexandre (Kaz)	**3rd**	+ 4"
18.	ZABEL Erik (Ger)	81st	+ 6'52"

LOTTO - DOMO

No.	Rider	Place	Time
21.	VAN PETEGEM Peter (Bel)	25th	+ 19"
22.	BAGUET Serge (Bel)	53rd	+ 1'32"
23.	BRANDT Christophe (Bel)	64th	+ 2'40"
24.	MARICHAL Thierry (Bel)	108th	+ 11'38"
25.	MERCKX Axel (Bel)	55th	+ 1'35"
27.	VERBRUGGHE Rik (Bel)	86th	+ 6'52"
28.	WADECKI Piotr (Pol)	51st	+ 1'09"
29.	D'HOLLANDER Glen (Bel)		*Abandon*

FASSA BORTOLO

No.	Rider	Place	Time
31.	VANDENBROUCKE Frank (Bel)	16th	+ 16"
32.	CIONI Dario (Ita)	68th	+ 2'57"
33.	CODOL Massimo (Ita)	63rd	+ 2'40"
34.	FLECHA Juan Antonio (Esp)	112nd	+ 11'38"
35.	KIRCHEN Kim (Lux)	42nd	+ 1'05"
36.	PETITO Roberto (Ita)	96th	+ 11'38"
37.	POZZATO Filippo (Ita)		*Abandon*
38.	SACCHI Fabio (Ita)	92nd	+ 11'38"

QUICK STEP - DAVITAMON

No.	Rider	Place	Time
41.	BETTINI Paolo (Ita)	22nd	+ 16"
42.	BRAMATI Davide (Ita)	131st	+ 13'28"
43.	DUFAUX Laurent (Sui)	46th	+ 1'05"
44.	NUYENS Nick (Bel)	129th	+ 13'28"
45.	PAOLINI Luca (Ita)	69th	+ 2'57"
46.	SINKEWITZ Patrik (Ger)	33rd	+ 53"
47.	TANKINK Bram (Ned)	82nd	+ 6'52"
48.	VAN GOOLEN Jurgen (Bel)	83rd	+ 6'52"

RABOBANK

No.	Rider	Place	Time
51.	BOOGERD Michael (Ned)	**2nd**	+ 2"
52.	DE WEERT Kevin (Bel)		*Abandon*
53.	DEKKER Erik (Ned)	**5th**	+ 12"
54.	DEN BAKKER Maarten (Ned)		*Abandon*
55.	FREIRE Oscar (Esp)	14th	+ 16"
56.	KROON Karsten (Ned)	126th	+ 13'28"
57.	LEIPHEIMER Levy (Usa)	72nd	+ 3'35"
58.	LOTZ Marc (Ned)	84th	+ 6'52"

US POSTAL - BERRY FLOOR

No.	Rider	Place	Time
61.	BELTRAN Manuel (Esp)	23rd	+ 19"
62.	AZEVEDO José (Por)	59th	+ 1'45"
63.	BARRY Michael (Can)	98th	+ 11'38"
64.	LANDIS Floyd (Usa)	19th	+ 16"
65.	MIKHAILOV Guennadi (Rus)		*Abandon*
66.	NOVAL Benjamin (Esp)	101st	+ 11'38"
67.	RUBIERA José Luis (Esp)	38th	+ 1'05"
68.	VAN DEN BROECK Jurgen (Bel)		*Abandon*

CSC

No.	Rider	Place	Time
71.	BARTOLI Michele (Ita)	27th	+ 21"
72.	ARVESEN Kurt-Asle (Nor)	78th	+ 5'34"
73.	BASSO Ivan (Ita)	**8th**	+ 12"
74.	JAKSCHE Jörg (Ger)	114th	+ 11'38"
75.	LUTTENBERGER Peter (Aut)		*Abandon*
76.	SASTRE Carlos (Esp)		*Abandon*
77.	SCHLECK Frank (Lux)	77th	+ 5'34"
78.	SØRENSEN Nicki (Den)	60th	+ 1'45"

ALESSIO - BIANCHI

No.	Rider	Place	Time
81.	PELLIZOTTI Franco (Ita)	29th	+ 27"
83.	BERTOLINI Alessandro (Ita)	37th	+ 1'05"
84.	IVANOV Ruslan (Mda)		*Abandon*
85.	MIHOLJEVIC Vladimir (Cro)		*Abandon*
86.	MORENI Cristian (Ita)	71st	+ 3'35"
87.	NOE' Andrea (Ita)	75th	+ 5'34"
88.	RASTELLI Ellis (Ita)	113rd	+ 11'38"

EUSKALTEL - EUSKADI

No.	Rider	Place	Time
91.	ETXEBARRIA David (Esp)	12nd	+ 12"
92.	ALBIZU Joseba (Esp)	104th	+ 11'38"
93.	ARTETXE Mikel (Esp)	88th	+ 6'52"
94.	CAMAÑO Iker (Esp)	102nd	+ 11'38"
95.	ETXEBARRIA Unai (Ven)	74th	+ 3'35"
96.	ISASI Iñaki (Esp)	123rd	+ 11'38"
97.	LANDALUZE Iñigo (Esp)	17th	+ 16"
98.	SANCHEZ Samuel (Esp)	**4th**	+ 8"

FDJEUX.COM

No.	Rider	Place	Time
101.	GILBERT Philippe (Bel)	40th	+ 1'05"
102.	BICHOT Freddy (Fra)		*Abandon*
103.	CASAR Sandy (Fra)	44th	+ 1'05"
104.	FRITSCH Nicolas (Fra)	66th	+ 2'40"
105.	LÖVKVIST Thomas (Swe)	117th	+ 11'38"
106.	ROBIN Jean-Cyril (Fra)	120th	+ 11'38"
107.	VOGONDY Nicolas (Fra)	119th	+ 11'38"

SAECO

No.	Rider	Place	Time
112.	CELESTINO Mirko (Ita)	24th	+ 19"
113.	GLOMSER Gerit (Aut)	85th	+ 6'52"
114.	MAZZOLENI Eddy (Ita)	13rd	+ 16"
115.	PETROV Evgueni (Rus)	73rd	+ 3'35"
116.	SABALIAUSKAS Marius (Ltu)		*Abandon*
117.	SPEZIALETTI Alessandro (Ita)	118th	+ 11'38"
118.	STANGELJ Gorazd (Slo)	50th	+ 1'05"

LAMPRE

No.	Rider	Place	Time
121.	BALLAN Alessandro (Ita)		*Abandon*
122.	BARBERO Sergio (Ita)		*Abandon*

124.	GARATE Juan Manuel (Esp)	20th	+ 16″
125.	PINOTTI Marco (Ita)	111st	+ 11'38″
126.	RIGHI Daniele (Ita)	58th	+ 1'45″
127.	SCOTTO D'ABUSCO Michele (Ita)	57th	+ 1'45″
128.	VILA Patxi (Esp)	52nd	+ 1'09″
130.	VAINSTEINS Romans (Lat)		*Abandon*

GEROLSTEINER

131.	REBELLIN Davide (Ita)	**1st**	**6h 20'09″**
132.	FARESIN Gianni (Ita)	34th	+ 1'04″
133.	HARDTER Uwe (Ger)		*Abandon*
134.	SERPELLINI Marco (Ita)		*Abandon*
135.	STRAUSS Marcel (Sui)	124th	+ 11'38″
136.	TOTSCHNIG Georg (Aut)	80th	+ 5'34″
137.	WEGMANN Fabian (Ger)	35th	+ 1'05″
138.	ZBERG Marcus (Sui)	21st	+ 16″

Chocolade JACQUES - WINCOR NIXDORF

141.	ABAKOUMOV Igor (Bel)		*Abandon*
143.	BRARD Florent (Fra)		*Abandon*
144.	PIATEK Zbigniew (Pol)	128th	+ 13'28″
145.	VAN DE WALLE Jurgen (Bel)		*Abandon*
146.	VAN VELZEN Jan (Ned)		*Abandon*
147.	VERHEYEN Geert (Bel)	47th	+ 1'05″
148.	VOSKAMP Bart (Ned)		*Abandon*
149.	BELOHVOSCIKS Raivis (Lat)		*Abandon*

LANDBOUWKREDIET - COLNAGO

151.	POPOVYCH Yaroslav (Ukr)	28th	+ 25″
152.	DE WAELE Bert (Bel)	67th	+ 2'57″
153.	DUMA Vladimir (Ukr)	121st	+ 11'38″
154.	GASPERONI Cristian (Ita)		*Abandon*
155.	MONFORT Maxime (Bel)		*Abandon*
157.	STREEL Marc (Bel)		*Abandon*
158.	VERSTREPEN Johan (Bel)		*Abandon*
159.	BILEKA Volodymir (Ukr)		*Abandon*

Brioches LA BOULANGÈRE

161.	ROUS Didier (Fra)	49th	+ 1'05″
162.	BENETEAU Walter (Fra)	130th	+ 13'28″
163.	BOUYER Franck (Fra)		*Abandon*
165.	CHAVANEL Sylvain (Fra)	89th	+ 6'52″
166.	HARY Maryan (Fra)		*Abandon*
167.	LEFÈVRE Laurent (Fra)		*Abandon*
168.	PINEAU Jérôme (Fra)	45th	+ 1'05″

Illes BALEARS - BANESTO

171.	MENCHOV Denis (Rus)	15th	+ 16'
172.	COLOM Antonio (Esp)		*Abandon*
173.	GUTIERREZ PALACIOS J. Ivan (Esp)	65th	+ 2'40″
174.	HORRACH Joan (Esp)		*Abandon*
175.	LASTRAS Pablo (Esp)	79th	+ 5'34″
176.	REYNES Vicente (Esp)		*Abandon*

SAUNIER DUVAL - PRODIR

181.	MORI Manuele (Ita)	41st	+ 1'05″
182.	BERTOGLIATI Rubens (Sui)	105th	+ 11'38″
183.	GOMEZ Angel "Litu" (Esp)		*Abandon*
184.	LOBATO Ruben (Esp)		*Abandon*
185.	MARTIN PERDIGUERO M. A. (Esp)	36th	+ 1'05″
186.	RODRIGUEZ OLIVER Joaquin (Esp)	70th	+ 2'57″
187.	VENTOSO Francisco (Esp)		*Abandon*
188.	ZAUGG Oliver (Sui)	103rd	+ 11'38″

LIBERTY Seguros

191.	SERRANO Marcos (Esp)	31st	+ 28″
192.	BARANOWSKI Dariusz (Pol)		*Abandon*
193.	CARUSO Giampaolo (Ita)	32nd	+ 46″
194.	GIL PEREZ Koldo (Esp)	125th	+ 11'50″
195.	HRUSKA Jan (Cze)	61st	+ 1'45″
196.	RAMIREZ ABEJA Javier (Esp)	110th	+ 11'38″
197.	SANCHEZ GIL Luis Leon (Esp)		*Abandon*
198.	VICIOSO Angel (Esp)	**10th**	+ 12″

Mr BOOKMAKER.COM - PALMANS

201.	VAN DE WOUWER Kurt (Bel)	91st	+ 8'16″
202.	COENEN Johan (Bel)		*Abandon*
203.	GABRIEL Frédéric (Fra)		*Abandon*
204.	LEUKEMANS Björn (Bel)	30th	+ 28″
205.	RENDERS Jens (Bel)	127th	+ 13'28″
206.	THIJS Erwin (Bel)	90th	+ 8'16″
207.	VAN HAECKE Michel (Bel)		*Abandon*
208.	WUYTS Peter (Bel)		*Abandon*

AG2R Prévoyance

211.	BROCHARD Laurent (Fra)	18th	+ 16″
212.	AGNOLUTTO Christophe (Fra)		*Abandon*
213.	ASTARLOZA Mikel (Esp)		*Abandon*
214.	CHAURREAU Iñigo (Esp)		*Abandon*
215.	GOUBERT Stéphane (Fra)		*Abandon*
216.	KRIVTSOV Yuriy (Ukr)		*Abandon*
217.	LAIDOUN Julien (Fra)		*Abandon*

CRÉDIT AGRICOLE

221.	MOREAU Christophe (Fra)		*Abandon*
222.	BOTCHAROV Alexandre (Rus)	48th	+ 1'05″
223.	FEDRIGO Pierrick (Fra)		*Abandon*
224.	HALGAND Patrice (Fra)		*Abandon*
225.	KASHECHKIN Andrey (Kaz)	56th	+ 1'35″
226.	LE MEVEL Christophe (Fra)		*Abandon*
227.	POILVET Benoît (Fra)	99th	+ 11'38″
228.	SALMON Benoît (Fra)		*Abandon*

Vini CALDIROLA - NOBILI Rubinetterie

231.	GARZELLI Stefano (Ita)	62nd	+ 2'17″
232.	BEUCHAT Roger (Sui)	109th	+ 11'38″
233.	CELLI Luca (Ita)		*Abandon*
234.	CHEULA Gianpaolo (Ita)		*Abandon*
235.	MASCIARELLI Simone (Ita)	115th	+ 11'38″
236.	MASON Oscar (Ita)	26th	+ 21″
237.	MILESI Marco (Ita)		*Abandon*
238.	ZAMPIERI Steve (Sui)	100th	+ 11'38″

DOMINA VACANZE

241.	SCARPONI Michele (Ita)	**7th**	+ 12″
242.	BAZHENOV Alexandr (Rus)	94th	+ 11'38″
243.	FAILLI Francesco (Ita)	132nd	+ 13'28″
244.	GENTILI Massimiliano (Ita)	93rd	+ 11'38″
245.	GIUNTI Massimo (Ita)	97th	+ 11'38″
246.	KOLOBNEV Alexandr (Rus)	39th	+ 1'05″
247.	SIMEONI Filippo (Ita)	76th	+ 5'34″
248.	VALOTI Paolo (Ita)	106th	+ 11'38″

TOTAL OF POINTS UCI OBTAINED IN THE RACE

RABOBANK	292 points
GEROLSTEINER	275 points
T.MOBILE	267 points
EUSKALTEL - EUSKADI	195 points
DOMINA VACANZE	107 points
CSC	88 points
LIBERTY Seguros	73 points
PHONAK	ditto
SAECO	66 points
FASSA BORTOLO	55 points
US POSTAL	51 points
QUICK STEP - DAVITAMON	48 points
LOTTO - DOMO	40 points
ILLES BALEARS - BANESTO	38 points
LAMPRE	37 points
FDJEUX.COM	30 points
Vini CALDIROLA - NOBILI Rubinetterie	29 points
ALESSIO - BIANCHI	26 points
SAUNIER DUVAL - PRODIR	25 points
AG2R Prévoyance	21 points
Brioches LA BOULANGÈRE	20 points
Mr BOOKMAKER - PALMANS	ditto
LANDBOUWKREDIET - COLNAGO	17 points
CRÉDIT AGRICOLE	15 points
Chocolade JACQUES - WINCOR NIXDORF	10 points

EX WINNERS AT THE START **5**

BARTOLI Michele	1997 &1998
BETTINI Paolo	2000 & 2002
VANDENBROUCKE Frank	1999
CAMENZIND Oscar	2001
HAMILTON Tyler	2003

RIDERS IN THE UCI TOP 100: ***49***

ROOKIES AT THE START
(LESS THAN ONE YEAR AS A PROFESSIONAL): ***13***

CLASSIFICATION OF WORLD CUP (AFTER 5 EVENTS)

1.	Davide Rebellin (Ita) Gerolsteiner	200 pts
2.	Michael Boogerd (Ned) Rabobank	146 pts
3.	Steffen Wesemann (Ger) T-Mobile	131 pts
4.	Oscar Freire (Esp) Rabobank	127 pts
5.	Erik Dekker (Ned) Rabobank	115 pts
6.	Magnus Backstedt (Swe) Alessio	100 pts
7.	Paolo Bettini (Ita) Quick Step	98 pts
8.	Peter van Petegem (Bel) Lotto-Domo	95 pts
9.	Leif Hoste (Bel) Lotto-Domo	84 pts
10.	Erik Zabel (Ger) T-Mobile	80 pts

Alexandre Vinokourov takes advantage of an opening left by Boogerd and Rebellin to take the lead in the last part of the race. But his strength leaves him wanting in his solo push for the line.

The rise of Australian cycle racing is emphasised by the victory in a World Cup classic by Stuart O'Grady .

Stuart O'Grady, the first

In recent years, Australia has joined the premier nations in the cycling world. The biggest island in the world can, it's true, count on an exceptional generation: Robbie Mc Ewen, Michael Rogers, not forgetting Baden Cooke, Allan Davis, Cadel Evans and also Stuart O'Grady. A few days before his 31st birthday, the rider from Adelaide became the first australian to win a World Cup event. True, Phil Anderson won the 1983 Amstel Gold Race, but at the time, that event was not yet admitted to the club. A pro for the last ten years, O' Grady was in the news in the closed season when he left the Credit Agricole team to join the troubled Cofidis in the Spring. Overcoming these problems, O' Grady confirms after this success that this is his best season since arriving in Europe.

Even though in the recent history of the only German Classic, no early breakaway has been successful, four men set out at the twentieth kilometre. Lars Michaelsen(CSC) , Roberto Lochowski (wiensenhof), Stefan Radochla (Illes Balears) and the immense Dutchman Rik Reinerink (Chocolade Jacques) won't find things easy: there are still 230 kilometers to go! Their effort soon pays off: 15 minutes lead at km 65. Too much as far as the local teams are concerned. T-Mobile and Gerolsteiner who, helped by Rabobank and the Quick Step team, set about reducing the gap. When the quartet starts its final lap (containing three ascentions of Waseberg, short but hard) their lead has been reduced to a mere two minutes. Obviously not enough, and at 55 kms from the line, Rik Reinerink- the only one to really put up a fight, is absorbed into the peloton, as were his companions a little earlier.

ELIMINATION FROM BEHIND

The first time at Waseberg, allows Bettini, followed by Di Luca, Pozzato and Rebellin to sort things out. A group of 18 riders take a few seconds lead, before, at the instigation of T Mobile and Gerolsteiner, a peloton forms. The crucial point of the race, Waseberg, is once again the scene of a major movement. At the second climb, it's Danilo Di Luca who fires things up. Igor Astarloa, the World Champion, Christian Moreni, the Italian champion and of course Davide Rebellin and Paolo Bettini, the two hot favourites, follow on. With 16 kilometers to go, it's the local rider Jan Ullrich who makes his move. Once again, Astarloa, Bettini and Rebellin are the first to take up the challenge. Thirty other riders follow them. This group will be fighting it out at the line, so there follow several attacks by those who would be out of the running in a sprint finish. Axel Merckx (Lotto- Domo), twice, and also Paolo Bossoni (Lampre) or Philippe Gilbert (Fdjeux.com) all finally fail. The sprint takes shape and Paolo Bettini makes a fatal mistake in pushing too soon, he's soon passed by Stuart O' Grady but manages to keep the second place, helping his placing in the World Cup series. His main rival, Davide Rebellin, passes the line in only the sixth place. ■

179 Competitors

QUICK STEP - DAVITAMON

1.	BETTINI Paolo (Ita)	**2nd**	s.t
2.	BOONEN Tom (Bel)	88th	+ 7'23"
3.	CRETSKENS Wilfried (Bel)		*Abandon*
4.	KNAVEN Servais (Ned)		*Abandon*
5.	NUYENS Nick (Bel)	49th	+ 4'04"
6.	PAOLINI Luca (Ita)	31st	s.t
7.	HULSMANS Kevin (Bel)	86th	+ 7'23"
8.	ZANINI Stefano (Ita)	96th	+ 7'23"

GEROLSTEINER

11.	HONDO Danilo (Ger)	32nd	+ 9"
12.	LANG Sebastian (Ger)		*Abandon*
13.	POLLACK Olaf (Ger)		*Abandon*
14.	REBELLIN Davide (Ita)	**6th**	s.t
15.	SCHOLZ Ronny (Ger)	33rd	+ 14"
16.	SERPELLINI Marco (Ita)	73rd	+ 7'23"
17.	WEGMANN Fabian (Ger)		*Abandon*
18.	ZBERG Markus (Sui)	35th	+ 4'04"

T.MOBILE

21.	ALDAG Rolf (Ger)	40th	+ 4'04"
22.	IVANOV Serguei (Rus)	58th	+ 7'23"
23.	KLIER Andreas (Ger)		*Abandon*
24.	KLÖDEN Andreas (Ger)	95th	+ 7'23"
25.	SCHAFFRATH Jan (Ger)		*Abandon*
26.	SCHRECK Stephan (Ger)		*Abandon*
27.	ULLRICH Jan (Ger)	30th	s.t
28.	ZABEL Erik (Ger)	**7th**	s.t

RABOBANK

31.	FREIRE Oscar (Esp)	**4th**	s.t
32.	DEKKER Erik (Ned)	11st	s.t
33.	HUNTER Robert (Rsa)		*Abandon*
34.	HAYMAN Mathew (Aus)	61st	+ 7'23"
35.	SENTJENS Roy (Ned)	109th	+ 11'40"
36.	DE JONGH Steven (Ned)	59th	+ 7'23"
37.	KROON Karsten (Ned)	43rd	+ 4'04"
38.	POSTHUMA Joost (Ned)		*Abandon*

LOTTO - DOMO

41.	VAN PETEGEM Peter (Bel)	87th	+ 7'23"
42.	MERCKX Axel (Bel)	20th	s.t
43.	HOSTE Leif (Bel)		*Abandon*
44.	MARICHAL Thierry (Bel)	55th	+ 4'09"
45.	VAN BON Leon (Ned)		*Abandon*
46.	VAN DIJK Stefan (Ned)		*Abandon*
47.	VANSEVENANT Wim (Bel)		*Abandon*
48.	VIERHOUTEN Aart (Ned)	66th	+ 7'23"

US POSTAL - BERRY FLOOR

51.	BARRY Michael (Can)	39th	+ 4'04"
52.	DEVOLDER Stijn (Bel)		*Abandon*
53.	JOACHIM Benoît (Lux)	76th	+ 7'23"
54.	MIKHAÏLOV Guennadi (Rus)	52nd	+ 4'04"
56.	VAN DEN BROECK Jurgen (Bel)		*Abandon*
57.	VAN HEESWIJK Max (Ned)	74th	+ 7'23"
58.	ZABRISKIE David (Usa)		*Abandon*

SAECO

61.	DI LUCA Danilo (Ita)	23rd	s.t
62.	BALDUCCI Gabriele (Ita)		*Abandon*
63.	BONOMI Giosue' (Ita)		*Abandon*
64.	CELESTINO Mirko (Ita)	12nd	s.t
65.	COMMESSO Salvatore (Ita)	34th	+ 4'04"
66.	LOOSLI David (Sui)		*Abandon*
67.	LUDEWIG Jörg (Ger)	37th	+ 4'04"
68.	SPEZIALETTI Alessandro (Ita)	99th	+ 11'40"

FASSA BORTOLO

71.	BRUSEGHIN Marzio (Ita)	104th	+ 11'40"
72.	CANCELLARA Fabian (Sui)	85th	+ 7'23"
73.	FLECHA Juan Antonio (Esp)	51st	+ 4'04"
74.	GUSTOV Volodymir (Ukr)	26th	s.t
75.	KIRCHEN Kim (Lux)	15th	s.t
76.	PETITO Roberto (Ita)	48th	+ 4'04"
77.	POZZATO Filippo (Ita)	56th	+ 4'11"
78.	TOSATTO Matteo (Ita)	14th	s.t

CSC

81.	GUIDI Fabrizio (Ita)	**8th**	s.t
82.	HØJ Frank (Den)	75th	+ 7'23"
83.	MICHAELSEN Lars (Den)		*Abandon*
84.	BARTOLI Michele (Ita)	57th	+ 4'11"
85.	BRUUN ERIKSEN Thomas (Den)	101st	+ 11'40"
86.	HOFFMAN Tristan (Ned)	92nd	+ 7'23"
87.	GOUSSEV Vladimir (Rus)	19th	s.t
88.	SANDSTØD Michael (Den)		*Abandon*

COFIDIS

91.	CASPER Jimmy (Fra)	113rd	+ 16'59"
92.	COYOT Arnaud (Fra)		*Abandon*
93.	ENGOULVENT Jimmy (Fra)		*Abandon*
94.	FARAZIJN Peter (Bel)		*Abandon*
95.	O'GRADY Stuart (Aus)	**1st**	**5h51'39"**
96.	WHITE Matthew (Aus)	25th	s.t
97.	TOMBAK Janek (Est)	106th	+ 11'40"
98.	VASSEUR Cédric (Fra)	46th	+ 4'04"

PHONAK

101.	ALBASINI Michael (Sui)	68th	+ 7'23"
102.	AEBERSOLD Niki (Sui)		*Abandon*
103.	CAMENZIND Oscar (Sui)	16th	s.t
104.	ELMIGER Martin (Sui)	79th	+ 7'23"
105.	DESSEL Cyril (Fra)		*Abandon*
106.	MURN Uros (Slo)	98th	+ 7'23"
107.	RAST Gregory (Sui)	94th	+ 7'23"
108.	USOV Alexandre (Blr)		*Abandon*

ALESSIO - BIANCHI

111.	BÄCKSTEDT Magnus (Swe)		*Abandon*
112.	BALDATO Fabio (Ita)	36th	+ 4'04"
113.	FURLAN Angelo (Ita)		*Abandon*
114.	HVASTIJA Martin (Slo)		*Abandon*
115.	IVANOV Ruslan (Mda)	27th	s.t
116.	MORENI Cristian (Ita)	89th	+ 7'23"
117.	RASTELLI Ellis (Ita)	90th	+ 7'23"
118.	SKELDE Michael (Den)	41st	+ 4'04"

FDJEUX.COM

131.	COOKE Baden (Aus)		*Abandon*
132.	DA CRUZ Carlos (Fra)	93rd	+ 7'23"
133.	EISEL Bernhard (Aut)		*Abandon*
134.	GILBERT Philippe (Bel)	13rd	s.t
135.	GUESDON Frédéric (Fra)	80th	+ 7'23"
136.	MENGIN Christophe (Fra)	53rd	+ 4'04"
137.	WILSON Matthew (Aus)		*Abandon*

LAMPRE

141.	ASTARLOA Igor (Esp)	**3rd**	s.t
142.	BORTOLAMI Gianluca (Ita)	54th	+ 4'04"
143.	BALLAN Alessandro (Ita)	71st	+ 7'23"
144.	BOSSONI Paolo (Ita)	**10th**	s.t
145.	BARBERO Sergio (Ita)	28th	s.t
146.	HAUPTMAN Andrej (Slo)	**9th**	s.t
148.	PICCOLI Mariano (Ita)		*Abandon*

Chocolade JACQUES - WINCOR NIXDORF

151.	BRARD Florent (Fra)		*Abandon*
152.	CAPPELLE Andy (Bel)		*Abandon*
153.	HIEMSTRA Bert (Ned)		*Abandon*
154.	LÖWIK Gerben (Ned)	**5th**	s.t
155.	PEERS Chris (Bel)	105th	+ 11'40"
156.	REINERINK Rik (Ned)		*Abandon*
157.	VAN VELZEN Jan (Ned)		*Abandon*
158.	VOSKAMP Bart (Ned)		*Abandon*

LANDBOUWKREDIET - COLNAGO

161.	STEELS Tom (Bel)	112nd	+ 11'40"
162.	DIERCKXSENS Ludo (Bel)		*Abandon*
163.	CAPELLE Ludovic (Bel)	111st	+ 11'40"
164.	VAN BONDT Geert (Bel)	110th	+ 11'40"
165.	BRACKE Tony (Bel)		*Abandon*
166.	VERSTREPEN Johan (Bel)		*Abandon*
167.	MITLUSHENKO Yuriy (Ukr)	114th	+ 16'59"
168.	TIMOCHINE Mikhaïl (Rus)	45th	+ 4'04"

Brioches LA BOULANGÈRE

171.	CHAVANEL Sébastien (Fra)		*Abandon*
172.	GESLIN Anthony (Fra)	38th	+ 4'04"
173.	HARY Maryan (Fra)	72nd	+ 7'23"
174.	KERN Christophe (Fra)		*Abandon*
175.	MARTIAS Rony (Fra)	102nd	+ 11'40"
176.	NAULLEAU Alexandre (Fra)		*Abandon*
177.	SPRICK Mathieu (Fra)	21st	s.t
178.	YUS Unai (Esp)	50th	+ 4'04"

ILLES BALEARS - BANESTO

181.	ARRIETA José Luis (Esp)		*Abandon*
182.	COLOM Antonio (Esp)	83rd	+ 7'23"
183.	HORRACH Joan (Esp)		*Abandon*
184.	LASTRAS Pablo (Esp)	42nd	+ 4'04"
185.	OSA Unai (Esp)	100th	+ 11'40"
186.	RADOCHLA Steffen (Ger)		*Abandon*
187.	REYNES Vicente (Esp)	69th	+ 7'23"
188.	TAULER Antonio (Esp)		*Abandon*

AG2R Prévoyance

191.	KIRSIPUU Jaan (Est)		*Abandon*
192.	BROCHARD Laurent (Fra)	18th	s.t
193.	AGNOLUTTO Christophe (Fra)	81st	+ 7'23"
194.	BERGÈS Stéphane (Fra)	78th	+ 7'23"
195.	NAZON Jean-Patrick (Fra)		*Abandon*
196.	PORTAL Nicolas (Fra)	84th	+ 7'23"
197.	PÜTSEP Erki (Est)	70th	+ 7'23"
198.	SCANLON Mark (Irl)	91st	+ 7'23"

CRÉDIT AGRICOLE

201.	DEAN Julian (Nzl)	108th	+ 11'40"
202.	HERVÉ Cédric (Fra)		*Abandon*
203.	HUSHOVD Thor (Nor)	97th	+ 7'23"
204.	JÉGOU Lilian (Fra)	82nd	+ 7'23"
205.	JOLY Sébastien (Fra)		*Abandon*
206.	KASHECHKIN Andrey (Kaz)	24th	s.t
207.	LEQUATRE Geoffroy (Fra)	77th	+ 7'23"
208.	NAZON Damien (Fra)		*Abandon*

DE NARDI

211.	HONCHAR Serhiy (Ukr)	17th	s.t
213.	GOBBI Michele (Ita)	22nd	s.t
214.	JURCO Matej (Svk)	67th	+ 7'23"
215.	LORENZETTO Mirco (Ita)		*Abandon*
216.	NURITDINOV Rafael (Uzb)	47th	+ 4'04"
217.	VANOTTI Alessandro (Ita)	107th	+ 11'40"
218.	WEGELIUS Charly (Gbr)		*Abandon*

DOMINA VACANZE

221.	DERGANC Martin (Slo)	63rd	+ 7'23"
222.	AUG Andrus (Est)		*Abandon*
223.	FAILLI Francesco (Ita)	29th	s.t
224.	FISCHER Murillo (Bra)	62nd	+ 7'23"
225.	LOMBARDI Giovanni (Ita)		*Abandon*
226.	BAZHENOV Alexandr (Rus)	65th	+ 7'23"
228.	NAUDUZS Andris (Lat)		*Abandon*

WIESENHOF

231.	HEPPNER Jens (Ger)		*Abandon*
232.	POITSCHKE Enrico (Ger)	44th	+ 4'04"
233.	GRABSCH Ralf (Ger)	103rd	+ 11'40"
234.	MÜLLER Martin (Ger)		*Abandon*
235.	SIEDLER Sebastian (Ger)	60th	+ 7'23"
236.	SCHRÖDER Björn (Ger)		*Abandon*
237.	KNEES Christian (Ger)	64th	+ 7'23"
238.	LOCHOWSKI Roberto (Ger)		*Abandon*

RIDERS AT THE START HAVING FINISHED THE TOUR DE FRANCE (258) — 45

PAST WINNERS AT THE START — 4

BETTINI Paolo	2003
ZABEL Erik	2001
CELESTINO Mirko	1999
VAN BON Leon	1998

3 YOUNGEST

JURCO Matej (Svk)	(19) 08/08/1984
FAILLI Francesco (Ita)	(20) 16/12/1983
VAN DEN BROECK Jurgen (Bel)	(21) 01/02/1983

3 OLDEST

DIERCKXSENS Ludo (Bel)	(39) 14/10/1964
HEPPNER Jens (Ger)	(39) 23/12/1964
VERSTREPEN Johan (Bel)	(36) 21/10/1967

CLASSIFICATION

1.	**Stuart O'Grady (Aus)**	**COF**	**5h 51'39"**
2.	Paolo Bettini (Ita)	QSD	s.t
3.	Igor Astarloa (Esp)	LAM	s.t
4.	Oscar Freire (Esp)	RAB	s.t
5.	Gerben Löwik (Ned)	CHO	s.t
6.	Davide Rebellin (Ita)	GST	s.t
7.	Erik Zabel (Ger)	TMO	s.t
8.	Fabrizio Guidi (Ita)	CSC	s.t
9.	Andrej Hauptman (Slo)	LAM	s.t
10.	Paolo Bossoni (Ita)	LAM	s.t

At the age of 31, Stuart O'Grady has the best season of an already eventful career.

Fourteen years in the coming!

A few years ago Miguel Angel Martin Perdiguero was remembered principally for the length of his name and also for a certain turn of speed. Since this first Saturday in August, he is also known as the Spaniard who finished a drought of home wins in the only Spanish round of the World Cup, the Clasica San Sebastian. After the success of Igor Astarloa in the Flèche Wallonne and Mondial 2003 and that of Oscar Freire in the Milan - san Remo, it seems that the Spanish competitors are no longer content to take stage wins but now have one day races in their sights.

The Alto de Garate , situated after 29 kms of the race, provokes the first movement of the day. A group of 25 (!) riders take advantage of the climb to distance themselves from the peloton. Moos (Phonak), Sgambelluri (Vini Caldirola), Barredo(Liberty), weening (Leipheimer, Kroon (Rabobank), Noval (US Postal), Canada (Saunier Duval), Christensen (CSC)? Moerenhout, Merckx (Lotto), Atienza, Fofonov (Cofidis), Nardello, Guerini (T Mobile), Inaudi, Chaurreau (Ag2r), Duaux, Sinkewitz (Quick Step), Gomez Marchante (Costa Almeria), Plaza Molina (Kelme), Stangelj (Saeco), Hauptman, Scotto d'Aabusco (Lampre) and Totschnig (Gerolsteiner) precede the main group by 2 mins 30 sec at the 55th kilometre at l'Alto de Azkarate, a second category climb. For a long time ,the peloton keeps the lead down to a reasonable level (around one minute) before a larger gap opens up following a refreshment stop, between them and leaders (now greatly reduced in number). However, with a lead of 4 mins 30 secs at sixty kilometers from the finish, things look far from easy for the leaders. Levi Leipheimer and the ex spanish champion Ruben Plaza Molina (Kelme) take things in hand at the typically Basque Alto de Gaintxurizketa, to overtake Jaizkibel, now with a reduced lead of just 1 min 12 sec, accompanied by the Slovenian Gorazd Stangelj, who had also broken out of a group. Jaizkibel, 8 kilometers long and with an average gradient of 5% (rising to nearly 8% in places) soon takes its toll on Levi Leipheimer, the sole survivor of the morning offensive, absorbed by the blue clad Gerolsteiner group. At the same moment, one of the favourites, Alejandro Valverde, recent winner of the Tour de Burgos falls victim to a mechanical failure after one kilometre of climbing. Forced to change cycles, he sees his chances of a win evaporate in seconds... The most difficult part of the climb sees last year's winner, Paolo Bettini, attack just as the sun is at its fiercest. Six men manage to follow him: World Cup leader , Davide Rebellinand his team mate Georg Totschnig (Gerolsteiner), Miguel Angel Martin Perdiguero (Saunier Duval), Marcos Serrano (Liberty), Ivan Basso (CSC) and Alberto Martinez Trinidad (Relax-Bodysol). Behind, the chasing riders have difficulty in organising a reply: having placed their number one rider at the head of the race, the saunier Duval team spend their time trying to disrupt any attempt at a

M. A Martin Perdiguero has anticipated the sprint. Here he leads Paolo Bettini, the partly hidden Davide Rebellin and Alberto Martinez over the line at San Sebastian.

On the left, Levi leipheimer and ruben Plaza (Kelme) held on until the first slopes of Jaizkibel... on which Jan Ullrich pullsout of the race with a broken saddle, the German was unable to make his presence felt.

counter attack. The Italians trapped!
We do not yet know, but begin to suspect, that this group is on its way to a victory.
At the summit of Jaizkibel the lead over a first peloton is one minute, but as they head towards San sebastian the lead increases.
At the front however, things are somewhat thrown into disarray by the attack of Alberto Martinez Trinidad. An attack wiped out soon after by Georg Totschnig. The final difficulty of the day, the Alto de Gerutze, 15 kilometers from the line, last year allowed Paolo Bettini and Ivan Basso to leave the rest of the field behind. Ivan Basso makes his move. There follows a marathon effort of more than three kilometers! Arriving in the streets of San Sebastian, the group loses its cohesion, each rider trying to force the first move from his opponents. Marcos Serrano makes the first move, soon followed by "Perdi" then Alberto Martinez and even Georg Totschnig. The brave Austrian clocks up at this moment more than 200kilometres at the head of the race! But, his strength is found to be lacking and it's a sprint that will decide the result of this 24th edition.
At 300 metres from the white line the pressure mounts even more. Bettini watches the man he considers his greatest rival, Davide "Tintin" Rebellin. This is noted by Miguel Angel Martin Perdiguero who uses this moment of inattention to start his challenge. The Spaniard knows how to take his chances, which Bettini and rebellin learn to their cost.

As with the preceding week, Paolo Bettini is beaten into second place, once again failing by a hair's breadth, whereas Rebellin, helped superbly by Totschnig, failed to make a single attack in the day. His legendary waiting game let him down once again... ■

188 Competitors

QUICK STEP - DAVITAMON

1.	BETTINI Paolo (Ita)	**2nd**	s.t
2.	VIRENQUE Richard (Fra)	17th	+ 1'39"
3.	DUFAUX Laurent (Sui)		*Abandon*
4.	PAOLINI Luca (Ita)	79th	+ 9'33"
5.	HORRILLO Pedro (Esp)	98th	+ 11'14"
6.	GARRIDO J. Antonio (Esp)		*Abandon*
7.	PECHARROMAN J. Antonio (Esp)	50th	+5'24"
8.	SINKEWITZ Patrik (Ger)	51st	+5'24"

FASSA BORTOLO

11.	GONZALEZ JIMENEZ Aitor (Esp)	60th	+ 5'24"
12.	CANCELLARA Fabian (Sui)		*Abandon*
13.	FLECHA Juan Antonio (Esp)	13rd	+ 1'39"
14.	CODOL Massimo (Ita)		*Abandon*
15.	CIONI Dario (Ita)	136th	+ 15'57"
16.	BRUSEGHIN Marzio (Ita)	65th	+ 9'33"
17.	GUSTOV Volodymir (Ukr)	29th	+ 1'39"
18.	KIRCHEN Kim (Lux)		*Abandon*

T.MOBILE

21.	ULLRICH Jan (Ger)		*Abandon*
22.	GUERINI Giuseppe (Ita)	121st	+ 11'14"
23.	KLÖDEN Andreas (Ger)		*Abandon*
24.	BOTERO Santiago (Col)	132nd	+ 15'57"
25.	NARDELLO Daniele (Ita)	70th	+ 9'33"
26.	IVANOV Serguei (Rus)	81st	+ 11'14"
27.	ZABEL Erik (Ger)	63rd	+ 9'33"

SAECO

31.	DI LUCA Danilo (Ita)	58th	+ 5'24"
32.	CUNEGO Damiano (Ita)	21st	+ 1'39"
33.	COMMESSO Salvatore (Ita)	124th	+ 11'14"
34.	FUENTES Juan (Esp)	78th	+ 9'33"
35.	PETROV Evgueni (Rus)	59th	+ 5'24"
36.	CELESTINO Mirko (Ita)	18th	+ 1'39"
37.	SPEZIALETTI Alessandro (Ita)	129th	+ 15'57"
38.	STANGELJ Gorazd (Slo)	88th	+ 11'14"

ILLES BALEARS - BANESTO

41.	LOPEZ GIL Antonio (Esp)		*Abandon*
42.	MENCHOV Denis (Rus)	76th	+ 9'33"
43.	KARPETS Vladimir (Rus)	77th	+ 9'33"

44. PRADERA Mikel (Esp) *Abandon*
45. ZANDIO Xabier (Esp) *Abandon*
46. OSA Aitor (Esp) *Abandon*
47. GARCIA ACOSTA J. Vicente (Esp) 33rd + 5'24"
48. GUTIERREZ PALACIOS J. Ivan (Esp) 41st + 5'24"

GEROLSTEINER

51. REBELLIN Davide (Ita) **3rd** s.t
52. TOTSCHNIG Georg (Aut) **6th** + 6"
53. STRAUSS Marcel (Sui) *Abandon*
54. ZBERG Marcus (Sui) **10th** + 1'39"
55. SCHOLZ Ronny (Ger) 106th + 11'14"
56. SERPELLINI Marco (Ita) 113rd + 11'14"
57. FARESIN Gianni (Ita) 38th + 5'24"
58. WEGMANN Fabian (Ger) 87th + 11'14"

COFIDIS

61. FARAZIJN Peter (Bel) *Abandon*
62. MONCOUTIÉ David (Fra) 55th + 5'24"
63. PEREZ RODRIGUEZ Luis (Esp) 103rd + 11'14"
64. CUESTA Iñigo (Esp) *Abandon*
65. ATIENZA Daniel (Esp) 91st + 11'14"
66. FOFONOV Dmitriy (Kaz) *Abandon*
67. TRENTIN Guido (Ita) 54th + 5'24"
68. VASSEUR Cédric (Fra) 35th + 5'24"

RABOBANK

71. FREIRE Oscar (Esp) 11st + 1'39"
72. BOOGERD Michael (Ned) 73rd + 9'33"
73. DEKKER Erik (Ned) 19th + 1'39"
74. LEIPHEIMER Levy (Usa) 66th + 9'33"
75. RASMUSSEN Michael (Den) 75th + 9'33"
76. WEENING Pieter (Ned) 115th + 11'14"
77. KROON Karsten (Ned) 117th + 11'14"
78. WAUTERS Marc (Bel) 114th + 11'14"

LIBERTY Seguros

81. BARREDO Carlos (Esp) *Abandon*
82. DAVIS Allan (Aus) 48th + 5'24"
83. NOZAL Isidro (Esp) *Abandon*
84. GONZALEZ de GALDEANO Alvaro (Esp) *Abandon*
85. RAMIREZ ABEJA Javier (Esp) *Abandon*
86. CARUSO Gianpaolo (Ita) 28th + 1'39"
87. SERRANO Marcos (Esp) **4th** s.t
88. SANCHEZ GIL Luis Leon (Esp) 120th + 11'14"

US POSTAL - BERRY FLOOR

91. AZEVEDO José (Por) 57th + 5'24"
92. HINCAPIE George (Usa) 56th + 5'24"
93. KLUCK Damon (Usa) *Abandon*
94. McCARTY P. Jonathan (Usa) *Abandon*
95. NOVAL Benjamin (Esp) 31st + 4'28"
96. PADRNOS Pavel (Cze) *Abandon*
97. RINCON Daniel (Col) 52nd + 5'24"

CSC

101. BASSO Ivan (Ita) **7th** + 6"
102. CHRISTENSEN Bekim (Den) *Abandon*
103. SØRENSEN Nicki (Den) *Abandon*
104. JULICH Bobby (Usa) 22nd + 1'39"
105. SCHLECK Frank (Lux) 34th + 5'24"
106. PERON Andrea (Ita) *Abandon*
107. CALVENTE Manuel (Esp) *Abandon*
108. LUTTENBERGER Peter (Aut) *Abandon*

ALESSIO - BIANCHI

111. SUNDERLAND Scott (Aus) 69th + 9'33"
112. BERTOLINI Alessandro (Ita) 86th + 11'14"
113. CAUCCHIOLI Pietro (Ita) 107th + 11'14"
114. FERRARA Raffaele (Ita) 135th + 15'57"
115. MIHOLJEVIC Vladimir (Cro) 93rd + 11'14"
116. NOE' Andrea (Ita) 84th + 11'14"
117. PELLIZOTTI Franco (Ita) 130th + 15'57"
118. MORENI Cristian (Ita) 14th + 1'39"

EUSKALTEL - EUSKADI

121. ARTETXE Mikel (Esp) *Abandon*
122. ZUBELDIA Haimar (Esp) 104th + 11'14"
123. ISASI Iñaki (Esp) 119th + 11'14"
124. ETXEBARRIA David (Esp) *Abandon*
125. MARTINEZ de ESTEBAN Egoi (Esp) 95th + 11'14"
126. SANCHEZ Samuel (Esp) *Abandon*
127. LANDALUZE Iñigo (Esp) 118th + 11'14"
128. GONZALEZ LARRANAGA Gorka (Esp) 97th + 11'14"

AG2R Prévoyance

131. BROCHARD Laurent (Fra) 67th + 9'33"
132. CHAURREAU Iñigo (Esp) 80th + 11'14"
133. ASTARLOZA Mikel (Esp) 100th + 11'14"
134. GOUBERT Stéphane (Fra) 53rd + 5'24"
135. KRIVTSOV Yuriy (Ukr) 72nd + 9'33"
136. ORIOL Christophe (Fra) 26th + 1'39"
137. INAUDI Nicolas (Fra) 134th + 15'57"

DOMINA VACANZE

141. SIMEONI Filippo (Ita) 25th + 1'39"
142. BAZHENOV Alexandr (Rus) *Abandon*
143. GENTILI Massimiliano (Ita) 96th + 11'14"
144. KOLOBNEV Alexandr(Rus) 101st + 11'14"
145. IANNETTI Massimo (Ita) 133rd + 15'57"
146. GIUNTI Massimo (Ita) *Abandon*
147. SCARPONI Michele (Ita) 137th + 15'57"
148. JONES Timothy (Zim) *Abandon*

PHONAK

151. FERTONANI Marco (Ita) 47th + 5'24"
152. RAST Gregory (Sui) *Abandon*
153. CAMENZIND Oscar (Sui) 39th + 5'24"
154. MOOS Alexandre (Sui) 116th + 11'14"
155. SCHNIDER Daniel (Sui) 71st + 9'33"
156. TSCHOPP Johann (Sui) 44th + 5'24"
157. VALJAVEC Tadej (Slo) 16th + 1'39"
158. BAYARRI Gonzalo (Esp) 83rd + 11'14"

LAMPRE

161. ASTARLOA Igor (Esp) 12nd + 1'39"
162. CASAGRANDE Francesco (Ita) *Abandon*
163. VILA Patxi (Esp) 40th +5'24"
164. BORTOLAMI Gianluca (Ita) *Abandon*
165. BARBERO Sergio (Ita) *Abandon*
166. BOSSONI Paolo (Ita) 37th + 5'24"
167. SCOTTO D'ABUSCO Michele (Ita) 108th + 11'14"
168. HAUPTMAN Andrej (Slo) 92nd + 11'14"

LOTTO - DOMO

171. MERCKX Axel (Bel) 27th + 1'39"
172. VERBRUGGHE Rik (Bel) **8th** + 1'19"
173. BAGUET Serge (Bel) 46th + 5'24"
174. MOERENHOUT Koos (Ned) *Abandon*
175. MARICHAL Thierry (Bel) *Abandon*
176. D'HOLLANDER Glen (Bel) 123rd + 11'14"
177. HOSTE Leif (Bel) 112nd + 11'14"
178. VANSEVENANT Wim (Bel) 111st + 11'14"

Vini CALDIROLA - NOBILI Rubinetterie

181. GARZELLI Stefano (Ita) 20th + 1'39"
182. TONKOV Pavel (Rus) 68th + 9'33"
183. ANDRIOTTO Dario (Ita) 125th + 11'14"
184. SGAMBELLURI Roberto (Ita) 82nd + 11'14"
185. GEROSA Mauro (Ita) 110th + 11'14"
186. ZINETTI Mauro (Ita) 139th + 15'57"
187. SIRONI Gianluca (Ita) 32nd + 5'24"
188. CALCAGNI Patrick (Sui) 74th + 9'33"

RELAX - BOSYSOL

191. MARTINEZ TRINIDAD J. Alberto (Esp) **5th** s.t
192. JUFRE Josep (Esp) 64th + 9'33"
193. FLORENCIO Xavier (Esp) 15th + 1'39"
194. DUEÑAS Moises (Esp) 102nd + 11'14"
195. BURGOS Nacor (Esp) 99th + 11'14"
196. VAN SUMMEREN Johan (Bel) 122nd + 11'14"
197. ROESEMS Bert (Bel) 90th + 11'14"
198. REBOLLO José Luis (Esp) 85th + 11'14"

SAUNIER DUVAL - PRODIR

201. MARTIN PERDIGUERO M. Angel (Esp) **1st** **5h18'35"**
202. PIEPOLI Leonardo (Ita) 62nd + 5'24"
203. JEKER Fabian (Sui) *Abandon*
204. DOMINGUEZ Juan Carlos (Esp) 49th + 5'24"
205. BELOKI Joseba (Esp) *Abandon*
206. CAÑADA David (Esp) 127th + 15'57"
207. ZABALLA Constantino (Esp) **9th** + 1'35"
208. RODRIGUEZ OLIVER Joaquin (Esp) 30th + 1'39"

Communitat VALENCIANA - KELME

211. VALVERDE Alejandro (Esp) 61st + 5'24"
212. PLAZA MOLINA Ruben (Esp) 45th + 5'24"
213. PASCUAL RODRIGUEZ Javier (Esp) *Abandon*
214. ODRIOZOLA Jon (Esp) *Abandon*
215. LATASA David (Esp) 105th + 11'14"
216. CABELLO Francisco (Esp) *Abandon*
217. GARCIA QUESADA Carlos (Esp) 23rd + 1'39"

COSTA de ALMERIA - PATERNINA

221. DEL RIO Jon (Esp) 128th + 15'57"
222. LOPEZ TORRELLA Joaquin (Esp) 36th + 5'24"
223. ORMAETXEA Jokin (Esp) 131st + 15'57"
224. ELGEZABAL Mikel (Esp) 89th + 11'14"
225. EUBA Lander (Esp) *Abandon*
226. GONZALEZ RIOS Jonathan (Esp) 109th + 11'14"
227. GOMEZ MARCHANTE José Angel (Esp) 138th + 15'57"
228. HERRERO LLORENTE David (Esp) 24th + 1'39"

CAFÉ BAQUE

231. ARREITUNANDIA Peio (Esp) 42nd + 5'24"
232. TORRES Fernando (Esp) *Abandon*
233. GAZTAÑAGA Mikel (Esp) *Abandon*
234. GARCIA MARIN Jorge (Esp) *Abandon*
235. LOPEZ GARCIA David (Esp) 43rd + 5'24"
236. PALACIO Francisco (Esp) 94th + 11'14"
237. PEREZ ARRIETA Aitor (Esp) 126th + 15'57"
238. SERRANO GONZALEZ Ricardo (Esp) *Abandon*

The first three, already neck and neck on the Jaizkibel...

FLECHA TO THE FORE...

Spanish rider Juan antonio Flecha of the Fassa Bortolo team emerges from the group of thirty riders after 241 kms of the race. Rebellin(6th), Fofonov (4th), Albasini (5th), Bettini (2nd) and Pineau (3rd) fight it out...

Bettini is decidedly no run of the mill rider. Author, last year of a memorable campaign through the summer, with successes at HEW, Cyclassics in Hamberg and the Spanish leg in San Sebastian, the Tuscan rider can only finish as runner up, for the third consecutive time in the August events. Happily for him, he can console himself with the gold medal won on the streets of Athens, and the fact that he trails the leader, Davide Rebellin by just six points. After having lost out in sprints to O' Grady (in Germany) and Martin Perdiguero (in the Basque country), Paolo Bettini is now beaten by Juan Antonio Flecha, the Spanish rider ,born in Argentina and riding for the Fassa Bortolo team.

The ninth victory in the career of Juan Antonio Flecha was a long time coming. Always in the top riders in one day events, (7th in the Gand - Wevelgem, 12th in the Tour Of Flanders, 13th in the Paris Roubaix), the rider laughingly declared "I followed the right man, that of the Canadian Michael Barry - at the right time, and I definitely came up with the best sprint of my career. Since the start of the season I have been anxious to bring a win to my new team. Now, I must say, it was well worth the wait". This patience did him no favours on several occasions in the Tour de France. Notably in Angers, when he was caught at the 1 kilometre mark, and on the way to Figeac, when he was surprised by David Moncoutié. It is also the first time that Juan Antonio Flecha has come out on top in front of thirty riders engaged in what could almost be called a mass sprint.

BARREDO AND ZABRISKIE, DID THEY BELIEVE?

Well before the race being decided, in perfect weather, things were shaken up by a joint attack by Carlos Barredo (Liberty Seguros) and David Zabriskie (US Postal). When the two had already put some distance between themselves and the pack, Christophe Mengin (Fdjeux.com) made an improbable attempt to go after them. At more than six minutes behind the duo, the rider from the Loraine finally had to admit defeat and was recuperated by the peloton with 80 kms left to ride. The two first attackers of the day gradually weakened as time went by, seeing their lead of 21 minutes fade away as the finish approached. The breakaway suffered a serious blow when the American rider accelerated on the climb at Pfannenstiel (km 177), leaving his companion behind.

Holding on for all he was worth, the Spaniard managed to catch up a little later, on the descent... and took his revenge by

attacking in turn while climbing at Forch (40kms from the finish). But, by that time, things were beginning to look bleak for the duo. A counter attack was led by Alexandre Vinocourov (T Mobile) along with Frabcesco Casagrande (Lampre), Marcus Zberg (Gerolsteiner) and Michael Rogers (Quick Step). The two riders who had led the race for so long were soon caught, but the group of four riders was split by the negative tactics of Michael Rogers on the pretext of riding in the interests of his leader Paolo Bettini. Their adventure came to an end 22 kilometers from the line on the last ascention of Pfannenstiel.

Immediately, Paolo Bettini shakes things up, reducing the peloton to thirty riders. Patxi Vila (Lampre) tries several times to break out of this group. In vain. On the other hand, Rik Verbrugghe (Lotto) and David Moncoutié (Cofidis) do manage to get away at the steepest part of the climb near the summit. Vinocourov followed a short distance behind, followed by small groups of 2 or 3 riders. The descent towards Zurich caused the groups to bunch up into a peloton of 30 contestants. Would the short climb to Wetzwil split up the riders once again? This could be going through the mind of Davide Rebellin as he accelerates up this last hill. Straight away, the world Cup leader is in the company of Paolo Bettini, as well as past winner Dario Frigo and Paolo Savoldelli who we had lost sight of for a long time. The Italian quartet can only stay ahead for two thousand metres. At 6 kilometers from the line a new group forms! Successively, Erik Dekker, Rik Verbrugghe then Michael Barry try to break out without success. Erik Dekker even has another go, as he did in san Sebastian some years before, before being caught again. Bettini goes for the sprint on the left hand side of the road, but soon realises his mistake. Before any reaction is possible, Juan Flecha is fired up, passing Michael Barry and fighting off the impressive Jerome Pineau, finally third. This year, second place in the august World Cup events is reserved for Mr Paolo Bettini... ■

David Zabriskie (left) and Carlos Barredo were in front for almost 200 kilometers!

172 Competitors

T.MOBILE			
1.	NARDELLO Daniele (Ita)	31st	+ 3"
2.	EVANS Cadel (Aus)	29th	s.t
3.	GUERINI Giuseppe (Ita)		*Abandon*
4.	WESEMANN Steffen (Ger)	63rd	+ 3'38"
5.	KONECNY Tomas (Cze)		*Abandon*
6.	SAVOLDELLI Paolo (Ita)	27th	s.t
7.	SCHRECK Stephan (Ger)	78th	+ 6'52"
8.	VINOKOUROV Alexandre	34th	+ 1'55"

QUICK STEP - DAVITAMON			
11.	BETTINI Paolo (Ita)	**2nd**	s.t
12.	DUFAUX Laurent (Sui)	73rd	+ 6'32"
13.	PAOLINI Luca (Ita)	52nd	+ 3'38"
14.	BRAMATI Davide (Ita)		*Abandon*
15.	ROGERS Michael (Aus)	71st	+ 6'32"
16.	SINKEWITZ Patrik (Ger)	33rd	+ 19"
17.	TANKINK Bram (Ned)	82nd	+ 6'52"
18.	GARRIDO J. Antonio (Esp)		*Abandon*

RABOBANK			
21.	DE WEERT Kevin (Bel)		*Abandon*
22.	DEKKER Erik (Ned)	32nd	+ 11"
23.	FREIRE Oscar (Esp)	**9th**	s.t
24.	LOTZ Marc (Ned)	39th	+ 3'38"
25.	NIERMANN Grischa (Ger)		*Abandon*
26.	LEIPHEIMER Levy (Usa)	46th	+ 3'38"
27.	WEENING Pieter (Ned)	86th	+ 6'52"
28.	DE GROOT Bram (Ned)		*Abandon*

FASSA BORTOLO			
31.	PETITO Roberto (Ita)		*Abandon*
32.	CIONI Dario (Ita)	48th	+ 3'38"
33.	CODOL Massimo (Ita)	51st	+ 3'38"
34.	FLECHA Juan Antonio (Esp)	**1st**	**6h13'30"**
35.	FRIGO Dario (Ita)	30th	s.t
36.	GUSTOV Volodymir (Ukr)	23rd	s.t
37.	GONZALEZ JIMENEZ Aitor (Esp)	54th	+ 3'38"
38.	SACCHI Fabio (Ita)	45th	+ 3'38"

LOTTO - DOMO			
41.	MERCKX Axel (Bel)	41st	+ 3'38"
42.	VERBRUGGHE Rik (Bel)	12nd	s.t
43.	D'HOLLANDER Glen (Bel)		*Abandon*
45.	BAGUET Serge (Bel)	20th	s.t
46.	DETILLOUX Christophe (Bel)		*Abandon*
47.	MOERENHOUT Koos (Ned)		*Abandon*
48.	VANSEVENANT Wim (Bel)		*Abandon*

SAECO			
51.	CELESTINO Mirko (Ita)	17th	s.t
52.	COMMESSO Salvatore (Ita)		*Abandon*

53.	DI LUCA Danilo (Ita)		*Abandon*
54.	STANGELJ Gorazd (Slo)	58th	+ 3'38"
55.	LOOSLI David (Sui)		*Abandon*
56.	SPEZIALETTI Alessandro (Ita)		*Abandon*
57.	MAZZOLENI Eddy (Ita)	90th	+ 6'52"

CSC

61.	PERON Andrea (Ita)	62nd	+ 3'38"
62.	SCHLECK Frank (Lux)		*Abandon*
63.	CALVENTE Manuel (Esp)	77th	+ 6'52"
64.	JAKSCHE Jörg (Ger)		*Abandon*
65.	BARTOLI Michele (Ita)	24th	s.t
66.	LÜTTENBERGER Peter (Aut)	59th	+ 3'38"
67.	SØRENSEN Nicki (Den)	60th	+ 3'38"

US POSTAL - BERRY FLOOR

71.	AZEVEDO José (Por)		*Abandon*
72.	BARRY Michael (Can)	**7th**	s.t
73.	BELTRAN Manuel (Esp)	40th	+ 3'38"
74.	HINCAPIE George (Usa)	**8th**	s.t
75.	VAN DEN BROECK Jurgen (Bel)		*Abandon*
76.	ZABRISKIE David (Usa)		*Abandon*
77.	NOVAL Benjamin (Esp)		*Abandon*
78.	PADRNOS Pavel (Cze)		*Abandon*

GEROLSTEINER

81.	FARESIN Gianni (Ita)	67th	+ 3'38"
82.	STRAUSS Marcel (Sui)	38th	+ 3'38"
83.	REBELLIN Davide (Ita)	**6th**	s.t
84.	SCHOLZ Ronny (Ger)	79th	+ 6'52"
85.	SERPELLINI Marco (Ita)	35th	+ 3'38"
86.	TOTSCHNIG Georg (Aut)	25th	s.t
87.	WEGMANN Fabian (Ger)	22nd	s.t
88.	ZBERG Marcus (Sui)	16th	s.t

COFIDIS

91.	ATIENZA Daniel (Esp)	69th	+ 6'32"
92.	CUESTA Iñigo (Esp)		*Abandon*
93.	FERNANDEZ BUSTINZA Bingen (Esp)	91st	+ 6'52"
94.	FOFONOV Dmitriy (Kaz)	**4th**	s.t
95.	MONCOUTIÉ David (Fra)	19th	s.t
96.	PEREZ RODRIGUEZ Luis (Esp)	93rd	+ 6'52"
97.	TRENTIN Guido (Ita)	55th	+ 3'38"
98.	WHITE Matthew (Aus)		*Abandon*

LAMPRE

101.	CASAGRANDE Francesco (Ita)	21st	s.t
102.	ASTARLOA Igor (Esp)	87th	+ 6'52"
103.	SCOTTO D'ABUSCO Michele (Ita)		*Abandon*
104.	QUINZIATO Manuel (Ita)	81st	+ 6'52"
105.	BORTOLAMI Gianluca (Ita)	44th	+ 3'38"
106.	BOSSONI Paolo (Ita)	49th	+ 3'38"
107.	VILA Patxi (Esp)	28th	s.t
108.	RIGHI Daniele (Ita)		*Abandon*

EUSKALTEL - EUSKADI

111.	ARTETXE Mikel (Esp)		*Abandon*
112.	ALBIZU Joseba (Esp)	15th	s.t
113.	ETXEBARRIA David (Esp)		*Abandon*
114.	GONZALEZ LARRAÑAGA Gorka (Esp)		*Abandon*
115.	ISASI Iñaki (Esp)	72nd	+ 6'32"
116.	MARTINEZ de ESTEBAN Egoi (Esp)		*Abandon*
117.	SANCHEZ Samuel (Esp)		*Abandon*
118.	SILLONIZ Aitor (Esp)		*Abandon*

PHONAK

121.	ALBASINI Michael (Sui)	**5th**	s.t
122.	ELMIGER Martin (Sui)	42nd	+ 3'38"
123.	MOOS Alexandre (Sui)	74th	+ 6'32"
124.	RAST Gregory (Sui)		*Abandon*
125.	SCHNIDER Daniel (Sui)	43rd	+ 3'38"
126.	TSCHOPP Johann (Sui)	64th	+ 3'38"
127.	VALJAVEC Tadej (Slo)	26th	s.t
128.	MURN Uros (Slo)	36th	+ 3'38"

ALESSIO - BIANCHI

131.	FERRARA Raffaele (Ita)	66th	+ 3'38"
132.	JØRGENSEN René (Den)		*Abandon*
133.	IVANOV Ruslan (Mda)		*Abandon*
134.	LJUNGQVIST Marcus (Swe)		*Abandon*
135.	FURLAN Angelo (Ita)		*Abandon*
136.	BERTOLINI Alessandro (Ita)		*Abandon*

LIBERTY Seguros

141.	BARREDO Carlos (Esp)	95th	+ 10'38"
142.	ANDRLE René (Cze)	50th	+ 3'38"
143.	DIAZ JUSTO Rafael (Esp)		*Abandon*
144.	HERNÁNDEZ BLAZQUEZ Jesus (Esp)	88th	+ 6'52"
145.	RAMIREZ ABEJA Javier (Esp)		*Abandon*
146.	SANCHEZ GIL Luis Leon (Esp)		*Abandon*
147.	VANDEVELDE Christian (Usa)		*Abandon*
148.	GONZALEZ de GALDEANO Alvaro (Esp)		*Abandon*

FDJEUX.COM

151	FRITSCH Nicolas (Fra)	85th	+ 6'52"
152.	GILBERT Philippe (Bel)	56th	+ 3'38"
153.	MENGIN Christophe (Fra)		*Abandon*
154.	MOUREY Francis (Fra)		*Abandon*
156.	DEREPAS David (Fra)		*Abandon*
157.	CASAR Sandy (Fra)	92nd	+ 6'52"

LANDBOUWKREDIET - COLNAGO

161.	POPOVYCH Yaroslav (Ukr)	68th	+ 3'38"
162.	DUMA Vladimir (Ukr)	61st	+ 3'38"
163.	GASPERONI Cristian (Ita)		*Abandon*
164.	GRYSCHENKO Ruslan (Ukr)		*Abandon*
165.	BILEKA Volodymir (Ukr)		*Abandon*
166.	LAGUTIN Serguey (Uzb)		*Abandon*
167.	ADVEYEV Serguey (Ukr)		*Abandon*
168.	BERNUCCI Lorenzo (Ita)	89th	+ 6'52"

DE NARDI

171.	HONCHAR Serhiy (Ukr)	13rd	s.t
172.	BORGHI Ruggero (Ita)	18th	s.t
174.	JURCO Matej (Svk)		*Abandon*
175.	GIORDANI Leonardo (Ita)	84th	+ 6'52"
176.	NURITDINOV Rafael (Uzb)	94th	+ 10'38"
177.	VANOTTI Alessandro (Ita)		*Abandon*
178.	LORENZETTO Mirko (Ita)		*Abandon*

The battle between Paolo Bettini (wearing a gold coloured jersey in celebration of his Olympic success) and Davide Rebellin, hots up after this eighth round of the World Cup.

Brioches LA BOULANGÈRE

181.	CHARTEAU Anthony (Fra)		*Abandon*
182.	CHAVANEL Sylvain (Fra)	57th	+ 3'38"
183.	HARY Maryan (Fra)	53rd	+ 3'38"
184.	KERN Christophe (Fra)		*Abandon*
185.	YUS Unai (Esp)	11st	s.t
186.	NAULLEAU Alexandre (Fra)		*Abandon*
187.	PINEAU Jérôme (Fra)	**3rd**	s.t
188.	SPRICK Mathieu (Fra)		*Abandon*

SAUNIER DUVAL - PRODIR

191.	BERTOGLIATI Rubens (Sui)		*Abandon*
192.	LODDO Alberto (Ita)		*Abandon*
193.	VENTOSO Francisco (Esp)		*Abandon*
194.	STRAZZER Massimo (Ita)		*Abandon*
195.	JOHNSON Tim (Usa)		*Abandon*
196.	DE LA FUENTE David (Esp)	83rd	+ 6'52"
197.	MORI Manuele (Ita)	37th	+ 3'38"
198.	ZAUGG Oliver (Sui)		*Abandon*

Vini CALDIROLA - NOBILI Rubinetterie

201.	ANDRIOTTO Dario (Ita)		*Abandon*
202.	BEUCHAT Roger (Sui)	65th	+ 3'38"
203.	MASCIARELLI Andrea (Ita)		*Abandon*
205.	GEROSA Mauro (Ita)	80th	+ 6'52"
206.	MASCIARELLI Simone (Ita)		*Abandon*
207.	SIRONI Gianluca (Ita)		*Abandon*
208.	ZAMPIERI Steve (Sui)		*Abandon*

AG2R Prévoyance

211.	LAIDOUN Julien (Fra)	70th	+ 6'32"
213.	CHAURREAU Iñigo (Esp)	76th	+ 6'52"
214.	GOUBERT Stéphane (Fra)		*Abandon*
215.	KRIVTSOV Yuriy (Ukr)		*Abandon*
216.	PORTAL Nicolas (Fra)		*Abandon*
217.	TURPIN Ludovic (Fra)		*Abandon*
218.	ORIOL Christophe (Fra)	47th	+ 3'38"

DOMINA VACANZE

221.	BAZHENOV Alexandr (Rus)		*Abandon*
222.	MORI Massimiliano (Ita)	75th	+ 6'32"
223.	GENTILI Massimiliano (Ita)	**10th**	s.t
224.	KOLOBNEV Alexandr (Rus)	14th	s.t
225.	SCARPONI Michele (Ita)		*Abandon*
228.	VALOTI Paolo (Ita)		*Abandon*

PAST WINNERS AT THE START	***7***
NARDELLO Daniele	2003
FRIGO Dario	2002
BETTINI Paolo	2001
DUFAUX Laurent	2000
BARTOLI Michele	1998
REBELLIN Davide	1997
BORTOLAMI Gianluca	1994

RIDERS IN THE U C I TOP 100 ***35***

ROOKIES AT THE START (LESS THAN ONE YEAR AS A PROFESSIONAL): ***19***

3 YOUNGEST	
JURCO Matej	1984/08/08
SANCHEZ GIL Luis Leon	1983/11/23
SCOTTO D'ABUSCO Michele	1983/03/05

3 OLDEST	
FARESIN Gianni	1965/07/16
BRAMATI Davide	1968/06/28
BORTOLAMI Gianluca	1968/08/28

TOTAL OF POINTS UCI OBTAINED IN THE RACE	
FASSA BORTOLO	277 points
QUICK STEP - DAVITAMON	175 points
Brioches LA BOULANGÈRE	173 points
GEROLSTEINER	152 points
COFIDIS	147 points
US POSTAL - BERRY FLOOR	137 points
PHONAK	130 points
DOMINA VACANZE	84 points
RABOBANK	73 points
DE NARDI	66 points
LOTTO - DOMO	61 points
LAMPRE	42 points
T.MOBILE	34 points
EUSKALTEL - EUSKADI	33 points
SAECO	
CSC	31 points
AG2R Prévoyance	15 points
FDJEUX.COM	
LANDBOUWKREDIET - COLNAGO	
LIBERTY Seguros	
SAUNIER DUVAL - PRODIR	10 points
Vini CALDIROLA - NOBILI Rubinetterie	
ALESSIO - BIANCHI	5 points

Bettini...

The risk, if there is a risk, it's that with teams limited to five riders, the medals can end up on the chest of an unknown. In the men's road race, that's what might well have happened if the devilish Paolo Bettini hadn't taken things in hand. At the start of a decisive attack he would only allow Sergio Paulinho to ride beside him. Who? A Portuguese rider aged 24 who'd just finished his national Tour which as in Athens was run in scorching temperatures. Even the high class field assembled at the foot of the Acropolis (without, of course Lance Armstrong, for whom the season gets shorter each year), didn't overwhelm him.

Taking place at the start of the Olympic Games, the men's road race inaugurated a circuit of 13.1 kms . A very different circuit to that in Sydney four years earlier. The peloton of 144 riders discovers a course with many bends, cobbles, road islands, rails and two tricky winding hills. And all this under a blazing sun...The day after the opening ceremony, the crowds have stayed away from the first of 18 cycling events. Even though it has always been an Olympic sport, cycle racing is a minority sport in Greece. And no local riders are present on the start line.
A strange atmosphere hangs over the start. The majestic surroundings perhaps have something to do with this. Strange also is the state of the Spanish team. Coming from their success in the world Championship, they suffer two retirements in the first ...5kms. Igor Astarloa and José Ivan Gutierrez are involved in a crash which also involves Michael Boogerd.

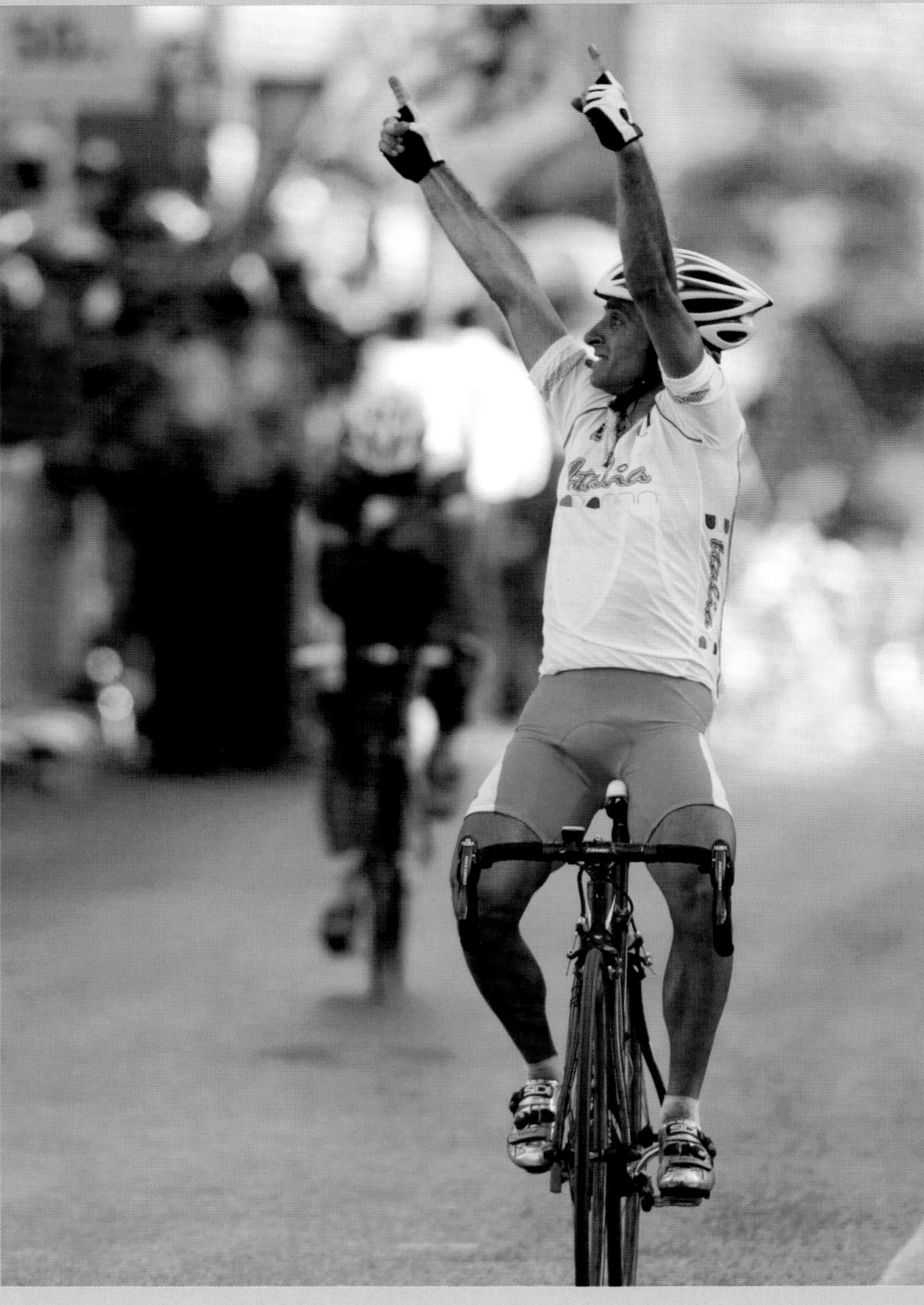

Paolo Bettini salutes his compatriots in the press box and gets ready to hug the Italian team manager Franco Ballerini. The tactics worked perfectly!

A WARRIORS SALUTE FROM VIRENQUE...
Magnus Backstedt, the giant Swede, hasn't come to Athens to see the sights. He waits just 23kms before launching into a suicidal attack (the race is over 222kms) in which no one joins him. A third of the way through the race the Scandinavian's lead stands at 3mins 20sec. This is the chosen moment for Richard Virenque to make his move. The Frenchman rapidly catches up with the Swede, but his counter attack looks more like a parting shot than anything else (Virenque knows well that these will be his last Olympics). He also knows he presents no real danger to the young guns in the peloton. Even with the help of the Hungarian Laszlo

Bodrogi (Team mate of the Frenchman for the rest of the year), things don't look promising. This turns out to be the truth. The Germans end up doing most of the work but wear themselves out 90kms from the line. Back to the drawing board!

The repeated climbs on the Lycabettus take their toll and the men left behind take longer and longer to catch up again. Another race begins. Abortive attempts at an attack come and go. The Americans Bobby Julich, Levi Leipheimer and Tyler Hamilton, the Belgians Philippe Gilbert and Axel Merckx, the Lettonian Romans Vainsteins are also making their presence felt. Less though than a quartet which pulls away at 60kms from the finish line. In it we find the Swiss rider Martin Elmiger, the South African Ryan Cox, Irishman Ciaran Power and the Australian Robbie Mc Ewen. The too well known reputation of the latter certainly condemns the group in its action. The tricky circuit doesn't help the riders in their decisions. Presented as tired after his Tour de France (understandably), Thomas Voeckler, the new French idol, goes into action. Straight away Hamilton and Nardello follow in his tracks. The attack peters out. Still bunched up at one and a half laps from the finish line, the peloton still hasn't been faced with a serious attack, when Paolo Bettini fires up. Alexandre Vinokourov or Jan Ullrich might be expected to be able to follow, but the two team mates from T Mobile seem stuck, unlike the surprising Portuguese rider Sergio Paulinho, the only one able to stay up front with Bettini. The Tuscan welcomes the arrival of the rider he has never or almost never come across before. He rapidly notes that the Portuguese rider has a job maintaining the pace when faced with a prolonged relay. Behind, no teams seem able to mount any kind of attack and if they were to, Daniele Nardello is watching with eagle eyes. The road is open for the leading duo. Without surprise and with little difficulty, Paolo Bettini gets the better of his adversary, seemingly already overwhelmed at the prospect of a silver medal. The bronze will go to a Belgian with a prestigious name: Axel Merckx, who pulled out of the pelotonin the final kilometers. That was a distinction his father never managed in the whole of his career!

For Richard Virenque, the important thing is not to take part, but to be seen. He puts this concept into action in Athens.

...A BAD FINGER FOR ARNDT

The day after the triumph of Bettini, the automobile still hasn't returned to the streets of Athens. 67 women representing any number of countries start out on the women's road race. The heat is just as unbearable, the Greek public just as absent and the race gets under way in an odd atmosphere. A few diversionary attacks, a crash of one of the favourites (the Duch Leontien van Moorseel who'd chosen Athens to bow out of competition) and a duo that fights it out for the Gold medal. The offensive from the Canadian Susan Palmer two laps from the finish has the effect of completely opening up the race. The brave Canadian is finally caught by Judith Arndt, the German, Nicole Cooke, the rider from Wales, Mirjam Melchers, the Dutchwoman, Joane Somarimba, the Spaniard, Olga Slyussareva, the Russian, and the Australians Oenone Wood and Sara Carrigan. The latter counter attacks immediately and supports only the return of Judith Arndt, in theory faster. But Sara Carrigan isn't worried by past form. She launches the sprint from a long way out and surprises the German, preoccupied by waving a finger at the German team officials (who, according to her made the mistake of leaving out her friend, Petra Rossner). The race was won at that point.

Judith Arndt, Sara Carrigan and Olga Slyussareva (left to right) show off their medals...

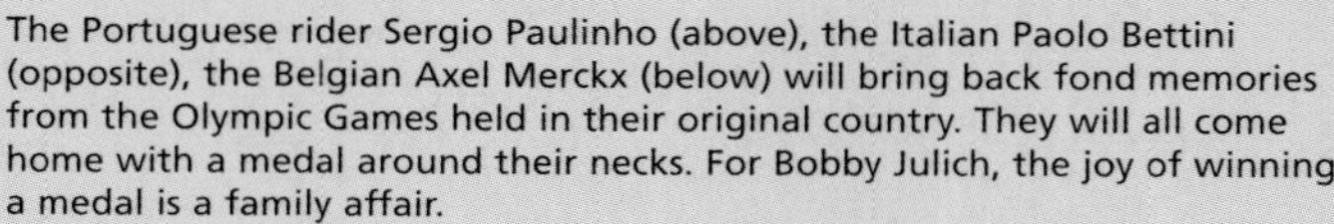

The Portuguese rider Sergio Paulinho (above), the Italian Paolo Bettini (opposite), the Belgian Axel Merckx (below) will bring back fond memories from the Olympic Games held in their original country. They will all come home with a medal around their necks. For Bobby Julich, the joy of winning a medal is a family affair.

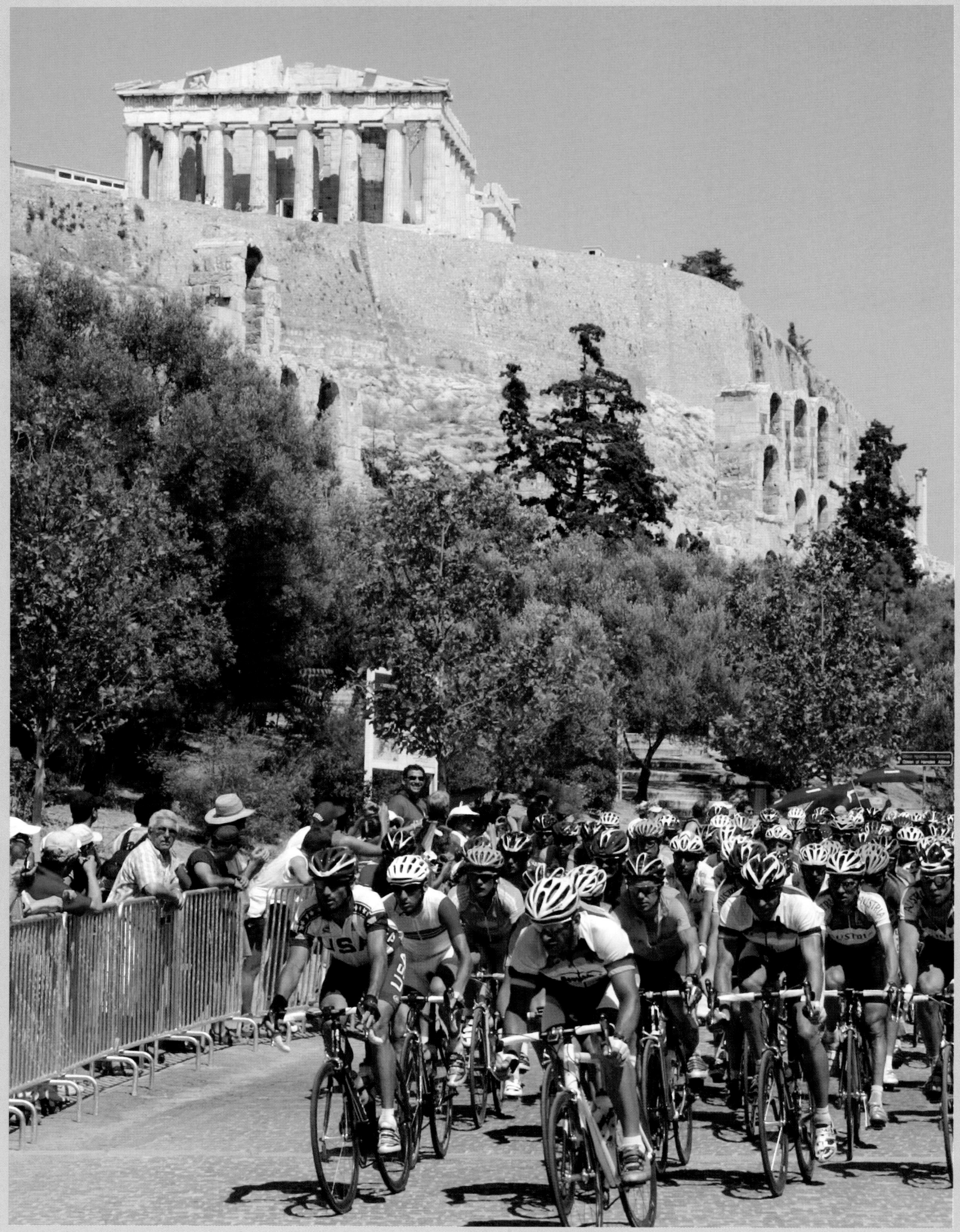

THE STAR SPANGLED BANNER FLIES OVER THE TIME TRIAL

Favourite, ultra favourite, Jan Ullrich could not be beaten in the Olympic time trial. All the attention being on the German rider meant that the media tended to forget that Hamilton, Rogers, Julich and Vinokourov hadn't come to Athens just to make up the numbers. Four years earlier in Sydney, it was also an outsider, the already experienced Russian Viatcheslav Ekimov who took the highest place on the podium. At 38 years old one of the trusted sidekicks of Lance Armstrong, is still very much a competitor and determined to go for the title. Finally, not much was missing to acheive his unthinkable challenge. Not accounting for Hamilton, he would have been able to collect a second Gold Medal. But Tyler Hamilton had prepared well for the event. Just the same, it was the veteran Russian who finished the first of the two laps with the fastest time. Mid way through the course, twenty kilometers outside Athens, the reigning Olympic champion was 4 seconds ahead of the Australian Michael Rogers, 5 seconds ahead of Tyler Hamilton, 10 seconds ahead of Michael Rich and Bobby Julich and already 38 seconds ahead of Jan Ullrich and 40seconds quicker than Alexandre Vinokourov. Christophe Moreau was already a long way from a first Olympic medal. He trailed by 1minute 04 seconds after 24 kilometers of the race! At this moment we could understand that Jan Ulrich would once again fail. And that this time trial would be somewhat in the image of his season: disappointing.

At 33 years old Tyler Hamilton has just signed up for the four year title of Olympic time trial Champion. The race, run near to Athens over two laps of a circuit.

The second lap of this lovely circuit, alas without any spectators, would be one too many for Viatcheslav Ekimov. The Russian begins to lose ground just as Tyler Hamilton, despite problems with his radio system, begins to eat up the kilometers at an impressive rate. At the line, the trend noted at the intermediary check points is confirmed: Tyler Hamilton pushes Ekimov 18 seconds down the order. Then another American, the strong finishing Bobby Julich pushes Michael Rogers off the Podium by just 3 seconds.

The harvest of medals is not finished for the American team. The women's time trial permits the wife of Michael Barry, the Canadian team mate of Lance Armstrong, Dierdre Demit – Barry to take the silver medal. The Gold medal goes to one of the big names of the last decade in women cycling, the Dutchwoman Leontien van Moorsel, who, at a little over 34 years old, had decided to retire after these Games. She retires on a high note with a new Gold medal to add to the three at Sydney four years before.

The only thing to cloud the horizon of the American team is the positive dope test of Tyler Hamilton a few weeks later in the Vuelta. Luckily for the rider from Massachusetts his B sample from Athens was frozen by mistake so another positive result was avoided...

The American could keep his medal and the IOC could save its honour. ■

Since his podium finish in the 1998 Tour de France, Bobby Julich had returned to relative obscurity. His closed season transfer to the CSC team put him back on the right track. His bronze medal in the time trial event confirmed his comeback.

TIME TRIAL RESULTS

Men - 48 km

1.	**Tyler Hamilton (Usa)**	**CSC**	**57'31"**
2.	Viatcheslav Ekimov (Rus)	USP	+ 18"
3.	Bobby Julich (Usa)	CSC	+ 26"
4.	Michael Rogers (Aus)	QSD	+ 29"
5.	Michael Rich (Ger)	GST	+ 37"
6.	Alexandre Vinokourov (Kaz)	TMO	+ 1'26"
7.	Jan Ullrich (Ger)	TMO	+ 1'30"
8.	Santiago Botero (Col)	TMO	+ 1'33"
9.	Igor Gonzalez de Galdeano (Esp)	LST	+ 1'55"
10.	Fabian Cancellara (Sui)	FAS	+ 2'10"
11.	Yuriy Krivtsov (Ukr)	A2R	+ 2'17"
12.	Christophe Moreau (Fra)	C.A	+ 2'18"
13.	Marc Wauters (Bel)	RAB	+ 2'27"
14.	Michal Hrazdira (Cze)	El2	+ 2'35"
15.	Victor Hugo Peña (Col)	USP	+ 2'38"
16.	J. Ivan Gutierrez Palacios (Esp)	IBB	+ 2'51"
17.	Rene Andrle (Cze)	LST	+ 2'55"
18.	Eric Wohlberg (Can)	SIE	+ 2'59"
19.	Peter van Petegem (Bel)	LOT	+ 3'03"
20.	Frank Høj (Den)	CSC	+ 3'05"
21.	Thomas Dekker (Ned)	RB3	+ 3'06"
22.	Laszlo Bodrogi (Hun)	QSD	+ 3'12"
23.	Serhiy Honchar (Ukr)	DEN	+ 3'28"
24.	Eugen Wacker (Kgz)	ATI	+ 3'49"
25.	Sergio Paulinho (Por)	LAP	+ 3'53"
26.	Benoît Joachim (Lux)	USP	+ 4'18"

27.	Rubens Bertogliati (Sui)	SDV	+ 4'44".
28.	Kurt-Asle Arvesen (Nor)	CSC	+ 4'49"
29.	Evgeni Petrov (Rus)	SAE	+ 5'18"
30.	Stuart Dangerfield (Gbr)	El2	+ 5'28"
31.	Dawid Krupa (Pol)	LEG	+ 5'35"
32.	Thor Hushovd (Nor)	C.A	+ 5'38"
33.	Heath Blackgrove (Nzl)	El2	+ 5'48"
34.	Thomas Lövkvist (Swe)	FDJ	+ 6'11"
35.	Gorazd Stangelj (Slo)	SAE	+ 6'14"
36.	Matej Jurco (Svk)	DEN	+ 6'50"
37.	Slawomir Kohut (Pol)	HOP	+ 8'47"

Women - 24 km

1.	**Leontien Zijlaard-Van Moorsel (Ned)**	**31'11"**
2.	Deidre Demet-Barry (Usa)	+ 24"
3.	Karin Thürig (Sui)	+ 43"
4.	Christine Thorburn (Usa)	+ 1'03"
5.	Lada Kozlikova (Cze)	+ 1'04"
6.	Oenone Wood (Aus)	+ 1'05"
7.	Joane Somarriba (Esp)	+ 1'14"
8.	Zoulfia Zabirova (Rus)	+ 1'19"
9.	Priska Doppmann (Sui)	+ 1'29"
10.	Edita Pucinskaite (Ltu)	+ 1'31"
11.	Judith Arndt (Ger)	+ 1'35"
12.	Olga Slyusareva (Rus)	+ 1'40"
13.	Mirjam Melchers (Ned)	+ 1'50"
14.	Jeannie Longo Ciprelli (Fra)	+ 1'54"
15.	Trixi Worrack (Ger)	s.t
16.	Lyne Bessette (Can)	+ 2'13"
17.	Susan Palmer-Komar (Can)	+ 2'15"
18.	Dori Ruano Sanchon (Spa)	+ 2'18"
19.	Nicole Cooke (Gbr)	+ 2'34"
20.	Edwige Pitel (Fra)	+ 2'34"
21.	Tatiana Guderzo (Ita)	+ 3'03"
22.	Anita Valen (Nor)	+ 3'20"
23.	Rasa Polikeviciute (Ltu)	+ 3'23"
24.	Nataliya Kachalka (Ukr)	+ 3'50"
25.	Susanne Ljungskog (Swe)	+ 4'06"

MEN'S ROAD RACE
144 Competitors

Germany

1.	ULLRICH Jan (TMO)	19th	+ 12"
2.	KLÖDEN Andreas (TMO)		*Abandon*
3.	RICH Michael (GST)		*Abandon*
4.	VOIGT Jens (CSC)	64th	+ 8'51"
5.	ZABEL Erik (TMO)	**4th**	+ 12"

Italy

6.	BETTINI Paolo (QSD)	**1st**	**5h41'44"**
7.	MORENI Cristian (ALB)	46th	+ 2'29"
8.	NARDELLO Daniele (TMO)	38th	+ 19"
9.	PAOLINI Luca (QSD)	39th	+ 19"
10.	POZZATO Filippo (FAS)	67th	+ 8'51"

Spain

11.	ASTARLOA Igor (LAM)		*Abandon*
12.	FREIRE Oscar (RAB)		*Abandon*
13.	GONZALEZ de GALDEANO Igor (LST)		*Abandon*
14.	GUTIERREZ PALACIOS José Ivan (IBB)		*Abandon*
15.	VALVERDE Alejandro (KEL)	47th	+ 2'29"

France

16.	BROCHARD Laurent (A2R)	44th	+ 2'29"
17.	CHAVANEL Sylvain (BLB)		*Abandon*
18.	MOREAU Christophe (C.A)		*Abandon*
19.	VIRENQUE Richard (QSD)	48th	+ 2'29"
20.	VOECKLER Thomas (BLB)	20th	+ 12"

U.S.A

21.	HAMILTON Tyler (PHO)	18th	+ 12"
22.	HINCAPIE George (USP)	24th	+ 12"
23.	JULICH Bobby (CSC)	28th	+ 12"
24.	LEIPHEIMER Levi (RAB)		
25.	McCARTNEY Jason (HNC)		

Belgium

26.	GILBERT Philippe (FDJ)	49th	+ 2'29"
27.	MERCKX Axel (LOT)	**3rd**	+ 8"
28.	VAN PETEGEM Peter (LOT)	40th	+ 19"

No.	Rider	Place	Gap
29.	VANSEVENANT Wim (LOT)		*Abandon*
30.	WAUTERS Marc (RAB)		*Abandon*
	Australia		
31.	COOKE Baden (FDJ)		*Abandon*
32.	McEWEN Robbie (LOT)	11st	+ 12"
33.	O'GRADY Stuart (COF)	33rd	+ 12"
34.	ROGERS Michael (QSD)		*Abandon*
35.	WHITE Matthew (COF)		*Abandon*
	Switzerland		
36.	BERTOGLIATI Rubens (SDV)		*Abandon*
37.	CANCELLARA Fabian (FAS)		*Abandon*
38.	ELMIGER Martin (PHO)	29th	+ 12"
39.	RAST Gregory (PHO)		*Abandon*
40.	ZBERG Marcus (GST)	12nd	+ 12"
	Netherlands		
41.	BOOGERD Michael (RAB)		*Abandon*
42.	DEKKER Erik (RAB)	41st	+ 45"
43.	KNAVEN Servais (QSD)		*Abandon*
44.	KROON Karsten (RAB)	52nd	+ 5'29"
45.	VAN HEESWIJK Max (USP)	17th	+ 12"
	Russia		
46.	EKIMOV Viatcheslav (USP)		*Abandon*
47.	KARPETS Vladimir (IBB)		*Abandon*
48.	KOLOBNEV Alexandr (DVE)	**10th**	+ 12"
49.	MENCHOV Denis (IBB)		*Abandon*
50.	PETROV Evgeni (SAE)	37th	+ 12"
	Denmark		
51.	HAMBURGER Bo (A&S)	25th	+ 12"
52.	HØJ Frank (CSC)	**8th**	+ 12"
53.	MICHAELSEN Lars (CSC)	55th	+ 8'51"
54.	RASMUSSEN Michael (RAB)		*Abandon*
55.	SØRENSEN Nicki (CSC)	60th	+ 8'51"
	Ukraine		
56.	DUMA Vladimir (LAN)		*Abandon*
57.	HONCHAR Serhiy (DEN)	21st	+ 12"
58.	KRIVTSOV Yuriy (A2R)		*Abandon*
59.	POPOVYCH Yaroslav (LAN)	68th	+ 8'51"
60.	POSPEEV Kyrylo (A&S)	23rd	+ 12"
	Poland		
61.	BROZYNA Tomasz (ATI)	56th	+ 8'51"
62.	KOHUT Slawomir (HOP)		*Abandon*
63.	KRUPA Dawid (LEG)	75th	+ 18'41"
64.	ROMANIK Radoslaw (HOP)		*Abandon*
65.	SZMYD Sylvester (SAE)		*Abandon*
	Great Britain		
66.	DANGERFIELD Stuart (El2)		Abandon
67.	HAMMOND Roger (MRB)	**7th**	+ 12"
68.	WEGELIUS Roger (DEN)		Abandon
69.	WINN Julian (El2)		Abandon
	Kazakstan		
70.	IGLINSKIY Maxim (CAP)		*Abandon*
71.	KASHECHKIN Andrey (C.A)	70th	+ 8'51"
72.	MIZOUROV Andrey (OKT)	73rd	+ 9'44"
73.	VINOKOUROV Alexandre (TMO)	35th	+ 12"
74.	YAKOVLEV Serguey (TMO)	53rd	+ 7'04"
	Austria		
75.	EISEL Bernhard (FDJ)		*Abandon*
76.	GLOMSER Gerrit (SAE)	51st	+ 3'37"
77.	TOTSCHNIG Georg (GST)	22nd	+ 12"
78.	TRAMPUSCH Gerhard (A&S)	30th	+ 12"
	Colombia		
79.	BOTERO Santiago (TMO)	31st	+ 12"
80.	LAVERDE Luis Felipe (FPF)	36th	+ 12"
81.	PEÑA Victor Hugo (USP)		*Abandon*
82.	PEREZ ARANGO Marlon (CLM)		*Abandon*
	Portugal		
83.	AMORIM Gonçalo (MIL)		*Abandon*
84.	BARBOSA Candido (LAP)		*Abandon*
85.	PAULINHO Sergio (LAP)	**2nd**	s.t
86.	RIBEIRO Nuno (LAP)	27th	+ 12"
	Czech Republic		
87.	ANDRLE René (LST)	58th	+ 8'51"
88.	HRAZDIRA Michal (El2)		*Abandon*
89.	SOSENKA Ondrej (A&S)	65th	+ 8'51"
90.	SVORADA Jan (LAM)	63rd	+ 8'51"
	Sweden		
91.	BÄCKSTEDT Magnus (ALB)		*Abandon*
92.	LARSSON Gustav Erik (FAS)	72nd	+ 9'44"
93.	LJUNGQVIST Marcus (ALB)	14th	+ 12"
94.	LÖVKVIST Thomas (FDJ)		*Abandon*
	Slovenia		
95.	HAUPTMAN Andrej (LAM)	**5th**	+ 12"
96.	MURN Uros (PHO)	50th	+ 2'29"
97.	STANGELJ Gorazd (SAE)	43rd	+ 1'36"
98.	VALJAVEC Tadej (PHO)	26th	+ 12"
	Estonia		
99.	AUG Andrus (DVE)		*Abandon*
100.	KIRSIPUU Jaan (A2R)		*Abandon*
101.	PÜTSEP Erki (A2R)		*Abandon*
102.	TOMBAK Janek (COF)	61st	+ 8'51"
	Norway		
103.	ARVESEN Kurt-Asle (CSC)	**9th**	+12"
104.	HEGREBERG Morten (JAR)		*Abandon*
105.	HUSHOVD Thor (C.A)		*Abandon*
106.	KAGGESTAD Mads (C.A)		*Abandon*
	New Zealand		
107.	BLACKGROVE Heath (El2)		*Abandon*
108.	DEAN Julian (C.A)	15th	+ 12"
109.	REID Robin (MPC)		*Abandon*
110.	YATES Jeremy (El2)		*Abandon*
	Luxembourg		
111.	JOACHIM Benoît (USP)	45th	+ 2'29"
112.	KIRCHEN Kim (FAS)	**6th**	+ 12"
113.	SCHLECK Frank (CSC)	16th	+ 12"
	Brazil		
114.	FISCHER Murillo (DVE)	62nd	+ 8'51"
115.	MAY Marcio (El2)		*Abandon*
116.	PAGLIARINI Luciano (LAM)		*Abandon*
	South Africa		
117.	COX Ryan (TBL)	69th	+ 8'51"
118.	HUNTER Robert (RAB)		*Abandon*
119.	KANNEMEYER Tiaan (TBL)		*Abandon*
	Canada		
120.	BARRY Michael (USP)	32nd	+ 12"
121.	FRASER Gordon (HNC)		*Abandon*
122.	WOHLBERG Eric (SIE)		*Abandon*

A great atmosphere on the Women's time trial podium: the American Dierdre Demit – Barry (silver medal), the Olympic Champion from Holland Leontien van Moorsel and the Swiss Karin Thurig (bronze medal) set the track alight.

Jan Ullrich disappoints once again... Did he get it wrong in the time trial?

Latvia		
123. NAUDUZS Andris (DVE)		*Abandon*
124. VAINSTEINS Romans (LAM)	42nd	+ 1'19"
Venezuela		
125. CHACON DIAZ José Isidro (El2)		*Abandon*
126. ETXEBARRIA Unai (EUS)	34th	+ 12"
Hungary		
127. BODROGI Laszlo (QSD)	74th	+ 15'01"
Ireland		
128. POWER Ciaran (NIC)	13rd	+ 12"
129. SCANLON Mark (A2R)		*Abandon*
Slovakia		
130. JURCO Matej (DEN)		*Abandon*
131. RISKA Martin (PSK)	71st	+ 9'44"
Moldavia		
132. IVANOV Ruslan (ALB)	54th	+ 8'51"
133. PUGACI Igor (DEN)	66th	+8'51"
Bulgaria		
134. GOSPODINOV Dimitar (El2)		*Abandon*
Ouzbekistan		
135. LAGUTIN Sergey (LAN)	59th	+ 8'51"
Belarus		
136. USOV Alexandre (PHO)		*Abandon*
Japan		
137. SUZUKI Shinri (SHI)		
138. TASHIRO Yasutaka (BGT)	57th	+ 8'51"
Kirghizistan		
139. WACKER Eugen (ATI)		*Abandon*
Iran		
140. SAEIDI TANHA Abbas (El2)		*Abandon*
141. ZARGARI Amir (El2)		*Abandon*
Chile		
142. ARRIAGADA Marcelo (El2)		*Abandon*
Hong-Kong		
143. WONG Kam-Po (El2)		*Abandon*
Serbia-Montenegro		
144. STEVIC Ivan (El2)		*Abandon*

224,4 km

1.	Paolo Bettini (Ita)	QSD	5h 41'44"
2.	Sergio Paulinho (Por)	LAP	s.t
3.	Axel Merckx (Bel)	LOT	+ 8"
4.	Erik Zabel (Ger)	TMO	+ 12"
5.	Andrej Hauptman (Slo)	LAM	s.t
6.	Kim Kirchen (Lux)	FAS	s.t
7.	Roger Hammond (Gbr)	MRB	s.t
8.	Frank Høj (Den)	CSC	s.t
9.	Kurt-Asle Arvesen (Nor)	CSC	s.t
10.	Alexandr Kolobnev (Rus)	DVE	s.t

WOMEN'S ROAD RACE

67 Competitors

Netherlands		
1. ZIJLAARD-VAN MOORSEL Leontien		*Abandon*
2. MELCHERS Mirjam	**6th**	+ 42"
3. VAN DER ZEE Anouska		*Abandon*
Germany		
4. ARNDT Judith	**2nd**	+ 7"
5. BRODTKA Angela		*Abandon*
6. WORRACK Trixi	25th	+ 1'18"
Australia		
7. CARRIGAN Sara	**1st**	**3h24'24"**
8. GOLLAN Olivia	12nd	+ 1'18"
9. WOOD Oenone	**4th**	+39"
Lithuania		
10. POLIKEVICIUTE Jolanta	31st	+ 1'18"
11. POLIKEVICIUTE Rasa	29th	+ 1'18"
12. PUCINSKAITE Edita	**9th**	+ 46"
Russia		
13. BOUBNENKOVA Svetlana		*Abandon*
14. SLYUSAREVA Olga	**3rd**	+ 39"
15. ZABIROVA Zoulfia0	39th	+ 4'15"
Sweden		
16. LARSSON Camilla		*Abandon*
17. LINDBERG Madeleine	49th	+ 9'11"
18. LJUNGSKOG Susanne	33rd	+ 1'18"
Canada		
19. BESSETTE Lyne		*Abandon*
20. JUTRAS Manon	30th	+ 1'18"
21. PALMER-KOMAR Susan	11st	+ 1'13"

Spain
22. ITURRIAGA Eneritz 34th + 4'15"
23. RUANO SANCHON Dori *Abandon*
24. SOMARRIBA Joane **7th** + 42"

Switzerland
25. BRÄNDLI Nicole 38th + 4'15"
26. DOPPMANN Priska 18th + 1'18"
27. HEEB Barbara 28th + 1'18"

U.S.A
28. ARMSTRONG Kristin **8th** + 42"
29. DEMET-BARRY Deirdre 16th + 1'18"
30. THORBURN Christine 15th + 1'18"

Italy
31. BRONZINI Giorgia 37th + 4'15"
32. CANTELE Noemi 13rd + 1'18"
33. GUDERZO Tatiana 26th + 1'18"

Great Britain
34. COOKE Nicole **5th** + 39"
35. HEAL Rachel 22nd + 1'18"
36. SYMINGTON Sara *Abandon*

France
37. HUGUET Sonia 40th + 6'06"
38. LONGO-CIPRELLI Jeannie **10th** +59"
39. PITEL Edwige 32nd + 1'18"

Norway
40. BYBERG Lene 48th + 9'11"
41. TORP Linn 53rd + 16'19"
42. VALEN Anita 14th + 1'18"

Ukraine
43. CHUZHYNOVA Iryna 23rd + 1'18"
44. KACHALKA Nataliya 36th + 4'15"
45. KARPENKO Valentyna 43rd + 9'11"

New Zealand
46. HOLT Melissa *Abandon*
47. HYLAND Michelle 56th + 16'19"
48. KIESANOWSKI Joanne 17th + 1'18"

Czech Republic
49. KOZLIKOVA Lada *Abandon*
50. RUZICKOVA Martina 52nd + 16'19"

Poland
51. MATUSIAK Bogumila 42nd + 7'31"
52. WYSOCKA Malgorzata 27th + 1'18"

Japan
53. KARAMI Miyoko 41st + 6'06"
54. OKI Miho 20th + 1'18"

Belarus
55. HAYEVA Volha 45th + 9'11"
56. STAHURSKAYA Zinaida 19th + 1'18"

Belgium
57. VANDROMME Sharon 21st + 1'18"

Austria
58. SOEDER Christiane 24th + 1'18"

Brazil
59. SILVA Janildes 54th + 16'19"

South Africa
60. SCHOEMAN Anriette 55th + 16'19"

Mexico
61. GUERRERO MENDEZ Belem 46th + 9'11"

China
62. QIAN Yunjuan 44th + 9'11"
63. ZHANG Junying 47th + 9'11"

El Salvador
64. GARCIA MARROQUIN Evelyn 35th + 4'15"

Estonia
65. MEIER Maaris *Abandon*

Guatemala
66. MOLINA Maria Dolores 50th + 16'19"

Korea
67. HAN Songhee 51st + 16'19"

Following her fall in the road race, Leontien van Moorsel (opposite) didn't want to retire on a negative note: she took the honours in the time trial to add another Gold medal to her collection.

Happiness with the Merckx family in the Athens night; the son receives the congratulations of the father.

Erik Dekker can enjoy his celebration. His race was *a veritable*

DEKKER ON TOP!

Rather like Richard Virenque three years earlier, Erik Dekker has held off the following peloton for... 227 kilometers! The Dutch champion has scored a third victory in a World Cup event (after La Clasica san Sebastian 2000 and the amstel Gold Race a year later) at the end of a fantastic show of strength that left his rivals in his wake...

Counting among its riders, the recent World Champion Oscar Freire, one of only a few top class sprinters engaged in this penultimate round of the World Cup, the Rabobank team decides to opt for a clear strategy in order to come out on top at the conclusion of the 252.5 kilometers separating St. Arnoult en Yvelines and Tours. The team must have a man in the breakaway sure to happen at the start of the day.

The Rabobank plan will be kept to without fail. Even before the morning mist has cleared, the inevitable skirmishes break out at the onset of the race. At km 25 seventeen riders find themselves out in front with a lead of some ten seconds. Four of their number keep up the effort: the Rabobank stalwart Erik Dekker, along with the young Russian Vladimir Goussev (CSC), The Italian Manuel Quinziato(Lampre) and his compatriot Bram Tankink (Quick Step). The lead over the peloton increases slowly but surely.

Opposite,on the avenue Grammont, the same Dekker accompanied by Kessler with the peloton in hot persuit!

BERTHOU SHOWS THE JERSEY

The Breton Eric Berthou (RAGT Semences-MG Rover) contests the first World Cup of his short career, started last year in a third division south african team, Barloworld. He wants to make his mark and begins his effort, albeit rather late, (the four men of the leading group already have a lead of 30 seconds). But he is very determined! After a chase of 46 kilometers (which he'll pay for later) he manages to catch the four leaders, who at km 71 lead the peloton by peloton approaches (less than one and a half minutes). When it is in view of Dekker and Goussev, now alone in front, the peloton suffers a crash, the principal victim being Luca Paolini. The team mate of Paolo Bettini and recent bronze medal winner in Verona suffers a broken hand. The foot of the Cote de l'Epan (situated at 8 kms from the finish) is fat al for Goussev who eases up after a new acceleration from the irresistible Erik Dekker. The Dutch champion is just the same caught at the summit by

The young Russian Goussev leads the main breakaway of the day. He precedes the Dutchman Tankink, the Italian Quinziato, the Frenchman Berthou and the hero of this 91st Paris-Tours, Erik Dekker.

eight minutes. It's the Cofidis team which leads the chase with three men fronting the peloton. A little later, Fritsch and Vogondy (Fdjeux;com) lend a helping hand, bringing the lead down to little more than two minutes, forty kilometers short of Tours.

Just as Eric Berthou loses control (a broken spoke ends his chances of success) and is absorbed into the peloton, the Cote de Crochu (km 226) puts an end to the hopes of Quinziato and Tankink. An acceleration by Erik Dekker finishes them off and the Astarloa (Lampre), Flecha (Fassa Bortolo), Kessler (T Mobile) and the rapid Allan Davis (Liberty seguros).

DEKKER KEEPS SOMETHING IN THE BAG...

The five men now have only a short lead over a peloton weakened by the crash.After the climb up the Cote du Petit-Pas-de l'Ane, three kilometers from the line, Erik Dekker finds new strength to accelerate at the moment the lead group is perturbed by the arrival of the Italian champion Cristan Moreni (Alessio) and Eddy Mazzoleni (Saeco). Only Matthias Kessler seems capable to catch Dekker at the beginning of the interminable avenue de Grammont. The two men join their effort but now have the peloton breathing down their necks. At 300 metres from the line , Dekker surprises (where does all this energy come from?) Kessler and triumphs. Danilo Hondo (Gerolsteiner) outpaces Freire and the following peloton of sixty riders. The tactics of the Rabobank team came up trumps even if it was not Erik Dekker who was imagined as victor. Adri Van Houwelingen, team manager, had thought to play the Oscar Freire card, but the circumstances of the race changed things. A thrilling finale decided by an athletic exploit despite a route that could never be called difficult (except in distance), Paris - Tours remains a first class Classic which once again managed to surprise. Only one mass sprint has decided the result in the last eight years.

For Erik Dekker, this victory marks something of a renaissance, despite his four wins this year when he has won the Tour of Drenthe and his national Tour... That of Holland in which he had a stage win to his name. When he was at the summit of his career at the start of the decade (with three stage wins in the 2000 Tour DeFrance and one the following year), the Dutch rider was the victim of a terrible crash at the end of the 2002 Milan - San Remo. The result was a multiple fracture of the femur. Ironically that very evening he became the number one rider in the UCI table due to his success in the Tirreno - Adriatico days before. A title he could of course not defend. He eased his way back into competition at the end of 2002 and just as his hopes were high for 2003 he suffered injury in a domestic accident. His premature comeback only serves to make his injuries worse. Another empty season. Such moments must be accepted in a long career (he turned pro in 1992) and forgotten in favour of his later triumph. ■

Oscar Freire is the first to congratulate Erik Dekker for his fantastic win. The two men on the podium bear witness to the excellent result for the Rabobank team.

188 Competitors

GEROLSTEINER			
1.	REBELLIN Davide (Ita)	13rd	s.t
2.	FÖRSTER Robert (Ger)	58th	+11"
3.	HONDO Danilo (Ger)	**2nd**	s.t
4.	LANG Sebastian (Ger)	110th	+ 4'44"
5.	SERPELLINI Marco (Ita)	60th	+28"
7.	ZBERG Marcus (Sui)	45th	s.t
8.	ZIEGLER Thomas (Ger)	98th	+ 2'53"
9.	FOTHEN Markus (Ger)	114th	+ 4'44"

T.MOBILE			
11.	WESEMANN Steffen (Ger)	86th	+ 2'53"
12.	ALDAG Rolf (Ger)	42nd	s.t
13.	BAUMANN Eric (Ger)	17th	s.t
14.	EVANS Cadel (Aus)	104th	+ 2'53"
15.	KESSLER Matthias (Ger)	**7th**	s.t
16.	KLIER Andreas (Ger)	49th	s.t
17.	NARDELLO Daniele (Ita)	55th	s.t
18.	SCHRECK Stephan (Ger)	129th	+ 4'44"

RABOBANK			
21.	FREIRE Oscar (Esp)	**3rd**	s.t
22.	DE JONGH Steven (Ned)	36th	s.t
23.	DEKKER Erik (Ned)	**1st**	**5h33'03"**
24.	HAYMAN Mathew (Aus)	40th	s.t
25.	KROON Karsten (Ned)	25th	s.t
26.	POSTHUMA Joost (Ned)	82nd	+ 2'27"
27.	SENTJENS Roy (Ned)	80th	+ 2'27"
28.	WAUTERS Marc (Bel)	46th	s.t

FASSA BORTOLO			
32.	CANCELLARA Fabian (Sui)	85th	+ 2'53"
33.	FLECHA Juan Antonio (Esp)	38th	s.t
34.	ONGARATO Alberto (Ita)	69th	+ 30"
35.	PETITO Roberto (Ita)	37th	s.t
36.	SACCHI Fabio (Ita)	52nd	s.t
37.	TRENTI Guido (Usa)	22nd	s.t
38.	VELO Marco (Ita)	57th	s.t
40.	CHICCHI Francesco (Ita)	70th	+ 30"

LOTTO - DOMO			
41.	VAN PETEGEM Peter (Bel)	16th	s.t
44.	STEEGMANS Geert (Bel)	24th	s.t
45.	VAN BON Leon (Ned)	133rd	+ 5'54"
46.	VAN DIJK Stefan (Ned)	11st	s.t
47.	VAN IMPE Kevin (Bel)	106th	+ 2'53"
48.	VIERHOUTEN Aart (Ned)	132nd	+ 5'54"
49.	BRANDT Christophe (Bel)	31st	s.t
50.	GARDEYN Gorik (Bel)	66th	+ 30"

QUICK STEP - DAVITAMON			
51.	BETTINI Paolo (Ita)	**6th**	s.t
52.	BRAMATI Davide (Ita)	138th	+ 5'54"
53.	CRETSKENS Wilfried (Bel)	63rd	+ 30"
54.	HULSMANS Kevin (Bel)	78th	+ 2'09"
55.	NUYENS Nick (Bel)		*Abandon*
56.	PAOLINI Luca (Ita)	152nd	+ 10'19"
57.	ROGERS Michael (Aus)	137th	+ 5'54"
58.	TANKINK Bram (Ned)	142nd	+ 7'31"

CSC			
61.	JAKSCHE Jörg (Ger)	100th	+ 2'53"
62.	ARVESEN Kurt-Asle (Nor)	88th	+ 2'53"
63.	BRUUN ERIKSEN Thomas (Den)	136th	+ 5'54"
64.	GOUSSEV Vladimir (Rus)	79th	+ 2'09"
65.	HOFFMAN Tristan (Ned)	71st	+ 30"
66.	HØJ Frank (Den)	101st	+ 2'53"
67.	MICHAELSEN Lars (Den)	64th	+ 30"
68.	VANDBØRG Brian (Den)	145th	+ 7'31"

US POSTAL - BERRY FLOOR			
71.	VAN HEESWIJK Max (Ned)	128th	+ 4'44"
72.	CREED Michael (Usa)	144th	+ 7'31"
73.	DEVOLDER Stijn (Bel)	30th	s.t
74.	JOACHIM Benoît (Lux)	43rd	s.t
75.	McCARTY Jonathan (Usa)	73rd	+ 30"
76.	MIKHAILOV Guennadi (Rus)		*Abandon*
78.	VAN DEN BROECK Jurgen (Bel)	53rd	s.t

SAECO			
81.	CELESTINO Mirko (Ita)	21st	s.t
83.	BONOMI Giosue' (Ita)	147th	+ 7'31"
84.	CASAGRANDA Stefano (Ita)		*Abandon*
85.	GAVAZZI Nicola (Ita)	156th	+ 12'11"
86.	GLOMSER Gerit (Aut)	28th	s.t
87.	MAZZOLENI Eddy (Ita)	**10th**	s.t

COFIDIS			
91.	O'GRADY Stuart (Aus)	**5th**	s.t
92.	BESSY Frédéric (Fra)	149th	+ 7'31"
93.	CASPER Jimmy (Fra)	154th	+ 12'11"
94.	ENGOULVENT Jimmy (Fra)	150th	+ 8'49"
95.	FARAZIJN Peter (Bel)	126th	+ 4'44"
96.	FOFONOV Dmitriy (Kaz)	51st	s.t
97.	VASSEUR Cédric (Fra)	48th	s.t
98.	WHITE Matthew (Aus)	153rd	+ 12'11"

LAMPRE			
101.	ASTARLOA Igor (Esp)	72nd	+ 30"
102.	BALLAN Alessandro (Ita)	120th	+ 4'44"
103.	BORTOLAMI Gianluca (Ita)	62nd	+ 30"
104.	BOSSONI Paolo (Ita)	32nd	s.t
105.	CORTINOVIS Alessandro (Ita)	119th	+ 4'44"
106.	HAUPTMAN Andrej (Slo)	23rd	s.t
107.	QUINZIATO Manuel (Ita)	141st	+ 7'31"
108.	VILA Patxi (Esp)	54th	s.t

PHONAK			
111.	AEBERSOLD Niki (Sui)		*Abandon*
112.	ALBASINI Michael (Sui)	59th	+ 20"
113.	DESSEL Cyril (Fra)	123rd	+ 4'44"
114.	ELMIGER Martin (Sui)	74th	+ 45"
115.	MURN Uros (Slo)	**8th**	s.t
116.	RAST Gregory (Sui)	33rd	s.t
117.	USOV Alexandre (Blr)	14th	s.t

LIBERTY Seguros			
121.	DAVIS Allan (Aus)	**4th**	s.t
122.	ANDRLE René (Cze)	109th	+ 4'44"
123.	BARANOWSKI Dariusz (Pol)	87th	+ 2'53"
124.	CARUSO Gianpaolo (Ita)	56th	s.t
125.	HRUSKA Jan (Cze)	115th	+ 4'44"
126.	NOZAL Isidro (Esp)	93rd	+ 2'53"
127.	RAMIREZ ABEJA Javier (Esp)	143rd	+ 7'31"

EUSKALTEL - EUSKADI			
131.	ARTETXE Mikel (Esp)	107th	+ 2'53"
132.	FERNANDEZ DE LARREA Koldo (Esp)		*Abandon*
133.	IRIZAR Markel (Esp)	113rd	+4'44"
134.	ISASI Iñaki (Esp)	19th	s.t
135.	PEÑA IZA Aketza (Esp)		*Abandon*
136.	SANCHEZ Samuel (Esp)	29th	s.t
137.	SILLONIZ Aitor (Esp)	94th	+ 2'53"
138.	SILLONIZ Josu (Esp)	95th	+ 2'53"

ALESSIO - BIANCHI			
141.	MORENI Cristian (Ita)	15th	s.t
142.	BALDATO Fabio (Ita)	130th	+ 4'44"
144.	FURLAN Angelo (Ita)	75th	+ 1'42"
145.	HVASTIJA Martin (Slo)	92nd	+ 2'53"
146.	IVANOV Ruslan (Mda)	35th	s.t
147.	RASTELLI Ellis (Ita)		*Abandon*
148.	TAFI Andrea (Ita)	61st	+ 30"

Brioches LA BOULANGÈRE

151.	PINEAU Jérôme (Fra)	39th	s.t
152.	BENETEAU Walter (Fra)		*Abandon*
153.	GESLIN Anthony (Fra)	18th	s.t
154.	HARY Maryan (Fra)	117th	+ 4'44"
155.	KERN Christophe (Fra)		*Abandon*
156.	MARTIAS Rony (Fra)	118th	+ 4'44"
157.	RENIER Franck (Fra)	44th	s.t
158.	SPRICK Mathieu (Fra)	103rd	+ 2'53"

FDJEUX.COM

161.	COOKE Baden (Aus)	108th	+ 3'20"
162.	BICHOT Freddy (Fra)		*Abandon*
163.	DA CRUZ Carlos (Fra)	84th	+ 2'27"
164.	FRITSCH Nicolas (Fra)	148th	+ 7'31"
165.	GILBERT Philippe (Bel)	12nd	s.t
166.	GUESDON Frédéric (Fra)	47th	s.t
167.	VOGONDY Nicolas (Fra)	83rd	+ 2'27"

Chocolade JACQUES - WINCOR NIXDORF

171.	BRARD Florent (Fra)	27th	s.t
172.	ARDILA Mauricio (Col)	140th	+ 7'28"
173.	KOSTYUK Denis (Ukr)	99th	+ 2'53"
174.	LÖWIK Gerben (Ned)	146th	+ 7'31"
175.	PIATEK Zbigniew (Pol)	34th	s.t
176.	VAN DE WALLE Jurgen (Bel)	127th	+ 4'44"
177.	VERHEYEN Geert (Bel)	125th	+ 4'44"
178.	ZAMANA Cezary (Pol)	77th	+ 1'58"

ILLES BALEARS - BANESTO

181.	GARCIA ACOSTA J. Vicente (Esp)	131st	+ 4'44"
183.	GUTIERREZ PALACIOS J. Ivan (Esp)	124th	+ 4'44"
184.	HORRACH Joan (Esp)		*Abandon*
185.	LASTRAS Pablo (Esp)	20th	s.t
186.	LOPEZ GIL Antonio (Esp)	76th	+ 1'52"
187.	OSA Unai (Esp)	151st	+ 10'19"
188.	PRADERA Mikel (Esp)	91st	+ 2'53"

CRÉDIT AGRICOLE

192.	HERVÉ Cédric (Fra)	116th	+ 4'44"
193.	HINAULT Sébastien (Fra)	81st	+ 2'27"
194.	JOLY Sébastien (Fra)		*Abandon*
195.	KAGGESTAD Mads (Nor)		*Abandon*
196.	LEBLACHER Eric (Fra)		*Abandon*
197.	LEQUATRE Geoffroy (Fra)	102nd	+ 2'53"
198.	NAZON Damien (Fra)		*Abandon*

SAUNIER DUVAL - PRODIR

202.	COBO Juan José (Esp)		*Abandon*
203.	GOMEZ Angel "Litu" (Esp)		*Abandon*
204.	GOMIS Juan (Esp)		*Abandon*
205.	HORNER Chris (Usa)	50th	s.t
206.	MORI Manuele (Ita)		*Abandon*
207.	VENTOSO Francisco (Esp)	112nd	+ 4'44"
208.	ZAUGG Oliver (Sui)		*Abandon*

AG2R Prévoyance

211.	KIRSIPUU Jaan (Est)	**9th**	s.t
212.	ASTARLOZA Mikel (Esp)	155th	+ 12'11"
213.	INAUDI Nicolas (Fra)		*Abandon*
214.	KRIVTSOV Yuriy (Ukr)	111st	+ 4'44"
215.	NAZON Jean-Patrick (Fra)		*Abandon*
216.	ORIOL Christophe (Fra)	121st	+ 4'44"
217.	PORTAL Nicolas (Fra)		*Abandon*
218.	PÜTSEP Erki (Est)	122nd	+ 4'44"

Mr BOOKMAKER - PALMANS

221.	DAY Ben (Aus)		*Abandon*
222.	DE SMET Andy (Bel)	26th	s.t
223.	GABRIEL Frédéric (Fra)	41st	s.t
224.	HUNT Jeremy (Gbr)	105th	+ 2'53"
225.	RENDERS Jens (Bel)	135th	+ 5'54"
226.	THIJS Erwin (Bel)	89th	+ 2'53"
228.	WUYTS Peter (Bel)	134th	+ 5'54"
230.	TROUVÉ Kristof (Bel)		*Abandon*

RAGT Semences - MG ROVER

231.	SEIGNEUR Eddy (Fra)		*Abandon*
232.	AUGER Guillaume (Fra)	90th	+ 2'53"
233.	BERTHOU Eric (Fra)		*Abandon*
234.	DION Renaud (Fra)	67th	+ 30"
235.	DULAC Nicolas (Fra)		*Abandon*
236.	FINOT Frédéric (Fra)		*Abandon*
237.	REYNAUD Nicolas (Fra)	139th	+ 7'28"
238.	RINERO Christophe (Fra)	65th	+ 30"

DOMINA VACANZE

241.	SCARPONI Michele (Ita)		*Abandon*
242.	BAZHENOV Alexandr (Rus)		*Abandon*
243.	FAILLI Francesco (Ita)	97th	+ 2'53"
244.	KOLOBNEV Alexandr (Rus)		*Abandon*
245.	MARINANGELI Sergio (Ita)	68th	+ 30"
246.	MORI Massimiliano (Ita)	96th	+ 2'53"

PAST WINNERS AT THE START — 2

TAFI Andrea	2000
WAUTERS Marc	1999

RIDERS AT THE START ARE IN THE UC I TOP 100 — 32

ROOKIES AT THE START (LESS THAN ONE YEAR AS A PROFESSIONAL): — 19

3 OLDEST

PIATEK Zbigniew (Pol)	(38 years) - 1966/05/01
TAFI Andrea (Ita)	(38 years) - 1966/05/07
ZAMANA Cezary (Pol)	(36 years) - 1967/11/14

3 YOUNGEST

FAILLI Francesco (Ita)	(20 years) - 1983/12/16
VAN DEN BROECK Jurgen (Bel)	(21 years) - 1983/02/01
GILBERT Philippe (Bel)	(22 years) - 1982/05/07

CLASSIFICATION

1.	**Erik Dekker (Ned) (average: 45,489 km/h)**	**RAB**	**5h 33'03"**
2.	Danilo Hondo (Ger)	GST	s.t
3.	Oscar Freire (Esp)	RAB	s.t
4.	Allan Davis (Aus)	LST	s.t
5.	Stuart O'Grady (Aus)	COF	s.t
6.	Paolo Bettini (Ita)	QSD	s.t
7.	Matthias Kessler (Ger)	TMO	s.t
8.	Uros Murn (Slo)	PHO	s.t
9.	Jaan Kirsipuu (Est)	A2R	s.t
10.	Eddy Mazzoleni (Ita)	SAE	s.t

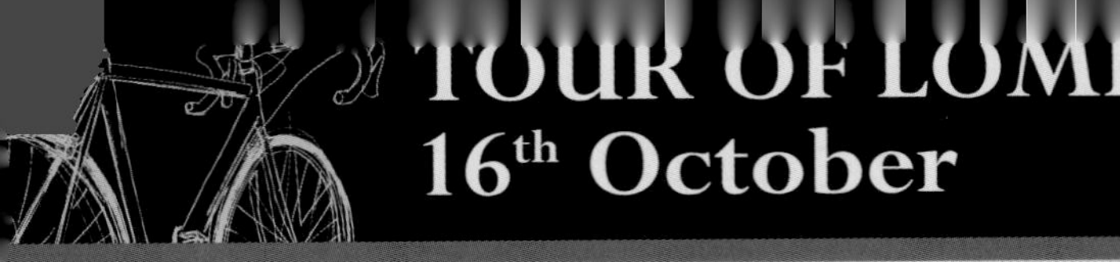

Cunego already...

The year 2004 will at least have shown the world a new star. A star who celebrates his 23rd birthday the 19th September soon after winning the Tour of Italy and eleven other events. The thirteenth is not to be sneezed at either. None other than one of the monuments of modern cycle racing, one of the five top one day races, the Tour of Lombardie. After playing a major part in the World Championship in his homeland, Damiano Cunego could look to the future with confidence.

The birth of the Pro-Tour brings about the demise of the World Cup. A competition that began fifteen years ago, often ignored by the top riders (who were only interested in the grand Tours) but which subsequently carved out an important place in the world of cycling. The world Cup consecrated, each year, the Classic rider who was the most consistent, if not the most brilliant. At the start of this 98th edition of the Tour of Lombardie (and the last ever round of the World Cup), two men can still reach for the top spot. Paolo Bettini who has taken the controls due to a good result (6th) in the Paris- Tours the previous week and Davide Rebellin,on top since mid April when he strung together a chain of successes , in particular the Amstel Gold Race then Liege-Bastogne- Liege (the Fleche Wallonne, which he also won, not counting for the World Cup). This duel almost eclipsed the importance of this final event of the season. The organisers of the event wished to get back to the good old days by including the famous Ghisallo (forty kilometers from the finish) and the Cote san Fermo Della Battaglia even closer to the line (less than five kilometers)!
A finishing line once again in the streets of Come whereas it was the old town of Bergame which, since 1995 greeted the riders in the final round of the season. The Ghisallo and san Fermo Della Battaglia which echoed to the exploits of Merckxs and Hinault more than twenty years ago. ..

BARTOLI SHOWS HIMSELF ... TOO SOON

Back to the old days then for the finishing line, but a start somewhat out of the ordinary, it being held in... Switzerland, at Mendrisio, on the Italian border. A large peloton for an end of season race (161 riders) set out under a cloudy sky but the weather is none the less pleasant. After only six kilometers the first action takes place. It's the work of the double winner Michele Bartoli (reputedly not on the top of his form), Robert Petito (Fassa Bortolo) and Allan Davis, the Australian winner of the Tour of Piemont two days earlier. A few kilometers later the trio is pulled back into the pack. Moments later, a much more numerous group (32 riders) breaks away. As in the Paris - Tours a week earlier, it's this group that will stay out in front for the greater part of the afternoon. One rider from Lampre, Manuel Quinziato (already member of a major attack in the Paris - Tours), another from the Panaria team, Paolo Toralongo, a World Cup event winner (Zurich in the month of August), Juan Antonio Flecha and the Swiss champion Gregory Rast make up the leading group. The action begins at the 25th kilometre. There are 221kms still to go. José Gutierrez Palacios (Illes Balears- Banesto) will take considerably less (32) to make the quartet a quintet.

LE GHISALLO AS JUDGE AND JURY

The peloton,generally led by the Gerolsteiner team of Davide Rebellin stays wary. It keeps the breakaway group of five at 4mins 30 sec (km 71) , the group now reduced to three

What a season for Damiano Cunego! At 23,he takes his first classic only months after dominating the Tour of Italy.

Cadel Evans, Ivan Basso,and Michael Boogerd forge up the San Fermo della Battaglia, but Damiano Cunego is hanging on. He won't waste time in catching them thanks to a terrific descent.

when Rast and Gutierrez fail to keep up with the pace. True to form ,the three remaining leaders are caught by the accelerating peloton as they approach the 8.6 kilometers of climb at Le Ghisallo, at times sloping at more than 14%! The CSC team show their strength by placing 6 men at the head of the pack. We can now expect an attack by their leader for the day, Ivan Basso. Having disposed of Francesco Casagrande, Basso takes the lead and at the summit is ten seconds ahead of a group including Boogerd, Casagrande, Rebellin, Cunego, Mazzoleni, Evans, Caruso and Fertonani. Paolo Bettini was slightly distanced at the moment Oscar Freire was found wanting. He would retire soon after.
At the bottom of the hill there is a partial regrouping of the riders. Basso was caught by his chasing group and the group led by Bettini was to follow...

CUNEGO PERSISTS... AND WINS

The calm before the storm does not last long. At 35 kms from Come, a new attacking group pulls away: Sosenka, Rasmussen, Nardello, Nozal, Rodriguez Oliver and Frigo quickly open a gap of one minute. But, disorganisation reigns in the lead group, and the fifteen who take up the chase. A strange state of affairs.

Perhaps fearing a first class debacle, Damiano Cunego takes up the chase alone. Soon realising he's wasting precious energy, he eases up. In the end it's Cedric Vasseur who is the first to join the leaders on the first slopes of Civiglio (2.8 kms at 6.9%), 17 kilometers from the line. The French rider is however passed by Basso, Boogerd, Cunego and several others in the last few hundred metres of the climb. Cunego launches another attack at the foot of the descent , leadind a group of ten riders by ten seconds as they enter the streets of Come. The "Petit Prince" as he is known locally is soon joined by the other riders before the start of the final hill, San Fermo della Battaglia. Basso, Boogerd and Evans show their strength at the hardest part of the climb. Cunego loses some ground but makes
it up on the descent. Another rider, Daniele Nardello makes a last minute challenge at just 2 kilometers from the finish. With Evans, the T Mobile team are in a majority in the group of five who will go for the line. Apparently the effort expended in the chase means Nordello will not come out on top in this final World Cup race. Damiano Cunego is capable of a great turn of speed when racing against a small group. The same can be said for Michael Boogerd. It's the young Italian however who is to have the last word. This Tour of Lombardie, touched with nostalgia, retracing its original course , brought to the fore a young winner who could signal a revival in the hopes of Italian cycling. ■

161 Competitors

CSC

No.	Rider	Place	Result
1.	BARTOLI Michele (Ita)		*Abandon*
2.	GOUSSEV Vladimir (Rus)	19th	+ 49"
3.	SØRENSEN Nicki (Den)		*Abandon*
4.	BASSO Ivan (Ita)	**3rd**	s.t
5.	JAKSCHE Jörg (Ger)	33rd	+ 2'10"
6.	ARVESEN Kurt-Asle (Nor)		*Abandon*
7.	CALVENTE Manuel (Esp)		*Abandon*
8.	LÜTTENBERGER Peter (Aut)		*Abandon*

ACQUA E SAPONE - MOKAMBO

No.	Rider	Place	Result
11.	NOCENTINI Rinaldo (Ita)	27th	+ 1'40"
12.	HAMBURGER Bo (Den)	56th	+ 11'43"
13.	MARZOLI Ruggero (Ita)		*Abandon*
14.	SOSENKA Ondrej (Cze)	13rd	+ 17"
15.	AREKEEV Alexandr (Rus)		*Abandon*
16.	DONATI Alessandro (Ita)		*Abandon*
17.	ASTOLFI Claudio (Ita)		*Abandon*
18.	KOBZARENKO Valeriy (Ukr)		*Abandon*

ALESSIO - BIANCHI

No.	Rider	Place	Result
21.	BALDATO Fabio (Ita)		*Abandon*
22.	HVASTIJA Martin (Slo)		*Abandon*
23.	IVANOV Ruslan (Mda)	21st	+ 49"
24.	BERTOLINI Alessandro (Ita)		*Abandon*
25.	NOE' Andrea (Ita)		*Abandon*
26.	PELLIZOTTI Franco (Ita)	**9th**	+ 17"
28.	TAFI Andrea (Ita)		*Abandon*

PANARIA - MARGRES

No.	Rider	Place	Result
31.	MAZZANTI Luca (Ita)	**10th**	+ 17"
32.	SELLA Emanuele (Ita)		*Abandon*
33.	TIRALONGO Paolo (Ita)		*Abandon*
34.	PEREZ CUAPIO J. Alberto (Mex)		*Abandon*
36.	LANFRANCHI Paolo (Ita)		*Abandon*
37.	MATVEYEV Serhiy (Ukr)		*Abandon*
38.	DAVIS Scott (Aus)		*Abandon*

COFIDIS

No.	Rider	Place	Result
41.	BESSY Frédéric (Fra)	60th	+ 11'43"
42.	EDALEINE Christophe (Fra)		*Abandon*
43.	FARAZIJN Peter (Bel)		*Abandon*
44.	FERNANDEZ BUSTINZA Bingen (Esp)		*Abandon*
45.	FOFONOV Dmitriy (Kaz)	38th	+ 3'39"
47.	TRENTIN Guido (Ita)		*Abandon*
48.	VASSEUR Cédric (Fra)	17th	+ 49"

DE NARDI

No.	Rider	Place	Result
51.	HONCHAR Serhiy (Ukr)	18th	+ 49"
52.	JURCO Matej (Svk)		*Abandon*
53.	GIORDANI Leonardo (Ita)		*Abandon*
54.	GOBBI Michele (Ita)		*Abandon*
55.	VANOTTI Alessandro (Ita)	58th	+ 11'43"
56.	MIORIN Devis (Ita)		*Abandon*
57.	NURITDINOV Rafael (Uzb)		*Abandon*
58.	PUGACI Igor (Mda)	31st	+ 1'40'

DOMINA VACANZE

No.	Rider	Place	Result
61.	BAZHENOV Alexandr (Rus)	51st	+ 9'21"
62.	GENTILI Massimiliano (Ita)		*Abandon*
63.	GIUNTI Massimo (Ita)		*Abandon*
64.	JONES Timothy (Zim)		*Abandon*
65.	KOLOBNEV Alexandr (Rus)		*Abandon*
66.	MARINANGELI Sergio (Ita)		*Abandon*
67.	SCARPONI Michele (Ita)		*Abandon*
68.	SIMEONI Filippo (Ita)	53rd	+ 9'21"

FASSA BORTOLO

No.	Rider	Place	Result
71.	BRUSEGHIN Marzio (Ita)	**6th**	+ 17"
72.	CIONI Dario (Ita)		*Abandon*
73.	CODOL Massimo (Ita)	39th	+ 4'33"
74.	FLECHA Juan Antonio (Esp)		*Abandon*
75.	FRIGO Dario (Ita)	**8th**	+ 17"
76.	GUSTOV Volodymir (Ukr)		*Abandon*
77.	LARSSON Gustav (Swe)		*Abandon*
78.	PETITO Roberto (Ita)		*Abandon*

GEROLSTEINER

No.	Rider	Place	Result
81.	FARESIN Gianni (Ita)		*Abandon*
82.	HARDTER Uwe (Ger)		*Abandon*
83.	REBELLIN Davide (Ita)	28th	+ 1'40"
84.	ZIEGLER Thomas (Ger)		*Abandon*
85.	SERPELLINI Marco (Ita)		*Abandon*
86.	STRAUSS Marcel (Sui)		*Abandon*
87.	WEGMANN Fabian (Ger)		*Abandon*
88.	ZBERG Marcus (Sui)		*Abandon*

Davide Bramati helps out his team leader Paolo Bettini, victim of a mechanical incident soon after the half way mark.

For Alex Zülle, this Tour of Lombardie brought to a close a long and glorious career which had started twelve years earlier.

ILLES BALEARS - BANESTO

No.	Rider	Place	Result
91.	ARRIETA José Luis (Esp)		*Abandon*
92.	GARCIA ACOSTA J. Vicente (Esp)		*Abandon*
93.	GUTIERREZ PALACIOS J. Ivan (Esp)		*Abandon*
94.	HORRACH Joan (Esp)		*Abandon*
95.	LASTRAS Pablo (Esp)	46th	+ 7'16"
96.	LOPEZ GIL Antonio (Esp)		*Abandon*
97.	OSA Unai (Esp)	43rd	+ 5'11"
98.	PRADERA Mikel (Esp)		*Abandon*

LAMPRE

No.	Rider	Place	Result
101.	ASTARLOA Igor (Esp)		*Abandon*
102.	BARBERO Sergio (Ita)		*Abandon*
103.	BORTOLAMI Gianluca (Ita)		*Abandon*
104.	GARATE Juan Manuel (Esp)		*Abandon*
105.	QUINZIATO Manuel (Ita)		*Abandon*
106.	RIGHI Daniele (Ita)		*Abandon*
107.	SCOTTO D'ABUSCO Michele (Ita)		*Abandon*
108.	VILA Patxi (Esp)	24th	+ 49"

LANDBOUWKREDIET - COLNAGO

No.	Rider	Place	Result
111.	ANZA Santo (Ita)		*Abandon*
112.	ADVEYEV Serguey (Ukr)	61st	+ 11'43"
113.	BERNUCCI Lorenzo (Ita)		*Abandon*
114.	DUMA Vladimir (Ukr)	16th	+ 44"
115.	GASPERONI Cristian (Ita)		*Abandon*
116.	POPOVYCH Yaroslav (Ukr)		*Abandon*
117.	GRYSCHENKO Ruslan (Ukr)	62nd	+ 11'43"
118.	MONFORT Maxime (Bel)	37th	+ 3'39"

LIBERTY Seguros

No.	Rider	Place	Result
121.	BARANOWSKI Dariusz (Pol)		*Abandon*
122.	CARUSO Gianpaolo (Ita)	15th	+ 25"
123.	DAVIS Allan (Aus)		*Abandon*
125.	HRUSKA Jan (Cze)		*Abandon*
126.	NOZAL Isidro (Esp)	14th	+ 17"
127.	RAMIREZ ABEJA Javier (Esp)		*Abandon*
128.	SERRANO Marcos (Esp)	44th	+ 5'11"

LOTTO - DOMO

No.	Rider	Place	Result
131.	VIERHOUTEN Aart (Ned)		*Abandon*
132.	BRANDT Christophe (Bel)	41st	+ 5'11"
134.	MOERENHOUT Koos (Ned)		*Abandon*
135.	VAN BON Leon (Ned)		*Abandon*
137.	GARDEYN Gorik (Bel)		*Abandon*
138.	MARICHAL Thierry (Bel)		*Abandon*

PHONAK

No.	Rider	Place	Result
141.	MURN Uros (Slo)	49th	+ 9'21"
142.	NOSE Tomas (Slo)	25th	+ 49"
143.	ELMIGER Martin (Sui)		*Abandon*
144.	FERTONANI Marco (Ita)	45th	+ 7'05"
145.	RAST Gregory (Sui)		*Abandon*
146.	SCHNIDER Daniel (Sui)	59th	+ 11'43"
147.	TSCHOPP Johann (Sui)		*Abandon*
148.	ZÜLLE Alex (Sui)		*Abandon*

QUICK STEP - DAVITAMON

151.	BETTINI Paolo (Ita)	29th	+ 1'40"
152.	BRAMATI Davide (Ita)		*Abandon*
153.	CRETSKENS Wilfried (Bel)		*Abandon*
154.	HULSMANS Kevin (Bel)		*Abandon*
155.	TANKINK Bram (Ned)	40th	+ 4'33"
156.	ROGERS Michael (Aus)	54th	+ 9'21"
157.	SINKEWITZ Patrik (Ger)	34th	+ 2'10"
158.	VAN GOOLEN Jurgen (Bel)	57th	+ 11'43"

RABOBANK

161.	FREIRE Oscar (Esp)		*Abandon*
162.	BOOGERD Michael (Ned)	**2nd**	s.t
163.	DEKKER Erik (Ned)	12nd	+ 17"
164.	RASMUSSEN Michael (Den)	23rd	+ 49"
165.	WEENING Pieter (Ned)	36eth	+ 3'06"
166.	VENEBERG Thorwald (Ned)		*Abandon*
167.	KROON Karsten (Ned)	50th	+ 9'21"
168.	DE GROOT Bram (Ned)		*Abandon*

SAECO

171.	CUNEGO Damiano (Ita)	**1st**	**6h 17'55"**
172.	BERTAGNOLLI Leonardo (Ita)	30th	+ 1'40"
173.	CELESTINO Mirko (Ita)		*Abandon*
174.	FUENTES Juan (Esp)	55th	+ 9'21"
175.	MAZZOLENI Eddy (Ita)	**7th**	+ 17"
176.	SABALIAUSKAS Marius (Ltu)		*Abandon*
177.	SZMYD Sylvester (Pol)	48th	+ 8'16"
178.	BONOMI Giosue' (Ita)		*Abandon*

SAUNIER DUVAL - PRODIR

181.	HORNER Chris (Usa)	11st	+ 17"
182.	CAÑADA David (Esp)		*Abandon*
183.	COBO Juan José (Esp)		*Abandon*
184.	RODRIGUEZ OLIVER Joaquin (Esp)	20th	+ 49"
185.	GOMEZ Angel "Litu" (Esp)		*Abandon*
186.	JEKER Fabian (Sui)	32nd	+ 1'54"
187.	VENTOSO Francisco (Esp)		*Abandon*
188.	ZAUGG Oliver (Sui)		*Abandon*

T-MOBILE

191.	EVANS Cadel (Aus)	**4th**	s.t
192.	GUERINI Giuseppe (Ita)		*Abandon*
193.	KLIER Andreas (Ger)		*Abandon*
194.	KESSLER Matthias (Ger)	22nd	+ 49"
195.	NARDELLO Daniele (Ita)	**5th**	+ 2"
196.	SCHRECK Stephan (Ger)		*Abandon*
197.	SAVOLDELLI Paolo (Ita)		*Abandon*
198.	WESEMANN Steffen (Ger)		*Abandon*

Vini CALDIROLA - NOBILI Rubinetterie

201.	CASAGRANDE Francesco (Ita)	26th	+ 1'25"
202.	ZAMPIERI Steve (Sui)	47th	+ 8'16"
203.	SGAMBELLURI Roberto (Ita)	42nd	+ 5'11"
204.	CALCAGNI Patrick (Sui)	52nd	+ 9'21"
205.	MASCIARELLI Andrea (Ita)	35th	+ 2'15"
206.	CHEULA Gianpaolo (Ita)		*Abandon*
207.	CAVALLARI Stefano (Ita)		*Abandon*
208.	LONGO BORGHINI Paolo (Ita)		*Abandon*

PAST WINNERS AT THE START	*4*
BARTOLI Michele (Ita)	2003, 2002
CELESTINO Mirko (Ita)	1999
TAFI Andrea (Ita)	1996
FARESIN Gianni (Ita)	1995

3 OLDEST	
FARESIN Gianni	(39) - 1965/07/16
TAFI Andrea	(38) - 1966/05/07
BALDATO Fabio	(36) - 1968/03/16

3 YOUNGEST:	
JURCO Matej	(20) - 1984/08/08
SCOTTO D'ABUSCO Michele	(21) - 1983/03/05
MONFORT Maxime	(21) - 1983/01/14

NATIONALITiES REPRESENTED:	*24*
Italy	59
Spain	24
Switzerland	11
Germany and Netherlands	9
Belgium and Ukraine	8
Australia and Russia	4
Denmark, France and Slovenia	3
Moldavia, Czeck Republic and Poland	2
Austria, Kazakstan, Lithuania, Mexico, Norway, Ouzbekistan, Slovakia, Sweden, USA and Zimbabwe	1

Separated by thirteen points at the start of this final World Cup race, Paolo Bettini and Davide Rebellin come out of it neck and neck, finishing down the field. For the third year running, the cup goes to Paolo Bettini!

History Repeats Itself

For the second time in five years ,the World Championship have set up shop on the banks of the Adige. For the fourth time in five years a Spanish rider has won the most prestigeous race, that of the Mens Elite. For the third time in five years, Oscar Freire took the supreme title. Is it déja vu in Verona?

27/09

YOUNG WOMENS' TIME TRIAL AND ESPOIRS MEN

THE EAST UP FRONT

In the young womens' category there are few chances for the competitors to race against each other, so any event tends to be open for all to shine in. The 2004 edition came up with the very young (just 16) Czeck Tereza Hurikova who dominated the american Rebecca Much, riding a borrowed cycle and the Australian Amanda Sprat. These three competitors were visibly in another class to the rest of the field, the forth placed rider - the German Sabine Fischer finishing the 15.5 kilometre course almost a minute slower than Hurikova. Things are very different for the young men in the "Espoirs" category (under 23s). The hot favourite, by the name of Thomas Dekker, from Holland, fresh from Olympic glory ,beat Rich, Peschel, Rogers etc. Veritable specialists in this sort of event in the GP Eddy Merckx. Having already suffered a setback last year, Thomas Dekker must once again play second fiddle to a rider from Slovenia. Janez Brajkovic proved himself a master of the 36.750 km course. With a reputation as an excellent climber, he already shone in the Italian Regions Race, this young Slovenian aged just 20, is anatural leader for a generation of talented cyclists from this ex Yougoslavian republic. Behind Brajkovic, Nose, Svab, Fajt and Bole are also jostling to make a name for themselves. For the first time since 1999 the bronze medal went to an Italian, by the name of Vincenzo Nibali, impressive on the main part of the course, but fading towards the end, as opposed to his compatriot Francesco Rivera, who, for a long time held the best time.

The swiss Karin Thurig breezed over the women's time trial.

The podium for the "Espoirs" time trial with from left to right, the Dutchman Thomas Dekker (2nd), the Slovenian Janez Brajkovic (gold medal), and the Italian Vincenzo Nibali (3rd) .

28/09
JUNIOR MEN'S TIME TRIAL AND WOMEN'S ELITE

THE CHAMPIONS SPEAK GERMAN

Two heavily built Germans, Patrick Gretsch and Stefan Schafer perpetuated the tradition of the German school in individual time trials. At a speed of 47kph the former snatched the title from the fancied Roman Kreuziger (son of the world cyclocross champion twenty years earlier) one of the most talented juniors of his generation. Equally impressive in persuit races, Patrick Gretsch will be able to defend his title next year in Madrid: this being only his first year in the junior category.

In the Elite women's event, the title holder Joane Sommariba must settle for fourth place despite an honorable performance. There was nothing anyone could do to compete against the Swiss Karin Thurig who wiped the floor with the opposition, leaving her nearest rival, the German Judith Arndt 51 seconds adrift! She, as last year, must console herself with the silver medal. The similarity with the podium at Hamilton doesn't stop there: the Russian Zoulfia Zabirova once again takes the bronze whereas Thurig and Somarriba simply change places...

With the races being run over the same distance, its interesting to compare the performances of the women and the young men. Interesting to note that Karin Thurig would have taken fifth place had the two categories run together. Last year, Somarriba would only have finished in 22nd place. Could this mean the women are making great progress? Or does it mean the men this year are mediocre?

29/09
ELITE MENS TIME TRIAL

ROGERS: THE RED CARPET AFTER THE GREEN

Some weeks before coming to Verona, Michael Rogers inherited the World Champions jersey for time trials following David Millar's doping confession. Not surprising then that the Australian should be fired up to win the same trophy here. A terrain that Rogers knows like the back of his hand as he resides for part of the year on the shores of Lac de Garde. His supporters (for the most part Italian) made the trip to the championship in the hope of seeing their man triumph. They would not be disappointed!

Starting last, Michael Rogers kept with the pace - conceding twelve seconds to Alexandre Vinokourov at the first intermediate point at the summit of the hill at Costermano, after 6.3 kms of the course. As the kilometers passed, the impression left by Michael Rogers left no-one in doubt. The Australian kept his fluidity, pedalling with apparent ease. This translated into a dominating position at the second intermediate: Vinokourov was now trailing by thirty seconds with the rest of the field a further ten seconds slower! The final part of the course served only to accentuate Rogers' advantage, finally finishing ahead not of Vinokourov (third place) but one of the other favourites, the German Michael Rich. For the third time in five years, the German

The crushing Elite time trial, Michael Rogers confirms an iris jersey won some weeks earlier...

found himself pipped at the post. After Honchar at Plouay in 2000, Botero in Zolder in 2002, his bogeyman this year goes by the name of Michael Rogers! As with every year, the World Championship brings new riders into the limelight. The 24 year old Swede Gustav Erik Larsson, just missing the podium and the American David Zabriskie, stage winner in the Vuelta, following a long solo attack, fall into this category. It only remains for them to confirm this form...

01/10

ROAD RACE JUNIOR GIRLS AND ESPOIRS MEN

CHANGE OF IDENTITY AND STATUS

Konstantin Siutsu comes from Bielorusse but has spent most of the year in Italy, his new home, where he rides for the Palazzago Vellutex team ,one of the best in Elite 2. Konstantin Suitsu is also the new World Champion in this category. An unusual world Champion as he has been in the ranks of the pros for three years. In 2001 he arrives in the only Russian team in Pro division 2, Itera. At the time his name is Konstantin Sivtsov. His only result is a fourth place in his own nation's championship. He would do better in the two following years (3rd in 2002 and 2nd in 2003), still with the Itera team and its successor Lokomotiv. This year he has split his time between his national team and his Italian team. Unnoticed for most of the season (we

can note only a 2nd place in the Tour of Lleida, run in Spain in June), he came to promenance by winning two races in Italy. These were his ticket for the World Championship.

Very wary since the start of the race, Konstanti Siutsou is the only rider able to keep up with Domenico Pozzovivo, one of the "Squadra azzura" riders, four laps from the line. He plays a waiting game before his devastating attack on the final ascent of the tiring climb at Torrincelle, when all thought the Italian more suited for the terrain. Pozzovivo, with a typically Italian build, seemed to have the better chance on this terrible climb which has decimated the peloton. All this was to change when the Bielorussian accelerated, the Italian could only watch him go. Behind, the Dutch favourite Thomas Dekker (third last year) , made the effort to join the two leaders. His attack however, came too late. Flanked by the Dane Mads Christensen, he manages to catch Pozzovivo on the descent towards the finishing line , beating the scandanavian. The line crossed more than a minute earlier by Siutsou, giving him the gold medal and winning him a contract with Fassa Bortolo for 2005!

Interrupted in 2002 in Zolder, by the Italian Francesco Chicchi, the list of world Champions "Espoirs" coming from the east grows longer year by year. Siutsou succeeds Petrov (crowned in 2000) , Popovych(in 2001), and Lagutin (last year). The same thing could be said with his club, Palazzago Vellutex, winning their fourth title with the help of Popovych, Lagutin and the Lithuanian Tomas Vaitkus, winner of the time trial in 2002.

The same series of successes can be noted in the Dutch team. For the third year running the "Oranges"take the honours thanks to the gold medal of Marianne Vos in the road race. Marianne Vos, 17 years old and therefore in her first year as a junior, succeeds Suzanne De Goede and Loes Markering. She forged her victory on the last lap with an acceleration on the climb at Torricelle. The Italian Marta Bastianelli sprinting into second place ahead of another Dutchwoman, Eleonara Van Dijk.

02/10

ROAD RACE
JUNIOR MEN AND ELITE WOMEN

ARNDT WITH AN EFFORT,
KREUZIGER WITH CLASS

Roman Kreuziger will be one of the lasting figures of the championship in Verona. For the first time in his short career, here he is, JuniorWorld Champion following several near misses. But this young eighteen year old had always come up against riders stronger than himself. The Belgian, Niels Albert, on the occasion of the European Cyclo cross championship, held on his home ground, the same man at the World Championship in Pontchateau and last but not least, the German Patrick Gretsch in the time trial three days earlier.

Roman Kreuziger played a waiting game before making his fatal attack in response to which only the Tunisian Rafaa Chtioui could

The Dutch rider Kai Reus finds himself in an uncomfortable position in his Espoirs time trial.

For his second success, Oscar Freire lines up his rivals: left to right, Stuart O' Grady, Michael Boogerd, Erik Zabel,Frank Schleck, Luca Paolini (partly hidden), Allan Davis and his compatriot Alejandro Valverde.

respond. The sprint between the two men seemed only a formality for Kreuziger, son of an ex moto cross champion. Leader of the UCI list for his category, the Slovenian simon Spilak takes the bronze after a sprint.

"It's a great day for German cycling" Declared Judith Arndt on dismounting her cycle. "We have not won for twenty years, and my team mates have worked very hard. It's a shame we can't shate the winner's jersey". The honours go to this girl who's actions on finishing the race at the Olympic Games a month and a half before. Her silver medal in hand after Athens she leaves these championship with two more medals, the gold for the road race and the silver for the time trial. Always near the front in a slow starting race, Judith Arndt profited from the descent towards the finish to put some distance between her and the few girls able to respond to the attack by Edita Pucinskaite in the climb. The valliant Italian Tatiana Guderzo made chase shortly after but was never able to reduce the gap of 50 metres which had opened up between the two girls. She was lucky to be able to keep the second place when the Norwegian Anita Valen continued an impressive sprint which had left a following group trailing in her wake. A group not including Jeannie Longo perhaps legitimately suggested the years were at last telling.

Judith Arndt, less provocative than in Athens some weeks earlier...

03/10

MENS ELITE ROAD RACE

OSCAR FREIRE? THE MAN FOR THE SITUATION

In the crowd around the circuit at Verona at around 3,30pm, the knee of Paolo Bettini was the subject of all the conversations. The number one favourite was languishing at the back of the peloton, surrounded by team mates taking frequent trips to the team manager's car. The confidence of the "Squadra azzurra" had taken a blow. Finally the olympic champion gave up the ghost and the serious business of the day could commence. When taking a second look at the situation, it seems obvious that

Erik Zabel and Luca Paolini take the places occupied five years earlier by Markus Zberg and Jean Cyril Robin. Oscar Freire for his part is still there...

the long minutes of dithering did no favours to the Italian strong men (Basso, Cunego and Garzelli), in favourising a waiting game that left the peloton with no hard work to do. Could this be the reason so many sprinters were among the leaders during the final lap? Or is it just that one day race specialists are able to adapt themselves to the varying terrains they come across in these events? Some of both ,in fact. Oscar Freire isn't worried about such things, he came, he won for the third time here, with some assistance from the Spanish team!

It all began with the offensive from the young Frenchman Christophe Le Mevel. Going it alone ,he is joined on the fifth lap by the Russian Vladimir Efimkin. The duo notch up a lead of 7 mins 20sec at one point. On the ninth lap, half way through the race - a group of thirty riders counter attack, catching the duo two laps later on the slopes of Torricelle. Another Frenchman, Sylvain Calzati then breaks out followed by the Swiss Steve Zampieri, the Dutchman Koos Moerenhout, the Pole Bartosz Huzarski and the Dane Frank Hoj. These five men finish the twelfth lap with a lead of almost a minute over a bunched peloton. After a lot of hard work from the Italians the peloton joins the lead group in the sixteenth lap.

David Moncoutié attempts another attack at the summit but his action provokes a chain reaction to which he becomes a victim. At this moment the Swiss Patrick Calcagni finds himself in the lead. For a short time. The penultimate climb of Torricelle permits a group of 25 of the strongest in the peloton to pull into a lead. No Frenchmen or Belgians are among this group though there are 6 Spaniards and 5 Italians. The final ascention takes place at frenetic pace. After several attacks, Michael Boogerd arrives at the top slightly ahead of Oscar Freire and Alejandro Valverde, Ivan Basso ,Damiano Cunego and Stuart O'Grady. At the end of the descent, under the influence of the German riders, the competitors regroup. Despite an attempted attack by Alexandre Vinokourov, the race is decided in a sprint. Weseman then Hondo devote all their efforts to helping Erik Zabel, Alejandro Valverde does as much for Oscar Freire. The final word goes to the Spanish Freire takes the race for the third time,followed by zabel and Paolini. ■

Oscar Freire: Makes a habit of climbing World Championship podiums..

WORLD CHAMPIONSHIP in Verona

Results

Chrono Women Juniors - 27/09 — 15,750 km

1.	**Tereza Hurikova (Cze) (average: 42,501 km/h)**	**22'14"**
2.	Rebecca Much (Usa)	+ 5"37
3.	Amanda Spratt (Aus)	+ 5"67
4.	Sabine Fischer (Ger)	+ 51"
5.	Marianne Vos (Ned)	+ 55"
6.	Roxane Knetemann (Ned)	+ 57"
7.	Alexandra Sontheimer (Ger)	+ 1'01"
8.	Natasha Mapley (Aus)	+ 1'09"
9.	Irina Zemlyanskaya (Rus)	+ 1'13"
10.	Emmanuelle Merlot (Fra)	+ 1'19"
11.	Aleksandra Dawidowicz (Pol)	+ 1'21"
12.	Martina Faccin (Ita)	s.t
13.	Florence Girardet (Fra)	+ 1'27"
14.	Ywona Pytel (Pol)	+ 1'28"
15.	Luydmila Zakirova (Rus)	s.t
16.	Marie Lindberg (Swe)	+ 1'29"
17.	Rebecca Bertolo (Ita)	+ 1'33"
18.	Joelle Numainville (Can)	+ 1'34"
19.	Anna Tratnyek (Can)	+ 1'35"
20.	Daiva Tuslaite (Ltu)	+ 1'37"
21.	Inga Cilvinaite (Ltu)	+ 1'38"
22.	Karen Verbeek (Bel)	+ 1'39"
23.	Olena Sharga (Ukr)	+ 1'40"
24.	Jarmila Marchacova (Cze)	+ 1'41"
25.	Alona Andruk (Ukr)	+ 1'46"
26.	Veronika Sprügel (Aut)	+ 1'51"
27.	Karin Metzler (Sui)	+ 1'52"
28.	M. Garcia Navas (Esp)	+ 1'56"
29.	Kata-Liina Normak (Est)	+ 2'09"
30.	Mayuko Hagiwara (Jpn)	+ 2'24"
31.	Jennifer Hohl (Sui)	+ 2'28"
32.	Silvia Tirado (Esp)	+ 2'40"
33.	Axelle Doisy (Bel)	+ 2'42"
34.	Mary Brennan (Irl)	+ 2'55"
35.	Katrine Josefsson (Swe)	+ 3'02"
36.	Veronika Vyrastka (Blr)	+ 3'26"
37.	Laura Lepasalu (Est)	+ 3'35"
38.	Stefanie Wiedner (Aut)	+ 4'03"

Chrono Men Espoirs - 27/09 — 36,750 km

1.	**Janez Brajkovic (Slo) (average: 46,975 km/h)**	**46'56"**
2.	Thomas Dekker (Ned)	+ 18"
3.	Vincenzo Nibali (Ita)	+ 19"
4.	Dominique Cornu (Bel)	+ 20"
5.	Christian Müller (Ger)	+ 47"
6.	Francesco Rivera (Ita)	+ 1'00"
7.	Piotr Mazur (Pol)	+ 1'21"
8.	Andriy Grivko (Ukr)	+ 1'23"
9.	Lukasz Bodnar (Pol)	+ 1'27"
10.	Stanislav Belov (Rus)	+ 1'33"
11.	Olivier Kaisen (Bel)	+ 1'35"
12.	Lasse Bøchmann (Den)	+ 1'50"
13.	Paul Martens (Ger)	+ 1'52"
14.	Andrei Kunitski (Blr)	+ 2'01"
15.	Miha Svab (Slo)	+ 2'03"
16.	Mads Christensen (Den)	+ 2'08"
17.	Ignas Konovalovas (Ltu)	+ 2'21"
18.	Alexey Esin (Rus)	s.t
19.	Ricardo Martins (Por)	+ 2'32"
20.	Dimitri Champion (Fra)	+ 2'34"
21.	Tyler Farrar (Usa)	+ 2'35"
22.	Alan Perez Lezaun (Esp)	+ 2'50"
23.	Eladio Sanchez Prado (Esp)	+ 2'53"
24.	Thomas Rohregger (Aut)	+ 3'27"
25.	Julian Muñoz Giraldo (Col)	+ 3'39"
26.	Florian Morizot (Fra)	+ 3'40"
27.	Peter Dawson (Aus)	+ 3'41"
28.	Bogdan Stoytchev (Bul)	+ 3'50"
29.	Tim Duggan (Usa)	+ 4'02"
30.	Kai Reus (Ned)	+ 4'03"
31.	Jeff Sherstobitoff (Can)	+ 4'14"
32.	Muradjan Khalmuratov (Uzb)	+ 4'16"
33.	João Cabreira (Por)	+ 4'24"
34.	Konstantin Sioutsou (Blr)	+ 4'27"
35.	Daryl Impey (Rsa)	+ 4'31"
36.	Rafael Infantino (Col)	+ 4'33"
37.	Steve Morabito (Sui)	+ 4'37"
38.	Andriy Pryschepa (Ukr)	s.t
39.	Peter Velits (Svk)	+ 4'44"
40.	Dominique Rollin (Can)	+ 4'46"
41.	Akos Haiszer (Hun)	+ 4'47"
42.	Andreas Schillinger (Ger)	s.t
43.	Martin Velits (Svk)	+ 4'53"
44.	Ruslan Sambris (Mda)	+ 5'04"
45.	Harald Berger (Aut)	+ 5'16"
46.	Aldis Abolins (Lat)	+ 5'24"
47.	Ryan Connor (Irl)	+ 5'26"
48.	Carlos Vargas (Col)	+ 5'27"
49.	Zolt Der (Scg)	s.t
50.	Byron Guama de la Cruz (Ecu)	+ 6'42"
51.	A. Kovaloczy (Hun)	+ 7'41"
DNF	Andrius Buividas (Ltu)	

Chrono Men Juniors - 28/09 — 24,05 km

1.	**Patrick Gretsch (Ger) (average: 47,328 km/h)**	**30'29"**
2.	Roman Kreuziger (Cze)	+ 15"
3.	Stefan Schäfer (Ger)	+ 16"
4.	Michael Schär (Sui)	+ 17"
5.	Viktor Renäng (Swe)	+ 18"
6.	Alexandr Pliushin (Mda)	+ 28"
7.	Anders Hansen (Den)	+ 37"
8.	Robert Gesink (Ned)	s.t
9.	Alexandr Slivkin (Rus)	+ 43"
10.	Jérôme Coppel (Fra)	+ 49"
11.	Maxime Bouet (Fra)	+ 59"
12.	Rafâa Chtioui (Tun)	s.t
13.	Simon Spilak (Slo)	+ 1'01"
14.	Edvald Boasson Hagen (Nor)	+ 1'11"
15.	Michiel van Aelbroeck (Bel)	+ 1'21"
16.	Maksym Kovalchuk (Ukr)	+ 1'24"
17.	Ben Hermans (Bel)	+ 1'25"
18.	Zdenek Machac (Cze)	+ 1'30"
19.	Kristjan Koren (Slo)	+ 1'31"
20.	Manuele Boaro (Ita)	+ 1'32"
21.	Yury Yazepchyk (Blr)	+ 1'35"
22.	Harley Goss (Aus)	s.t
23.	Janis Ozols (Lat)	+ 1'37"
24.	Johan Lindgren (Swe)	+ 1'41"
25.	Thijs van Amerongen (Ned)	+ 1'43"
26.	Jacques van Rensburg (Rsa)	+ 1'46"
27.	Alessandro Carretti (Ita)	s.t
28.	Gatis Smukulis (Lat)	+ 1'48"
29.	André Steensen (Den)	s.t
30.	Fabio Duarte (Col)	+ 1'49"
31.	Tanel Kangert (Est)	+ 1'51"
32.	Ian Stannard (Gbr)	+ 1'52"
33.	Yevhen Nikolenko (Ukr)	+ 1'54"
34.	Timofey Kritskiy (Rus)	+ 1'56"
35.	Lukasz Modzelewski (Pol)	+ 1'58"
36.	Bolat Raimbekov (Kaz)	+ 1'59"
37.	Nick Clesen (Lux)	+ 2'01"
38.	Andreas Simon (Aut)	+ 2'05"
39.	Panagiotis Potsakis (Gre)	+ 2'07"
40.	Alberto Ibañez (Esp)	+ 2'12"
41.	Adam Switters (Usa)	+ 2'15"
42.	Duncan Viljoen (Rsa)	+ 2'20"
43.	Egoitz Garcia Echeguibel (Esp)	+ 2'21"
44.	Ervin Korts-Laur (Est)	s.t
45.	Chris Stockburger (Usa)	+ 2'26"
46.	Carlos Quintero (Col)	s.t
47.	Raphaël Tremblay (Can)	+ 2'28"
48.	Eric Boily (Can)	+ 2'35"
49.	Alexander Egger (Aut)	+ 2'38"
50.	Martin Munroe (Irl)	+ 2'44"
51.	Ciaran Kelly (Irl)	s.t
52.	Roman Kireyev (Kaz)	+ 2'50"
53.	Rodrick Muscat (Mlt)	s.t
54.	Jaroslaw Marycz (Pol)	+ 2'56"
55.	Dejan Stefanovic (Scg)	+ 2'58"
56.	Egidijus Jursys (Ltu)	+ 2'59"
57.	Edwin Crossling (Nzl)	s.t
58.	Julien Schopfer (Sui)	+ 3'13"
59.	Andrew Thompson (Nzl)	+ 3'21"
60.	Slavomir Benc (Svk)	+ 3'33"
61.	Laszlo Madaras (Rom)	+ 3'36"
62.	Ruslan Karimov (Uzb)	s.t
63.	Marius-Nicolae Stoica (Rom)	+ 3'38"
64.	Eligijus Dalisanskas (Ltu)	+ 3'41"
65.	Samuel Coelho (Por)	+ 3'42"
66.	Ante Radic (Cro)	+ 3'43"
67.	Giorgi Nadiradze (Geo)	+ 4'18"
68.	Aleksei Sakavets (Blr)	+ 4'39"
69.	Archil Makharashvili (Geo)	+ 4'44"
70.	Ryuta Morimoto (Jpn)	+ 4'59"
71.	Shawn Pullicino (Mlt)	+ 5'27"
72.	Tal Eizinbad (Isr)	+ 5'42"
73.	Anton Mikhailov (Isr)	+ 5'50"
74.	Luis Pulido (Mex)	+6'40"

Chrono Women Elites - 28/09 — 24,05 km

1.	**Karin Thürig (Sui) (average: 46,708 km/h)**	**30'53"**
2.	Judith Arndt (Ger)	+ 51"
3.	Zoulfia Zabirova (Rus)	+ 56"

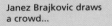

Janez Brajkovic draws a crowd...

Nice nugget, Michael!

4.	Joane Somarriba (Esp)	+ 1'15"
5.	Edita Pucinskaite (Ltu)	+ 1'32"
6.	Mirjam Melchers (Ned)	+ 1'41"
7.	Christine Thorburn (Usa)	+ 1'44"
8.	Priska Doppmann (Sui)	+ 1'54"
9.	Oenone Wood (Aus)	+ 2'07"
10.	Tatiana Guderzo (Ita)	+ 2'11"
11.	Anita Valen (Nor)	+ 2'16"
12.	Svetlana Bubnenkova (Rus)	s.t
13.	Trixi Worrack (Ger)	s.t
14.	Deirdre Demet-Barry (Usa)	+ 2'17"
15.	Jeannie Longo-Ciprelli (Fra)	+ 2'29"
16.	Olivia Gollan (Aus)	+ 2'38"
17.	Bogumila Matusiak (Pol)	+ 2'44"
18.	Dori Ruano Sanchon (Esp)	+ 2'49"
19.	Anna Zugno (Ita)	+ 3'02"
20.	Edwige Pitel (Fra)	+ 3'03"
21.	Susan Palmer-Komar (Can)	+ 3'15"
22.	Blaza Klemencic (Slo)	+ 3'16"
23.	Tatiana Shishkova (Mda)	+ 3'31"
24.	Natacha Maes (Bel)	+ 3'34"
25.	Jolanta Polikeviciute (Ltu)	+ 3'41"
26.	Evy van Damme (Bel)	+ 3'42"
27.	Ana-Paola Madrinan (Col)	+ 3'46"
28.	Malgorzata Wysocka (Pol)	+ 3'57"
29.	Natalya Kachalka (Ukr)	+ 4'02"
30.	Maria M. Cagigas (Esp)	+ 4'04"
31.	Loes Gunnewijk (Ned)	+ 4'26"
32.	Tiina Nieminen (Fin)	+ 4'31"
33.	Amy Moore (Can)	+ 5'09"
34.	Veronica Leal (Mex)	+ 7'20"

Chrono Men Elites - 29/09 — ***46,750 km***

1.	**Michael Rogers (Aus) (average: 48,78 km/h)**	**QSD**	**57'30"**
2.	Michael Rich (Ger)	GST	+ 1'12"
3.	Alex. Vinokourov (Kaz)	TMO	+ 1'25"
4.	Gustav E. Larsson (Swe)	FAS	+ 1'34"
5.	David Zabriskie (Usa)	USP	+ 1'36"
6.	Marzio Bruseghin (Ita)	FAS	+ 1'37"
7.	Marc Wauters (Bel)	RAB	+ 1'56"
8.	Fabian Cancellara (Sui)	FAS	+ 2'10"
9.	J. Ivan Gutierrez (Esp)	IBB	+ 2'23"
10.	Uwe Peschel (Ger)	GST	+ 2'28"
11.	Andrea Peron (Ita)	CSC	+ 2'32"
12.	Brian Vandbørg (Den)	CSC	+ 2'34"
13.	Bert Roesems (Bel)	REB	+ 2'36"
14.	Eddy Seigneur (Fra)	RAG	+ 2'41"
15.	David McCann (Irl)	GNT	+ 2'44"
16.	Przemyslaw Niemec (Pol)	MIE	+ 2'59"
17.	Dmitri Semov (Rus)	MIE	+ 3'05"
19.	Ivailo Gabrovski (Bul)	OKT	+ 3'16"
20.	Serhiy Matveyev (Ukr)	PAN	+ 3'38"
21.	Laszlo Bodrogi (Hun)	QSD	+ 3'40"
22.	Frédéric Finot (Fra)	RAG	+ 3'42"
23.	Eric Wohlberg (Can)	SIE	+ 3'48"
24.	Joost Posthuma (Ned)	RAB	+ 3'50"
25.	Ruslan Ivanov (Mda)	ALB	+ 3'54"
26.	Bradley McGee (Aus)	FDJ	+ 4'08"
27.	Ivan Parra (Col)	BAQ	+ 4'11"
28.	Jean Nuttli (Sui)	VOL	+ 4'15"
29.	Michael Blaudzun (Den)	CSC	+ 4'19"
30.	Victor Hugo Peña (Col)	USP	+ 4'22"
31.	Michal Hrazdira (Cze)	EI2	+ 4'24"
32.	Marcus Ljungvist (Swe)	ALB	+ 4'27"
33.	Svein Tuft (Can)	EI2	+ 4'46"
34.	Gregor Gazvoda (Slo)	PER	+ 4'57"
35.	Isidro Nozal (Esp)	LST	+ 5'02"
36.	Tom Danielson (Usa)	FAS	+ 5'06"
37.	Benoît Joachim (Lux)	USP	+ 5'07"
38.	Denis Shkarpeta (Uzb)	EI2	+ 5'31"
39.	David O'Loughlin (Irl)	EI2	+ 5'32"
40.	Oleg Joukov (Rus)	NIP	+ 5'45"
41.	Yuriy Krivtsov (Ukr)	A2R	+ 5'48"
42.	Raivis Belohvosciks (Lat)	CHO	+ 5'57"
43.	Krzysztof Ciesielski (Pol)	DHL	+ 6'07"
44.	Martin Prazdnovksy (Svk)	EI2	+ 6'48"
45.	Csaba Szekeres (Hun)	EI2	+ 7'19"
46.	Rafael Nuritdinov (Uzb)	DEN	+ 7'52"
47.	Dean Podgornik (Slo)	TEN	+ 8'33"

Bart Voskamp (Ned) CHO was disqualified for sheltering behind another competitor for too long.

Road Race Women Juniors — ***73,750 km***

1.	**Marianne Vos (Ned) (average: 33,591 km/h)**	**2h 11'44"**
2.	Marta Bastianelli (Ita)	+ 30"
3.	Eleonora van Dijk (Ned)	s.t
4.	Olena Andruk (Ukr)	s.t
5.	Roxane Knetemann (Ned)	s.t
6.	Daiva Tuslaite (Ltu)	s.t
7.	Ekaterina Tretiakova (Rus)	s.t
8.	Savrina Bernardi (Ita)	s.t
9.	Amanda Spratt (Aus)	s.t
10.	Suzanne van Veen (Ned)	s.t

66 Competitors

Netherlands			
1.	Roxane Knetemann	**5th**	+ 30"
2.	Eleonora van Dijk	**3rd**	+ 30"
3.	Suzanne van Veen	**10th**	+ 30"
4.	Marianne Vos	**1st**	**2h 11'44"**
Russia			
5.	Diana Dzemikavichyute	54th	+ 14'26"
6.	Maria Kazachenko	23rd	+ 1'58"
7.	Irina Tolmacheva	52nd	+ 13'52"
8.	Ekaterina Tretiakova	**7th**	+ 30"
Germany			
9.	Sabine Fischer	19th	+ 1'58"
10.	Virgina Hennig	16th	+ 37"
11.	Caroline Ibele	13rd	+ 30"
12.	Franziska Kniesche		*Abandon*
Italy			
13.	Francesca Andina	29th	+ 2'02"
14.	Federica Balestri	32nd	+ 3'18"
15.	Marta Bastianelli	**2nd**	+ 30"
16.	Savrina Bernardi	**8th**	+ 30"
Australia			
17.	Hannah Banks	34th	+ 7'29"
18.	Natasha Mapley	41st	+ 9'25"
19.	Amanda Spratt	**9th**	+ 30"
Poland			
20.	Aleksandra Dawidowicz	22nd	+ 1'58"
21.	Barbara Gromaszek	26th	+ 1'58"
22.	Magdalena Pyrgies		*Abandon*
23.	Jwona Pytel	18th	+ 1'41"
Switzerland			
24.	Jennifer Hohl	31st	+ 3'15"
25.	Karin Metzler	28th	+ 1'58"
26.	Ramona Weder	56th	+ 15'28"
27.	Andrea Wolfer	38th	+ 9'25"
Belgium			
28.	Ine Beyen	40th	+ 9'25"
29.	Axelle Doisy	57th	+ 18'56"
30.	Kim Schoonbaert	24th	+ 1'58"
Lithuania			
31.	Inga Cilvinaite	27th	+ 1'58"
32.	Agne Maracinskaite	25th	+ 1'58"
33.	Simona Muraskaite	59th	+ 19'51"
34.	Daiva Tuslaite	**6th**	+ 30"

UKRAINE		
35. Olena Andruk	**4th**	+ 30″
36. Olha Polkhovska	14th	+ 33″
37. Olena Sharha	11st	+ 30″
CANADA		
38. Naomi Cooper	42nd	+ 9′25″
39. Mylène Laliberté	55th	+ 14′40″
40. Joelle Numainville	50th	+ 13′52″
41. Anna Tratnyek	49th	+ 11′32″
FRANCE		
42. Sandrine Allais	47th	+ 10′24″
43. Florence Girardet	20th	+ 1′58″
44. Marie Le Moing	51st	+ 13′52″
45. Emmanuelle Merlot	17th	+ 1′19″
ESTONIA		
46. Laura Lepasalu	53rd	+ 14′26″
47. Kata-Liina Normak	58th	+ 19′41″
SPAIN		
48. M. Garcia-Navas		*Abandon*
49. Maria Martin Morales		*Abandon*
50. Patricia Perez Jimenez	43rd	+ 9′25″
51. Anna Sanchis	46th	+ 9′31″
SWEDEN		
52. Catrine Josefsson	36th	+ 7′30″
53. Marie Lindberg	37th	+ 9′25″
U.S.A		
54. Rebecca Much	15th	+ 33″
HUNGARY		
55. Gabriella Palotai	60th	+ 20′31″
BELARUS		
56. Veronika Vyrastka	45th	+ 9′25″
CZECH REPUBLIC		
57. Andrea Babunkova	48th	+ 11′18″
61. Tereza Hurikova	12nd	+ 30″
62. Jarmila Machacova	35th	+ 7′30″
MEXICO		
58. Berenice Castro Plaza	39th	+ 9′25″
VENEZUELA		
59. Danielys Garcia	33rd	+ 7′13″
63. Blendys Rojas	44th	+ 9′25″
JAPAN		
60. Mayuko Hagiwara	21st	+ 1′58″
AUSTRIA		
64. Veronika Sprügel	30th	+ 3′15″
65. Stefanie Wiedner		*Abandon*
IRELAND		
66. Mary Brennan		*Abandon*

Road Race Men Espoirs — ***177 km***

1.	**Konstantin Siutsou (Blr) (average: 38,823 km/h)**	**4h 33′33″**
2.	Thomas Dekker (Ned)	+ 1′01″
3.	Mads Christensen (Den)	+ 1′02″
4.	Domenico Pozzovivo (Ita)	+ 1′09″
5.	Vincenzo Nibali (Ita)	+ 1′30″
6.	Matti Breschel (Den)	+ 1′38″
7.	Giovanni Visconti (Ita)	s.t
8.	Marc de Maar (Ned)	+ 1′41″
9.	Andreas Dietziker (Sui)	+ 1′50″
10.	Nic Ingels (Bel)	+ 1′51″

171 Competitors

OUZBEKISTAN		
1. Muradjan Khalmuratov	63rd	+ 11′49″
BELGIUM		
2. Dominique Cornu		*Abandon*
3. Nic Ingels	**10th**	+ 1′51″
4. Serge Pauwels	24th	+ 2′40″
5. Jean-Paul Simon		*Abandon*
6. Wouter Weylandt		*Abandon*
NETHERLANDS		
7. Koen de Kort	21st	+ 2′40″
8. Marc de Maar	**8th**	+ 1′41″
9. Thomas Dekker	**2nd**	+ 1′01″
10. Bastiaan Giling		*Abandon*
11. Kai Reus		*Abandon*
SLOVENIA		
12. Janez Brajkovic	13rd	+ 2′24″
13. Tomas Nose	37th	+ 2′47″
14. Andrej Omulec		*Abandon*
15. Matic Strgar	12nd	+ 2′23″
16. Miha Svab		*Abandon*
RUSSIA		
17. Sergey Firsanov	57th	+ 6′08″
18. Dmitriy Kozantchouk	56th	+ 6′04″
19. Ivan Shchegolev		*Abandon*
20. Boris Shpilevsky	61st	+ 10′41″
21. Eduard Vorganov	15th	+ 2′40″
GERMANY		
22. Marcus Burghardt	42nd	+ 4′25″
23. Heinrich Haussler	58th	+ 7′08″
24. Paul Martens	26th	+ 2′40″
25. Konstantin Schubert		*Abandon*
26. Carlo Westphal	75th	+ 16′16″
ITALY		
27. Claudio Corioni		*Abandon*
28. Vincenzo Nibali	**5th**	+ 1′30″
29. Domenico Pozzovivo	**4th**	+ 1′09″
30. Elia Rigotto	51st	+ 5′57″
31. Giovanni Visconti	**7th**	+ 1′38″
SPAIN		
32. Igor Anton	38th	+ 2′50″
33. Jorge Azanza		*Abandon*
34. Ivan Gilmartin		*Abandon*
35. José Antonio Redondo	43rd	+ 4′25″
36. J. Joaquin Rojas Gil	47th	+ 5′56″
SWITZERLAND		
37. Laurent Arn	62nd	+ 10′41″
38. Andreas Dietziker	**9th**	+ 1′50″
39. Daniel Gysling		*Abandon*
40. Hubert Schwab		*Abandon*
41. Florian Stalder		*Abandon*
SLOVAKIA		
42. Milan Branicky	46th	+ 5′56″
43. Marjan Hecl		*Abandon*
44. Robert Mitosinka		*Abandon*
45. Martin Velits		*Abandon*
46. Peter Velits		*Abandon*
KAZAKSTAN		
47. Sergey Danniker		*Abandon*
48. Valeriy Dmitriyev		*Abandon*
49. Alexandr Kovdiy		*Abandon*
FINLAND		
50. Juha-Matti Alaluusua		*Abandon*
51. Jukka Vastaranta		*Abandon*
FRANCE		
52. Olivier Bonnaire	73rd	+ 16′12″
53. Rémy Di Gregorio		*Abandon*
54. Arnaud Gérard	67th	+ 14′05″
55. Julien Loubet		*Abandon*
56. Sébastien Minard		*Abandon*
AUSTRIA		
57. Markus Eibegger	48th	+ 5′56″
58. Bernhard Kohl		*Abandon*
59. Michael Pichler		*Abandon*
60. Thomas Rohregger	33rd	+ 2′42″
JAPAN		
61. Fumiyuki Beppu		*Abandon*
62. Masahiro Shinagawa		*Abandon*
PORTUGAL		
63. João Cabreira		*Abandon*
64. Filipe Cardoso	11st	+ 2′03″
65. Micael Isidoro	49th	+ 5′57″
66. Antonio Jesus		*Abandon*
67. Ricardo Martins	34th	+ 2′42″
SWEDEN		
68. Jonas Holmkvist		*Abandon*
69. Andreas Johansson		*Abandon*
IRELAND		
70. Timothy Cassidy		*Abandon*
71. Philip Deignan	17th	+ 2′40″
72. Andrew McQuaid		*Abandon*
73. Paidi O'Brien	68th	+ 16′12″
74. Nicholas Roche	22nd	+ 2′40″
COLOMBIA		
75. Alex Cano Ardila	53rd	+ 5′57″
76. Rafael Infantino		*Abandon*
77. Julian Muñoz Giraldo	35th	+ 2′42″
78. Fredy Piamonte	66th	+ 14′04″
79. Carlos Vargas	65th	+ 14′02″
CROATIA		
80. Alan Dumic		*Abandon*
81. Emanuel Kiserlovski	82nd	+ 25′36″
82. Zvonimir Pokupec		*Abandon*
83. Ivan Sever	32nd	+ 2′40″
U.S.A		
84. Kevin Bouchard-Hall	64th	+ 12′31″
85. Matthew Crane		*Abandon*
86. Timothy Duggan	78th	+ 19′42″
87. Tyler Farrar	28th	+ 2′40″
88. Saul Raisin	36th	+ 2′42″
DENMARK		
89. Matti Breschel	**6th**	+ 1′38″
90. Mads Christensen	**3rd**	+ 1′02″
91. Kasper Kløstergaard		*Abandon*
92. Anders Lund		*Abandon*
93. Martin Pedersen	18th	+ 2′40″
AUSTRALIA		
94. Peter Dawson		*Abandon*
95. Ashley Humbert	50th	+ 5′57″
96. Benjamin Johnson	44th	+ 5′48″
97. Aaron Kemps		*Abandon*
98. Nicholas Sanderson		*Abandon*
SOUTH AFRICA		
99. Eckard Bergh		*Abandon*
100. Daryl Impey		*Abandon*
101. Jaco Odendaal		*Abandon*
102. Waylon Woolcock		*Abandon*
UKRAINE		
103. Andriy Buchko		*Abandon*
104. Andriy Grivko	14th	+ 2′31″
105. Volodymyr Kogut		*Abandon*
106. Dmytro Novosad		*Abandon*
107. Andriy Pryshchepa	69th	+ 16′12″
POLAND		
108. Lukasz Bodnar		*Abandon*
109. Blazej Janiaczyk	40th	+ 3′10″
110. Artur Krol		*Abandon*
111. Tomasz Marczynski		*Abandon*
112. Piotr Mazur	55th	+ 6′04″
CANADA		
113. Cameron Evans		*Abandon*
114. Chris Isaac		*Abandon*
115. Dustin McBurnie		*Abandon*
116. François Parisien	27th	+ 2′40″
GREAT BRITAIN		
117. Dan Fleeman		*Abandon*
118. Evan Oliphant		*Abandon*
119. Kieran Page		*Abandon*
120. Jonathan Tiernan-Lock		*Abandon*
ESTONIA		
121. Caspar Austa		*Abandon*
122. Andrei Laptsenkov	77th	+ 19′42″
123. René Mandri	19th	+ 2′40″
MOLDAVIA		
124. Denis Cioban	74th	+ 16′12″
125. Dumitru Creciun	79th	+ 22′51″
126. Evghenii Gutalov	30th	+ 2′40″
127. Ruslan Sambris	83rd	+ 25′38″
NORWAY		
128. Christopher Myhre		*Abandon*
129. Haavard Nybö		*Abandon*
130. Stian Remme		*Abandon*
LATVIA		
131. Igors Dobrovolskis	60th	+ 10′41″
132. Kalvis Eisaks		*Abandon*
133. Olegs Melehs	41st	+ 3′10″
134. Kristofers Racenajs	76th	+ 19′42″
135. Aleksejs Saramotins	23rd	+ 2′40″
HUNGARY		
136. Akos Haiszer		*Abandon*
137. Peter Kusztor		*Abandon*
138. Barnabas Vizer	84th	+ 25′38″
139. Daniel Zsombok		*Abandon*
VENEZUELA		
140. Miguel Chacon Sosa		*Abandon*
141. Artur Garcia Rincon		*Abandon*
142. Honorio Machado	20th	+ 2′40″
143. Richard Ochoa Quintero		*Abandon*
ROMANIA		
144. Marin Andrei		*Abandon*
CZECH REPUBLIC		
145. Jan Barta	72nd	+ 16′12″
149. Lukas Fus	25th	+ 2′40″
155. Martin Mares	52nd	+ 5′57″
ARGENTINA		
146. Anibal Borrajo		*Abandon*
151. Lucas Haedo		*Abandon*
159. Maximiliano Richeze		*Abandon*
LITHUANIA		
147. Andrius Buividas	70th	+ 16′12″
167. Justas Volungevicius		*Abandon*
168. Karolis Volungevicius	80th	+ 25′09″
ISRAEL		
148. Dor Dviri		*Abandon*
ECUADOR		
150. Byron Guama		*Abandon*
157. Segundo Navarrete		*Abandon*
161. Carlos Sanchez		*Abandon*
SERBIA-MONTENEGRO		
152. Nebosja Jovanovic	54th	+ 6′02″
165. Goran Smelcerovic	81st	+ 25′36″
166. Dragan Spasic		*Abandon*
BELARUS		
153. Andrei Kunitski	45th	+ 5′56″
160. Branislau Samoilau	59th	+ 10′41″
164. Konstantin Siutsou	**1st**	**4h 33′33″**

Alone out front... The Bielorussian Konstantin Siutsov.

In obtaining the silver medal, the Tunisian raises the profile of North african cycling.

No.	Rider	Place	Time
64.	Lukas Hanus	101st	+ 17'48"
65.	Michal Prachar	91st	+ 16'01"
66.	Branislav Zachar	75th	+ 14'59"
	Poland		
67.	Lukasz Bujko		*Abandon*
68.	Pawel Cieslik	62nd	+ 8'56"
69.	Jaroslaw Marycz		*Abandon*
70.	Lukasz Modzelewski		*Abandon*
71.	Piotr Pyszny		*Abandon*
	Australia		
72.	Simon Clarke	13rd	+ 47"
73.	Matthew Goss	63rd	+ 8'56"
74.	Patrick Shaw	84th	+ 15'14"
75.	Andrew Wade	98th	+ 16'01"
	Great Britain		
76.	Daniel Martin	67th	+ 9'14"
77.	Ian Stannard		*Abandon*
78.	Alistair Stoddart		*Abandon*
79.	Geraint Thomas	14th	+ 54"
	U.S.A		
80.	Zachary Bolian	121st	+ 23'47"
81.	Alexander Boyd		*Abandon*
82.	Chris Stockburger	104th	+ 19'49"
83.	Adam Switters		*Abandon*
84.	Zachary Taylor	122nd	+ 23'47"
	Luxembourg		
85.	Nick Clesen	105th	+ 21'55"
86.	Jempy Drucker	61st	+ 8'22"
87.	Ben Gastauer	94th	+ 16'01"
88.	Cyrille Heymans	77th	+ 15'10"
89.	Robert Schmitt	120th	+ 23'47"
	Latvia		
90.	Daniels Ernestovskis	68th	+ 11'19"
91.	Janis Ozols	108th	+ 23'40"
92.	Herberts Pudans	31st	+ 3'40"
93.	Gints Reinolds	125th	+ 28'56"
94.	Gatis Smukulis	21st	+ 3'30"
	New Zealand		
95.	Clinton Avery	46th	+ 4'12"
96.	Edwin Crossling		*Abandon*
97.	Andrew Pollock	85th	+ 15'30"
98.	Andrew Thompson	88th	+ 15'59"
99.	Calvin Wilson		*Abandon*
	Ukraine		
100.	Vitaliy Buts	71st	+ 12'23"
101.	Yevgeniy Nykolenko	70th	+ 11'59"
102.	Nikolay Onysechko	97th	+ 16'01"
103.	Oleg Opryshko		*Abandon*
104.	Anatoliy Yugov		*Abandon*
	Austria		
105.	Stefan Denifl		*Abandon*
106.	Heimo Flechl		*Abandon*
107.	Franz Grassmann	64th	+ 8'56"
109.	Christoph Sokoll	92nd	+ 16'01"
176.	Philipp Ludescher	89th	+ 16'01"
	Portugal		
110.	Marcio Barbosa		*Abandon*
111.	Samuel Coelho		*Abandon*
112.	Rui Costa	69th	+ 11'51"
113.	Jorge Pereira		*Abandon*
114.	Vitor Rodrigues	16th	+ 1'42"
	Canada		
115.	Eric Boily		*Abandon*
116.	Brooke Boocock		*Abandon*
117.	Adam Thuss	112nd	+ 23'40"
118.	Raphael Tremblay		*Abandon*
	Kazakstan		
119.	Roman Kireyev	28th	+ 3'40"
120.	Bolat Raimbekov		*Abandon*
121.	Ruslan Tleubayev	93rd	+ 16'01"
122.	Ivan Zhiyentayev		*Abandon*
	Japan		
123.	Ryuta Morimoto	103rd	+ 18'28"
124.	Makoto Shimada	119th	+ 23'40"
	Hungary		
125.	David Balogh		*Abandon*
126.	Istvan Cziraki	102nd	+ 18'28"
127.	Sandor Koczka		*Abandon*
128.	Gergely Liska		*Abandon*
	Moldavia		
129.	Oleg Berdos	80th	+ 15'10"
130.	Sergiu Catan	123rd	+ 27'31"
131.	Andrei Mironov		*Abandon*
132.	Alexandr Pliushin	55th	+ 6'28"
	Lithuania		
133.	Marius Bernatonis	90th	+ 16'01"
134.	Eligijus Dalisanskas	106th	+ 23'40"
135.	Egidijus Jursys	52nd	+ 6'21"
136.	Tomas Tareilis	86th	+ 15'37"
	Bulgaria		
137.	Martin Grashev		*Abandon*
138.	Spas Gyurov	100th	+ 17'16"
139.	Petar Panayotov		*Abandon*
	South Africa		
140.	John-Lee Augustyn	27th	+ 3'40"
141.	Jacques Janse van Rensburg	57th	+ 6'28"
142.	Juan van Heerden	87th	+ 15'59"
143.	Duncan Viljoen	45th	+ 3'58"
	Croatia		
144.	Kristijan Durasek	83rd	+ 15'10"
145.	Matej Fonovic		*Abandon*
146.	Robert Kiserlovski	37th	+ 3'40"
147.	Vedran Vitasovic		*Abandon*
	Norway		
148.	Edvald Boasson Hagen	23rd	+ 3'40"
149.	Alexander Kristoff	107th	+ 23'40"
	Estonia		
150.	Janar Jermakov	113rd	+ 23'40"
151.	Tanel Kangert	40th	+ 3'40"
152.	Ervin Korts-Laur	76th	+ 15'10"
	Malta		
153.	Roderick Muscat	60th	+ 7'08"
154.	Shawn Pullicino		*Abandon*
	Israel		
155.	Tal Eizinbad		*Abandon*
	Belarus		
156.	Artur Tarasau	33rd	+ 3'40"
157.	Yury Yazepchyk	32nd	+ 3'40"
158.	Siarhei Zatonenka		*Abandon*
	Georgia		
159.	Archil Makharashvili	114th	+ 23'40"
160.	Giorgi Nadiradze	49th	+ 5'29"
	Greece		
161.	Ilias Periklis	124th	+ 27'34"
162.	Panagiotis Potsakis	115th	+ 23'40"
	Mexico		
154.	Juan Pablo Magallanes	39th	+ 3'10"
158.	Marco Ortega		*Abandon*
162.	Ignacio Sarabia		*Abandon*
	San Marino		
156.	Marco Mauri		*Abandon*
	Luxembourg		
163.	Andy Schleck	31st	+ 2'40"
169.	Ben Würth	71st	+ 16'12"
	New Zealand		
170.	Jeremy Yates	16th	+ 2'40"
	Armenia		
171.	Tigran Korkotyan		*Abandon*

Road Race Men Juniors — ***132,750 km***

1.	**Roman Kreuziger (Cze) (average: 38,731 km/h)**	**3h 25'39"**
2.	Rafâa Chtioui (Tun)	s.t
3.	Simon Spilak (Slo)	+ 6"
4.	Eros Capecchi (Ita)	s.t
5.	Pieter Jacobs (Bel)	s.t
6.	Robert Gesink (Ned)	s.t
7.	Ben Hermans (Bel)	s.t
8.	Alexandre Binet (Fra)	+ 32"
9.	Ivan Rovnyi (Rus)	s.t
10.	Cyril Gautier (Fra)	s.t

174 Competitors

No.	Rider	Place	Time
	Netherlands		
1.	Robert Gesink	**6th**	+ 6"
2.	Michel Kreder	73rd	+ 13'09"
3.	Rob Ruigh	47th	+ 4'13"
4.	Thijs van Amerongen	54th	+ 6'21"
5.	Cornelius van Ooijen	96th	+ 16'01"
	Denmark		
6.	Anders Berendt	44th	+ 3'56"
7.	Jonas Follmann	95th	+ 16'01"
8.	Troels Ronning		*Abandon*
9.	André Steensen	22nd	+ 3'40"
10.	Thomas Vedel	11st	+ 32"
	Czech Republic		
11.	Leopold König	36th	+ 3'40"
12.	Roman Kreuziger	**1st**	**3h 25'39"**
13.	Zdenek Machac		*Abandon*
14.	Petr Novotny	53rd	+ 6'21"
	Spain		
15.	David Abal		*Abandon*
16.	Arkaitz Duran		*Abandon*
17.	Egoitz Garcia Echeguibel	82nd	+ 15'10"
18.	Hector Gonzalez Baeza		*Abandon*
19.	Ruben Reig	38th	+ 3'40"
	Sweden		
20.	Jonas Bjelkmark		*Abandon*
21.	Fredrik Johansson	118th	+ 23'40"
22.	Johan Lindgren	17th	+ 1'42"
23.	Viktor Renäng	25th	+ 3'40"
	Belgium		
24.	Ben Hermans	**7th**	+ 6"
25.	Pieter Jacobs	**5th**	+ 6"
26.	Nikolas Maes	24th	+ 3'40"
27.	Kevin Seeldrayers	18th	+ 3'09"
28.	Michiel van Albroeck	19th	+ 3'09"
	Slovenia		
29.	Marko Hlebanja	78th	+ 15'10"
30.	Kristjan Koren	48th	+ 5'20"
31.	Joze Senekovic	20th	+ 3'29"
32.	Simon Spilak	**3rd**	+ 6"
	France		
34.	Alexandre Binet	**8th**	+ 32"
35.	Mikael Cherel	56th	+ 6'28"
36.	Cyril Gautier	**10th**	+ 32"
37.	Blel Kadri	72nd	+ 13'09"
38.	Pierre Rolland	15th	+ 1'42"
	Italy		
39.	Eros Capecchi	**4th**	+ 6"
40.	Marco Corti	50th	+ 5'47"
41.	Fabio Donesana		*Abandon*
42.	Federico Masiero	58th	+ 6'28"
43.	Simone Ponzi	59th	+ 6'28"
	Russia		
44.	Pavel Kochetkov	39th	+ 3'40"
45.	Anton Reshetnikov	43rd	+ 3'40"
46.	Ivan Rovnyi	**9th**	+ 32"
47.	Alexander Slivkin	66th	+ 8'56"
48.	Alexander Urychev		*Abandon*
	Tunisia		
49.	Rafâa Chtioui	**2nd**	s.t
	Germany		
50.	Marcel Barth	74th	+ 13'11"
51.	Mathias Belka	26th	+ 3'40"
52.	Michael Franzl	29th	+ 3'40"
53.	Sebastian Hans	79th	+ 15'10"
54.	Phillip Seubert	65th	+ 8'56"
	Colombia		
55.	Fabio Duarte	41st	+ 3'40"
56.	Carlos Quintero	34th	+ 3'40"
	Switzerland		
57.	Tobias Eggli	30th	+ 3'40"
58.	Mathias Frank	51st	+ 5'47"
59.	Rafael Nick	35th	+ 3'40"
60.	Michael Schär	12nd	+ 32"
61.	Marcel Wyss	42nd	+ 3'40"
	Slovakia		
62.	Slavomir Benc	116th	+ 23'40"
63.	Patrik Fabian		*Abandon*

The junior Roman Kreuziger sizes up his opponents before launching an attack.

No.	Name	Place	Time
	Ireland		
163.	Martin Munroe	109th	+ 23'40"
164.	Mark Nestor	99th	+ 16'01"
165.	Maurice O'Brien		*Abandon*
	Mexico		
166.	Luis Pulido	81st	+ 15'10"
	Morocco		
167.	Mouhim Hayani		*Abandon*
	Romania		
168.	Laszlo Madaras	117th	+ 23'40"
169.	Marius Nicolae Stoica	111st	+ 23'40"
	San Marino		
170.	Lorenzo Antonini		*Abandon*
171.	Simone Podeschi	110th	+ 23'40"
172.	Marco Zafferani		*Abandon*
	Serbia-Montenegro		
173.	Dejan Stefanovic		*Abandon*
174.	Milos Velickovic		*Abandon*
	Ouzbekistan		
175.	Ruslan Karimov		*Abandon*

Road Race Women Elites — *132,75 km*

1.	**Judith Arndt (Ger) (average: 35,458 km/h)**	**3h 44'38"**
2.	Tatiana Guderzo (Ita)	+ 10"
3.	Anita Valen (Nor)	+ 12"
4.	Trixi Worrack (Ger)	s.t
5.	Modesta Vzesniauskaite (Ltu)	s.t
6.	Nicole Brändli (Sui)	s.t
7.	Joane Sommariba (Esp)	s.t
8.	Svetlana Bubnenkova (Rus)	s.t
9.	Mirjam Melchers (Ned)	s.t
10.	Edita Pucinskaite (Ltu)	s.t

118 Competitors

No.	Name	Place	Time
	Sweden		
1.	Susanne Ljungskog	26th	+ 1'11"
2.	Monica Holler		*Abandon*
3.	Camilla Larsson	68th	+ 22'51"
4.	Madeleine Lindberg		*Abandon*
	Netherlands		
5.	Chantal Beltman	29th	+ 3'30"
6.	Ghita Beltman	59th	+ 11'12"
7.	Arenda Grimberg		*Abandon*
8.	Loes Gunnewijk		*Abandon*
9.	Mirjam Melchers	**9th**	+ 12"
10.	Elisabeth Vink	55th	+ 6'09"
	Great Britain		
11.	Nicole Cooke	24th	+ 1'07"
12.	Charlotte Goldsmith		*Abandon*
13.	Rachel Heal	36th	+ 6'09"
14.	Frances Newstead		*Abandon*
	Lithuania		
15.	Edita Kubelskiene		*Abandon*
16.	Jolanta Polikeviciute	19th	+ 41"
17.	Rasa Polikeviciute	17th	+ 41"
18.	Edita Pucinskaite	**10th**	+ 12"
19.	Zita Urbonaite		*Abandon*
20.	Modesta Vzesniauskaite	**5th**	+ 12"
	Russia		
21.	Natalia Boyarskaya	69th	+ 22'51"
22.	Svetlana Bubnenkova	**8th**	+ 12"
23.	Julia Martissova		*Abandon*
24.	Valentina Polkhanova	11st	+ 12"
25.	Olga Slyusareva		*Abandon*
26.	Zoulfia Zabirova	12nd	+ 12"
	France		
27.	Elisabeth Chevanne-Brunel	43rd	+ 6'09"
28.	Sonia Huguet	52nd	+ 6'09"
29.	Marina Jaunatre	71st	+ 22'51"
30.	Magali Le Floc'h	28th	+ 3'30"
31.	Jeannie Longo-Ciprelli	21st	+ 1'07"
32.	Edwige Pitel	23rd	+ 1'07"
	Norway		
33.	Lene Byberg		*Abandon*
34.	Linn Torp		*Abandon*
35.	Anita Valen	**3rd**	+ 12"
	Germany		
36.	Judith Arndt	**1st**	**3h 44'38"**
37.	Tina Liebig	57th	+ 6'13"
38.	Madeleine Sandig		*Abandon*
39.	Regina Schleicher		*Abandon*
40.	Theresa Senff	30th	+ 3'38"
41.	Trixi Worrack	**4th**	+ 12"
	Poland		
42.	Paulina Brzezna	74th	+ 28'08"
43.	Bogumila Matusiak	35th	+ 6'09"
44.	Malgorzata Wysocka	60th	+ 11'23"
45.	Aleksandra Zabrocka		*Abandon*
	U.S.A		
46.	Kristin Armstrong	58th	+ 11'12"
47.	Kimberly Bruckner	49th	+ 6'09"
48.	Deirdre Demet-Barry	16th	+ 41"
49.	Tina Mayolo-Pic	67th	+ 21'23"
50.	Amber Neben	45th	+ 6'09"
51.	Christine Thorburn	20th	+ 41"
	Italy		
52.	Tania Belvederesi		*Abandon*
53.	Noemi Cantele	27th	+ 2'08"
54.	Daniela Fusar Poli		*Abandon*
55.	Tatiana Guderzo	**2nd**	+ 10"
56.	Silvia Parietti		*Abandon*
57.	Anna Zugno	41st	+ 6'09"
	Canada		
58.	Lyne Bessette	14th	+ 41"
59.	Nicole Demars		*Abandon*
60.	Manon Jutras	50th	+ 6'09"
61.	Amy Moore	33rd	+ 6'09"
62.	Susan Palmer-Komar	18th	+ 41"
63.	Erinne Willock	53rd	+ 6'09"
	Czech Republic		
64.	Lada Kozlikova	32nd	+ 6'09"
	Spain		
65.	Cristian Alcalde		*Abandon*
66.	Eneritz Iturriaga	15th	+ 41"
67.	Maribel Moreno	51st	+ 6'09"
68.	Anna Ramirez		*Abandon*
69.	Dori Ruano	54th	+ 6'09"
70.	Joane Somarriba	**7th**	+ 12"
	Austria		
71.	Andrea Graus	72nd	+ 22'51"
72.	Christiane Soeder	38th	+ 6'09"
	Australia		
73.	Nathalie Bates		
74.	Olivia Gollan	56th	+ 6'09"
75.	Margaret Hemsley	48th	+ 6'09"
76.	Hayley Rutherford		*Abandon*
77.	Oenone Wood	13rd	+ 41"
78.	Alison Wright		*Abandon*
	Switzerland		
79.	Annette Beutler	22nd	+ 1'07"
80.	Nicole Brändli	**6th**	+ 12"
81.	Sarah Grab	47th	+ 6'09"
82.	Barbara Heeb	31st	+ 3'38"
83.	Irene Hostettler		*Abandon*
84.	Sereina Trachsel		*Abandon*
	Ukraine		
85.	Iryna Chuzhynova		*Abandon*
86.	Natalya Kachalka	62nd	+ 11'23"
87.	Valentina Karpenko	66th	+ 21'21"
88.	Oxana Kashchyshyna	64th	+ 20'52"
	Belgium		
89.	Sofie Goor		*Abandon*
90.	Corine Hierckens	42nd	+ 6'09"
91.	Veerle Ingels	63rd	+ 12'14"
92.	Cindy Pieters		*Abandon*
93.	Evy van Damme	39th	+ 6'09"
94.	Sharon van Dromme		*Abandon*
	Japan		
95.	Miho Oki	34th	+ 6'09"
	Denmark		
96.	Lise Christensen	70th	+ 22'51"
97.	Trine Hansen	44th	+ 6'09"
98.	Linda Villumsen Serup	25th	+1'07"
	Jamaica		
99.	Iona Wynter		*Abandon*
	Mexico		
100.	Veronica Leal		*Abandon*
	Argentina		
101.	Noelia Fernandez		*Abandon*
	Belarus		
102.	Volha Hayeva		*Abandon*
103.	Tatsiana Sharakova		*Abandon*
104.	Zinaida Stahurskaya	46th	+ 6'09"
	Brazil		
105.	Rosane Kirch	61st	+ 11'23"
106.	Clemilda Silva Fernandes	37th	+ 6'09"
107.	Janildes Silva Fernandes		*Abandon*
108.	Maria Silva		*Abandon*
109.	Uenia Souza		*Abandon*
	Colombia		
110.	Ana Paola Madrinan	73rd	+ 23'32"
	Estonia		
111.	Grete Treier	65th	+ 21'21"
	Finland		
112.	Tiina Nieminen		*Abandon*
	Hungary		
113.	Veronika Jeger		*Abandon*
114.	Monika Kiraly		*Abandon*
	Ireland		
115.	Louise Moriarty		*Abandon*
116.	Colette Swift		*Abandon*
	Moldavia		
117.	Tatiana Shishkova	40th	+ 6'09"
	South Africa		
118.	Diane Emery		*Abandon*

Road Race Men Elites — *261 km*

1.	**Oscar Freire (Esp) (average: 38,179 km/h)**	**6h 57'15"**
2.	Erik Zabel (Ger)	s.t
3.	Luca Paolini (Ita)	s.t
4.	Stuart O'Grady (Aus)	s.t
5.	Allan Davis (Aus)	s.t
6.	Alejandro Valverde (Esp)	s.t
7.	Michael Boogerd (Ned)	s.t
8.	Chris Horner (Usa)	s.t
9.	Damiano Cunego (Ita)	s.t
10.	Frank Schleck (Lux)	s.t

200 Competitors

No.	Name	Place	Time
	Spain		
1.	Igor Astarloa (LAM)	64th	+ 4'34"
2.	J. Antonio Flecha (FAS)	69th	+ 6'23"
3.	Oscar Freire (RAB)	**1st**	**6h 57'15"**
4.	J.Ivan Gutierrez (IBB)		*Abandon*
5.	Pedro Horrillo (QSD)		*Abandon*
6.	Eladio Jimenez (KEL)		*Abandon*
7.	Francisco Mancebo (IBB)	12nd	s.t
8.	Isidro Nozal (LST)	63rd	+ 4'34"
9.	Luis Perez Rodriguez (COF)	17th	+ 9"
10.	J.Luis Rubiera (USP)		*Abandon*
11.	Marcos Serrano (LST)	15th	s.t
12.	Alejandro Valverde (KEL)	**6th**	s.t
13.	Constantino Zaballa (SDV)	45th	+ 4'26"
	Belgium		
14.	Serge Baguet (LOT)	51st	+ 4'26"
15.	Tom Boonen (QSD)		*Abandon*
16.	Philippe Gilbert (FDJ)		*Abandon*
17.	Maxime Monfort (LAN)		*Abandon*
18.	Nick Nuyens (QSD)	84th	+ 4'57"
19.	Nico Sijmens (LAN)	83rd	+ 4'57"
20.	Jurgen van Goolen (QSD)		*Abandon*
21.	Wim van Huffel (VLA)		*Abandon*
22.	Peter van Petegem (LOT)	29th	+ 4'26"
23.	Johan van Summeren (REB)	52nd	+ 4'26"
24.	Geert Verheyen (CHO)	31st	+ 4'26"
25.	Marc Wauters (RAB)		*Abandon*
	Italy		
26.	Ivan Basso (CSC)	11st	s.t
27.	Leonardo Bertagnolli (SAE)	23rd	+ 1'41"
28.	Paolo Bettini (QSD)		*Abandon*
29.	Damiano Cunego (SAE)	**9th**	s.t
30.	Dario Frigo (FAS)	22nd	+ 1'41"
31.	Stefano Garzelli (VIN)		*Abandon*
32.	Luca Mazzanti (PAN)	59th	+ 4'26"
33.	Cristian Moreni (ALB)	62nd	+ 4'26"
34.	Daniele Nardello (TMO)	67th	+ 4'34"
35.	Luca Paolini (QSD)	**3rd**	s.t
36.	Franco Pellizotti (ALB)	65th	+ 4'34"
37.	Roberto Petito (FAS)		*Abandon*
38.	Filippo Simeoni (DVE)		*Abandon*
	Netherlands		
39.	Michael Boogerd (RAB)	**7th**	s.t
40.	Jan Boven (RAB)		*Abandon*
41.	Bram de Groot (RAB)		*Abandon*
42.	Erik Dekker (RAB)		*Abandon*
43.	Maarten den Bakker (RAB)		*Abandon*
44.	Karsten Kroon (RAB)	20th	+ 1'39"
45.	Marc Lotz (RAB)		*Abandon*
46.	Gerben Löwik (CHO)		*Abandon*
47.	Koos Moerenhout (LOT)		*Abandon*
48.	Bram Tankink (QSD)	82nd	+ 9'54"
49.	Thorwald Veneberg (RAB)		*Abandon*
50.	Pieter Weening (RAB)		*Abandon*
	Denmark		
51.	Lars Ytting Bak (BGL)		*Abandon*
52.	Michael Blaudzun (CSC)		*Abandon*
53.	Frank Høj (CSC)	85th	+ 10'30"
54.	René Jørgensen (ALB)		*Abandon*
55.	Allan Johansen (BGL)		*Abandon*
56.	Michael Rasmussen (RAB)	13rd	s.t
57.	Michael Skelde (ALB)		*Abandon*
58.	Nicki Sørensen (CSC)	39th	+ 4'26"

No.	Rider	Place	Result
Canada			
59.	Michael Barry (USP)		*Abandon*
60.	Charles Dionne (WEB)	87th	+ 28'45"
Germany			
61.	Rolf Aldag (TMO)	66th	+ 4'34"
62.	Markus Fothen (GST)		*Abandon*
63.	Danilo Hondo (GST)	14th	s.t
64.	Matthias Kessler (TMO)	19th	+ 58"
65.	Sebastian Lang (GST)		*Abandon*
66.	Ronny Scholz (GST)		*Abandon*
67.	Stephan Schreck (TMO)		*Abandon*
68.	Stefan Schumacher (TLM)		*Abandon*
69.	Fabian Wegmann (GST)	33rd	+ 4'26"
70.	Christian Werner (TMO)		*Abandon*
71.	Stefan Wesemann (TMO)	18th	+ 26"
72.	Erik Zabel (TMO)	**2nd**	s.t
Australia			
73.	Paul Crake (CAA)		*Abandon*
74.	Allan Davis (LST)	**5th**	s.t
75.	Scott Davis (PAN)		*Abandon*
76.	Cadel Evans (TMO)		*Abandon*
77.	Simon Gerrans (EI2)		*Abandon*
78.	Mathew Hayman (RAB)		*Abandon*
79.	David McPartland (TEN)		*Abandon*
80.	Stuart O'Grady (COF)	**4th**	s.t
81.	Luke Roberts (COM)		*Abandon*
82.	Michael Rogers (QSD)	81st	+ 9'54"
83.	Matthew White (COF)		*Abandon*
Switzerland			
84.	Michael Albasini (PHO)		*Abandon*
85.	Roger Beuchat (VIN)	38th	+ 4'26"
86.	Patrick Calcagni (VIN)	80th	+ 9'54"
87.	Fabian Cancellara (FAS)		*Abandon*
88.	Martin Elmiger (PHO)	26th	+ 4'26"
89.	Fabian Jeker (SDV)	60th	+ 4'26"
90.	Gregory Rast (PHO)	35th	+ 4'26"
91.	Daniel Schnider (PHO)	43rd	+ 4'26"
92.	Marcel Strauss (GST)		*Abandon*
93.	Johann Tschopp (PHO)		*Abandon*
94.	Steve Zampieri (VIN)	71st	+ 6'23"
95.	Marcus Zberg (GST)		*Abandon*
Russia			
96.	Alexandr Arekeev (A&S)		*Abandon*
97.	Alexandr Bazhenov (DVE)	54th	+ 4'26"
98.	Alexandre Botcharov (C.A)	40th	+ 4'26"
99.	Vladimir Efimkin (EI2)		*Abandon*
100.	Viatcheslav Ekimov (USP)		*Abandon*
101.	Vladimir Goussev (CSC)	70th	+ 6'23"
102.	Serguei Ivanov (TMO)		*Abandon*
103.	Andrey Klyuev (EI2)		*Abandon*
104.	Alexandr Kolobnev (DVE)		*Abandon*
105.	Dmitri Konyshev (LPR)	25th	+ 4'26"
106.	Mikhail Timochine (LAN)		*Abandon*
107.	Oleg Zhukov (NIP)		*Abandon*
U.S.A			
108.	Chris Baldwin (NIC)		*Abandon*
109.	Michael Creed (USP)		*Abandon*
110.	Tom Danielson (FAS)		*Abandon*
111.	Chris Horner (WEB)	**8th**	s.t
112.	Jonathan McCarty (USP)		*Abandon*
113.	Jason McCartney (HNC)		*Abandon*
114.	Kirk O'Bee (NIC)		*Abandon*
115.	Fred Rodriguez (A&S)		*Abandon*
116.	Guido Trenti (FAS)	79th	+ 9'54"
117.	Christian Vandevelde (LST)		*Abandon*
Slovenia			
118.	Kristjan Fajt (TEN)		*Abandon*
119.	Jure Golcer (FPF)	58th	+ 4'26"
120.	Matej Mugerli (EI2)	42nd	+ 4'26"
121.	Uros Murn (PHO)	30th	+ 4'26"
Belarus			
122.	Aleksandr Kuchynski (AMO)		*Abandon*
Austria			
123.	Peter Luttenberger (CSC)	53rd	+ 4'26"
124.	Harald Morscher (VOL)	41st	+ 4'26"
125.	Gerhard Trampusch (A&S)		*Abandon*
126.	Peter Wrolich (GST)		*Abandon*
France			
127.	Laurent Brochard (A2R)		*Abandon*
128.	Sylvain Calzati (RAG)		*Abandon*
129.	Sandy Casar (FDJ)		*Abandon*
130.	Cyril Dessel (PHO)		*Abandon*
131.	Christophe Le Mével (C.A)		*Abandon*
132.	Eric Leblacher (C.A)	75th	+ 9'54"
133.	David Moncoutié (COF)	46th	+ 4'26"
134.	Jérôme Pineau (BLB)	32nd	+ 4'26"
135.	Franck Renier (BLB)		*Abandon*
136.	Christophe Rinero (RAG)	68th	+ 6'23"
137.	Yannick Talabardon (AUB)		*Abandon*
138.	Nicolas Vogondy (FDJ)	48th	+ 4'26"
Luxembourg			
139.	Benoît Joachim (USP)		*Abandon*
140.	Frank Schleck (CSC)	**10th**	s.t
Great Britain			
141.	Tom Southam (AMO)		*Abandon*
142.	Charles Wegelius (DEN)		*Abandon*
Colombia			
143.	Mauricio Ardila (CHO)	21st	+ 1'39"
144.	Leonardo Duque (JAR)		*Abandon*
145.	Fr. Gonzalez Martinez (CLM)	47th	+ 4'26"
146.	Luis Felipe Laverde (FPF)	36th	+ 4'26"
147.	Ivan Parra (BAQ)	24th	+ 3'09"
Hungary			
148.	Laszlo Garamszegi (EI2)		*Abandon*
Ukraine			
149.	Volodymyr Bileka (LAN)		*Abandon*
150.	Vladimir Duma (LAN)	72nd	+ 6'23"
151.	Volodymyr Gustov (FAS)	55th	+ 4'26"
152.	Mikhaylo Khalilov (ICT)	28th	+ 4'26"
153.	Denys Kostyuk (CHO)		*Abandon*
154.	Yuriy Krivtsov (A2R)		*Abandon*
155.	Yaroslav Popovych (LAN)		*Abandon*
156.	Kyrylo Pospeev (A&S)		*Abandon*
Norway			
157.	Kurt-Asle Arvesen (CSC)	37th	+ 4'26"
158.	Morten Hegreberg (JAR)	88th	+ 28'45"
159.	Mads Kaggestad (C.A)		*Abandon*
Portugal			
160.	Nuno Alves (BAR)		*Abandon*
161.	Pedro Cardoso (MIL)	76th	+ 9'54"
162.	Helder Miranda (WBP)		*Abandon*
163.	Hugo Sabido (MIL)		*Abandon*
164.	Nelson Vitorino (WBP)		*Abandon*
Kazakstan			
165.	Dmitriy Fofonov (COF)		*Abandon*
166.	Andrey Kashechkin (C.A)		*Abandon*
167.	Alexandre Vinokourov (TMO)	16th	+ 5"
168.	Serguei Yakovlev (TMO)		*Abandon*
Poland			
169.	Krzysztof Ciesielski (CHL)		*Abandon*
170.	Bartosz Huzarski (ATI)		*Abandon*
171.	Mateusz Mroz (AMO)	77th	+ 9'54"
172.	Przemyslaw Niemec (MIE)		*Abandon*
173.	Marek Rutkiewicz (ATI)		*Abandon*
174.	Sebastian Skiba (LEG)		*Abandon*
175.	Jaroslaw Welniak (LEG)		*Abandon*
176.	Cezary Zamana (CHO)	34th	+ 4'26"
Ireland			
177.	David McCann (GNT)	74th	+ 9'54"
178.	David O'Loughlin (EI2)	50th	+ 4'26"
Czech Republic			
179.	Tomas Konecny (TMO)	57th	+ 4'26"
180.	Ondrej Sosenka (A&S)	56th	+ 4'26"
Argentina			
181.	Alejandro Borrajo (PAN)		*Abandon*
Brazil			
182.	Murilo Fischer (DVE)		*Abandon*
183.	Luciano Pagliarini (LAM)		*Abandon*
Estonia			
184.	Mirko Pöldmä (KCT)		*Abandon*
185.	Erki Pütsep (A2R)	27th	+ 4'26"
Finland			
186.	Kjell Carlström (AMO)		*Abandon*
Japan			
187.	Shinri Suzuki (SHI)		*Abandon*
Latvia			
188.	Raivis Belohvosciks (CHO)		*Abandon*
189.	Romans Vainsteins (LAM)	61st	+ 4'26"
Lithuania			
190.	Raimondas Rumsas (A&S)		*Abandon*
191.	Marius Sabaliauskas (SAE)	73rd	+ 8'06"
Mexico			
192.	Julio Alberto Perez Cuapio (PAN)		*Abandon*
Moldavia			
193.	Ruslan Ivanov (ALB)	44th	+ 4'26"
194.	Igor Pugaci (DEN)	49th	+ 4'26"
Slovakia			
195.	Matej Jurco (DEN)	86th	+ 28'45"
Sweden			
196.	Stefan Adamsson (TBL)		*Abandon*
197.	Gustav Erik Larsson (FAS)	78th	+ 9'54"
198.	Jonas Ljungblad (AMO)		*Abandon*
199.	Marcus Ljungqvist (ALB)		*Abandon*
Ouzbekistan			
200.	Sergey Lagutin (LAN)		*Abandon*

STAGE RACES

WINNERS TABLE

MAJOR TOURS

TOUR DE FRANCE

1. Lance Armstrong (Usa)
2. A. Klöden (Ger)
3. I. Basso (Ita)

STAGE WINNERS

Lance Armstrong (Usa)	5
Tom Boonen (Bel)	2
Robbie McEwen (Aus)	2
Ivan Basso (Ita)	1
Fabian Cancellara (Sui)	1
Aitor Gonzalez Jimenez (Esp)	1
Thor Hushovd (Nor)	1
Jaan Kirsipuu (Est)	1
Juan Miguel Mercado (Esp)	1
David Moncoutié (Fra)	1
Jean-Patrick Nazon (Fra)	1
Stuart O'Grady (Aus)	1
Filippo Pozzato (Ita)	1
Richard Virenque (Fra)	1
US POSTAL - BERRY FLOOR	1

TOUR OF ITALY

1. Damiano Cunego (Ita)
2. S. Honchar (Ukr)
3. G. Simoni (Ita)

STAGE WINNERS

Alessandro Petacchi (Ita)	9
Damiano Cunego (Ita)	4
Stefano Garzelli (Ita)	1
Serhiy Honchar (Ukr)	1
Robbie McEwen (Aus)	1
Bradley McGee (Aus)	1
Fred Rodriguez (Usa)	1
Emanuele Sella (Ita)	1
Gilberto Simoni (Ita)	1
Pavel Tonkov (Rus)	1

TOUR OF SPAIN

1. Roberto Heras (Esp)
2. S. Perez (Esp)
3. F. Mancebo (Esp)

STAGE WINNERS

Alessandro Petacchi (Ita)	4
Santi Perez Fernandez (Esp)	3
Félix Cardenas (Col)	1
Oscar Freire (Esp)	1
J. Enrique Gutierrez (Esp)	1
Tyler Hamilton (Usa)	1
Roberto Heras (Esp)	1
Eladio Jimenez (Esp)	1
José Cayetano Julia (Esp)	1
Denis Menchov (Rus)	1
Javier Pascual Rodriguez (Esp)	1
Leonardo Piepoli (Ita)	1
Alejandro Valverde (Esp)	1
Constantino Zaballa (Esp)	1
David Zabriskie (Usa)	1
US POSTAL - BERRY FLOOR	1

OTHER TOURS

PARIS-NICE

1. Jörg Jaksche (Ger)
2. D. Rebellin (Ita)
3. B. Julich (Usa)

STAGE WINNERS

Alexandre Vinokourov (Kaz)	3
Pedro Horrillo (Esp)	1
Jörg Jaksche (Ger)	1
Denis Menchov (Rus)	1
Leon van Bon (Ned)	1

TIRRENO-ADRIATICO

1. Paolo Bettini (Ita)
2. O. Freire (Esp)
3. E. Zabel (Ger)

STAGE WINNERS

Alessandro Petacchi (Ita)	3
Paolo Bettini (Ita)	2
Oscar Freire (Esp)	1
Roberto Petito (Ita)	1

TOUR OF ROMANDIE

1. Tyler Hamilton (Usa)
2. F. Jeker (Sui)
3. L. Piepoli (Ita)

STAGE WINNERS

Stefano Garzelli (Ita)	1
Tyler Hamilton (Usa)	1
Fabian Jeker (Sui)	1
Bradley McGee (Aus)	1
Alexandre Moos (Sui)	1
Jan Svorada (Cze)	1

TOUR OF LANGUEDOC

1. Christophe Moreau (Fra)
2. V. Ekimov (Rus)
3. I. Flores (Esp)

STAGE WINNERS

Thor Hushovd (Nor)	2
Lance Armstrong (Usa)	1
Martin Elmiger (Sui)	1
Christophe Moreau (Fra)	1

CRITERIUM DU DAUPHINÉ

1. Iban Mayo (Esp)
2. T. Hamilton (Usa)
3. O. Sevilla (Esp)

STAGE WINNERS

Iban Mayo (Esp)	2
Stuart O'Grady (Aus)	2
J. Enrique Gutierrez (Esp)	1
Thor Hushovd (Nor)	1
Nicolas Portal (Fra)	1
Michael Rasmussen (Den)	1

TOUR OF SWITZERLAND

1. Jan Ullrich (Ger)
2. F. Jeker (Sui)
3. D. Cioni (Ita)

Stage winners

Robert Hunter (Rsa)	2
Robbie McEwen (Aus)	2
Jan Ullrich (Ger)	2
Niki Aebersold (Sui)	1
Paolo Bettini (Ita)	1
Georg Totschnig (Aut)	1

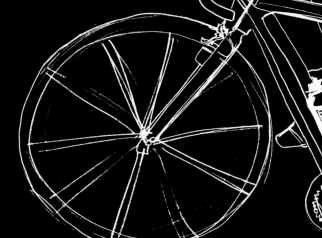

Damiano Cunego, not yet 23 and already at the summit of his art.

BIRTH OF AN IDOL

An angelic face, eyes always bright, clear skin, even after three weeks of racing: Damiano Cunego is the successor to Marco Pantani in the hearts of the Italian people. The rider from Verona showed his class in a Giro marked by a battle between brothers with Gilberto Simoni, his Saeco team mate and team leader.

At first compared with the ex World champion Guiseppi Saronni, the 22 year old winner of the Giro showed such qualities in the mountains that comparisons with Pantani were bound to be made. Even if the pirate from Cesenatico was a tragic hero and not a model, as the Gazzetta Dello Sport, organiser of the Giro, put it. Cunego was to reply that there was no comparison, but the Tifosi had made their decision. They had scrawled graffiti on the roads comparing the two riders, something unimaginable weeks before.

But, in 40 days the rider from Verona, with ten victories (including the significant Tour of Trentin a few days before the Giro) had taken off. His ease at attacking and prolonging his effort, his level headedness and his cold bloodedness impress. He also shows an amazing ability to recover. The natural level of hematocrite, very high at 52% may have something to do with it, but with an authorisation from the cycling authorities he risks no disciplinary action.

Damiano Cunego has had an already illustrious career. He becomes Junior World Champion in 1999, after just three years of riding. He wins the Giro after only three years as a pro. In his new life as a champion he has also learnt quickly. His confidence when dealing with the media, his way with words, witness this. Replying to questions from journalists asking if he was intimidated by the Gavia, one of the great climbs of the Giro, he replied; "I was concentrating hard, I couldn't admire the view, which pass were you referring to? The first or the second stage"? Now he must show if he can stand the limelight and not be consumed by it like others. It's a tall order for a young man who's tastes and habits are now known by all. His passion for the Doors and their charismatic singer Jim Morrison, his culinary preferences (spaghetti with honey), his rather ordinary teenage years are endlessly mulled over in the press. Even down to his butcher in his home town of Cerro Veronese who talks about " His" Damiano. A star is born.

MISSION ACCOMPLISHED FOR MCGEE

Deprived of two of its protagonists (the Slovenian Jure Golcer of the Pinzolo Fiavé Team and the Colombian Uberlino Mesa of the Colombia – Selle Italia team) who both had hematocrite levels above the permitted maximum, the 87th Giro starts with a prologue in the sunny streets of Genoa. Coming from a Tour of Romandie where he had played a leading role... And not only in the time trials, Bradley McGee, the Australian from the Fdjeux.com, hadn't

hidden his intentions for this prologue. The Antipodean rider doesn't do things by half: his immediate rival, the German Olaf Pollack is relegated to a 10 second deficit, Yaroslav Popovych, a favourite for the podium is at 20 seconds, Simoni at 35 seconds, Garzelli even further back at 46 seconds. Mc Gee then, takes the first Pink jersey of the Giro. A shirt he won't keep for long. The next day it's Olaf Pollack who takes it over. Just as at home in sprints as in time trials, the German from the Gerolsteiner team benefits from points gained in intermediary sprints to finish second in the stage. Second behind who? The obvious answer is , the first road racing day of the Giro , finishing in a mass sprint, and " Ale Jet" also known as Alessandro Petacchi turned the chain red hot to beat off all his rivals...

In Genoa, the peloton doesn't let itself be taken for a ride...

ENTER CUNEGO

The next day, the Giro turns towards the South, going from Novi Ligure, the town of Fausto Coppi to Pontremoli, the region of Bruno Raschi, legend of the Giro in the post war years. The course passes the Passo del Bratello (953 metres) situated 20 kilometers from the line. A good place for the first sort out to take place. 40 riders arrive together at Pontremoli, and Damiano Cunego shows his turn of speed. He leads with little trouble Bradley Mc Gee who takes the consolation of recuperating the Pink Jersey lost the day before. For Olaf Pollack, as for most of the sprinters, the final difficulty of the day was really too much.

The fourth stage ending at Corno Alle Scale is also the first finishing at altitude. Gilberto Simoni, the title holder, leaves no one the opportunity to get ahead, and takes the win by a margin of 16 seconds over a group of four riders led in by yesterdays winner Damiano Cunego. Simoni attacks three kilometers from the line, on the steepest part of the 12 kilometre climb, after having fought off acceleration from... Damiano Cunego. Gilberto Simoni takes the Pink jersey thanks to his win. Stefano Garzelli, his main rival, in trailing by more than 30 seconds, shows the first worrying signs of weakness.

AND PETACCHI GOES FOR A SERIES...

Nothing but crashes in this rainy fourth stage taking the peloton to Civitella Val di Chiana. First it's Alessandro Petacchi who falls at the 110th kilometre. Waited for by the major part of the riders, he comes back into the peloton complaining only of a sore coccyx. A problem which in the end is of no great consequence. On the other hand, the fall of his great rival Mario Cipollini (a crash provoked by his own team mate, Andris Aug) is much more serious. It forces the rider from the Domina Vacanze team and his team mate to leave the race two days later. The few timid attacks through the day are not enough to avoid another mass arrival. With a team completely dedicated to his cause, "Ale jet" finishes the stage with style to take his second bouquet in four days. And the series has only just begun.

The 5th stage joining Tuscany to Umbria on a flat course of 177 kilometers is the theatre for a good number of attacks. But the attackers (Magnus Backstedt, Bo Hamburger, Manuele Mori, Michael Albasini, Thomas Ziegler, and Dean Podgornik) arrive at the 7.3 kilometre circuit they must complete three times with a too slim advance of no more than 30seconds. The result is another bunching of the pack 15 kilometers from the line. The final attackers (Bradley Mc Gee, Alexandre Moos, and Ruggero Marzoli, at first, Igor Astarloa later) fail in the same way despite the difficult little hill at the finish. Hot favourite to take another win, Alessandro Petacchi finds himself boxed in by one of his team mates at the final bend. He has no time to position himself for the sprint which is won by the Australian Robby

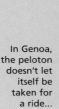

In Pontremoli, Damiano Cunega goes into action. He leads Bradley Mc Gee (centre) and forty other riders to take charge of the race.

The Pink jersey (here Bradley Mc Gee) is treated in ways the other riders can only dream about...

Mc Ewen. This is his fifth win in a Giro after two stage wins in 2002 and two more the following year. Arriving in the same time as the winner, Gilberto Simoni keeps his Pink jersey by the same margin (13 seconds) over his team mate Damiano Cunego. Once again starting in the rain, the sixth stage (Spoleto/ Valmontone), a run of 164 kilometers finishes once again in a sprint. Meticulously respecting the carefully orchestrated scenario, the Fassa Bortolo team propulses in the last few hundred yards, Alessandro Petacchi, who doesn't even need to dig into his deep reserves to beat off the German Olaf Pollack- decidedly getting into the habit of finishing second- and the surprising Argentinian Alejandro Borrajo. The stage was for a long time animated by one of his team mates, Fortunato Baliani, who was unable to open a lead of more than five minutes. Not enough to have in hand to prevent a counter attack from the peloton as it passed the banner marking the last 20 kilometers. ..

CUNEGO TAKES COMMAND

Damiano Cunego hammers his message home. Pulling ahead of the impressive Bradley Mc Gee and his compatriots Franco Pellizoti and Giuliano Figueras at the end of a 17 kilometre climb finishing at Montevergine, Cunego shows his intentions. As he had already shown in the Tour of Trentin, his accelerations up hill were devastating. Passed, as is his great rival Stefano Garzelli, the Pink jersey Gilberto Simoni crosses the line just 3 seconds after his young team mate, but with the extra points (20 seconds) going to the winner of the stage, he takes the leader's jersey. A good sport, Simoni tells the waiting journalists "This was a good team effort. The main thing is the Pink jersey stays with Saeco". After having recuperated the final elements of the morning breakaway, Niki Aebersold and Luca Mazzanti, after an attack lasting 191 kilometers, the favourites were to fight it out on the regular slopes of Montevergine. In the front of a small peloton of about twenty men, Gilberto Simoni accelerates twice, the first time at 8 kilometers from the line, a second time after the sign indicating the final two kilometers. The reaction of Garzelli, following closely, is immediate and the

Alessandro Petacchi wins in all weathers...

group of riders reforms. Giulano Figueras, the local boy, is also held in check. Each time he attempts to accelerate, Cunego is right behind him and in the end he is resigned to waiting for the upcoming sprint. But in this kind of exercise Cunego has nothing to fear from anyone. ..

Take the same riders, shuffle them around and here we are for the 8th stage. For the 4th time in this race and the 10th in his career, Alessandro Petacchi (Fassa Bortolo) wins with a sprint, once again with ease, ahead of Robbie Mc Ewen sanctioned for an irregularity (finally demoted to the 117th place), the Lithuanian Tomas Vaitkus and the German Olaf Pollack In this transitional stage the only notable action is an attack by Alessandro Bertolini, J. Alberto Perez Cuapio, Jacky Durand, Mariano Piccoli and Marco Velo – team mate of Petacchi – soon joined by Marlon Perez Arango. An escapade which at one point held a lead of seven minutes before being caught in the last 20 kilometers.

"It's my fault. I pushed too late. I was afraid of the effects of the wind. I came back well but was a few metres short. When Velo set me off, he was in the middle of the road and he was slowed down by the wind. It would have been beter to have been near the side of the road. That would have prevented me being overtaken on both sides". A rare enough explanation coming from Alessandro Petacchi after his defeat in the sprint ending the 9th stage between Policoro and Carovigno. It's the American Fred Rodriguez who ends up as winner at the end of another transitional stage , short and windy, marked by several falls, one of which caused the retirement of the Colombian rider Freddy Gonzalez Martinez, winner for the past two years of the best climber prize.

Petacchi on the road to the record books! The determination shown by Bo Hamburger, Fabian Wegman, Daniele Righi, Raffaele Illiano, Oliver Zaugg, Giuseppe Muraglia and Kyrylo Pospeev was not enough! Once again, the attack of the day was condemned to failure by the hard work of the Fassa Bortolo team, exclusively devoted to Alessandro Petacchi. It's necessary here to praise the work of Dario Cioni. Taking his share of the work in catching the breakaway group, this native of Reading in England also managed to take the 4th place without having any privileged place in the team. A valuable performance. As far as the rest is concerned, and for the 5th time since leaving Genoa, Petacchi justified the confidence placed in him. He takes the sprint, very fast in its late stages (67.1kph average) ahead of Marco Zanotti and Andris Nauduzs.

Emanuele Sella triumphs at Cesena in the 11th stage

SELLA WITH PANTANI

Neo pro and aged 23, Emanuele Sella was the man who went out in front on a solo attack lasting for 50kilometres on a hilly final section of this stage of 234 kilometers finishing in Cesena, the home town of Marco Pantani. Young and promising, the rider from the Panaria team leads a group of chasers led by Cristian Morini and Steve Zampieri by thirty seconds. Damiano Cunego arrives in the group of the favourites with a retard of 50 seconds. The offensive from Sella comes on the climb to Saint – Marin (km 163) in a small group behind the twenty riders in the lead. After joining them he advances towards his first professional success, this despite a minor fall not far from the finish. Small (1.64 metres and 52kg) Emanuele Sella last year won three stages in the prestigious Tour du Val d' Aoste in the Elite 2 division. This unusual stage was also marked by numerous graffitis to the glory of Marco Pantani, dead from an overdose of cocaine three months earlier.

Invariably on the Giro, stages without big climbs end with a mass sprint. Almost invariably it's Alessandro Petacchi who wins them. For the sixth time, the sprinter from La Spezia wins comfortably, ahead of Robbie Mc Ewen and Alexandre Usov, while Marco Zanotti found himself on the ground after a fall on the long straight before the line. No luck then for Leonardo Scarselli, the Croatian champion Radoslav Rogina and the Belgian Gert Steegmans (who further prolonged the adventure). They led the race for most of the day with no reward. No prizes for taking the offensive in this Tour of Italy.

WHEN THE UKRAINE IS KING...

Waiting in ambush at 40 seconds from Damiano Cunego, the ex World Champion Espoirs Yaroslav Popovych has, until now had a discrete but efficient Giro. In the morning of this time trial of 52 kilometers around Trieste, he's among the fancied riders but is kept in the shade by the media circus around the two riders from the Saeco team, where separate clans are apparently forming. It's another Ukrainian, the experienced Serhiy Honchar, well known in Italy where he has spent most of his career, who takes the honours. Making a superb time of 46.741kph, he takes his 5th stage win in the Giro. All the victories taken in his favourite discipline, the time trial. Honchar leads Bradley Mc Gee by just 8 seconds and his compatriot Yaroslav Popovych by 34 seconds even though the two men were neck and neck at the mid way point. Popovych takes consolation from the fact that with 3 seconds advance he takes the Pink jersey. Two Ukrainians in the first two places in the Giro. Now that's unusual! But the Italian hill specialists, outridden today are not far behind: Pellizoti at 2mins 18 sec, Garzelli at 2mins 30 sec, Simoni at 2 mins 31 sec (victim of a minor crash) and Cunego at 3 mins 02 sec haven't had their last word. For the Swiss rider Sven Montgomery though, the Giro ends here. Victim of a heavy fall, he breaks his shoulder.

SEVENTH AND EIGHTH HEAVEN FOR PERACCHI!

In winning the sprint in the Croatian town of Pula, Alessandro Petacchi not only takes his seventh stage win, but also enters the record books for the most wins in a Giro, where he joins Roger De Vlaeminck (1975), Freddy Maertens (1977), and Beppe Saronni (1980). Clear proof that the Fassa Bortolo dominates in sprints, it's Marco Velo, the rider in charge of bringing the star to the front for the finale who takes third place. The second place being saved by the Anerican Fred Rodriguez. The stage, for most of the day on the roads of Croatia, permits once again Raffaele Illiano, Ruggero Marzoli and Giuseppi Muraglia – for a long time accompanied by Andrej Hauptman and Pavel Tonkov who revealed their presence near the end, to show what they're made of. Not enough however to prevent the return of the peloton.
Controlling the race for 234 kilometers, the longest stage of this Giro, doesn't seem to worry the invincible team of Alessandro Petacchi. Sure, the white jerseyed men let go, around the 40th kilometre, a quartet of volunteers composed of the veteran Mario Scirea, orphan of his friend Mario Cipollini and who melted into the peloton, the Australian Russel van Hout, and the Italians Giancarlo Ginestri and Daniele Righi. A little more than 10 minutes is accorded to them by the peloton. The work of Petacchi's team mates is so efficient that the attackers are caught with 50 kilometers still to go! The Fassa Bortolo team ease up a little and let the leaders keep a small lead before absorbing them with 12 kilometers to go. 180 kilometers in front and nothing to show for it? Yes, it's Alessandro Petacchi who takes over the race to score his eighth success. Another win which takes him one step closer to the record of Alfredo Binda who scored 12 stage wins from 15 stages in 1927.

THE INSOLENCE OF CUNEGO

Attacking at 59 kilometers from the line, in a difficulty feared by many, the Passo Furcia, it's how Damiano Cunego decided to go for the win in this stage, and an action that will stay in the memory of many for a long time to come. Between insouciance and insolence. This first stage in the Dolomites won't have gone to a worthless winner. The winner who recuperates the Pink jersey lost days before to Yaroslav Popovych visibly at the end of his tether (the Ukrainian loses 3mins 20sec on the line along with most of his hopes for victory). The tactic worked out by the Saeco team, who more than ever hold the key to success is effective. Eddy Mazzolini and Andrea Tonti infiltrated a group of riders decided to attack in the mountains. The two men play their roles to perfection as a relay between the descent of Passo Furcia, where Cunego places his attack, and the foot of Passo Di Terento, the last climb of the day. The gap between Cunego and his chasers opens up to three minutes. The Giro was changing. One by one, Cunego passes the seventeen in the leading group leaving just the lowly Rinaldo Noncentini...Who he leaves in his wake shortly before the line. Such a victory can only be celebrated solo. The overall lead once again was up for grabs. Damiano Cunego once again led the Ukrainians by 1 min 14 sec (Honchar) – 2 mins 22 sec (Popovych). After a second rest day there is a renaissance. That of the always young Pavel Yonkov, who in a solo effort takes the 17th stage in Fondo Sarnonico, with a lead of more than two minutes over Alessandro Bertolini, who he distanced twenty kilometers before the finish. The third place, three minutes after the winner had crossed the line, a winner who presented no danger to the overall standings, going to Brad Mc Gee who led the Pink jersey rider for most of

In the Dolomites, Damiano Cunego leads the way, ahead of Gilberto Simoni. The pupil passes the master!

the stage. The out of touch Giuliano Figueras, on the road to Passo della Mendola suffered a fall. This happens in the same place, 53 kilometers from the line, that Tonkov choses to pull out of the peloton after a first attack by his team leader Stefano Garzelli. The Russian, winner of the 1996 Giro, soon joins the breakaway group (Alessandro Bertolini and Oscar Pozzi) before the summit, then distances himself from Bertolini, who had kept in contact in the valley. In Fondo Sarnonico he takes the victory in the seventh stage of the Tour of Italy, his first success since the stage at Passo Coe in the 2002 Giro.

CUNEGO'S FINAL TOUCH

The last but one stage takes in the famous Gavia and ends in Bormio, no great difference in the time gaps between the principal players comes about, but Damiano Cunego manages to comfort his position a little. It's with a time advantage of 5 seconds that the rider from Verona wins, over Cioni and Honchar. Gilberto Simoni, who had given his all on the ascent of the final hill, has a setback, losing 9 seconds ,but most of all he must admit that if all goes as planned, his young team mate will win the 2004 Giro. Another candidate for the throne, Stefano Garzelli has set himself the objective of winning this prestigious stage. In attacking 9 kilometers from the summit, the leader of the Vini Caldirola team opens up a lead of 1 min 48 sec over the Cunego group, still led by his team mates Szmyd and in particular Mazzoleni. On his own, Garzelli is unable to catch the Croat Vladimir Miholjevec, sole survivor of an attack launched at the start of the day. The Italian finishes by capitulating 18 kilometers from the line, before the climb towards Bormio. Miholjevic, who still has a lead of 2 mins 15 sec at the foot of this final ascention (9.9 km at 7.5%) suffers the same fate, passed six kilometers from the finish. He will not see his name written in the record books as winner of a stage in the 2004 Giro...

GARZELLI FIGHTS BACK

Having had, so far, a mediocre Giro, Stefano Garzelli had only one more occasion to stop the rot. This final mountain stage containing the terrifying Mortirolo – certainly one of the most difficult passes in Europe, used by the ex Tour of Italy winner to his advantage. With there being no real danger to his Pink jersey, Damiano Cunego took a back seat. Gilberto Simoni would accompany team leader Vini Caldirola. At the summit of Mortirolo, the two men along with the Slovenian Valjavec (Phonak) Have two minutes lead over Cunego who is meanwhile keeping a keen eye on his two rivals Honchar and Cioni. The descent of the famous col permits the Cunego group to close the gap before the climb at Passo di Vivione. When Alessandro Bertolini and Raffaele Illiano, the two last survivors of the ritual morning breakaway are caught by the trio Garzelli/ Simoni/ Valjavec at the foot of the descent, it's the adversaries of Cunego that are obliged to put in an effort to limit the damage. The young Pink jersey is floating on air! In a surreal atmosphere, a particularly wild crowd see Garzelli start his last effort at the two kilometre mark. Simoni reacts! Valjavec cannot answer the call. At the finish in Presolana, the speed of Garzelli triumphs over the pugnacity of Simoni. Cunego, who's had a fairly easy day of it, follows Cioni over the line 52 seconds later. The young man from Verona can now shout aloud "I've won the Giro".

The convoy towards Milan for the final stage of the race gets off to a steady start. The time comes for those watching to go over the high points of the race so far. The coming of age of Damiano Cunego who begins to look like a great. The temperament, the speed and the strength of Alessandro Petacchi. The great stamina of the 33 year old Gilberto Simoni, managing to take third place. The parting shot of Stefano Garzelli, ferocious attacker of the last week. The consistance of Serhiy Honchar, weeks before his 34th birthday taking his best overall position.(2nd this year, 4th in 2001, 5th in 1997, 7th in 1999, 8th in 2003, 9th in 2000,10th in 1998)! Some new faces (Emanuele Sella, Fabian Wegman- best climber- and Raffaele Illiano ,and also the regularity of Bradley Mc Gee no longer afraid of the mountains. Not forgetting the crowning glory of the ninth stage win for Alessandro Petacchi, who crossed the line in yet another sprint, head and shoulders above the competition.
All that could be asked for by the Tifosi here to cheer their heros in this soap opera in the month of May. ■

The peloton passes through Brunico on the 17th stage.

FINAL OVERALL STANDINGS

1.	Damiano Cunego (Ita)	**SAE**	**88h 40'43"**
2.	Serhiy Honchar (Ukr)	DEN	+ 2'02"
3.	Gilberto Simoni (Ita)	SAE	+ 2'05"
4.	Dario Cioni (Ita)	FAS	+ 4'36"
5.	Yaroslav Popovych (Ukr)	LAN	+ 5'05"
6.	Stefano Garzelli (Ita)	VIN	+ 5'31"
7.	Wladimir Belli (Ita)	LAM	+ 6'12"
8.	Bradley McGee (Aus)	FDJ	+ 6'15"
9.	Tadej Valjavec (Slo)	PHO	+ 6'34"
10.	Juan Manuel Garate (Esp)	LAM	+ 7'47"
11.	Franco Pellizotti (Ita)	ALB	+ 9'45"
12.	Emanuele Sella (Ita)	PAN	+ 10'26"
13.	Pavel Tonkov (Rus)	VIN	+ 10'43"
14.	Christophe Brandt (Bel)	LOT	+ 10'50"
15.	Luis Felipe Laverde (Col)	FPF	+ 13'43"

Prologue in Genova - 7 km

1.	Bradley McGee (Aus)	FDJ	8'30"
2.	Olaf Pollack (Ger)	GST	+ 10"
3.	Yaroslav Popovych (Ukr)	LAN	+ 20"
4.	Gerhard Trampusch (Aut)	A&S	+ 24"
5.	Davide Rebellin (Ita)	GST	+ 27"

1st stage: Genova/Alba - 143 km

1.	Alessandro Petacchi (Ita)	FAS	3h 41'56"
2.	Olaf Pollack (Ger)	GST	s.t
3.	Crescenzo D'Amore (Ita)	A&S	s.t
4.	Robbie McEwen (Aus)	LOT	s.t
5.	Marco Zanotti (Ita)	VIN	s.t

Leader - Olaf Pollack (Ger)	GST	3h 50'24"
Points - Alessandro Petacchi (Ita)	FAS	25 pts
Mountain - Fabian Wegmann (Ger)	GST	3 pts

2nd stage: Novi Ligure/Pontremoli - 184 km

1.	Damiano Cunego (Ita)	SAE	4h 37'08"
2.	Bradley McGee (Aus)	FDJ	s.t
3.	Cristian Moreni (Ita)	ALB	s.t
4.	Igor Astarloa (Esp)	LAM	s.t
5.	Eddy Mazzoleni (Ita)	SAE	s.t

Leader - Bradley McGee (Aus)	FDJ	8h 27'22"
Points - Damiano Cunego (Ita)	SAE	25 pts
Mountain - Alexandre Moos (Sui)	PHO	5 pts

3rd stage: Pontremoli/Corno alle Scale - 191 km

1.	Gilberto Simoni (Ita)	SAE	5h 46'09"
2.	Damiano Cunego (Ita)	SAE	+ 15"
3.	Franco Pellizotti (Ita)	ALB	+ 16"
4.	Giuliano Figueras (Ita)	PAN	s.t
5.	Yaroslav Popovych (Ukr)	LAN	s.t

Leader - Gilberto Simoni (Ita)	SAE	14h 13'58"
Points - Damiano Cunego (Ita)	SAE	45 pts
Mountain - Gilberto Simoni (Ita)	SAE	16 pts

4th stage: Porretta Terme/Civitella in Val di Chiana - 184 km

1.	Alessandro Petacchi (Ita)	FAS	4h 55'40"
2.	Robbie McEwen (Aus)	LOT	s.t
3.	Simone Cadamuro (Ita)	DEN	s.t
4.	Marco Zanotti (Ita)	VIN	s.t
5.	Fred Rodriguez (Usa)	A&S	s.t

Leader - Gilberto Simoni (Ita)	SAE	19h 09'38"
Points - Alessandro Petacchi (Ita)	FAS	51 pts
Mountain - Gilberto Simoni (Ita)	SAE	16 pts

5th stage: Civitella in Val di Chiana/Spoleto - 177 km

1.	Robbie McEwen (Aus)	LOT	4h 24'57"
2.	Olaf Pollack (Ger)	GST	s.t
3.	Marco Zanotti (Ita)	VIN	s.t
4.	Alexandre Usov (Blr)	BLR	s.t
5.	Crescenzo D'Amore (Ita)	A&S	s.t

Leader - Gilberto Simoni (Ita)	SAE	23h 34'35"
Points - Robbie McEwen (Aus)	LOT	59 pts
Mountain - Gilberto Simoni (Ita)	SAE	16 pts

6th stage: Spoleto/Valmontone - 164 km

1.	Alessandro Petacchi (Ita)	FAS	4h 00'56"
2.	Olaf Pollack (Ger)	GST	s.t
3.	Alejandro Borrajo (Arg) PAN	s.t	
4.	Eddy Mazzoleni (Ita)	SAE	s.t
5.	Andris Nauduzs (Lat)	DVE	s.t

Leader - Gilberto Simoni (Ita)	SAE	27h 35'31"
Points - Alessandro Petacchi (Ita)	FAS	80 pts
Mountain - Fabian Wegmann (Ger)	GST	16 pts

7th stage: Frosinone/Montevergine - 214 km

1.	Damiano Cunego (Ita)	SAE	5h 26'25"
2.	Bradley McGee (Aus)	FDJ	s.t
3.	Franco Pellizotti (Ita)	ALB	s.t
4.	Giuliano Figueras (Ita)	PAN	s.t
5.	Stefano Garzelli (Ita)	VIN	+ 3"

Leader - Damiano Cunego (Ita)	SAE	33h 01'48"
Points - Alessandro Petacchi (Ita)	FAS	80 pts
Mountain - Damiano Cunego (Ita)	SAE	28 pts

8th stage: Giffoni Valle Piana/Policoro - 214 km

1.	Alessandro Petacchi (Ita)	FAS	3h 41'56"
2.	Tomas Vaitkus (Ltu)	LAN	s.t
3.	Olaf Pollack (Ger)	GST	s.t
4.	Marco Zanotti (Ita)	VIN	s.t
5.	Jan Svorada (Cze)	LAM	s.t

Leader - Damiano Cunego (Ita)	SAE	37h 54'37"
Points - Alessandro Petacchi (Ita)	FAS	105 pts
Mountain - Damiano Cunego (Ita)	SAE	28 pts

9th stage: Policoro/Carovigno - 142 km

1.	Fred Rodriguez (Usa)	A&S	4h 04'38"
2.	Alessandro Petacchi (Ita)	FAS	s.t
3.	Angelo Furlan (Ita)	ALB	s.t
4.	Robbie McEwen (Aus)	LOT	s.t
5.	Jan Svorada (Cze)	LAM	s.t

Leader - Damiano Cunego (Ita)	SAE	41h 59'15"
Points - Alessandro Petacchi (Ita)	FAS	120 pts
Mountain - Damiano Cunego (Ita)	SAE	28 pts

10th stage: Porto Sant'Elpidio/Ascoli Piceno - 146 km

1.	Alessandro Petacchi (Ita)	FAS	3h 24'17"
2.	Marco Zanotti (Ita)	VIN	s.t
3.	Andris Nauduzs (Lat)	DVE	s.t
4.	Magnus Bäckstedt (Swe)	ALB	s.t
5.	Alejandro Borrajo (Arg)	PAN	s.t

Leader - Damiano Cunego (Ita)	SAE	45h 23'32"
Points - Alessandro Petacchi (Ita)	FAS	150 pts
Mountain - Damiano Cunego (Ita)	SAE	28 pts

11st stage: Porto Sant'Elpidio/Cesena - 228 km

1.	Emanuele Sella (Ita)	PAN	5h 19'08"
2.	Cristian Moreni (Ita)	ALB	+ 30"
3.	Steve Zampieri (Sui)	VIN	s.t
4.	Bo Hamburger (Den)	A&S	s.t
5.	Ruben Lobato (Esp)	SDV	s.t

Leader - Damiano Cunego (Ita)	SAE	50h 43'29"
Points - Alessandro Petacchi (Ita)	FAS	150 pts
Mountain - Fabian Wegmann (Ger)	GST	30 pts

12nd stage: Cesena/Treviso - 210 km

1.	Alessandro Petacchi (Ita)	FAS	4h 48'12"
2.	Robbie McEwen (Aus)	LOT	s.t
3.	Alexandre Usov (Blr)	PHO	s.t
4.	Zoran Klemencic (Slo)	TEN	s.t
5.	Olaf Pollack (Ger)	GST	s.t

Leader - Damiano Cunego (Ita)	SAE	55h 31'41"
Points - Alessandro Petacchi (Ita)	FAS	175 pts
Mountain - Fabian Wegmann (Ger)	GST	30 pts

13rd stage: Trieste/Altopiano Carsico - 52 km (Team time trial)

1.	Serhiy Honchar (Ukr)	DEN	1h 06'45"
2.	Bradley McGee (Aus)	FDJ	+ 18"
3.	Yaroslav Popovych (Ukr)	LAN	+ 34"
4.	Marzio Bruseghin (Ita)	TMO	+ 44"
5.	Rubens Bertogliati (Sui)	SDV	+ 1'32"

Leader - Yaroslav Popovych (Ita)	LAN	56h 39'40"
Points - Alessandro Petacchi (Ita)	FAS	175 pts
Mountain - Fabian Wegmann (Ger)	GST	30 pts

14th stage: Trieste/Pula - 175 km

1.	Alessandro Petacchi (Ita)	FAS	4h 08'58"
2.	Fred Rodriguez (Usa)	A&S	s.t
3.	Marco Velo (Ita)	FAS	s.t
4.	Olaf Pollack (Ger)	GST	s.t
5.	Alexandre Usov (Blr)	PHO	s.t

Leader - Yaroslav Popovych (Ita)	LAN	60h 48'38"
Points - Alessandro Petacchi (Ita)	FAS	200 pts
Mountain - Fabian Wegmann (Ger)	GST	30 pts

15th stage: Porec/San Vendemiano - 234 km

1.	Alessandro Petacchi (Ita)	FAS	5h 59'52"
2.	Robbie McEwen (Aus)	LOT	s.t
3.	Olaf Pollack (Ger)	GST	s.t
4.	Andris Nauduzs (Lat)	DVE	s.t
5.	Alexandre Usov (Blr)	PHO	s.t

Leader - Yaroslav Popovych (Ita)	LAN	66h 48'30"
Points - Alessandro Petacchi (Ita)	FAS	225 pts
Mountain - Fabian Wegmann (Ger)	GST	30 pts

16th stage: San Vendemiano/Falzes - 217 km

1.	Damiano Cunego (Ita)	SAE	6h 11'23"
2.	Rinaldo Nocentini (Ita)	A&S	+ 1'16"
3.	Alexandre Moos (Sui)	PHO	+ 1'38"
4.	Raffaele Illiano (Ita)	CLM	s.t
5.	Giuseppe Di Grande (Ita)	FPF	s.t

Leader - Damiano Cunego (Ita)	SAE	73h 01'21"
Points - Alessandro Petacchi (Ita)	FAS	225 pts
Mountain - Fabian Wegmann (Ger)	GST	45 pts

17th stage: Brunico/Fondo Sarnonico - 153 km

1.	Pavel Tonkov (Rus)	VIN	3h 40'05"
2.	Alessandro Bertolini (Ita)	ALB	+ 2'15"
3.	Bradley McGee (Aus)	FDJ	+ 2'49"
4.	Damiano Cunego (Ita)	SAE	s.t
5.	Franco Pellizotti (Ita)	ALB	s.t

Leader - Damiano Cunego (Ita)	SAE	76h 44'15"
Points - Alessandro Petacchi (Ita)	FAS	225 pts
Mountain - Fabian Wegmann (Ger)	GST	45 pts

18th stage: Cles Val Di Non/Bormio 2000 - 118 km

1.	Damiano Cunego (Ita)	SAE	3h 56'31"
2.	Dario Cioni (Ita)	FAS	+ 5"
3.	Serhiy Honchar (Ukr)	DEN	s.t
4.	Gilberto Simoni (Ita)	SAE	+ 9"
5.	J. Alberto Perez Cuapio (Mex)	RAB	+ 17"

Leader - Damiano Cunego (Ita)	SAE	80h 38'46"
Points - Alessandro Petacchi (Ita)	FAS	225 pts
Mountain - Damiano Cunego (Ita)	SAE	53 pts

19th stage: Bormio/Presolana - 122 km

1.	Stefano Garzelli (Ita)	VIN	3h 52'16"
2.	Gilberto Simoni (Ita)	SAE	+ 2"
3.	Tadej Valjavec (Slo)	PHO	+ 23"
4.	Dario Cioni (Ita)	FAS	+ 52"
5.	Damiano Cunego (Ita)	SAE	s.t

Leader - Damiano Cunego (Ita)	SAE	84h 33'34"
Points - Alessandro Petacchi (Ita)	FAS	225 pts
Mountain - Fabian Wegmann (Ger)	GST	56 pts

20th stage: Clusone/Milano - 149 km

1.	Alessandro Petacchi (Ita) FAS	4h 07'01"	
2.	Marco Zanotti (Ita)	VIN	s.t
3.	Aart Vierhouten (Ned) GST	s.t	
4.	Olaf Pollack (Ger)	GST	s.t
5.	Alejandro Borrajo (Arg)	PAN	s.t

POSITIONS ON POINTS...

1.	Alessandro Petacchi (Ita)	FAS	250 pts
2.	Damiano Cunego (Ita)	SAE	153 pts
3.	Olaf Pollack (Ger)	GST	148 pts
4.	Alexandre Usov (Blr)	PHO	111 pts
5.	Marco Zanotti (Ita)	VIN	102 pts

POSITIONS IN THE MOUNTAINS...

1.	Fabian Wegmann (Ger)	GST	56 pts
2.	Damiano Cunego (Ita)	SAE	54 pts
3.	Gilberto Simoni (Ita)	SAE	36 pts
4.	Stefano Garzelli (Ita)	VIN	33 pts
5.	Alexandre Moos (Sui)	PHO	27 pts

PRINCIPAL ASCENTION OF THE GIRO 2004

Stage 3
Corno alle Scale: Gilberto Simoni (Ita)

Stage 7
Montevergine di Mercogliano: Damiano Cunego (Ita)

Stage 16
Passo di Valparola: Fabian Wegmann (Ger)
Passo Furcia: Niki Aebersold (Sui)
Terento: Damiano Cunego (Ita)

Stage 18
Passo di Gavia: Vladimir Miholjevic (Cro)
Bormio 2000: Damiano Cunego (Ita)

Stage 19
Passo del Mortirolo: Raffaele Illiano (Ita)
Passo del Vivione: Stefano Garzelli (Ita)
Passo della Presolana: Gilberto Simoni (Ita)

169 Competitors

SAECO

1.	SIMONI Gilberto (Ita)	**3rd**	+ 2'05"
2.	BERTAGNOLLI Leonardo (Ita)	37th	+ 1h07'10"
3.	CUNEGO Damiano (Ita)	**1st**	**88 h 40'43"**
4.	FORNACIARI Paolo (Ita)	100th	+ 2h30'09"
5.	MAZZOLENI Eddy (Ita)	21st	+ 27'44"
6.	SPEZIALETTI Alessandro (Ita)	66th	+ 1h54'06"
7.	STANGELJ Gorazd (Slo)	95th	+ 2h24'36"
8.	SZMYD Sylvester (Pol)	43rd	+ 1h15'54"
9.	TONTI Andrea (Ita)	29th	+ 47'11"

ACQUA E SAPONE - MOKAMBO

11.	MARZOLI Ruggero (Ita)	23rd	+ 31'41"
12.	FERRIGATO Andrea (Ita)	84th	+ 2h15'21"
13.	NOCENTINI Rinaldo (Ita)	34th	+ 58'53"
14.	HAMBURGER Bo (Den)	38th	+ 1h07'49"
15.	D'AMORE Crescenzo (Ita)	123rd	+ 2h49'38"
16.	RODRIGUEZ Fred (Usa)	99th	+ 2h28'10"
17.	POSPEEV Kyrylo (Ukr)	42nd	+ 1h13'05"
18.	SOSENKA Ondrej (Cze)	NP	7th stage
19.	TRAMPUSCH Gerhard (Aut)	26th	+ 39'16"

ALESSIO - BIANCHI

21.	BÄCKSTEDT Magnus (Swe)	*Abandon*	15th stage
22.	FURLAN Angelo (Ita)	128th	+ 3h00'46"
23.	BERTOLINI Alessandro (Ita)	53rd	+ 1h39'29"
24.	LJUNGQVIST Marcus (Swe)	63rd	+ 1h51'37"
25.	MIHOLJEVIC Vladimir (Cro)	24th	+ 32'06"
26.	MORENI Cristian (Ita)	25th	+ 35'24"
27.	NOE' Andrea (Ita)	17th	+ 22'33"
28.	PELLIZOTTI Franco (Ita)	11st	+ 9'45"
29.	RASTELLI Ellis (Ita)	73rd	+ 2h03'26"

PANARIA - MARGRES

31.	FIGUERAS Giuliano (Ita)	NP	18th stage
32.	PEREZ CUAPIO J. Alberto (Mex)	33rd	+ 58'21"
33.	DAVIS Scott (Aus)	90th	+ 2h21'33"
34.	LANCASTER Brett (Aus)	124th	+ 2h50'32"
35.	LANFRANCHI Paolo (Ita)	61st	+ 1h50'25"
36.	MAZZANTI Luca (Ita)	46th	+ 1h26'22"
37.	SELLA Emanuele (Ita)	12nd	+ 10'26"
38.	BALIANI Fortunato (Ita)	39th	+ 1h09'35"
39.	BORRAJO Alejandro (Arg)	79th	+ 2h12'03"

Chocolade JACQUES - WINCOR NIXDORF

41.	ARANAGA Andoni (Esp)	*Abandon*	6th stage
42.	ARDILA Mauricio (Col)	31st	+ 51'05"
43.	BRARD Florent (Fra)	108th	+ 2h39'04"
44.	KOSTYUK Denis (Ukr)	60th	+ 1h49'17"
45.	GADRET John (Fra)	*Abandon*	4th stage
46.	RUDENKO Maxim (Ukr)	133rd	+ 3h22'09"
47.	VAN DE WALLE Jurgen (Bel)	*Abandon*	3rd stage
48.	VERHEYEN Geert (Bel)	49th	+ 1h34'21"
49.	VAN VELZEN Jan (Ned)	122nd	+ 2h49'28"

COLOMBIA - SELLE ITALIA

51.	GONZALEZ MARTINEZ Freddy (Col)	*Abandon*	9th stage
52.	PEREZ ARANGO Marlon (Col)	40th	+ 1h11'58"
53.	MARIN Ruber Alveiro (Col)	83rd	+ 2h15'08"
55.	ILLIANO Raffaele (Ita)	35th	+ 1h05'13"
56.	SCARSELLI Leonardo (Ita)	*Abandon*	16th stage
57.	SCHNYDER Philippe (Sui)	129th	+ 3h03'50"
58.	VAN HOUT Russel (Aus)	134th	+ 3h25'27"
59.	WILSON Trent (Aus)	126th	+ 2h54'57"

DE NARDI

61.	HONCHAR Serhiy (Ukr)	**2nd**	+ 2'02"
62.	BORGHI Ruggero (Ita)	28th	+ 47'02"
63.	CADAMURO Simone (Ita)	120th	+ 2h48'28"
64.	GASPARRE Graziano (Ita)	78th	+ 2h10'47"
65.	GIORDANI Leonardo (Ita)	75th	+ 2h05'22"
66.	GOBBI Michele (Ita)	93rd	+ 2h24'26"
67.	PUGACI Igor (Mda)	70th	+ 1h56'20"
68.	VANOTTI Alessandro (Ita)	44th	+ 1h20'55"
69.	WEGELIUS Charly (Gbr)	48th	+ 1h32'14"

DOMINA VACANZE

71.	CIPOLLINI Mario (Ita)	NP	7th stage
72.	AUG Andrus (Est)	NP	7th stage
73.	COLOMBO Gabriele (Ita)	117th	+ 2h46'59"
74.	DERGANC Martin (Slo)	127th	+ 3h00'23"
75.	GALLETTI Alessio (Ita)	89th	+ 2h21'16"
76.	IANNETTI Massimo (Ita)	NP	12nd stage
77.	LOMBARDI Giovanni (Ita)	119th	+ 2h48'06"
78.	NAUDUZS Andris (Lat)	106th	+ 2h37'29"
79.	SCIREA Mario (Ita)	121st	+ 2h48'41"

FASSA BORTOLO

81.	BRUSEGHIN Marzio (Ita)	58th	+ 1h46'46"
82.	CIONI Dario (Ita)	**4th**	+ 4'36"
83.	CODOL Massimo (Ita)	69th	+ 1h56'19"
84.	ONGARATO Alberto (Ita)	109th	+ 2h39'50"
85.	PETACCHI Alessandro (Ita)	97th	+ 2h27'44"
86.	SACCHI Fabio (Ita)	102nd	+ 2h34'12"
87.	TOSATTO Matteo (Ita)	107th	+ 2h37'41"
88.	GUSTOV Volodymir (Ukr)	103rd	+ 2h34'26"
89.	VELO Marco (Ita)	101st	+ 2h30'41"

FDJEUX.COM

91.	BICHOT Freddy (Fra)	*Abandon*	10th stage
92.	DEREPAS David (Fra)	85th	+ 2h15'45"
93.	FRITSCH Nicolas (Fra)	51st	+ 1h36'22"
94.	GILBERT Philippe (Bel)	32nd	+ 57'58"
95.	McGEE Bradley (Aus)	**8th**	+ 6'15"
96.	MOUREY Francis (Fra)	104th	+ 2h35'51"
97.	VAUGRENARD Benoît (Fra)	136th	+ 3h30'00"
98.	VOGONDY Nicolas (Fra)	81st	+ 2h14'10"
99.	WILSON Matthew (Aus)	132nd	+ 3h22'02"

Formaggi PINZOLO PIAVE'

101.	QUARANTA Ivan (Ita)	*Abandon*	10th stage
102.	MANZONI Mario (Ita)	135th	+ 3h26'45"
103.	MERVAR Bostjan (Slo)	130th	+ 3h07'33"
105.	GUALDI Domenico (Ita)	139th	+ 3h55'37"
106.	DI GRANDE Giuseppe (Ita)	20th	+ 26'05"
107.	MURAGLIA Giuseppe (Ita)	57th	+ 1h45'37"
108.	LAVERDE Luis Felipe (Col)	15th	+ 13'43"
109.	SERINA Corrado (Ita)	140th	+ 4h03'22"

GEROLSTEINER

111.	FARESIN Gianni (Ita)	NP	10th stage
112.	FÖRSTER Robert (Ger)	116th	+ 2h45'24"
113.	MONTGOMERY Sven (Sui)	NP	14th stage
114.	POLLACK Olaf (Ger)	112nd	+ 2h42'01"
115.	REBELLIN Davide (Ita)	NP	8th stage
116.	SERPELLINI Marco (Ita)	71st	+ 1h56'52"
117.	STRAUSS Marcel (Sui)	105th	+ 2h36'19"
118.	WEGMANN Fabian (Ger)	36th	+ 1h06'50"
119.	ZIEGLER Thomas (Ger)	64th	+ 1h53'33"

LAMPRE

121.	GARATE Juan Manuel (Esp)	**10th**	+ 7'47"
122.	BELLI Wladimir (Ita)	**7th**	+ 6'12"
123.	ASTARLOA Igor (Esp)	56th	+ 1h42'08"
124.	SVORADA Jan (Cze)	*Abandon*	17th stage
125.	HAUPTMAN Andrej (Slo)	82nd	+ 2h14'38"
126.	PAGLIARINI Luciano (Bra)	*Abandon*	17th stage
127.	PICCOLI Mariano (Ita)	59th	+ 1h48'33"
128.	RIGHI Daniele (Ita)	96th	+ 2h26'05"
129.	VILA Patxi (Esp)	22nd	+ 30'50"

LANDBOUWKREDIET - COLNAGO

131.	BILEKA Volodymir (Ukr)	50th	+ 1h35'31"
132.	DUMA Vladimir (Ukr)	65th	+ 1h53'45"
133.	DURAND Jacky (Fra)	*Abandon*	18th stage
134.	GASPERONI Cristian (Ita)	*Abandon*	2nd stage
135.	POPOVYCH Yaroslav (Ukr)	**5th**	+ 5'05"
136.	SIJMENS Nico (Bel)	68th	+ 1h56'13"
137.	VAITKUS Tomas (Ltu)	NP	10th stage
138.	VERSTREPEN Johan (Bel)	94th	+ 2h24'34"
139.	ADVEYEV Serguey (Ukr)	86th	+ 2h16'12"

LOTTO - DOMO

141.	McEWEN Robbie (Aus)	NP	16th stage
142.	BRANDT Christophe (Bel)	14th	+ 10'50"
143.	GARDEYN Gorik (Bel)	125th	+ 2h51'16"
144.	WADECKI Piotr (Pol)	*Abandon*	15th stage
145.	VIERHOUTEN Aart (Ned)	110th	+ 2h40'13"
146.	DETILLOUX Christophe (Bel)	*Abandon*	16th stage
147.	GATES Nick (Aus)	113rd	+ 2h42'48"
148.	STEEGMANS Geert (Bel)	131st	+ 3h11'11"
149.	VERBRUGGHE Ief (Bel)	115th	+ 2h44'56"

PHONAK

151.	ALBASINI Michael (Sui)	88th	+ 2h18'18"
152.	AEBERSOLD Niki (Sui)	41st	+ 1h12'52"
153.	BENNATI Daniele (Ita)	*Abandon*	2nd stage
154.	FERTONANI Marco (Ita)	55th	+ 1h40'51"
155.	MOOS Alexandre (Sui)	27th	+ 46'16"
156.	MURN Uros (Slo)	92nd	+ 2h23'26"
157.	SCHNIDER Daniel (Sui)	45th	+ 1h22'38"
158.	USOV Alexandre (Blr)	98th	+ 2h27'48"
159.	VALJAVEC Tadej (Slo)	**9th**	+ 6'34"

SAUNIER DUVAL - PRODIR

161.	BERTOGLIATI Rubens (Sui)	52nd	+ 1h38'22"
162.	CAÑADA David (Esp)	18th	+ 22'52"
163.	DOMINGUEZ Juan Carlos (Esp)	NP	8th stage
164.	GOMIS Juan (Esp)	67th	+ 1h55'39"
165.	LOBATO Ruben (Esp)	16th	+ 21'11"
166.	LODDO Alberto (Ita)	*Abandon*	17th stage
167.	MORI Manuele (Ita)	76th	+ 2h09'30"
168.	ZAUGG Oliver (Sui)	47th	+ 1h27'53"
169.	STRAZZER Massimo (Ita)	NP	10th stage

TENAX

171.	BOSISIO Gabriele (Ita)	137th	+ 3h30'36"
172.	GINESTRI Giancarlo (Ita)	118th	+ 2h47'03"
173.	KLEMENCIC Zoran (Slo)	NP	14th stage
174.	LODA Nicola (Ita)	74th	+ 2h03'33"
175.	MAZZOLENI Renzo (Ita)	111st	+ 2h41'06"
176.	PIETROPOLLI Daniele (Ita)	80th	+ 2h13'39"
177.	PODGORNIK Dean (Slo)	138th	+ 3h46'50"
178.	POZZI Oscar (Ita)	72nd	+ 2h01'24"
179.	ROGINA Radoslav (Cro)	87th	+ 2h17'10"

Vini CALDIROLA - NOBILI Rubinetterie

181.	GARZELLI Stefano (Ita)	**6th**	+ 5'31"
182.	TONKOV Pavel (Rus)	13rd	+ 10'43"
183.	ANDRIOTTO Dario (Ita)	54th	+ 1h40'16"
184.	GEROSA Mauro (Ita)	62nd	+ 1h50'43"
185.	MASCIARELLI Simone (Ita)	91st	+ 2h21'36"
186.	MASON Oscar (Ita)	30th	+ 50'02"
187.	SIRONI Gianluca (Ita)	77th	+ 2h09'36"
188.	ZAMPIERI Steve (Sui)	19th	+ 25'53"
189.	ZANOTTI Marco (Ita)	114th	+ 2h43'02"

EX WINNERS AT THE START — *3*

SIMONI Gilberto	2003 - 2001
GARZELLI Stefano	2000
TONKOV Pavel	1996

3 OLDEST

SCIREA Mario (39 ans)	1964/08/07
FARESIN Gianni (38 ans)	1965/07/16
DURAND Jacky (37 ans)	1967/02/10

3 YOUNGEST

IANNETTI Massimo (21 ans)	1982/12/22
GILBERT Philippe (21 ans)	1982/07/05
KOSTYUK Denis (22 ans)	1982/05/13

-28 different nationalities were represented. The majority were Italians (75 riders) , followed by the Belgians and the swiss (10 riders), the Ukrainians and the frenchs (9 riders), the Australians, the spaniards et Slovènes (8 riders).

-79 riders at the start of Giro 2004 (soit 47%) were here last year.

In Fondo Sarnonico, Pavel Tonkov back on the road to success with a gesture to all those who had him dead and buried too soon...

NO SUSPENSE NO EXCITEMENT...

Lance Armstrong has then, won his sixth consecutive Tour de France. For this reason he enters the history books, but many would have liked to see him have to fight a little harder for this latest win. But this 2004 edition was cruelly lacking in suspense. Despite the pre race declarations of several of his adversaries, there was to be no real competition. And from the first real test in the mountains, that of La Mongie, all knew that, excluding accidents, nothing, or no one could prevent Armstrong from taking this sixth victory. From reconaissance to advance planning, the Texan and his team left nothing to chance which could prevent him passing the records of Anquetil, Merckx, Hinault and Indurain.

In Liege, the tour got off to an optimistic start, talk being of epic battles to come (revenge for last year's terrific duel between Lance Armstrong and Jan Ullrich, pre race challenges by Tyler Hamilton, Roberto Heras and particularly Iban Mayo). All the same the atmosphere was a little subdued despite the well known ability of the Belgian supporters enjoy the occasion. Hot from the presses a few days before, the book "L A Confidential" accuses the champion and visibly irritates him. For its part, the tour organisation announces a clean up campaign.

The Italian rider Danilo Luca is sent home in disgrace due to a forthcoming judgement in a case dating from several years in the past. Forty eight hours before the Prologue, the Basque rider Gorka Gonzalez Larranaga fails a dope test. His Euskaltel team will therefore start the Tour with only eight riders! After a few stages, the Slovenian Martin Hvastija (Alassio Boanchi) and the Italian Stefano Casagranda (Saeco) must also leave the race: also due to coming court cases. For some obscure reason however the same sanction does not apply to Pavel Padrnos (US Postal) or Stafano Zanini 5Quick Step...

THEY'RE OFF, WITH A SPRINT!

The Tour begins with a prologue in the streets of Liege. Even at this point it's plain for all to see that last year's winner is on the pace. Just the same he is just beaten by a specialist in this kind of stage by the Swiss youngster Fabian Cancellara. Jan Ullrich trails by 17 seconds, Hamilton a further second behind, Mayo limits the damage 21 seconds behind the winner who wears the first Yellow Jersey.

Under a cloudy sky, leaking the occasional light drizzle, more like the weather for a spring Classic than a summer's day, the sprinters didn't miss their first chance for glory. One of the most experienced (soon to celebrate his 35th birthday), the Estonian Jaan Kirsipuu showed a clean pair of heels to Robbie Mc Ewen and to the Norwegian champion Thor Hushovd in an incident packed day. A day started with aplomb by Paolo Bettini, Bernhard Eisel, Franck Renier, Janek Tombak and Jens Voight, for a long time out front before leaving the work to the duo of Dane Jakob Piil with the Belgian Marc Wauters. But the numerous sprinters present at the start of this tour soon make their presence felt. Much to the pleasure of Fabian Cancellara who conserves the leader's jersey.

It couldn't last for the man from the Fassa Bortolo team, because of the points collected by Thor Hushovt the day before (third on the stage), and those won on this third day, taking the peloton to Namur. Sure, the Scandinavian rider lost out to Robbie Mc Ewen, but took the Yellow Jersey from Cancellara with an advantage of eight seconds. This, with the help of an excellent Prologue, (5th at 10 seconds from the winner) two days earlier. The day before, the breakout of Lang, Pineau, Edaleine,Piil,Scanlon and Mengin was insufficient to build up a lead over the peloton.

Fabian Cancellara, the fatal weapon in the Prologue.

The third stage , starting on the plain of Waterloo, was much criticised by many in the tour. This stage brought back the old tradition of including some of the less hazardous cobbled section of the Paris – Roubaix into the day's ride. The old expression "We won't know the winner, but we may know the loser at the end of the day" came back into play. Iban Mayo and all of his Euskaltel team mates, as well as Christophe Moreau and the Russian Denis Menchov saw their chances for the podium evaporate after only four days of the event. A deficit of 3minutes 53 seconds is too much to lose in such a stage. Robbie Mc Ewen inherits the Yellow Jersey but knows only too well that the next day's time trial will make it hard for him to keep it on his back.

The US Postal team were the favourites for the team time trial which they had won for the first time last year. After their text book ride over the cobbles the day before, Lance Armstrong and his team did just enough to take the victory and at the same time, the Yellow Jersey. Luck also played its part, allowing the US Postal team to run its race in dry weather as opposed to the teams who started in rain earlier in the day. This could explain the average speed of 53.71 kph, the third fastest in the history of the Tour de France(the record of 54.93 being held by the Gewiss – Ballan team since 1995. The Phonak team was not so lucky, suffering punctures and mechanical

The French teams dominate the sprint in Charleroi, the first day. Jaan Kirsipuu (centre) shows himself stronger than Thor Hushovd (left) and his team mate Jean Patrick Nazon.

problems on their run. Thanks to a superb final third of the stage, the surviving five riders of the Swiss team were promoted to second place due to a recent rule change. A change that helped some, but not others such as Gilberto Simoni, victim of a fall on the final bend, meaning his actual time, 2 mins 42 sec behind U S Postal.

FOR VOECKLER, THE STORY BEGINS IN CHARTRES...

On the road between Amiens and Chartres, the teams of the sprinters don't seem to have decided to make the race their own. Boonen,the man named as one of the main contenders in the sprints. Set up perfectly by his team mates for the finales in Charleroi and Namur, but both times set back by mechanical problems and relegated to 14th place. At Wasquehal, he makes some progress, finishing 4th. In Angers, having taken the precaution of fitting stronger pedals, things begin to look better. The breakaway of the day, composing of Flecha, Engoulvent, Bertolini, Lotz, Da Cruz and Arvesen cannot build up a sufficient lead, and the work of the team mates of Tom Boonen bear fruit a few kilometers from the line. Juan Antonio Victim of a fall on the wasquehal stage, the nine times stage winner of the Giro would be forced to retire from the Tour without ever showing his hand. Luckily for them, his team had other cards up their sleeves. Once the attack of the day (Dekker and Marichal), had been beaten off, and the sprinters were making ready their pushes for the line, several riders,encouraged by a slight climb, decided to attack in their turn. The decisive attack is begun at 3 kilometers from the line by Laurent Brochard, followed by several others, including... Pozzato. Beating off the attack from Iker Flores, he finds

So much the better for the opportunists. These go by the name of Magnus Backstedt, Sandy Casar, Stuart O'Grady, Jakob Piil and Thomas Voeckler. The latter does not yet imagine he is about to live the maddest two weeks of his existance. In fact the quintet have an advantage of 12 minutes 30 seconds as they enter the streets of Chartres. To no one's surprise it's the strongest of the lot, Stuart O' Grady who takes the win. To no one's surprise, Lance Armstrong leaves the Yellow Jersey to Thomas Voeckler, too soon on his back ,with the mountains still well over the horizon... He was beginning to get annoyed,Tom Flecha, the last of the attacking group being caught under the Red Flame. At this very place ,a serious pile up didn't help the chances of several leading riders, among them Tyler Hamilton. Several sprinters (Nazon, Hushovd, Kirsipuu and Mc Ewen) are also involved. All this leaves the road open to Boonen who shows his superiority to O' Grady and Zabel to take a first stage win on the Tour... The Fassa Bortolo team arrived in the area with just one objective: to help their star sprinter Alessandro Petacchi to add to his list of stage wins. Four times a winner in 2003, he remained modest and humble when setting off in Liege. The future was to prove him right! himself in the company of two Spaniards (Mancebo completing the trio) at 500 metres from the finish. "Pipo" doesn't miss the chance to show his speed.

The second Brittany stage of the Tour comes the day before a rest day for the remaining 176 riders. After the team mates of Hushovd, helped by those of Tom Boonen, wiped out the attack of the day, (Piil, Tossato, and Scholz, caught 10kms from the line) , the peloton presents itself bunched at the foot of a gentle climb towards the finish in Quimper.Bettini and Mc Ewen try to team up with the sprinters and also with the champion of Luxembourg Kim Kirchen, who makes an apparently

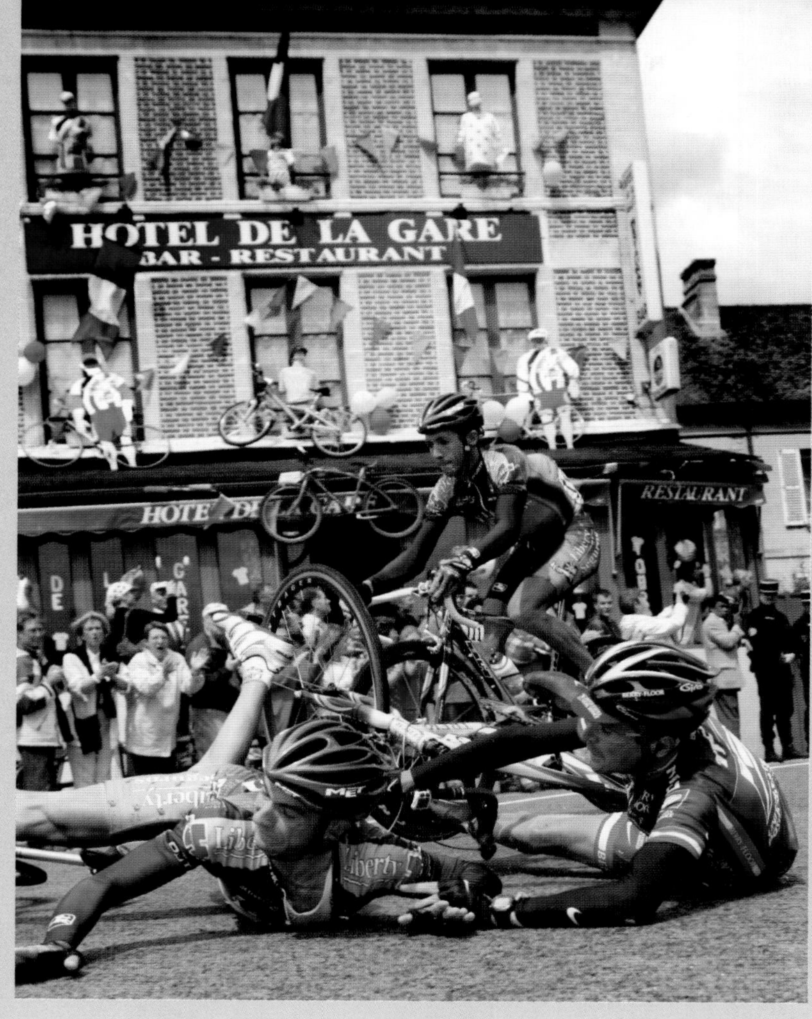

Angel Vicioso and Benjamin Noval touchdown.

irresistible push for the line at the 500 metre mark. That's not accounting for the finishing power of Thor Hushovd, strong as a... Viking, overtaking Kirchen at the last minute and raising his arms in a victory salute. All this does nothing to threaten the Yellow Jersey of Thomas Voeckler, who can savour his leadership on the rest day whilst transfering to Limoges.

THE FIRST MOUNTAINS AS HORS D'OEUVRE

Inigo Landaluze and Filipo Simeoni must be kicking themselves! Impatient for the finish, with 15 seconds lead at the last kilometre mark, the two riders were swept aside by the peloton, from which emerged the australian Robbie Mc Ewen, taking his second stage win and increasing his points lead in the Tour. The Spaniard (Landaluz) and the Italian (Simeoni) fall at the last hurdle after an escapade of 125 kilometers on the rustic roads of La Creuse, the only French department which had up till now never seen the finish of a Tour de France stage in its hundred year history. On this 14th July the sunshine reappears on the route of the Tour. Something guaranteed to please Richard Virenque, up until now discreetly hidden in the peloton. Nine climbs are in line for the stage, and as the rider from the Var has already expressed his wish to wear the red and white jersey in Paris, this is too good an opportunity to miss. With 237 kilometers to ride, this is also the longest stage of this years race. There are 202 kms left when Richard Virenque takes off on his own for one of his speciality lone attacks. In this exercise he has found a companion, axel Merckx, unafraid by the hilly nature of the stage. The two men help each other along for the first six climbs, but the Puy Mary proves too much for the Belgian rider. Counting ten minutes lead over a peloton in which the favourites seem satisfied to watch each other's moves, the Varois waits a little on the descent for Meckx before deciding to go it alone for the rest of the route. The only problem being the fact that there are 67 kms left to the line! At the limit of his strenght and with a great show of strenght, Richard Virenque becomes the 14th French rider to win on the 14th July. Though not feeling at his best, Thomas Voeckler manages to come in a remarkable fifth. Those thinking he would lose his Yellow Jersey on this day were to be proved wrong. After a French victory on the 14th July, it was now time for a victory for a local boy! The Figeac stage will crown David Moncoutié, who from the start of this strange day is on the tips of his toes. At first he tries to hitch a ride with the first attacks of the day. These come to nothing. However, soon after the ascention of the Cote de Therondels (km 48.5), the rider from the Lot region takes the bull by the horns and sets off after the Basque Egoi Martinez de Esteban. Seeing his chance, Juan Antonio Flecha ,another Spaniard, stage winner last year in Toulouse, takes chase and joins them a few kilometers later. As the "Brioches" are concentrating on protecting the Yellow Jersey of Thomas Voeckler, the trio is set for an easy time up front. Reaching the final ten kilometre mark, Flecha (even though the fastest) goes first.

"Pippo" Pozzato in the Spanish coalition in St. Brieuc.

Thomas Voeckler: once again surprised by an unexpected celebrity.

and to a lesser extent Ivan Mayo (1 min 03 sec) or Gilberto Simoni (1 min 32 sec). Just the same, Thomas Voeckler, losing only (!) 3 mins 59 sec can still count a lead of 5 mins 24 sec overall. But God knows, this sort of treasure is hard to hang on to. The stage goes to Ivan Basso, the only one able to follow the acceleration of the American on this run finishing in La Mongie. A rather limp stage, at first animated by an attack (Finot, Vansevenant, Kirchen and Ljungqvist), wiped out even before the real racing began, then an attempt by the dane Michael Rasmussen on the ascent of the Col d'Aspin before the "Blue train" got to work. Hicapie

Despite the rain, it's a great day in Brittany.

David Moncoutié follows, leaving the two Spaniards standing. The Frenchman's dream comes true minutes later, winning in front of his home crowd on the streets of Figeac.

THE KNOCKOUT BLOW

Just as we suspected. The confirmation was quick in coming. Lance Armstrong takes this Tour de France by the scruff of the neck. Creating alliances of convenience(Basso and the CSC team on this stage) before wiping the floor with his rivals. At least, those who thought themselves to be rivals. This first high altitude finish went by the book, some losing a little, others losing a great deal. The first victims of these first hills in the Pyrenees? Jan Ullrich of course (mins 30 sec conceded), but also Tyler Hamilton (3 mins 27 sec) or Roberto Heras (2 mins 57 sec)

A seventh stage win for Richard Virenque before taking a seventh red and white jersey in Paris.

Jan Ullrich: in trouble on the Mongie stage.

Lance Armstrong and Ivan Basso: inseparable on the Pyreneen pass.

then, in particular Azevedo pull the leading group apart before the awaited attack from the number 1 rider.The rest we know...

VOECKLER RESISTS!

After the bad news of the day before, the 13th stage already seemed like the final chance for his rivals to stop the five times winner running away with this year's race. However, if there are some out of touch riders in the peloton, they are the adversaries of Armstrong. Haimar Zubeldia (5th in 2003) and Denis Menchov drop out soon after the start. Then Tyler Hamilton follows at a refreshment break.

Carrying a back injury since his fall in Angers, also upset by the death of his dog, the American prefers to abandon the race. The same idea comes into the mind of Iban Mayo, left behind by the peloton during the ascention of the Col de Latrape, 75 kilometers from the line, the Basque rider no longer able to make the mental effort to continue. In his moment of pain he first comes to a halt and passes his cycle to a mechanic. But his team mates encourage him to make another effort. Back in the saddle, Mayo reaches the end with a time gap of 37 mins 40sec... For Roberto Heras, the day is just as bad. Victim of a crash just before the climb to the Col d'agnes, the going is too hard and he arrives with a gap of 21 mins 25 sec.

Three brave men have less trouble. Sylvain Chavenel and Jens Voight joined by the infatigable Michael Rasmussen at the Portet d'Aspet, are in the lead for a long time and are still there at the start of the climb to the Plateau de Beille, the last difficulty of a hard day. Their adventure, however, ends on the steep slopes of the Pyreneen pass. Lance Armstrong is now protected by four team members and begins to up the pace. Of the now thinned out leading group, it's Jan Ullrich who cracks first (he'll lose even more time on La Mongie: 2mins 42 sec as against 2 mins 30 sec). The Austrian Georg Totchnig has a good climb to finish 3rd at 1 min 05 sec. Andreas Kloden and Francisco Mancebo put up a good fight but trail Lance Armstrong by 1 min 27 sec. Armstrong leading in the company of... Ivan Basso. Armstrong takes his opponent by surprise at the finish to take the stage. Just the same ,he is not yet to wear the Yellow Jersey. Showing a great deal of courage, Voeckler manages to maintain an overall lead over Armstrong of 22 seconds. What a show!

After the Pyrenees and before a rest day, the main part of the peloton hopes to take things easy. There are, however, thirty or so riders who attempt to mount the attack of the day which will go up to the line. This is a tradition in what are known as "Etapes de transition". This one between Carcassone and Nimes is no exception. After 98 kilometers of the stage, ten riders are still in the frame. Who from Santiago Botero, Nicolas Jalabert, Inigo Landaluze, Igor Gonzalez de Galdeano, Egoi Martinez de Esteban, Aitor Gonzalez Jimenez, Pierrick Fedrigo, Peter Wrolich, Marc Lotz and Christophe Mengin can take it? The peloton seems unconcerned (the highest placed rider overall , Egoi Martinez de Esteban being 37 minutes behind Armstrong).
The answer comes less than ten kilometers from Nimes. Aitor Gonzalez makes a determined attack, Nicolas Jalabert and Christophe Mengin hesitate for a few seconds before taking up the chase, and that's that. The spanish have their first success of the 2004 Tour.

VILLARS-DE LANCE

And finally Lance Armstrong is wearing the jersey he usually has on in July. Thomas Voeckler can take consolation in wearing the white jersey of the "Best young rider" after having the honour of wearing the Yellow jersey for ten days. The start of the stage sees the outsiders in the driving seat. All hoping that today will be their lucky day.

After a good hour of more or less serious attempts, a group of 14 riders break away at km 56. We find the usual suspects for this kind of operation, like Richard Virenque, Jens Voight and the Dane Michael Rasmussen, men at ease with this sort of terrain (Brochard, Fofonov, Santos Gonzalez or Vandervelde), a few old timers (Dufaux, Sunderland) or even some sprinters not afraid of the mountains (Hushovd, O' Grady), the courageous Garcia Acosta, a team mate of the leader, Anthony Charteau and also the stage winner the day before, Aitor Gonzalez. On the climbs, particularly the Col des Limouches, the group shakes off the weaker elements. And at the foot of the Col de l'Echarasson, the most difficult of the day, only Virenque, Rasmussen, Voigt and Santos Gonzalez are still in the chase. The two latter soon disappear on the steeper slopes. It's from behind that the challenge will come. Jan Ullrich, relegated at more than six minutes from Lance Armstrong goes on the offensive 60 kilometers from the line. The thinned out peloton shatters. Roberto Heras is quickly in difficulty soon to be followed by Thomas Voeckler. Francisco Mancebo lets go a little later (he crosses the line in 17th position having lost 2 mins 13 secs). Soon enough Jan Ullrich joins the duo Virenque/Rasmussen at the summit and crosses the line 50 seconds ahead of Lance Armstrong, who, accompanied by team mates Azevido and Landis shows no sign of panic. His second in command Ivan Basso neither. Team manager Bjarne Riis tells Jens Voigt to await his leader in order to put a final effort into the persuit of Jan Ullrich who could claim a place on the podium. Voigt goes into action, and with the gap standing at 1 min 10 sec the winner of the 1997 Tour, lets up and is caught at the foot of the Col de Chalimont, 25 kilometers from the line. On this last climb of the day, Richard Virenque and Michael Rasmussen suffer the same fate a little later. Finally it's a quartet (Armstrong, Basso, Kloden, Ullrich) which shows itself at the entry to Villars-de Lans. The Germans no longer have the energy to go for the stage win and Armstrong easily gets away from Ivan Basso.

Even before the much awaited stage at the Alpes d'Huez is run, the outcome of the 91st Tour de France is decided! The only doubt is who will take second and third places on the final podium. A feeling of *déjà vu*.

How many are waiting on the Alpe d'Huez and its famous hairpin bends, its slopes sometimes up to 11% and its 13.8 kms climb? 500,000, 1,000,000? We'll never know. Of course the stakes are not the same as a week ago. The Pyrenees saw to that. Exit therefore, Mayo (winner here last year but retired this time around), Hamilton, Heras (languishing down the order), and even Ullrich, 6 mins 58 sec behind Armstrong. Ullrich has the objective of winning this stage if only to please the thousands of his supporters lining the route. Once again he fails. Even with a very good time, he is beaten by 1 min 01 sec by Armstrong. Andreas Kloden comes in third 1 min 41 sec after the American. Ivan Basso, not doing so well as in recent days is 8th at 2 mins 23 sec. Times are hard also for the young ex Yellow Jersey Thomas Voeckler, visibly exhausted by his effort in the last week, he takes the 88th place 6 mins 36 sec behind the winner. A hard return to reality.

"PAS DE CADEAU"!

One less but one more. Of the four big rivals lined up against the American in Liege, only Ullrich remains, even though the German can now only hope for third place, he's still there. As opposed to the three others, Hamilton, Mayo and Roberto heras who will not be present at the start of this 17th stage, the last in the mountains and also considered as the hardest, with no less than 70 kms of climbing. This does not sap the morale of five competitors: simoni and simeoni, Frenchman Ludovic Martin, the German Rolf Aldag and Michele Bartoli, very discreet for the last twenty days, who attack after only 2 kilometers. The pack let them go. With the exception of two men.

Richard Virenque and Christophe Moreau take chase at the Col de Glandon 169 kilometers from the line! They catch up on the summit of the Col de la Madeleine, too tough for Simeoni and even more so for Bartoli who retires soon after. It's on the next climb at the Col de Tamié that Ludovic Martin gets into trouble, and the next, Forclaz, that Rolf Aldag comes unstuck. This leaves just the three best climbers out in front, moreau, Simoni and Virenque, but the group of the favourites is on their heels. And now the Col de la Croix Fry is looming on the horizon, it's summit 13 kilometers from the finish at Grand Bornand. Under the guidance of Floyd Landis, the Yellow Jersey group catch the last of the morning attackers at the 20 kilometre mark.

But Richard Virenque is un worried, knowing he is assured of keeping the red and white jersey of the best climber for a record breaking seventh time. Another record is about to be broken. On the brink of asixth consecutive victory on the Tour, Lance Armstrong doesn't tremble on the col de la Croix Fry, where Carlos sastre attempts a last ditch attack. Now the leading group is reduced to five men, the Yellow Jersey can count on the reliable Floyd Landis. To reward his precious team mate, Lance Armstrong lets him pull ahead on the descent to Grand Bornand. But the team mate of Armstrong is counter attacked by Basso, Kloden, and Ullrich. The five will fight it out in a sprint. After another attempt from Landis, it's Andreas Kloden who goes, a few hundred metres short of the line. But the German champion seems stuck to the tarmac. Armstrong overtakes Kloden just before the line. When asked later about his series of stage wins, the Texan quoted the words of Bernard Hinault who was standing at the foot of the podium, "Pas de cadeau"!

With only three days left before the arrival in Paris, a stage many had been waiting for is upon us. For the "Baroudeurs" their day has come, as only the second time trial and the last stage, favouring the sprinters remain. The legs are tired, the teams often decimated, making it difficult to control this stage across the Ain and finishing in the capital of the Jura. Very quickly the attack which turns out to be the good one takes shape. The Spaniards Flecha, Garcia Acosta and Mercado, the Dutchman Lotz, the Khazak Fofonov, and the Frenchman Joly contribute to putting it out of danger from the peloton. Not without difficulty. With the lead reduced to 30 seconds an unusual incident takes place. The Italian Filippo Simeoni comes out of the peloton to join the group of leaders. Yes, but Lance Armstrong gives him a glaring stare.

In the dock of the tribunal in Bologna in 2002, Filippi Simeoni had admitted doping himself with EPO on the recommendation of Michele Ferrari. The Doctor is of course the personal trainer of Lance Armstrong who has always claimed the practitioner to be honest and a great professional. With the possibility legal action in the air, there is no love lost between the two riders. And if Armstrong had tolerated the Italian's presence at the head of certain stages in "his" race, today was not the day. Armstrong follows the Italian, therefore ruining the chances of the six other riders at the front of the pack. The only solution is to give up. Simeoni realises this and leaves the others to their fate. Armstrong them sticks to him like glue until the two men are reabsorbed into the peloton. The six attackers take advantage of the situation to pull ahead of a peloton more interested in the Armstrong/Simeoni situation than a counter attack. Knowing a sprint would go against him, Sebastien Joly makes his move 15 kms from the line. He is immediately followed by Juan Miguel Mercado, who soon receives the help of his compatriot

José Vincente Garcia Acosta. The two men who are the best of friends and team mates pull out to put an end to any thoughts of a counter attack. Though the stronger sprinter, Garcia Acosta makes the error of not anticipating the attack of Mercado metres from the line. The winner of the Draguignan stage in 2000 could well hammer on his handlebars, he was beaten by a man sharper than he...

Basso against Kloden is one of the matches of the day with the prize being that of dauphin to Lance Armstrong who is in another class to the others. Separated by 1 min 02 sec in the overall standings, (to the advantage of the Italian), the confrontation rapidly turns to the advantage of the German, who, at 29, is one of the few revelations of the 2004 race. The German champion finishes with a show of force, takes third place in the stage, beating his adversary by 1 min 23 sec, 21 seconds overall. The other fight is for the title of best young rider (less than 25). Three riders are in the frame for this honour: Thomas Voeckler, wearing the white jersey at the start of this stage, the Russian Vladimir Karpets and another Frenchman, Sandy Casar. The Russian is favourite. He confirms this confidence. On the 55 kms around Besancon he takes a lead over Voeckler of more than six minutes and more than two minutes over Sandy Casar. Karpets wears the white jersey then, as he did for several days in the centenary tour. This stage has also known a winner. As in 1999 at the Futuroscope, in 2000 at Mulhouse, in St. Amand-Montrond in 2001, and in 2002 in Macon, Lance Armstrong takes the second time trial, his fifth stage win this year. Cannibalism? The stage commences for with a slip up. Filippo Simeoni doesn't appreciate the attention of Armstrong (and a sizeable number in the peloton) since the incident 48 hours earlier. Decided to upset the party, the Italian of the Domina Vacanze team goes out of the traps like a hare. The game doesn't last long, but Simeoni has another go as the race enters Paris. With the same negative result. The real racing begins as the riders enter the Champs Elysees. Ten men, including Thomas Voeckler, apparently having found new strenght, Paolo Bettini or Juan Antonio Flecha pull away from a insouciant peloton. On the final lap things sort themselves out. The only thing yet to be decided is who will be the points winner. A mass sprint terminates the Tour: a sprint pulled out of the hands of the master by Tom Boonen who beats off Jean Patrick Nazon, Danilo Hondo and the wearer of the Green Jersey, Robbie Mc Ewen, who, in consequence keeps his status: his last rival Thor Hushovd finishing behind him. ■

Lance Armstrong passes Ivan Basso on the Alpes d'Huez time trial. A wipeout?

The first alpine stage confirms the dominance already noticed in the Pyrenees of Lance Armstrong and Ivan Basso.

CLASSIFICATION

Prologue in Liege - 6,1 km (Team time trial)

1.	Fabian Cancellara (Sui)	FAS	6'50"
2.	Lance Armstrong (Usa)	USP	+ 1"
3.	J. Ivan Gutierrez (Esp)	IBB	+ 7"
4.	Bradley McGee (Aus)	FDJ	+ 8"
5.	Thor Hushovd (Nor)	C.A	+ 10"

1st stage: Liege/Charleroi - 202,5 km

1.	Jaan Kirsipuu (Est)	A2R	4h 40'29"
2.	Robbie McEwen (Aus)	LOT	s.t
3.	Thor Hushovd (Nor)	C.A	s.t
4.	Danilo Hondo (Ger)	GST	s.t
5.	Jean-Patrick Nazon (Fra)	A2R	s.t

Yellow jersey - Fabian Cancellara (Sui)	FAS	4h 47'11"
Green jersey - Thor Hushovd (Nor)	C.A	38 pts
Red and white jersey - Paolo Bettini (Ita)	QSD	13 pts
White jersey - Fabian Cancellara (Sui)	FAS	4h 47'11"

2nd stage: Charleroi/Namur - 197 km

1.	Robbie McEwen (Aus)	LOT	4h 18'39"
2.	Thor Hushovd (Nor)	C.A	s.t
3.	Jean-Patrick Nazon (Fra)	A2R	s.t
4.	Danilo Hondo (Ger)	GST	s.t
5.	Stuart O'Grady (Aus)	COF	s.t

Yellow jersey - Thor Hushovd (Nor)	C.A	9h 05'42"
Green jersey - Thor Hushovd (Nor)	C.A	68 pts
Red and white jersey - Paolo Bettini (Ita)	QSD	16 pts
White jersey - Fabian Cancellara (Sui)	FAS	9h 05'50"

3rd stage: Waterloo/Wasquehal - 210 km

1.	Jean-Patrick Nazon (Fra)	A2R	4h 36'45"
2.	Erik Zabel (Ger)	TMO	s.t
3.	Robbie McEwen (Aus)	LOT	s.t
4.	Tom Boonen (Bel)	QSD	s.t
5.	Kim Kirchen (Lux)	FAS	s.t

Yellow jersey - Robbie McEwen (Aus)	LOT	13h 42'34"
Green jersey - Robbie McEwen (Aus)	LOT	93 pts
Red and white jersey - Paolo Bettini (Ita)	QSD	19 pts
White jersey - Fabian Cancellara (Sui)	FAS	13h 42'35"

4th stage: Cambrai/Arras - 64,5 km (Team time trial)

1.	US POSTAL-BERRY FLOOR	USP	1h 12'03"
2.	PHONAK	PHO	+ 1'07"
3.	ILLES BALEARS	IBB	+ 1'15"
4.	T. MOBILE	TMO	+ 1'19"
5.	CSC	CSC	+ 1'45"

Yellow jersey - Lance Armstrong (Usa)	USP	14h 54'53"
Green jersey - Robbie McEwen (Aus)	LOT	93 pts
Red and white jersey - Paolo Bettini (Ita)	QSD	19 pts
White jersey - Matthias Kessler (Ger)	TMO	14h 56'07"

5th stage: Amiens/Chartres - 200,5 km

1.	Stuart O'Grady (Aus)	COF	5h 05'58"
2.	Jakob Piil (Den)	CSC	s.t
3.	Sandy Casar (Fra)	FDJ	s.t
4.	Thomas Voeckler (Fra)	BLB	s.t
5.	Magnus Bäckstedt (Swe)	ALB	+ 3"

Yellow jersey - Thomas Voeckler (Fra)	BLB	20h 03'49"
Green jersey - Robbie McEwen (Aus)	LOT	113 pts
Red and white jersey - Paolo Bettini (Ita)	QSD	19 pts
White jersey - Thomas Voeckler (Fra)	BLB	20h 03'49"

6th stage: Bonneval/Angers - 196 km

1.	Tom Boonen (Bel)	QSD	4h 33'41"
2.	Stuart O'Grady (Aus)	COF	s.t
3.	Erik Zabel (Ger)	TMO	s.t
4.	Danilo Hondo (Ger)	GST	s.t
5.	Baden Cooke (Aus)	FDJ	s.t

Yellow jersey - Thomas Voeckler (Fra)	BLB	24h 37'30"
Green jersey - Stuart O'Grady (Aus)	COF	115 pts
Red and white jersey - Paolo Bettini (Ita)	QSD	19 pts
White jersey - Thomas Voeckler (Fra)	BLB	24h 37'30"

7th stage: Châteaubriant/St-Brieuc - 204,5 km

1.	Filippo Pozzato (Ita)	FAS	4h 31'34"
2.	Iker Flores (Esp)	EUS	s.t
3.	Francisco Mancebo (Esp)	IBB	s.t
4.	Laurent Brochard (Fra)	A2R	+ 10"
5.	Sébastien Hinault (Fra)	C.A	s.t

Yellow jersey - Thomas Voeckler (Fra)	BLB	29h 09'14"
Green jersey - Stuart O'Grady (Aus)	COF	131 pts
Red and white jersey - Paolo Bettini (Ita)	QSD	20 pts
White jersey - Thomas Voeckler (Fra)	BLB	29h 09'14"

8th stage: Lamballe/Quimper - 168 km

1.	Thor Hushovd (Nor)	C.A	3h 54'22"
2.	Kim Kirchen (Lux)	FAS	s.t
3.	Erik Zabel (Ger)	TMO	s.t
4.	Robbie McEwen (Aus)	LOT	s.t
5.	Andreas Klöden (Ger)	TMO	s.t

Yellow jersey - Thomas Voeckler (Fra)	BLB	33h 03'36"
Green jersey - Robbie McEwen (Aus)	LOT	158 pts
Red and white jersey - Paolo Bettini (Ita)	QSD	20 pts
White jersey - Thomas Voeckler (Fra)	BLB	33h 03'36"

9th stage: St-Léonard de Noblat/Guéret - 160,5 km

1.	Robbie McEwen (Aus)	LOT	3h 32'55"
2.	Thor Hushovd (Nor)	C.A	s.t
3.	Stuart O'Grady (Aus)	COF	s.t
4.	Jérôme Pineau (Fra)	BLB	s.t
5.	Erik Zabel (Ger)	TMO	s.t

Yellow jersey - Thomas Voeckler (Fra)	BLB	36h 36'31"
Green jersey - Robbie McEwen (Aus)	LOT	195 pts
Red and white jersey - Paolo Bettini (Ita)	QSD	20 pts
White jersey - Thomas Voeckler (Fra)	BLB	36h 36'31"

10th stage: Limoges/St-Flour - 237 km

1.	Richard Virenque (Fra)	QSD	6h 00'24"
2.	Andreas Klöden (Ger)	TMO	+ 5'19"
3.	Erik Zabel (Ger)	TMO	s.t
4.	Francisco Mancebo (Esp)	IBB	s.t
5.	Thomas Voeckler (Fra)	BLB	s.t

Yellow jersey - Thomas Voeckler (Fra)	BLB	42h 42'14"
Green jersey - Robbie McEwen (Aus)	LOT	195 pts
Red and white jersey - Richard Virenque (Fra)	QSD	73 pts
White jersey - Thomas Voeckler (Fra)	BLB	42h 42'14"

11st stage: St-Flour/Figeac - 164 km

1.	David Moncoutié (Fra)	COF	3h 54'58"
2.	Juan Antonio Flecha (Esp)	FAS	+ 2'15"
3.	Egoi Martinez de Esteban (Esp)	EUS	+ 2'17"
4.	Thor Hushovd (Nor)	C.A	+ 5'58"
5.	Erik Zabel (Ger)	TMO	s.t

Yellow jersey - Thomas Voeckler (Fra)	BLB	46h 43'10"
Green jersey - Robbie McEwen (Aus)	LOT	210 pts
Red and white jersey - Richard Virenque (Fra)	QSD	84 pts
White jersey - Thomas Voeckler (Fra)	BLB	46h 43'10"

12nd stage: Castelsarrasin/La Mongie - 197,5 km

1.	Ivan Basso (Ita)	CSC	5h 03'58"
2.	Lance Armstrong (Usa)	USP	s.t
3.	Andreas Klöden (Ger)	TMO	+ 20"
4.	Francisco Mancebo (Esp)	IBB	+ 24"
5.	Carlos Sastre (Esp)	CSC	+ 33"

Yellow jersey - Thomas Voeckler (Fra)	BLB	51h 51'07"
Green jersey - Robbie McEwen (Aus)	LOT	210 pts
Red and white jersey - Richard Virenque (Fra)	QSD	95 pts
White jersey - Thomas Voeckler (Fra)	BLB	51h 51'07"

13rd stage: Lannemezan/Plateau de Beille - 205,5 km

1.	Lance Armstrong (Usa)	USP	6h 04'38"
2.	Ivan Basso (Ita)	CSC	s.t
3.	Georg Totschnig (Aut)	GST	+ 1'05"
4.	Andreas Klöden (Ger)	TMO	+ 1'27"
5.	Francisco Mancebo (Esp)	IBB	s.t

Yellow jersey - Thomas Voeckler (Fra)	BLB	58h 00'27"
Green jersey - Robbie McEwen (Aus)	LOT	210 pts
Red and white jersey - Richard Virenque (Fra)	QSD	128 pts
White jersey - Thomas Voeckler (Fra)	BLB	58h 00'27"

14th stage: Carcassonne/Nîmes - 192,5 km

1.	Aitor Gonzalez Jimenez (Esp)	FAS	4h 18'32"
2.	Nicolas Jalabert (Fra)	PHO	+ 25"
3.	Christophe Mengin (Fra)	FDJ	s.t
4.	Pierrick Fedrigo (Fra)	C.A	+ 29"
5.	Peter Wrolich (Aut)	GST	+ 31"

Yellow jersey - Thomas Voeckler (Fra)	BLB	62h 33'11"
Green jersey - Robbie McEwen (Aus)	LOT	225 pts
Red and white jersey - Richard Virenque (Fra)	QSD	128 pts
White jersey - Thomas Voeckler (Fra)	BLB	62h 33'11"

15th stage: Valréas/Villard-de-Lans - 180,5 km

1.	Lance Armstrong (Usa)	USP	4h 40'30"
2.	Ivan Basso (Ita)	CSC	s.t
3.	Jan Ullrich (Ger)	TMO	+ 3"
4.	Andreas Klöden (Ger)	TMO	+ 6"
5.	Levi Leipheimer (Usa)	RAB	+ 13"

Yellow jersey - Lance Armstrong (Usa)	USP	67h 13'43"
Green jersey - Robbie McEwen (Aus)	LOT	225 pts
Red and white jersey - Richard Virenque (Fra)	QSD	177 pts
White jersey - Thomas Voeckler (Fra)	BLB	67h 23'11"

16th stage: Bourg d'Oisans/L'Alpe d'Huez - 15,5 km (Team time trial)

1.	Lance Armstrong (Usa)	USP	39'41"
2.	Jan Ullrich (Ger)	TMO	+ 1'01"
3.	Andreas Klöden (Ger)	TMO	+ 1'41"
4.	José Azevedo (Por)	USP	+ 1'45"
5.	Santos Gonzalez Capilla (Esp)	PHO	+ 2'11"

Lance Armstrong takes the Grand Slam in the alpes. His latest victim? Andreas Kloden, passed in the final metres at Grand Bornand.

Just as effective in the time trials as in the mountains...

Yellow jersey - Lance Armstrong (Usa)	USP	67h 53'24"
Green jersey - Robbie McEwen (Aus)	LOT	225 pts
Red and white jersey - Richard Virenque (Fra)	QSD	177 pts
White jersey - Thomas Voeckler (Fra)	BLB	68h 09'28"

17th stage: Bourg d'Oisans/Le Grand-Bornand - 204,5 km

1.	Lance Armstrong (Usa)	USP	6h 11'52"
2.	Andreas Klöden (Ger)	TMO	s.t
3.	Jan Ullrich (Ger)	TMO	+ 1"
4.	Ivan Basso (Ita)	CSC	s.t
5.	Floyd Landis (Usa)	USP	+ 13"

Yellow jersey - Lance Armstrong (Usa)	USP	74h 04'56"
Green jersey - Robbie McEwen (Aus)	LOT	225 pts
Red and white jersey - Richard Virenque (Fra)	QSD	226 pts
White jersey - Thomas Voeckler (Fra)	BLB	74h 26'08"

18th stage: Annemasse/Lons-le-Saunier - 166,5 km

1.	Juan Miguel Mercado (Esp)	QSD	4h 04'03"
2.	J. Vicente Garcia Acosta (Esp)	IBB	s.t
3.	Dmitriy Fofonov (Kaz)	COF	+ 11"
4.	Sébastien Joly (Fra)	C.A	s.t
5.	Marc Lotz (Ned)	RAB	s.t

Yellow jersey - Lance Armstrong (Usa)	USP	78h 20'28"
Green jersey - Robbie McEwen (Aus)	LOT	238 pts
Red and white jersey - Richard Virenque (Fra)	QSD	226 pts
White jersey - Thomas Voeckler (Fra)	BLB	78h 41'40"

19th stage: Team time trial à Besançon - 55 km

1.	Lance Armstrong (Usa)	USP	1h 06'49"
2.	Jan Ullrich (Ger)	TMO	+ 1'01"
3.	Andreas Klöden (Ger)	TMO	+ 1'27"
4.	Floyd Landis (Usa)	USP	+ 2'25"
5.	Bobby Julich (Usa)	CSC	+ 2'48"

Yellow jersey - Lance Armstrong (Usa)	USP	79h 27'17"
Green jersey - Robbie McEwen (Aus)	LOT	238 pts
Red and white jersey - Richard Virenque (Fra)	QSD	226 pts
White jersey - Vladimir Karpets (Rus)	IBB	79h 52'28"

20th stage: Montereau/Paris (Champs Élysées) - 163 km

1.	Tom Boonen (Bel)	QSD	4h 08'26"
2.	Jean-Patrick Nazon (Fra)	A2R	s.t
3.	Danilo Hondo (Ger)	GST	s.t
4.	Robbie McEwen (Aus)	LOT	s.t
5.	Erik Zabel (Ger)	TMO	s.t

POINTS TABLE

1.	Robbie McEwen (Aus)	LOT	272 pts
2.	Thor Hushovd (Nor)	C.A	247 pts
3.	Erik Zabel (Ger)	TMO	245 pts

MOUNTAIN STANDINGS

1.	Richard Virenque (Fra)	QSD	226 pts
2.	Lance Armstrong (Usa)	USP	172 pts
3.	Michael Rasmussen (Den)	RAB	119 pts

ALL ASCENTION OF THE 2004 TOUR

(classed as 2nd, 1st and "Hors category)

STAGE **10**
Col de Neronne /2nd cat. : Richard Virenque (Fra)
Col du Pas de Peyrol / 1st cat. : Richard Virenque (Fra)
Col de Prat de Bouc / 2nd cat. : Richard Virenque (Fra)

STAGE **11**
Côte de Montsalvy / 2nd cat. : David Moncoutié (Fra)

STAGE **12**
Col d'Aspin / 1st cat. : Michael Rasmussen (Den)
La Mongie / 1st cat. : Ivan Basso (Ita)

STAGE **13**
Col du Portet d'Aspet / 2nd cat. : Sylvain Chavanel (Fra)
Col de la Core / 1st cat. : Sylvain Chavanel (Fra)
Col de Latrape / 2nd cat. : Sylvain Chavanel (Fra)
Col d'Agnès / 1st cat. : Michael Rasmussen (Den)
Plateau de Beille / Hors cat. : Lance Armstrong (Usa)

STAGE **15**
Col des Limouches / 2nd cat. : Richard Virenque (Fra)
Col de l'Echarasson - 1st cat. : Richard Virenque (Fra)
Col de Chalimont - 2nd cat. : Richard Virenque (Fra)
Villard-de-Lans - 2nd cat. : Lance Armstrong (Usa)

STAGE **16**
Alpe d'Huez - Hors cat. : Lance Armstrong (Usa)

STAGE **17**
Col du Glandon - 1st cat. : Gilberto Simoni (Ita)
Col de la Madeleine - Hors cat. : Gilberto Simoni (Ita)
Col de Tamié - 2nd cat. : Richard Virenque (Fra)
Col de la Forclaz - 1st cat. : Richard Virenque (Fra)
Col de la Croix-Fry - 1st cat. : Lance Armstrong (Usa)

STAGE **18**
Col de la Faucille - 2nd cat. : Juan Miguel Mercado (Esp)

FINAL OVERALL CLASSIFICATIONS

1.	**Lance Armstrong (Usa) (average: 40,560 km/h)**	**USP**	**83h 36'02"**
2.	Andreas Klöden (Ger)	TMO	+ 6'19"
3.	Ivan Basso (Ita)	CSC	+ 6'40"
4.	Jan Ullrich (Ger)	TMO	+ 8'50"
5.	José Azevedo (Por)	USP	+ 14'30"
6.	Francisco Mancebo (Esp)	IBB	+ 18'01"
7.	Georg Totschnig (Aut)	GST	+ 18'27"
8.	Carlos Sastre (Esp)	CSC	+ 19'51"
9.	Levi Leipheimer (Usa)	RAB	+ 20'12"
10.	Oscar Pereiro (Esp)	PHO	+ 22'54"
11.	Pietro Caucchioli (Ita)	ALB	+ 24'21"
12.	Christophe Moreau (Fra)	C.A	+ 24'36"
13.	Vladimir Karpets (Rus)	IBB	+ 25'11"
14.	Michael Rasmussen (Den)	RAB	+ 27'16"
15.	Richard Virenque (Fra)	QSD	+ 28'11"

188 Competitors

US POSTAL - BERRY FLOOR

1.	ARMSTRONG Lance (Usa)	**1st**	**en 83h36'02"**
2.	AZEVEDO José (Por)	**5th**	+ 14'30"
3.	BELTRAN Manuel (Esp)	46th	+ 1h26'28"
4.	EKIMOV Viatcheslav (Rus)	80th	+ 2h16'44"
5.	HINCAPIE George (Usa)	33rd	+ 1h04'09"
6.	LANDIS Floyd (Usa)	23rd	+ 42'55"
7.	NOVAL Benjamin (Esp)	66th	+ 1h57'41"
8.	PADRNOS Pavel (Cze)	79th	+ 2h16'19"
9.	RUBIERA José Luis (Esp)	19th	+ 32'50"

T.MOBILE

11.	ULLRICH Jan (Ger)	**4th**	+ 8'50"
12.	ALDAG Rolf (Ger)	69th	+ 2h02'55"
13.	BOTERO Santiago (Col)	75th	+ 2h12'32"
14.	GUERINI Giuseppe (Ita)	25th	+ 47'07"
15.	IVANOV Serguei (Rus)	57th	+ 1h49'51"
16.	KESSLER Matthias (Ger)	DNS	11st stage
17.	KLÖDEN Andreas (Ger)	**2nd**	+ 6'19"
18.	NARDELLO Daniele (Ita)	48th	+ 1h35'26"
19.	ZABEL Erik (Ger)	59th	+ 1h50'21"

PHONAK

21.	HAMILTON Tyler (Usa)	*Abandon*	13rd stage
22.	ELMIGER Martin (Sui)	108th	+ 2h47'22"
23.	GONZALEZ CAPILLA Santos (Esp)	31st	+ 1h01'01"
24.	GRABSCH Bert (Ger)	81st	+ 2h17'14"
25.	GUTIERREZ CATALUÑA J. Enrique (Esp)	28th	+ 50'39"
26.	JALABERT Nicolas (Fra)	82nd	+ 2h18'42"
27.	PEREIRO Oscar (Esp)	**10th**	+ 22'54"
28.	PEREZ FERNANDEZ Santi (Esp)	49th	+ 1h35'54"
29.	SEVILLA Oscar (Esp)	24th	+ 45'19"

EUSKALTEL - EUSKADI

31.	MAYO Iban (Esp)	DNS	15th stage
32.	CAMAÑO Iker (Esp)	26th	+ 47'14"
33.	ETXEBARRIA David (Esp)	77th	+ 2h14'42"
34.	ETXEBARRIA Unai (Ven)	91st	+ 2h30'47"
35.	FLORES Iker (Esp)	60th	+ 1h50'49"
36.	LANDALUZE Iñigo (Esp)	52nd	+ 1h39'52"
37.	MARTINEZ de ESTEBAN Egoi (Esp)	41st	+ 1h15'10"
38.	ZUBELDIA Haimar (Esp)	*Abandon*	13rd stage

FASSA BORTOLO

41.	PETACCHI Alessandro (Ita)	DNS	6th stage
42.	BRUSEGHIN Marzio (Ita)	68th	+ 1h59'21"
43.	CANCELLARA Fabian (Sui)	109th	+ 2h48'42"
44.	FLECHA Juan Antonioi (Esp)	93rd	+ 2h33'38"
45.	GONZALEZ JIMENEZ Aitori (Esp)	45th	+ 1h17'23"
46.	KIRCHEN Kim (Lux)	63rd	+ 1h55'52"
47.	POZZATO Filippo (Ita)	116th	+ 2h54'55"
48.	TOSATTO Matteo (Ita)	110e	+ 2h49'06"
49.	VELO Marco (Ita)	*Abandon*	3rd stage

CRÉDIT AGRICOLE

51.	MOREAU Christophe (Fra)	12nd	+ 24'36"
52.	BOTCHAROV Alexandre (Rus)	36th	+ 1h10'54"
53.	DEAN Julian (Nzl)	127th	+ 3h02'09"
54.	FEDRIGO Pierrick (Fra)	76th	+ 2h13'14"
55.	HALGAND Patrice (Fra)	39th	+ 1h12'24"
56.	HINAULT Sébastien (Fra)	*Abandon*	10th stage
57.	HUSHOVD Thor (Nor)	104th	+ 2h42'45"
58.	JOLY Sébastien (Fra)	146th	+ 3h43'18"
59.	SALMON Benoît (Fra)	83rd	+ 2h24'49"

CSC

61.	BASSO Ivan (Ita)	**3rd**	+ 6'40"
62.	ARVESEN Kurt-Asle (Nor)	123rd	+ 3h00'35"
63.	BARTOLI Michele (Ita)	*Abandon*	17th stage
64.	JULICH Bobby (Usa)	40th	+ 1h12'42"
65.	PERON Andrea (Ita)	64th	+ 1h56'29"
66.	PIIL Jakob (Den)	DNS	15th stage
67.	SASTRE Carlos (Esp)	**8th**	+ 19'51"
68.	SØRENSEN Nicki (Den)	88th	+ 2h27'39"
69.	VOIGT Jens (Ger)	35th	+ 1h07'07"

ILLES BALEARS - BANESTO

71.	MANCEBO Francisco (Esp)	**6th**	+ 18'01"
72.	BECKE Daniel (Ger)	*Abandon*	17th stage
73.	GARCIA ACOSTA J. Vicente (Esp)	86th	+ 2h26'14"
74.	GUTIERREZ PALACIOS J. Ivan (Esp)	51st	+ 1h39'16"
75.	KARPETS Vladimir (Rus)	13rd	+ 25'11"
76.	MENCHOV Denis (Rus)	*Abandon*	13rd stage
77.	OSA Aitor (Esp)	50th	+ 1h38'38"
78.	PRADERA Mikel (Esp)	*Abandon*	12nd stage
79.	ZANDIO Xabier (Esp)	97th	+ 2h35'48"

...For Lance Armstrong, the sixth consecutive success in the Tour de France came with no serious adversaries in sight.

GEROLSTEINER

81. TOTSCHNIG Georg (Aut)	**7th**	+ 18'27"
82. HASELBACHER René (Aut)	DNS	7th stage
83. HONDO Danilo (Ger)	106th	+ 2h46'54"
84. LANG Sebastian (Ger)	78th	+ 2h15'31"
85. MONTGOMERY Sven (Sui)	*Abandon*	7th stage
86. PESCHEL Uwe (Ger)	125th	+ 3h01'36"
87. SCHOLZ Ronny (Ger)	53rd	+ 1h42'44"
88. WEGMANN Fabian (Ger)	*Abandon*	13rd stage
89. WROLICH Peter (Aut)	113rd	+ 2h51'06"

COFIDIS

91. O'GRADY Stuart (Aus)	61st	+ 1h51'41"
92. BESSY Frédéric (Fra)	DNS	3rd stage
93. CASPER Jimmy (Fra)	147th	+ 3h55'49"
94. EDALEINE Christophe (Fra)	141st	+ 3h22'39"
95. ENGOULVENT Jimmy (Fra)	138th	+ 3h13'55"
96. FOFONOV Dmitriy (Kaz)	87th	+ 2h26'22"
97. MONCOUTIÉ David (Fra)	34th	+ 1h04'37"
98. TOMBAK Janek (Est)	*Abandon*	17th stage
99. FARAZIJN Peter (Bel)	107th	+ 2h46'56"

QUICK STEP - DAVITAMON

101. VIRENQUE Richard (Fra)	15th	+ 28'11"
102. BETTINI Paolo (Ita)	58th	+ 1h50'10"
103. BOONEN Tom (Bel)	120th	+ 2h59'07"
104. BRAMATI Davide (Ita)	TC	16th stage
105. DUFAUX Laurent (Sui)	67th	+ 1h58'22"
106. KNAVEN Servais (Ned)	142nd	+ 3h23'07"
107. MERCADO Juan Miguel (Esp)	37th	+ 1h11'31"
108. ROGERS Michael (Aus)	22nd	+ 41'39"
109. ZANINI Stefano (Ita)	126th	+ 3h01'39"

LIBERTY Seguros

111. HERAS Roberto (Esp)	DNS	17th stage
112. BARANOWSKI Dariusz (Pol)	94th	+ 2h33'54"
113. DAVIS Allan (Aus)	98th	+ 2h36'16"
114. GONZALEZ de GALDEANO Igor (Esp)	44th	+ 1h16'45"
115. HRUSKA Jan (Cze)	117th	+ 2h56'01"
116. NOZAL Isidro (Esp)	73rd	+ 2h10'33"
117. SERRANO Marcos (Esp)	54th	+ 1h42'53"
118. VANDEVELDE Christian (Usa)	56th	+ 1h48'11"
119. VICIOSO Angel (Esp)	*Abandon*	10th stage

Brioches LA BOULANGÈRE

121. CHAVANEL Sylvain (Fra)	30th	+ 54'43"
122. BENETEAU Walter (Fra)	102nd	+ 2h38'36"
123. CHARTEAU Anthony (Fra)	103rd	+ 2h41'31"
124. HARY Maryan (Fra)	TC	5th stage
125. LEFÈVRE Laurent (Fra)	DNS	17th stage
126. PINEAU Jérôme (Fra)	27th	+ 47'53"
127. RENIER Franck (Fra)	114th	+ 2h53'16"
128. ROUS Didier (Fra)	*Abandon*	17th stage
129. VOECKLER Thomas (Fra)	18th	+ 31'12"

ALESSIO - BIANCHI

131. BÄCKSTEDT Magnus (Swe)	*Abandon*	11st stage
132. BALDATO Fabio (Ita)	135th	+ 3h10'46"
133. BERTOLINI Alessandro (Ita)	DNS	17th stage
134. CAUCCHIOLI Pietro (Ita)	11st	+ 24'21"
135. HVASTIJA Martin (Slo)	DNS	9th stage
136. LJUNGQVIST Marcus (Swe)	132nd	+ 3h07'51"
137. MØLLER Claus Michael (Den)	70th	+ 2h04'01"
138. NOE' Andrea (Ita)	99th	+ 2h36'36"
139. SUNDERLAND Scott (Aus)	96th	+ 2h35'20"

AG2R Prévoyance

141. BROCHARD Laurent (Fra)	29th	+ 51'35"
142. ASTARLOZA Mikel (Esp)	62nd	+ 1h55'04"
143. DUMOULIN Samuel (Fra)	DNS	9th stage
144. GOUBERT Stéphane (Fra)	20th	+ 37'11"
145. KIRSIPUU Jaan (Est)	*Abandon*	9th stage
146. KRIVTSOV Yuriy (Ukr)	95th	+ 2h34'16"
147. NAZON Jean-Patrick (Fra)	137th	+ 3h13'10"
148. PORTAL Nicolas (Fra)	72nd	+ 2h09'45"
149. SCANLON Mark (Irl)	89th	+ 2h27'49"

RABOBANK

151. LEIPHEIMER Levy (Usa)	**9th**	+ 20'12"
152. BOOGERD Michael (Ned)	74th	+ 2h10'39"
153. DE GROOT Bram (Ned)	111st	+ 2h49'33"
154. DEKKER Erik (Ned)	133rd	+ 3h07'54"
155. KROON Karsten (Ned)	115th	+ 2h53'22"
156. LOTZ Marc (Ned)	90th	+ 2h29'48"
157. NIERMANN Grischa (Ger)	65th	+ 1h57'25"
158. RASMUSSEN Michael (Den)	14th	+ 27'16"
159. WAUTERS Marc (Bel)	112nd	+ 2h50'16"

FDJEUX.COM

161. McGEE Bradley (Aus)	*Abandon*	5th stage
162. CASAR Sandy (Fra)	16th	+ 28'53"
163. COOKE Baden (Aus)	139th	+ 3h15'45"
164. DA CRUZ Carlos (Fra)	85th	+ 2h25'43"
165. EISEL Bernhard (Aut)	131st	+ 3h05'44"
166. GUESDON Frédéric (Fra)	129th	+ 3h03'40"
167. MENGIN Christophe (Fra)	84th	+ 2h25'08"
168. ROBIN Jean-Cyril (Fra)	47th	+ 1h32'06"
169. WILSON Matthew (Aus)	144th	+ 3h36'31"

SAECO

171. SIMONI Gilberto (Ita)	17th	+ 29'00"
172. CASAGRANDA Stefano (Ita)	DNS	9th stage
173. CELESTINO Mirko (Ita)	*Abandon*	10th stage
174. COMMESSO Salvatore (Ita)	124th	+ 3h01'21"
175. GLOMSER Gerrit (Aut)	*Abandon*	13rd stage
176. LOOSLI David (Sui)	105th	+ 2h44'24"
177. LUDEWIG Jörg (Ger)	55th	+ 1h44'57"
178. PETROV Evgueni (Rus)	38th	+ 1h12'24"
179. SABALIAUSKAS Marius (Ltu)	42nd	+ 1h15'15"

LOTTO - DOMO

181. McEWEN Robbie (Aus)	122nd	+ 2h59'18"
182. BRANDT Christophe (Bel)	DNS	7th stage
183. GATES Nick (Aus)	TC	1st stage
184. MARICHAL Thierry (Bel)	101st	+ 2h37'58"
185. MERCKX Axel (Bel)	21st	+ 39'54"
186. MOERENHOUT Koos (Ned)	100th	+ 2h36'48"
187. VANSEVENANT Wim (Bel)	140th	+ 3h22'15"
188. VERBRUGGHE Rik (Bel)	43rd	+ 1h16'42"
189. VIERHOUTEN Aart (Ned)	TC	16th stage

DOMINA VACANZE

191. CIPOLLINI Mario (Ita)	DNS	6th stage
192. FAGNINI GianMatteo (Ita)	*Abandon*	2nd stage
193. GIUNTI Massimo (Ita)	*Abandon*	17th stage
194. MARINANGELI Sergio (Ita)	DNS	13rd stage
195. MORI Massimiliano (Ita)	121st	+ 2h59'12"
196. SCARPONI Michele (Ita)	32nd	+ 1h03'01"
197. SECCHIARI Francesco (Ita)	143rd	+ 3h25'37"
198. SIMEONI Filippo (Ita)	118th	+ 2h56'30"
199. VALOTI Paolo (Ita)	*Abandon*	15th stage

RAGT Semences - MG ROVER

201. RINERO Christophe (Fra)	92nd	+ 2h31'34"
202. AUGER Guillaume (Fra)	136th	+ 3h11'10"
203. BOURQUENOUD Pierre (Sui)	130th	+ 3h04'47"
204. BOUVARD Gilles (Fra)	128th	+ 3h03'28"
205. CALZATI Sylvain (Fra)	71st	+ 2h09'34"
206. FINOT Frédéric (Fra)	145th	+ 3h39'31"
207. LAURENT Christophe (Fra)	134th	+ 3h09'38"
208. MARTIN Ludovic (Fra)	119th	+ 2h59'00"
209. SEIGNEUR Eddy (Fra)	TC	4th stage

PARTICIPATION

- 38 riders took part in their first Tour de France. Viatcheslav Ekimov took part in his 14th Tour, Richard Virenque and Marc Wauters in their 12th.

3 OLDEST

EKIMOV Viatcheslav (38 ans)	04/02/1966
SUNDERLAND Scott (37 ans)	28/11/1966
CIPOLLINI Mario (37 ans)	22/03/1967

3 YOUNGEST

POZZATO Filippo (22 ans)	10/09/1981
CANCELLARA Fabian (23 ans)	18/03/1981
EISEL Bernhard (23 ans)	17/02/1981

EX WINNERS OF THE TOUR TAKING THE START — 2

Jan Ullrich (1997) and of course Lance Armstrong (1999, 2000, 2001, 2002 and 2003)

STAGE WINNERS AT THE START — 45

ARMSTRONG Lance (Usa)	16 + 5 (2004)
CIPOLLINI Mario (Ita)	12
ZABEL Erik (Ger)	12
ULLRICH Jan (Ger)	7
VIRENQUE Richard (Fra)	6 + 1 (2004)
DEKKER Erik (Ned)	4
PETACCHI Alessandro (Ita)	4
BOTERO Santiago (Col)	3
KIRSIPUU Jaan (Est)	3 + 1 (2004)
McEWEN Robbie (Aus)	3 + 2 (2004)

- 57 riders at the start are in the UCI top 100.

-26 different nationalities were represented. The majority were French (40 riders), followed by the spaniards (31), the Italians (28) the Germans (16) the Australians (9) the Belgians and Dutch (8

THE METAMORPHOSIS OF HERAS!

Out of contention two months earlier on the Tour de France for which he had proclaimed himself a favourite, the rider from Bejar won the Tour of Spain for the third time, even though he was troubled throughout by the challenge of Santi Perez.

For the last few years La Vuelta has begun with a team time trial. Already crowned in the Tour de France, the US Postal team comes with a very different face to that present in the French event, only Betran and Landis being here – beat off T Mobile, led by Alexandre Vinokourov, absent in France, and the Illes Balears – Banesto team led by " Paco" Mancebo and the Russian Denis Menchov. This success by the American postmen permits them to keep the lead for the first half of this Vuelta. Johan Bruyneel's men have fun sharing the leader's jersey between them until Floyd Landis, who wore it on the first day, claimed it on a more permenant basis.

US POSTAL KEEP IT TO THEM

Max van Heeswijk, the flying Dutchman (for a day), then Benoit Joachim, the brave Luxembourg rider (for forty eight hours) and Manuel Beltran (leader of the 5th and 7th stages) swap the jersey before it once again sits on the shoulders of Floyd Landis, following a first time trial around Almussafes. Between times, the sprinters had some fun. Alessandro Petacchi, seeking revenge after pulling out of the Tour de France, shows his dominance 300 metres from the line, impeccably helped by his devoted team mates Ongarato, Velo and Trenti. At Soria, under driving rain, a dispersed peloton shows itself. Alejandro Valverde, the young rider from Mercia makes easy going of passing a group of ten riders who lead the main group by a few seconds. Benoit Joachim, member (with Kevin Hulsmans, Andy Flickinger and Thorwald Veneberg) of a breakaway with a lead of up to 9 mins 40sec, scored enough points in the sprints to snatch the leader's jersey from his Dutch team mate. After the always impressive Alessandro Petacchi takes the honours at Saragossa, the first mountain stage comes. Even if the climb of Puerto de Torremiro (2nd category) followed by that at Morella (3rd category) is nothing to write home about, this day is rich in information. First, there's a repeat of the PDM affair of the 1990's, with the retirements of the T-Mobile riders, Botero, Hiekmann, and Wesemann on the fourth day, at the same time that Alexandre Vinokourov, one of the hot favourites is relegated along with team mate Andreas Klier to a deficit of more than 17 minutes at the line! The cause of this massacre? Opinions vary but it seems there was a problem with the food at their hotel. The only member of the team to come through with no problems is the vegetarian Cadel Evans!

The other big news of the day is the stage win for the Russian Denis Menchov, who's push for the line 500 metres out left those following breathless. And they were numerous. With the exception of Garzelli, Di Luca and Jaksche, nearly a minute behind, the rest of the favourites come in bunched and as could be expected, this stage is too complicated for Benoit Joachim, having to pass his leader's jersey to team mate Manuel Beltran.
The waltz continues at US Postal.

The next day's finish at Castellon de la Plana is too steep for Alessandro Petacchi. But Erik Zabel, the only one seeming capable of troubling the Italian, finds refuge with Oscar Freire, who with a magnificent sprint deprives the German of victory.

Four different leaders in five days for US Postal!
Floyd Landis (top left , first to wear the leader's jersey, left it the next day to team mate Max van Heeswijk (top right), himself displaced by Benoit Joachim (bottom left), who keeps it just two days before giving it up to Manuel Beltran...

WHEN PETACCHI FEELS GOOD...

"Today, for the first time since the start, I felt really good"... With this sentence, Alessandro Petacchi commented on his third stage win of this Vuelta. A very conventional seventh stage, with an attack of seven men, caught up 16 kilometers from the line, where the Italian from the Fassa Bortolo team once again beat Eric Zabel to the honours.

The first time trial arrives after a week of racing. A flat course around the Ford factory (one of the sponsors of the event), in Almussafes. Recently declared Olympic Champion, Tyler Hamilton confirms his form by taking first place, in front of two US Postal riders, the Colombian Victor Hugo Pena and the gold jersey rider from the first day, Floyd Landis, who limits the damage, takes back that same jersey. A logical victory then for the leader of the Phonak team. But a victory completely devalued a few days later when he is tested positive for blood doping, following a new type of test. The same type of cheating was probably responsible for his success in Athens, but the "B" sample was spoilt in the laboratory so the result stands.
Coming back to the Vuelta time trial, it's now time to sort things out. Mancebo concedes 57 sec to the disqualified winner, forty less

Whether it be on the Tour of Aragon or the Vuelta, Alessandro Petacchi keeps to his habits in Saragossa: he raises his arms!

Joachim, Flickinger, Hulsmansand Veneberg animated one of the early stages of the Vuelta. Efforts always reduced to nothing by the sprinting teams...

than to Alejandro Valverde and Roberto Heras. These men seem to be ahead of the pack when we take into account the problems of Hamilton and Vinokourov…

The day after the first time trial, a real mountain stage takes place. The Alto de Aicana, perched on the heights over Alicante, permits Roberto Heras, with the magnificent help of Isidro Nozal to seriously mount in the overall ratings. The final kilometers of the ascention permit the two Liberty Seguros riders, Heras and Nozal as well as the tiny but surprising Jorge Ferrio (Paternina), and the Italian Leonardo Piepoli to make their mark. The latter attacks in the last 400metres to take a first win in a Grand Tour, to add to his many successes in less prestigious races. This high altitude finish leaves many by the wayside, such as Tyler Hamilton (who retires anyway a few days later), Damiana Cunego, and even Floyd Landis, who just the same manages to keep his leader's jersey.

We don't completely quit the mountains in the next day's stage to Xorret deCati. It's the third time that the Vuelta comes here and it is also the third time that a Jimenez takes the win. After the late José Maria won in 1998, Eladio (no relation) took his first win as a pro. Apparently motivated in coming back to the scene of past glory, he slips into the right breakaway in the company of three sprinters, Freire, O'Grady, and Zabel. It's O'Grady who crosses the line in second place, seconds before Oscar Freire! A wait of more than four minutes is needed before seeing the overall leaders appear. Valverde and Heras take advantage of the situation to claw back thirty seconds from their main rivals. Every little bit counts! Floyd Landis keeps the leader's jersey, much longed after by Alejandro Valverde who reduces his deficit to just nine seconds.

SANTI PEREZ SHOWS HIS FACE

Going towards Caravaca de la Cruz, Alejandro Valverde has a fright and David Zabriskie, the talented young rider for U S Postal finds some happiness. The happiness coming with a good attack lasting 160 kilometers on his own. There were echoes of Thierry Marie and his famous exploit in Le Havre in the 1991 Tour de France. On the other hand, we feared the worse for the principal attraction of the Spanish media, Alejandro Valverde, victim of a crash at the start of the stage, after Zabriskie had pulled away. With the help of his team mates the young rider from Murcia was able to catch up with the peloton which was to finish on the heels of Zabriskie despite his one time lead of 18 mins 40 sec! The rest day which follows is also the occasion of the transfer to the region of Extremadure, not far from the Portugese

Alejandro Valverde, a little less at ease than in 2003?

border. The next day's menu is not easy to digest for many in the peloton. A finish at altitude for a start, a hard day's work. This will cause no problems for Roberto Heras, at the summit of his art on the final ascention of Calar alto. After a lot of effort from Nozal, revelation and adversary of his leader in the 2003 Vuelta, but still as unsuited to the mountains as ever. Heras doesn't spare the horses just short of the summit and builds up an unbeatable lead. It's also on this stage that we discover a certain Santi Perez, known only to the specialists and fairly discrete since his arrival in the Phonac team in 2003. He comes in second on the stage, preceding "Paco" Mancebo by 19 seconds and Alejandro Valverde who seems to be feeling the effects of his earlier accident, by almost a minute. Roberto Heras, who takes the jersey of the Leader on this occasion, is left wondering whether a new rival is going to be snapping at his heels!

If there's only one left, what is it? The final chance to shine for the sprinters (not including Freire at this stage). Sewn up by the Fassa Bortrolo team, the Malaga stage ends as predicted with a mass sprint... Of which Alessandro Petacchi comes out winner!

THE THREAT BECOMES EVIDENT...

The stage taking the peloton to Granada is a difficult one. A problem by the name of Alto de Monachil stands 22 kilometers from the line. Santi Perez uses this as a springboard for his show. He passes the summit with an advance of 33seconds, increasing to 46 seconds at the line, ahead of Valverde, Heras, Nozaland Mancebo. Out of form for the past two years following the death of his partnerin a road accident, at last things seem to be coming into place. Something to cheer up his Phonak team manager after the Tyler Hamilton affair.

Inspired by the time trial at the Alpe d'Huez, the Vuelta now has its own mountain time trial. Relatively rare in the French event this is a style of stage more often seen in these parts.

Transformed since his success the day before, Santi Perez uses the stage to increase his lead. He does the 29 kilometers from Granada to the summit of the Sierra Nevada in little more than an hour, distancing Alejandro Valverde by 1min 07 sec, Roberto Heras, visibly out of touch at 1min 31 sec and Francisco Mancebo at more than three minutes! Not to mention the others, who are simply not in the same race. A race in which Santi Perez rides, at

The tactics employed this year in the Vuelta by the Liberty Seguros team is resumed here: Isidro Nozal does the hard work and Roberto Heras takes the glory.

A happy band at the depart from Malaga.

1 min 45 sec from Roberto Heras who just manages to keep his jersey with a lead of five seconds. The lead he has over Valverde!

Behind him however the main subject in the minds of the riders is the confirmation of the positive drug test on Tyler Hamilton. Once again, scandal takes over from sport...

Who would have thought the final days of the Vuelta would come down to a duel between Roberto Heras (left) and Santi Perez?

JULIA IN THE SHADOW OF HAMILTON

The stage at Caceres, the 16th on the race, suits the sprinters. The only problem being they're now very thin on the ground! With the notable exception of Erik Zabel, wearing the jersey of the leader on points. From now on it's the long distance specialists that have the advantage. Among them, a certain José Cayetano Julia, in his first Vuelta, and wearing the jersey of the Comunidad Valenciana–Kelme team. The young rider finds himself in the better half of a group of thirteen men which breaks up into several parts at the finishing line. However, in an attack by Pablo Lastras (Illes Balears), he finds himself distanced by a group including the Italians Di Luca and Spezialetti, the Slovenian Valjavec, the Colombian Ivan Parra, the American Cruz and the Basque Isasi. With a terrific effort he wipes out the deficit and mounts a counter attack. He then has two kilometers to ride for a superb victory, a month after his first on the Tour of Portugal.

The next stage passes the heights of Bejar, the home town of leader Roberto Heras. Will the ascention to the ski resort of La Covatilla permit the local hero to increase his overall lead? It's the question many are asking.
Very discrete this year, the compact Colombian hill specialist Felix Cardenas, has just one thing on his mind: to slip into an attack and increase his chances of taking the jersey of the best climber.
The first part of his plan works out. In the first kilometre! In the company of Zaballa, Gustov, Valjavec, Lopez de Munain and Arrieta, he goes for the solid attack which will continue until the line. As in 2000 and 2003, takes his mountain stage. The highlight of the day comes to pass 1200metres from the line, Santi Perez pulls away from Roberto Heras who until that moment looked in form and distances him by 32 seconds. Valverde, obviously not at his best, concedes three minutes to Perez who climbs to second place overall at 1 min 13 sec from Heras.

The traditional stage at Avila is a good one for Javier Pascual Rodriguez, who's thankless work in favour of Alejandro Valverde this year is rewarded with a sprint win over Ivan Parra, the Colombian ex team mate who now rides for the Café Baque team. The overall leaders finish in the same group. It's status quo.
D'Avila to Collado Villalba is the same sort of stage as that which will follow the next day. A big group, from which Constantino Zaballa extracts himself early on, precedes the peloton of the leaders by six minutes at the line. Things would then be sorted out the next day at the summit of Puerto de Navacerrada! The last finish at altitude, the last chance for Santi Perez to reverse the course of the race. Effectively, the Asturian

accelerates ahead of Heras 2kms from the summit. But Heras does not give up, losing thirty seconds but still keeping a lead of forty three before the final time trial in Madrid. The stage win goes to Guitierrez, team mate of Santi Perez and last survivor of an attack begun at the 10th kilometre.

INCERTITUDE UP TO THE LINE

Santi Perez doesn't consider himself a time trial specialist. And can he wipe out the lead of 43 seconds held by Roberto Heras. The 119 remaining contestants discover the sumptuous course to be used in the 2005 World Championship. In the shadows of the Casa de Campo, the survivors (the term seems fitting) of an exhausting Vuelta make their final effort of the competition. The German Bert Grabsch (Phonak Hearing Systems) for a long time holds the best time, but the following battle between the leaders will soon eclipse the performance of the German, finally to finish sixth. Of the four riders going for the podium, Alejandro Valverde is probably the fastest.

But the end of the season looms. The riders are tired, their enthusiasm worn. Valverde is exhausted, quite simply, and it's with a great deal of pain that he takes 14th place of the day at 1 min 17 sec from the winner. He will then, have to settle for 4th place in the Vuelta. Francisco Mancebo is more surprising. The Spanish champion confirms his third place in taking second in the time trial at seven seconds from the winner. But who will mount the highest step of the podium: Heras or Perez? The two riders set off at an electrifying pace on the final 28.2 kilometers of the Vuelta. The Jersey de Oro is at stake. He grits his teeth, shakes his head. The pain marks his reddened face and the first times are in the favour of Roberto Heras.

Roberto Heras makes a better start than Santiago Perez, who, more regular, takes a few seconds from his rival. The difference between the two riders never exceeds eight seconds. Heras and Perez fight it out. Santiago Perez comes out on top in the struggle making the best time of the day. Roberto Heras struggles a little towards the end. He finishes 4th conceding 13 seconds. The Jersey De Oro conserves a lead of 30 seconds over his rival to take the 59th Tour of Spain. Before ending we should note the fine performance of the young pro from Spain, Angel Gomez (Paternina- Costa de Almeria), at 24, taking eighth place in his first Vuelta at 13mins 08 sec from Roberto Heras. The succession is assured. ■

Carlos Sastre, Isidro Nozal, Francisco Mancebo, Luis Perez Rodriguez: as usual, the Spaniards take the honours in their national tour.

CLASSIFICATIONS

1st stage: Leon/Leon - 28 km (Team time trial)

1.	US POSTAL-BERRY FLOOR	USP	30'45"
2.	T.MOBILE	TMO	+ 31"
3.	ILLES BALEARS	IBB	+ 56"
4.	Com. Valenciana-KELME	KEL	+ 58"
5.	PHONAK	PHO	+ 1'01"
	Leader: Floyd Landis (Usa)	USP	30'45"

2nd stage: Leon/Burgos - 206 km

1.	Alessandro Petacchi (Ita)	FAS	5h 02'05"
2.	Erik Zabel (Ger)	TMO	m.t
3.	Oscar Freire (Esp)	RAB	s.t
4.	Stuart O'Grady (Aus)	COF	s.t
5.	Pedro Horrillo (Esp)	QSD	s.t
	Leader - Max van Heeswijk (Ned)	USP	5h 32'44"
	Points - Erik Zabel (Ger)	TMO	28 pts
	Mountain- Floyd Landis (Usa)	USP	6 pts

3rd stage: Burgos/Soria - 156 km

1.	Alejandro Valverde (Esp)	KEL	3h 43'17"
2.	Stuart O'Grady (Aus)	COF	s.t
3.	Denis Menchov (Rus)	IBB	s.t
4.	Oscar Freire (Esp)	RAB	s.t
5.	Roberto Heras (Esp)	LST	s.t
	Leader - Benoît Joachim (Lux)	USP	9h 16'00"
	Points - Stuart O'Grady (Aus)	COF	34 pts
	Mountain- Floyd Landis (Usa)	USP	6 pts

4e stage: Soria/Zaragoza - 174 km

1.	Alessandro Petacchi (Ita)	FAS	4h 23'01"
2.	Erik Zabel (Ger)	TMO	s.t
3.	Oscar Freire (Esp)	RAB	s.t
4.	Stuart O'Grady (Aus)	COF	s.t
5.	Angelo Furlan (Ita)	ALB	s.t
	Leader - Benoît Joachim (Lux)	USP	13h 38'59"
	Points - Erik Zabel (Ger)	TMO	52 pts
	Mountain- Floyd Landis (Usa)	USP	6 pts

5th stage: Zaragoza/Morella - 191 km

1.	Denis Menchov (Rus)	IBB	5h 07'44"
2.	Aitor Gonzalez Jimenez (Esp)	FAS	+ 3"
3.	Alejandro Valverde (Esp)	KEL	s.t
4.	Leonardo Piepoli (Ita)	SDV	s.t
5.	Carlos Sastre (Esp)	CSC	s.t
	Leader - Manuel Beltran (Esp)	USP	18h 47'16"
	Points - Stuart O'Grady (Aus)	COF	60 pts
	Mountain- Juan Manuel Garate (Esp)	LAM	10 pts

6th stage: Benicarló/Castellón de la Pl.-157 km

1.	Oscar Freire (Esp)	RAB	3h 48'23"
2.	Erik Zabel (Ger)	TMO	s.t
3.	Stuart O'Grady (Aus)	COF	s.t
4.	Cristian Moreni (Ita)	ALB	s.t
5.	M.A Martin Perdiguero (Esp)	SDV	s.t
	Leader - Manuel Beltran (Esp)	USP	22h 55'39"
	Points - Stuart O'Grady (Aus)	COF	76 pts
	Mountain- Francisco Mancebo (Esp)	IBB	17 pts

7th stage: Castellón de la Pl./Valencia - 170 km

1.	Alessandro Petacchi (Ita)	FAS	5h 02'05"
2.	Erik Zabel (Ger)	TMO	s.t
3.	Oscar Freire (Esp)	RAB	s.t
4.	Stuart O'Grady (Aus)	COF	s.t
5.	Luca Paolini (Ita)	QSD	s.t
	Leader - Manuel Beltran (Esp)	USP	26h 28'43"
	Points - Erik Zabel (Ger)	TMO	92 pts
	Mountain- Francisco Mancebo (Esp)	IBB	17 pts

8th stage: Team time trial in Almussafes - 40,1 km

*1.	Tyler Hamilton (Usa)	PHO	47'16"
2.	Victor Hugo Peña (Col)	USP	+ 15"
3.	Floyd Landis (Usa)	USP	+ 18"
4.	Manuel Beltran (Esp)	USP	+ 28"
5.	Isidro Nozal (Esp)	LST	+ 37"
	Leader - Floyd Landis (Usa)	USP	27h 16'17"
	Points - Erik Zabel (Ger)	TMO	92 pts
	Mountain- Francisco Mancebo (Esp) IBB		17 pts

* Positive dope test after this stage, Tyler Hamilton must logically give up his victory in favour of the second placed V H Pena.

9th stage: Xátiva/Alto de Aitana -170 km

1.	Leonardo Piepoli (Ita)	SDV	4h 29'36"
2.	Roberto Heras (Esp)	LST	+ 4"
3.	Isidro Nozal (Esp)	LST	+ 10"
4.	Francisco Mancebo (Esp)	IBB	+ 15"
5.	Jorge Ferrio (Esp)	ALM	+ 25"
	Leader - Floyd Landis (Usa)	USP	31h 46'48"
	Points - Erik Zabel (Ger)	TMO	92 pts
	Mountain - David Fernandez Domingo (Esp)	ALM	35 pts

10th stage: Alcoy/Xorret de Catí -159 km

1.	Eladio Jimenez (Esp)	KEL	4h 31'57"
2.	Stuart O'Grady (Aus)	COF	+ 32"
3.	Oscar Freire (Esp)	RAB	+ 48"
4.	Ruslan Ivanov (Mda)	ALB	s.t
5.	Juan Fuentes (Esp)	SAE	+1'04"
	Leader - Floyd Landis (Usa)	USP	36h 23'51"
	Points - Stuart O'Grady (Aus)	COF	114 pts
	Mountain - José Miguel Elias (Esp)	REB	48 pts

11e stage: San Vicente del Raspeig / Caravaca de la Cruz - 165,8 km

1.	David Zabriskie (Usa)	USP	4h 05'31"
2.	Alessandro Petacchi (Ita)	FAS	+ 1'11"
3.	Stuart O'Grady (Aus)	COF	s.t
4.	Marco Zanotti (Ita)	VIN	s.t
5.	Erik Zabel (Ger)	TMO	s.t
	Leader - Floyd Landis (Usa)	USP	40h 30'33"
	Points - Stuart O'Grady (Aus)	COF	130 pts
	Mountain - José Miguel Elias (Esp)	REB	48 pts

12nd stage: Almeria/Calar Alto - 150 km

1.	Roberto Heras (Esp)	LST	4h 19'30"
2.	Santi Perez Fernandez (Esp)	PHO	+ 34"
3.	Francisco Mancebo (Esp)	IBB	+ 53"
4.	Alejandro Valverde (Esp)	KEL	+ 1'27"
5.	Isidro Nozal (Esp)	LST	s.t
	Leader - Roberto Heras (Esp)	LST	44h 50'50"
	Points - Stuart O'Grady (Aus)	COF	130 pts
	Mountain - Roberto Heras (Esp)	LST	57 pts

13rd stage: El Ejido/Málaga - 170 km

1.	Alessandro Petacchi (Ita)	FAS	4h 01'55"
2.	Erik Zabel (Ger)	TMO	s.t
3.	Pedro Horrillo (Esp)	QSD	s.t
4.	Stuart O'Grady (Aus)	COF	s.t
5.	Cristian Moreni (Ita)	ALB	s.t
	Leader - Roberto Heras (Esp)	LST	48h 52'45"
	Points - Erik Zabel (Ger)	TMO	148 pts
	Mountain - Roberto Heras (Esp)	LST	57 pts

14th stage: Málaga/Granada - 170 km

1.	Santi Perez Fernandez (Esp)	PHO	4h 06'34"
2.	Alejandro Valverde (Esp)	KEL	+ 46"
3.	Luis Perez Rodriguez (Esp)	COF	s.t
4.	Francisco Mancebo (Esp)	IBB	s.t
5.	Isidro Nozal (Esp)	LST	s.t
	Leader - Roberto Heras (Esp)	LST	53h 00'05"
	Points - Erik Zabel (Ger)	TMO	148 pts
	Mountain - Roberto Heras (Esp)	LST	67 pts

15th stage: Granada/Sierra Nevada - 29 km (Team time trial)

1.	Santi Perez Fernandez (Esp)	PHO	1h 02'29"
2.	Alejandro Valverde (Esp)	KEL	+1'07"
3.	Roberto Heras (Esp)	LST	+1'51"
4.	Alexandre Vinokourov (Kaz)	TMO	+3'06"
5.	Francisco Mancebo (Esp)	IBB	+3'18"
	Leader - Roberto Heras (Esp)	LST	54h 04'25"
	Points - Erik Zabel (Ger)	TMO	148 pts
	Mountain - Roberto Heras (Esp)	LST	87 pts

16th stage: Olivenza/Cáceres - 170 km

1.	J. Cayetano Julia (Esp)	KEL	4h 19'23"
2.	Tadej Valjavec (Slo)	PHO	+12"
3.	Danilo Di Luca (Ita)	SAE	+ 35"
4.	Antonio Cruz (Usa)	USP	s.t
5.	Pablo Lastras (Esp)	IBB	s.t
	Leader - Roberto Heras (Esp)	LST	58h 35'32"
	Points - Erik Zabel (Ger)	TMO	148 pts
	Mountain - Roberto Heras (Esp)	LST	87 pts

17th stage: Plasencia/La Covatilla - 178 km

1.	Félix Cardenas (Col)	BAQ	4h 52'08"
2.	Santi Perez Fernandez (Esp)	PHO	+ 29"
3.	Roberto Heras (Esp)	LST	+ 1'01"
4.	Francisco Mancebo (Esp)	IBB	+ 1'15"
5.	Luis Perez Rodriguez (Esp)	COF	+ 2'05"
	Leader - Roberto Heras (Esp)	LST	63h 28'41"
	Points - Erik Zabel (Ger)	TMO	148 pts
	Mountain - Félix Cardenas (Col)	BAQ	126 pts

18th stage: Béjar /Avila - 196 km

1.	Javier Pascual Rodriguez (Esp)	KEL	5h 02'59"
2.	Ivan Parra (Col)	BAQ	s.t
3.	Joan Horrach (Esp)	IBB	+19"
4.	Hernan Buenahora (Col)	BAQ	s.t
5.	Patrick Calcagni (Sui)	VIN	+ 24"
	Leader - Roberto Heras (Esp)	LST	68h 33'04"
	Points - Erik Zabel (Ger)	TMO	152 pts
	Mountain - Félix Cardenas (Col)	BAQ	132 pts

19th stage: Avila/Collado Villalba - 150 km

1.	Constantino Zaballa (Esp)	SDV	3h 33'32"
2.	Ruslan Ivanov (Mda)	ALB	+1'23"
3.	Damiano Cunego (Ita)	SAE	s.t
4.	José Luis Arrieta (Esp)	IBB	s.t
5.	Eddy Mazzoleni (Ita)	SAE	s.t
	Leader - Roberto Heras (Esp)	LST	72h 13'01"
	Points - Erik Zabel (Ger)	TMO	152 pts
	Mountain - Félix Cardenas (Col)	BAQ	167 pts

20th stage: Alcobendas/Navacerrada - 175 km

1.	J. Enrique Gutierrez (Esp)	PHO	4h 52'20"
2.	Eladio Jimenez (Esp)	KEL	+28"
3.	David Latasa (Esp)	KEL	+1'25"
4.	Santi Perez Fernandez (Esp)	PHO	+1'37"
5.	Aitor Perez Arrieta (Esp)	BAQ	+2'03"
	Leader - Roberto Heras (Esp)	LST	77h 07'28"
	Points - Erik Zabel (Ger)	TMO	152 pts
	Mountain - Félix Cardenas (Col)	BAQ	167 pts

21th stage: Team time trial in Madrid - 30 km

1.	Santi Perez Fernandez (Esp)	PHO	35'05"
2.	Francisco Mancebo (Esp)	IBB	+7"
3.	Carlos Sastre (Esp)	CSC	+8"
4.	Roberto Heras (Esp)	LST	+13"
5.	David Blanco Rodriguez (Esp)	KEL	+18"

POINTS TABLE

1.	Erik Zabel (Ger)	TMO	152 pts
2.	Alejandro Valverde (Esp)	KEL	144 pts
3.	Roberto Heras (Esp)	LST	142 pts

MOUNTAIN STANDING

1.	Félix Cardenas (Col)	BAQ	167 pts
2.	Roberto Heras (Esp)	LST	111 pts
3.	Santi Perez Fernandez (Esp)	PHO	110 pts

ALL ASCENTION TO VUELTA 2004

(classed as 2nd, 1st and " No category)

STAGE 5
Puerto de Torremiró /2nd cat.: J.Manuel Garate (Esp)

STAGE 6
Coll de la Bandereta /2nd cat.: Manuel Quinziato (Ita)
Alto del desierto de las Palmas /2nd cat.: F. Mancebo (Esp)

STAGE 7
Puerto de Montemayor /2nd cat.: J.Miguel Elias (Esp)

STAGE 9
Alto de Tollos /2nd cat.: D. Fernandez Domingo (Esp)
Puerto de Tudons /2nd cat. : D. Fernandez Domingo (Esp)
Alto de Torremanzanas /2nd cat.: Félix Cardenas (Col)
Alto de Aitana / Hors cat.: Leonardo Piepoli (Ita)

STAGE 10
Puerto de la Carrasqueta /2ndcat.: J.Miguel Elias (Esp)
Xorret de Catí /1st cat.: Eladio Jimenez (Esp)

STAGE 12
Alto de Velefique/1st cat.: Francisco Lara (Esp)
Alto de Calar Alto /1st cat.: Francisco Lara (Esp)
Observatorio Calar Alto / Hors cat.: Roberto Heras (Esp)

STAGE 14
Alto Ventas Zafarraya /2nd cat.: Jorge Ferrio (Esp)
Alto de Monachil /1st cat.: Santi Perez Fernandez (Esp)

STAGE 15
Sierra Nevada / Hors cat. : Santi Perez Fernandez (Esp)

STAGE 16
Puerto de Piornal /1th cat.: Félix Cardenas (Col)
Puerto de Honduras /1th cat.: Félix Cardenas (Col)
La Covatilla / Hors cat.: Félix Cardenas (Col)

STAGE 18
Puerto de la Peña Negra /1th cat.: Juan Fuentes (Esp)
Puerto de Serranillos /1th cat.: Juan Fuentes (Esp)
Puerto de Navalmoral /2ndcat.: Ivan Parra (Col)

STAGE 19
Puerto de Santa María /2ndcat.: Constantino Zaballa (Esp)
Alto de Abantos /1th cat.: Constantino Zaballa (Esp)

STAGE 20
Puerto de la Morcuera /1th cat.: Eladio Jimenez (Esp)
Puerto de Cotos /1th cat.: Eladio Jimenez (Esp)
Alto del Leon /1th cat.: Eladio Jimenez (Esp)
Puerto de Navacerrada /1th cat.: J. Enrique Gutierrez (Esp)

FINAL CLASSIFICATION

1.	**Roberto Heras (Esp)**	**LST**	**77h 42'46"**
2.	Santi Perez Fernandez (Esp)	PHO	+ 30"
3.	Francisco Mancebo (Esp)	IBB	+ 2'13"
4.	Alejandro Valverde (Esp)	KEL	+ 3'30"
5.	Carlos Garcia Quesada (Esp)	KEL	+ 7'44"
6.	Carlos Sastre (Esp)	CSC	+ 8'11"
7.	Isidro Nozal (Esp)	LST	+ 8'32"
8.	Angel Gomez Marchante (Esp)	ALM	+ 13'08"
9.	Luis Perez Rodriguez (Esp)	COF	+ 13'24"
10.	David Blanco Rodriguez (Esp)	KEL	+ 15'15"
11.	Stefano Garzelli (Ita)	VIN	+ 16'33"
12.	Marcos Serrano (Esp)	LST	+ 17'14"
13.	Manuel Beltran (Esp)	USP	+ 17'43"
14.	Francisco Lara (Esp)	ALM	+ 24'16"
15.	Samuel Sanchez (Esp)	EUS	+ 29'23"

187 Competitors

LIBERTY Seguros

1.	HERAS Roberto (Esp)	**1st**	**77h42'46"**
2.	NOZAL Isidro (Esp)	**7th**	+ 8'32"
3.	ANDRLE René (Cze)	110th	+ 3h36'56"
4.	CARUSO Gianpaolo (Ita)	72nd	+ 2h04'49"
5.	GIL Koldo (Esp)	61st	+ 1h48'53"
6.	GONZALEZ de GALDEANO Igor (Esp)	96th	+ 3h03'23"
7.	HRUSKA Jan (Cze)	99th	+ 3h11'46"
8.	SERRANO Marcos (Esp)	12nd	+ 17'14"
9.	BARANOWSKI Dariusz (Pol)	33rd	+ 1h00'03"

Communitat VALENCIANA - KELME

11.	VALVERDE Alejandro (Esp)	**4th**	+ 3'30"
12.	BLANCO RODRIGUEZ David (Esp)	**10th**	+ 15'15"
13.	CABELLO Francisco (Esp)	102nd	+ 3h13'11"
14.	GARCIA QUESADA Carlos (Esp)	**5th**	+ 7'44"
15.	JIMENEZ Eladio (Esp)	19th	+ 34'35"
16.	JULIA J. Cayetano (Esp)	100th	+ 3h12'47"
17.	LATASA David (Esp)	50th	+ 1h37'51"
18.	PASCUAL RODRIGUEZ Javier (Esp)	53rd	+ 1h40'41"
19.	PLAZA MOLINA Ruben (Esp)	*Abandon*	19th stage

AG2R Prévoyance

21.	ASTARLOZA Mikel (Esp)	*Abandon*	14th stage
22.	BERGÈS Stéphane (Fra)	*Abandon*	9th stage
23.	CHAURREAU Iñigo (Esp)	55th	+ 1h42'03"
24.	FLICKINGER Andy (Fra)	*Abandon*	9th stage
25.	GOUBERT Stéphane (Fra)	*Abandon*	12nd stage
26.	INAUDI Nicolas (Fra)	*Abandon*	9th stage
27.	ORIOL Christophe (Fra)	*Abandon*	12nd stage
28.	PÜTSEP Erki (Est)	*Abandon*	17th stage
29.	LAIDOUN Julien (Fra)	*Abandon*	9th stage

ALESSIO - BIANCHI

31.	CAUCCHIOLI Pietro (Ita)	*Abandon*	14th stage
32.	FURLAN Angelo (Ita)	DNS	9th stage
33.	HVASTIJA Martin (Slo)	*Abandon*	9th stage
34.	IVANOV Ruslan (Mda)	77th	+ 2h21'02"
35.	MIHOLJEVIC Vladimir (Cro)	78th	+ 2h21'43"
36.	MØLLER Claus Michael (Den)	80th	+ 2h28'24"
37.	MORENI Cristian (Ita)	*Abandon*	18th stage
38.	RASTELLI Ellis (Ita)	*Abandon*	19th stage
39.	SUNDERLAND Scott (Aus)	*Abandon*	5th stage

Cafés BAQUE

41.	CARDENAS Félix (Col)	29th	+ 52'55"
42.	ARREITUNANDIA Peio (Esp)	*Abandon*	17th stage
43.	BUENAHORA Hernan (Col)	32nd	+ 58'44"
44.	GARCIA RODRIGUEZ Fr. Tomas (Esp)	41st	+ 1h26'16"
45.	GUTIERREZ GARCIA Herbert (Col)	111st	+ 3h43'08"
46.	PARRA Ivan (Col)	34th	+ 1h00'10"
47.	PLAZA David (Esp)	18th	+ 31'24"
48.	PEREZ ARRIETA Aitor (Esp)	66th	+ 2h00'36"
49.	SERRANO GONZALEZ Ricardo (Esp)	TC	12nd stage

COFIDIS

51.	ATIENZA Daniel (Esp)	25th	+ 48'29"
52.	CUESTA Iñigo (Esp)	*Abandon*	9th stage
53.	FERNANDEZ BUSTINZA Bingen (Esp)	67th	+ 2h02'26"
54.	O'GRADY Stuart (Aus)	DNS	14th stage
55.	PEREZ RODRIGUEZ Luis (Esp)	**9th**	+ 13'24"
56.	COYOT Arnaud (Fra)	*Abandon*	12nd stage
57.	TRENTIN Guido (Ita)	76th	+ 2h19'55"
58.	VASSEUR Cédric (Fra)	36th	+ 1h13'30"
59.	WHITE Matthew (Aus)	119th	+ 4h16'42"

EUSKALTEL - EUSKADI

61.	ZUBELDIA Haimar (Esp)	40th	+ 1h25'56"
62.	ALBIZU Joseba (Esp)	*Abandon*	12nd stage
63.	ARTETXE Mikel (Esp)	108th	+ 3h27'35"
64.	ISASI Iñaki (Esp)	89th	+ 2h50'25"
65.	LAISEKA Roberto (Esp)	54th	+ 1h41'44"
66.	LOPEZ de MUNAIN Alberto (Esp)	91st	+ 2h51'36"
67.	SANCHEZ Samuel (Esp)	15th	+ 29'23"
68.	SILLONIZ Aitor (Esp)	118th	+ 4h12'11"
69.	SILLONIZ Josu (Esp)	*Abandon*	7th stage

FASSA BORTOLO

71.	GONZALEZ JIMENEZ Aitor (Esp)	DNS	18th stage
72.	PETACCHI Alessandro (Ita)	DNS	15th stage
73.	CIONI Dario (Ita)	52nd	+ 1h39'08"
74.	TRENTI Guido (Usa)	113rd	+ 3h51'15"
75.	SANCHEZ PIMIENTA Julian (Esp)	105th	+ 3h23'18"
76.	SACCHI Fabio (Ita)	*Abandon*	14th stage
77.	GUSTOV Volodymir (Ukr)	97th	+ 3h04'25"
78.	ONGARATO Alberto (Ita)	*Abandon*	17th stage
79.	VELO Marco (Ita)	114th	+ 3h52'36"

ILLES BALEARS - BANESTO

81.	MANCEBO Francisco (Esp)	**3rd**	+ 2'13"
82.	MENCHOV Denis (Rus)	*Abandon*	14th stage
83.	ARRIETA José Luis (Esp)	28th	+ 51'48"
84.	COLOM Antonio (Esp)	101st	+ 3h13'06"
85.	GARCIA ACOSTA J. Vicente (Esp)	106th	+ 3h23'57"
86.	HORRACH Joan (Esp)	24th	+ 46'17"
87.	LASTRAS Pablo (Esp)	38th	+ 1h18'12"
88.	OSA Unai (Esp)	21st	+ 38'06"
89.	PRADERA Mikel (Esp)	83rd	+ 2h38'45"

LAMPRE

92.	ASTARLOA Igor (Esp)	DNS	12nd stage
93.	BERTOLETTI Simone (Ita)	*Abandon*	6th stage
94.	CORTINOVIS Alessandro (Ita)	82nd	+ 2h38'41"
95.	GARATE Juan Manuel (Esp)	23rd	+ 40'09"
96.	PICCOLI Mariano (Ita)	115th	+ 3h25'40"
97.	QUINZIATO Manuel (Ita)	94th	+ 2h58'55"
98.	SCOTTO D'ABUSCO Michele (Ita)	*Abandon*	12nd stage
99.	RIGHI Daniele (Ita)	107th	+ 3h26'28"

COSTA de ALMERIA - PATERNINA

101.	DEL RIO Jon (Esp)	*Abandon*	12nd stage
102.	FERNANDEZ DOMINGO David (Esp)	TC	19th stage
104.	FERRIO Jorge (Esp)	17th	+ 30'49"
105.	GOMEZ MARCHANTE J. Angel (Esp)	**8th**	+ 13'08"
106.	LARA Francisco (Esp)	14th	+ 24'16"
107.	HERRERO LLORENTE David (Esp)	73rd	+ 2h04'56"
108.	LOPEZ TORRELLA Joaquin (Esp)	69th	+ 2h03'22"
109.	TORRENT Carlos (Esp)	*Abandon*	9th stage

PHONAK

111.	SEVILLA Oscar (Esp)	22nd	+ 39'01"
112.	HAMILTON Tyler (Usa)	DNS	13rd stage
113.	BAYARRI Gonzalo (Esp)	*Abandon*	12nd stage
114.	GONZALEZ CAPILLA Santos (Esp)	*Abandon*	14th stage
115.	GRABSCH Bert (Ger)	86th	+ 2h44'35"
116.	GUTIERREZ CATALUÑA J. Enrique (Esp)	31st	+ 58'28"
117.	JALABERT Nicolas (Fra)	*Abandon*	10th stage
118.	PEREZ FERNANDEZ Santi (Esp)	**2nd**	+ 30"
119.	VALJAVEC Tadej (Slo)	26th	+ 49'23"

QUICK STEP - DAVITAMON

121.	PECHARROMAN J. Antonio (Esp)	49th	+ 1h37'18"
122.	BODROGI Laszlo (Hun)	*Abandon*	10th stage
123.	GARRIDO J. Antonio (Esp)	98th	+ 3h10'48"
124.	HORRILLO Pedro (Esp)	88th	+ 2h49'25"
125.	HULSMANS Kevin (Bel)	104th	+ 3h22'54"
126.	PAOLINI Luca (Ita)	DNS	19th stage
127.	SINKEWITZ Patrik (Ger)	DNS	9th stage
128.	TANKINK Bram (Ned)	64th	+ 1h57'01"
129.	VAN GOOLEN Jurgen (Bel)	56th	+ 1h45'13"

RABOBANK

131.	FREIRE Oscar (Esp)	*Abandon*	12nd stage
132.	BOVEN Jan (Ned)	*Abandon*	17th stage
133.	DE WEERT Kevin (Bel)	71st	+ 2h04'39"
134.	DEN BAKKER Maarten (Ned)	84th	+ 2h40'07"
135.	HUNTER Robert (Rsa)	*Abandon*	9th stage
136.	MUTSAARS Ronald (Ned)	*Abandon*	12nd stage
137.	POSTHUMA Joost (Ned)	92nd	+ 2h53'23"
138.	WEENING Pieter (Ned)	59th	+ 1h48'37"
139.	VENEBERG Thorwald (Ned)	48th	+ 1h36'19"

RELAX - BOSYSOL

141.	MARTINEZ TRINIDAD Alberto (Esp)	*Abandon*	17th stage
142.	ELIAS José Miguel (Esp)	39th	+ 1h21'01"
143.	FLORENCIO Xavier (Esp)	90th	+ 2h50'51"
144.	JUFRE Josep (Esp)	62nd	+ 1h51'10"
145.	BURGOS Nacor (Esp)	*Abandon*	17th stage
146.	PASAMONTES Luis (Esp)	20th	+ 37'49"
147.	REBOLLO José Luis (Esp)	51st	+ 1h37'53"
148.	ROESEMS Bert (Bel)	*Abandon*	14th stage
149.	VAN SUMMEREN Johan (Bel)	35th	+ 1h13'19"

SAECO

151.	CUNEGO Damiano (Ita)	16th	+ 29'51"
152.	DI LUCA Danilo (Ita)	*Abandon*	19th stage
153.	FORNACIARI Paolo (Ita)	117th	+ 4h06'31"
154.	FUENTES Juan (Esp)	81st	+ 2h34'06"
155.	SABALIAUSKAS Marius (Ltu)	87th	+ 2h48'45"
156.	BONOMI Giosue' (Ita)	*Abandon*	9th stage
157.	MAZZOLENI Eddy (Ita)	70th	+ 2h03'30"
158.	SPEZIALETTI Alessandro (Ita)	116th	+ 3h54'54"
159.	SZMYD Sylvester (Pol)	74th	+2h07'59"

SAUNIER DUVAL - PRODIR

161.	BELOKI Joseba (Esp)	*Abandon*	16th stage
162.	CAÑADA David (Esp)	47th	+ 1h36'05"
163.	CASERO Rafael (Esp)	75th	+ 2h09'21"
164.	DOMINGUEZ Juan Carlos (Esp)	*Abandon*	12nd stage
165.	JEKER Fabian (Sui)	*Abandon*	10th stage
166.	MARTIN PERDIGUERO M.A (Esp)	*Abandon*	19th stage
167.	PIEPOLI Leonardo (Ita)	27th	+ 50'28"
168.	RODRIGUEZ OLIVER Joaquin (Esp)	42nd	+ 1h27'08"
169.	ZABALLA Constantino (Esp)	30th	+ 55'37"

CSC

171.	SASTRE Carlos (Esp)	**6th**	+ 8'11"
172.	BRUUN ERIKSEN Thomas (Den)	*Abandon*	12nd stage
173.	CALVENTE Manuel (Esp)	37th	+ 1h13'36"
174.	GOUSSEV Vladimir (Rus)	93rd	+ 2h57'17"
175.	JAKSCHE Jörg (Ger)	44th	+ 1h29'25"
176.	LÜTTENBERGER Peter (Aut)	85th	+ 2h42'45"
177.	HØJ Frank (Den)	112nd	+ 3h46'52"
178.	SCHLECK Frank (Lux)	46th	+ 1h35'10"
179.	VANDBØRG Brian (Den)	*Abandon*	17th stage

T-MOBILE

181.	VINOKOUROV Alexandre (Kaz)	DNS	18th stage
182.	BOTERO Santiago (Col)	*Abandon*	5th stage
183.	EVANS Cadel (Aus)	60th	+ 1h48'46"
184.	HIEKMANN Torsten (Ger)	*Abandon*	5th stage
185.	KLIER Andreas (Ger)	*Abandon*	6th stage
186.	KONECNY Tomas (Cze)	*Abandon*	9th stage
187.	SCHRECK Stephan (Ger)	58th	+ 1h47'25"
188.	WESEMANN Steffen (Ger)	*Abandon*	5th stage
189.	ZABEL Erik (Ger)	43rd	+ 1h29'02"

US POSTAL - BERRY FLOOR

191.	BARRY Michael (Can)	DNS	18th stage
192.	BELTRAN Manuel (Esp)	13rd	+ 17'43"
193.	JOACHIM Benoît (Lux)	57th	+ 1h45'14"
194.	LANDIS Floyd (Usa)	*Abandon*	18th stage
195.	MIKHAILOV Guennadi (Rus)	63rd	+ 1h53'40"
196.	PEÑA Victor Hugo (Col)	45th	+ 1h31'14"
197.	CRUZ Antonio (Usa)	68th	+ 2h02'39"
198.	VAN HEESWIJK Max (Ned)	*Abandon*	9th stage
199.	ZABRISKIE David (Usa)	*Abandon*	17th stage

Vini CALDIROLA - NOBILI Rubinetterie

201.	GARZELLI Stefano (Ita)	11st	+ 16'33"
202.	ANDRIOTTO Dario (Ita)	103rd	+ 3h15'18"
203.	CALCAGNI Patrick (Sui)	65th	+ 2h00'01"
204.	GEROSA Mauro (Ita)	95th	+ 3h00'20"
205.	MILESI Marco (Ita)	109th	+ 3h31'30"
206.	SGAMBELLURI Roberto (Ita)	79th	+ 2h27'20"
207.	ZANOTTI Marco (Ita)	*Abandon*	14th stage
208.	TONKOV Pavel (Rus)	*Abandon*	12nd stage
209.	ZAMPIERI Steve (Sui)	*Abandon*	9th stage

A GOOD WEEK FOR JAKSCHE

In the lead from start to finish, the German Jorg Jaksche has taken the 62nd edition of the Paris Nice. An exploit that only a few of his illustrious predecessors, such as Eddy Merckx, Freddy Maertens, Laurent Jalabert or Frank Vandenbroucke (the last, in 1998) have managed.

On the podium, Alexandre Vinokourov, winner of the last two editions, passed the torch to Jaksche, who is the second German rider in four years to take the honours. Transferring from the ONCE team to CSC in the closed season, Jaksche showed his superiority throughout the week. This with the help of a team that placed two other riders at the top of the rankings, Bobby Julich finishing 3rd and his countryman Jens Voigt 4th.

Two operations mounted by his team wreaked havoc among its rivals. Twice, on the road to Montargis (2nd stage) then to Rasteau (5th stage), the riders of Bjarne Riis made good use of adverse wind conditions to wipe out adversarial moves.

Out of the reckoning from the second day, Alexandre Vinokourov, winner of the last two editions, concentrated on stage wins. He dedicated his first success in Rasteau, the day after a cancellation due to snow, to the memory of his friend Andrei Kivilev, who died a year before, and renewed his exploit the day before the finish at Nice. Before making it three at the end of the race. Even though he was to finish down the field in the overall rankings, he was surely the most charismatic of the riders present.

Much more than the rather ordinary Jaksche and Rebellin in any case...

Finally we should note the sub standard performances of the French riders, true, upset by the rash of doping cases at the start of the season, as well as the decision to replace the usual technical assistants with physiotherapists, made hours before the race. A ministerial decision which visibly made no one happy.

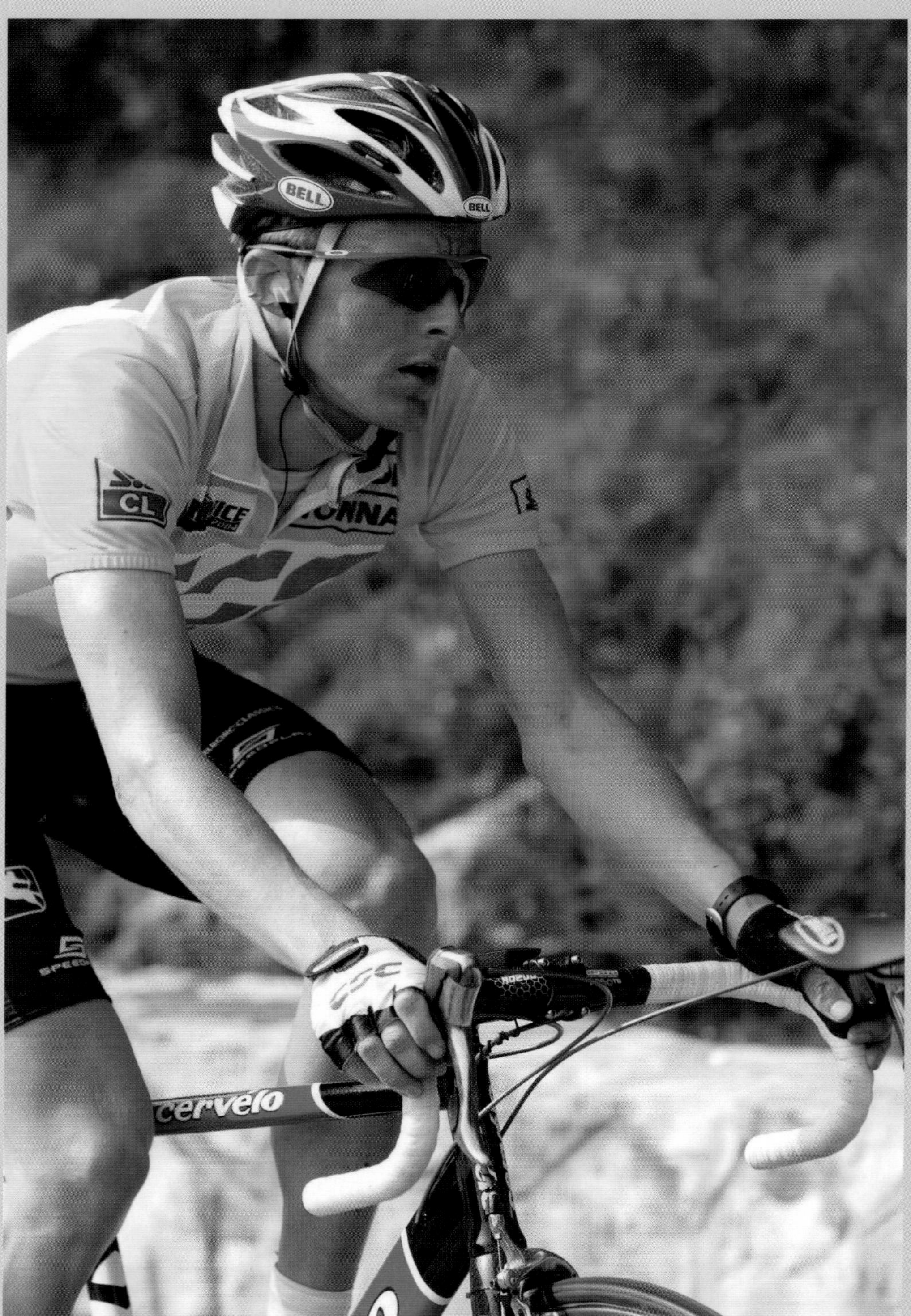

1st Stage:

Chaville / Vanves – 13.2 kms Time trial

Jaksche gets off to a strong start

13.2 kilometers in the south Paris suburbs is all the competitors in the 62ndParis – Nice have to worry about on this first day. In effect, the traditional prologue is replaced by a slightly longer course which gives us the chance to see who is and who is not in form. For Davide Rebellin everything is looking good. For a long time it looks as though his time will stand as the best of the day. That's not reckoning with Jorg Jaksche, coming from his win in the Tour Med, who is a tough customer in time trial stages. Not benefiting from as favourable weather conditions as the Italian, (rain having made an appearance in the second part of the stage), the CSC rider finished the course at a good enough speed of 45.74 kph. This gave him a lead over Davide Rebellin of 4 seconds, enough to ensure the win and therefore take the leader's jersey. Of the best placed riders, the remarkable return to form of Erik Dekker (who since his crash in the 2002 Milan – San Remo had been looking to find his previous level of performance) should be applauded, as should that of World Champion David Millar, that of the young Iberian Alberto Contador (Liberty Seguros) 5th at 13 seconds and the return of veteran Alex Zulle (Phonak) 6th at 14 seconds. These men were satisfied with their performances, others were less so: Alexandre Vinokourov, winner for the past two years, was 26 seconds adrift, Michael Rogers at 30 seconds Leipheimer at 40 seconds and Sylvain Chavanel at a distant 1 min 03 sec!

2nd stage:
Chaville / Montargis – 166.5 kms
The day of the losers!

The day after the time trial won at Vanves by Jorg Jaksche, his CSC team has a sort out on the second stage of the Paris – Nice. At the end of 166.5 kilometers between Chaville and Montargis, the Spaniard Pedro Horrillo (Quick Step) takes the win ahead of Beat Zberg (Gerolsteiner) and Michele Bartoli (CSC). But it's particularly the show of strength shown by the riders of Bjarne Riis around Malesherbes which impresses. On a wind swept road, ideal for a collective attack. Put in the picture by Alain Gallopin, one of the team originating from the region, of the possibility of making a mark on this stage, the CSC riders regrouped half way through the course and stepped up the pace. Excepting Bobby Julich, the totality of the team were present in the first breakaway in which were also to be found the young French Credit Agricole riders Christophe Le Mevel and Geoffroy Lequatre (the latter coming from the nearby town of Pithiviers) and two Belgians from the Chocolat Jaques team, Geert Verheyen and Jurgen van de Walle. Behind it's every man for himself in a peloton shattered on an interminable straight section of road. Early on, only Frank Vandenbroucke (Fassa Bortolo) and René Jorgensen (Alessio – Bianchi) were the only ones able to join them. Later a further 23 riders manage to join them. With two team mates, Alexandre Vinokourov put up a strong fight. In vain. The same can be said of the unique Cofidis rider, David Millar, or Sandy Casar, victim of a roundabout just as things were hotting up, and his team mate Baden Cooke. And what can be said of Tyler Hamilton, with a deficit of more than thirteen minutes at the finish.

Coming to the line, an attack by Mathew Hyman (Rabobank) was soon quashed and the sprint looked as if it would go to Thor Hushovd, but up the hill to the finish, Pedro Horillo counter attacked to take the stage. Solidly supported by his seven team mates Jorg Jaksche of course kept the yellow and white jersey of the leader. Perhaps he would be reminded of the last situation of this type in a Paris – Nice: between Nangis and Sens, in the rain, when the Rabobank team had pulverised the opposition. In Nice, their leader Michael Boogerd went on to take the win...

3rd stage:
La Chapelle St Ursin / Roanne- 227.5 kms
Van Bon in the cold

In glacial temperatures (0°), several aborted attacks take place before The German Thomas Ziegler (Gerolsteiner) pulls away in the company of Dutchman Leon Van Bon (Lotto – Domo). The two men rapidly open up a lead of 15 minutes (km 80) before the men from CSC take things in hand and reduce the deficit to nine minutes. Things seem already to be decided. But the team mates of the leader, not receiving the help they were counting on ease up. The result being the gap reopeningto fifteen minutes. For better or for worse, the chase gets underway once again in the final third of the stage. The teams Fdjeux.com (to favour the ambitions of their sprinter Baden Cooke), Credit Agricole (working for Thor Hushovd) and Liberty Seguros (for Allan Davis) hot up the pace towards the climb at Chatel Montaigne, the summit of which is situated 46 kilometers from Roanne. A climb too many for the two Frenchmen Christophe Le Mevel and Geoffroy Lequatre (Credit Agricole) who shone the day before. The two leaders have a lead of 3 mins 50 sec at the summit, not normally enough here, but the peloton seems unable to reduce the gap in the final kilometers. The duo, after a long breakaway has kept enough in reserve to be able to fight out the finish between themselves. In this game, the crafty Leon Van Bon plays (not without difficulty) on the inexperience of Thomas Ziegler. A few seconds later, the peloton is brought home in style by Tom Boonen. The overall leadership stays unchanged.

4th stage:
Roanne / Le Puy en Velay – 184.5 kms
Le Puy deprived of its race

For the third time in the history of the race, a stage of the Paris Nice is cancelled. Already, in 1995 the stage between Clermont Ferrand and Chalvignac had been cancelled due to snow. In 1960, floods had washed out the stage between Manosque and Frejus. Snow is already falling in Roanne in the morning, and the organisers are worried that the section at altitude at the Col de l' Homme Mort will be too dangerous for the riders. At first, the organisers decide to delay the start by thirty minutes and organise a convoy of riders for the first part of the stage, but finding that the snow was strengthening the decision was taken to cancel the stage and send the cyclists back to their hotels.

5th stage:
Le Puy en Velay / Rasteau – 215 kms
The tribute of "Vino"

What better tribute could Alexandre Vinokourov pay to his friend Andrei Kivilev, victim last year of a fatal crash, than to win this stage? Clearly not at the best of his form (the Tour de France, Olympic Games and World Championship having taken their toll), Alexandre Vinokourov just the same made a point of honour of taking a victory from under the noses of the still impressive CSC team. Tricked out of the honours on the Montargis stage, the Kazakh rider found himself in a good position when the stage was at its decisive point, Dariusz Baranowski, Unai Etxebarria and Aitor Osa who had been leading for most of the day, were caught 25 kms from Rasteau when the Danish team stepped up the pace. For ten kilometers or so, the acceleration does no great harm to the peloton, but as soon as the terrain began to get more difficult the effect was catastrophic. Only ten men find themselves in a favourable position. And among them, six from CSC! The Yellow jersey, of course, but also his inevitable team mates Voigt, Bartoli, Julich, Piil and the young Schleck. Only the vigilant Davide Rebellin, George Hincapie but also Alexandre Vinokourov and Baden Cooke were able to follow this TGV heading for the line. Making use of the climb at Buisson, eight kilometers from the finish, last year's winner attacked and even Jaksche was unable to follow. The T Mobile rider manages to maintain a short lead over the final kilometers to lead a group by four seconds at the line. A group led by none other than the race leader himself, who collects some valuable points on the way. Members of the leading group on the second stage, Vandenbroucke, Chavanel, Pereiro and Rogers trail home thirty seconds later. Gilbert, a little later, and Victor hugo Pena minutes later. The circle of pretenders to the podium in Nice was reduced in size when the race passed from winter to springtime, from a glacial 4° in Le Puy to the mild provencale climate of Rasteau and its famous vines.

6th stage: Rasteau/Gap – 173.5 kms
Jaksche in charge

With a major difficulty, the Col de Manse (6.3 kms of climb at 6.8 % average) with its summit situated at less than ten kilometers from the finish at Gap, this stage promised to be hard one for the indisputed leader, Jorg Jaksche. Sure, his team was less in control than at the start, but never was his only serious rival Davide Rebellin able to contest his leadership. Trailing in the overall rankings by nearly a minute, Frank Vandenbroucke set the cat amongst the pigeons with an attack in the final

Alexandre Vinokourov was unable to defend his title but took revenge with three stage wins.

kilometre of the Col de Manse, but the first to react was of course Jorg Jaksche in person. It should be said that most of his team mates, themselves well placed, were at the time a little off the pace. At the line however, the German consolidated his position thanks to points won in the intermediate sprints!

A day which really got under way after forty kilometers of racing. Aitor Osa (Illes Baleares) pushed the pace along in the last metres of the Col de Fontaube (he was after the jersey of the best climber) and pulled away. Soon after it's Nicolas Portal (AG2R) who went after the leader. The two men set off on a long adventure that was to end on the first slopes of the Col de la Sentinelle (31 kms from the line) when the rider from the Gerse region was unable to keep up with the Basque rider. Aitor Osa arrived at the top of the last but one obstacle of the day with a slim lead over a peloton deprived of half its elements. A few rare attempts at an attack followed (in which the young Spanish rider Alberto Contador several times took part) but all were without consequence as the race approached the Col de Manse. Alexandre Moos (Phonak) lit the fuse on the first slopes. Dave Bruylandts (Chocolat Jaques) joined him, then Samuel Sanchez (Euskaltel) and Floyd Landis (U S Postal). Moos pulled away rapidly and the leading trio took a lead of no more than 20 seconds over a peloton from which Denis Menchov had escaped. The Russian rider joined the leaders less than a kilometre from the summit. Behind, VDB launched his offensive, catching Alex Zulle, but unable to trouble Jorg Jaksche. In the descent (the same which had proved fatal to Joseba Beloki in the 2003 Tour de France), the leaders managed to maintain their substantial lead despite an attack from Samuel Sanchez 3 kilometers from the line. Bruylandts launched the sprint too far from the finish to hope for a positive result. He was caught by Menchov who resisted the return of Sanchez. The White jersey rider of the Centenary Tour took the victory on a day of mourning in his adopted country, Spain.

7th stage:
Digne les Bains / Cannes – 185.5 kms
Unlucky Sanchez!

Still looking for a first pro victory in his fifth season in the elite, Samuel Sanchez once again came close on this last but one day of the race. Second the day before, third at the Col d'Eze in 2002 – where only Dario Frigo and Cadel Evans led him – or fifth last year in this same town of Cannes, he would have needed another three kilometers to gain his first success here. But an alert AlexandreVinokourov decided otherwise. At 5 kilometers from the line, he pulled ahead of a small group in persuit of the leader. Already crowned two days earlier, the Kazakh managed (after catching and leaving behind Sanchez) to resist the attacks by his rivals as well as the violent wind on the coast in Cannes. The strong man, though by his own condition not at the top of his form, scored his forth stage win.
This day plagued with difficulties (no less than seven climbs) saw ,at first, a trio looking to make a reputation for themselves, open the route at the Col d'Ayen (km 60). David Moncoutié (Cofidis), Erik Dekker (Rabobank) and Inigo Landaluze (Euskaltel) were never going to get themselves into an unassailable position ahead of the chasing peloton. Shortly before the final climb of the day, that of the Col du Tanneron, they were caught by a peloton split by the rigours of the road. The traditional ascention of Tanneron was the

scene of several attacks (les Boulangers, then Bruylandts, then Vinokourov followed by Sanchez, Menchov, Leipheimer, Zulle) but it was the one of Frank Vandenbroucke, mounted in the last part of the climb that was to do the most damage. The Belgian started his descent with a lead of several metres over Samuel Sanchez. A little behind was a group including Jaksche, Rebellin, Vinokourov and Voigt. From the start of the difficult descent of Tanneron, Sanchez, taking many a risk, opened a lead of 25 seconds over the Yellow (and white) jersey group, while speeding past VDB at the same time. Unfortunately for him, his strength diminished as he approached Cannes and Vino once again showed his force...

8th stage:
Nice/Nice – 144 kms

Hat trick for Vinokourov!

Not since the four victories of Tom Steels in 1997 had anyone managed such a score in the race to the sun. Alexandre Vinokourov has then, achieved a third success in four days. Not bad for someone claiming to be out of form the week before. And the yellow (and white) jersey of Jorg Jaksche was not in the least danger. As we were expecting.

Just the same, Frank Vandenbroucke, still menacing at one minute from the leader at the start of this stage – didn't wait long before showing his hand: on the first slopes of the Col d'Eze at the eighth kilometre , he had a go.. But the CSC team were on their toes. Just a moment later, five men (Mario Aerts, Marcos Serrano, Inigo Cuesta, Tyler Hamilton and the points leader Aitor Osa) go to the head of the race. After amassing a lead of 2mins 20sec on the first ascention of the Col de Chateauneuf (km 40) the timid quartet came back into the sights of those following the second time around (km 100). Aitor Osa and Tyler Hamilton managed to hitch a ride with a good group of riders including three T Mobiles, Vinokourov, Hiekmann and Kessler – the latter would fade away soon after – but also Benoit Poilvet, David Moncoutié, Levi Leipheimer, Gorka Gonzalez Larranaga and Denis Menchov. At the foot of the third and final ascent of the Cold' Eze, 20 kilometers from the line, the breakaways achieved a lead of 1 min 07 sec. This would be enough to resist any attack coming from the peloton containing all the overall leaders. A peloton not impressed by a half hearted attack from Davide Rebellin which is soon brought to an end. After various movements, Vinokourov and Menchov, the winners of the last two stages, open up a gap at the front. It's in the sprint that things are sorted out between these two men who have dominated the second half of this Paris – Nice. A sprint that is to the advantage of "Vino" forcing through. The Kazakh, riding on what has become his home ground since his moving to Monaco some years before. Jorg Jaksche crosses the line over two minutes later and immediately stops to join in celebrations. Ah. The taste of victory. ■

CLASSIFICATIONS

1st stage: Chaville/Vanves - 13,2 km (Team time trial)

1.	Jörg Jaksche (Ger)	CSC	17'19"
2.	Davide Rebellin (Ita)	GST	+ 4"
3.	Erik Dekker (Ned)	RAB	s.t
4.	David Millar (Gbr)	COF	+ 13"
5.	Alberto Contador (Esp)	LST	s.t
6.	Alex Zülle (Sui)	PHO	+ 14"
7.	Bobby Julich (Usa)	CSC	+ 16"
8.	Grischa Niermann (Ger)	RAB	+ 22"
9.	Jens Voigt (Ger)	CSC	s.t
10.	Laurent Brochard (Fra)	A2R	s.t

2nd stage: Chaville/Montargis - 166,5 km

1.	Pedro Horrillo (Esp)	QSD	3h 47'55"
2.	Beat Zberg (Sui)	GST	s.t
3.	Michele Bartoli (Ita)	CSC	s.t
4.	Philippe Gilbert (Bel)	FDJ	s.t
5.	Aart Vierhouten (Ned)	LOT	s.t
6.	Davide Rebellin (Ita)	GST	s.t
7.	Gerben Löwik (Ned)	CHO	s.t
8.	Thor Hushovd (Nor)	C.A	s.t
9.	George Hincapie (Usa)	USP	s.t
10.	Jens Voigt (Ger)	CSC	s.t
Leader:	Jörg Jaksche (Ger)		4h 05'12"
2.	Davide Rebellin (Ita)		+ 6"
3.	Bobby Julich (Usa)		+ 18"

3rd stage: La Chapelle St Ursin/Roanne - 227,5 km

1.	Leon van Bon (Ned)	LOT	5h 38'18"
2.	Thomas Ziegler (Ger)	GST	s.t
3.	Tom Boonen (Bel)	QSD	+ 25"
4.	Robert Hunter (Rsa)	RAB	s.t
5.	Pietro Cauchioli (Ita)	ALB	s.t
6.	Jens Voigt (Ger)	CSC	s.t
7.	Kim Kirchen (Lux)	FAS	s.t
8.	Thor Hushovd (Nor)	C.A	s.t
9.	Fabian Wegmann (Ger)	GST	s.t
10.	Pablo Lastras (Esp)	IBB	s.t
Leader:	Jörg Jaksche (Ger)		9h 43'55"
2.	Davide Rebellin (Ita)		+ 6"
3.	Bobby Julich (Usa)		+ 18"

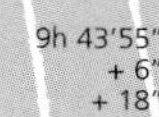

In Gap, Denis Menchov beats off Samuel Sanchez, Dave Bruylandts and Floyd Landis, the breakaway group which pulled away at the Col de Manse.

4th stage: Roanne/ Le Puy en Velay - 184,5 km

Cancelled stage

5th stage: Le Puy en Velay/Rasteau - 215 km

1.	Alexandre Vinokourov (Kaz)	MOB	5h 06'15"
2.	Jörg Jaksche (Ger)	CSC	+ 4"
3.	Michele Bartoli (Ita)	CSC	s.t
4.	Davide Rebellin (Ita)	GST	s.t
5.	Jens Voigt (Ger)	CSC	s.t
6.	George Hincapie (Usa)	USP	s.t
7.	Bobby Julich (Usa)	CSC	s.t
8.	Baden Cooke (Aus)	FDJ	s.t
9.	Frank Schleck (Lux)	CSC	+ 11"
10.	Allan Davis (Aus)	LST	+ 29"

Leader:	Jörg Jaksche (Ger)	14h 50'07"
2.	Davide Rebellin (Ita)	+ 10"
3.	Bobby Julich (Usa)	+ 25"

6th stage: Rasteau/Gap - 173,5 km

1.	Denis Menchov (Rus)	IBB	4h 52'22"
2.	Samuel Sanchez (Esp)	EUS	s.t
3.	Floyd Landis (Usa)	USP	s.t
4.	Dave Bruylandts (Bel)	CHO	s.t
5.	Kim Kirchen (Lux)	FAS	+ 24"
6.	Frank Vandenbroucke (Bel)	FAS	s.t
7.	Davide Rebellin (Ita)	GST	s.t
8.	Jörg Jaksche (Ger)	CSC	s.t
9.	Iñigo Landaluze (Esp)	EUS	s.t
10.	Oscar Pereiro (Esp)	PHO	s.t

Leader:	Jörg Jaksche (Ger)	19h 42'49"
2.	Davide Rebellin (Ita)	+ 14"
3.	Bobby Julich (Usa)	+ 42"

7th stage: Digne les Bains/Cannes - 185,5 km

1.	Alexandre Vinokourov (Kaz)	MOB	4h 39'02"
2.	Kim Kirchen (Lux)	FAS	+ 18"
3.	Jens Voigt (Ger)	CSC	s.t
4.	Beat Zberg (Sui)	GST	s.t
5.	Davide Rebellin (Ita)	GST	s.t
6.	George Hincapie (Usa)	USP	s.t
7.	Dmitriy Fofonov (Kaz)	COF	s.t
8.	Oscar Pereiro (Esp)	PHO	s.t
9.	Philippe Gilbert (Bel)	FDJ	s.t
10.	Sylvain Chavanel (Fra)	BLB	s.t

Leader:	Jörg Jaksche (Ger)	24h 22'08"
2.	Davide Rebellin (Ita)	+ 15"
3.	Bobby Julich (Usa)	+ 43"

8th stage: Nice/Nice - 144 km

1.	Alexandre Vinokourov (Kaz)	MOB	3h35'43"
2.	Denis Menchov (Rus)	IBB	s.t
3.	Torsten Hiekmann (Ger)	MOB	+ 1'37"
4.	Gorka Gonzalez Larranaga (Esp)	EUS	+ 1'48"
5.	Levi Leipheimer (Usa)	RAB	s.t
6.	David Moncoutié (Fra)	COF	s.t
7.	Alberto Contador (Esp)	LST	s.t
8.	Tyler Hamilton (Usa)	PHO	s.t
9.	Samuel Sanchez (Esp)	EUS	+ 2'10"
10.	Kim Kirchen (Lux)	FAS	s.t

FINAL OVERALL STANDINGS

1.	Jörg Jaksche (Ger)	CSC	28h 00'01"
2.	Davide Rebellin (Ita)	GST	+ 15"
3.	Bobby Julich (Usa)	CSC	+ 43"
4.	Jens Voigt (Ger)	CSC	s.t
5.	George Hincapie (Usa)	USP	+ 46"
6.	Frank Vandenbroucke (Bel)	FAS	+ 57"
7.	Oscar Pereiro (Esp)	PHO	+ 1'01"
8.	Michael Rogers (Aus)	QSD	+ 1'09"
9.	Frank Schleck (Lux)	CSC	+ 1'36"
10.	José Azevedo (Por)	USP	+ 1'46"
11.	Ivan Basso (Ita)	CSC	+ 1'53"
12.	Denis Menchov (Rus)	IBB	+ 3'55"
13.	Beat Zberg (Sui)	GST	+ 4'02"
14.	Sylvain Chavanel (Fra)	BLB	+ 4'35"
15.	Torsten Hiekmann (Ger)	MOB	+ 5'14"

POINTS TABLE

1.	Davide Rebellin (Ita)	GST	96 pts
2.	Jens Voigt (Ger)	CSC	85 pts
3.	Alexandre Vinokourov (Kaz)	MOB	80 pts
4.	Jörg Jaksche (Ger)	CSC	74 pts
5.	Kim Kirchen (Lux)	FAS	66 pts
6.	George Hincapie (Usa)	USP	55 pts

MOUNTAIN STANDINGS

1.	Aitor Osa (Esp)	IBB	82 pts
2.	Erik Dekker (Ned)	RAB	30 pts
3.	David Moncoutié (Fra)	COF	28 pts
4.	Denis Menchov (Rus)	IBB	25 pts
5.	Alberto Contador (Esp)	LST	23 pts
6.	Iñigo Landaluze (Esp)	EUS	20 pts

BEST YOUNG STANDINGS

1.	Michael Rogers (Aus)	28h 01'10"
2.	Frank Schleck (Lux)	+ 25"
3.	Kim Kirchen (Lux)	+ 5'16"

TEAM STANDINGS

1.	CSC	84h 01'53"
2.	US POSTAL - BERRY FLOOR	+ 1'20"
3.	QUICK STEP - DAVITAMON	+ 7'05"
4.	PHONAK	+ 8'57"
5.	GEROLSTEINER	+ 15'04'

160 Competitors

T-MOBILE

1.	VINOKOUROV Alexandre (Kaz)	46th	+ 19'04"
2.	AERTS Mario (Bel)	59th	+ 33'10"
3.	BOTERO Santiago (Col)	*Abandon*	6th stage
4.	HIEKMANN Torsten (Ger)	15th	+ 5'14"
5.	KESSLER Matthias (Ger)	54th	+ 30'14"
6.	SCHRECK Stephan (Ger)	*Abandon*	8th stage
7.	WERNER Christian (Ger)	50th	+ 24'32"
8.	YAKOVLEV Serguey (Kaz)	*Abandon*	3rd stage

RABOBANK

11.	LEIPHEIMER Levy (Usa)	22nd	+ 7'00"
12.	DE GROOT Bram (Ned)	74th	+ 47'32"
13.	DE WEERT Kevin (Bel)	*Abandon*	8th stage
14.	DEKKER Erik (Ned)	57th	+ 31'01"
15.	HAYMAN Mathew (Aus)	*Abandon*	8th stage
16.	HUNTER Robert (Rsa)	*Abandon*	8th stage
17.	LOTZ Marc (Ned)	66th	+ 42'29"
18.	NIERMANN Grischa (Ger)	DNS	6th stage

CSC

21.	BASSO Ivan (Ita)	11st	+ 1'53"
22.	BARTOLI Michele (Ita)	*Abandon*	7th stage
23.	BLAUDZUN Michael (Den)	DNS	7th stage
24.	JAKSCHE Jörg (Ger)	**1st**	**48h 00'01"**
25.	JULICH Bobby (Usa)	**3rd**	+ 43"
26.	PIIL Jakob (Den)	*Abandon*	7th stage
27.	SCHLECK Frank (Lux)	**9th**	+ 1'36"
28.	VOIGT Jens (Ger)	**4th**	+ 43"

COFIDIS

31.	MILLAR David (Gbr)	82nd	+ 1h 11'39"
32.	BESSY Frédéric(Fra)	*Abandon*	6th stage
33.	CUESTA Iñigo(Esp)	78th	+ 58'49"
34.	EDALEINE Christophe (Fra)	*Abandon*	7th stage
35.	FOFONOV Dmitriy (Kaz)	33rd	+ 11'49"
36.	MONCOUTIÉ David (Fra)	53rd	+ 29'52"
37.	VASSEUR Cédric (Fra)	43rd	+ 17'36"
38.	WHITE Matthew (Aus)	*Abandon*	7th stage

US POSTAL - BERRY FLOOR

41.	LANDIS Floyd (Usa)	16th	+ 5'55"
42.	AZEVEDO José (Por)	**10th**	+ 1'46"
43.	EKIMOV Viatcheslav (Rus)	40th	+ 16'49"
44.	HINCAPIE George (Usa)	**5th**	+ 46"
45.	JOACHIM Benoît (Lux)	61st	+ 34'17"
46.	NOVAL Benjamin (Esp)	35th	+ 15'04"
47.	PEÑA Victor Hugo (Col)	*Abandon*	8th stage
48.	ZABRISKIE David (Usa)	*Abandon*	8th stage

QUICK STEP - DAVITAMON

51.	ROGERS Michael (Aus)	**8th**	+ 1'09"
52.	BOONEN Tom (Bel)	*Abandon*	7th stage
53.	CRETSKENS Wilfried (Bel)	*Abandon*	8th stage
54.	HORRILLO Pedro (Esp)	29th	+ 8'58"
55.	HULSMANS Kevin (Bel)	*Abandon*	8th stage
56.	SINKEWITZ Patrik (Ger)	30th	+ 10'58"
57.	TANKINK Bram (Ned)	17th	+ 6'02"
58.	VIRENQUE Richard (Fra)	*Abandon*	7th stage

FDJEUX.COM

61.	CASAR Sandy (Fra)	44th	+ 18'37"
62.	COOKE Baden (Aus)	DNS	6th stage

63.	DA CRUZ Carlos (Fra)	*Abandon*	8th stage
64.	EISEL Bernhard (Aut)	*Abandon*	5th stage
65.	GILBERT Philippe (Bel)	19th	+ 6'08"
66.	GUESDON Frédéric (Fra)	*Abandon*	8th stage
67.	LÖVKVIST Thomas (Swe)	56th	+ 30'37"
68.	WILSON Matthew (Aus)	*Abandon*	8th stage

EUSKALTEL - EUSKADI

71.	SANCHEZ Samuel (Esp)	18th	+ 6'08"
72.	ARRIZABALAGA Gorka (Esp)	*Abandon*	8th stage
73.	ARTETXE Mikel (Esp)	TC	5th stage
74.	ETXEBARRIA Unai (Ven)	*Abandon*	8th stage
75.	GALPARSORO Dionisio (Esp)	28th	+ 8'27"
76.	GONZALEZ LARRANAGA Gorka (Esp)	21st	+ 6'44"
77.	IRIZAR Markel (Esp)	84th	+ 1h 26'08"
78.	LANDALUZE Iñigo (Esp)	27th	+ 8'21"

LOTTO - DOMO

81.	McEWEN Robbie (Aus)	DNS	5th stage
82.	DE CLERCQ Hans (Bel)	*Abandon*	8th stage
83.	DETILLOUX Christophe (Bel)	*Abandon*	5th stage
84.	MERCKX Axel (Bel)	47th	+ 21'28"
85.	MOERENHOUT Koos (Ned)	*Abandon*	5th stage
86.	VAN BON Leon (Ned)	*Abandon*	5th stage
87.	VERBRUGGHE Rik (Bel)	42nd	+ 17'31"
88.	VIERHOUTEN Aart (Ned)	72nd	+ 46'47"

AG2R Prévoyance

91.	BROCHARD Laurent (Fra)	23rd	+ 7'04"
92.	ASTARLOZA Mikel (Esp)	TC	5th stage
93.	DUMOULIN Samuel (Fra)	69th	+ 44'00"
94.	GOUBERT Stéphane (Fra)	DNS	6th stage
95.	KRIVTSOV Yuriy (Ukr)	*Abandon*	7th stage
96.	NAZON Jean-Patrick (Fra)	*Abandon*	6th stage
97.	PORTAL Nicolas (Fra)	*Abandon*	8th stage
98.	SCANLON Mark (Irl)	75th	+ 54'18"

CRÉDIT AGRICOLE

101.	HALGAND Patrice	*Abandon*	8th stage
102.	HUSHOVD Thor	*Abandon*	8th stage
103.	KASHECHKIN Andrey	37th	+ 15'16"
104.	LE MEVEL Christophe	55th	+ 30'26"
105.	LEQUATRE Geoffroy	81st	+ 1h 08'28"
106.	POILVET Benoît	31st	+ 11'14"
107.	SALMON Benoît	80th	+ 1h 02'29"
108.	WIGGINS Bradley	*Abandon*	8th stage

FASSA BORTOLO

111.	FRIGO Dario (Ita)	DNS	6th stage
112.	CANCELLARA Fabian (Sui)	*Abandon*	8th stage
113.	CIONI Dario (Ita)	*Abandon*	8th stage
114.	GUSTOV Volodymir (Ukr)	*Abandon*	6th stage
115.	KIRCHEN Kim (Lux)	20th	+ 6'25"
116.	LARSSON Gustav (Swe)	*Abandon*	8th stage
117.	ONGARATO Alberto (Ita)	*Abandon*	8th stage
118.	VANDENBROUCKE Frank (Bel)	**6th**	+ 57"

LIBERTY Seguros

121.	NOZAL Isidro (Esp)	45th	+ 18'41"
122.	BARANOWSKI Dariusz (Pol)	67th	+ 42'45"
123.	CONTADOR Alberto (Esp)	26th	+ 7'43"
124.	DAVIS Allan (Aus)	*Abandon*	8th stage
125.	GONZALEZ de GALDEANO Alvaro (Esp)	*Abandon*	8th stage
126.	RAMIREZ ABEJA Javier (Esp)	39th	+ 16'45"
127.	SANCHEZ GIL Luis Leon (Esp)	73rd	+ 47'27"
128.	SERRANO Marcos (Esp)	34th	+ 12'48"

GEROLSTEINER

131.	REBELLIN Davide (Ita)	**2nd**	+ 15"
132.	POLLACK Olaf (Ger)	*Abandon*	5th stage
133.	SCHOLZ Ronny (Ger)	60th	+ 33'42"
134.	SERPELLINI Marco (Ita)	79th	+ 59'57"
135.	TOTSCHNIG Georg (Aut)	36th	+ 15'04"
136.	WEGMANN Fabian (Ger)	71st	+ 46'12"
137.	ZBERG Beat (Sui)	13rd	+ 4'02"
138.	ZIEGLER Thomas (Ger)	*Abandon*	7th stage

ILLES BALEARS - Banco Santander

141.	MENCHOV Denis (Rus)	12nd	+ 3'55"
142.	BECKE Daniel (Ger)	*Abandon*	5th stage
143.	KARPETS Vladimir (Rus)	24th	+ 7'07"
144.	LASTRAS Pablo (Esp)	64th	+ 39'34"
145.	OSA Aitor (Esp)	70th	+ 45'47"
146.	RADOCHLA Steffen Ger)	*Abandon*	8th stage
147.	REYNES Vicente (Esp)	*Abandon*	8th stage
148.	ZANDIO Xabier (Esp)	63rd	+ 38'18"

Chocolade JACQUES - WINCOR NIXDORF

151.	BRARD Florent (Fra)	49th	+ 22'20"
152.	BELOHVOSCIKS Raivis (Lat)	*Abandon*	7th stage
153.	BRUYLANDTS Dave(Bel)	48th	+ 21'43"
154.	LÖWIK Gerben (Ned)	52nd	+ 25'35"
155.	PEERS Chris (Bel)	DNS	6th stage
156.	PIATEK Zbigniew (Pol)	62nd	+ 37'56"
157.	VAN DE WALLE Jurgen (Bel)	*Abandon*	8th stage
158.	VERHEYEN Geert (Bel)	*Abandon*	7th stage

ALESSIO - BIANCHI

161.	CAUCCHIOLI Pietro (Ita)	*Abandon*	8th stage
162.	JØRGENSEN René (Den)	DNS	5th stage
163.	LJUNGQVIST Marcus (Swe)	DNS	6th stage
164.	MIHOLJEVIC Vladimir (Cro)	41st	+ 16'57"
165.	MØLLER Claus Michael (Den)	32nd	+ 11'44"
166.	PELLIZOTTI Franco (Ita)	*Abandon*	8th stage
167.	RASTELLI Ellis (Ita)	*Abandon*	7th stage
168.	SUNDERLAND Scott (Aus)	76th	+ 56'37"

Brioches LA BOULANGÈRE

171.	ROUS Didier (Fra)	*Abandon*	8th stage
172.	BENETEAU Walter (Fra)	*Abandon*	8th stage
173.	BOUYER Franck (Fra)	77th	+ 57'54"
174.	CHAVANEL Sylvain (Fra)	14th	+ 4'35"
175.	GESLIN Anthony (Fra)	*Abandon*	7th stage
176.	PINEAU Jérôme (Fra)	*Abandon*	7th stage
177.	RENIER Franck (Fra)	68th	+ 42'49"
178.	VOECKLER Thomas (Fra)	*Abandon*	7th stage

PHONAK

181.	HAMILTON Tyler (Usa)	38th	+ 16'14"
182.	DESSEL Cyril (Fra)	*Abandon*	7th stage
183.	JALABERT Nicolas (Fra)	*Abandon*	8th stage
184.	MOOS Alexandre (Sui)	51st	+ 25'02"
185.	PEREIRO Oscar (Esp)	**7th**	+ 1'01"
186.	SCHNIDER Daniel (Sui)	58th	+ 32'12"
187.	VALJAVEC Tadej (Slo)	*Abandon*	7th stage
188.	ZÜLLE Alex (Sui)	25th	+ 7'27"

RAGT Semences - MG ROVER

181.	RINERO Christophe (Fra)	*Abandon*	8th stage
182.	AUGER Guillaume (Fra)	*Abandon*	8th stage
183.	BERTHOU Eric (Fra)	85th	+ 1h 08'28"
184.	BUFFAZ Mickaël (Fra)	*Abandon*	8th stage
185.	LE BOULANGER Yoann (Fra)	65th	+ 42'03"
186.	MUTSCHLER Klaus (Ger)	83rd	+ 1h 20'43"
187.	SEIGNEUR Eddy (Fra)	*Abandon*	8th stage
188.	THIBOUT Bruno (Fra)	*Abandon*	5th stage

TABLE POINTS UCI IN STAGE

CSC	173
GEROLSTEINER	103
T.MOBILE	70
QUICK STEP - DAVITAMON	50
LOTTO - DOMO	40
ILLES BALEARS - BANESTO	35
FASSA BORTOLO	33
EUSKALTEL - EUSKADI	25
RABOBANK	25
US POSTAL	21
Chocolade JACQUES/WINCOR NIXDORF	10
COFIDIS	10
FDJEUX.COM	10
ALESSIO - BIANCHI	5
LIBERTY Seguros	5
PHONAK	3
AG2R Prévoyance	0
Brioches LA BOULANGÈRE	0
CRÉDIT AGRICOLE	0
RAGT Semences - MG ROVER	0

EX WINNERS TAKING THE START **4**

VINOKOUROV Alexandre	2002 & 2003
FRIGO Dario	2001
VANDENBROUCKE Frank	1998
ZÜLLE Alex	1993

In Torre San Patrizio as elsewhere, Paolo Bettini(Middle) didn't rest on his laurels. Every second counts on the Tirreno - Adriatico!

Bettini avoids the traps

The race between the Tyrrhenian coast and the Adriatic is a stressful one even if the course is less difficult than that of the Paris – Nice which takes place at the same time. A high class field, a full peloton, the ends of stages often tricky, a few demanding hills, these are some of the characteristics of this race, which, there's no hiding the fact is a sort of rehearsal for the Primavera. Recent statistics prove the fact: the winner on the Via Roma in San Remo, has for most of the time, warmed up on the Tirreno – Adriatico a few days earlier...

Paolo Bettini, winner of the first round of the World Cup did just this last year, even if he was forced to stop at the end of a particularly confused stage. This year "il Grillo" has managed to avoid the incidents which always affect this race and pushed aside Alessandro Petacchi, winner of three stages and always imperial in the final 300metres.

Since last year everybody knows, Alessandro Petacchi is the best sprinter in the World at the moment. Coming to Tirreno – Adriatico with already two victories under his belt (in the Tour du Luca, now run in February), the rider from La Spezia didn't miss the chance to take his first hat trick of the year, three sprints ending in three wins. With a team completely dedicated to his success, it seemed almost foolish to try to upset his plans. The Italians, Gerosa and Giordani, the Frenchmen Clain and Hervé, the Spaniards Flecha and Igor Gonzalez de Galdeano, the Swiss riders Bertogliati and the Dutchman Mutsaars will all try. But fail fifteen kilometers from the line. Zabel, Hondo or Pagliarini won't have much more luck in the final sprint. Of Petacchi they'll only see the number on his back…

The rain which accompanies the riders for most of the stage didn't encourage the riders to attack but more likely to stay cosily in the middle of the peloton. All this is to the advantage of "Ale Jet" who beat all comers in one sided sprints, no discussion possible with the man who takes the place at the top of the sprinter's pyramid of Mario Cipolini...

DOUBLE BLOW FOR FREIRE...

The day after the terrible terrorist attack in Madrid, the Spaniards found an ounce of comfort, just a small one, in the face of the

tragedy they had known.
This hilly stage suited perfectly those who are rapid but can at the same time cope with hills. Oscar Freire, but also Erik Zabel responded to these criteria. The sprint which would string out the thirty riders who'd got away from the peloton, would clearly go to the Spaniard, perfectly aided by Michael Boogerd. The Ukrainian Vladimir Duma going into a surprising second place when Zabel could only manage to come home in fifth. The winner of the day taking the leader's jersey from Petacchi who shows his weakness when it comes to the climbs...

...AND FOR BETTINI!

Andrea Tafi has remembered something he had forgotten: the Italian is the rider who goes for the longest breakaway of the day. But that's far from enough to take the stage in the small town of Paglieta, nestling in a niche in the mountains. The final circuit to be completed three times would be the occasion for the big guys to do their stuff. The hill of 3.8 kilometers at 7% average would be the ideal trampoline for a Bettini in unbeatable form. Finally he led two World Champions, the reigning one Igor Astarloa and the one from 1999 and 2001, Oscar Freire. For 3 seconds, Bettini takes command.

PETITO, THE COMEBACK

Winner of the same race seven years earlier, Roberto Petito doesn't have too many occasions to get out in front these days. Too occupied being the organiser of the team (he's now aged 33), the Fassa Bortolo captain went on the attack early on and although presenting no real danger for the leaders, resisted well, petito would not leave himself to be manoeuvred in the final kilometers. Backstedt, Calcagni and Matveyev unable to counter when he goes for his 7th victory in a career which started in 19...?

Bettini doesn't forget the second coat
Coming back at several cheeky attackers at five kilometers from home, the peloton, led by the Quick Step team of Paolo Bettini had played its cards well. An uphill sprint, just as the race leader likes them concluded this day spent in the Marches. With the few seconds won in the sprint, the Tuscan could go into the final stage more relaxed. Even if nothing was as yet decided!

PETACCHI TO WIND THINGS UP

For Paolo Bettini it was the ideal scenario. A mass sprint to conclude this edition of the Tirreno – Adriatico, and the extra bonus points amassed by a breakaway. And that's exactly what came to pass. Rony Martias, the West Indian rider for the La Boulangere team, would take a front seat in the race for quite a few kilometers but would give in to the peloton headed by the Fassa Bortolo team of Alessandro Petacchi. He would not disappoint in taking a third stage on this race of the two seas; Paolo Bettini can now breathe easy, the day went as planned. It's in the bag! The hot favourite for the Milan-San Remo doesn't hide his ambitions. ■

Alessandro Petacchi dominates the mass sprints of the Tirreno – Adriatico. He'll do the same thing a few months later in the Giro.

5th stage: Paglieta /Torricella Sicura - 215 km

1.	R. Petito (Ita)	FAS	5h 20'51"
2.	S. Matveyev (Ukr)	PAN	+ 10"
3.	M. Bäckstedt (Swe)	ALB	+ 1'06"
4.	P. Calcagni (Sui)	VIN	+ 1'07"
5.	P. Bettini (Ita)	QSD	+ 3'10"

6th stage: Monte S.Pietrangeli/Torre S.Patrizio - 185 km

1.	P. Bettini (Ita)	QSD	5h 23'41"
2.	O. Freire (Esp)	RAB	s.t
3.	E. Zabel (Ger)	TMO	s.t
4.	M. Lorenzetto (Ita)	DEN	s.t
5.	S. O'Grady (Aus)	COF	s.t

7th stage: S.Benedetto Del Tronto/S.Benedetto Del Tronto - 162 km

1.	A. Petacchi (Ita)	FAS	4h 43'29"
2.	E. Zabel (Ger)	TMO	s.t
3.	G. Balducci (Ita)	SAE	s.t
4.	D. Hondo (Ger)	GST	s.t
5.	A. Aug (Est)	DVE	s.t

FINAL OVERALL STANDINGS

1.	**P. Bettini (Ita)**	**QSD**	**33h 47'06"**
2.	O. Freire (Esp)	RAB	+ 5"
3.	E. Zabel (Ger)	TMO	+ 11"
4.	I. Astarloa (Esp)	COF	+ 18"
5.	S. O'Grady (Aus)	COF	+ 21"
6.	M. Boogerd (Ned)	RAB	+ 22"
7.	R. Aldag (Ger)	TMO	+ 26"
8.	G. Figueras (Ita)	PAN	s.t
9.	A. Vicioso (Esp)	LST	+ 27"
10.	J. Rodriguez Oliver (Esp)	SDV	+ 28"

CLASSIFICATIONS

1st stage: Sabaudia/Sabaudia - 160 km

1.	A. Petacchi (Ita)	FAS	3h 55'31"
2.	E. Zabel (Ger)	TMO	s.t
3.	D. Hondo (Ger)	GST	s.t
4.	L. Pagliarini (Bra)	LAM	s.t
5.	S. Zanini (Ita)	QSD	s.t

2nd stage: Latina /Maddaloni - 164 km

1.	A.Petacchi (Ita)	FAS	4h 53'25"
2.	M. Cipollini (Ita)	DVE	s.t
3.	L. Pagliarini (Bra)	LAM	s.t
4.	S. O'Grady (Aus)	COF	s.t
5.	E. Zabel (Ger)	TMO	s.t

3rd stage: Maddaloni/Isernia - 168 km

1.	O. Freire (Esp)	RAB	4h 47'55"
2.	V. Duma (Ukr)	LAN	s.t
3.	M. Boogerd (Ned)	RAB	s.t
4.	D. Hondo (Ger)	GST	s.t
5.	E. Zabel (Ger)	TMO	s.t

4th stage: Isernia/Paglieta -179 km

1.	P. Bettini (Ita)	QSD	4h 39'31"
2.	I. Astarloa (Esp)	COF	s.t
3.	O. Freire (Esp)	RAB	s.t
4.	J. Rodriguez Oliver (Esp)	LST	s.t
5.	G. Figueras (Ita)	PAN	s.t

Rain, snow, this year the weather conditions were capricious on the Tirreno – Adriatico. But of all that, Paolo Bettini (opposite with Figueras and Honchar, closely following) doesn't worry. He stays focused on one thing, victory.

160 Competitors

FASSA BORTOLO

1.	POZZATO Filippo (Ita)	35th	1'20"
2.	FLECHA Juan Antonio (Esp)	47th	4'22"
3.	PETACCHI Alessandro (Ita)	75th	13'36"
4.	PETITO Roberto (Ita)	90th	8'55"
5.	SACCHI Fabio (Ita)	48th	4'37"
6.	TOSATTO Matteo (Ita)	88th	17'50"
7.	TRENTI Guido (Usa)	95th	21'26"
8.	VELO Marco (Ita)	49th	5'03"

ALESSIO - BIANCHI

11.	BALDATO Fabio (Ita)	50th	5'21"
12.	BERTOLINI Alessandro (Ita)	*Abandon*	6th stage
13.	FURLAN Angelo (Ita)	114th	32'08"
14.	IVANOV Ruslan (Mda)	44th	3'06"
15.	BÄCKSTEDT Magnus (Swe)	100th	24'17"
16.	SKELDE Michael (Den)	94th	19'58"
17.	MORENI Cristian (Ita)	60th	8'03"
18.	TAFI Andrea (Ita)	119th	34'30"

Brioches LA BOULANGÈRE

21.	CHARTEAU Anthony (Fra)	93rd	19'54"
22.	CHAVANEL Sébastien (Fra)	131st	1h09'24"
23.	KERN Christophe (Fra)	*Abandon*	5th stage
24.	LEFÈVRE Laurent (Fra)	56th	7'43"
25.	MARTIAS Rony (Fra)	126th	42'27"
26.	NAULLEAU Alexandre (Fra)	*Abandon*	6th stage
27.	PICHON Mickaël (Fra)	20th	29"
28.	SPRICK Mathieu (Fra)	102nd	25'05"

PANARIA - MARGRES

31.	FIGUERAS Giuliano (Ita)	**8th**	26"
32.	MAZZANTI Luca (Ita)	32nd	1'05"
33.	TIRALONGO Paolo (Ita)	*Abandon*	5th stage
34.	MATVEYEV Serhiy (Ukr)	84th	16'20"
35.	BALIANI Fortunato (Ita)	DNS	5th stage
36.	BONGIORNO Guillermo (Arg)	*Abandon*	4th stage
37.	BORRAJO Alejandro (Arg)	113rd	13'59"
38.	LANCASTER Brett (Aus)	118th	34'23"

COFIDIS

41.	ASTARLOA Igor (Esp)	**4th**	18"
42.	CLAIN Médéric (Fra)	107th	28'35"
43.	FARAZIJN Peter (Bel)	19th	29"
44.	FERNANDEZ BUSTINZA Bingen (Esp)	13rd	29"
45.	O'GRADY Stuart (Aus)	**5th**	21"
46.	LELLI Massimiliano (Ita)	52nd	6'04"
47.	TRENTIN Guido (Ita)	58th	7'51"
48.	TOMBAK Janek (Est)	83rd	16'06"

CRÉDIT AGRICOLE

51.	AUGÉ Stéphane (Fra)	130th	55'44"
52.	BOTCHAROV Alexandre (Rus)	18th	29"
53.	DEAN Julian (Nzl)	DNS	7th stage
54.	HINAULT Sébastien (Fra)	87th	17'48"
55.	JÉGOU Lilian (Fra)	99th	23'56"
56.	LEBLACHER Eric (Fra)	*Abandon*	6th stage
57.	NAZON Damien (Fra)	DNS	2nd stage
58.	HERVÉ Cédric (Fra)	26th	44"

DE NARDI

61.	HONCHAR Serhiy (Ukr)	28th	50"
62.	LORENZETTO Mirco (Ita)	82nd	15'52"
63.	GASPARRE Graziano (Ita)	*Abandon*	6th stage
64.	GIORDANI Leonardo (Ita)	*Abandon*	6th stage
65.	GOBBI Michele (Ita)	101st	25'04"
66.	PUGACI Igor (Mda)	109th	31'37"
67.	MIORIN Devis (Ita)	128th	42'59"
68.	BORGHI Ruggero (Ita)	33rd	1'07"

DOMINA VACANZE

71.	CIPOLLINI Mario (Ita)	*Abandon*	6th stage
72.	AUG Andrus (Est)	127th	42'46"
73.	COLOMBO Gabriele (Ita)	DNS	5th stage
74.	DERGANC Martin (Slo)	110th	31'45"
75.	FAGNINI GianMatteo(Ita)	115th	32'48"
76.	GALLETTI Alessio (Ita)	111st	31'45"
77.	LOMBARDI Giovanni (Ita)	106th	27'57"
78.	SCIREA Mario (Ita)	78th	14'25"

GEROLSTEINER

81.	FÖRSTER Robert (Ger)	103rd	27'18"
82.	HONDO Danilo (Ger)	24th	32"
83.	LANG Sebastian (Ger)	92nd	19'34"
84.	MONTGOMERY Sven (Sui)	*Abandon*	4th stage
85.	ORDOWSKI Volker (Ger)	*Abandon*	6th stage
86.	HARDTER Uwe (Ger)	*Abandon*	5th stage
87.	STRAUSS Marcel (Sui)	16th	29"
88.	ZBERG Marcus (Sui)	12nd	29"

LAMPRE

91.	BORTOLAMI Gianluca (Ita)	120th	34'43"
92.	BELLI Wladimir (Ita)	DNS	5th stage
93.	BOSSONI Paolo (Ita)	39th	1'47"
94.	BARBERO Sergio (Ita)	21st	29"
95.	HAUPTMAN Andrej (Slo)	*Abandon*	4th stage
96.	CARRARA Matteo (Ita)	38th	1'26"
97.	VAINSTEINS Romans (Lat)	62nd	9'25"
98.	PAGLIARINI Luciano (Bra)	122nd	37'30"

LANDBOUWKREDIET - COLNAGO

101.	BERNUCCI Lorenzo (Ita)	70th	12'15"
102.	DUMA Vladimir (Ukr)	23rd	30"
103.	DIERCKXSENS Ludo (Bel)	76th	14'08"
104.	GASPERONI Cristian (Ita)	65th	11'30"
105.	BILEKA Volodymir (Ukr)	29th	58"
106.	POPOVYCH Yaroslav (Ukr)	61st	9'11"
107.	DURAND Jacky (Fra)	129th	43'47"
108.	VAN BONDT Geert (Bel)	51st	5'29"

LIBERTY Seguros

111.	CARUSO Giadnsaolo (Ita)	37th	1'21"
112.	ANDRLE René (Cze)	91st	19'18"
113.	BARREDO Carlos (Esp)	41st	2'03"
114.	DIAZ JUSTO Rafael (Esp)	*Abandon*	4th stage
115.	GONZALEZ de GALDEANO Igor (Esp)	81st	15'35"
116.	HERNANDEZ BLAZQUEZ Jesus (Esp)	*Abandon*	4th stage
117.	HRUSKA Jan (Cze)	46th	4'13"
118.	VICIOSO Angel (Esp)	**9th**	27"

LOTTO - DOMO

121.	VAN PETEGEM Peter (Bel)	22nd	29"
122.	BRANDT Christophe (Bel)	55th	7'39"
123.	WADECKI Piotr (Pol)	96th	22'18"
124.	VAN DIJK Stefan (Ned)	*Abandon*	6th stage
125.	BAGUET Serge (Bel)	*Abandon*	5th stage
126.	VANSEVENANT Wim (Bel)	71st	12'19"
127.	MARICHAL Thierry (Bel)	85th	17'10"
128.	HOSTE Leif (Bel)	97th	22'21"

PHONAK

131.	AEBERSOLD Niki (Sui)	34th	1'18"
132.	CAMENZIND Oscar (Sui)	14th	29"
133.	ELMIGER Martin (Sui)	11st	29"
134.	ALBASINI Michael (Sui)	27th	48"
135.	GRABSCH Bert (Ger)	30th	1'03"
136.	RAST Gregory (Sui)	67th	11'54"
137.	TSCHOPP Johann (Sui)	45th	3'38"
138.	USOV Alexandre (Blr)	89th	18'25"

QUICK STEP - DAVITAMON

141.	BETTINI Paolo (Ita)	**1st**	**33h 17'06"**
142.	BRAMATI Davide (Ita)	108th	30'32"
143.	KNAVEN Servais (Ned)	74th	13'28"
144.	NUYENS Nick (Bel)	105th	27'30"
145.	PAOLINI Luca (Ita)	43rd	3'05"
146.	BODROGI Laszlo (Hun)	73rd	12'51"
147.	MUSEEUW Johan (Bel)	68th	12'03"
148.	ZANINI Stefano (Ita)	86th	17'27"

RABOBANK

151.	BOOGERD Michael (Ned)	**6th**	22"
152.	BOVEN Jan (Ned)	64th	11'13"
153.	DE JONGH Steven (Ned)	98th	22'46"
154.	BARTKO Robert (Ger)	112nd	31'54"
155.	FREIRE Oscar (Esp)	**2nd**	5"
156.	KROON Karsten (Ned)	72nd	12'39"
157.	MUTSAARS Ronald (Ned)	104th	27'22"
158.	WAUTERS Marc (Bel)	66th	11'48"

SAECO

161.	DI LUCA Danilo (Ita)	25th	34"
162.	BALDUCCI Gabriele (Ita)	117th	33'32"
163.	CELESTINO Mirko (Ita)	*Abandon*	6th stage
164.	COMMESSO Salvatore (Ita)	124th	41'29"
165.	FORNACIARI Paolo (Ita)	123rd	38'29"
166.	PETROV Evgueni (Rus)	36th	1'20"
167.	PIERI Dario (Ita)	*Abandon*	6th stage
168.	SPEZIALETTI Alessandro (Ita)	69th	12'12"

SAUNIER DUVAL - PRODIR

171.	BERTOGLIATI Rubens (Sui)	79th	15'09"
172.	LOBATO Ruben (Esp)	15th	29"
173.	COBO Juan José (Esp)	*Abandon*	6th stage
174.	RODRIGUEZ OLIVER Joaquin (Esp)	**10th**	28"
175.	LODDO Alberto (Ita)	*Abandon*	5th stage
176.	ZAUGG Oliver (Sui)	40th	1'59"
177.	STRAZZER Massimo (Ita)	125th	41'53"
178.	JOHNSON Tim (Usa)	DNS	5th stage

T-MOBILE

181.	ALDAG Rolf (Ger)	**7th**	26"
182.	IVANOV Serguei (Rus)	59th	7'54"
183.	KLIER Andreas (Ger)	42nd	2'37"
184.	KLÖDEN Andreas (Ger)	77th	14'12"
185.	NARDELLO Daniele (Ita)	53rd	6'39"
186.	SCHAFFRATH Jan (Ger)	54th	7'05"
187.	WESEMANN Steffen (Ger)	17th	29"
188.	ZABEL Erik (Ger)	**3rd**	11"

Vini CALDIROLA - NOBILI Rubinetterie

181.	TONKOV Pavel (Rus)	63rd	10'13"
182.	ZANOTTI Marco (Ita)	121st	35'07"
183.	MILESI Marco (Ita)	80th	15'21"
184.	CALCAGNI Patrick (Sui)	57th	7'45"
185.	MASCIARELLI Simone (Ita)	DNS	6th stage
186.	SGAMBELLURI Roberto (Ita)	31st	1'03"
187.	GEROSA Mauro (Ita)	116th	33'08"
188.	ZINETTI Mauro (Ita)	DNS	5th stage

EX WINNERS TAKING THE START — 2

POZZATO Filippo	2003
PETITO Roberto	1997

3 OLDEST

SCIREA Mario	1964/08/07
DIERCKXSENS Ludo	1964/10/14
MUSEEUW Johan	1965/10/13

3 YOUNGEST

TSCHOPP Johann	1982/07/01
KERN Christophe	1981/11/18
SPRICK Mathieu	1981/09/29

NATIONALITIES REPRESENTED — 24

Italy	57
France	16
Germany	13
Belgium, Spain and Switzerland	12
Netherlands	7
Ukraine	5
Russia	4
Argentina, Australia, Czech Republic, Estonia, Moldavia, Slovenia and U.S.A	2
Belarus, Brazil, Denmark, Hungary, Latvia, New Zealand, Poland and Sweden	1

On this day the gods of cycle racing were with Roberto petito, winner in Toricella Sicura.

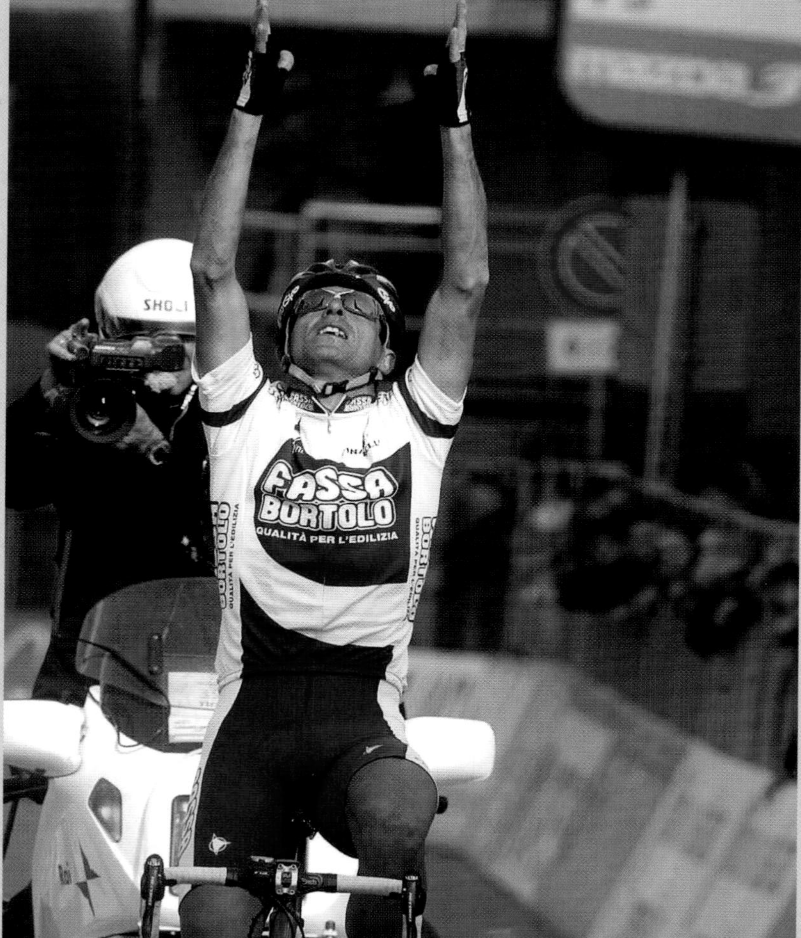

HAMILTON AGAIN

Before the start of this Tour of Romandie the Phonak team can count only two victories (a stage of the Tour of Valencia and the minor Tour of Berne) taken by the rapid Bielarussian Alexandre Usov. Considering the recruiting effort of the closed season the results are more than modest. Tyler Hamilton, but also Oscar Camenzind, Alexandre Moos and Alex Zulle now knew what was needed to put the team back on the right track. The mission was brilliantly accomplished, in particular by Hamilton who repeated the success he'd had with the CSC team.

1st stage: Yverdon / Yverdon – 175.2 kms

Petacchi, thinking of something else?

Sprinting for the victory on the Tour of Romandie has become a luxury since the traditional road race of the final day was replaced by a time trial in the streets of Lausanne. That's to say the kings of the sprint had no intention of missing their only chance to shine, before the mountain specialists would take over. Just the same, the Ukrainian Yuriy Krivtsov (AG2R) thought he could create a surprise with an attack at the tenth kilometre, but his talent (which notably gave him the victory last year) would not go unnoticed this time around. His at one time lead of 14 mins 10 sec which he had laboriously constructed was wiped out when the teams of the sprinters went into action. The rider from the East was caught 20 kilometers from Yverdon following a breakaway of 145 kilometers. A desperate attempt by Rubens Bertogliati (Saunier Duval) shortly before the finish would end in the same way. The sprinters would fight things out among themselves. The most successful of them, Alessandro Petacchi, was of course, the favourite. But a sprint is never over before the line. The now famous final rush of the rider from La Spezia was late in coming. In fact, it was never to come! It's the experienced Jan Svorada who takes the win, on the line, ahead of Marco Zanotti, Petacchi settling for fifth place after easing up in the final metres. Bradley Mc Gee also took part in the sprint, but in a second group, in which he followed closely his nearest challenger, Olaf Pollack. If he was unable to win any points in the final sprint, the Australian made sure of keeping his lead by fighting hard in the intermediate sprints.

2nd stage: Romont / Romont – 156 kms

Garzelli reassures

For the protagonists of the Giro, the Tour of Romandie is ideally placed in the calendar to test their strength before launching into three weeks racing on the roads of Italy. That said, the least that can be said is that the favourites for the Giro are keeping a low profile here in Geneva. One had, however shown his presence. Stefano Garzelli, winner a fortnight earlier in the Tour of Aragon, did not show much in the Liege – Bastogne – Liege and a few doubts about his condition were beginning to surface. Doubts that were soon dissipated when he came in first, ahead of a group of twenty riders who had survived the several climbs of the day.

The first offensive of the day comes from Alessandro Petacchi, doubtless wanting to tackle the day's difficulties with a certain lead under his belt, but his effort is soon wiped out. It's at the 35th kilometre that a more serious offensive takes shape. Nine men, (O. Camenzind, F. Mourey, I. Landaluze, M Calvente, T. Danieson, J. Svorada, R. Forster, R. Bertgliati, and V. Dumas) quickly open up a lead of two minutes... but only a little more the first time at the line in Romont (2.43) when Camenzind and Dalielson are left behind. The second time at the line, one man, the Basque Inigo Landaluze (Euskaltel) is alone in the lead, just ahead of Calvente and a little more than two minutes ahead of a group lead by the Phonak team. With 37 kilometers left to race, Landaluze knows he will be unable to resist the fate that awaits in just a few minutes. In fact, it's a reduced peloton of thirty riders that race for the finish line. Marco Pinotti tries an attack 4 kms from the line but fades at the last climb and is caught by a group 500metres from the line, not noticing Stefano Garzelli pull out from behind Piepoli less than 100 metres from the line. The leader of Vini Caldirola takes the win ahead of Ivan Basso and Gerrit Glomser. Bradley Mc Gee, who follows in with the peloton of the leaders (he finishes 7th in the stage) keeps his leader's jersey.

3rd stage: Romont / Morgins – 145 kms

Tears of joy in Morgins

With two first category climbs on the menu, this stage promised to be the most difficult of the week. This probably incites a few riders to set up a lead at the outset. Among them, the two "Oscars" from Phonak, the Swiss Camenzind, the Spaniard Sevilla, and also Alessandro Petacchi, Sandy Casar, Alberto Lopez de Munain and Rubens Bertogliati. After setting up a lead of more than five minutes, the group disintegrates. Oscar Camenzind attacks alone the first slopes of the Col des Mosses with a lead of forty seconds over Casar, Calcagni, Blaudzun, Sevilla, Rudenko, Petacchi and Bertogliati and of a little more than two minutes over a peloton led by the canary yellow shirted men of the Saunier Duval team. A peloton which absorbed in between riders in the valley preceding the final ascent to Morgins. The case of Camenzind being sorted out after 3kms of the climb. The struggle of the men looking for victory could now take place. It's the exciting Leonardo Piepoli (Saunier Duval) who lights the fuse. Alexandre Moos (Phonak) at first, then his leader Tyler Hamilton and at last Ivan Basso (CSC) and Fabian Jeker (Saunier Duval) go to the front, momentarily as far as the last two are concerned. On the final slight slope to the line, Tyler Hamilton makes a final effort to assure victory. Sandwiched, Piepoli eased up before an irresistible Alexandre Moos. The Valaisan rider broke down in tears, winning for the first time on home soil and at the same time taking the leader's jersey.

4th stage: Sion / Sion – 127 kms

Saunier Duval Vs Phonak

Mayens de Chamoson, Veysonnaz and Crans- Montana, this is the plat de resistance on this short but very difficult penultimate stage. After a nice parting shot from Sven Montgomery (Gerolsteiner) and Stefano Garzelli on the two first climbs, it's finally a quartet that pulls away in the last kilometers before the ascention towards Crans – Montana. A perfectly balanced group as it contains two Saunier Duval (Jeker and Piepoli) and two Phonak (Hamilton and...Valuate). In effect, Alexandre Moos, wearing the leader's jersey eased up at 3 kilometers from the summit, abandoning any hope of taking the win. At first reticent, Tyler Hamilton and the Slovenian champion Tadej Valjavec work with the Saunier Duval duo. Very impressive throughout the day, Fabian Jeker even took the liberty of beating his adversaries in the following sprint. The Leader's jersey came to rest on the shoulders of Tyler Hamilton (and therefore stayed in the same team), Alexandre Moos having conceded 1 min 18 sec to his American team mate in Sion.

5th stage:

Time trial in Lausanne – 20 kilometers

The finishing touches

The logical favourite for the difficult time trial that now concludes the Tour of Romandie, Tyler Hamilton confirmed his position. Beating the winner of the prologue, Bradley Mc Gee by 35 seconds the Massachusetts rider removed any suspense at the outcome , his principal rival, Fabian Jeker being relegated down the rankings at all the intermediate timing points. As last year, Tyler Hamilton waited until the final day before definitively marking his domination of a race which seems to fit him like a glove. ■

In Morgins, Alexandre Moos is unbeatable. He sweeps Leonardo Piepoli aside to take the Leader's Jersey.

CLASSIFICATIONS

Prologue in Geneva - 3,4 km

1.	Bradley McGee (Aus)	FDJ	4'24"38
2.	Olaf Pollack (Ger)	GST	+ 3"14
3.	Martin Elmiger (Sui)	PHO	+ 6"98
4.	Alexandre Moos (Sui)	PHO	+ 7"45
5.	Tyler Hamilton (Usa)	PHO	+ 8"58

1st stage: Yverdon/Yverdon - 175,2 km

1.	Jan Svorada (Cze)	LAM	4h 15'12"
2.	Marco Zanotti (Ita)	VIN	s.t
3.	Luciano Pagliarini (Bra)	LAM	s.t
4.	Massimo Strazzer (Ita)	SDV	s.t
5.	Alessandro Petacchi (Ita)	FAS	s.t

Leader: Bradley McGee (Aus) 4h 19'32"

2nd stage: Romont/Romont - 156 km

1.	Stefano Garzelli (Ita)	VIN	3h 46'01"
2.	Ivan Basso (Ita)	CSC	s.t
3.	Gerrit Glomser (Aut)	SAE	s.t
4.	David Etxebarria (Esp)	EUS	s.t
5.	Manuele Mori (Ita)	SDV	s.t

Leader: Bradley McGee (Aus) 4h 19'32"

3rd stage: Romont/Morgins - 145 km

1.	Alexandre Moos (Sui)	PHO	3h 32'45"
2.	Leonardo Piepoli (Ita)	SDV	s.t
3.	Tyler Hamilton (Usa)	PHO	s.t
4.	Alex Zülle (Sui)	PHO	+ 25"
5.	Dario Cioni (Ita)	FAS	+ 26"

Leader: Alexandre Moos (Sui) 11h 38'19"

4th stage: Sion/Sion - 127 km

1.	Fabian Jeker (Sui)	SDV	3h 40'54"
2.	Dario Cioni (Ita)	FAS	s.t
3.	Tadej Valjavec (Slo)	PHO	s.t
4.	Tyler Hamilton (Usa)	PHO	s.t
5.	Leonardo Piepoli (Ita)	SDV	+ 3"

Leader: Tyler Hamilton (Usa) 15h 19'15"

5th stage: Team time trial in Lausanne - 20 km

1.	Tyler Hamilton (Usa)	PHO	26'29"
2.	Bradley McGee (Aus)	FDJ	+ 35"
3.	Ronny Scholz (Ger)	GST	+ 53"
4.	Ivan Basso (Ita)	CSC	+ 57"
5.	Stefano Garzelli (Ita)	VIN	+ 1'00"

FINAL OVERALL STANDINGS

1.	**Tyler Hamilton (Usa)**	**PHO**	**15h 45'44"**
2.	Fabian Jeker (Sui)	SDV	+ 1'43"
3.	Leonardo Piepoli (Ita)	SDV	+ 2'18"
4.	Tadej Valjavec (Slo)	PHO	+ 2'19"
5.	Dario Cioni (Ita)	FAS	+ 2'33"
6.	Alexandre Moos (Sui)	PHO	+ 2'39"
7.	Ivan Basso (Ita)	CSC	+ 3'31"
8.	Francisco Mancebo (Esp)	IBB	+ 4'32"
9.	Bradley McGee (Aus)	FDJ	+ 5'08"
10.	Steve Zampieri (Sui)	VIN	+ 5'53"
11.	Georg Totschnig (Aut)	GST	+ 6'00"
12.	Marco Pinotti (Ita)	LAM	+ 7'38"
13.	Sylvester Szmyd (Pol)	SAE	+ 8'27"
14.	Jörg Jaksche (Ger)	CSC	+ 9'00"
15.	Bert de Waele (Bel)	LAN	+ 10'17"

POINTS TABLE

1.	Tyler Hamilton (Usa)	PHO	50 pts
2.	Bradley McGee (Aus)	FDJ	47 pts
3.	Ivan Basso (Ita)	CSC	40 pts
4.	Alexandre Moos (Sui)	PHO	38 pts
5.	Stefano Garzelli (Ita)	VIN	33 pts
6.	Fabian Jeker (Sui)	SDV	31 pts

MOUNTAIN STANDINGS

1.	Sven Montgomery (Sui)	GST	20 pts
2.	Steve Zampieri (Sui)	VIN	19 pts
3.	Tyler Hamilton (Usa)	PHO	18 pts
4.	Fabian Jeker (Sui)	SDV	16 pts
5.	Manuel Calvente (Esp)	CSC	16 pts
6.	Oscar Camenzind (Sui)	PHO	15 pts

BEST YOUNG STANDINGS

1.	Michael Rogers (Aus)	28h 01'10"
2.	Frank Schleck (Lux)	+ 25"
3.	Kim Kirchen (Lux)	+ 5'16"

TEAM STANDINGS

1.	CSC	84h 01'53"
2.	US POSTAL - BERRY FLOOR	+ 1'20"
3.	QUICK STEP - DAVITAMON	+ 7'05"
4.	PHONAK	+ 8'57"
5.	GEROLSTEINER	+ 15'04'

117 Competitors

PHONAK

1.	HAMILTON Tyler (Usa)	**1st**	**15h 45'44"**
2.	ZÜLLE Alex (Sui)	DNS	5th stage
3.	VALJAVEC Tadej (Slo)	**4th**	+ 2'19"
4.	CAMENZIND Oscar (Sui)	52nd	+ 36'54"
5.	ELMIGER Martin (Sui)	*Abandon*	4th stage
6.	MOOS Alexandre (Sui)	**6th**	+ 2'39"
7.	SCHNIDER Daniel (Sui)	33rd	+ 22'55"
8.	SEVILLA Oscar (Esp)	24th	+ 16'58"

AG2R Prévoyance

11.	ASTARLOZA Mikel (Esp)	83rd	+ 1h 13'56"
12.	CHAURREAU Iñigo (Esp)	54th	+ 41'24"
13.	DUMOULIN Samuel (Fra)	67th	+ 56'24"
14.	GOUBERT Stéphane (Fra)	37th	+ 25'47"
15.	KRIVTSOV Yuriy (Ukr)	60th	+ 48'43"
16.	ORIOL Christophe (Fra)	86th	+ 1h 24'00"
17.	PORTAL Nicolas (Fra)	*Abandon*	4th stage
18.	INAUDI Nicolas (Fra)	DNS	2nd stage

Chocolade JACQUES - WINCOR NIXDORF

21.	ARANAGA Andoni (Esp)	64th	+ 53'07"
22.	ARDILA Mauricio (Esp)	23rd	+ 15'02"
23.	BRARD Florent (Fra)	*Abandon*	4th stage
24.	GADRET John (Fra)	35th	+ 24'13"
25.	PIATEK Zbigniew (Pol)	*Abandon*	4th stage
26.	KOSTYUK Denis (Ukr)	26th	+ 18'25"
27.	VERHEYEN Geert (Bel)	61st	+ 50'21"
28.	RUDENKO Maxim (Ukr)	*Abandon*	4th stage

CSC

41.	JAKSCHE Jörg (Ger)	14th	+ 9'00"
42.	BLAUDZUN Michael (Den)	*Abandon*	4th stage
43.	CALVENTE Manuel (Esp)	41st	+ 29'00"
44.	SCHLECK Frank (Lux)	*Abandon*	4th stage
45.	LUTTENBERGER Peter (Aut)	42nd	+ 30'25"
46.	BASSO Ivan (Ita)	**7th**	+ 3'31"
47.	SASTRE Carlos (Esp)	31st	+ 21'53"
48.	SØRENSEN Nicki (Den)	16th	+ 10'47"

EUSKALTEL - EUSKADI

51.	LAISEKA Roberto (Esp)	21st	+ 13'54"
52.	ALBIZU Joseba (Esp)	*Abandon*	4th stage
53.	ETXEBARRIA David (Esp)	28th	+ 19'17"
54.	CAMAÑO Iker (Esp)	19th	+ 12'52"
55.	LOPEZ de MUNAIN Alberto (Esp)	34th	+ 23'43"
56.	LANDALUZE Iñigo (Esp)	58th	+ 47'21"
57.	GONZALEZ LARRAÑAGA Gorka (Esp)	*Abandon*	4th stage

FASSA BORTOLO

61.	CIONI Dario (Ita)	**5th**	+ 2'33"
62.	DANIELSON Tom (Usa)	18th	+ 12'16"
63.	FACCI Mauro (Ita)	73rd	+ 58'50"
64.	GONZALEZ JIMENEZ Aitor (Esp)	*Abandon*	4th stage
65.	GUSTOV Volodymir (Ukr)	44th	+ 31'47"
66.	LARSSON Gustav (Swe)	57th	+ 46'28"
67.	PETACCHI Alessandro (Ita)	DNS	4th stage
68.	SANCHEZ PIMIENTA Julian (Esp)	48th	+ 34'08"

FDJEUX.COM

71.	CASAR Sandy (Fra)	*Abandon*	4th stage
72.	VAUGRENARD Benoît (Fra)	81st	+ 1h 04'39"
73.	FRITSCH Nicolas (Fra)	17th	+ 10'57"
74.	McGEE Bradley (Aus)	**9th**	+ 5'08"
75.	MOUREY Francis (Fra)	70th	+ 58'00"
76.	SANCHEZ Fabien (Fra)	80th	+ 1h 01'08"
77.	VOGONDY Nicolas (Fra)	53rd	+ 41'10"
78.	WILSON Matthew (Aus)	85th	+ 1h 19'03"

GEROLSTEINER

81.	FÖRSTER Robert (Ger)	77th	+ 59'46"
82.	HARDTER Uwe (Ger)	82nd	+ 1h 10'56"
83.	MONTGOMERY Sven (Sui)	30th	+ 20'41"
84.	ORDOWSKI Volker (Ger)	*Abandon*	4th stage
85.	PESCHEL Uwe (Ger)	DNS	5th stage
86.	POLLACK Olaf (Ger)	68th	+ 57'07"
87.	SCHOLZ Ronny (Ger)	45th	+ 31'50"
88.	TOTSCHNIG Georg (Aut)	11st	+ 6'00"

ILLES BALEARS - BANESTO

91.	COLOM Antonio (Esp)	DNS	2nd stage
93.	HORRACH Joan (Esp)	51st	+ 36'15"
94.	LASTRAS Pablo (Esp)	22nd	+ 14'56"
95.	MANCEBO Francisco (Esp)	**8th**	+ 4'32"
96.	RADOCHLA Steffen (Ger)	84th	+ 1h 16'32"
97.	REYNES Vicente (Esp)	66th	+ 56'18"
98.	ZANDIO Xabier (Esp)	*Abandon*	1st stage

LAMPRE

101.	BELLI Wladimir (Ita)	47th	+ 33'23"
102.	PINOTTI Marco (Ita)	12nd	+ 7'38"
103.	BERTOLETTI Simone (Ita)	39th	+ 26'55"
104.	KVACHUK Oleksandr (Ukr)	63rd	+ 52'36"
105.	PICCOLI Mariano (Ita)	DNS	5th stage
106.	QUINZIATO Manuel (Ita)	72nd	+ 58'38"
107.	SVORADA Jan (Cze)	59th	+ 47'54"
108.	PAGLIARINI Luciano (Bra)	*Abandon*	4th stage

LANDBOUWKREDIET - COLNAGO

111.	ANZA Santo (Ita)	*Abandon*	2nd stage
112.	ADVEYEV Serguey (Ukr)	55th	+ 44'02"
113.	BILEKA Volodymir (Ukr)	50th	+ 36'09"
114.	DE WAELE Bert (Bel)	15th	+ 10'17"
115.	DUMA Vladimir (Ukr)	25th	+ 16'58"
116.	GRYSCHENKO Ruslan (Ukr)	56th	+ 44'19"
118.	VERSTREPEN Johan (Bel)	DNS	4th stage

RAGT Semences - MG ROVER

121.	BERNARD Jérôme (Fra)	79th	+ 59'54"
122.	BERTHOU Eric (Fra)	*Abandon*	1st stage
123.	BOURQUENOUD Pierre (Sui)	62nd	+ 51'31"
124.	MARTIN Ludovic (Fra)	40th	+ 28'13"
125.	BUFFAZ Mickaël (Fra)	75th	+ 59'17"
126.	LAURENT Christophe (Fra)	65th	+ 54'31"
127.	SEIGNEUR Eddy (Fra)	69th	+ 57'43"
128.	RINERO Christophe (Fra)	74th	+ 59'17"

SAECO

131.	BALDUCCI Gabriele (Ita)	*Abandon*	2nd stage
132.	GLOMSER Gerrit (Aut)	*Abandon*	3rd stage
133.	LOOSLI David (Sui)	20th	+ 13'06"
134.	CASAGRANDA Stefano (Ita)	*Abandon*	4th stage
135.	SABALIAUSKAS Marius (Ltu)	43rd	+ 30'51"
136.	STANGELJ Gorazd (Slo)	27th	+ 19'09"
137.	SZMYD Sylvester (Pol)	13rd	+ 8'27"
138.	MATZBACHER Andreas (Aut)	76th	+ 59'30"

SAUNIER DUVAL - PRODIR

141.	BERTOGLIATI Rubens (Sui)	38th	+ 26'48"
142.	JEKER Fabian (Sui)	**2nd**	+ 1'43"
143.	PIEPOLI Leonardo (Ita)	**3rd**	+ 2'18"
144.	RODRIGUEZ OLIVER Joaquin (Esp)	*Abandon*	4th stage
145.	MORI Manuele (Ita)	49th	+ 34'26"
146.	DE LA FUENTE David (Esp)	*Abandon*	2nd stage
147.	STRAZZER Massimo (Ita)	DNS	5th stage
148.	ZAUGG Oliver (Sui)	32nd	+ 21'57"

Vini CALDIROLA - NOBILI Rubinetterie

151.	BEUCHAT Roger (Sui)	36th	+ 25'42"
152.	CALCAGNI Patrick (Sui)	71st	+ 58'30"
153.	CHEULA Giadnsaolo (Ita)	DNS	3rd stage
154.	GARZELLI Stefano (Ita)	29th	+ 20'00"
155.	SGAMBELLURI Roberto (Ita)	78th	+ 59'47"
156.	MILESI Marco (Ita)	46th	+ 32'50"
157.	ZANOTTI Marco (Ita)	*Abandon*	4th stage
158.	ZAMPIERI Steve (Sui)	**10th**	+ 5'53"

EX WINNERS TAKING THE START — **0**

RIDERS IN THE UCI TOP 100 — **13**

TABLE POINTS UCI IN STAGE

T.MOBILE	402

3 OLDEST

SCIREA Mario	1964/08/07
DIERCKXSENS Ludo	1964/10/14
MUSEEUW Johan	1965/10/13

3 YOUNGEST

TSCHOPP Johann	1982/07/01
KERN Christophe	1981/11/18
SPRICK Mathieu	1981/09/29

NATIONALITIES REPRESENTED	**24**
Italy	57
France	16
Germany	13
Belgium, Spain and Switzerland	12
Netherlands	7
Ukraine	5
Russia	4
Argentina, Australia, Czech Republic, Estonia, Moldavia, Slovenia and U.S.A	2
Belarussia, Brazil, Denmark, Hungary, Latvia, New Zealand, Poland and Sweden	1

Tyler Hamilton Keeps his title in Romandie; Much to the pleasure of his new Swiss employer Phonak.

A radiant Christophe Moreau had his best day in the Languedoc and the Roussillon

Moreau, in style

After an interruption of a year, the ex Grand Prix du Midi Libre is brought back to life by the ASO organisation which also runs the Tour de France under the name of Tour of Languedoc – Roussillon.

The race is more than ever seen as a springboard for the Tour de France and for this reason draws the stars such as Lance Armstrong, back in Europe after a break of several weeks, and Christophe Moreau who takes pleasure in alternating warm (victory in the Trophée des Grimpers) and the cold (successive retirements in the 4Jours de Dunkerque and the Tour of Asturies). After a particularly intense Tour of Languedoc – Roussillon we can see him fighting hard for his sprinter Thor Hushovd, but also on the final two days with successes at Mende and Mont Saint Clair, where the terrain suits him, Christophe Moreau comes out of the race with a renewed confidence. The star of a great show on the steep slopes of the Mont Saint Clair (he seems less at ease on the Cote de Mendes), the Texan, winner of this race two years ago, showed himself satisfied with his return to racing.

1st stage:
Maury / Port – Vendres – 167 kms

The most Catalan of Norwegians!

The reasonably straight forward nature of this first stage encourages the long distance specialists. After a few false starts, three men manage to escape the pack. Three Frenchmen at that! The experienced Walter Beneteau, the young Jeremy Roy and Philippe Koehler, quickly open up a lead of up to eight minutes in front of a peloton seemingly unconcerned by their escape. At the front, the rhythm remains rapid, this excludes Koehler when the catch up has only just begun, under the guidance of the Credit Agricole team and that of AG2R which, theoretically count in their number the two fastest men in the race, that's to say Thor Hushovd, the solid Norwegian, now living in the area, and the muscular Samuel Dumoulin. Still holding a lead of 5 mins 30 sec at 35 kilometers from Port - Vendres, the leading duo can still believe in their chances. But things quickly change and the hill near the end of the stage proves fatal for the two men visibly worn by their adventure. The final few metres seem to allow Samuel Dumoulin to surprise the imposing Thor Hushovd, but summoning all of his strength the Scandinavian comes back to take the win and the first Yellow jersey of this almost new race.

Only Egoi Martinez de Esteban (Euskaltel) can stay with Lance Armstrong on the steep slopes of Mont saint Clair. But the Spaniard will soon buckle after a new acceleration from the US Postal leader, who seemed to want to reassert himself on this stage.

2nd stage:

Port Leucate / Narbonne – 187 kms

The same old faces…

It's a sufficiently rare occurrence to merit note: the winning trio of Port Vendres take the same places in a sprint which in many ways resembles that of the day before.
If certain sprinters are capable of several victories in a row, it's much rarer to see the same three riders sprint home in the same order two days running. That's just what happened in Narbonne after the two animators of the day, Anthony Charteau and Christophe Edaleine (once again a breakaway 100% French) were caught fifteen kilometers from the line. A peloton orchestrated by a U S Postal team, complete and impressive when, using the wind to their advantage, they break up the peloton near the end of the course. They were only 51 riders who managed to arrive in Narbonne in the same time as winner Thor Hushovd, (who as before leads Dumoulin and Pineau). Among the victims of the U S Postal strategy we can count David Moncoutié, Patrice Halgand or the Swiss riders Oscar Camenzind and Alex Zulle. No stage is won before it's run.

3rd stage:

Ganges / Aigues Mortes – 162kms

Elmiger on the line

Twelve men decide to change the way the race has run for the first two days. Getting away at km 44, Moncoutié, (Cofidis), Beltran (U S Postal), Yakovlev (T Mobile), Martinez de Estaban and Fernandez de Larrea (Euskaltel), Brochard (AG2R), Pineau (La Boulangere), Robin (Fdjeux.com), Calzati (Ragt), Serri(Barloworld) and two men sent up front by the Yellow jersey, Fedrigo and Muravyev organise (with the exception, of course, of the last two) a breakaway culminating in a lead of 4mins 45 sec a little later. The Phonak team, not represented in the leading group set up the chase and at less than ten kilometers from Aigues Mortes the group is caught. Just the same, Calzati and Robin resist. That said, the peloton finally pulls them in at the last kilometre point Once again a sprint decides who will win, but this time the huge form of Thor Hushovd is passed by Yuriy Krivtsov and Martin Elmiger. A photo finish gives the win to the Swiss rider. A victory coming as a reward for the work done by his team mates some hours before.

4th stage:

Pont du Gard / Mende – 161 kms

The new strength of Christophe Moreau

At the end of his tether, and his streignth, Christophe Moreau, with a final push, has managed to take a victory from the grasp of the "old" Viat cheslav Ekimov. With a dramatic come back on the terrifying Cote de la Croix Neuve in Mende (3.5 kms at 8.8%) the rider from Belfort, weakening earlier, comes back progressively to overhaul Steinhauser, then Iker Flores and in the end, Ekimov...50 metres from

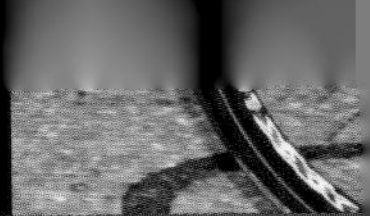

the finish which also gives him the Yellow jersey. Parting in the company of eighteen other riders at the start of the stage, Christophe Moreau, perfectly supported throughout the day by a superb Pierrick Fedrigo, upset the plans of U S Postal who were unable to bring a weak peloton including Lance Armstrong, Laurent Brochard and Sandy Casar back into contention. Still with a lead of 3 minutes at the foot of the final climb of the day, the Moreau group (or what was left of it) would fight out the finish and take the lead in the overall standings. Accompanied by José Azevedo, Lance Armstrong took a lowly 15th place at 1min 21sec from the new Yellow jersey. Who would have believed that a few hours before!

5th stage:
Florac / Sete (Mont saint Clair) – 203 kms
The reaction from Armstrong

It's in the ascension of the Col de Rey, the first climb of this final stage, situated at km 11, that the attack of the day forms. Daniel Atienza (Cofidis), Anthony Charteau (La Boulangere), the South African champion Ryan Cox (Barloworld), Koldo Fernandez de Larrea (Muscatel) and Stephane Goubert (AG2R) soon joined by Oscar Camenzind (Phonak) go into a lead of 6 minutes at km 111. But under the influence of the Credit Agricole team, which has the race leader in its ranks, the gap narrows to 2 mins 50 sec at Marseillan, 30 kilometers from the line. Before even arriving at the Mont Saint Clair (climbed twice), the attackers are brought back into the pack 14 kilometers from the finish. From the start of the first ascension, Lance Armstrong, helped by team mate José Azevedo, makes his presence felt. Only an orange jerseyed rider manages to stay with them. His name is Egoi Martinez de Esteban, winner of the Tour De l'Avenir 2003. The first time crossing the line, the duo precedes Missaglia by 15 seconds, himself followed a few seconds behind by Casar, Brochard and Flores. The Yellow jerseyed Christophe Moreau trailling at 25 seconds. The two leaders work together on the descent but the second climb proves fatal to the Basque rider. The multiple winner of the Tour de France wins on his own ahead of Laurent Brochard who pips Egoi Martinez at the post. Christophe Moreau finishes in 10th place having conceded 37 seconds, but still keeping the advantage over his direct rivals, Ekimov and Flores. He also takes the jersey for the best climber whereas the points prize stays with Thor Hushovd, first leader of the race and team mate. Sandy Casar, though victim of a crash in the descent of the Mont saint Clair is rewarded with the white jersey of the best young rider. ■

The signs of the crash at the foot of the descent of Mont Saint Clair can be seen on Sandy Casar. This does nothing to dampen the enthusiasm of the Parisian rider who takes the white jersey of the best young rider in this new version of the Tour of Languedoc Roussillon.

CLASSIFICATIONS

1st stage: Maury/Port-Vendres - 168 km

1.	Thor Hushovd (Nor)	C.A	4h 20'23"
2.	Samuel Dumoulin (Fra)	A2R	s.t
3.	Jérôme Pineau (Fra)	BLB	s.t
4.	Martin Elmiger (Sui)	PHO	s.t
5.	Bernhard Eisel (Aut)	FDJ	s.t

2nd stage: Port-Leucate/Narbonne - 195 km

1.	Thor Hushovd (Nor)	C.A	4h 47'25"
2.	Samuel Dumoulin (Fra)	A2R	s.t
3.	Jérôme Pineau (Fra)	BLB	s.t
4.	Enrico Degano (Ita)	TBL	s.t
5.	Franck Renier (Fra)	BLB	s.t

Leader:	Thor Hushovd (Nor)	9h 07'27"
2.	Samuel Dumoulin (Fra)	+ 8"
3.	Jérôme Pineau (Fra)	+ 13"

3rd stage: Ganges/Aigues-Mortes - 180 km

1.	Martin Elmiger (Sui)	PHO	3h 30'00"
2.	Yuriy Krivtsov (Ukr)	A2R	s.t
3.	Iñaki Isasi (Esp)	EUS	s.t
4.	Thor Hushovd (Nor)	C.A	s.t
5.	Bernhard Eisel (Aut)	FDJ	s.t

Leader:	Thor Hushovd (Nor)	12h 03'27"
2.	Jérôme Pineau (Fra)	+ 8"
3.	Samuel Dumoulin (Fra)	s.t

4th stage: Pont-du-Gard/Mende - 180 km

1.	Christophe Moreau (Fra)	C.A	4h 16'44"
2.	Viatcheslav Ekimov (Rus)	USP	s.t
3.	Iker Flores (Esp)	EUS	+ 18"
4.	Tobias Steinhauser (Ger)	TMO	+ 39"
5.	Pierrick Fedrigo (Fra)	C.A	+ 48"

Leader:	Christophe Moreau (Fra)	16h 54'24"
2.	Viatcheslav Ekimov (Rus)	+ 12"
3.	Iker Flores (Esp)	+ 27"

5th stage: Florac/Sète (Mont St Clair) - 209 km

1.	Lance Armstrong (Usa)	USP	4h 42'08"
2.	Laurent Brochard (Fra)	A2R	+ 19"
3.	Egoi Martinez de Esteban (Esp)	EUS	s.t
4.	Wim van Huffel (Bel)	VLA	+ 27"
5.	Laurent Lefèvre (Fra)	BLB	+ 32"

FINAL OVERALL STANDINGS:

1.	**Christophe Moreau (Fra)**	**C.A**	**21h 37'09"**
2.	Viatcheslav Ekimov (Rus)	USP	+ 19"
3.	Iker Flores (Esp)	EUS	+ 46"
4.	Egoi Martinez de Esteban (Esp)	EUS	+ 1'24"
5.	Laurent Brochard (Fra)	A2R	+ 1'34"
6.	Lance Armstrong (Usa)	USP	+ 1'44"
7.	Laurent Lefèvre (Fra)	BLB	+ 2'14"
8.	Sandy Casar (Fra)	FDJ	+ 2'31"
9.	José Azevedo (Por)	USP	+ 2'34"
10.	Gabriele Missaglia (Ita)	TBL	+ 2'47"
11.	Frédéric Bessy (Fra)	COF	+ 2'57"
12.	Benoît Salmon (Fra)	C.A	+ 3'03"
13.	Yuriy Krivtsov (Ukr)	A2R	+ 3'09"
14.	Dmitriy Fofonov (Kaz)	COF	+ 3'09"
15.	Jean-Cyril Robin (Fra)	FDJ	+ 3'14"

POINTS TABLE

1.	Thor Hushovd (Nor)	C.A	69 pts
2.	Martin Elmiger (Sui)	PHO	58 pts
3.	Jérôme Pineau (Fra)	BLB	57 pts

MOUNTAIN STANDINGS

1.	Christophe Moreau (Fra)	C.A	36 pts
2.	Maryan Hary (Fra)	BLB	32 pts
3.	Anthony Charteau (Fra)	BLB	32 pts

BEST YOUNGS STANDINGS

1.	Sandy Casar (Fra)	FDJ	21h39'40"
2.	Yuriy Krivtsov (Ukr)	A2R	+ 38"
3.	Wim van Huffel (Bel)	VLA	+ 2'08"

TEAM STANDINGS

1.	US POSTAL - BERRY FLOOR	64h56'06"
2.	CREDIT AGRICOLE	+ 49"
3.	AG2R Prévoyance	+ 2'32"

107 Competitors

US POSTAL - BERRY FLOOR

1.	ARMSTRONG Lance (Usa)	**6th**	+ 1'44"
2.	AZEVEDO José (Por)	**9th**	+ 2'34"
3.	BELTRAN Manuel (Esp)	*Abandon*	5th stage
4.	EKIMOV Viatcheslav (Rus)	**2nd**	+ 19"
5.	JOACHIM Benoît (Lux)	25th	+ 6'33"
6.	NOVAL Benjamin (Esp)	*Abandon*	5th stage
7.	PADRNOS Pavel (Cze)	*Abandon*	5th stage
8.	RUBIERA José Luis (Esp)	*Abandon*	5th stage

T.MOBILE

11.	AERTS Mario (Bel)	72nd	+ 35'34"
12.	EVANS Cadel (Aus)	Disqualified	4th stage
13.	KONECNY Tomas (Cze)	78th	+ 59'11"
14.	KORFF André (Ger)	*Abandon*	5th stage
15.	STEINHAUSER Tobias (Ger)	18th	+ 4'20"
16.	YAKOVLEV Serguey (Kaz)	57th	+ 16'32"

QUICK STEP - DAVITAMON

21.	BODROGI Laszlo (Hun)	22nd	+ 6'03"
22.	AMORISON Frédéric (Bel)	47th	+ 14'38"
23.	BRAMATI Davide (Ita)	51st	+ 15'34"
24.	PECHARROMAN J. Antonio (Esp)	68th	+ 24'19"
25.	VANTHOURENHOUT Sven (Bel)	38th	+ 10'38"

PHONAK

31.	CAMENZIND Oscar (Sui)	*Abandon*	5th stage
32.	BAYARRI Gonzalo (Esp)	*Abandon*	3rd stage
33.	DESSEL Cyril (Fra)	24th	+ 6'31"
34.	ELMIGER Martin (Sui)	16th	+ 3'39"
35.	JALABERT Nicolas (Fra)	33rd	+ 9'17"
36.	RAST Gregory (Sui)	35th	+ 10'01"
37.	TSCHOPP Johann (Sui)	53rd	+ 15'52"
38.	ZÜLLE Alex (Sui)	*Abandon*	5th stage

EUSKALTEL - EUSKADI

41.	MARTINEZ de ESTEBAN Egoi (Esp)	**4th**	+ 1'24"
42.	ARRIZABALAGA Gorka (Esp)	66th	+ 22'17"
43.	FERNANDEZ de LARREA Koldo (Esp)	65th	+ 21'49"
44.	FLORES Iker (Esp)	**3rd**	+ 46"
45.	GALPARSORO Dionisio (Esp)	*Abandon*	3rd stage
46.	ISASI Iñaki (Esp)	48th	+ 14'40"
47.	PEÑA IZA Aketza (Esp)	42nd	+ 12'50"
48.	SILLONIZ Aitor (Esp)	43rd	+ 13'28"

COFIDIS

51.	MILLAR David (Gbr)	*Abandon*	4th stage
52.	ATIENZA Daniel (Esp)	29th	+ 8'29"
53.	BESSY Frédéric (Fra)	11st	+ 2'57"
54.	EDALEINE Christophe (Fra)	60th	+ 20'03"
55.	FOFONOV Dmitriy (Kaz)	14th	+ 3'09"
56.	MONCOUTIÉ David (Fra)	37th	+ 10'37"
57.	PEREZ RODRIGUEZ Luis (Esp)	27th	+ 7'40"
58.	TRENTIN Guido (Ita)	*Abandon*	3rd stage

AG2R Prévoyance

61.	BROCHARD Laurent (Fra)	**5th**	+ 1'34"
62.	CHAURREAU Iñigo (Esp)	41st	+ 12'10"
63.	DUMOULIN Samuel (Fra)	21st	+ 5'57"
64.	FLICKINGER Andy (Fra)	76th	+ 43'21"
65.	GOUBERT Stéphane (Fra)	20th	+ 4'49"
66.	PORTAL Nicolas (Fra)	54th	+ 15'54"
67.	KRIVTSOV Yuriy (Ukr)	13rd	+3'09"
68.	ORIOL Christophe (Fra)	71st	+ 33'53"

Brioches LA BOULANGÈRE

71.	ROUS Didier (Fra)	45th	+ 14'32"
72.	BENETEAU Walter (Fra)	46th	+ 14'33"
73.	CHARTEAU Anthony (Fra)	69th	+ 25'20"
74.	HARY Maryan (Fra)	23rd	+6'12"
75.	LEFÈVRE Laurent (Fra)	**7th**	+ 2'14"
76.	PICHON Mickaël (Fra)	49th	+ 15'22"
77.	PINEAU Jérôme (Fra)	34th	+9'24"
78.	RENIER Franck (Fra)	52nd	+ 15'44"

FDJEUX.COM

81.	CASAR Sandy (Fra)	**8th**	+ 2'31"
82.	DA CRUZ Carlos (Fra)	TC	3rd stage
83.	EISEL Bernhard (Aut)	55th	+ 16'14"
84.	GUESDON Frédéric (Fra)	63rd	+ 21'39"
85.	LÖVKVIST Thomas (Swe)	*Abandon*	1st stage
86.	MENGIN Christophe (Fra)	73rd	+ 39'40"
87.	ROBIN Jean-Cyril (Fra)	15th	+ 3'14"
88.	ROY Jérémy (Fra)	50th	+ 15'28"

Mr BOOKMAKER.COM - PALMANS

91.	CASTRESANA Angel (Esp)	*Abandon*	5th stage
92.	COENEN Johan (Bel)	44th	+ 13'52"
93.	DAY Ben (Aus)	*Abandon*	4th stage
94.	GABRIEL Frédéric (Fra)	62nd	+ 20'37"
95.	KOEHLER Philippe (Fra)	*Abandon*	4th stage
96.	LEMBO Eddy (Fra)	*Abandon*	5th stage
97.	ROODHOOFT Christoph (Bel)	*Abandon*	1st stage
98.	WUYTS Peter (Bel)	*Abandon*	4th stage

CRÉDIT AGRICOLE

101.	MOREAU Christophe (Fra)	**1st**	**21h 37'09"**
102.	BOTCHAROV Alexandre (Rus)	17th	+ 4'15"
103.	FEDRIGO Pierrick (Fra)	31st	+ 9'02"
104.	HALGAND Patrice (Fra)	*Abandon*	5th stage
105.	HUSHOVD Thor (Nor)	59th	+ 20'00"
106.	JÉGOU Lilian (Fra)	*Abandon*	4th stage
107.	MURAVYEV Dmitriy (Kaz)	*Abandon*	4th stage
108.	SALMON Benoît (Fra)	12nd	+ 3'03"

RAGT Semences - MG ROVER

111.	RINERO Christophe (Fra)	30th	+ 8'38"
112.	BERNARD Jérôme (Fra)	64th	+ 21'44"
113.	CALZATI Sylvain (Fra)	32nd	+ 9'15"
114.	FINOT Frédéric (Fra)	74th	+ 41'08"
115.	LAURENT Christophe (Fra)	56th	+ 16'15"
116.	MARTIN Ludovic (Fra)	*Abandon*	5th stage
117.	REYNAUD Nicolas (Fra)	67th	+ 22'35"
118.	SEIGNEUR Eddy (Fra)	61st	+ 20'07"

BARLOWORLD - ANDRONI GIOCATTOLI

121.	GEORGE David (Rsa)	28th	+ 8'06"
122.	BELLOTTI Francesco (Ita)	26th	+ 6'38"
123.	COX Ryan (Rsa)	39th	+ 11'46"
124.	DEGANO Enrico (Ita)	*Abandon*	4th stage
125.	LILL Darren (Rsa)	75th	+ 41'34"
126.	MISSAGLIA Gabriele (Ita)	**10th**	+ 2'47"
127.	RAVAIOLI Ivan (Ita)	*Abandon*	4th stage
128.	SERRI Eddy (Ita)	*Abandon*	5th stage

VLAANDEREN - T INTERIM

131.	VAN HUFFEL Wim (Bel)	19th	+ 4'39"
132.	BARBÉ Koen (Bel)	77th	+ 53'35"
133.	CAETHOVEN Steven (Bel)	70th	+ 26'38"
134.	MERTENS Pieter (Bel)	*Abandon*	4th stage
135.	PEETERS Jef (Bel)	*Abandon*	4th stage
136.	VAN DER LINDEN Wesley (Bel)	40th	+ 11'50"
137.	VEUCHELEN Frederik (Bel)	58th	+ 17'08"
138.	WILLEMS Frederik (Bel)	36th	+ 10'11"

POINTS TABLE UCI IN STAGE

CRÉDIT AGRICOLE	324
US POSTAL - BERRY FLOOR	286
EUSKALTEL - EUSKADI	229
AG2R Prévoyance	193
Brioches LA BOULANGÈRE	112
FDJEUX.COM	87
COFIDIS	74
PHONAK	61
BARLOWORLD	60
VLAANDEREN - T INTERIM	28
T.MOBILE	20
QUICK STEP - DAVITAMON	19
RAGT Semences - MG ROVER	10
Mr BOOKMAKER - PALMANS	5

EX WINNERS TAKING THE START 3

ARMSTRONG Lance	2002
ROUS Didier	2000
SALMON Benoît	1999

* Of course they are former winners of the Midi Libre GP

3 OLDEST

EKIMOV Viatcheslav (38 ans)	04/02/1966
BROCHARD Laurent (36 ans)	26/03/1968
BRAMATI Davide (35 ans)	28/06/1968

3 YOUNGEST

LÖVKVIST Thomas (20 ans)	04/04/1984
ROY Jérémy (20 ans)	22/06/1983
LILL Darren (21 ans)	20/08/1982

- 9 néo-pros participated in Tour du Languedoc-Roussillon 2004.

- 13 riders at the start are in the U C I top 100, 5 don't classed.

- 20 different nationalities were represented. The majority were French (41 riders), followed by the spaniards (17 riders), the Belgians (14 riders), the Italians (7) et les Swiss (5).

THE WRONG ROAD

Between Lance Armstrong and Iban Mayo the entente is cordial. Why think otherwise.

From Lance Armstrong, in the event to try out new equipment, but also his stamina on the Ventoux, to Ivan Basso (who pulls out of the final stage to catch a plane) and to Tyler Hamilton and his team, the majority of the stars taking part in this edition of the Criterium du Dauphiné Liberé had other priorities in mind than the excellent course designed by Charly Mottet.

One rider could not be accused of this attitude: Iban Mayo, second last year and the man who took command in the time trial on the slopes of the Ventoux and never let go on the following stages. In the end this was a disappointing "Dauphiné" even if Stuart O'Grady did show us what he was made of and showed us his skills in the mountains.

Prologue in Megeve – 5.4 kms

The course of this race through the streets of Megeve was not as simple as could be imagined, because a hill of 1200metres with portions at slope of 9% was to be found at the half way mark. This is where Iban Mayo made the difference, simply going faster than his rivals. The Basque rider just avoided a crash on the final corner and then recorded the fastest time. The signal to the other stars was clear: he was not there to build up his stamina, already impressive several weeks before when winning the Clasica Alcobendas (two stage wins and the overall title) the hill climb at the Cote Naranco and the Tour des Asturies.

Tyler Hamilton, whos form was uncertain since his win in the Tour de Romandie, proved that racing against the clock was one of his strong points. The American finishes second, 72 hundredths of a second behind Mayo and precedes the man all are looking at, his compatriot Lance Armstrong by the same margin (69 hundredths of a second). Hamilton could count on his highly impressive Phonak team to back him up in this month of June: it places five riders in the first eight in this prologue: apart from Hamilton, Pereiro finishes 2nd at 2seconds, Sevilla 6th at 6 seconds, Dessel 7th at 8seconds and Gutierrez 8th also at 8 seconds. Others met with less success in Megeve. This is the case with David Millar, 11th at 12 seconds, Jorg Jaksche 13th at 13seconds, Christophe Moreau 23rd at 21 seconds or Richard Virenque 52nd at 40 seconds. But the week was only just beginning...

1st stage: Megeve / Bron – 231 kms

Jimmy Casper was not born yesterday. Just as confident in an attack (victory in the 4 days of Dunkerque) as in a mass sprint (victory in the Tour of Picardie), the man universally known as a sprinter attacks after 4 kms of racing. No one goes with the rider from Picardie on this mad adventure. There are still 227 kilometers to ride!

The solitude of the Cofidis rider lasts for a long time. The peloton lets him go. Even e wait at a level crossing does nothing to cut his lead, standing at 17mins 50sec just before the half way point. It's the chosen moment for the teams of the sprinters to begin to close the gap. The fdjeux.com and the Credit Agricole teams along with the men from Euskaltel take it in turns to do the work. Quickly, perhaps too quickly the lead begins to reduce. It is only one minute at 50kilometres from the finish. Jimmy Casper finds help in the form of Christophe Laurent (RAGT Semences) coming out of the pack in a counter attack. The rider from the Lozere brings new blood to the attack which pushes ahead once again. The peloton plays the game, leaving the leading duo to take the lead to 3 mins 30 sec. The two men are still 1 min 20 sec ahead at the 10 kilometre mark but are caught in the final 1500metres. Jimmy Casper had stayed in front for 225 kilometers, mostly on his own. The Cofidis rider could have hoped that his team mate Stuart O'Grady would go on to take the sprint, but this was not to be. His ex team mate, the Norwegian Thor Hushovd taking his seventh win since the start of the year.

2nd stage: Bron / St Etienne- 181 kms

After the warm up the previous day, this stage seems perfect to sort out the peloton. Including at its end, the familiar Col de la Croix de Chabouret which overlooks St Etienne. As can be imagined, the riders do not want to wait until this final difficulty before making a move. A group of five men form a group at the exit from Bron (km 4) and counts in its number several riders specialising in this sort of action: the Dutchmen Erik Dekker and Karsten Kroon (both with Rabobank) and the three Frenchmen Guillaume Auger (RAGT Semences) , Andy Flickinger (AG2R) , and Anthony Geslin (La Boulangere). The Euskaltel team of leader Iban Mayo keep an eye on the situation and the lead never exceeds 4 mins 50sec. The first few hundred metres of the Col de la Croix de Chabouret are fatal for the breakaway group excepting Geslin who left them just before the end of their attack. It's Ludovic Martin who takes it upon himself to chase after him ,and the RAGT rider soon dashes past. Martin in turn suffers the same fate at the hands of José Enrique Gutierrez (Phonak) 2 kilometers from the summit. The Spaniard is 25 seconds ahead of his rivals as ha descends towards St Etienne. Despite a determined chase by Iban Mayo, he stays seven seconds ahead on the Cours Fauriel where the finishing line awaits. This is enough

Day of glory for Nicolas Portal in Aubenas.

The first of two successes for Stuart O'Grady in the Dauphiné Liberé. This time he fights off George Hincapie at the finish in Sisteron.

to also take the leader's jersey. Winner of the last stage, that of Geneva on the 2002 Dauphiné, Gutierrez appreciates this event... And the event seems to like him too!

3rd stage: St Etienne / Aubenas – 173 kms

For his first victory since turning pro, Nicolas Portal would doubtless have preferred that no unfortunate incidents come to spoil his moment in the limelight. But the road is full of traps and surprises for the racers. As it happened, it was the rider from Nantes, Mickael Pichon who was the subject of all the conversations on the evening of the stage. Victim of a spectacular crash on the descent of the Cote de Mezillac, the La Boulangere rider fell into a ravine fifteen metres below the road. He was later taken by helicopter to the hospital in Grenoble. The diagnosis of the doctors was that the rider was suffering from concussion, cuts and bruises and fractures of the jaw, and an open fracture of the tibia ...the list of injuries spoke for itself. Compared to this, the recurring back pain of Nicolas Portal seemed a minor problem. Today he went from the start in a breakaway group soon after the start. A group including Jerome Pineau, who was just seconds behind the leaders in the overall standings. Feeling that this presence would compromise any attack, Pineau eased up to let Portal, Tombak and Flores go it alone. A Flores who took advantage of the Cote de Mezillac to leave his two rivals standing. Tombak, much better than Portal in a sprint, took the bull by the horns and went after Flores, catching him up twenty kilometers later. Nicolas Portal then went for a counter attack. Flores and Tombak not wishing to work together, Portal went on to take the stage by a winning margin of one minute.

4th stage: Bedoin – Mont Ventoux – 21.6 kms Time trial

Since his first victory in the 1999 Tour de France, Lance Armstrong had never had such a setback: fifth on the Mont Ventoux time trial in the Dauphiné Liberé, the Texan was almost two minutes behind the winner, Iban Mayo and one and a half minutes behind his countryman Tyler Hamilton, this in the stage that had motivated his participation in the event.

No one knows what was going through the mind of Lance Armstrong, sitting in the team manager's car after the climb , but we can guess he was worried as he was using the same ultra lightweight equipment he would have a month later on the Alpe d'Huez. But also to lose by two minutes to the man who took the Alpe d'Huez stage in 2003, is too much, much too much!

"Lance didn't have a bad day, insisted team manager Bruyneel, but he wasn't at his very best. After fifteen kilometers of effort and

already a minute behind Mayo, he didn't persist. He is not here to win the Criterium du Dauphiné Liberé but to prepare himself". He's not yet ready" confirmed Charly Mottet standing next to him. "I didn't think he'd lose two minutes, but he obviously isn't yet 100% fit. It should come as no surprise as he always says he wants to attack the Tour de France feeling fresh".

Looking at the famous climb up the Alpe d'Huez (15.51kms) from this point of view, a stage Lance Armstrong himself considers the key to success in the 2004 Tour de France, the test at the Ventoux poses several questions. For a start, that posed by the stage winner (and new overall leader) Iban Mayo, who says" I'd heard he'd go for this time trial flat out, therefore he must have been below par. For my part, I controlled this stage well, managing to accelerate from Chalet Reynard. It's true to say I was also in form last year in this race and faded in the final week of the Tour de France. If the same were to happen in this year's event it would be a shame as the Tour will be won or lost in the final week this time; But I feel stronger and more experienced now".
The new holder of the record on the Ventoux, in 55mins 51sec (the precedent record of 56mins 50sec was held by Jonathan Vaughters since 1999 , the year Lance Armstrong took 5th place at a little more than a minute from the winner) took the race in hand , confirming himself as the number one favourite.

5th stage: Bollene / Sisteron –149 kms

Second in Bron, third in St Etienne, fourth in Aubenas, Stuart O'Grady well knew he had nothing to look forward to in the final two stages around Grenoble. He therefore had to put everything into the remaining stages on the roads of the Drome, and with a deal of authority he did what was called for to take the stage win he was looking for in the Dauphiné.

If O'Grady realised he'd have to attack, the peloton had the same idea. 48 kilometers were covered in the first hour and it's only at the 41st that the winning attack sees the light of day, nine strong, and full of favourites.
There were two sprinters, Stuart O'Grady and Baden Cooke, and five others , mostly with a good turn of speed: George Hincapie, Jerome Pineau, Nicolas Jalabert, Pierrick Fedrigo and the Colombian Victor Hugo Pena.
The peloton took a certain time to give up the chase, keeping the lead down to a minute for twenty kilometers before it was to open up to a more comfortable distance for the leaders. The Euskaltel team of overall leader Iban Mayo charged itself with controlling the situation. The lead went to 6 mins 40sec. There were now just nine men at the front to fight it out. "I knew when I climbed the final hill that I had the race won, I attacked a long way out because I knew the others would soon stop riding along with me. I did the opposite to what a sprinter should do, but it was fun" declared Stuart O'Grady on the finish line at Sisteron.
Winner ten days before in the GP de Villers – Cotterets in the Coupe de France , Stuart O'Grady shows he's in good condition a few weeks before the start of the Tour de France on which he'll once again go for the Green Jersey that has until now always eluded him.

Watched from the corner of his eye by Oscar Sevilla (Phonak) and Lance Armstrong, Iban Mayo will just the same not be troubled on the last two stages around Grenoble.

6th stage: Gap / Grenoble - 144 kms

The 144 kilometers that separate Gap from Grenoble via the Cols of Bayard, Malissol, La Morte and Luitel as well as the climbs at Motty, Mure Villeneuve d' Uriage and the four Seigneurs, permitted an ex World Mountain Bike Champion (in 1999), Michael Rasmussen to sign a veritable exploit at the end of a long attack that started at the third kilometre! At first accompanied bi Ivan Basso (CSC) ,who, victim of a mechanical incident on the Col de la Morte lost touch, the blonde Dane found himself with a lead of more than eight minutes twenty kilometers from the line. A situation which would put him in contention with the overall leaders. Maintaining a lead of nearly seven minutes at the finishing line in Grenoble, he rose to an overall seventh place ...with a stage victory as an added bonus!

7th stage: Grenoble / Grenoble - 200 kms

Kept out of competition for several weeks because of a rib injury contracted on the GP E3in Harebeke, Stuart O'Grady showed a new temperament on the Travers de Morbihan (5th) where he was one of the main animators of the event and in winning the GP de Villers – Cotterets forty eight hours later. The 5th stage of the Dauphiné (that of Sisteron)

It's in the lunar landscape of Mont Ventoux that Iban Mayo showed his domination of the Dauphiné 2004.

This stage including several lesser known but difficult passes such as the Luitel, narrow and invaded by abundant vegetation, was also marked by the retirement of Christophe Moreau, suffering from tendonitis and a minor crash by Tyler Hamilton a short time after that of his team mate Santos Gonzalez Capilla. It was also marked by the neutral performances of the principal rivals of Iban Mayo, who seemed to all be looking for a restful day.

went to him after a breakaway of 108 kms. But the antipodean rider is insatiable and as a bonus can count on a perfect physical condition.

It's no surprise then to find the Cofidis rider in the first attack of the day which takes place in the first kilometre!

Sandy Casar (Fdjeux.com) is the instigator, soon followed by Anthony geslin (La Boulangere), Pedro Horillo (Quick step), Dmitriy Muravyev (Credit Agricole) ,Nicolas Reynaud (RAGT Semences), David Millar (Cofidis) and of course Stuart O'Grady. As the day before the peloton shows itself to be particularly passive... and comprehensive to those with a will to win. It concedes 12mins 50sec to the leaders, reduced to six after the leaving a failing David Millar on the ascent of the Col de l'Echarasson (2nd category). The leaders work together for some time, but the Col de Sarcenas (1st category), situated thirty kilometers from the line marks the end of the pact of non aggression. Dmitriy Muravyev attacks on the first slopes but burns out and sees Stuart O'Grady and Sandy Casar pass ahead of him. Then sandy Casar attacks. He tries to distance his Australian rival on the pass, but O'Grady holds on and comes back at the leader before the summit. He decides to take the descent flat out and leaves the Parisian behind ten kilometers before the finish. In Grenoble, six years after his Tour de France triumph there, Stuart O'Grady takes the big mountain stage in the Criterium du Dauphiné Liberé. The peloton of the favourites, led by Lance Armstrong comes in 6minutes 44 seconds behind. Iban Mayo wins therefore the 56th edition of the Criterium du Dauphiné Liberé without being troubled by his adversaries, among which the Phonak team, (4 members in the top 10 overall ratings) were very much present. The Swiss team left us craving for more...■

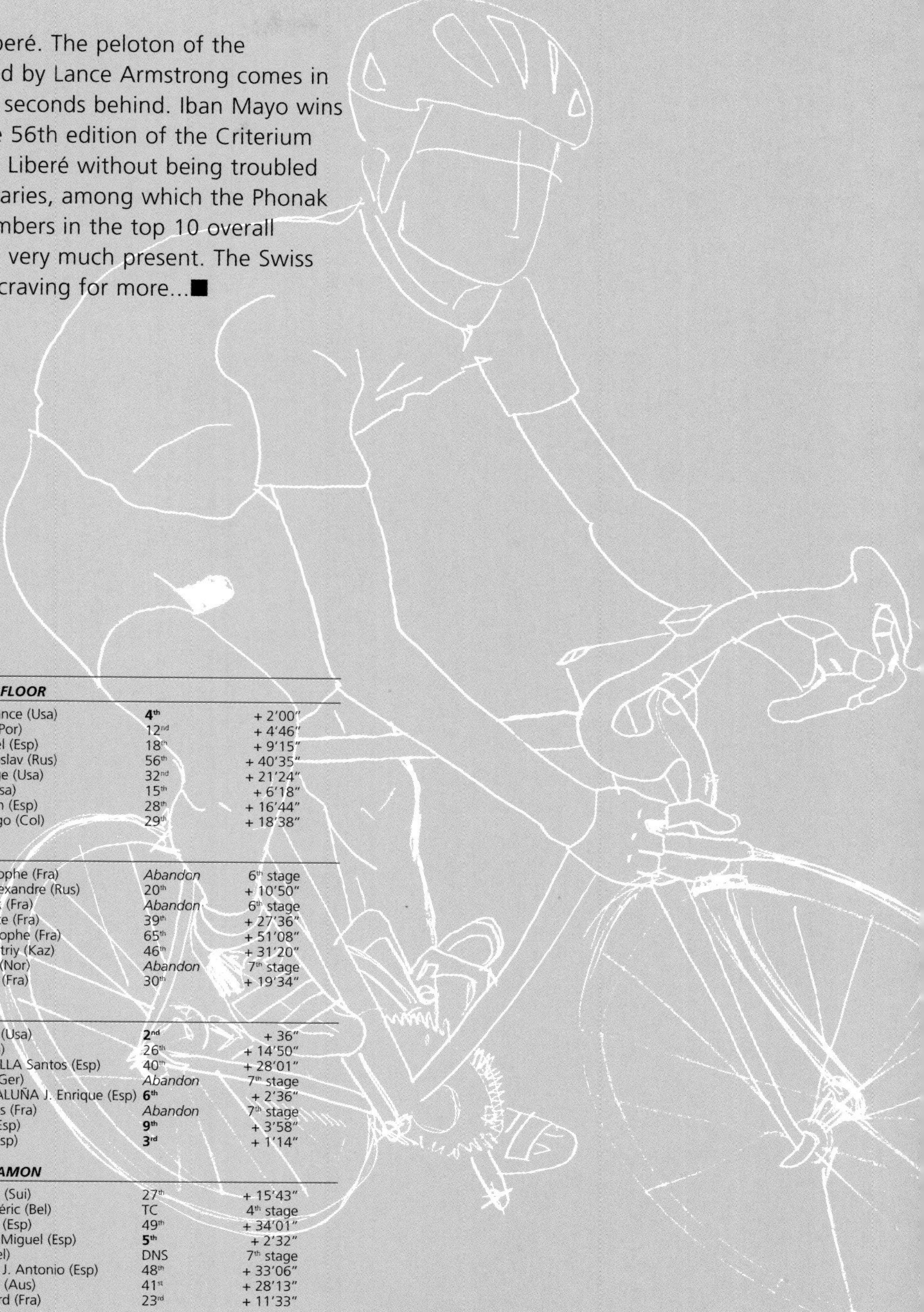

CLASSIFICATIONS

Prologue in Megève - 5,4 km

1.	Iban Mayo (Esp)	EUS	7'51"
2.	T. Hamilton (Usa)	PHO	+ 0"72
3.	L. Armstrong (Usa)	USP	+ 1"41
4.	O. Pereiro (Esp)	PHO	+ 2"49
5.	M. Rogers (Aus)	QSD	+ 5"85

Megève/Bron - 231 km

1.	Thor Hushovd (Nor)	C.A	6h03'47"
2.	S. O'Grady (Aus)	COF	s.t
3.	S. Dumoulin (Fra)	A2R	s.t
4.	B. Cooke (Aus)	FDJ	s.t
5.	O. Freire (Esp)	RAB	s.t
Leader:	Iban Mayo		6h 11'38"

Bron/Saint-Etienne - 167 km

1.	J.E Gutierrez (Esp)	PHO	4h36'44"
2.	C. Dessel (Fra)	PHO	+ 7"
3.	S. O'Grady (Aus)	COF	s.t
4.	J. Pineau (Fra)	BLB	s.t
5.	A. Botcharov (Rus)	C.A	s.t
Leader:	J. Enrique Gutierrez		10h 48'21"

Saint-Etienne/Aubenas - 173 km

1.	Nicolas Portal (Fra)	A2R	4h41'52"
2.	J. Tombak (Est)	COF	+ 51"
3.	Iker Flores (Esp)	EUS	s.t
4.	S. O'Grady (Aus)	COF	+ 1'49"
5.	T. Voeckler (Fra)	BLB	s.t
Leader:	J. Enrique Gutierrez		15h 31'52"

Bédoin/Mont Ventoux - 21,8 km (Team time trial)

1.	Iban Mayo (Esp)	EUS	55'51"
2.	T. Hamilton (Usa)	PHO	+ 35"
3.	O. Sevilla (Esp)	PHO	+ 1'03"
4.	J.M Mercado (Esp)	QSD	+ 1'48"
5.	L. Armstrong (Usa)	USP	+ 1'57"
Leader:	Iban Mayo		16h27'51"

Bollène /Sisteron - 149 km

1.	Stuart O'Grady (Aus)	COF	3h12'21"
2.	George Hincapie (Usa)	USP	s.t
3.	Baden Cooke (Aus)	FDJ	+ 1'33"
4.	Jérôme Pineau (Fra)	BLB	s.t
5.	Nicolas Jalabert (Fra)	PHO	+ 2'14"
Leader:	Iban Mayo		19h 47'24"

Gap/Grenoble - 144 km

1.	Michael Rasmussen(Den)	RAB	4h04'44"
2.	Ivan Basso (Ita)	CSC	+ 5'20"
3.	Th. Voeckler (Fra)	BLB	+ 6'43"
4.	J. Enrique Gutierrez (Esp)	PHO	s.t
5.	J.M Mercado (Esp)	QSD	s.t
Leader:	Iban Mayo		23h58'51"

Grenoble/Grenoble - 200 km

1.	Stuart O'Grady (Aus)	COF	5h21'40"
2.	S. Casar (Fra)	FDJ	+ 19"
3.	P. Horrillo (Esp)	QSD	+ 3'14"
4.	D. Muravyev (Kaz)	C.A	s.t
5.	N. Reynaud (Fra)	RAG	+ 4'53"

FINAL OVERALL STANDINGS

1.	Iban Mayo (Esp)	EUS	29h 27'15"
2.	T. Hamilton (Usa)	PHO	+ 36"
3.	O. Sevilla (Esp)	PHO	+ 1'14"
4.	L. Armstrong (Usa)	USP	+ 2'00"
5.	J.M Mercado (Esp)	QSD	+ 2'32"
6.	J.E Gutierrez Cataluña (Esp)	PHO	+ 2'36"
7.	Michael Rasmussen (Den)	RAB	+ 2'39"
8.	Levi Leipheimer (Usa)	RAB	+ 3'33"
9.	Oscar Pereiro (Esp)	PHO	+ 3'58"
10.	Iñigo Landaluze (Esp)	EUS	+ 4'02"
11.	David Moncoutié (Fra)	COF	+ 4'25"
12.	José Azevedo (Por)	USP	+ 4'46"
13.	Stéphane Goubert (Fra)	A2R	+ 5'36"
14.	Carlos Sastre (Esp)	CSC	+ 5'41"
15.	Floyd Landis (Usa)	USP	+ 6'18"

95 Competitors

US POSTAL - BERRY FLOOR

1.	ARMSTRONG Lance (Usa)	**4th**	+ 2'00"
2.	AZEVEDO José (Por)	12nd	+ 4'46"
3.	BELTRAN Manuel (Esp)	18th	+ 9'15"
4.	EKIMOV Viatcheslav (Rus)	56th	+ 40'35"
5.	HINCAPIE George (Usa)	32nd	+ 21'24"
6.	LANDIS Floyd (Usa)	15th	+ 6'18"
7.	NOVAL Benjamin (Esp)	28th	+ 16'44"
8.	PEÑA Victor Hugo (Col)	29th	+ 18'38"

CRÉDIT AGRICOLE

11.	MOREAU Christophe (Fra)	*Abandon*	6th stage
12.	BOTCHAROV Alexandre (Rus)	20th	+ 10'50"
13.	FEDRIGO Pierrick (Fra)	*Abandon*	6th stage
14.	HALGAND Patrice (Fra)	39th	+ 27'36"
15.	LE MÉVEL Christophe (Fra)	65th	+ 51'08"
16.	MURAVYEV Dmitriy (Kaz)	46th	+ 31'20"
17.	HUSHOVD Thor (Nor)	*Abandon*	7th stage
18.	SALMON Benoît (Fra)	30th	+ 19'34"

PHONAK

21.	HAMILTON Tyler (Usa)	**2nd**	+ 36"
22.	DESSEL Cyril (Fra)	26th	+ 14'50"
23.	GONZALEZ CAPILLA Santos (Esp)	40th	+ 28'01"
24.	GRABSCH Bert (Ger)	*Abandon*	7th stage
25.	GUTIERREZ CATALUÑA J. Enrique (Esp)	**6th**	+ 2'36"
26.	JALABERT Nicolas (Fra)	*Abandon*	7th stage
27.	PEREIRO Oscar (Esp)	**9th**	+ 3'58"
28.	SEVILLA Oscar (Esp)	**3rd**	+ 1'14"

QUICK STEP - DAVITAMON

31.	DUFAUX Laurent (Sui)	27th	+ 15'43"
32.	AMORISON Frédéric (Bel)	TC	4th stage
33.	HORRILLO Pedro (Esp)	49th	+ 34'01"
34.	MERCADO Juan Miguel (Esp)	**5th**	+ 2'32"
35.	NUYENS Nick (Bel)	DNS	7th stage
36.	PECHARROMAN J. Antonio (Esp)	48th	+ 33'06"
37.	ROGERS Michael (Aus)	41st	+ 28'13"
38.	VIRENQUE Richard (Fra)	23rd	+ 11'33"

EUSKALTEL - EUSKADI

41.	MAYO Iban (Esp)	**1st**	**29h 27'15"**
42.	ALBIZU Joseba (Esp)	69th	+ 1h13'53"
43.	CAMAÑO Iker (Esp)	22nd	+ 11'30"
44.	FLORES Iker (Esp)	36th	+ 25'21"
45.	ISASI Iñaki (Esp)	70th	+ 1h15'10"
46.	LANDALUZE Iñigo (Esp)	**10th**	+ 4'02"
47.	MARTINEZ de ESTEBAN Egoi (Esp)	16th	+ 7'12"
48.	SILLONIZ Josu (Esp)	71st	+ 1h30'28"

COFIDIS

51.	MILLAR David (Gbr)	*Abandon*	7th stage
52.	BESSY Frédéric (Fra)	34th	+ 23'45"
53.	CASPER Jimmy (Fra)	TC	4th stage
54.	EDALEINE Christophe (Fra)	*Abandon*	6th stage
55.	MONCOUTIÉ David (Fra)	11st	+ 4'25"
56.	O'GRADY Stuart (Aus)	21st	+ 11'06"
57.	TOMBAK Janek (Est)	63rd	+ 50'41"
58.	WHITE Matthew (Aus)	64th	+ 51'03"

CSC

61.	BASSO Ivan (Ita)	*Abandon*	7th stage
62.	BARTOLI Michele (Ita)	54th	+ 38'19"
63.	CALVENTE Manuel (Esp)	38th	+ 27'26"
65.	JAKSCHE Jörg (Ger)	*Abandon*	7th stage
66.	PERON Andrea (Ita)	33rd	+ 23'07"
67.	SASTRE Carlos (Esp)	14th	+ 5'41"
68.	SØRENSEN Nicki (Den)	60th	+ 47'18"

AG2R Prévoyance

71.	CHAURREAU Iñigo (Esp)	43rd	+ 29'51"
72.	ASTARLOZA Mikel (Esp)	35th	+ 25'00"
73.	DUMOULIN Samuel (Fra)	*Abandon*	3rd stage
74.	FLICKINGER Andy (Fra)	*Abandon*	7th stage
75.	GOUBERT Stéphane (Fra)	13rd	+ 5'36"
76.	INAUDI Nicolas (Fra)	TC	4th stage
77.	KRIVTSOV Yuriy (Ukr)	44th	+ 30'18"
78.	PORTAL Nicolas (Fra)	42nd	+ 28'34"

RABOBANK

81.	LEIPHEIMER Levy (Usa)	**8th**	+ 3'33"
82.	DE GROOT Bram (Ned)	66th	+ 52'26"
83.	DE WEERT Kevin (Bel)	68th	+ 54'10"
84.	DEKKER Erik (Ned)	67th	+ 52'31"
85.	FREIRE Oscar (Esp)	TC	4th stage
86.	KROON Karsten (Ned)	TC	4th stage
87.	LOTZ Marc (Ned)	58th	+ 42'40"
88.	RASMUSSEN Michael (Den)	**7th**	+ 2'39"

FDJEUX.COM

91.	COOKE Baden (Aus)	57th	+ 41'41"
92.	CASAR Sandy (Fra)	25th	+ 14'20"
93.	DA CRUZ Carlos (Fra)	*Abandon*	7th stage
94.	EISEL Bernhard (Aut)	DNS	7th stage
95.	GUESDON Frédéric (Fra)	52nd	+ 37'54"
96.	LÖVKVIST Thomas (Swe)	17th	+ 8'07"
97.	MENGIN Christophe (Fra)	50th	+ 37'15"
98.	ROBIN Jean-Cyril (Fra)	24th	+ 14'01"

Brioches LA BOULANGÈRE

101.	PINEAU Jérôme (Fra)	*Abandon*	7th stage
102.	BENETEAU Walter (Fra)	47th	+ 32'17"
103.	GESLIN Anthony (Fra)	45th	+ 31'19"
104.	HARY Maryan (Fra)	51st	+ 37'47"
105.	LEFÈVRE Laurent (Fra)	37th	+ 26'17"
106.	PICHON Mickaël (Fra)	*Abandon*	3rd stage
107.	RENIER Franck (Fra)	53rd	+ 38'18"
108.	VOECKLER Thomas (Fra)	19th	+ 5'41"

RAGT Semences - MG ROVER

111.	AUGER Guillaume (Fra)	*Abandon*	6th stage
112.	BOURQUENOUD Pierre (Sui)	59th	+ 44'47"
113.	BOUVARD Gilles (Fra)	55th	+ 38'49"
114.	CALZATI Sylvain (Fra)	TC	4th stage
115.	LAURENT Christophe (Fra)	61st	+ 47'57"
116.	MARTIN Ludovic (Fra)	31st	+ 21'21"
117.	REYNAUD Nicolas (Fra)	62nd	+ 48'02"
118.	SEIGNEUR Eddy (Fra)	*Abandon*	6th stage

Cruel second

We can all still remember the 8 seconds that crucity Laurent Fignon at the end of the Tour in 1989. Lile the Parisian fifteen years earlier, Fabian Jeker must have had the same empty feeling on the banks of Lake Lugano. It's in fact for one tiny second that the Swiss lost, at the end of 1434 kilometers, in the race that has haunted for several months, his number one objective for the season, and even for the end of his career (he is now 35), his Tour of Switzerland. German born, but living in Switzerland, it's a certain Jan Ullrich who took the glory. In preparation for the coming Tour de France, Ullrich finds himself in the country of banks and expensive watches and chocolate to get into shape, already better than at the same period in previous years. The winner of the 1997 Tour de France showed remarkable form particularly considering his less than perfect state just a month before. We didn't yet know, but this advanced state of preparation would be paid for some weeks later, in the Tour de France. Had Jan Ullrich dug too deep in the Tour of Switzerland? Many think this may have been the case.

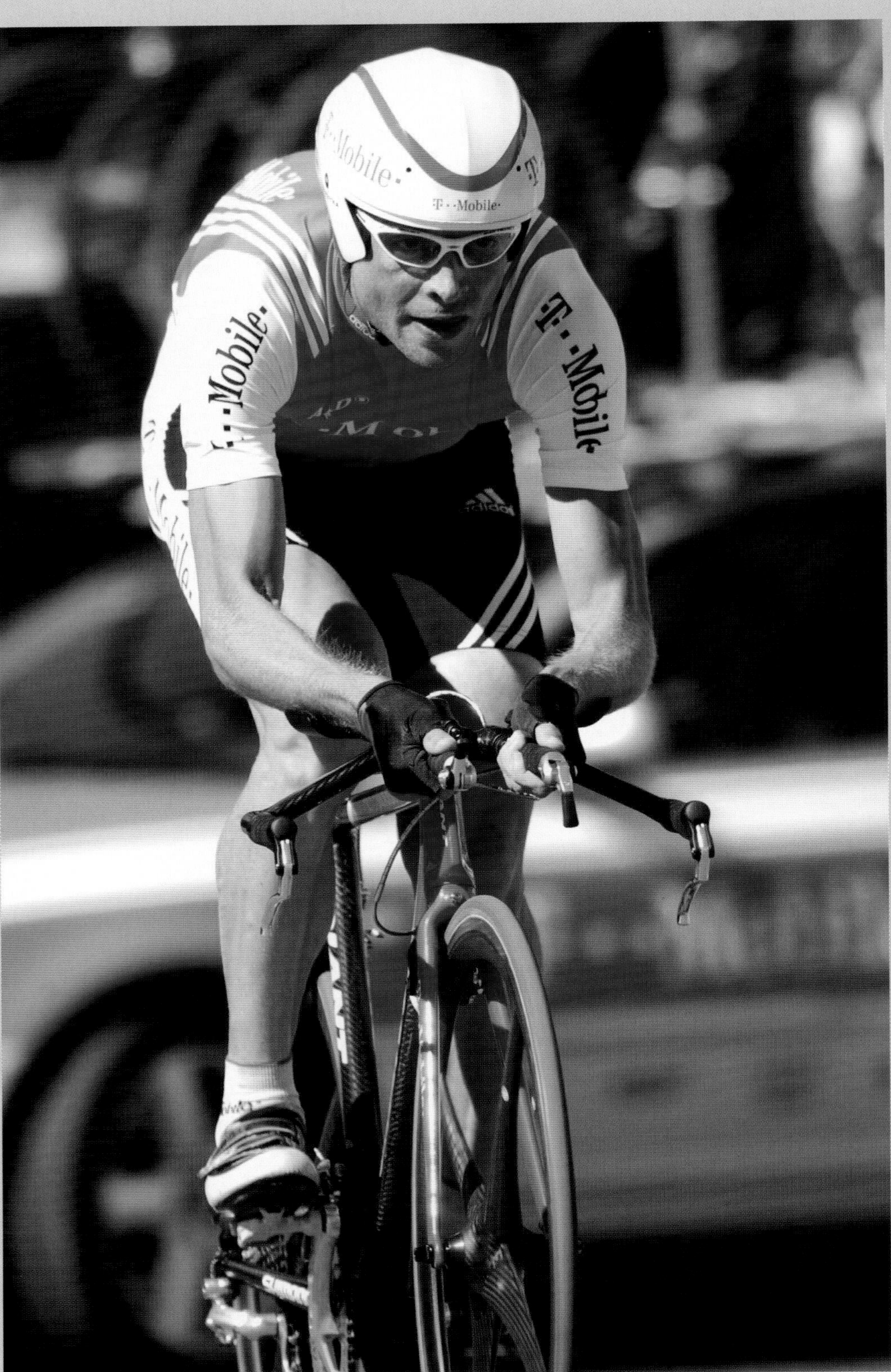

It's in the one and only time trial that Jan Ullrich manages to snatch victory from the grasp of Fabian Jeker. The Yellow jersey changing hands for a matter of one second.

Nothing would give a clue to a first stage as unconventional as the one to come. Sure, the twisting course around the canton of Lucerne was not without difficulty, but there was a surprise in store for those expecting the stage to end in a mass sprint. Sebastien Joly (Credit Agricole) and Roger Beuchat (Vini Caldirola) couldn't have imagined they'd light the fuse to such a bomb. Coming out of the peloton in the first few kilometers, the two men provoke such a reaction that 30 kilometers later, 39 men had split from the pack. We could pose the question whether it was not in fact the peloton that had broken away!
The names in this group leave us breathless: from Vinokourov to Ullrich and Cioni, Totschnig, Merckx, Julich, Tonkov, Jeker, Camenzind, Moos and Inkewitz. All the favourites had leapt onto the same wagon. Apart from Stefano Garzelli and Alex Zulle who must submit to the tactics of Tonkov for the first, and Zampieri and Moos for the second. The lead, which grows to five minutes (km74) begins to reduce when suddenly the peloton throws in the towel. At km140 the gap between the two groups stands at more than seven minutes. The winner of the Tour of Switzerland and of the stage is to be found in the star studded leading group, it's now a certainty.
At twenty kilometers from the line, some attacks begin to take place. The most serious coming from David Canada (Saunier Duval)and Steve Zampieri (Vini Caldirola). It's Jan Ullrich in person who sets up the chase along with the ex World Champion Oscar Camenzind following in his wake. The two stars soon have the leading duo in their sights. There now only remains one obstacle, the Herlisberg, at 10 kilometers

Crowned Champion of the World Espoirs in Zolder 2002, Francesco Chicchi thought he had victory in his hands among the elite of Batterkinden, end of the 4th stage of the Tour of Switzerland. That was not accounting for the final "Jump" of Robbie Mc Ewen, taking a second win unthinkable just seconds before.

from the line. A difficulty used by Fabian Jeker (Saunier Duval) to join the leading four riders. The others, between 15 and 25 seconds behind cannot manage this. It's now time to think about winning the stage. Jan Ullrich takes the lead at 300 metres to be the first into the final bend placed at 150 metres from the line. No one is in a position to catch him. The group of Vinokourov finishes 15 seconds later, the peloton finally comes in 18 minutes after.

VINO MARKED BY FATE

It had to happen. The riders who had missed the boat the day before came to life in the 2nd stage. Nothing unusual then that the first attack comes from those left behind the previous day. And not for all that , just anybody: Stefano Garzelli, Paolo Bettini, Markus Zberg, (Gerolsteiner), and Martin Elmiger (Phonak), Erik Leblacher (Credit Agricole), Jan Boven (Rabobank) and Michael Blaudzun (CSC) will stay in front for most of the stage before the Lotto – Domo team of Robbie McEwen decide to put them in their place. At 6 kilometers from Rheinfelden, the group was compact. And to reward his team, Robbie McEwen comes home victorious, containing Olaf Pollack (Gerolsreiner), decidedly attached to second places, and the South African Robert Hunter... who we'll be talking about later. The big news of the day is less happy: Alexandre Vinokourov is the victim of a crash and is transported to hospital. The rider from the T Mobile team must, the next day, admit he will not be able to take part in the Tour de France. Exactly as in 2002. In the future the Kazakh rider must absolutely not take part in the Tour of Switzerland on even years...

THIS CHAP IS UNUSUAL!

Robert hunter, this 27 year old South African rider is what is often called a second division sprinter. That's to say, he's quick but lacks that little something extra to be up there with the big boys, Petacchi, McEwen, Cooke, Zabel and company. To find success then he is obliged to be inventive an opportunist. In form at the start of the year, winning the Your of Qatar in January, he can perhaps surprise the well known sprinters at this time of the year. This is exactly what happens on this 3rd stage finishing in Juraparc above the town of Vallorbe. In the company of the red headed Peter Wuyts (Mr. Bookmaker.com), of Gregory Rast (Phonak), local boy Jurgen van Goolen (Quick Step) and Alberto Ongarato (Fassa Bortilo), one of the launch pads for the Petacchi missile, Robert Hunter goes rapidly into a lead over the peloton. The case is won at 20 kilometers from the line when the gap is nine minutes. The uphill end to the stage doesn't displease Robert Hunter who is now accompanied only by Gregory Rast, who is disposed of a few metres before the line. An unexpected win. Rob isn't allergic to the mountains!

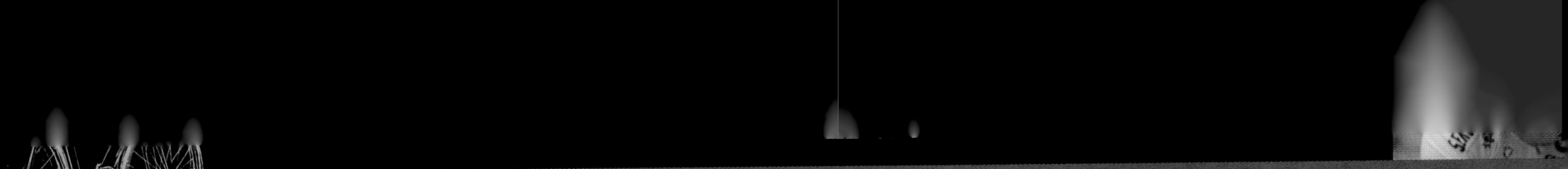

A BEGINNERS ERROR FOR CHICCHI

The accident of Alexandre Vinokourov was still the principal subject of conversation the next day at the start of the 4th stage. And unfortunately it's another medical report that makes the news in the first hours of the stage. A crash involving five riders leaves us fearing the worse for Marcus Zberg (Gerolsteiner). The news gets better however a few days later. Forster (team mate of Marcus Zberg), Amorim, Nauduzs and Steinhauser (team mate and friend of Jan Ullrich) are also taken to hospital even though their injuries seem less serious. This upsetting moment passed, four men launch for real, the race. But tom Danielson (Fassa Bortolo), Geert Verheyen (Chocolade Jaques), Maarten den Bakker (Rabobank) and Juan Manuel Garate (Lampre) never manage to get far enough ahead of the peloton (5mins at km145). At 15 kilometers from Batterkinden things get back to normal. The sprinters make ready. Just the same the short climb situated at Buchegg, 5.6 kilometers from the line, inspires, one after the other, Rik Verbrugghe, Paolo Bettini and last but not least, Gregory Rast (second the day previous) who don't however manage to open up a big enough gap. It's therefore a mass sprint that will decide the stage. A sprint that the young Francesco Chicchi, going for his first pro win, thought he'd won. But that's not accounting for Robbie McEwen, who in the manner of Oscar Freire in the Milan – San Remo throws his cycle at the line to win a second stage much to the disappointment of Francesco Chicchi, who, arms raised in victory, counted his chickens too soon. Let's hope he's learnt his lesson!

HUNTER AGAIN

The match between the sprinters continues. After the second success for Robbie McEwen, Robert Hunter doesn't want to leave things at that. But he does things in a different way: blocked by the Australian and certain others in the sprints, he would have to use his imagination to make his effort work. He launches an attack a long way out along with two other riders, the Dane Michael Blaudzun (CSC) and the Brazilian Murilo Fischer (Domina Vacanze). The stage finishing in the ski resort of Adelboden is not the ideal place for the operation, but arriving at the thirty kilometre mark the trio still have a lead of six minutes. The steady climb towards the finish is taken advantage of by Robert Hunter to pull away from his two companions. The South African takes his second stage victory on a terrain not normally suited to his style of riding. We have discovered a complete competitor.

The two gestures are the same but the frequency at which they are used is very different for Paolo Bettini (below), winner in Bellinzona, and the Swiss rider Niki Aebersold, starved of victories for six years before this Tour of Switzerland.

FIVE YEARS WAITING

With the Sustenpass and the Klausenpess awaiting, the day looks like being a difficult one for those not in love with the mountains. This doesn't seem to be the case of Niki Aebersold (Phonak), Stephane Augé (Credit Agricole), Alexandr Bazhenov (Domina Vacanze), Roger Beuchat (Vini Caldirola), Salvatore Commesso (Saeco), and Thorwald Veneberg (Rabobank) who take the race in hand at the 6th kilometre. At the summit of Sustenpass (km91), there are only three left: the Swiss riders Aebersold and Beuchat and Veneberg who maintain a substantial lead (11 mins) at the foot of the imposing Klausenpass. Niki Aebersold uses the difficulty to push for the line, leaving his two rivals behind and taking the win in Linthal. With this win he puts behind him a long period of waiting; his last success coming in 1998 (Milan – Turin). At the finish a big clear out takes place. Aided by the ever helpful Giuseppe Guerini, Jan Ullrich, uncontested leader since the first day, could no longer tolerate the presence of a privileged few: Georg Totschnig, Fabian Jeker, Dario cioni and Txema Del Olmo. The circle of those hoping to win is reduced.

ULLRICH LETS GO

With this incursion in Lichtenstein, the real mountain specialists had their chance. Despite the various difficulties along the route, it's the final climb towards Malbun (13km at almost 9% average) which is the strong point of the stage. Until then the day was animated by the two team mates from Mr Bookmaker.com, the Belgian Erwin Thijs and the Australian Ben Day. At the ten kilometre board the two men are engulfed by a group of strong men into which infiltrated Georg Totschnig. The Austrian managed to contain the effort of the impressive Jeker to take this prestigious stage. Jeker took the leader's jersey from the shoulders of Jan Ullrich who had known a moment of doubt 3 kilometers from the finish, before pulling himself together and conceding 39 seconds to the stage winner.

"IL GRILLO" SAVES FACE

They attack 14 strong and end up at the foot of the savage Cote de Artore as a duo, just before the finish at Bellinzona. The duel between the duo, Paolo Bettini and the Swiss rider Patrick Calcagni (riding on home ground on this stage), doesn't last long. As soon as the first slopes arrive, the Italian champion pulls away. He increases his lead on the rain soaked descent. With a reasonable lead he can ease up as he enters the town. He knows he has saved his Tour of Switzerland as he raises his arms in a victory salute. The overall ratings not being his priority. The peloton takes the descent to the line at a more casual pace. Just the same, there are some falls. The leaders cross the line with a deficit of a good three minutes from Bettini. All the leaders? No: Georg Totschnig is distanced on the descent and comes in 42 seconds after his rivals.

ULLRICH, BY MILLIMETRES

The suspense was to last until the final seconds. A final second fatal to the hopes of Fabian Jeker who has a lead of 41 seconds on the starting ramp, but loses 42 seconds in the course of the race. It's the same story in the battle between Georg Totschnig and Dario Cioni fighting it out for third place. Finally it's the Italian who takes the advantage over his rival by six seconds. Since turning pro, Jan Ullrich takes his first stage race before tackling the Tour de France. Good for his morale but less so for his physical condition. July will confirm this...But this win on his adopted home ground will permit him to save an otherwise disappointing season. ■

Stuck between his unfortunate rival, Fabian Jeker (left) and Dario Cioni, Jan Ullrich enjoys his victory in the Tour of Switzerland.

CLASSIFICATIONS

1st stage: Sursee/Beromünster - 176,3 km

1.	Jan Ullrich (Ger)	TMO	4h07'56"
2.	Oscar Camenzind (Sui)	PHO	s.t
3.	Fabian Jeker (Sui)	SDV	s.t

2nd stage: Dürrenroth/Rheinfelden - 169,9 km

1.	Robbie McEwen (Aus)	LOT	3h44'57"
2.	Olaf Pollack (Ger)	GST	s.t
3.	Robert Hunter (Rsa)	RAB	s.t

3rd stage: Rheinfelden/Juraparc - 185 km

1.	Robert Hunter (Rsa)	RAB	4h05'07"
2.	Gregory Rast (Sui)	PHO	+2"
3.	Jurgen van Goolen (Bel)	QSD	+19"

4e stage: Le Sentier/Bätterkinden - 211,6 km

1.	Robbie McEwen (Aus)	LOT	4h51'50"
2.	Francesco Chicchi (Ita)	FAS	s.t
3.	Olaf Pollack (Ger)	GST	s.t

5e stage: Bätterkinden/Adelboden - 161,7 km

1.	Robert Hunter (Rsa)	RAB	4h45'16"
2.	Murilo Fischer (Bra)	SDV	+35"
3.	Michael Blaudzun (Den)	CSC	+37"

6e stage: Frutigen/Linthal - 185,4 km

1.	Niki Aebersold (Sui)	PHO	5h04'07"
2.	Thorwald Veneberg (Ned)	RAB	+2'51"
3.	Roger Beuchat (Sui)	VIN	+3'00"

7e stage: Linthal/Malbun - 133,7 km

1.	Georg Totschnig (Aut)	GST	3h22'45"
2.	Fabian Jeker (Sui)	SDV	+7"
3.	Frank Schleck (Lux)	CSC	+14"

8e stage: Team time trial in Lugano - 25,6 km

1.	Jan Ullrich (Ger)	TMO	31'36"
2.	Laszlo Bodrogi (Hun)	QSD	+8"
3.	Fabian Cancellara (Sui)	FAS	+10"

FINAL OVERALL STANDINGS

1.	**Jan Ullrich (Ger)**	**TMO**	**34h19'25"**
2.	Fabian Jeker (Sui)	SDV	+1"
3.	Dario Cioni (Ita)	FAS	+1'20"
4.	Georg Totschnig (Aut)	GST	+1'26"
5.	Evgeni Petrov (Rus)	SAE	+2'14"
6.	Txema Del Olmo (Esp)	MIL	+2'17"
7.	Patrik Sinkewitz (Ger)	QSD	+3'18"
8.	Giuseppe Guerini (Ita)	TMO	+3'20"
9.	Oscar Camenzind (Sui)	PHO	+4'38"
10.	David Cañada (Esp)	SDV	+ 4'46"

144 Competitors

T.MOBILE

1.	VINOKOUROV Alexandre (Kaz)	*Abandon*	2nd stage
2.	BOTERO Santiago (Col)	55th	+ 46'59"
3.	GUERINI Giuseppe (Ita)	**8th**	+ 3'20"
4.	IVANOV Serguei (Rus)	64th	+ 56'58"
5.	NARDELLO Daniele (Ita)	53rd	+ 46'03"
6.	STEINHAUSER Tobias (Ger)	*Abandon*	4th stage
7.	ULLRICH Jan (Ger)	**1st**	**34h19'25"**
8.	WESEMANN Steffen (Ger)	DNS	6th stage

ALESSIO - BIANCHI

11.	BALDATO Fabio (Ita)	88th	+ 1h19'39"
12.	CAUCCHIOLI Pietro (Ita)	35th	+ 32'35"
13.	FERRARA Raffaele (Ita)	93rd	+ 1h22'53"
14.	HVASTIJA Martin (Slo)	94th	+ 1h23'05"
15.	JØRGENSEN René (Den)	67th	+ 1h04'07"
16.	MØLLER Claus Michael (Den)	DNS	5th stage
17.	SUNDERLAND Scott (Aus)	44th	+ 36'25"
18.	IVANOV Ruslan (Mda)	62nd	+ 56'30"

CRÉDIT AGRICOLE

21.	AUGÉ Stéphane (Fra)	105th	+ 1h40'50"
22.	DEAN Julian (Nzl)	71st	+ 1h07'15"
23.	HINAULT Sébastien (Fra)	89th	+ 1h19'59"
24.	WIGGINS Bradley (Gbr)	99th	+ 1h29'49"
25.	KASHECHKIN Andrey (Kaz)	22nd	+ 12'28"
26.	LEBLACHER Eric (Fra)	36th	+ 33'40"
27.	JOLY Sébastien (Fra)	28th	+ 20'59"
28.	NAZON Damien (Fra)	104th	+ 1h37'50"

Chocolade JACQUES - WINCOR NIXDORF

31.	ARANAGA Andoni (Esp)	*Abandon*	8th stage
32.	HIEMSTRA Bert (Ned)	92nd	+ 1h22'23"
33.	STEVENS Christophe (Bel)	*Abandon*	8th stage
34.	GADRET John (Fra)	*Abandon*	3rd stage
35.	LÖWIK Gerben (Ned)	85th	+ 1h17'44"
36.	PIATEK Zbigniew (Pol)	42nd	+ 36'04"
37.	VOSKAMP Bart (Ned)	70th	+ 1h06'57"
38.	VERHEYEN Geert (Bel)	51st	+ 45'24"

CSC

41.	JULICH Bobby (Usa)	13rd	+ 6'30"
42.	BLAUDZUN Michael (Den)	31st	+ 24'59"
43.	CHRISTENSEN Bekim (Den)	59th	+ 51'50"
44.	GUIDI Fabrizio (Ita)	DNS	6th stage
45.	HOFFMAN Tristan (Ned)	100th	+ 1h31'22"
46.	LUTTENBERGER Peter (Aut)	*Abandon*	6th stage
47.	SCHLECK Frank (Lux)	30th	+ 23'08"
48.	GOUSSEV Vladimir (Rus)	65th	+ 59'59"

DOMINA VACANZE

51.	FAGNINI GianMatteo (Ita)	98th	+ 1h29'29"
52.	BAZHENOV Alexandr (Rus)	*Abandon*	8th stage
53.	CLINGER David (Usa)	*Abandon*	3rd stage
54.	FISCHER Murillo (Bra)	69th	+ 1h06'01"
55.	GENTILI Massimiliano (Ita)	48th	+ 40'22"
56.	JONES Timothy (Zim)	*Abandon*	8th stage
57.	KOLOBNEV Alexandr (Rus)	15th	+ 7'13"
58.	NAUDUZS Andris (Lat)	*Abandon*	4th stage

FASSA BORTOLO

61.	CANCELLARA Fabian (Sui)	63rd	+ 56'55"
62.	CHICCHI Francesco (Ita)	106th	+ 1h52'42"
63.	CODOL Massimo (Ita)	39th	+ 34'11"
64.	DANIELSON Tom (Usa)	*Abandon*	8th stage
65.	KIRCHEN Kim (Lux)	26th	+ 18'33"
66.	ONGARATO Alberto (Ita)	103rd	+ 1h37'02"
67.	CIONI Dario (Ita)	**3rd**	+ 1'20"
68.	GUSTOV Volodymir (Ukr)	19th	+ 10'18"

GEROLSTEINER

71.	TOTSCHNIG Georg (Aut)	**4th**	+ 1'26"
72.	FOTHEN Markus (Ger)	40th	+ 34'25"
73.	FÖRSTER Robert (Ger)	*Abandon*	4th stage
74.	FARESIN Gianni (Ita)	*Abandon*	5th stage
75.	POLLACK Olaf (Ger)	*Abandon*	6th stage
76.	SERPELLINI Marco (Ita)	58th	+ 51'33"
77.	STRAUSS Marcel (Sui)	66th	+ 1h02'40"
78.	ZBERG Marcus (Sui)	*Abandon*	4th stage

LAMPRE

81.	CASAGRANDE Francesco (Ita)	DNS	7th stage
82.	BARBERO Sergio (Ita)	43rd	+ 36'16"
83.	BELLI Wladimir (Ita)	*Abandon*	4th stage
84.	BORTOLAMI Gianluca (Ita)	81st	+ 1h16'32"
85.	CORTINOVIS Alessandro (Ita)	32nd	+ 25'11"
86.	BERTOLETTI Simone (Ita)	86th	+ 1h18'32"
87.	GARATE Juan Manuel (Esp)	60th	+ 52'34"
88.	VILA Patxi (Esp)	11st	+ 5'41"

LOTTO - DOMO

91.	MERCKX Axel (Bel)	18th	+ 9'07"
92.	VERBRUGGHE Rik (Bel)	27th	+ 20'04"
93.	McEWEN Robbie (Aus)	DNS	7th stage
94.	DETILLOUX Christophe (Bel)	DNS	6th stage
95.	MARICHAL Thierry (Bel)	95th	+ 1h23'11"
96.	D'HOLLANDER Glenn (Bel)	101st	+ 1h32'53"
97.	VANSEVENANT Wim (Bel)	87th	+ 1h19'27"
98.	VAN IMPE Kevin (Bel)	*Abandon*	6th stage

MILANEZA - MAIA

101.	BERNABEU David (Esp)	52nd	+ 45'56"
102.	ZINTCHENKO Andrei (Rus)	23rd	+ 12'59"
103.	LAVARINHAS Rui (Por)	16th	+ 7'16"
104.	CARDOSO Pedro (Por)	41st	+ 34'40"
105.	SOUSA Rui (Por)	33rd	+ 29'02"
106.	DEL OLMO Txema (Esp)	**6th**	+ 2'17"
107.	AMORIM Gonçalo (Por)	*Abandon*	4th stage
108.	CASTANHEIRA Bruno (Por)	74th	+ 1h10'59"

Mr BOOKMAKER - PALMANS

111.	CASTRESANA Angel (Esp)	38th	+ 34'04"
112.	COENEN Johan (Bel)	57th	+ 49'44"
113.	COMMEYNE Davy (Bel)	47th	+ 40'16"
114.	HAMMOND Roger (Gbr)	73rd	+ 1h09'31"
115.	HUNT Jeremy (Gbr)	96th	+ 1h24'35"
116.	THIJS Erwin (Bel)	75th	+ 1h11'34"
117.	DAY Ben (Aus)	79th	+ 1h15'19"
118.	WUYTS Peter (Bel)	84th	+ 1h17'17"

PHONAK

121.	ZÜLLE Alex (Sui)	54th	+ 46'22"
122.	AEBERSOLD Niki (Sui)	49th	+ 41'10"
123.	CAMENZIND Oscar (Sui)	**9th**	+ 4'38"
124.	ELMIGER Martin (Sui)	45th	+ 37'37"
125.	MOOS Alexandre (Sui)	14th	+ 6'44"
126.	PEREZ FERNANDEZ Santi (Esp)	29th	+ 21'26"
127.	RAST Gregory (Sui)	56th	+ 47'36"
128.	SCHNIDER Daniel (Sui)	25th	+ 14'52"

QUICK STEP - DAVITAMON

131.	BETTINI Paolo (Ita)	DNS	9th stage
132.	BODROGI Laszlo (Hun)	24th	+ 13'42"
133.	BRAMATI Davide (Ita)	91st	+ 1h22'07"
134.	CLERC Aurélien (Sui)	83rd	+ 1h17'17"
135.	TANKINK Bram (Ned)	*Abandon*	3rd stage
136.	PAOLINI Luca (Ita)	*Abandon*	3rd stage
137.	SINKEWITZ Patrik (Ger)	**7th**	+ 3'18"
138.	VAN GOOLEN Jurgen (Bel)	DNS	9th stage

RABOBANK

141.	WAUTERS Marc (Bel)	76th	+ 1h13'53"
142.	BOVEN Jan (Ned)	80th	+ 1h15'36"
143.	DEN BAKKER Maarten (Ned)	78th	+ 1h14'35"
144.	HAYMAN Mathew (Aus)	97th	+ 1h26'58"
145.	HUNTER Robert (Rsa)	61st	+ 56'07"
146.	NIERMANN Grischa (Ger)	17th	+ 8'55"
147.	VENEBERG Thorwald (Ned)	34th	+ 30'37"
148.	WEENING Pieter (Ned)	DNS	7th stage

SAECO

151.	COMMESSO Salvatore (Ita)	77th	+ 1h13'54"
152.	BUCCIERO Antonio (Ita)	*Abandon*	6th stage
153.	GLOMSER Gerrit (Aut)	DNS	9th stage
154.	LOOSLI David (Sui)	*Abandon*	7th stage
155.	FUENTES Juan (Esp)	82nd	+ 1h17'06"
156.	LUDEWIG Jörg (Ger)	46th	+ 38'52"
157.	PETROV Evgueni (Rus)	**5th**	+ 2'14"
158.	SABALIAUSKAS Marius (Ltu)	21st	+ 12'18"

SAUNIER DUVAL - PRODIR

161.	JEKER Fabian (Sui)	**2nd**	+ 1"
162.	BERTOGLIATI Rubens (Sui)	90th	+ 1h20'03"
163.	GOMIS Juan (Esp)	*Abandon*	1st stage
164.	COBO Juan José (Esp)	102nd	+ 1h33'38"
165.	LOBATO Ruben (Esp)	*Abandon*	8th stage
166.	LODDO Alberto (Ita)	*Abandon*	3rd stage
167.	CAÑADA David (Esp)	**10th**	+ 4'46"
168.	ZAUGG Oliver (Sui)	*Abandon*	7th stage

Vini CALDIROLA - NOBILI Rubinetterie

171.	GARZELLI Stefano (Ita)	*Abandon*	4th stage
172.	BEUCHAT Roger (Sui)	37th	+ 33'59"
173.	CALCAGNI Patrick (Sui)	72nd	+ 1h08'23"
174.	GEROSA Mauro (Ita)	50th	+ 43'25"
175.	MILESI Marco (Ita)	68th	+ 1h05'45"
176.	TONKOV Pavel (Rus)	20th	+ 10'53"
177.	ZAMPIERI Steve (Sui)	12nd	+ 6'23"
178.	ZANOTTI Marco (Ita)	DNS	6th stage

EX WINNERS TAKING THE START — 7

VINOKOUROV Alexandre	2003
ZÜLLE Alex	2002
CAMENZIND Oscar	2000
CASAGRANDE Francesco	1999
GARZELLI Stefano	1998
LÜTTENBERGER Peter	1996
TONKOV Pavel	1995

3 OLDEST

PIATEK Zbigniew	(38) - 1966/05/01
SUNDERLAND Scott	(37) - 1966/11/28
BALDATO Fabio	(36) - 1968/03/16

3 YOUNGEST

GOUSSEV Vladimir	(21) - 1982/07/04
FOTHEN Markus	(22) - 1981/09/09
ZAUGG Oliver	(23) - 1981/05/09

NATIONALITIES REPRESENTED — 28

Italy	30
Switzerland	18
Belgium	15
Spain	12
Germany and Netherlands	9
Russia	7
France	6
Portugal	5
Australia and Denmark	4
Autstria, Great Britain and U.S.A	3
Kazakstan & Luxembourg	2
South Africa, Brazil, Colombia, Hungary, Latvia, Lithuania, Moldavia, New Zealand, Poland, Slovenia, Ukraine and Zimbabwe	1

COUPE DE FRANCE

17 ROUNDS 17 PODIUMS

TOUR DU HAUT-VAR
1. Marc Lotz (Ned)
2. D. Fofonov (Kaz)
3. S. Devolder (Bel)

CLASSIC HARIBO
1. Thor Hushovd (Nor)
2. G. Balducci (Ita)
3. S. Hinault (Fra)

GP CHOLET - PAYS DE LOIRE
1. Bert de Waele (Bel)
2. D. Rous (Fra)
3. T. Hushovd (Nor)

ROUTE ADÉLIE
1. Anthony Geslin (Fra)
2. S. Marinangeli (Ita)
3. P. Fedrigo (Fra)

GP DE RENNES
1. Andrus Aug (Est)
2. S. Ruskys (Ltu)
3. K. O'Bee (Usa)

PARIS-CAMEMBERT
1. Franck Bouyer (Fra)
2. T. Lövkvist (Swe)
3. J. Coenen (Bel)

GP DE DENAIN
1. Thor Hushovd (Nor)
2. M. Scanlon (Irl)
3. N. Sijmens (Bel)

TOUR DE VENDÉE
1. Thor Hushovd (Nor)
2. J. Kirsipuu (Est)
3. S. Hinault (Fra)

TRO BRO LÉON
1. Samuel Dumoulin (Fra)
2. C. Mengin (Fra)
3. B. Scheirlinckx (Bel)

TROPHÉE DES GRIMPEURS
1. Christophe Moreau (Fra)
2. P. Gilbert (Bel)
3. J. Pineau (Fra)

À TRAVERS LE MORBIHAN
1. Thomas Voeckler (Fra)
2. L. Paumier (Fra)
3. P. Fedrigo (Fra)

GP DE VILLERS-COTTERÊTS
1. Stuart O'Grady (Aus)
2. G. Omloop (Bel)
3. B. Cooke (Aus)

CLASSIQUE DES ALPES
1. Oscar Pereiro (Esp)
2. I. Mayo (Esp)
3. J.E Gutierrez (Esp)

POLYNORMANDE
1. Sylvain Chavanel (Fra)
2. G. Trentin (Ita)
3. C. Oriol (Fra)

BOUCLES DE L'AULNE
1. Frédéric Finot (Fra)
2. A. Naulleau (Fra)
3. S. Krushevskiy (Uzb)

FINAL INDIVIDUAL RATINGS

1. Thor Hushovd (Nor)	199
2. Pierrick Fedrigo (Fra)	135
3. Jérôme Pineau (Fra)	111
4. Thomas Voeckler (Fra)	98
5. Sylvain Chavanel (Fra)	86
6. Franck Bouyer (Fra)	79
7. Stuart O'Grady (Aus)	68
8. Frédéric Guesdon (Fra)	67
9. Frédéric Finot (Fra)	61
10. Anthony Geslin (Fra)	60

FINAL TEAM RATINGS

1. Crédit Agricole	133
2. Brioches La Boulangère	115
3. Fdjeux.com	101
4. Oktos	77
5. Auber 93	75
6. AG2R Prévoyance	65
7. RAGT Semences-MG Rover	61
8. Cofidis	55

GP D'ISBERGUES

1. Ludovic Capelle (Bel)
2. F. Guesdon (Fra)
3. C. Zamana (Pol)

PARIS-BOURGES

1. Jérôme Pineau (Fra)
2. M. Elmiger (Sui)
3. D. Rebellin (Ita)

WATER AND LOTZ

Marc Lotz and Levi Leipheimer have already had something in common. It was in the first stage of the Tour de France 2003. The two competitors were forced to retire following a crash in the streets of Meaux. Some months later, they were together again for a happier occasion, but the action took place in difficult circumstances. And in torrential rain!

Marc Lotz (born in Valkenburg) would have to wait seven seasons of his professional career with Rabobank for his first victory. Thirty years of age, his only results until now were a 3rd place in the Clasica de Almeria (2002), a 4th place in a stage of the Tour of Spain (2001), a 6th place in the Fleche Brabanconne the same year as well as a 12th place in his favourite , The Amstel Gold Race (2001). Considered by his leaders as the perfect team member, the rider took his chance to at last win a race known for its difficulty. It was particularly so this year. In fact, from the start of the race, the 196 competitors were affected dry the weather conditions: the heavens opened forcing the riders to wear whatever waterproof clothing they could find. This situation seemed to suit however one rider, the Basque Andoni Aranaga, who, wearing the jersey of the newly formed Chocolat Jacques team was new to the pro scene. We soon realise that he is clearing the way for his team leader Dave Bruylandts to make a first attack on the slopes of the Col de Marjoris at km 50. After the traditional passage through the streets of Montauroux, a group of 11 men make use of the Col de Mons (km 75) to take the lead. We can notice the presence of several riders already visible in Marjoris, such as Stijn Devolder (US Postal), Frederic Bessy (Cofidis) or Levi Leipheimer (Rabobank). Progressively, the group which had a lead over the peloton of 1 min 30 sec at the summit of the Col de Mons, lost its members, victims of the cold , the rain and the fast pace for an early season race; The Poilvet's Wegmann, Abakoumov, Rast and Calzati would have to let a group of five riders composed of the three men mentioned above , accompanied by the Dutchman Bram Tankink (Quick Step) and the surprising Italian Massimo Iannetti (Domina Vacanze) , 21 years old and a brand new pro. These two must just the same let Bessy, Devolder and Leipheimer pull away on the terrifying Cote des Tuileires, placed much further from the finish this year. At the summit (km 144) the trio headed the peloton by 58 seconds. A peloton shaken by several attacks such as that by Sylvain Chavanel, the recent winner over Paolo Bettini. It's finally a couple formed by Dmitriy Fofonov (Cofidis) and Marc Lotz (Rabobank) who manage to break away from the now thinning peloton. Two men having team mates up front and therefore who should not be participating in the chase of the last 100 kilometers by their adversaries. At 16 kilometers from the line the counter attackers join the leading trio, giving this group an odd look, with two Cofidis, two Rabobank and the sole US Postal in the person of Devolder. Still leading by more than a minute entering the final ten kilometers, the leaders could now concentrate on winning this first round of the Coupe de France. No one was in a position to leave his rivals behind entering Draguignan, and finally Devolder decided to go for the sprint at 400 metres. He was first passed by Fofonov...himself passed by a joyful Marc Lotz. We now know why. Present at the head of the race for most of the day, the Cofidis team was to finish with no points in the Coupe de France: none of its other riders managing to finish the race! However, they could take comfort in the provisional first place of the individual rankings before the second round to be run the next day! ■

194 Competitors

Brioches LA BOULANGÈRE

No.	Rider	Place	
1.	CHAVANEL Sylvain (Fra)	18th	
2.	CHARTEAU Anthony (Fra)		*Abandon*
3.	BOUYER Franck (Fra)		*Abandon*
4.	HARY Maryan (Fra)		*Abandon*
6.	PICHON Mickaël (Fra)		*Abandon*
7.	PINEAU Jérôme (Fra)		*Abandon*
8.	SPRICK Mathieu (Fra)		*Abandon*

COFIDIS

No.	Rider	Place	
11.	VASSEUR Cédric (Fra)		*Abandon*
13.	BESSY Frédéric (Fra)	**4th**	
14.	CLAIN Médéric (Fra)		*Abandon*
15.	EDALEINE Christophe (Fra)		*Abandon*
16.	FOFONOV Dmitriy (Kaz)	**2nd**	
17.	CASPER Jimmy (Fra)		*Abandon*
18.	ROULSTON Hayden (Nzl)		*Abandon*

RABOBANK

No.	Rider	Place	
21.	RASMUSSEN Michael (Den)		*Abandon*
22.	WIELINGA Remmert (Ned)		*Abandon*
23.	VENEBERG Thorwald (Ned)		*Abandon*
24.	TRAKSEL Bobbie (Ned)		*Abandon*
25.	DE WEERT Kevin (Bel)		*Abandon*
26.	LEIPHEIMER Levy (Usa)	**5th**	
27.	MUTSAARS Ronald (Ned)		*Abandon*
28.	LOTZ Marc (Ned)	**1st**	

RAGT Semences - MG ROVER

No.	Rider	Place	
31.	BOURQUENOUD Pierre (Sui)		*Abandon*
32.	RINERO Christophe (Fra)	28th	
33.	BOUVARD Gilles (Fra)		*Abandon*
34.	BUFFAZ Mickaël (Fra)		*Abandon*
35.	DION Renaud (Fra)		*Abandon*
36.	LE BOULANGER Yoann (Fra)		*Abandon*
37.	MARTIN Ludovic (Fra)		*Abandon*
38.	REYNAUD Nicolas (Fra)		*Abandon*

AG2R Prévoyance

No.	Rider	Place	
41.	BROCHARD Laurent (Fra)	20th	
43.	GOUBERT Stéphane (Fra)	43rd	
44.	KRIVTSOV Yuriy (Ukr)		*Abandon*
45.	AGNOLUTTO Christophe (Fra)		*Abandon*
46.	BERGÈS Stéphane (Fra)		*Abandon*
47.	PORTAL Nicolas (Fra)		*Abandon*
48.	FLICKINGER Andy (Fra)		*Abandon*

QUICK STEP - DAVITAMON

No.	Rider	Place	
51.	BETTINI Paolo (Ita)	13rd	
52.	VIRENQUE Richard (Fra)		*Abandon*
53.	AMORISON Frédéric (Bel)	34th	
54.	BODROGI Laszlo (Hun)	31st	
55.	BRAMATI Davide (Ita)		*Abandon*
56.	NUYENS Nick (Bel)		*Abandon*
57.	ROGERS Michael (Aus)	36th	
58.	TANKINK Bram (Ned	**8th**	

Just for a change, the Tour du Haut - Var 2004 was run in pouring rain. A bunched peloton takes on the first climb of the Cote des Tuilieres under the leadership of Belgians Christophe Brandt (Lotto) and Jurgen van de Walle (Chocolat Jaques), but soon the strong men will show themselves...

CRÉDIT AGRICOLE

61.	BOTCHAROV Alexandre (Rus)	23th	
62.	HALGAND Patrice (Fra)		*Abandon*
63.	SALMON Benoît (Fra)		*Abandon*
64.	FEDRIGO Pierrick (Fra)		*Abandon*
65.	KAGGESTAD Mads (Nor)	32nd	
66.	KASHECHKIN Andrey (Kaz)	11st	
67.	LE MEVEL Christophe (Fra)	25th	
68.	POILVET Benoît (Fra)		

VLAANDEREN - T INTERIM

71.	DEMEYERE Geoffrey (Bel)		*Abandon*
72.	DE SCHROODER Benny (Bel)		*Abandon*
73.	PEETERS Jef (Bel)		*Abandon*
74.	WILLEMS Frederik (Bel)		*Abandon*
75.	MERTENS Pieter (Bel)		*Abandon*
76.	DE SPIEGELAERE Bart (Bel)		*Abandon*
77.	VAN HUFFEL Wim (Bel)	17th	
78.	VEUCHELEN Frederik (Bel)		*Abandon*

FDJEUX.COM

81.	DA CRUZ Carlos (Fra)		*Abandon*
82.	VOGONDY Nicolas (Fra)		*Abandon*
83.	McGEE Bradley (Aus)		*Abandon*
84.	CASAR Sandy (Fra)	41st	
85.	FRITSCH Nicolas (Fra)		*Abandon*
86.	GILBERT Philippe (Bel)	33rd	
87.	SANCHEZ Fabien (Fra)		*Abandon*
88.	WILSON Matthew (Aus)		*Abandon*

SAECO

91.	CELESTINO Mirko (Ita)	**7th**	
92.	COMMESSO Salvatore (Ita)		*Abandon*
93.	BONOMI Giosue' (Ita)		*Abandon*
94.	GAVAZZI Nicola (Ita)		*Abandon*
95.	BUCCIERO Antonio (Ita)		*Abandon*
96.	CASAGRANDA Stefano (Ita)		*Abandon*
97.	GLOMSER Gerrit (Aut)		*Abandon*
98.	FORNACIARI Paolo (Ita)		*Abandon*

GEROLSTEINER

101.	REBELLIN Davide (Ita)	**6th**	
102.	SERPELLINI Marco (Ita)		*Abandon*
103.	ZBERG Marcus (Sui)		*Abandon*
104.	LANG Sebastian (Ger)		*Abandon*
105.	MONTGOMERY Sven (Sui)		*Abandon*
106.	SCHOLZ Ronny (Ger)		*Abandon*
107.	WEGMANN Fabian (Ger)		*Abandon*
108.	ZIEGLER Thomas (Ger)		*Abandon*

LOTTO - DOMO

111.	VERBRUGGHE Ief (Bel)		*Abandon*
112.	DETILLOUX Christophe (Bel)		*Abandon*
113.	DE CLERCQ Hans (Bel)		*Abandon*
114.	BRANDT Christophe (Bel)	21st	
115.	D'HOLLANDER Glen (Bel)		*Abandon*
116.	HOSTE Leif (Bel)		*Abandon*
117.	GATES Nick (Aus)		*Abandon*
118.	STEEGMANS Geert (Bel)		*Abandon*

PHONAK

121.	JALABERT Nicolas (Fra)		*Abandon*
122.	MURN Urosl (Slo)		*Abandon*
123.	DESSEL Cyril (Fra)		*Abandon*
124.	ALBASINI Michael (Sui)		*Abandon*
125.	CAMENZIND Oscarl (Sui)	15th	
126.	RAST Gregoryl (Sui)		*Abandon*
127.	SCHNIDER Daniell (Sui)		*Abandon*
128.	AEBERSOLD Nikil (Sui)		*Abandon*

US POSTAL - BERRY FLOOR

131.	EKIMOV Viatcheslav (Rus)		*Abandon*
132.	KLUCK Damon (Usa)		*Abandon*
133.	VAN HEESWIJK Max (Ned)		*Abandon*
134.	CRUZ Antonio (Usa)		*Abandon*
135.	DEVOLDER Stijn (Bel)	**3rd**	
136.	JOACHIM Benoît (Lux)		*Abandon*
138.	ZABRISKIE David (Usa)		*Abandon*

NAVIGATORS

141.	McKENZIE David (Aus)		*Abandon*
142.	LOUDER Jeff (Usa)		*Abandon*
143.	BALDWIN Chris (Usa)		*Abandon*
144.	O'BEE Kirk (Usa)		*Abandon*
145.	POWER Ciaran (Irl)		*Abandon*
146.	SWINDLEHURST Burke (Usa)		*Abandon*
147.	WALTERS Mark (Can)		*Abandon*
148.	ZAJICEK Phil (Usa)		*Abandon*

Mr BOOKMAKER - PALMANS

151.	VAN DE WOUWER Kurt (Bel)		*Abandon*
152.	HAMMOND Roger (Gbr)		*Abandon*
153.	GABRIEL Frédéric (Fra)		*Abandon*
154.	COENEN Johan (Bel)	14th	
155.	OMLOOP Geert (Bel)		*Abandon*
156.	PLANCKAERT Jo (Bel)		*Abandon*
157.	THIJS Erwin (Bel)		*Abandon*
158.	VAN HAECKE Michel (Bel)		*Abandon*

Vini CALDIROLA - NOBILI Rubinetterie

161.	TONKOV Pavel (Rus)		*Abandon*
162.	ZAMPIERI Steve (Sui)		*Abandon*
163.	BEUCHAT Roger (Sui)		*Abandon*
164.	ZANOTTI Marco (Ita)		*Abandon*
165.	LONGO BORGHINI Paolo (Ita)		*Abandon*
166.	SGAMBELLURI Roberto (Ita)		*Abandon*
167.	CHEULA Gianpaolo (Ita)	26th	
168.	MILESI Marco (Ita)		*Abandon*

ALESSIO - BIANCHI

171.	BÄCKSTEDT Magnus (Swe)		*Abandon*
172.	PELLIZOTTI Franco (Ita)	16th	
173.	FURLAN Angelo (Ita)		*Abandon*
174.	BALDATO Fabio (Ita)		*Abandon*
175.	BERTOLINI Alessandro (Ita)		*Abandon*
176.	CAUCCHIOLI Pietro (Ita)	**10th**	
177.	IVANOV Ruslan (Mda)		*Abandon*
178.	SKELDE Michael (Den)		*Abandon*

Chocolade JACQUES - WINCOR NIXDORF

181.	VAN DE WALLE Jurgen (Bel)		*Abandon*
182.	BRUYLANDTS Dave (Bel)	38th	
183.	ABAKOUMOV Igor (Bel)		*Abandon*
184.	BRARD Florent (Fra)		*Abandon*
185.	KOSTUYK Denis (Ukr)		*Abandon*
186.	ARANAGA Andoni (Esp)		*Abandon*
187.	RUDENKO Maxim (Ukr)		*Abandon*
188.	VERHEYEN Geert (Bel)	22nd	

DOMINA VACANZE

191.	IANNETTI Massimo (Ita)	**9th**	
192.	KOLOBNEV Alexandr (Rus)	12nd	
193.	SIMEONI Filippo (Ita)		*Abandon*
194.	JONES Timothy (Zim)		*Abandon*
195.	FISCHER Murillo (Bra)		*Abandon*
196.	NAUDUZS Andris (Lat)		*Abandon*
197.	GENTILI Massimiliano (Ita)	19th	
198.	GIUNTI Massimo (Ita)	35th	

LPR - PIACENZA

201.	LUCCHINI Claudio (Ita)		*Abandon*
202.	KARPATCHEV Andrei (Rus)		*Abandon*
203.	AGGIANO Elio (Ita)		*Abandon*
204.	SANTAMBROGIO Mauro (Ita)	27th	
205.	MASOLINO Daniele (Ita)		*Abandon*
206.	HERNANDEZ GUTIERREZ Aitor (Esp)		*Abandon*
207.	NARDELLO Luca (Ita)		*Abandon*
208.	BOGLIA Massimo (Ita)		*Abandon*

ACQUA e SAPONE - Caffé MOKAMBO

211.	HAMBURGER Bo (Den)		*Abandon*
212.	FERRIGATO Andrea (Ita)		*Abandon*
213.	AREKEEV Alexandr (Rus)		*Abandon*
214.	ASTOLFI Claudio (Ita)		*Abandon*
215.	DONATI Alessandro (Ita)		*Abandon*
216.	KOBZARENKO Valeriy (Ukr)	24th	
217.	PALUMBO Giuseppe (Ita)		*Abandon*
218.	NOCENTINI Rinaldo (Ita)		*Abandon*

MICHE

221.	ROTHMER Balasz (Hun)	30th	
222.	VARINI Maurizio (Ita)		*Abandon*
224.	SEMOV Dimitri (Rus)		*Abandon*
226.	NIEMEC Przemyslaw (Pol)		*Abandon*
227.	MUTO Pasquale (Ita)		*Abandon*
228.	MURRO Cristian (Ita)		*Abandon*

OKTOS - St QUENTIN

231.	MIZOUROV Andrei (Kaz)		*Abandon*
232.	CALZATI Sylvain (Fra)		*Abandon*
233.	GABROVSKI Ivaïlo (Bul)		*Abandon*
234.	GUROV Maxim (Kaz)		*Abandon*
235.	KRUSHEVSKIY Serhiy (Uzb)		*Abandon*
236.	PENCOLÉ Franck (Fra)	29th	
237.	LEVECOT Benjamin (Fra)		*Abandon*
238.	RUSKYS Saulius (Ltu)		*Abandon*

AUBER 93

241.	AUGER Ludovic (Fra)		*Abandon*
242.	NILSSON John (Swe)		*Abandon*
243.	TALABARDON Yannick (Fra)		*Abandon*
244.	BRÉARD David (Fra)		*Abandon*
245.	LAMOULLER Loïc (Fra)	37th	
246.	OLIVIER Lénaïc (Fra)		*Abandon*
247.	PAUMIER Laurent (Fra)		*Abandon*
248.	VALENTIN Tristan (Fra)		*Abandon*

CLASSIFICATION

Draguignan/Draguignan - 180 km

1.	**Marc Lotz (Ned)**	**RAB**	**4h 49'10"**
2.	**Dmitriy Fofonov (Kaz)**	**COF**	**s.t**
3.	**Stijn Devolder (Bel)**	**USP**	**s.t**
4.	Frédéric Bessy (Fra)	COF	s.t
5.	Levy Leipheimer (Usa)	RAB	+ 10"
6.	Davide Rebellin (Ita)	GST	+ 1'10"
7.	Mirko Celestino (Ita)	SAE	s.t
8.	Bram Tankink (Ned)	QSD	s.t
9.	Massimo Iannetti (Ita)	DVE	s.t
10.	Pietro Caucchioli (Ita)	ALB	+ 1'12"

COUPE DE FRANCE RANKINGS AFTER 1 ROUND

1.	**Dmitriy Fofonov (Kaz)**	**COF**	**35 pts**
2.	Frédéric Bessy (Fra)	COF	20 pts
3.	Andrey Kashechkin (Kaz)	C.A	6 pts

HUSHOVD DOESN'T SPARE THE HORSES!

Two weeks after a stage win in the Etoile de Besseges, the "Viking" Thor Hushovd (Credit Agricole) has once again found victory at the end of a damp Classic Haribo.

Reputedly easier than the previous day's Tour du Haut Var, the Classic Haribo has however a start far from easy, in the form of the always magnificent ascent of the Baux de Provence. Usually run under a generous winter sun which doesn't exclude a few strong gusts of wind, the second round of the Coupe de France this year was marked by incessant rain from Uzes to Marseilles. This does not discourage the neo pro Russian Alexandre Arekeev (Acqua&Sapone), Nicolas Jalabert, now wearing the Phonak jersey and... the Kazakh Dmitry Fofonov (Cofidis) already second the day before! Coming out of the peloton around the 40th kilometre, the three men will animate the major part of the day, obtaining a lead of 6 minutes before seeing it come down as they approach la Canebiere. Arekeev will fade first, Nicolas Jalabert next (twenty kilometers from the line) and Fofonov on his own could not fight against a peloton which had controlled the situation well. The duo Bramati / Traksel racing between the two groups were also caught in the final half hour of the race. At this moment the race looks wide open for the sprinters. Mc Ewen, Kirsipuu (three times winner of the race), Cooke and Van Dijk eat up the kilometers at high speed despite the wet road surface. The final, right angle, bend situated at 400metres from the finish will however be fatal to their chances: the slippery surface slides the cycle from under Stefan van Dijk and the others will find themselves either unseated or obliged to stop. The riders following this group now find themselves in the front line. Franck Pencolé (Oktos) pushes for the line but cannot sweep aside the massive Thor Hushovd, who goes on to take the lead 200metres from the line and takes the win ahead of the Italian Gabriele Balducci and his team mate Sebastien Hinault who obtains an excellent third place crossing the line with arms raised in a victory salute for his team. Member of a French team (this since turning pro), the Credit Agricole, Thor Hushovd takes the lead in the Coupe de France by fifteen points over Dmitry Fofonov. But the road is long and scattered with problems until the final Paris – Bourges... ■

Thor Hushovd was better at negotiating the final bend than Mc Ewen, Kirsipuu or Van Dijk who found themselves unseated. The Norwegian rider leads Gabriele Balducci (Saeco) and his team mate Sebastien Hinault (hidden by the Italian) by several lengths.

192 Competitors

*** Riders finishing outside of the time limit.**

AG2R Prévoyance

1.	KIRSIPUU Jaan (Est)	120th	+ 1'13"
2.	AGNOLUTTO Christophe (Fra)	144th	+ 8'42"
3.	BERGÈS Stéphane(Fra)	47th	+ 13"
4.	BROCHARD Laurent (Fra)	26th	s.t
5.	FLICKINGER Andy (Fra)	66th	+ 21"
6.	KRIVTSOV Yuriy (Ukr)	55th	+ 21"
7.	NAZON Jean-Patrick (Fra)	49th	+ 19"
8.	PORTAL Nicolas (Fra)	150th	+ 29'58"*

QUICK STEP - DAVITAMON

11.	BODROGI Laszlo(Hun)	48th	+ 13"
12.	AMORISON Frédéric (Bel)	53rd	+ 21"
13.	BRAMATI Davide (Ita)	113rd	+ 1'00"
15.	HULSMANS Kevin (Bel)	13rd	s.t
16.	NUYENS Nick (Bel)	16th	s.t
18.	TANKINK Bram (Ned)	128th	+ 5'46"

SAECO

21.	BALDUCCI Gabriele (Ita)	**2nd**	s.t
22.	BONOMI Giosue' (Ita)		*Abandon*
23.	BUCCIERO Antonio (Ita)	95th	+ 40"
24.	CASAGRANDA Stefano (Ita)	85th	+ 29"
25.	COMMESSO Salvatore (Ita)	19th	s.t
26.	GAVAZZI Nicola (Ita)	20th	s.t
27.	GLOMSER Gerrit (Aut)	81st	+ 27"
28.	PIERI Dario (Ita)		*Abandon*

GEROLSTEINER

31.	WEGMANN Fabian (Ger)		*Abandon*
32.	FÖRSTER Robert (Ger)	**10th**	s.t
33.	LANG Sebastian (Ger)	149th	+ 28'19"
34.	MONTGOMERY Sven (Sui)		*Abandon*
35.	POLLACK Olaf (Ger)		*Abandon*
36.	SCHOLZ Ronny (Ger)	91st	+ 40"
37.	SERPELLINI Marco (Ita)	77th	+ 29"
38.	ZIEGLER Thomas (Ger)	56th	+ 21"

COFIDIS

41.	CASPER Jimmy (Fra)	**7th**	s.t
42.	BESSY Frédéric (Fra)	80th	+ 29"
43.	CLAIN Médéric (Fra)	134th	+ 5'46"
44.	EDALEINE Christophe (Fra)	133rd	+ 5'46"
45.	FOFONOV Dmitriy (Kaz)	123rd	+ 2'00"
46.	ROULSTON Hayden (Nzl)	**6th**	s.t
47.	VASSEUR Cédric (Fra)	76th	+ 29"

RABOBANK

51.	LEIPHEIMER Levy (Usa)	98th	+ 40"
52.	DE WEERT Kevin (Bel)	41st	+ 13"
53.	DEKKERS Hans (Ned)	117th	+ 1'06"
54.	LOTZ Marc (Ned)	97th	+ 40"
55.	MUTSAARS Ronald (Ned)	68th	+ 21"
56.	RASMUSSEN Michael (Den)		*Abandon*
57.	TRAKSEL Bobbie (Ned)	132nd	+ 5'46"
58.	VENEBERG Thorwald (Ned)	79th	+ 29"

US POSTAL - BERRY FLOOR

61.	VAN HEESWIJK Max (Ned)	60ththth	+ 21"
63.	CRUZ Antonio (Usa)	121st	+ 1'20"
64.	DEVOLDER Stijn (Bel)	99th	+ 40"
65.	EKIMOV Viatcheslav (Rus)		*Abandon*
66.	JOACHIM Benoît (Lux)	63rd	+ 21"
67.	KLUCK Damon (Usa)	114th	+ 1'00"
68.	ZABRISKIE David (Usa)	103rd	+ 40"

ALESSIO - BIANCHI

71.	BALDATO Fabio (Ita)	90th	+ 40"
73.	BERTOLINI Alessandro (Ita)		*Abandon*
74.	FURLAN Angelo (Ita)	**4th**	s.t
75.	IVANOV Ruslan (Mda)	92nd	+ 40"
76.	SKELDE Michael (Den)	34th	+ 8"

FDJEUX.COM

81.	COOKE Baden (Aus)	30th	s.t
83.	DA CRUZ Carlos (Fra)	64th	+ 21"
84.	GILBERT Philippe (Bel)	73rd	+ 21"
85.	McGEE Bradley (Aus)		*Abandon*
86.	ROBIN Jean-Cyril (Fra)	136th	+ 5'46"
87.	VOGONDY Nicolas (Fra)	140th	+ 5'46"
88.	WILSON Matthew (Aus)	106th	+ 48"
90.	SANCHEZ Fabien (Fra)	143rd	+ 8'41"

PHONAK

91.	CAMENZIND Oscar (Sui)	51st	+ 21"
92.	AEBERSOLD Niki (Sui)		*Abandon*
93.	ALBASINI Michael (Sui)		*Abandon*
94.	DESSEL Cyril (Fra)	78th	+ 29"
95.	JALABERT Nicolas (Fra)	146th	+ 8'44"
96.	MURN Uros (Slo)	29th	s.t
97.	RAST Gregory (Sui)	27th	s.t
98.	SCHNIDER Daniel (Sui)	46th	+ 13"

Vini CALDIROLA - NOBILI Rubinetterie

101.	TONKOV Pavel (Rus)	141st	+ 5'46"
102.	BEUCHAT Roger (Sui)	75th	+ 29"
103.	CHEULA Gianpaolo (Ita)		*Abandon*
104.	LONGO BORGHINI Paolo (Ita)	137th	+ 5'46"
105.	MILESI Marco (Ita)	86th	+ 29"
106.	SGAMBELLURI Roberto (Ita)	135th	+ 5'46"
107.	ZAMPIERI Steve (Sui)	124th	+ 2'02"
108.	ZANOTTI Marco (Ita)	38th	+ 10"

Brioches LA BOULANGÈRE

111.	BOUYER Franck (Fra)	65th	+ 21"
112.	CHARTEAU Anthony (Fra)	94th	+ 40"
113.	CHAVANEL Sébastien (Fra)	14th	s.t
114.	GESLIN Anthony (Fra)	40th	+ 13"
115.	KERN Christophe (Fra)		*Abandon*
116.	MARTIAS Rony (Fra)		*Abandon*
117.	NAULLEAU Alexandre (Fra)	110th	+ 51"
118.	RENIER Franck (Fra)	**8th**	s.t

LOTTO - DOMO

121.	McEWEN Robbie (Aus)	126th	+ 2'34"
122.	BRANDT Christophe (Bel)	54th	+ 21"
123.	DE CLERCQ Hans (Bel)	89th	+ 36"
124.	EECKHOUT Nico (Bel)	62nd	+ 21"
125.	GARDEYN Gorik (Bel)	127th	+ 5'46"
126.	HOSTE Leif (Bel)	100th	+ 40"
127.	VAN DIJK Stefan (Ned)	33rd	s.t
128.	VIERHOUTEN Aart (Ned)	111st	+ 55"

CRÉDIT AGRICOLE

131.	HUSHOVD Thor (Nor)	**1st**	**4h 49'27"**
132.	AUGÉ Stéphane (Fra)	138th	+ 5'46"
133.	DEAN Julian (Nzl)		*Abandon*
134.	HINAULT Sébastien (Fra)	**3rd**	s.t
135.	JÉGOU Lilian (Fra)	28th	s.t
136.	LEQUATRE Geoffroy (Fra)	145th	+ 8'42"
137.	NAZON Damien (Fra)		*Abandon*
138.	WIGGINS Bradley (Gbr)	125th	+ 2'02"

Chocolade JACQUES - WINCOR NIXDORF

141.	KOERTS Jans (Ned)		*Abandon*
142.	HIEMSTRA Bert (Ned)		*Abandon*
143.	LÖWIK Gerben (Ned)	31st	s.t
144.	PEERS Chris (Bel)	22nd	s.t
145.	PLANCKAERT Francesco (Bel)		*Abandon*
146.	REINERINK Rik (Ned)	**5th**	s.t
147;	VAN VELZEN Jan (Ned)	82nd	+ 29"
148.	VOSKAMP Bart (Ned)		*Abandon*

RAGT Semences - MG ROVER

151.	SEIGNEUR Eddy (Fra)	70th	+ 21"
152.	BOURQUENOUD Pierre (Sui)	50th	+ 19'
153.	BOUVARD Gilles (Fra)	88th	+ 29"
154.	BUFFAZ Mickaël (Fra)	122nd	+ 1'56"
155.	DION Renaud (Fra)	147th	+ 25'00"*
156.	LE BOULANGER Yoann (Fra)	109th	+ 51"
157.	REYNAUD Nicolas (Fra)		*Abandon*
158.	RINERO Christophe (Fra)	36th	+ 10"

DOMINA VACANZE

161.	FISCHER Murillo (Bra)	37th	+ 10"
162.	GENTILI Massimiliano (Ita)	39th	+ 10"
163.	GIUNTI Massimo (Ita)		*Abandon*
164.	IANNETTI Massimo (Ita)	84th	+ 29"
165.	JONES Timothy (Zim)		*Abandon*
166.	KOLOBNEV Alexandr (Rus)		*Abandon*
167.	NAUDUZS Andris (Lat)	24th	s.t
168.	SIMEONI Filippo (Ita)		*Abandon*

LANDBOUWKREDIET - COLNAGO

171.	DURAND Jacky (Fra)	43rd	+ 13"
172.	BILEKA Volodymir (Ukr)	52nd	+ 21"
173.	BRACKE Tony (Bel)	108th	+ 48"
174.	CAPELLE Ludovic (Bel)	**9th**	s.t
175.	GRYSCHENKO Ruslan (Ukr)	116th	+ 1'06"
176.	LAGUTIN Serguey (Uzb)	115th	+ 1'06"
177.	MITLUSHENKO Yuriy (Ukr)	59th	+ 21"
178.	DIERCKXSENS Ludo (Bel)	45th	+ 13"

Mr BOOKMAKER - PALMANS

181.	PLANCKAERT Jo (Bel)	32nd	s.t
182.	DE SMET Andy (Bel)	74th	+ 21"
183.	HAMMOND Roger (Gbr)	119th	+ 1'10"
184.	OMLOOP Geert (Bel)	102nd	+ 40"
185.	THIJS Erwin (Bel)	72nd	+ 21"
186.	TROUVÉ Kristof (Bel)	67th	+ 21"
187.	VAN HAECKE Michel (Bel)		*Abandon*
188.	VANDERAERDEN Gert (Bel)	61st	+ 21"

ACQUA e SAPONE - Caffé MOKAMBO

191.	FERRIGATO Andrea (Ita)	71st	+ 21"
192.	AREKEEV Alexandr (Rus)	129th	+ 5'46"
193.	ASTOLFI Claudio (Ita)		*Abandon*
194.	DONATI Alessandro (Ita)		*Abandon*
195.	HAMBURGER Bo (Den)	57th	+ 21"
196.	KOBZARENKO Valeriy (Ukr)	93rd	+ 40"
197.	NOCENTINI Rinaldo (Ita)	107th	+ 48"
198.	PALUMBO Giuseppe (Ita)	139th	+ 5'46"

VLAANDEREN - T INTERIM

201.	SCHOONACKER Jehudi (Bel)	44th	+ 13"
202.	CAETHOVEN Steven (Bel)		*Abandon*
204.	KUYCKX Jan (Bel)	23rd	s.t
205.	MEYS David (Bel)	87th	+ 29"
206.	VAN HYFTE Paul (Bel)	42nd	+ 13"
207.	VAN MECHELEN Wouter (Bel)		*Abandon*
208.	VAN SPEYBROECK Wesley (Bel)	17th	s.t
209.	BARBÉ Koen (Bel)	25th	s.t

AUBER 93

211.	AUGER Ludovic (Fra)	11st	s.t
212.	BRÉARD David (Fra)		*Abandon*
213.	LAMOULLER Loïc (Fra)	83rd	+ 29"
214.	NILSSON John (Swe)	35th	+ 10"
215.	OLIVIER Lénaïc (Fra)		*Abandon*
216.	PAUMIER Laurent (Fra)	69th	+ 21"
217.	TALABARDON Yannick (Fra)	118th	+ 1'10"
218.	VALENTIN Tristan (Fra)		*Abandon*

NAVIGATORS

221.	O'BEE Kirk (Usa)	101st	+ 40"
222.	CAMPONOGARA Siro (Ita)	148th	+ 25'13"*
223.	DAVIDENKO Vassili (Rus)		*Abandon*
224.	LOUDER Jeff (Usa)	104th	+ 40"
225.	McKENZIE David (Aus)		*Abandon*
226.	POWER Ciaran (Irl)	15th	s.t
227.	RAPINSKI Viktor (Blr)	131st	+ 5'46"
228.	WALTERS Mark (Can)	130th	+ 5'46"

OKTOS - St QUENTIN

231.	CALZATI Sylvain (Fra)	96th	+ 40"
232.	GABROVSKI Ivaïlo (Bul)		*Abandon*
233.	GUROV Maxim (Kaz)	112nd	+ 55"
234.	KRUSHEVSKIY Serhiy (Uzb)	142nd	+ 7'35"
235.	LEVECOT Benjamin (Fra)		*Abandon*
236.	MIZOUROV Andrei (Kaz)		*Abandon*
237.	PENCOLÉ Franck (Fra)	21st	s.t
238.	RUSKYS Saulius (Ltu)	58th	+ 21"

LPR - PIACENZA

242.	AGGIANO Elio (Ita)	12nd	s.t
243.	BOGLIA Massimo (Ita)		*Abandon*
244.	HERNANDEZ GUTIERREZ Aitor (Esp)	18th	s.t
246.	MASOLINO Daniele (Ita)	105th	+ 40"
247.	NARDELLO Luca (Ita)		*Abandon*
248.	SANTAMBROGIO Mauro (Ita)		*Abandon*
249.	KARPATCHEV Andrei (Rus)		*Abandon*

CLASSIFICATION

Uzès/Marseille - 204 km

1.	**Thor Hushovd (Nor)**	**C.A**	**4h 49'27"**
2.	**Gabriele Balducci (Ita)**	**SAE**	**s.t**
3.	**Sébasti Hinault (Fra)**	**C.A**	**s.t**
4.	Angelo Furlan (Ita)	ALB	s.t
5.	Rik Reinerink (Ned)	CHO	s.t
6.	Hayden Roulston (Nzl)	COF	s.t
7.	Jimmy Casper (Fra)	COF	s.t
8.	Franck Renier (Fra)	BLB	s.t
9.	Ludovic Capelle (Bel)	LAN	s.t
10.	Robert Förster (Ger)	GST	s.t

COUPE DE FRANCE RANKINGS AFTER 2 ROUNDS

1.	**Thor Hushovd (Nor)**	**C.A**	**50 pts**
2.	Dmitriy Fofonov (Kaz)	COF	35 pts
3.	Sébastien Hinault (Fra)	C.A	25 pts
4.	Frédéric Bessy (Fra)	COF	20 pts
5.	Hayden Roulston (Nzl)	COF	16 pts

De Waele at a throw of the dice

Pure Flemmish, Bert de Waele speaks French with some difficulty. He would be advised to take a few lessons because France seems to be a country which brings him a certain amount of success. Having started his winning ways in the Tour de Doubs 2003, he's managed a second success in the country by surprising the favourites in the Cholet – Pays de Loire, the third round of the Coupe de France.

Traditionally run the day after the Milan – San Remo, the "Classic des Mauges" rarely benefits from the participation of the riders who raced on the Via Roma just hours earlier. Such is life. The peloton present on this windy day, where the sun just manages to break through heavy cloud, contains many French riders anxious to make amends for a disappointing ride in the Paris – Nice. Just the same, it's a Belgian rider who is the first to mount a serious attack. Frederik Willems (Vlaanderen – T Interim) pulls away after an hour of the race. He's soon reinforced by Frederic Guesdon (Fdjeux.com) and Thomas Voeckler (La Boulangere) then his compatriot Jurgen van de Walle (Chocolat Jaques) and Patrice Halgand (Credit Agricole). The five men work well together and by mid race have a lead of 4 mins 50sec. In the peloton and with the help of a strong wind, the strong men get to work. A group of twenty riders forms. In this first counter attack some teams are over represented. It's the case of CSC, Brioches La Boulangere, and Credit Agricole , who can each count on four men. There are also three men from Cofidis (Bessy, Clain and Moncoutié). The lead of the leading group is greatly diminished, coming down to half a minute coming to the final difficulty of the day. The hill at St Georges des Gardes (km 161). Having visibly held more in reserve than their co attackers, Frederic Guesdon and Jurgen van de Walle take advantage of the climb to pull away from the others. They are soon joined by a Frank Schlek (CSC) in great form as proved by his 9th place in the recent Paris – Nice. The approach towards Cholet (which presents no problems) permits other members of the counter attack group (Thor Hushovd, Bert de Waele, and Didier Rous) to join the leaders. At the entrance to the urban circuit (5.3 kms to be taken three times), the group of six lead a following group of thirteen by 1 min 20sec. Despite a counter attack launched by the young Russian Vladimir Goussev (CSC), Pierrick Fedrigo (C. A) and Jan Kuyckx (Vlaanderen), the leaders were no longer worried by those following. Logical favourite in a sprint, Thor Hushovd, leader of the Coupe de France after his victory in the Classic Haribo a few weeks earlier, is feared by his rivals who can only apply one tactic against him: make him work on the final lap in order to wear him down. That's the intention of Didier Rous. The French champion decides to accelerate 1500 metres from the line but is much too closely watched to make anything of it. Bert de Waele is much less watched and uses a slight descent to join the leaders. There are 1200metres left to race and the other five don't seem ready to make a move. Thor Hushovd decides belatedly to go after the rider, but with no real conviction. De waele keeps his lead and announces on crossing the line "To win such a big race as this is a terrific thing for a rider like me". Five seconds behind, Didier Rous, visibly feeling much better after recent illnesses even takes the liberty of beating Thor Hushovd to take second place. The Norwegian however consolidates his position in the Coupe de France. ■

The helmet at a jaunty angle and with a wide smile, it's Bert de Waele who crosses the line first. Did someone say surprise winner?

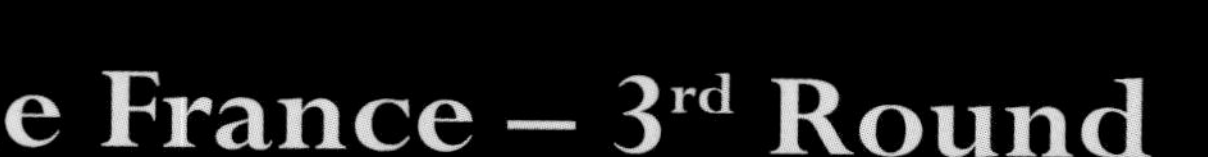

Under the watchful eye of Daniel Mangeas (with the microphone) and the watching crowd, the leading group must complete another lap before the finish. Bert de Waele leads the group followed by the French champion Didier Rous. At the line they finish in the same order!

125 Competitors

FDJEUX.COM

1.	MENGIN Christophe (Fra)	24th	+ 1'39"
2.	BICHOT Freddy (Fra)		*Abandon*
3.	CASAR Sandy (Fra)	13rd	+ 1'08"
4.	VAUGRENARD Benoît (Fra)		*Abandon*
5.	GUESDON Frédéric (Fra)	**5th**	+ 6"
6.	ROBIN Jean-Cyril (Fra)	25th	+ 1'39"
7.	ROY Jérémy (Fra)		*Abandon*
8.	VOGONDY Nicolas (Fra)	30th	+ 1'39"

Brioches LA BOULANGÈRE

11.	BOUYER Franck (Fra)	11st	+ 1'08"
12.	BENETEAU Walter (Fra)	22nd	+ 1'39"
13.	CHARTEAU Anthony (Fra)	26th	+ 1'39"
14.	CHAVANEL Sébastien (Fra)		*Abandon*
15.	ROUS Didier (Fra)	**2nd**	+ 5"
16.	SPRICK Mathieu (Fra)		*Abandon*
17.	YUS Unai (Esp)	36th	+ 1'39"
18.	VOECKLER Thomas (Fra)	18th	+ 1'34"

Mr BOOKMAKER - PALMANS

21.	COENEN Johan (Bel)	29th	+ 1'39"
22.	DAY Ben (Aus)		*Abandon*
23.	GABRIEL Frédéric (Fra)	40th	+ 6'27"
24.	HUNT Jeremy (Gbr)	64th	+ 6'45"
25.	RENDERS Jens (Bel)	61st	+ 6'45"
26.	LEUKEMANS Björn (Bel)		*Abandon*
27.	VAN DE WOUWER Kurt (Bel)	63rd	+ 6'45"
28.	WUYTS Peter (Bel)	62nd	+ 6'45"

CSC

31.	ARVESEN Kurt-Asle (Nor)	12nd	+ 1'08"
32.	SCHLECK Frank (Lux)	**4th**	+ 5"
33.	HOFFMAN Tristan (Ned)	32nd	+ 1'39"
34.	MADSEN Jimmi (Den)	28th	+ 1'39"
36.	SANDSTØD Michael (Den)		*Abandon*
37.	GOUSSEV Vladimir (Rus)	**7th**	+ 54"

Chocolade JACQUES - WINCOR NIXDORF

41.	ZAMANA Cezary (Pol)		*Abandon*
42.	VERHEYEN Geert (Bel)	49th	+ 6'27"
43.	KOSTYUK Denis (Ukr)		*Abandon*
44.	RUDENKO Maxim (Ukr)		*Abandon*
45.	BELOHVOSCIKS Raivis (Lat)	47th	+ 6'27"
46.	PEERS Chris (Bel)	14th	+ 1'14"
47.	VAN DE WALLE Jurgen (Bel)	**6th**	+ 10"
48.	ARANAGA Andoni (Esp)	19th	+ 1'37"

VLAANDEREN - T INTERIM

51.	VAN HYFTE Paul (Bel)	17th	+ 1'31"
52.	DEMEYERE Geoffroy (Bel)		*Abandon*
53.	DE SCHROODER Benny (Bel)		*Abandon*
54.	KUYCKX Jan (Bel)	**9th**	+ 54"
55.	MERTENS Pieter (Bel)		*Abandon*
56.	VEUCHELEN Frederik (Bel)	44th	+ 6'27"
57.	VAN HUFFEL Wim (Bel)	23rd	+ 1'39"
58.	WILLEMS Frederik (Bel)	60th	+ 6'45"

AG2R Prévoyance

61.	KIRSIPUU Jaan (Est)	21st	+ 1'39"
62.	AGNOLUTTO Christophe (Fra)		*Abandon*
63.	BERGÈS Stéphane (Fra)	51st	+ 6'39"
65.	LAIDOUN Julien (Fra)		*Abandon*
67.	TURPIN Ludovic (Fra)		*Abandon*
68.	PÜTSEP Erki (Est)		*Abandon*

RAGT Semences - MG ROVER

71.	BERNARD Jérôme (Fra)		*Abandon*
72.	DION Renaud (Fra)	48th	+ 6'27"
73.	LAURENT Christophe (Fra)		*Abandon*
74.	BOUVARD Gilles (Fra)		*Abandon*
75.	FINOT Frédéric (Fra)	55th	+ 6'45"
76.	LUHOVYY Roman (Ukr)		*Abandon*
78.	REYNAUD Nicolas (Fra)		*Abandon*

COFIDIS

81.	CASPER Jimmy (Fra)	27th	+ 1'39"
82.	BESSY Frédéric (Fra)	38th	+ 6'02"
83.	CLAIN Médéric (Fra)		*Abandon*
84.	FOFONOV Dmitriy (Kaz)		*Abandon*
85.	EDALEINE Christophe (Fra)	58th	+ 6'45"
86.	MONCOUTIÉ David (Fra)		*Abandon*
87.	MONIER Damien (Fra)		*Abandon*

CRÉDIT AGRICOLE

91.	HUSHOVD Thor (Nor)	**3rd**	+ 5"
92.	FEDRIGO Pierrick (Fra)	**8th**	+ 54"
93.	LE MÉVEL Christophe (Fra)	33rd	+ 1'39"
94.	HERVÉ Cédric (Fra)	46th	+ 6'27"
95.	HALGAND Patrice (Fra)	57th	+ 6'45"
96.	HINAULT Sébastien (Fra)		*Abandon*
97.	KAGGESTAD Mads (Nor)		*Abandon*
98.	POILVET Benoît (Fra)	37th	+ 1'39"

OKTOS - St QUENTIN

101.	CALZATI Sylvain (Fra)		*Abandon*
102.	GABROVSKI Ivaïlo (Bul)		*Abandon*
103.	GUROV Maxim (Kaz)		*Abandon*
104.	LEVECOT Benjamin (Fra)		*Abandon*
105.	MIZOUROV Andrey (Kaz)	43rd	+ 6'27"
106.	PENCOLÉ Franck (Fra)	**10th**	+ 1'08"
107.	TESSIER Jean-Michel (Fra)		*Abandon*
108.	RUSKYS Saulius (Ltu)	20th	+ 1'39"

AUBER 93

111.	AUGER Ludovic (Fra)		*Abandon*
112.	BRÉARD David (Fra)		*Abandon*
113.	LAMOULLER Loïc (Fra)	53rd	+ 6'42"
114.	NILSSON John (Swe)	41st	+ 6'27"
115.	OLIVIER Lénaïc (Fra)	39th	+ 6'27"
116.	PAUMIER Laurent (Fra)	42nd	+ 6'27"
117.	TALABARDON Yannick (Fra)	50th	+ 6'33"
118.	VALENTIN Tristan (Fra)	45th	+ 6'27"

WÜRTH - BOM PETISCO

121.	VITORINO Nelson (Por)	31st	+ 1'39"
122.	FITAS Vidal (Por)		*Abandon*
123.	MARTA Nuno (Por)		*Abandon*
124.	ANDRADE Joaquim (Por)	34th	+ 1'39"
125.	VASILEV Krasimir (Bul)		*Abandon*
126.	COSTA Ricardo (Por)		*Abandon*

ED'SYSTEM - ZVVZ

131.	BENCIK Petr (Cze)		*Abandon*
132.	KEJVAL Lubomir (Cze)		*Abandon*
133.	PFANNBERGER Christian (Aut)	54th	+ 6'45"
134.	PRECECHTEL Michal (Cze)		*Abandon*
135.	TESAR Lubor (Cze)		*Abandon*
136.	TRKAL Frantisek (Cze)		*Abandon*
137.	VALACH Jan (Cze)		*Abandon*
138.	BRONIS Roman (Cze)		*Abandon*

AMORE e VITA - BERETTA

142.	KUCHYNSKI Aleksandr (Blr)		*Abandon*
144.	SOUTHAM Tom (Gbr)	56th	+ 6'45"
145.	CARLSTRÖM Kjell (Fin)	52nd	+ 6'41"
146.	GRÖNQVIST Thomas (Swe)		*Abandon*
147.	GRÖNQVIST Anders (Swe)		*Abandon*
148.	LJUNGBLAD Jonas (Swe)		*Abandon*

LANDBOUWKREDIET - COLNAGO

151.	SIJMENS Nico (Bel)	66th	+ 6'45"
152.	GRYSCHENKO Ruslan (Ukr)	16th	+ 1'23"
153.	DE WAELE Bert (Bel)	**1st**	**5h 09'07"**
154.	BRACKE Tony (Bel)		*Abandon*
155.	MONFORT Maxime (Bel)	65th	+ 6'45"
156.	MITLUSHENKO Yuriy (Ukr)		*Abandon*
157.	VAITKUS Tomas (Ltu)	15th	+ 1'23"

CARVALHELHOS - BOAVISTA

161.	MARQUE Alejandro (Esp)		*Abandon*
162.	VITAL André (Por)		*Abandon*
163.	VAZ José (Por)		*Abandon*
164.	RODRIGUES SILVA José (Por)	35th	+ 1'39"
165.	SOEIRO Pedro (Por)		*Abandon*
166.	SOUSA Celio (Por)	59th	+ 6'45"
167.	MOSQUERA Ezequiel (Esp)		*Abandon*
168.	PALOMARES Adrian (Esp)	67th	+ 6'57"

CLASSIFICATION

202 km

1.	**Bert de Waele (Bel)**	**LAN**	**5h 09'07"**
2.	**Didier Rous (Fra)**	**BLB**	**+ 5"**
3.	**Thor Hushovd (Nor)**	**C.A**	**s.t**
4.	Franck Schleck (Lux)	CSC	s.t
5.	Frédéric Guesdon (Fra)	FDJ	+ 6"
6.	Jurgen van de Walle (Bel)	CHO	+ 10"
7.	Vladimir Goussev (Rus)	CSC	+ 54"
8.	Pierrick Fedrigo (Fra)	C.A	s.t
9.	Jan Kuyckx (Bel)	VLA	s.t
10.	Franck Pencolé (Fra)	OKT	+ 1'08"

COUPE DE FRANCE RANKINGS AFTER 3 ROUNDS

1.	**Thor Hushovd (Nor)**	**C.A**	**75 pts**
2.	Dmitriy Fofonov (Kaz)	COF	35 pts
-	Didier Rous (Fra)	BLB	35 pts
4.	Sébastien Hinault (Fra)	C.A	25 pts
5.	Frédéric Bessy (Fra)	COF	20 pts
6.	Frédéric Guesdon (Fra)	FDJ	18 pts
7.	Hayden Roulston (Nzl)	COF	16 pts
8.	Jimmy Casper (Fra)	COF	14 pts
9.	Pierrick Fedrigo (Fra)	C.A	12 pts
-	Franck Renier (Fra)	BLB	12 pts

GESLIN IS A CLEVER CHAP

"I'd decided to base my race on that of Pierrick Fedrigo who I thought to be the fastest in our group. I was right"! Economising his energy in the final kilometers, Anthony Geslin, pro since 2002, manifestly had more left in him than his rivals in the final sprint of this 9th Route Adelie, run around the town of Vitré.

The judicial problems of Cedric Vasseur and Mederic Clain, coming to light a day before this 4th round of the Coupe de France fuelled the conversations of many at the start of the Route Adelie. But, once the flag dropped, attention switched to the race. Eddy Seigneur, captain of a more than discrete RAGT Semences team at the start of the season, is the first to show, in the company of Samuel Dumoulin (AG2R).Their escapade was to end at the 45th kilometre. But the race is now well and truly under way. Nicolas Fritsch (FDJ) accompanied by Denis Robin wearing the jersey of the French team, goes to the front. The duo is then joined by eleven other riders determined to make a race if it: the three Credit Agricole, Kashenchkin, Le Mevel and Halgand but also Agnolutto, Failliand Secchiari, Marzoli, Davidenko, Voeckler, Valentinand Fofonov. Trapped behind, the Barloworld and Mr Bookmaker teams take up the chase and keep the lead down to one and a half minutes. The two Kazakhs of the attacking group then put their cards on the table: Kashechkin and Fofonov find themselves in command but are unable to avoid the return of a counter attack in which we can see the names of Franck Pencolé, Anthony Geslin, Alessandro Bertolini, Sergio Marinangeli, Christophe Edaleine and Pierick Fedrigo, the latter only just managing to join them. After Fofonov, relegated down the field, it's the turn of his team mate Edaleine to suffer the same fate moments later. The now six leaders start their last lap of 8.3kms with a lead of 36 seconds and begin to think about victory. An attack by Pencolé six kilometers from the line knocks out Kashechkin but does not dislodge the leading group. That of Bertolini under the "Flamme Rouge" is fatal to ...Pencolé. Finally, it's Anthony Geslin who goes for the sprint, always difficult here due to an uphill slope for the final 200metres. Neither Marinangeli nor Fedrigo are able to claw back the few metres that separate them from the lead and the La Boulangere rider takes a second victory for his team this season, the first being taken by his friend Jerome Pineau in the Clasica de Almeria a few weeks earlier.. ■

120 Competitors

AG2R Prévoyance			
1.	BROCHARD Laurent (Fra)	15th	+ 1'08"
2.	AGNOLUTTO Christophe (Fra)	58th	+ 5'25"
3.	BERGÈS Stéphane (Fra)	65th	+ 8'06"
4.	DUMOULIN Samuel (Fra)	56th	+ 3'05"
5.	GOUBERT Stéphane (Fra)	51st	+ 2'56"
6.	KIRSIPUU Jaan (Est)	28th	+ 1'14"
7.	PORTAL Nicolas (Fra)	64th	+ 8'06"
8.	TURPIN Ludovic (Fra)	55th	+ 3'02"
NAVIGATORS			
11.	BALDWIN Chris (Usa)	48th	+ 2'56"
12.	McKENZIE David (Aus)		*Abandon*
13.	O'BEE Kirk (Usa)	34th	+ 1'14"
14.	POWER Ciaran (Irl)		*Abandon*
15.	RAPINSKI Viktor (Blr)		*Abandon*
16.	VOGELS Henk (Aus)		*Abandon*
17.	WALTERS Mark (Can)		*Abandon*
18.	ZAJICEK Phil (Usa)		*Abandon*
OKTOS			
21.	CALZATI Sylvain (Fra)	36th	+ 1'14"
22.	GABROVSKI Ivaïlo (Bul)		*Abandon*
23.	GUROV Maxim (Kaz)	40th	+ 2'56"
24.	LEVECOT Benjamin (Fra)		*Abandon*
25.	MIZOUROV Andrei (Kaz)	43rd	+ 2'56"
26.	PENCOLÉ Franck (Fra)	**5th**	+ 8"
27.	RUSKYS Saulius (Ltu)	66th	+ 8'06"
28.	TESSIER Jean-Michel (Fra)	41st	+ 2'56"
DOMINA VACANZE			
31.	DERGANC Martin (Slo)	23rd	+ 1'12"
32.	FAILLI Francesco (Ita)	57th	+ 4'39"
33.	FISCHER Murillo (Bra)		*Abandon*
34.	GENTILI Massimiliano (Ita)	20th	+ 1'12"
35.	MARINANGELI Sergio (Ita)	**2nd**	s.t
36.	SECCHIARI Francesco (Ita)		*Abandon*
37.	VALOTI Paolo (Ita)	29th	+ 1'14"
RAGT Semences - MG ROVER			
41.	AUGER Guillaume (Fra)	39th	+ 2'56"
42.	BERNARD Jérôme (Fra)		*Abandon*
43.	BOURQUENOUD Pierre (Sui)		*Abandon*
44.	LAURENT Christophe (Fra)		*Abandon*
45.	LE BOULANGER Yoann (Fra)	12nd	+ 1'08"
46.	MARTIN Ludovic (Fra)		*Abandon*
47.	RINERO Christophe (Fra)	22nd	+ 1'12"
48.	SEIGNEUR Eddy (Fra)		*Abandon*
BARLOWORLD - ANDRONI Giocattoli			
51.	ADAMSSON Stefan (Swe)		*Abandon*
52.	DEGANO Enrico (Ita)		*Abandon*
53.	GEORGE David (Rsa)		*Abandon*
54.	GREEN Rodney (Rsa)		*Abandon*
55.	KANNEMEYER Tiaan (Rsa)	35th	+ 1'14"
56.	MISSAGLIA Gabriele (Ita)	49th	+ 2'56"
57.	SALOMONE Antonio (Ita)	31st	+ 1'14"
58.	SERRI Eddy (Ita)		*Abandon*
AUBER 93			
61.	AUGER Ludovic (Fra)	16th	+ 1'08"
62.	BRÉARD David (Fra)	45th	+ 2'56"
63.	VALENTIN Tristan (Fra)		*Abandon*
64.	LAMOULLER Loïc (Fra)	46th	+ 2'56"
65.	NILSSON John (Swe)	42nd	+ 2'56"
66.	OLIVIER Lénaïc (Fra)	11st	+ 1'08"
67.	PAUMIER Laurent (Fra)	26th	+ 1'12"
68.	TALABARDON Yannick (Fra)	18th	+ 1'08"
ACQUA & SAPONE - Caffe MOKAMBO			
71.	ASTOLFI Claudio (Ita)		*Abandon*
72.	FERRIGATO Andrea (Ita)	54th	+ 2'56"
73.	HAMBURGER Bo (Den)		*Abandon*
74.	MARZOLI Ruggero (Ita)		*Abandon*
75.	PALUMBO Giuseppe (Ita)		*Abandon*
76.	POSPEEV Kyrylo (Ukr)	37th	+ 1'27"
77.	RODRIGUEZ Fred (Usa)		*Abandon*
78.	TRAMPUSCH Gerhard (Aut)		*Abandon*
COFIDIS			
81.	BESSY Frédéric (Fra)	24th	+ 1'12"
83.	FOFONOV Dmitriy (Kaz)		*Abandon*
84.	EDALEINE Christophe (Fra)	44th	+ 2'56"
85.	MONCOUTIÉ David (Fra)	32nd	+ 1'14"
86.	MONIER Damien (Fra)		*Abandon*
Mr BOOKMAKER - PALMANS			
91.	DAY Ben (Aus)		*Abandon*
92.	GABRIEL Frédéric (Fra)	47th	+ 2'56"
93.	KOEHLER Philippe (Fra)		*Abandon*
94.	LEMBO Eddy (Fra)		*Abandon*
95.	LEUKEMANS Björn (Bel)	**9th**	+ 1'06"
96.	RENDERS Jens (Bel)		*Abandon*
97.	VAN DE WOUWER Kurt (Bel)	**6th**	+ 18"
98.	VANDERAERDEN Gert (Bel)		*Abandon*
FDJEUX.COM			
101.	BICHOT Freddy (Fra)	63rd	+ 6'55"
102.	CASAR Sandy (Fra)	**10th**	+ 1'08"
103.	FRITSCH Nicolas (Fra)		*Abandon*
104.	LÖVKVIST Thomas (Swe)	25th	+ 1'12"
105.	ROBIN Jean-Cyril (Fra)	14th	+ 1'08"
107.	VAUGRENARD Benoît (Fra)		*Abandon*
108.	VOGONDY Nicolas (Fra)	52nd	+ 2'56"
ALESSIO - BIANCHI			
111.	BERTOLINI Alessandro (Ita)	**4th**	s.t
112.	FURLAN Angelo (Ita)		*Abandon*
113.	MØLLER Claus Michael (Den)	33rd	+ 1'14"
114.	NOE' Andrea (Ita)	17th	+ 1'08"
115.	RASTELLI Ellis (Ita)		*Abandon*
116.	PELLIZOTTI Franco (Ita)		*Abandon*
CRÉDIT AGRICOLE			
121.	BOTCHAROV Alexandre (Rus)	30th	+ 1'14"
122.	FEDRIGO Pierrick (Fra)	**3rd**	s.t
123.	HALGAND Patrice (Fra)		*Abandon*
124.	KASHECHKIN Andrey (Kaz)	**7th**	+ 24"
125.	LE MEVEL Christophe (Fra)		*Abandon*
126.	MOREAU Christophe (Fra)		*Abandon*
127.	POILVET Benoît (Fra)	21st	+ 1'12"
128.	SALMON Benoît (Fra)	59th	+ 5'25"
Chocolade JACQUES - WINCOR NIXDORF			
131.	ABAKOUMOV Igor (Bel)	**8th**	+ 1'06"
132.	BLANCHY Michael (Bel)		*Abandon*
133.	CAPPELLE Andy (Bel)		*Abandon*
134.	GADRET John (Fra)	50th	+ 2'56"
135.	PLANCKAERT Francesco (Bel)		*Abandon*
136.	RONDELEZ Björn (Bel)		*Abandon*
137.	STEVENS Christophe (Bel)		*Abandon*
Brioches LA BOULANGÈRE			
141.	BENETEAU Walter (Fra)	38th	+ 1'35"
142.	BOUYER Franck (Fra)	13rd	+ 1'08"
143.	GESLIN Anthony (Fra)	**1st**	**4h 21'25"**
144.	HARY Maryan (Fra)	53rd	+ 2'56"
145.	MARTIAS Rony (Fra)		*Abandon*
146.	RENIER Franck (Fra)		*Abandon*
147.	ROUS Didier (Fra)	27th	+ 1'12"
148.	VOECKLER Thomas (Fra)		*Abandon*
Equipe de FRANCE			
151.	BOUQUET Camille (Fra)		*Abandon*
152.	COUTOULY Cédric (Fra)	19th	+ 1'12"
153.	DUPONT Hubert (Fra)	60th	+ 6'55"
154.	DURET Sébastien (Fra)	62nd	+ 6'55"
155.	GÈNE Yohann (Fra)		*Abandon*
156.	MANGEL Laurent (Fra)		*Abandon*
157.	ROBIN Denis (Fra)		*Abandon*
158.	STAELEN Marc (Fra)		*Abandon*

CLASSIFICATION

185,3 km

1.	**Anthony Geslin (Fra)**	**BLB**	**4h21'25"**
2.	**Sergio Marinangeli (Ita)**	**DVE**	**s.t**
3.	**Pierrick Fedrigo (Fra)**	**C.A**	**s.t**
4.	Alessandro Bertolini (Ita)	ALB	s.t
5.	Franck Pencolé (Fra)	OKT	+ 8"

THE INEVITABLE SPRINT!

For a long time run in the town centre, for the past three years the Grand Prix de Rennes takes in the surrounding terrain and includes several difficulties in its new form. Invariably the race finishes in a mass sprint...

If the final form of the race is not in doubt, this does nothing to change the tactics of those who wish to have a go. This time around they go by the name of, Christophe Le Mevel (Credit Agricole) and Nicolas Inaudi (AG2R) who take advantage of a slow start to race off in front. At mid race, at the summit of the Cote de Talensac, they are almost thirteen minutes ahead of the pack. Turning back towards Rennes, things start to get harder and the lead slips to two minutes as the two enter the final lap. The teams of the sprinters go hell for leather in the persuit of Le Mevel and Inaudi. The two runaways finish one lap then another, but are caught on their third, at 15 kilometers from the line after a breakaway of 150kilometres.

Thomas Voeckler (La Boulangere) tries to avoid a mass sprint by pulling a few metres ahead of the pack, but they will have the last word. Once again it's a mass sprint that finishes the race. Sergio Marinangeli launches his team mate from the Domina Vacanze – the team of Mario Cipollini needs lessons from no one in this sort of situation- Andrus Aug towards the victory. At 31, the Estonian rider takes his first win on the French scene following wins in such divers places as Morrocco, Finland and Poland.

If this victory surprised the casual observer, what would they have thought if the fourth placed Japanese rider Takehiro Mizutani had taken the win? It's true that many 3rd division teams field riders of talent such as Mizutani, who for the past few years rides for the French Besson Caussures team. ■

110 Competitors

NAVIGATORS

1.	O'BEE Kirk (Usa)	**3rd**	s.t
2.	BALDWIN Chris (Usa)	61st	+ 56"
3.	DAVIDENKO Vassili (Rus)	43rd	+ 16"
4.	McKENZIE David (Aus)		*Abandon*
5.	POWER Ciaran (Irl)	73rd	+ 2'38"
6.	LOUDER Jeff (Usa)	26th	s.t
7.	VOGELS Henk (Aus)	58th	+ 35"
8.	WALTERS Mark (Can)	59th	+ 48"

AG2R Prévoyance

11.	AGNOLUTTO Christophe (Fra)	28th	s.t
12.	GOUBERT Stéphane (Fra)	76th	+ 4'36"
13.	DUMOULIN Samuel (Fra)	19th	s.t
14.	INAUDI Nicolas (Fra)	69th	+ 1'51"
15.	LAIDOUN Julien (Fra)		*Abandon*
17.	PORTAL Nicolas (Fra)		*Abandon*
18.	TURPIN Ludovic (Fra)		*Abandon*

Brioches LA BOULANGÈRE

31.	BOUYER Franck (Fra)	42nd	+ 16"
32.	CHAVANEL Sébastien (Fra)	33rd	s.t
33.	GESLIN Anthony (Fra)	**9th**	s.t
34.	BENETEAU Walter (Fra)	38th	s.t
35.	MARTIAS Rony (Fra)	32nd	s.t
36.	NAULLEAU Alexandre (Fra)	25th	s.t
37.	PICHON Mickaël (Fra)	22nd	s.t
38.	VOECKLER Thomas (Fra)	63rd	+ 1'11"

Mr BOOKMAKER - PALMANS

41.	DAY Ben (Aus)	75th	+ 4'36"
42.	GABRIEL Frédéric (Fra)	78th	+ 4'36"
43.	KOEHLER Philippe (Fra)		*Abandon*
44.	LEMBO Eddy (Fra)	74th	+ 2'53"
45.	LEÜKEMANS Björn (Bel)	12nd	s.t
46.	RENDERS Jens (Bel)	53rd	+ 35"
47.	VAN DE WOUWER Kurt (Bel)	52nd	+ 35"
48.	VANDERAERDEN Gert (Bel)	13rd	s.t

COFIDIS

52.	COYOT Arnaud (Fra)		*Abandon*
53.	EDALEINE Christophe (Fra)	17th	s.t
54.	MONCOUTIÉ David (Fra)	87th	+ 4'36"
55.	MONIER Damien (Fra)		*Abandon*
56.	ROULSTON Hayden (Nzl)		*Abandon*

ALESSIO - BIANCHI

61.	BERTOLINI Alessandro (Ita)	**10th**	s.t
62.	JØRGENSEN René (Den)		*Abandon*
63.	FURLAN Angelo (Ita)		*Abandon*
65.	NOE' Andrea (Ita)	47th	+ 31"
66.	MØLLER Claus Michael (Den)	40th	+ 8"

CRÉDIT AGRICOLE

71.	FEDRIGO Pierrick (Fra)		*Abandon*
72.	KASHECHKIN Andrey (Kaz)	82nd	+ 4'36"
73.	MURAVYEV Dmitriy (Kaz)	80th	+ 4'36"
74.	LE MEVEL Christophe (Fra)		*Abandon*
75.	LEBLACHER Eric (Fra)	24th	s.t
76.	LEQUATRE Geoffroy (Fra)	15th	s.t
77.	MOREAU Christophe (Fra)	79th	+ 4'36"
78.	POILVET Benoît (Fra)	44th	+ 27"

ACQUA & SAPONE - Caffe MOKAMBO

81.	BERTOLINI Denis (Ita)	64th	+ 1'38"
82.	FERRIGATO Andrea (Ita)		*Abandon*
83.	NOCENTINI Rinaldo (Ita)	67th	+ 1'38"
84.	MARZOLI Ruggero (Ita)		*Abandon*
85.	D'AMORE Crescenzo (Ita)	**5th**	s.t
86.	POSPEEV Kyrylo (Ukr)	68th	+ 1'38"
87.	RODRIGUEZ Fred (Usa)	14th	s.t

FDJEUX.COM

91.	CASAR Sandy (Fra)	20th	s.t
92.	DEREPAS David (Fra)	71st	+ 2'00"
93.	BICHOT Freddy (Fra)	**8th**	s.t
94.	ROY Jérémy (Fra)	88th	+ 4'36"
95.	RENSHAW Mark (Aus)		*Abandon*
96.	ROBIN Jean-Cyril (Fra)	60th	+ 53"
97.	VAUGRENARD Benoît (Fra)	89th	+ 4'36"
98.	VOGONDY Nicolas (Fra)	55th	+ 35"

DOMINA VACANZE

101.	AUG Andrus (Est)	**1st**	**4h 50'31"**
102.	DERGANC Martin (Slo)	31st	s.t
103.	FAILLI Francesco (Ita)	66th	+ 1'38"
104.	FISCHER Murillo (Bra)	65th	+ 1'38"
105.	GENTILI Massimiliano (Ita)	56th	+ 35"
106.	MARINANGELI Sergio (Ita)	**7th**	s.t
107.	SECCHIARI Francesco (Ita)	62nd	+ 1'04"
108.	VALOTI Paolo (Ita)	37th	s.t

RAGT Semences - MG ROVER

111.	BERTHOU Eric (Fra)	27th	s.t
112.	BOUVARD Gilles (Fra)	50th	+ 35"
113.	FINOT Frédéric (Fra)	86th	+ 4'36"
114.	DION Renaud (Fra)	72nd	+ 2'21"
115.	LE BOULANGER Yoann (Fra)	30th	s.t
116.	LUHOVYY Roman (Ukr)	**6th**	s.t
117.	RINERO Christophe (Fra)	48th	+ 35"
118.	THIBOUT Bruno (Fra)	54th	+ 35"

BARLOWORLD - ANDRONI Giocattoli

121.	ADAMSSON Stefan (Swe)	23rd	s.t
122.	DEGANO Enrico (Ita)	39th	s.t
123.	GEORGE David (Rsa)	81st	+ 4'36"
124.	LILL Darren (Rsa)		*Abandon*
125.	KANNEMEYER Tiaan (Rsa)	46th	+ 27"
126.	MISSAGLIA Gabriele (Ita)	41st	+ 8"
127.	SALOMONE Antonio (Ita)	70th	+ 1'51"
128.	SERRI Eddy (Ita)	57th	+ 35"

AUBER 93

131.	AUGER Ludovic (Fra)	11st	s.t
132.	VALENTIN Tristan (Fra)	34th	s.t
133.	BROUZES Niels (Fra)		*Abandon*
134.	LAMOULLER Loïc (Fra)		*Abandon*
135.	NILSSON John (Swe)	45th	+ 27"
136.	OLIVIER Lénaïc (Fra)	18th	s.t
137.	PAUMIER Laurent (Fra)		*Abandon*
138.	TALABARDON Yannick (Fra)	29th	s.t

BRIDGESTONE - ANCHOR

141.	FUKUSHIMA Koji (Jpn)	83rd	+ 4'36"
143.	INOUE Kazuo (Jpn)	77th	+ 4'36"
144.	MIYAZAKI Keisuke (Jpn)		*Abandon*
145.	MIZUTANI Takehiro (Jpn)	**4th**	s.t
146.	KANO Tomoya (Jpn)		*Abandon*
147.	SHIBUYA Junichi (Jpn)	90th	+ 4'36"
148.	TASHIRO Yasutaka (Jpn)	51st	+ 35"

OKTOS

151.	CALZATI Sylvain (Fra)	84th	+ 4'36"
152.	LEVECOT Benjamin (Fra)	49th	+ 35"
153.	GUROV Maxim (Kaz)	21st	s.t
155.	MIZOUROV Andrei (Kaz)	36th	s.t
156.	PENCOLÉ Franck (Fra)	35th	s.t
157.	RUSKYS Saulius (Ltu)	**2nd**	s.t
158.	TESSIER Jean-Michel (Fra)	16th	s.t

CLASSIFICATION

185,3 km

1.	**Andrus Aug (Est)**	**DVE**	**4h50'31"**
2.	**Saulius Ruskys (Ltu)**	**OKT**	**s.t**
3.	**Kirk O'Bee (Usa)**	**NIC**	**s.t**
4.	Takehiro Mizutani (Jpn)	BGT	s.t
5.	Crescenzo D'Amore (Ita)	A&S	s.t
6.	Roman Luhovyy (Ukr)	RAG	s.t
7.	Sergio Marinangeli (Ita)	DVE	s.t
8.	Freddy Bichot (Fra)	FDJ	s.t
9.	Anthony Geslin (Fra)	BLB	s.t
10.	Alessandro Bertolini (Ita)	ALB	s.t

COUPE DE FRANCE RANKINGS AFTER 5 ROUNDS

1.	**Thor Hushovd (Nor)**	**C.A**	**75 pts**
2.	Anthony Geslin (Fra)	BLB	50 pts
3.	Pierrick Fedrigo (Fra)	C.A	37 pts
4.	Dmitriy Fofonov (Kaz)	COF	35 pts
-	Didier Rous (Fra)	BLB	16 pts

Bouyer plays his trump card

After an attack of more than 60 kilometers, Franck Bouyer found in the finale of the difficult Normandy round, the resources to accompany the young and talented Swede Thomas Lovkvist and in the end to beat him in the sprint. These two riders took the first two places (but in reverse order) on the circuit of the Sarthe just days before...

This 65th Paris – Camembert starts with protests and negotiations. At the centre of it all, the Normandy based rider Franck Pencolé, who, through the past weeks has confirmed his reputation as being difficult to deal with. Not admitted to take part in this round of the Coupe de France (which takes place on his home ground) the leader of the Oktos team infiltrates the peloton wearing a false number which he fabricated himself. At the start the race organisers refuse to let the race start until Pencolé quits the peloton. This he does after a certain time but not before trying to get the other riders involved in the dispute ...

Half an hour late, the riders start the race under a sky which has become cloudy following a start to the day in bright sunshine. The inevitable attacks come soon after but none are to be of any consequence. At kilometre 20 though, thirteen men manage to get away and set up a lead of almost a minute. Looking at the names involved in this group one could think the race was settled. There are 4 Boulangeres, (Charteau, Sy, Chavanel, Geslinand Lefevre), 2 AG2R (Agnolutto, and Caurreau), two Fdjeux.com (Fritsch and Lovkvist), as well as Coenen(Mr Bookmaker.com), L Auger (Auber93), Poilvet (Credit Agricole) , Finot (RAGT) and Nauduzs (Domina Vacanze).

Just as well for the race, the following riders don't give up. The teams, Oktos, Ed'System and also AG2R (who apparently don't rate the chances of Agnolutto and Chaurreau) set up the chase which ends in success thirty kilometers later. When the peloton begins to break up, nine men break away. Christophe moreau and sylvain Chavanel find themselves at the front, accompanied by Dumoulin, one of the locals, Breard, Kashechkin, Klimov, Gilbert, Ruskys and Charteau. Without being able to pull away from the pack the attack is aborted soon after the mid way point.

A DAZZLING FRANCK BOUYER

The end of the race with its hills (Canapville, Roiville, Moulin Neuf and Champeaux) will once again sort things out. The peloton, already worn by the attacks at the beginning of the race, shrinks again as the rain starts to fall. The Lettonian champion, Andris Nauduzs pulls away from the peloton only to be caught by a trio of strong men on the first ascencion of Canapville. The three men: Franck Bouyer, his team mate Jerome Pineau and Sandy Casar. There are 70 kilometers left to race and the three Frenchmen (Nauduzs couldn't keep up!) stay a minute ahead for many a kilometre. We must wait for the final climb of the day, the Mur de Champeau (less than 7 kilometers from the line), before last year's winner Laurent Brochard brings a group of about ten riders up to the leading group. Caught at the summit, Franck Bouyer takes stock and pushes once again. This time alone. Just the same, he is unable to resist the comeback of the Impressive Swede Thomas Lovkvist, at twenty years old, the winner of the Circuit de Sarthe, on which he had dethroned... Franck Bouyer on the last day! The long distance duel becomes close combat, but before fighting it out for the win, the two men must work together to keep their rivals in the pack at bay. This done, the two men enter the final kilometre feeling sure of their situation.

The experience and the power of Franck Bouyer (Lovkvist is ten years younger) show their value in the final sprint. The rider from Cholet takes his revenge little by little becomes a specialist in the Coupe de France (he has already triumphed on the Trophée des Grimpeurs and the Tour de Vendée in recent years). A competition that obviously suits him! ■

The winner is always honoured in Vimoutiers, the finish of the Paris - Camembert.

84 Competitors

AG2R Prévoyance

1.	BROCHARD Laurent (Fra)	**7th**	+ 20"
2.	AGNOLUTTO Christophe (Fra)	20th	+ 1'11"
3.	CHAURREAU Iñigo (Esp)	34th	+ 7'20"
4.	DUMOULIN Samuel (Fra)		*Abandon*
5.	GOUBERT Stéphane (Fra)	27th	+ 2'41"
6.	LAIDOUN Julien (Fra)		*Abandon*
7.	KRIVTSOV Yuriy (Ukr)	32nd	+ 4'56"
8.	TURPIN Ludovic (Fra)		*Abandon*

Mr BOOKMAKER - PALMANS

11.	COENEN Johan (Bel)	**3rd**	+ 20"
13.	GABRIEL Frédéric (Fra)	37th	+ 7'21"
14.	KOEHLER Philippe (Fra)		*Abandon*
15.	LEMBO Eddy (Fra)	22nd	+ 1'14"
17.	TROUVÉ Kristof (Bel)		*Abandon*
18.	VANDERAERDEN Gert (Bel)		*Abandon*

AUBER 93

21.	AUGER Ludovic (Fra)	23rd	+ 1'14"
22.	BRÉARD David (Fra)	38th	+ 7'21"
23.	BROUZES Niels (Fra)		*Abandon*
24.	NILSSON John (Swe)		*Abandon*
25.	OLIVIER Lénaïc (Fra)	25th	+ 2'41"
26.	PAUMIER Laurent (Fra)		*Abandon*
27.	TALABARDON Yannick (Fra)		*Abandon*
28.	VALENTIN Tristan (Fra)	28th	+ 2'41"

ELK Haus - SIMPLON

31.	BRADLEY Andrew (Aut)		*Abandon*
33.	HÖLLER Mario (Aut)		*Abandon*
34.	MURER Wolfgang (Aut)		*Abandon*
36.	SCHERZER Ralph (Aut)		*Abandon*
37.	SUMMER Jochen (Aut)		*Abandon*
38.	TOTSCHNIG Harald (Aut)		*Abandon*

CRÉDIT AGRICOLE

41.	BOTCHAROV Alexandre (Rus)	21st	+ 1'11"
42.	FEDRIGO Pierrick (Fra)	**9th**	+ 1'11"
43.	HALGAND Patrice (Fra)	17th	+ 1'11"
44.	KASHECHKIN Andrey (Kaz)	**6th**	+ 20"
45.	LE MEVEL Christophe (Fra)	36th	+ 7'21"
46.	MOREAU Christophe (Fra)		*Abandon*
47.	POILVET Benoît (Fra)	35th	+ 7'21"
48.	SALMON Benoît (Fra)		*Abandon*

RAGT Semences - MG ROVER

51.	BERNARD Jérôme (Fra)		*Abandon*
52.	BOURQUENOUD Pierre (Sui)	30th	+ 2'41"
53.	BOUVARD Gilles (Fra)	13rd	+ 1'11"
54.	FINOT Frédéric (Fra)	**10th**	+ 1'11"
55.	MARTIN Ludovic (Fra)		*Abandon*
56.	BERTHOU Eric (Fra)	31st	+ 2'45"
57.	LE BOULANGER Yoann (Fra)		*Abandon*
58.	REYNAUD Nicolas (Fra)		*Abandon*

LOKOMOTIV

61.	KULAKOV Serguei (Rus)		*Abandon*
62.	KLIMOV Serguei (Rus)		*Abandon*
63.	BRUTT Pavel (Rus)		*Abandon*
64.	MINDLIN Anton (Rus)		*Abandon*
65.	ESKOV Nikita (Rus)		*Abandon*
66.	TROUSSOV Nikolai (Rus)		*Abandon*
67.	POSTERNAK Alexandr (Rus)		*Abandon*
68.	AVERIN Maxim (Rus)		*Abandon*

FDJEUX.COM

71.	CASAR Sandy (Fra)	**4th**	+ 20"
72.	FRITSCH Nicolas (Fra)	18th	+ 1'11"
73.	GILBERT Philippe (Bel)	14th	+ 1'11"
74.	BICHOT Freddy (Fra)		*Abandon*
75.	ROBIN Jean-Cyril (Fra)	11st	+ 1'11"
76.	ROY Jérémy (Fra)	26th	+ 2'41"
77.	LÖVKVIST Thomas (Swe)	**2nd**	+ 1"
78.	VOGONDY Nicolas (Fra)	33rd	+ 4'56"

DOMINA VACANZE

81.	BAZHENOV Alexandre (Rus)	**8th**	+ 28"
82.	FISCHER Murilo (Bra)		*Abandon*
83.	CLINGER David (Usa)		*Abandon*
84.	DERGANC Martin (Slo)	15th	+ 1'11"
85.	FAILLI Francesco (Ita)	19th	+ 1'11"
86.	NAUDUZS Andris (Lat)		*Abandon*

ED'SYSTEM - ZVVZ

91.	KUPKA David (Cze)		Abandon
92.	PFANNBERGER Christian (Aut)		Abandon
94.	ZERZAN Pavel (Cze)		Abandon
95.	TESAR Lubor (Cze)	29th	+ 2'41"
98.	VALACH Jan (Svk)		Abandon

OKTOS - St QUENTIN

101.	CALZATI Sylvain (Fra)		*Abandon*
103.	GUROV Maxim (Kaz)		*Abandon*
104.	LEVECOT Benjamin (Fra)		*Abandon*
105.	MIZOUROV Andrey (Kaz)		*Abandon*
107.	RUSKYS Saulius (Ltu)		*Abandon*

Brioches LA BOULANGÈRE

111.	BENETEAU Walter (Fra)	16th	+ 1'11"
112.	BOUYER Franck (Fra)	**1st**	**4h 29'19"**
113.	CHARTEAU Anthony (Fra)	12nd	+ 1'11"
114.	CHAVANEL Sylvain (Fra)	**5th**	+ 20"
115.	LEFÈVRE Laurent (Fra)		Abandon
116.	GESLIN Anthony (Fra)		Abandon
117.	PINEAU Jérôme (Fra)	24th	+ 1'20"
118.	HARY Maryan (Fra)		Abandon

CLASSIFICATION

200 km

1.	**Franck Bouyer (Fra)**	**BLB**	**4h 29'19"**
2.	Thomas Lövkvist (Swe)	FDJ	+ 1"
3.	Johan Coenen (Bel)	MRB	+ 20"
4.	Sandy Casar (Fra)	FDJ	s.t
5.	Sylvain Chavanel (Fra)	BLB	s.t
6.	Andrey Kashechkin (Kaz)	C.A	s.t
7.	Laurent Brochard (Fra)	A2R	s.t
8.	Alexandr Bazhenov (Rus)	DVE	+ 28"
9.	Pierrick Fedrigo (Fra)	C.A	+ 1'11"
10.	Frédéric Finot (Fra)	RAG	s.t

COUPE DE FRANCE RANKINGS AFTER 6 ROUNDS

1.	**Thor Hushovd (Nor)**	**C.A**	**75 pts**
2.	Anthony Geslin (Fra)	BLB	60 pts
3.	Franck Bouyer (Fra)	BLB	59 pts
4.	Pierrick Fedrigo (Fra)	C.A	47 pts
5.	Andrey Kashechkin (Kaz)	C.A	36 pts
6.	Dmitriy Fofonov (Kaz)	COF	35 pts
-	Thomas Lövkvist (Swe)	FDJ	35 pts
-	Didier Rous (Fra)	BLB	35 pts
-	Saulius Ruskys (Ltu)	OKT	35 pts
10.	Sandy Casar (Fra)	FDJ	31 pts

HUSHOVD CAPITALISES

To the contrary of what this photo may suggest, Thor Hushovd didn't finish the race through the streets of Denain on his own, but his superiority over the Irish champion Mark Scanlon was so great that the sprint was a mere formality.

Beating the young Irishman Mark Scanlon in the sprint, Thor Hushovd consolidates his position of leader in the Coupe de France. A position he occupies since his success in the Classic Haribo at the end of February. The GP de Denain was only the third round of the Coupe de France the Scandinavian rider took part in, and he could already envisage being honoured...in six months with his two successes and a third place!

If two months earlier the Paris – Camembert could only muster 85 participants, the start of the 45th GP de Denain is another story. In effect, no less than 21 teams presented themselves at the Place de l'Hotel de Ville in Raismes from where this event has started for the last few years. True, therewere eight 3rd division teams in the number but "the more the merrier" as they say...

The impressive peloton, despite its number soon explodes. After a few kilometers of the race, a good twenty riders are already forcing ahead. If the leader of the Coupe de France is in this group, the same cannot be said of his second place man, Anthony Geslin, who was surprised by the speed of the attack so soon after the start. The Oktos team, at the centre of all the conversations two days before, was not caught out, because Franck Pencolé, Benjamin Levecot and Jean Michel Tessier are up front, along with JP Nazon (AG2R), B McGee and F. Sanchez (Fdjeux.com), the rapid Mitlushenko (Landbouwkrediet) and the neo pro Alexandre Naulleau (La Boulangere) the only representative of his team. The 50th kilometre is not reached before the shape of the race once again changes. The leading group loses several members and some ground to a chasing group of 25 riders escaped from the peloton. This chasing group, including Jaan Kirsipuu and Mark Scanlon catch the leaders before reaching the traditional circuit of 13.8kms around Denain to be completed nine times.

THE PELOTON ABDICATES...

The race now takes another turn, in the peloton , the Brioches La Boulangere team eases up. The attackers increase their lead. The peloton (thinned out) will later finish outside the time limit at more than 17 minutes. Meanwhile, up front, the kilometers of effort are beginning to take their toll. Only the toughest will survive. Twelve men are in this category in the last laps: Ludovic Auger (Auber 93), Borut Bozic (Perutnina Ptuj), Thor Hushovd and Dmitry Muravyev (Credit Agricole), Bradley McGee(Fdjeux.com), Franck Pencolé and Jean Michel Tessier (Oktos –MBK), Mark Scanlon (AG2R), Nico Sijmens (Landbouwkrediet), Erwin Thijs (Mr Bookmaker), Eelke van der Wal (Bankgiroloterij) and Jurgen van de Walle (Chocolat Jaques). Judged as the fastest rider in this sort of situation Thor Hushovd had learnt his lesson in the Cholet – Pays de Loire, where faced with a similar configuration he was attacked from all sides and finally came in only third. The ex World Champion Espoirs surprises everyone and particularly his companions in the leading group by attacking at the start of the final lap. Only the Irish champion Mark Scanlon can follow the Norwegian, whereas Bradley McGee, victim of a cramp, loses ground. Together, the two men go to a lead of 46 seconds over their erstwhile companions. In Denain, the time comes to fight it out. Scanlon leaves Hushovd to launch the sprint but is unable to follow. The leader of the Coupe de France takes the win with no trouble and seems also to take a decisive step towards the overall victory. True there are still ten rounds to go, but what's done is done...■

155 Competitors

Mr BOOKMAKER - PALMANS

1.	COENEN Johan (Bel)		*Abandon*
2.	GABRIEL Frédéric (Fra)	74th	+ 17'24"
3.	HUNT Jeremy (Gbr)		*Abandon*
4.	LEMBO Eddy (Fra)		*Abandon*
5.	THIJS Erwin (Bel)	**6th**	+ 46"
6.	TROUVÉ Kristof (Bel)	82nd	+ 17'29"
8.	VANDERAERDEN Gert (Bel)		*Abandon*

Chocolade JACQUES - WINCOR NIXDORF

21.	BLANCHY Michael (Bel)	29th	+ 17'12"
22.	GADRET John (Fra)		*Abandon*
23.	ABAKOUMOV Igor (Bel)		*Abandon*
24.	PLANCKAERT Francesco (Bel)	25th	+ 17'12"
25.	VAN DE WALLE Jurgen (Bel)	**9th**	+ 59"
26.	CAPPELLE Andy (Bel)		*Abandon*
27.	VERHEYEN Geert (Bel)	16th	+ 5'56"
28.	RUDENKO Maxim (Ukr)		*Abandon*

FDJEUX.COM

31.	BICHOT Freddy (Fra)		*Abandon*
32.	DEREPAS David (Fra)	39th	+ 17'12"
33.	EISEL Bernhard (Aut)		*Abandon*
34.	McGEE Bradley (Aus)	12nd	+ 4'08"
35.	SANCHEZ Fabien (Fra)	51st	+ 17'12"
36.	RENSHAW Mark (Aus)	53rd	+ 17'12"
37.	ROY Jérémy (Fra)		*Abandon*
38.	VOGONDY Nicolas (Fra)	79th	+ 17'29"

AG2R Prévoyance

41.	AGNOLUTTO Christophe (Fra)	19th	+ 5'56"
42.	BERGÈS Stéphane (Fra)		*Abandon*
43.	FLICKINGER Andy (Fra)		*Abandon*
44.	INAUDI Nicolas (Fra)		*Abandon*
45.	KIRSIPUU Jaan (Est)		*Abandon*
46.	NAZON Jean-Patrick (Fra)	61st	+ 17'20"
47.	PÜTSEP Erki (Est)		*Abandon*
48.	SCANLON Mark (Irl)	**2nd**	s.t

LANDBOUWKREDIET - COLNAGO

51.	CAPELLE Ludovic (Bel)	91st	+ 17'29"
52.	SIJMENS Nico (Bel)	**3rd**	+ 46"
53.	TIMOCHINE Mikhail (Rus)		*Abandon*
54.	DURAND Jacky (Fra)	89th	+ 17'29"
55.	MITLUSHENKO Yuriy (Ukr)	92nd	+ 17'29"
56.	MONFORT Maxime (Bel)	21st	+ 5'56"
57.	STREEL Marc (Bel)		*Abandon*
58.	VAN BONDT Geert (Bel)		*Abandon*

CRÉDIT AGRICOLE

61.	DEAN Julian (Nzl)	93rd	+ 17'29"
62.	AUGÉ Stéphane (Fra)	87th	+ 17'29"
63.	HINAULT Sébastien (Fra)	83rd	+ 17'29"
64.	HUSHOVD Thor (Nor)	**1st**	**4h 29'33"**
65.	JÉGOU Lilian (Fra)	66th	+ 17'24"
66.	LEBLACHER Eric (Fra)	43rd	+ 17'12"
67.	LEQUATRE Geoffroy (Fra)	15th	+ 5'56"
68.	MURAVYEV Dmitriy (Kaz)	11st	+ 1'48"

Brioches LA BOULANGÈRE

71.	LEFÈVRE Laurent (Fra)	38th	+ 17'12"
72.	CHAVANEL Sébastien (Fra)		*Abandon*
73.	GESLIN Anthony (Fra)	88th	+ 17'29"
74.	RENIER Franck (Fra)	57th	+ 17'12"
75.	MARTIAS Rony (Fra)		*Abandon*
76.	NAULLEAU Alexandre (Fra)	90th	+ 17'29"
77.	YUS Unai (Esp)	13rd	+ 5'36"
78.	VOECKLER Thomas (Fra)		*Abandon*

BANKGIROLOTERIJ

81.	ANDRESEN Allan Bo (Den)	30th	+ 17'12"
82.	BAK Lars Ytting (Den)		*Abandon*
83.	BOS Marco (Ned)		*Abandon*
84.	ENGELS Addy (Ned)		*Abandon*
85.	SMINK Julien (Ned)		*Abandon*
86.	TEN DAM Laurens (Ned)		*Abandon*
87.	VAN DER WAL Eelke (Ned)	**8th**	+ 46"
88.	VAN DULMEN Frank (Ned)	36th	+ 17'12"

RAGT Semences - MG ROVER

91.	BUFFAZ Mickaël (Fra)	46th	+ 17'12"
92.	DION Renaud (Fra)	50th	+ 17'12"
93.	LUHOVYY Roman (Ukr)		*Abandon*
94.	FINOT Frédéric (Fra)	14th	+ 5'36"
95.	LAURENT Christophe (Fra)	40th	+ 17'12"
96.	MUTSCHLER Klaus (Ger)		*Abandon*
97.	REYNAUD Nicolas (Fra)	18th	+ 5'56"
98.	THIBOUT Bruno (Fra)		*Abandon*

LOKOMOTIV

101.	AVERIN Maxim (Rus)	44th	+ 17'12"
102.	BRUTT Pavel (Rus)	52nd	+ 17'12"
103.	MINDLIN Anton (Rus)		*Abandon*
104.	IGNATIEV Mikhail (Rus)		*Abandon*
105.	KLIMOV Serguei (Rus)	42nd	+ 17'12"
106.	POSTERNAK Alexander (Rus)		*Abandon*
107.	SEROV Alexander (Rus)		*Abandon*
108.	TROUSSOV Nikolaï (Rus)		*Abandon*

WIESENHOF

111.	GRABSCH Ralf (Ger)		*Abandon*
112.	HEPPNER Jens (Ger)	22nd	+ 5'56"
113.	KNEES Christian (Ger)	73rd	+ 17'24"
114.	POITSCHKE Enrico (Ger)		*Abandon*
115.	MEINKE Daniel (Ger)	78th	+ 17'28"
116.	PODLESCH Carsten (Ger)	86th	+ 17'29"

ED'SYSTEM - ZVVZ

121.	PRECECHTEL Michal (Cze)		*Abandon*
123.	KEJVAL Lubomir (Cze)	84th	+ 17'29"
124	KUPKA David (Cze)		*Abandon*
126.	TRKAL Frantisek (Cze)		*Abandon*
127.	VRANA Jindrich (Cze)		*Abandon*
128.	ZERZAN Pavel (Cze)		*Abandon*

ACTION - ATI

131.	BONDARIEV Bogdan (Ukr)	76th	+ 17'24"
132.	PAWLYTA Michal (Pol)		*Abandon*
133.	LEWANDOWSKI Marcin (Pol)	32nd	+ 17'12"
134.	JERECZEK Pawel (Pol)	71st	+ 17'24"
135.	KRAFT Dennis (Ger)		*Abandon*
136.	KRZYWY Krzysztof (Pol)	60th	+ 17'20"
137.	OSINSKI Marcin (Pol)	34th	+ 17'12"
138.	WADECKI Adam (Pol)		*Abandon*

AC SPARTA PRAHA

143.	HEBIK Martin (Cze)	77th	+ 17'24"
144.	HEKELE Emil (Cze)	95th	+ 17'39"
145.	MLYNAR Zdenek (Cze)	24th	+ 17'12"
146.	PECENKA Martin (Cze)	94th	+ 17'39"
147.	PUCELIK Petr (Cze)	55th	+ 17'12"

AUBER 93

151.	AUGER Ludovic (Fra)	**4th**	+ 46"
152.	BROUZES Niels (Fra)	81st	+ 17'29"
153.	BREARD David (Fra)	33rd	+ 17'12"
154.	NILSSON John (Swe)	17th	+ 5'56"
155.	OLIVIER Lénaïc (Fra)		*Abandon*
156.	PAUMIER Laurent (Fra)	80th	+ 17'29"
157.	TALABARDON Yannick (Fra)	64th	+ 17'20"
158.	VALENTIN Tristan (Fra)		*Abandon*

FLANDERS - A.FIN.COM

161.	ASSEZ Ronny (Bel)		*Abandon*
162.	DELIENS Yoeri (Bel)		*Abandon*
163.	LEPRON Jérôme (Fra)	63rd	+ 17'20"
164.	GALLAGHER Stephen (Irl)		*Abandon*
165.	MASSCHELEIN Thierry (Bel)	31st	+ 17'12"
166.	MATTOZZA Sébastien (Bel)	54th	+ 17'12"
167.	SCHEIRLINCKX Bert (Bel)		*Abandon*
168.	VANSTRAELEN Stijn (Bel)		*Abandon*

OKTOS

171.	CALZATI Sylvain (Fra)		*Abandon*
172.	GABROVSKI Ivailo (Bul)		*Abandon*
173.	GOUROV Maxim (Kaz)	20th	+ 5'56"
174.	LEVECOT Benjamin (Fra)		*Abandon*
175.	MIZOUROV Andrei (Kaz)	59th	+ 17'20"
176.	PENCOLÉ Franck (Fra)	**7th**	+ 46"
177.	RUSKYS Saulius (Ltu)	26th	+ 17'12"
178.	TESSIER Jean-Michel (Fra)	**10th**	+ 1'48"

PERUTNINA PTUJ

181.	GAZVODA Gregor (Slo)	69th	+ 17'24"
182.	BOZIC Borut (Slo)	**5th**	+ 46"
183.	KRANJEC Igor (Slo)		*Abandon*
186.	FILIP Branko (Slo)	67th	+ 17'24"
187.	ILESIC Aldo Ino (Slo)		*Abandon*
188.	KELNER Miran (Slo)	45th	+ 17'12"

COMNET - SENGES

191.	DRESSLER Frank (Ger)	48th	+ 17'12"
192.	WOOLDRIDGE Stephen (Aus)		*Abandon*
193.	JURETZEK Hans-Jürgen (Ger)	27th	+ 17'12"
194.	SENGEWALD Uwe (Ger)	68th	+ 17'24"
195.	ROBERTS Luke (Aus)	75th	+ 17'24"
196.	SCHILD René (Ger)	47th	+ 17'12"
197.	SWEET Corey (Aus)		*Abandon*
198.	COHNEN Stefan (Ned)		*Abandon*

CYCLINGNEWS.COM - Team Down Under

201.	BARRAS Tom (Gbr)	49th	+ 17'12"
202.	CLARKE Hilton (Aus)		*Abandon*
203.	JENNINGS Cameron (Aus)	23rd	+ 5'56"
204.	LIEVENS Erik (Bel)		*Abandon*
205.	RICE Matthew (Aus)	58th	+ 17'12"
206.	RUSSEL Nathan (Aus)	28th	+ 17'12"
207.	THUAUX Phillip (Aus)	65th	+ 17'24"
208.	DE WEERDT Sven (Bel)	35th	+ 17'12"

WINFIX - Arnold SICHEREIT

211.	GAJEK Arthur (Pol)	41st	+ 17'12"
212.	HOLSCHE Patrick (Ger)	56th	+ 17'12"
213.	LEDER Manuel (Ger)	37th	+ 17'12"
214.	ODEBRECHT Felix (Ger)	62nd	+ 17'20"
216.	RUND Thorsten (Ger)	70th	+ 17'24"
217.	SCHOLZ Timo (Ger)	85th	+ 17'29"
218.	WILLWOHL Gregor (Ger)	72nd	+ 17'24"

* All the riders finishing below the 23rd place finished outside of the time limit.

COUPE DE FRANCE RANKINGS AFTER 7 ROUNDS

1.	**Thor Hushovd (Nor)**	**C.A**	**125 pts**
2.	**Anthony Geslin (Fra)**	**BLB**	**60 pts**
3.	**Franck Bouyer (Fra)**	**BLB**	**59 pts**
4.	Pierrick Fedrigo (Fra)	C.A	47 pts
5.	Franck Pencolé (Fra)	OKT	40 pts
6.	Andrey Kashechkin (Kaz)	C.A	36 pts
7.	Dmitriy Fofonov (Kaz)	COF	35 pts
-	Thomas Lövkvist (Swe)	FDJ	35 pts
-	Didier Rous (Fra)	BLB	35 pts
-	Saulius Ruskys (Ltu)	OKT	35 pts

Mark Scanlon, Thor Hushovd, Jurgen van de Walle, Eelke van der Wal, Ludovic Auger and Franck Pencolé (left to right in this photo): the survivors of the first breakaway will take the honours in this G P de Denain.

THOR … NEVER A FOOT WRONG!

The performances of Thor Hushovd in this year's Coupe de France are surprising this year. Winner in Marseille (Classic Haribo) and in Denain, 3rd in Cholet, and here he is again on the podium in La Roche / Yon, finish of this 33rd Tour de Vendée, three days after his triumph in the north. Practically 100% success. The only problem being: where's the suspense?

There were whispers suggesting that the foreign riders taking part being a little weak, the French were free to run away with the race. It's true, the three 3rd division Portuguese teams, and the Polish Atlas Hoop Polsat or the Russian Lokomotiv didn't set the world on fire in this race started in pouring rain with a gusting wind and finishing in only slightly better conditions. Once again it's five Frenchmen who set up the first part of the race: Freddy Bichot (Fd.com) accompanied by two duos, Fedrigo and Le Mevel (Credit Agricole) as well as Charteau and Voeckler (La Boulangere), a team which operates in this region. After 100 kilometers of the race, things evolve somewhat. First, it's an ex winner of this race (it was in 2002) Franck Bouyer, who goes to the front before leaving the task to his team mate Sylvain Chavanel closely followed by Benoit Poilvet. At this time there are only 40 kilometers to race.
The peloton worn by the fast pace and the bad weather is reduced to a series of small groups. The one chasing the two leaders is composed of 4 riders from La Boulangere (Bouyer, Charteau, Pineau and Rous) and two men from Credit Agricole (Hushovd and Hinault) therefore the two teams already represented up front, but also last year's winner Jaan Kirsipuu, very active in the persuit, Calzati (Oktos) and Berthou (RAGT Semences). The work done by Kirsipuu is rewarded by the formation of a group of fifteen men at the head of the race. Once again the La Boulangere team is over represented at the front, but this doesn't stop them being caught out by Thor Hushovd, who, as three days earlier in Denain, decides to avoid the dangers of a sprint by attacking 18kms from the finish. The Norwegian constructs a good lead so as to be able to do the final three laps in the streets of La Roche sur Yon without any challenges. The Scandinavian beats four times winner Jaan Kirsipuu by more than a minute.

These considerations were far from the mind of Brioches La Boulangere leader Joseba Beloki, who was using the race to make a third attempt to get back into competition. But after his failures in the Criterium International and the Tour du Pays Basque, the rider from Vitoria retired after only 40 kilometers... The first signs of worry began to surface on the faces of some of his team managers. 80days (the time separating him from the start of the Tour de France) passes quickly! ■

100 Competitors

AG2R Prévoyance			
1.	KIRSIPUU Jaan (Est)	**2nd**	+ 1'07"
2.	BERGÈS Stéphane (Fra)		*Abandon*
3.	ASTARLOZA Mikel (Esp)		*Abandon*
4.	FLICKINGER Andy (Fra)	18th	+ 3'40"
5.	INAUDI Nicolas (Fra)	39th	+ 4'41"
6.	AGNOLUTTO Christophe (Fra)	12nd	+ 3'40"
7.	NAZON Jean-Patrick (Fra)		*Abandon*
8.	PÜTSEP Erki (Est)		*Abandon*
FDJEUX.COM			
11.	BICHOT Freddy (Fra)		*Abandon*
12.	GUESDON Frédéric (Fra)		*Abandon*
13.	FRITSCH Nicolas (Fra)	37th	+ 4'41"
14.	ROBIN Jean-Cyril (Fra)	16th	+ 3'40"
15.	ROY Jérémy (Fra)		*Abandon*
16.	SANCHEZ Fabien (Fra)		*Abandon*
17.	VAUGRENARD Benoît (Fra)		*Abandon*
18.	VOGONDY Nicolas (Fra)	33rd	+ 4'41"
Brioches LA BOULANGÈRE			
21.	BELOKI Joseba (Esp)		*Abandon*
22.	BENETEAU Walter (Fra)	22nd	+ 4'21"
23.	BOUYER Franck (Fra)	**4th**	+ 1'31"
24.	CHARTEAU Anthony (Fra)	14th	+ 3'40"
25.	CHAVANEL Sylvain (Fra)	23rd	+ 4'21"
26.	PINEAU Jérôme (Fra)	**5th**	+ 1'31"
27.	ROUS Didier (Fra)	31st	+ 4'41"
28.	VOECKLER Thomas (Fra)	**7th**	+ 2'02"
CRÉDIT AGRICOLE			
41.	DEAN Julian (Nzl)		*Abandon*
42.	FEDRIGO Pierrick (Fra)	**6th**	+ 2'00"
43.	HALGAND Patrice (Fra)	21st	+ 4'12"
44.	HINAULT Sébastien (Fra)	**3rd**	+ 1'20"
45.	HUSHOVD Thor (Nor)	**1st**	**4h 55'27"**
46.	KAGGESTAD Mads (Nor)	32nd	+ 4'41"
47.	LE MEVEL Christophe (Fra)	36th	+ 4'41"
48.	POILVET Benoît (Fra)		*Abandon*
RAGT Semences - MG ROVER			
51.	AUGER Guillaume (Fra)	19th	+ 3'40"
52.	BERNARD Jérôme (Fra)		*Abandon*
53.	BERTHOU Eric (Fra)	15th	+ 3'40"
54.	BOURQUENOUD Pierre (Sui)		*Abandon*
55.	BOUVARD Gilles (Fra)		*Abandon*
56.	FINOT Frédéric (Fra)		*Abandon*
57.	LE BOULANGER Yoann (Fra)	34th	+ 4'41"
58.	MARTIN Ludovic (Fra)	**10th**	+ 2'11"
AUBER 93			
61.	AUGER Ludovic (Fra)	13rd	+ 3'40"
62.	BROUZES Niels (Fra)		*Abandon*
63.	BRÉARD David (Fra)		*Abandon*
64.	NILSSON John (Swe)	41st	+ 9'38"
65.	OLIVIER Lénaïc (Fra)	40th	+ 7'15"
66.	PAUMIER Laurent (Fra)		*Abandon*
67.	TALABARDON Yannick (Fra)	11st	+ 3'40"
68.	VALENTIN Tristan (Fra)		*Abandon*
OKTOS - St QUENTIN			
71.	CALZATI Sylvain (Fra)	38th	+ 4'41"
72.	GABROVSKI Ivaïlo (Bul)		*Abandon*
73.	LEVECOT Benjamin (Fra)		*Abandon*
75.	MIZOUROV Andrei (Kaz)		*Abandon*
76.	PENCOLÉ Franck (Fra)	29th	+ 4'41"
77.	TESSIER Jean-Michel (Fra)	**9th**	+ 2'06"
78.	RUSKYS Saulius (Ltu)	25th	+ 4'36"
ASC - VILA DO CONDÉ			
81.	COSTA Pedro (Por)		*Abandon*
82.	FERNANDEZ Victoriano (Esp)		*Abandon*
83.	NUÑEZ BATICON Israel (Esp)		*Abandon*
84.	CARNEIRO Carlos (Por)		*Abandon*
85.	VIEIRA Hermano (Por)		*Abandon*
86.	SERRANO ALONSO Oscar (Esp)	27th	+ 4'39"
CARVALHELHOS - BOAVISTA			
91.	SAMPAIO Joaquim (Por)	35th	+ 4'41"
92.	RODRIGUES SILVA José (Por)	20th	+ 3'40"
93.	VAZ José (Por)		*Abandon*
94.	VITAL André (Por)	42nd	+ 9'38"
95.	MARQUE Alejandro (Esp)		*Abandon*
96.	SOEIRO Pedro (Por)	24th	+ 4'36"
97.	PALOMARES Adrian (Esp)		*Abandon*
98.	PETROV ANDONOV Daniel (Bul)		*Abandon*
WÜRTH - BOM PETISCO			
101.	ANDRADE Joaquim (Por)	30th	+ 4'41"
102.	PETROV Daniel (Bul)		*Abandon*
103.	VITOR Hugo Manuel (Por)		*Abandon*
104.	JIMENEZ DIAZ José Antonio (Esp)		*Abandon*
105.	BARTOLOMEU Luis (Por)		*Abandon*
106.	VASSILIEV Krassimir (Bul)		*Abandon*
107.	MIRANDA Helder (Por)		*Abandon*
108.	FITAS Vidal (Por)		*Abandon*
ATLAS - HOOP - POLSAT			
111.	RODRIGUES Quintino (Por)		*Abandon*
112.	NIWCZYK Robert (Pol)		*Abandon*
113.	KOHUT Seweryn (Pol)		*Abandon*
114.	KOHUT Slawomir (Pol)		*Abandon*
115.	SAWKO Lukasz (Pol)		*Abandon*
116.	MARKOV Alexei (Rus)		*Abandon*
118.	SIVAKOV Alexei (Rus)	17th	+ 3'40"
LOKOMOTIV			
121.	MINDLIN Anton (Rus)		*Abandon*
122.	KLIMOV Serguei (Rus)		*Abandon*
123.	BRUTT Pavel (Rus)	28th	+ 4'41"
124.	SEROV Alexandre (Rus)		*Abandon*
125.	POSTERNAK Alexandre (Rus)		*Abandon*
126.	TROUSSOV Nikolai (Rus)		*Abandon*
127.	IGNATIEV Mikhail (Rus)		*Abandon*
128.	AVERIN Maxim (Rus)		*Abandon*
Equipe de Russie			
131.	GRISHKIN Oleg (Rus)		*Abandon*
132.	VORGANOV Eduard (Rus)	**8th**	+ 2'03"
133.	PONOMAREV Konstantin (Rus)		*Abandon*
134.	SOKOLOV Evgueni (Rus)		*Abandon*
135.	KUDENTSOV Sergey (Rus)		*Abandon*
136.	TERENIN Ivan (Rus)	26th	+ 4'36"
137.	MINACHKIN Andrey (Rus)		*Abandon*
138.	KARPATCHEV Maxim (Rus)		*Abandon*

CLASSIFICATION

193 km

1.	**Thor Hushovd (Nor)**	**C.A**	**4h55'27"**
2.	**Jaan Kirsipuu (Est)**	**A2R**	**+ 1'07"**
3.	**Sébasti Hinault (Fra)**	**C.A**	**+ 1'20"**
4.	Franck Bouyer (Fra)	BLB	+ 1'31"
5.	Jérôme Pineau (Fra)	BLB	s.t
6.	Pierrick Fedrigo (Fra)	C.A	+ 2'00"
7.	Thomas Voeckler (Fra)	BLB	+ 2'02"
8.	Eduard Vorganov (Rus)	El2	+ 2'03"
9.	Jean-Michel Tessier (Fra)	OKT	+ 2'06"
10.	Ludovic Martin (Fra)	RAG	+ 2'11"

From the end of April, Thor Hushovd removes any suspense as to the outcome of the 2004 Coupe de France...

SAME AGAIN

Brought forward this year because of it's inclusion in the Coupe de France, the Tro Bro Leon, an unusual race, which includes sections on miniscule lanes across the Finistere countryside was won for the second year running by the rider from Lyon, Samuel Dumoulin.

Even if he has changed teams in the closed season, going from Jean Delatour to AG2R Prevoyance, Jean Delatour rode like a master to win on a course he loves so much. "I avoided making the same mistakes I made last year. This time I saved my strength till the end of the race and had a lot in reserve for the final kilometers. That's what made the difference", he said after beating off Christophe Mengin and the Belgian Bert Scherlinckx, the last survivors of an eventful day on the wild roads of Tro Bro.

The man with the number one on his back knew how to play the waiting game, and heaven knows patience was needed on this 21st edition of the Brittany version of the Paris – Roubaix, which only really got started when the leaders approached Lannilis. Christophe Oriol (AG2R) and Ludovic Auger (Auber 93), had signalled the start of the battle as they left Gouesnou (km60) but after playing to the gallery for a couple of hours with a maximum lead of 4 mins 55 sec the two were pulled back into the pack near Kervaro (km 140).

The linking of sectors 9 and 14, tackled in a deluge of dust decimated the pack and at section 15 only six riders came through unscathed: Samuel Dumoulin (AG2R), the surprising Spaniard Unai Yus (La Boulangere), Christophe Mengin (Fdjeux.com),the Belgian Bert Scheirlinckx (Flanders), the Kazakh Andrey Mizourov (Oktos) and Yoann Le Boulanger (RAGT).

The latter, already victim of a first puncture was not to have an easy day: Le Boulanger, very aggressive and once again in the thick of the action, had three more punctures (!) on the final circuit, the last causing him to crash. A crash which didn't prevent him crossing the line with a suspected fractured knee cap that would side line him for the rest of the season!

Le Boulanger and Yus (also eliminated with a puncture) out of the way, the rapid Samuel Dumoulin could now concentrate on his remaining rivals. Coming out on top after a head to head race last year against the Belgian Phillipe Gilbert, Dumoulin- the experience helping!- negotiated the sprint perfectly to collect his first win of the season. ■

86 Competitors

AG2R Prévoyance			
1.	DUMOULIN Samuel (Fra)	**1st**	**5h 02'26"**
2.	ORIOL Christophe (Fra)	43rd	+ 7'49"
3.	BERGÈS Stéphane (Fra)		*Abandon*
4.	PORTAL Nicolas (Fra)	35th	+ 4'58"
5.	INAUDI Nicolas (Fra)	**5th**	+ 46"
6.	PÜTSEP Erki (Est)	**8th**	+ 55"

FDJEUX.COM			
12.	DEREPAS David (Fra)	24th	+ 2'10"
13.	ROY Jérémy (Fra)	45th	+ 7'49"
14.	GUESDON Frédéric (Fra)	**7th**	+ 55"
15.	MENGIN Christophe (Fra)	**2nd**	+ 2"
16.	MOUREY Francis (Fra)		*Abandon*
17.	RENSHAW Mark (Aus)	12nd	+ 55"

CRÉDIT AGRICOLE			
21.	AUGÉ Stéphane (Fra)		*Abandon*
22.	HERVÉ Cédric (Fra)	39th	+ 7'49"
23.	HINAULT Sébastien (Fra)		*Abandon*
24.	JÉGOU Lilian (Fra)	30th	+ 3'52"
25.	JOLY Sébastien (Fra)		*Abandon*
26.	LEBLACHER Eric (Fra)	37th	+ 7'49"
27.	LEQUATRE Geoffroy (Fra)	28th	+ 3'45"
28.	MURAVYEV Dmitriy (Kaz)	19th	+ 1'20"

Brioches LA BOULANGÈRE			
32.	CHAVANEL Sébastien (Fra)		*Abandon*
33.	GESLIN Anthony (Fra)	33rd	+ 4'58"
34.	YUS Unai (Esp)	18th	+ 1'00"
35.	MARTIAS Rony (Fra)		*Abandon*
36.	NAULLEAU Alexandre (Fra)		*Abandon*
37.	RENIER Franck (Fra)	**10th**	+ 55"
38.	VOECKLER Thomas (Fra)	**6th**	+ 49"

RAGT Semences - MG ROVER			
41.	AUGER Guillaume (Fra)	21st	+ 1'40"
42.	BERTHOU Eric (Fra)	32nd	+ 4'14"
43.	LAURENT Christophe (Fra)		*Abandon*
44.	LE BOULANGER Yoann (Fra)	36th	+ 6'19"
45.	BUFFAZ Mickaël (Fra)	38th	+ 7'49"
46.	LUHOVYY Roman (Ukr)		*Abandon*
47.	SEIGNEUR Eddy (Fra)		*Abandon*

OKTOS - St QUENTIN			
53.	GUROV Maxim (Kaz)		*Abandon*
55.	MIZOUROV Andrei (Kaz)	**4th**	+ 14"
56.	PENCOLÉ Franck (Fra)	17th	+ 55"
57.	TESSIER Jean-Michel (Fra)	13rd	+ 55"
58.	RUSKYS Saulius (Ltu)	20th	+ 1'20"
59.	DUMONT David (Fra)		*Abandon*

AUBER 93			
61.	AUGER Ludovic (Fra)	34th	+ 4'58"
62.	OLIVIER Lénaïc (Fra)		*Abandon*
63.	NILSSON John (Swe)	16th	+ 55"
64.	VALENTIN Tristan (Fra)		*Abandon*
65.	TALABARDON Yannick (Fra)	26th	+ 3'45"

FLANDERS - AFIN.COM			
71.	GERMER Gregg (Usa)		*Abandon*
72.	ASSEZ Ronny (Bel)		*Abandon*
73.	SCHEIRLINCKX Bert (Bel)	**3rd**	+ 5"
74.	VERSTICHELEN Dimitri (Bel)		*Abandon*
75.	MASSCHELEIN Thierry (Bel)		*Abandon*
76.	LEPRON Jérôme (Fra)		*Abandon*
77.	LANDRIE Jurgen (Bel)		*Abandon*

JONGE VLAANDEREN 2016			
81.	STEURS Geert (Bel)	14th	+ 55"
82.	DE NEEF Steven (Bel)		*Abandon*
83.	RENDERS Sven (Bel)	23rd	+ 2'09"
84.	HOVELYNCK Kurt (Bel)	25th	+ 3'45"
85.	UYTTERHOEVEN Peter (Bel)		*Abandon*
86.	WIJNANDS Stefan (Bel)		*Abandon*
87.	HUYSMANS Aron (Bel)		*Abandon*
88.	VAN DE GEHUCHTE Tommy (Bel)	40th	+ 7'49"

VAN HEMERT Groep - EUROGIFTS			
91.	CURVERS Roy (Ned)		*Abandon*
94.	VAN GROEZEN Jelle (Ned)		*Abandon*
96.	HOOGERLAND Johnny (Ned)		*Abandon*
97.	VAN HUMMEL Kenny (Ned)	44th	+ 7'49"
99.	JEURISSEN Cees (Ned)		*Abandon*
100.	VAN RIJN Vincent (Ned)	22nd	+ 1'40"

HSBC			
101.	WHITE Nicholas (Rsa)		*Abandon*
102.	McDONALD Neil (Rsa)	42nd	+ 7'49"
103.	McLEOD Ian (Rsa)	29th	+ 3'45"
104.	BALL Jamie (Rsa)		*Abandon*
105.	SPENCE Daniel (Rsa)		*Abandon*
106.	HOWES Jeff (Rsa)		*Abandon*
107.	ESCH Christopher (Rsa)		*Abandon*
108.	PAVLOV Alex (Rsa)		*Abandon*

WÜRTH - BOM PETISCO			
112.	MARTA Nuno (Por)	27th	+ 3'45"
113.	MIRANDA Helder (Por)	41st	+ 7'49"
114.	COSTA Ricardo Jorge (Por)	15th	+ 55"
115.	LOURENÇO Mário (Por)		*Abandon*
116.	PETROV Daniel (Bul)		*Abandon*
117.	BARTOLOMEU Luis (Por)		*Abandon*

Mr BOOKMAKER - PALMANS			
121.	DE SMET Andy (Bel)		*Abandon*
122.	HUNT Jeremy (Gbr)		*Abandon*
123.	PLANCKAERT Jo (Bel)	**9th**	+ 55"
125.	TROUVÉ Kristof (Bel)	31st	+ 4'01"
126.	LEMBO Eddy (Fra)		Abandon
127.	VANDERAERDEN Gert (Bel)	11st	+ 55"

CLASSIFICATION

195,2 km

1.	**Samuel Dumoulin (Fra)**	**A2R**	**5h02'26"**
2.	**Christophe M gin (Fra)**	**FDJ**	**s.t**
3.	**Bert Scheirlinckx (Bel)**	**FLA**	**s.t**
4.	Andrey Mizourov (Kaz)	OKT	+ 14"
5.	Nicolas Inaudi (Fra)	A2R	+ 46"
6.	Thomas Voeckler (Fra)	BLB	+ 49"
7.	Frédéric Guesdon (Fra)	FDJ	+ 55"
8.	Erki Pütsep (Est)	A2R	s.t
9.	Jo Planckaert (Bel)	MRB	s.t
10.	Franck Renier (Fra)	BLB	s.t

Moreau was not prepared for this!

For several years now, Christophe Moreau has seen his early seasons perturbed by various physical problems. This year it's a persistent pain in the knee which forced him to delay the start of his season until mid March, in the Classic Loire- Atlantic. The rider from Belfort was therefore not expecting too much at the start of this Trophée des Grimpeurs which brought together a meagre peloton of 69 riders in front of the Mairie of Argenteuil in the suburbs of Paris. A few minutes before the start on this tricky circuit (including the famous Cote de l'Ermitage with its slopes rising at 15%), he declared that he would wait until the Tour of Languedoc – Roussillon a few weeks later to really test his form , and today, he would be content to help his team mates Patrice Halgand and Christophe le Mevel. But a race is never run in advance. This was proved once again on this chilly but sunny first Sunday in May.

Things get off to a brisk start! As early as the first of the seventeen laps to be covered, Christophe Moreau takes the lead, accompanied only by the Irish champion Mark Scanlon (AG2R) and Jean Cyril Robin (Fdjeux.com). Unbeaten for three years, Jean René Berneadeau, team manager of Brioches La Boulangere calls up his troops who get to work reducing the lead of the trio. This is achieved after a few laps when nine riders (among them, Putsep, Gilbert, S. Auger, Roy and Pineau) arrive at the front. The race then explodes into action. In the fifth lap, Phillipe Gilbert along with Erki Putsep and Jerome Pineau lead the peloton by a minute, but the situation evolves in the following laps. The French champion Didier Rous who we thought caught out, comes to the front accompanied by his team mate Laurent Lefevre and Patrice Halgand.

Christophe Moreau had waited ten years before winning his first one day road race!

GILBRT- PINEAU: THE IMPERFECT ARRANGEMENT

It takes much more to discourage Phillipe Gilber, full of vitality and at ease on this hilly course. The rider re- takes the lead with only Jerome Pineau for company. The rivalry between the La Boulangere and Fdjeux.com teams, much talked about before the start, now comes out into the open. The two men engage in a waiting game which helps the return of Christophe Moreau, who, once up there with the leading duo, goes on to lead the race. The game of cat and mouse between the now chasing pair allows Christophe Moreau to pull into a lead and he spares no effort in making it as wide as possible. Without easing up, he can enjoy his final lap, knowing that the two are trailing by a minute and are now only interested in fighting it out for the second place.
A fight which ends up favouring the Belgian rider, who outguns Jerome Pineau on the final ascension of the Cote de l'Ermitage. The rider from the La Boulangere team will just the same make it clear on the podium that the attitude of his opponent, refusing to take any relays in the final ten kilometers, did not help either of them! None of this matters to Christophe Moreau who had waited for ten years as a pro before winning his first big road race. A victory which comes at just the right moment to lift the sometimes fragile morale of a rider now looking with impatience towards the Tour de France. A victory which also rewards the efforts of the past weeks and also puts behind him the disappointing performances in the Ardennaises, the Fleche Wallon and the Liege- Bastogne- Liege.

With the confidence of a winner, the leader of the Credit Agricole team will start the 4 Jours de Dunkerque three days later. A race he won in 2003. Trailing badly, he'll come to a halt on the first stage and retire from the race. A new setback for the rider from Belfort who's team mate Thor Hushovd, absent from the Trophée des Grimpeurs, with his qualities as a sprinter, stays the solid leader of the Coupe de France. ■

69 Competitors

Brioches LA BOULANGÈRE

No.	Rider	Place	Time
1.	ROUS Didier (Fra)	**6th**	+4'46"
2.	CHAVANEL Sylvain (Fra)	**5th**	+3'59"
3.	GESLIN Anthony (Fra)	31st	+ 8'38"
4.	LEFÈVRE Laurent (Fra)	**8th**	+4'49"
5.	MARTIAS Rony (Fra)		*Abandon*
7.	PINEAU Jérôme (Fra)	**3rd**	+1'23"
8.	BOUYER Franck (Fra)	29th	+ 8'29"

AUBER 93

No.	Rider	Place	Time
11.	AUGER Ludovic (Fra)		*Abandon*
12.	BRÉARD David (Fra)	33rd	+ 8'44"
13.	OLIVIER Lénaïc (Fra)		*Abandon*
14.	BROUZES Niels (Fra)		*Abandon*
15.	NILSSON John (Swe)	21st	+ 5'28"
16.	PAUMIER Laurent (Fra)	27th	+ 8'27"
17.	TALABARDON Yannick (Fra)	14th	+ 5'04"
18.	VALENTIN Tristan (Fra)	35th	+ 8'52"

FDJEUX.COM

No.	Rider	Place	Time
21.	BICHOT Freddy (Fra)	12nd	+ 4'57"
22.	DEREPAS David (Fra)	30th	+ 8'29"
23.	GILBERT Philippe (Bel)	**2nd**	+1'10"
24.	ROBIN Jean-Cyril (Fra)		*Abandon*
25.	LÖVKVIST Thomas (Swe)	**9th**	+ 4'51"
26.	MENGIN Christophe (Fra)	20th	+ 5'19"
28.	ROY Jérémy (Fra)	19th	+ 5'17"

CRÉDIT AGRICOLE

No.	Rider	Place	Time
31.	AUGÉ Stéphane (Fra)	34th	+ 8'44"
32.	FEDRIGO Pierrick (Fra)	**7th**	+ 4'46"
33.	HALGAND Patrice (Fra)	**10th**	+ 4'51"
34.	LEBLACHER Eric (Fra)	16th	+ 5'09"
35.	LE MEVEL Christophe (Fra)	11st	+ 4'54"
36.	MOREAU Christophe (Fra)	**1st**	**3h 09'57"**
37.	POILVET Benoît (Fra)		*Abandon*
38.	SALMON Benoît (Fra)	32nd	+ 8'40"

OKTOS - St QUENTIN

No.	Rider	Place	Time
41.	CALZATI Sylvain (Fra)		*Abandon*
42.	GABROVSKI Ivaïlo (Bul)		*Abandon*
43.	MIZOUROV Andrei (Kaz)	15th	+ 5'06"
44.	PENCOLÉ Franck (Fra)		*Abandon*
45.	TESSIER Jean-Michel (Fra)	26th	+ 8'22"
46.	RUSKYS Saulius (Ltu)	13rd	+ 4'59"
47.	LEVECOT Benjamin (Fra)		*Abandon*
48.	GUROV Maxim (Kaz)		*Abandon*

AG2R Prévoyance

No.	Rider	Place	Time
51.	AGNOLUTTO Christophe (Fra)	18th	+ 5'14"
52.	BROCHARD Laurent (Fra)	25th	+ 8'19"
55.	MONDORY Lloyd (Fra)		*Abandon*
56.	PÜTSEP Erki (Est)	23rd	+ 7'30"
57.	SCANLON Mark (Irl)	**4th**	+ 3'52"
58.	LAIDOUN Julien (Fra)		*Abandon*

ROSSO Sport

No.	Rider	Place	Time
61.	HERZ Serge (Ger)		*Abandon*
62.	HUDSON Ron (Usa)		*Abandon*
63.	McGEE Michael (Aus)		*Abandon*
64.	MERTS Vitaliy (Ger)		*Abandon*
65.	SCHWARZER Jan-Eric (Ger)		*Abandon*
66.	PRENGEL Sebastian (Ger)		*Abandon*

RAGT Semences - MG ROVER

No.	Rider	Place	Time
71.	AUGER Guillaume (Fra)	17th	+ 5'12"
72.	DION Renaud (Fra)	24th	+ 8'19"
73.	FINOT Frédéric (Fra)		*Abandon*
74.	LUHOVYY Roman (Ukr)		*Abandon*
75.	REYNAUD Nicolas (Fra)	22nd	+ 5'54"
76.	BERTHOU Eric (Fra)		*Abandon*
77.	THIBOUT Bruno (Fra)		*Abandon*
78.	MUTSCHLER Klaus (Ger)		*Abandon*

AC SPARTA PRAHA

No.	Rider	Place	Time
82.	BECKA Radek (Cze)		*Abandon*
83.	PUCELIK Petr (Cze)		*Abandon*
85.	MLYNAR Zdenek (Cze)		*Abandon*
87.	SLAJCHRT Filip (Cze)		*Abandon*
88.	HEBIK Martin (Cze)		*Abandon*

Team RSH

No.	Rider	Place	Time
91.	GOLLHARDT Yves (Ger)		*Abandon*
93.	HAUEISEN Dennis (Ger)	28th	+ 8'27"
95.	POKRANDT Jan (Ger)		*Abandon*
96.	SCZEPUREK Robert (Ger)		*Abandon*
97.	STRAUCH Daniel (Ger)		*Abandon*
98.	WILK Jens (Ger)		*Abandon*

CLASSIFICATION

1.	**Christophe Moreau (Fra)**	**C.A**	**3h 09'57"**
2.	**Philippe Gilbert (Bel)**	**FDJ**	**+ 1'10"**
3.	**Jérôme Pineau (Fra)**	**BLB**	**+ 1'23"**
4.	Mark Scanlon (Irl)	A2R	+ 3'52"
5.	Sylvain Chavanel (Fra)	BLB	+ 3'59"
6.	Didier Rous (Fra)	BLB	+ 4'46"
7.	Pierrick Fedrigo (Fra)	C.A	s.t
8.	Laurent Lefèvre (Fra)	BLB	+ 4'49"
9.	Thomas Lövkvist (Swe)	FDJ	+ 4'51"
10.	Patrice Halgand (Fra)	C.A	s.t

COUPE DE FRANCE RANKINGS AFTER 10 ROUNDS

1.	**Thor Hushovd (Nor)**	**C.A**	**125 pts**
2.	Anthony Geslin (Fra)	BLB	60 pts
3.	Franck Bouyer (Fra)	BLB	59 pts
4.	Pierrick Fedrigo (Fra)	C.A	47 pts
5.	Franck Pencolé (Fra)	OKT	40 pts
6.	Andrey Kashechkin (Kaz)	C.A	36 pts
7.	Dmitriy Fofonov (Kaz)	COF	35 pts
-	Thomas Lövkvist (Swe)	FDJ	35 pts
-	Didier Rous (Fra)	BLB	35 pts
-	Saulius Ruskys (Ltu)	OKT	35 pts

Jerome Pineau tries his chances a few laps before the finish but Christophe Moreau resists well.

Even in a Coupe de France race, victory doesn't come easy!

IN MAY, VOECKLER DOES AS HE PLEASES!

The splendid winner of the Tour of Luxembourg 2003, a victory coming with two stage wins, the Alsatian from the Antilles (he was born in Schiltigheim but brought up in Guadeloupe) Thomas Voeckler found new honours in winning a competitive A Travers le Morbihan. A year to the day after his triumph in Luxembourg.

Thomas Voeckler has been working as a super team member since the start of this season. A few days before this 11th round of the Coupe de France, he had largely contributed to the success of his team leader Sylvain Chavanel on the Tour of Belgium, as well as the same man's triumph on the Quatre Jours de Dunkerque. In the absence of the "Boss" he had carte blanche and didn't miss the occasion to add to his own successes.

From the 25th kilometre of the race, 11 men decide to attack. Voeckler is of course present, as is Mickael Buffez (RAGT), the Australian Matthew White, the duo Mr Bookmaker, Lembo/ Koehler, the South African Mc Leod (HSBC), but also Pierrick Fedrigo (Credit Agricole); Laurent Paumier (Auber 93), Boggia (ICET), the indispensable Franck Pencolé (Oktos), and last but not least, Maxime Mederel (Equipe de France). O'Grady, Ludovic Martin and the Briton Tom Southam fearing their chances may be slipping away, join the group rapidly. All is not finished however. The peloton is not resigned to its fate and never lets the lead pass the 1minute 30 second mark. At each passage of the impressive Cote de Cadoudal at Plumelec, the group of fourteen riders loses some members but manages to contain the peloton, also weakened by the effort. Infatigable animator of the Coupe de France races, Franck Pencolé decides to give his all, one lap from the finishing line. But his seven ex companions of the attack don't see things his way. Metre by metre, they claw back the gap between them and the rider from Normandy. It's the final climb of the Cote de Cadoudal that will sort things out. Thomas Voeckler anticipates a sprint from O'Grady or from Fedrigo, stronger in this sort of situation, and resists the fiery return of Laurent Paumier, very much in form throughout the day. Less than a minute later, the front of the peloton is dominated by Thor Hushovd, gaining points which comfort his position as leader of the Coupe de France... ■

100 Competitors

AG2R Prévoyance

1.	KIRSIPUU Jaan (Est)	**2nd**	+ 1'07"
2.	BERGÈS Stéphane (Fra)		*Abandon*
3.	ASTARLOZA Mikel (Esp)		*Abandon*
4.	FLICKINGER Andy (Fra)	18th	+ 3'40"
5.	INAUDI Nicolas (Fra)	39th	+ 4'41"
6.	AGNOLUTTO Christophe (Fra)	12nd	+ 3'40"
7.	NAZON Jean-Patrick (Fra)		*Abandon*
8.	PÜTSEP Erki (Est)		*Abandon*

FDJEUX.COM

11.	BICHOT Freddy (Fra)		*Abandon*
12.	GUESDON Frédéric (Fra)		*Abandon*
13.	FRITSCH Nicolas (Fra)	37th	+ 4'41"
14.	ROBIN Jean-Cyril (Fra)	16th	+ 3'40"
15.	ROY Jérémy (Fra)		*Abandon*
16.	SANCHEZ Fabien (Fra)		*Abandon*
17.	VAUGRENARD Benoît (Fra)		*Abandon*
18.	VOGONDY Nicolas (Fra)	33rd	+ 4'41"

Brioches LA BOULANGÈRE

21.	BELOKI Joseba (Esp)		*Abandon*
22.	BENETEAU Walter (Fra)	22nd	+ 4'21"
23.	BOUYER Franck (Fra)	**4th**	+ 1'31"
24.	CHARTEAU Anthony (Fra)	14th	+ 3'40"
25.	CHAVANEL Sylvain (Fra)	23rd	+ 4'21"
26.	PINEAU Jérôme (Fra)	**5th**	+ 1'31"
27.	ROUS Didier (Fra)	31st	+ 4'41"
28.	VOECKLER Thomas (Fra)	**7th**	+ 2'02"

CRÉDIT AGRICOLE

41.	DEAN Julian (Nzl)		*Abandon*
42.	FEDRIGO Pierrick (Fra)	**6th**	+ 2'00"
43.	HALGAND Patrice (Fra)	21st	+ 4'12"
44.	HINAULT Sébastien (Fra)	**3rd**	+ 1'20"
45.	HUSHOVD Thor (Nor)	**1st**	**4h 55'27"**
46.	KAGGESTAD Mads (Nor)	32nd	+ 4'41"
47.	LE MEVEL Christophe (Fra)	36th	+ 4'41"
48.	POILVET Benoît (Fra)		*Abandon*

RAGT Semences - MG ROVER

51.	AUGER Guillaume (Fra)	19th	+ 3'40"
52.	BERNARD Jérôme (Fra)		*Abandon*
53.	BERTHOU Eric (Fra)	15th	+ 3'40"
54.	BOURQUENOUD Pierre (Sui)		*Abandon*
55.	BOUVARD Gilles (Fra)		*Abandon*
56.	FINOT Frédéric (Fra)		*Abandon*
57.	LE BOULANGER Yoann (Fra)	34th	+ 4'41"
58.	MARTIN Ludovic (Fra)	**10th**	+ 2'11"

AUBER 93

61.	AUGER Ludovic (Fra)	13rd	+ 3'40"
62.	BROUZES Niels (Fra)		*Abandon*
63.	BRÉARD David (Fra)		*Abandon*
64.	NILSSON John (Swe)	41st	+ 9'38"
65.	OLIVIER Lénaïc (Fra)	40th	+ 7'15"
66.	PAUMIER Laurent (Fra)		*Abandon*
67.	TALABARDON Yannick (Fra)	11st	+ 3'40"
68.	VALENTIN Tristan (Fra)		*Abandon*

OKTOS - St QUENTIN

71.	CALZATI Sylvain (Fra)	38th	+ 4'41"
72.	GABROVSKI Ivaïlo (Bul)		*Abandon*
73.	LEVECOT Benjamin (Fra)		*Abandon*
75.	MIZOUROV Andrei (Kaz)		*Abandon*
76.	PENCOLÉ Franck (Fra)	29th	+ 4'41"
77.	TESSIER Jean-Michel (Fra)	**9th**	+ 2'06"
78.	RUSKYS Saulius (Ltu)	25th	+ 4'36"

ASC - VILA DO CONDÉ

81.	COSTA Pedro (Por)		*Abandon*
82.	FERNANDEZ Victoriano (Esp)		*Abandon*
83.	NUÑEZ BATICON Israel (Esp)		*Abandon*
84.	CARNEIRO Carlos (Por)		*Abandon*
85.	VIEIRA Hermano (Por)		*Abandon*
86.	SERRANO ALONSO Oscar (Esp)	27th	+ 4'39"

CARVALHELHOS - BOAVISTA

91.	SAMPAIO Joaquim (Por)	35th	+ 4'41"
92.	RODRIGUES SILVA José (Por)	20th	+ 3'40"
93.	VAZ José (Por)		*Abandon*
94.	VITAL André (Por)	42nd	+ 9'38"
95.	MARQUE Alejandro (Esp)		*Abandon*
96.	SOEIRO Pedro (Por)	24th	+ 4'36"
97.	PALOMARES Adrian (Esp)		*Abandon*
98.	PETROV ANDONOV Daniel (Bul)		*Abandon*

WÜRTH - BOM PETISCO

101.	ANDRADE Joaquim (Por)	30th	+ 4'41"
102.	PETROV Daniel (Bul)		*Abandon*
103.	VITOR Hugo Manuel (Por)		*Abandon*
104.	JIMENEZ DIAZ José Antonio (Esp)		*Abandon*
105.	BARTOLOMEU Luis (Por)		*Abandon*
106.	VASSILIEV Krassimir (Bul)		*Abandon*
107.	MIRANDA Helder (Por)		*Abandon*
108.	FITAS Vidal (Por)		*Abandon*

ATLAS - HOOP - POLSAT

111.	RODRIGUES Quintino (Por)		*Abandon*
112.	NIWCZYK Robert (Pol)		*Abandon*
113.	KOHUT Seweryn (Pol)		*Abandon*
114.	KOHUT Slawomir (Pol)		*Abandon*
115.	SAWKO Lukasz (Pol)		*Abandon*
116.	MARKOV Alexei (Rus)		*Abandon*
118.	SIVAKOV Alexei (Rus)	17th	+ 3'40"

LOKOMOTIV

121.	MINDLIN Anton (Rus)		*Abandon*
122.	KLIMOV Serguei (Rus)		*Abandon*
123.	BRUTT Pavel (Rus)	28th	+ 4'41"
124.	SEROV Alexandre (Rus)		*Abandon*
125.	POSTERNAK Alexandre (Rus)		*Abandon*
126.	TROUSSOV Nikolai (Rus)		*Abandon*
127.	IGNATIEV Mikhail (Rus)		*Abandon*
128.	AVERIN Maxim (Rus)		*Abandon*

Equipe de Russie

131.	GRISHKIN Oleg (Rus)		*Abandon*
132.	VORGANOV Eduard (Rus)	**8th**	+ 2'03"
133.	PONOMAREV Konstantin (Rus)		*Abandon*
134.	SOKOLOV Evgueni (Rus)		*Abandon*
135.	KUDENTSOV Sergey (Rus)		*Abandon*
136.	TERENIN Ivan (Rus)	26th	+ 4'36"
137.	MINACHKIN Andrey (Rus)		*Abandon*
138.	KARPATCHEV Maxim (Rus)		*Abandon*

CLASSIFICATION

181 km

1.	**Thomas Voeckler (Fra)**	**BLB**	**4h23'16"**
2.	**Laur t Paumier (Fra)**	**AUB**	**+ 2"**
3.	**Pierrick Fedrigo (Fra)**	**C.A**	**s.t**
4.	Ludovic Martin (Fra)	RAG	+ 4"
5.	Stuart O'Grady (Aus)	COF	+ 7"
6.	Ian McLeod (Rsa)	HSB	+ 9"
7.	Franck Pencolé (Fra)	OKT	+ 44"
8.	Thor Hushovd (Nor)	C.A	+ 59"
9.	Mykhaylo Khalilov (Ukr)	ICT	s.t
10.	Stefano Boggia (Ita)	ICT	+ 1'01"

COUPE DE FRANCE RANKINGS AFTER 11 ROUNDS

1.	**Thor Hushovd (Nor)**	**C.A**	**187 pts**
2.	Pierrick Fedrigo (Fra)	C.A	102 pts
3.	Thomas Voeckler (Fra)	BLB	80 pts
4.	Franck Bouyer (Fra)	BLB	79 pts
5.	Anthony Geslin (Fra)	BLB	60 pts

Only the Belgian champion Geert Omloop was able to follow Stuart O'Grady in the finale, but the Australian will show his superiority in the final 100 metres...

Fifteen months of waiting...

A little "short" two days earlier in the A Travers de Morbihan race, the Australian Stuart O'Grady worked like the devil to win, in the land of Alexandre Dumas, his first bouquet of the season, adding to the successes of the Cofidis team, decidedly inspired when racing on its home ground.

The first to attack are often rewarded in the GP Villers-Cotterets. This was also the case this year. In effect, from the end of the first lap of a thirteen kilometre circuit to be completed fourteen times...a quarter of the pack constituted a leading group which would, until the middle of the race, keep the main peloton at bay. Unable to close the gap, the peloton soon capitulates, leaving the leaders to fight things out among themselves. Up front, some teams are better represented than others. This is the case with Credit Agricole with Hushovd, Fedrigo and Muravyev; Cofidis with Casper, O'Grady, Edaleine and Moncoutié; La Boulangere with Renier, Sebastien Chavanel and Naulleau, Mr Bookmaker.com with the Belgian champion Geert Omloop and the Frenchmen Gabriel, Koehler and Lembo, AG2R with Dumoulin, Flickinger and Portal, RAGT Semences with G. Auger, Dion and Mutschler, or Auber 93 with L. Auger, Lamouller and Talabardon. On the other hand Fdjeux.com can only count on Baden Cooke and Oktos has only sent up Jean Michel Tessier. But the hill at Haramont thins out the leading group and after several laps it's a rider from Australia, Stuart O'Grady who finds an opening. Only Geert Omloop has enough in reserve to follow the rider from Adelaide. The duo work well together and fight off the disorganised attacks from chasing groups. The logical favourite in a sprint, Stuart O'Grady doesn't even need to show his turn of speed. Omloop doesn't contest the victory. A win coming after a wait of 15 months for the red headed Australian, his thoughts already turning to the Tour de France, where he will once again be fighting for the Green Jersey of the winner on Points. ■

116 Competitors

COFIDIS

1.	CASPER Jimmy (Fra)	17th	+ 7'15"
2.	BESSY Frédéric (Fra)		*Abandon*
3.	EDALEINE Christophe (Fra)	16th	+ 7'10"
5.	MONCOUTIÉ David (Fra)	**7th**	+ 16"
6.	MONIER Damien (Fra)		*Abandon*
7.	O'GRADY Stuart (Aus)	**1st**	**4h 16'38"**
8.	WHITE Matthew (Aus)		*Abandon*

CRÉDIT AGRICOLE

12.	FEDRIGO Pierrick (Fra)	**5th**	+ 16"
13.	HUSHOVD Thor (Nor)	**8th**	+ 1'56"
14.	KAGGESTAD Mads (Nor)		*Abandon*
15.	JOLY Sébastien (Fra)		*Abandon*
16.	LE MÉVEL Christophe (Fra)		*Abandon*
17.	LEQUATRE Geoffroy (Fra)		*Abandon*
18.	MURAVYEV Dmitriy (Kaz)	23rd	+ 7'15"

FDJEUX.COM

21.	CASAR Sandy (Fra)		*Abandon*
22.	COOKE Baden (Aus)	**3rd**	+ 16"
23.	DA CRUZ Carlos (Fra)		*Abandon*
24.	BICHOT Freddy (Fra)		*Abandon*
26.	LÖVKVIST Thomas (Swe)		*Abandon*
27.	MENGIN Christophe (Fra)		*Abandon*
29.	ROY Jérémy (Fra)		*Abandon*

AG2R Prévoyance

31.	ASTARLOZA Mikel (Esp)		*Abandon*
32.	DUMOULIN Samuel (Fra)		*Abandon*
33.	FLICKINGER Andy (Fra)	18th	+ 7'15"
34.	GOUBERT Stéphane (Fra)		*Abandon*
37.	PORTAL Nicolas (Fra)	24th	+ 7'17"

RAGT Semences - MG ROVER

41.	AUGER Guillaume (Fra)	22nd	+ 7'15"
43.	BUFFAZ Mickaël (Fra)		*Abandon*
44.	DION Renaud (Fra)	19th	+ 7'15"
46.	LAURENT Christophe (Fra)		*Abandon*
47.	MUTSCHLER Klaus (Ger)	14th	+ 7'10"
48.	THIBOUT Bruno (Fra)		*Abandon*
49.	SEIGNEUR Eddy (Fra)		*Abandon*
50.	REYNAUD Nicolas (Fra)		*Abandon*

Brioches LA BOULANGÈRE

51.	CHAVANEL Sébastien (Fra)		*Abandon*
53.	GESLIN Anthony (Fra)		*Abandon*
54.	KERN Christophe (Fra)		*Abandon*
55.	MARTIAS Rony (Fra)		*Abandon*
56.	NAULLEAU Alexandre (Fra)		*Abandon*
57.	RENIER Franck (Fra)	**4th**	+ 16"
58.	PICHON Mickaël (Fra)		*Abandon*

AUBER 93

61.	AUGER Ludovic (Fra)	15th	+ 7'10"
62.	BREARD David (Fra)		*Abandon*
63.	BROUZES Niels (Fra)		*Abandon*
64.	LAMOULLER Loïc (Fra)		*Abandon*
65.	NILSSON John (Swe)		*Abandon*
66.	OLIVIER Lénaïc (Fra)	11st	+ 3'41"
67.	PAUMIER Laurent (Fra)		*Abandon*
68.	TALABARDON Yannick (Fra)		*Abandon*

OKTOS

71.	LEVECOT Benjamin (Fra)		*Abandon*
73.	GOUROV Maxim (Kaz)		*Abandon*
74.	KRUSHEVSKIY Serhiy (Uzb)		*Abandon*
75.	MIZOUROV Andrey (Kaz)		*Abandon*
76.	PENCOLÉ Franck (Fra)		*Abandon*
77.	TESSIER Jean-Michel (Fra)	13rd	+ 5'53"
78.	RUSKYS Saulius (Ltu)		*Abandon*
80.	BOUCHER David (Fra)		*Abandon*

Chocolade JACQUES - WINCOR NIXDORF

81.	BLANCHY Michael (Bel)		*Abandon*
82.	GADRET John (Fra)		*Abandon*
83.	CAPPELLE Andy (Bel)		*Abandon*
84.	STEVENS Christophe (Bel)		*Abandon*
85.	KOERTS Jans (Ned)		*Abandon*
87.	PEERS Chris (Bel)		*Abandon*
89.	ABAKOUMOV Igor (Bel)		*Abandon*
90.	LÖWIK Gerben (Ned)		*Abandon*

Mr BOOKMAKER.COM - PALMANS

91.	PLANCKAERT Jo (Bel)		*Abandon*
92.	LEMBO Eddy (Fra)	**10th**	+ 1'59"
93.	GABRIEL Frédéric (Fra)	**9th**	+ 1'56"
94.	KOEHLER Philippe (Fra)	12nd	+ 5'53"
95.	OMLOOP Geert (Bel)	**2nd**	+ 4"
96.	RENDERS Jens (Bel)		*Abandon*
98.	TROUVÉ Kristof (Bel)		*Abandon*

MICHE Components

101.	BESPALOV Alexandre (Rus)		*Abandon*
102.	CANESCHI Leonardo (Ita)		*Abandon*
103.	CARTA Maurizio (Ita)		*Abandon*
104.	TACCONI Alberto (Ita)		*Abandon*
109.	MARTELLA Massimiliano (Ita)		*Abandon*
110.	VARINI Maurizio (Ita)		*Abandon*

ICET

111.	BALESTRI Daniele (Ita)		*Abandon*
112.	BRANCHI Leonardo (Ita)		*Abandon*
113.	BOGGIA Stefano (Ita)		*Abandon*
114.	CIPOLLETTA Francesco (Ita)		*Abandon*
115.	DI BIASE Moreno (Ita)		*Abandon*
116.	GAYNITDINOV Dmitri (Rus)		*Abandon*
117.	KHALILOV Mikhaylo (Ukr)	**6th**	+ 16"
120.	GOLOUBEV Kirill (Rus)		*Abandon*

AMORE & VITA - BERETTA

121.	CIUFFI Stefano (Ita)		*Abandon*
122.	FANELLI Ivan (Ita)		*Abandon*
123.	BURROW Jamie (Gbr)		*Abandon*
124.	SOUTHAM Tom (Gbr)	20th	+ 7'15"
126.	PASSUELLO Domenico (Ita)		*Abandon*
127.	POMIETLO Michal (Pol)		*Abandon*
129.	KRZESZOWIEC Artur (Pol)		*Abandon*
130.	KUCHYNSKI Aleksandr (Blr)		*Abandon*

CAPEC

131.	BAZAYEV Assan (Kaz)		*Abandon*
132.	IGLINSKIY Maxim (Kaz)		*Abandon*
133.	BAIGUDINOV Kairat (Kaz)		*Abandon*
134.	MAMYROV Bakhtyiar (Kaz)		*Abandon*
136.	SHESTAKOV Viktor (Kaz)		*Abandon*
137.	DYMOVSHIKH Alexandr (Kaz)		*Abandon*

USA Espoirs

141.	MILNE Shawn (Usa)		*Abandon*
142.	KING Austin (Usa)		*Abandon*
143.	BOUCHARD-HALL Kevin (Usa)		*Abandon*
144.	VOIGT Michael (Usa)		*Abandon*
145.	FARRAR Tyler (Usa)		*Abandon*
146.	JANKOWIAK Dane (Usa)		*Abandon*
147.	FERGUSON Walker (Usa)		*Abandon*
148.	MITCHELL Nathan (Usa)		*Abandon*

RUSSIE

151.	SOKOLOV Evgueny (Rus)		*Abandon*
152.	VORGANOV Eduard (Rus)	21st	+ 7'15"
153.	PTCHELKIN Andrei (Rus)		*Abandon*
154.	PARAMONOV Roman (Rus)		*Abandon*
156.	TERENIN Ivan (Rus)		*Abandon*
157.	POLUKHIN Sergey (Rus)		*Abandon*
158.	KARPATCHEV Maxim (Rus)		*Abandon*

CLASSIFICATION

193,2 km

1.	**Stuart O'Grady (Aus)**	**COF**	**4h16'38"**
2.	**Geert Omloop (Bel)**	**MRB**	**+ 4"**
3.	**Bad Cooke (Aus)**	**FDJ**	**+ 16"**
4.	Franck Renier (Fra)	BLB	s.t
5.	Pierrick Fedrigo (Fra)	C.	
6.	Mikhaylo Khalilov (Ukr)	ICT	s.t
7.	David Moncoutié (Fra)	COF	s.t
8.	Thor Hushovd (Nor)	C.A	+ 1'56"
9.	Frédéric Gabriel (Fra)	MRB	s.t
10.	Eddy Lembo (Fra)	MRB	+ 1'59'

D-Day for Phonak

Out of the limelight since the start of the year- with the exception of the Tour de Romandie fought on its home ground- the Swiss team Phonak shot back onto the scene in the 14th Classique des Alpes which could well be the last edition...

Volontarily leaving out its leader Tyler Hamilton- who preferred to save himself for the Criterium du Dauphiné Liberé starting the following day, the Phonak team counted on a strong Spanish contingent for success in this 13th round of the Coupe de France. The choice was a good one. At the line in Aix-Les-Bains no less than four men wearing the yellow, white and green jerseys of the team were among the first ten finishers!

From the first of the six climbs of the day, the Swiss team sends José Enrique Gutierrez out as a scout. Accompanied by his compatriot Inigo Landaluze (Euskaltel), he does not manage to create a consequent lead and at the refreshment point in La Rivoire (km75) a group of ten riders takes the lead. Soon after, a now thinned out peloton closes up the gap. But the Col des Près (km99) redesigns the shape of the race; Just the same, it's J. E Gutierrez that reaches the summit of this little known but difficult pass in the lead. He precedes Egoi Martinez (Euskaltel), Ruslan Gryschenko (Landbouwkrediet) and Patrice halgand (Credit Agricole), the peloton being relegated at four minutes.

CSC in the chase

The Col de Plaimpalais (km 133) is an insurmountable obstacle for Martinez, Gryschenko and Halgand who let Gutierrez go it alone in front. But the Spaniard is still under the menace of the CSC team which is chasing furiously. Gutierrez conserves a slight lead at the summit of the Col de Revard, situated twenty kilometers from the line, but is caught by a group containing two of his team mates (Pereiro and Sevilla) as well as the Euskaltel riders Mayo and Landaluze, Botcharov (Credit agricole), Sastre (CSC) and Thomas Voeckler (La Boulangere). The latter has several attempts in the streets of Aix- Les-Bains but each time, another rider pulls back the Alsatian, victorious the week before in the Coupe de France. The sprint is launched at 400 metres and in a final effort Pereiro takes the win ahead of Mayo and the ever present Gutierrez. ■

91 Competitors

EUSKALTEL - EUSKADI

No.	Rider	Place	Time
1.	MAYO Iban (Esp)	**2nd**	s.t
2.	ALBIZU Joseba (Esp)		*Abandon*
3.	CAMAÑO Iker (Esp)	18th	+ 1'07"
4.	FLORES Iker (Esp)		*Abandon*
5.	ISASI Iñaki (Esp)		*Abandon*
6.	LANDALUZE Iñigo (Esp)	**7th**	s.t
7.	MARTINEZ de ESTEBAN Egoi (Esp)	29th	+ 8'44"
8.	SILLONIZ Josu (Esp)		*Abandon*

CSC

No.	Rider	Place	Time
11.	BASSO Ivan (Ita)		*Abandon*
12.	BARTOLI Michele (Ita)		*Abandon*
13.	CALVENTE Manuel (Esp)	28th	+ 8'42"
14.	JAKSCHE Jörg (Ger)		*Abandon*
15.	PERON Andrea (Ita)		Hors délais
16.	SASTRE Carlos (Esp)	**4th**	s.t
17.	SCHLECK Frank (Lux)		*Abandon*
18.	SØRENSEN Nicki (Den)		*Abandon*

PHONAK Hearing Systems

No.	Rider	Place	Time
21.	SEVILLA Oscar (Esp)	**6th**	s.t
22.	DESSEL Cyril (Fra)	**10th**	+ 1'07"
23.	GONZALEZ CAPILLA Santos (Esp)		*Abandon*
24.	GRABSCH Bert (Ger)		*Abandon*
25.	GUTIERREZ CATALUÑA José Enrique (Esp)	**3rd**	s.t
26.	JALABERT Nicolas (Fra)		*Abandon*
27.	PEREIRO Oscar (Esp)	**1st**	**4h 32'23"**
28.	TSCHOPP Johann (Sui)	22nd	+ 6'56"

COFIDIS

No.	Rider	Place	Time
31.	MILLAR David (Gbr)		*Abandon*
32.	BESSY Frédéric (Fra)	31st	+ 11'43"
33.	COYOT Arnaud (Fra)		*Abandon*
34.	EDALEINE Christophe (Fra)		*Abandon*
35.	MONCOUTIÉ David (Fra)	17th	+ 1'07"
36.	TOMBAK Janek (Est)		*Abandon*
37.	WHITE Matthew (Aus)	26th	+ 8'42"

LANDBOUWKREDIET - COLNAGO

No.	Rider	Place	Time
41.	POPOVYCH Yaroslav (Ukr)	16th	+ 1'07"
42.	ADVEYEV Serguey (Ukr)		*Abandon*
43.	BILEKA Volodymir (Ukr)		*Abandon*
46.	GASPERONI Cristian (Ita)	33rd	+ 11'48"
47.	GRYSCHENKO Ruslan (Ukr)	24th	+ 6'56"
48.	LAGUTIN Serguey (Uzb)		*Abandon*
50.	MONFORT Maxime (Bel)		*Abandon*

FDJEUX.COM

No.	Rider	Place	Time
51.	CASAR Sandy (Fra)		*Abandon*
52.	BICHOT Freddy (Fra)		*Abandon*
54.	GILBERT Philippe (Bel)	25th	+ 8'42"
55.	MENGIN Christophe (Fra)		*Abandon*
56.	ROBIN Jean-Cyril (Fra)	13rdrd	+ 1'07"
57.	ROY Jérémy (Fra)	34th	+ 13'15"
58.	VOGONDY Nicolas (Fra)	15th	+ 1'07"
59.	GUESDON Frédéric (Fra)		*Abandon*

DOMINA VACANZE

No.	Rider	Place	Time
61.	COLOMBO Gabriele (Ita)		*Abandon*
62.	GIUNTI Massimo (Ita)	12nd	+ 1'07"
63.	MORI Massimiliano (Ita)		*Abandon*
64.	SCARPONI Michele (Ita)		*Abandon*
65.	SIMEONI Filippo (Ita)	35th	+ 13'15"
66.	VALOTI Paolo (Ita)	**9th**	+ 1'07"

AG2R Prévoyance

No.	Rider	Place	Time
71.	GOUBERT Stéphane (Fra)	23rd	+ 6'56"
72.	ASTARLOZA Mikel (Esp)	19th	+ 4'55"
73.	CHAURREAU Iñigo (Esp)	30th	+ 11'43"
74.	DUMOULIN Samuel (Fra)		*Abandon*
75.	FLICKINGER Andy (Fra)		*Abandon*
76.	INAUDI Nicolas (Fra)		*Abandon*
77.	KRIVTSOV Yuriy (Ukr)	32nd	+ 11'43"
78.	PORTAL Nicolas (Fra)		*Abandon*

Brioches LA BOULANGÈRE

No.	Rider	Place	Time
81.	PINEAU Jérôme (Fra)		*Abandon*
82.	BENETEAU Walter (Fra)	21st	+ 6'56"
83.	GESLIN Anthony (Fra)		*Abandon*
84.	HARY Maryan (Fra)		*Abandon*
85.	LEFÈVRE Laurent (Fra)		*Abandon*
86.	PICHON Mickaël (Fra)		*Abandon*
87.	RENIER Franck (Fra)		*Abandon*
88.	VOECKLER Thomas (Fra)	**5th**	s.t

CRÉDIT AGRICOLE

No.	Rider	Place	Time
91.	HALGAND Patrice (Fra)		*Abandon*
92.	BOTCHAROV Alexandre	**8th**	s.t
93.	FEDRIGO Pierrick (Fra)	14th	+ 1'07"
94.	JOLY Sébastien (Fra)	20th	+ 6'56"
95.	LE MEVEL Christophe (Fra)		*Abandon*
96.	LEQUATRE Geoffroy (Fra)		*Abandon*
97.	MURAVYEV Dmitriy (Kaz)	11st	+ 1'07"
98.	SALMON Benoît (Fra)		*Abandon*

Chocolade JACQUES - WINCOR NIXDORF

No.	Rider	Place	Time
101.	ABAKOUMOV Igor (Bel)		*Abandon*
102.	ARANAGA Andoni (Esp)		*Abandon*
103.	ARDILA Mauricio (Col)		*Abandon*
104.	BRARD Florent (Fra)		*Abandon*
105.	GADRET John (Fra)		*Abandon*
106.	KOSTYUK Denis (Ukr)		*Abandon*
107.	RUDENKO Maxim (Ukr)		*Abandon*

RAGT Semences - MG ROVER

No.	Rider	Place	Time
111.	RINERO Christophe (Fra)		*Abandon*
112.	BOUVARD Gilles (Fra)		*Abandon*
113.	BUFFAZ Mickaël (Fra)		*Abandon*
114.	DION Renaud (Fra)		*Abandon*
115.	FINOT Frédéric (Fra)		*Abandon*
116.	LAURENT Christophe (Fra)		*Abandon*
117.	MARTIN Ludovic (Fra)		*Abandon*
119.	BOURQUENOUD Pierre (Sui)	27th	+ 8'42"

CLASSIFICATION

Chambéry/Aix les Bains - 165 km

1.	Oscar Pereiro (Esp)	PHO	4h32'23"
2.	Iban Mayo (Esp)	EUS	s.t
3.	J.Enrique Gutierrez (Esp)	PHO	s.t
4.	Carlos Sastre (Esp)	CSC	s.t
5.	Thomas Voeckler (Fra)	BLB	s.t
6.	Oscar Sevilla (Esp)	PHO	s.t
7.	Iñigo Landaluze (Esp)	EUS	s.t
8.	Alexandre Botcharov (Rus)	C.A	s.t
9.	Paolo Valoti (Ita)	DVE	+ 1'07"
10.	Cyril Dessel (Fra)	PHO	s.t

COUPE DE FRANCE RANKINGS AFTER 13 ROUNDS

1.	Thor Hushovd (Nor)	C.A	199 pts
2.	Pierrick Fedrigo (Fra)	C.A	102 pts
3.	Thomas Voeckler (Fra)	BLB	98 pts
4.	Franck Bouyer (Fra)	BLB	79 pts
5.	Anthony Geslin (Fra)	BLB	60 pts

CHAVANEL IN TRANSIT

The PolyNormandie has for a long time been one of the most respected Criteriums in France. Since last year, the race founded by Daniel Mangeas, the legendary commentator of the Tour de France, has become a road race. This year it became part of the Coupe de France series.

A rather strange two way sprint marks the Polynormandie the finish of which is always in the small town of St Martin de Landelles. The logical favourite in the sprint, Sylvain Chavanel seeming to push his adversary, the Italian Guido Trentin, who, it must be said, deviates in his trajectory. The act is finally of no consequence, the La Boulangere rider being obviously much stronger.

Coming to this race to get back into competition and to warm up for the Olympic Games where he will ride for the French national team, Sylvain Chavanel had taken a break after the Tour de France in which he is rarely able to ride for himself, being too occupied in defending the Yellow Jersey of his team mate Thomas Voeckler. Just the same, he's in the thick of it as soon as the first attack takes place. Eleven men- the only riders to finish the race in the time limit! – resist all attempts from the peloton to pull them back. A peloton which will soon implode. In the final part of the race, the Belgian Bjorn Leukemans (MrBookmaker.com) and last year's winner Jerome Pineau (La Boulangere) manage to pull away in front but are unable to resist the return of Christophe Oriol (AG2R), Sylvain Chavanel and Guido Trentin. In a position of strength, the riders from La Boulangere play their cards well. An attack by Trentin on one of the many gentle slopes of the race where the famous Cote de la Pigeonniere has a devastating effect is used by Sylvain Chavanel to take the lead in the company of the Italian rider for Cofidis. "Rincé" Oriol is unable to respond. It's therefore for the lone Leukemans to set off in persuit, the man who was in the leading group moments before! The Belgian must however admit defeat and watch Christophe Oriol pedal into the distance to take second place. As far as the victory is concerned it's Sylvain Chavanel who takes the honours. ■

96 Competitors

Brioches LA BOULANGÈRE			
1.	PINEAU Jérôme (Fra)	**5th**	+ 1'06"
2.	BENETEAU Walter (Fra)		*Abandon*
4.	CHAVANEL Sylvain (Fra)	**1st**	**3h40'34"**
5.	RENIER Franck (Fra)	**9th**	+ 3'54"
6.	ROUS Didier (Fra)	40th	+ 14'57"

AG2R Prévoyance			
11.	TURPIN Ludovic (Fra)	44th	+ 15'14"
12.	ORIOL Christophe (Fra)	**3rd**	+ 36"
13.	LAIDOUN Julien (Fra)	30th	+ 14'57"
14.	KRIVTSOV Yuriy (Ukr)	15th	+ 14'57"
15.	INAUDI Nicolas (Fra)	16th	+ 14'57"
16.	CHAURREAU Iñigo (Esp)	29th	+ 14'57"
17.	FLICKINGER Andy (Fra)	43rd	+ 15'06"

COFIDIS			
21.	ATIENZA Daniel (Esp)	38th	+ 14'57"
22.	FOFONOV Dmitriy (Kaz)		*Abandon*
23.	EDALEINE Christophe (Fra)	18th	+ 14'57"
24.	FERNANDEZ BUSTINZA Bingen (Esp)		*Abandon*
26.	MONCOUTIÉ David (Fra)		*Abandon*
28.	TRENTIN Guido (Ita)	**2nd**	s.t

CRÉDIT AGRICOLE			
31.	AUGÉ Stéphane (Fra)		*Abandon*
32.	FÉDRIGO Pierrick (Fra)	**8th**	+ 3'54"
33.	HALGAND Patrice (Fra)	19th	+ 14'57"
34.	LEBLACHER Eric (Fra)	**6th**	+ 1'46"
35.	LE MÉVEL Christophe (Fra)	**10th**	+ 4'10"
36.	BOTCHAROV Alexandre (Rus)	34th	+ 14'57"
37.	KAGGESTAD Mads (Nor)	31st	+ 14'57"
38.	SALMON Benoît (Fra)		*Abandon*

FDJEUX.COM			
41.	BICHOT Freddy (Fra)		*Abandon*
42.	CASAR Sandy (Fra)	23rd	+ 14'57"
43.	DEREPAS David (Fra)		*Abandon*
44.	ROBIN Jean-Cyril (Fra)	11st	+ 8'24"
45.	ROY Jérémy (Fra)	32nd	+ 14'57"
46.	VAUGRENARD Benoît (Fra)		*Abandon*
47.	VOGONDY Nicolas (Fra)	12nd	+ 14'57"
48.	LÖVKVIST Thomas (Swe)	46th	+ 15'14"

RAGT Semences - MG ROVER			
51.	AUGER Guillaume (Fra)	25th	+ 14'57"
52.	BOUVARD Gilles (Fra)		*Abandon*
53.	CALZATI Sylvain (Fra)		*Abandon*
54.	DULAC Nicolas (Fra)	33rd	+ 14'57"
55.	FINOT Frédéric (Fra)		*Abandon*
56.	MARTIN Ludovic (Fra)		*Abandon*
57.	RINERO Christophe (Fra)	22nd	+ 14'57"
58.	SEIGNEUR Eddy (Fra)		*Abandon*

AUBER 93			
61.	AUGER Ludovic (Fra)	42nd	+ 14'57"
62.	BRÉARD David (Fra)	13rd	+ 14'57"
63.	BROUZES Niels (Fra)		*Abandon*
64.	VALENTIN Tristan (Fra)	45th	+ 15'14"
65.	NILSSON John (Swe)	20th	+ 14'57"
66.	OLIVIER Lénaïc (Fra)		*Abandon*
67.	PAUMIER Laurent (Fra)		*Abandon*
68.	TALABARDON Yannick (Fra)	24th	+ 14'57"

FLANDERS - AFIN.COM			
71.	MASSCHELEIN Thierry (Bel)		*Abandon*
72.	GERMER Gregg (Usa)		*Abandon*
73.	LLOYD Daniel (Gbr)		*Abandon*
74.	COUTTS Alex (Gbr)	37th	+ 14'57"
75.	GALLAGHER Stephen (Irl)		*Abandon*
76.	LANDRIE Jurgen (Bel)	21st	+ 14'57"
77.	LEPRON Jérôme (Fra)		*Abandon*
78.	GUALANDI Alex (Ita)		*Abandon*

OKTOS - St QUENTIN			
82.	GOUROV Maxim (Kaz)		*Abandon*
83.	BOUCHER David (Fra)	17th	+ 14'57"
84.	MIZOUROV Andrei (Kaz)	28th	+ 14'57"
85.	RUSKYS Saulius (Ltu)		*Abandon*
86.	LEVECOT Benjamin (Fra)		*Abandon*
87.	BARTHE Stéphane (Fra)	36th	+ 14'57"
88.	LEMBO Eddy (Fra)		*Abandon*

Mr BOOKMAKER - PALMANS			
91.	COENEN Johan (Bel)	14th	+ 14'57"
92.	COMMEYNE Davy (Bel)		*Abandon*
93.	GABRIEL Frédéric (Fra)	**7th**	+ 2'12"
94.	KOEHLER Philippe (Fra)		*Abandon*
96.	LEUKEMANS Björn (Bel)	**4th**	+ 1'06"
97.	THIJS Erwin (Bel)	26th	+ 14'57"
98.	TROUVÉ Kristof (Bel)		*Abandon*

HSBC			
101.	BALL Jamie (Rsa)		*Abandon*
102.	ESCH Christopher (Rsa)		*Abandon*
103.	HOWES Jeff (Rsa)		*Abandon*
104.	McDONALD Neil (Rsa)		*Abandon*
105.	McLEOD Ian (Rsa)	27th	+ 14'57"
106.	PAVLOV Alex (Rsa)		*Abandon*
107.	SPENCE Daniel (Rsa)		*Abandon*
108.	WHITE Nicholas (Rsa)	39th	+ 14'57"

BRIDGESTONE - ANCHOR			
111.	TASHIRO Yasutaka (Jpn)		Abandon
112.	FUKUSHIMA Shinichi (Jpn)		Abandon
113.	FUKUSHIMA Koiji (Jpn)	41st	+ 14'57"
114.	MIZUTANI Takehiro (Jpn)		Abandon
115.	SANO Tomoya (Jpn)		Abandon
116.	MIYAZAKI Keisuke (Jpn)		*Abandon*
117.	SHIMIZU Yusuke (Jpn)		*Abandon*
118.	SHIMIZU Miyataka (Jpn)		*Abandon*

Equipe de France Elite 2			
121.	ROBIN Denis (Fra)		*Abandon*
122.	DELPECH Jean-Luc (Fra)		*Abandon*
123.	BOUQUET Camille (Fra)		*Abandon*
124.	COUTOULY Cédric (Fra)		*Abandon*
125.	DURET Sébastien (Fra)		*Abandon*
126.	MÉDÉREL Maxime (Fra)	35th	+ 14'57"
127.	RIBLON Christophe (Fra)		*Abandon*
128.	BOUCHET Jérôme (Fra)		*Abandon*

CLASSIFICATION

157 km

1.	Sylvain Chavanel (Fra)	BLB	3h40'34"
2.	Guido Trentin (Ita)	COF	s.t
3.	Christophe Oriol (Fra)	A2R	+ 36"
4.	Björn Leukemans (Bel)	MRB	+ 1'06"
5.	Jérôme Pineau (Fra)	BLB	s.t
6.	Eric Leblacher (Fra)	C.A	+ 1'46"
7.	Frédéric Gabriel (Fra)	MRB	+ 2'12"
8.	Pierrick Fedrigo (Fra)	C.A	+ 3'54"
9.	Franck Renier (Fra)	BLB	s.t
10.	Christophe Le Mével (Fra)	C.A	+ 4'10"
11.	Jean-Cyril Robin (Fra)	FDJ	+ 8'24"

N.B: All riders classified 11th and lower finished outside the time limit.

BOUCLES DE L'AULNE A CHATEAULIN
30th August

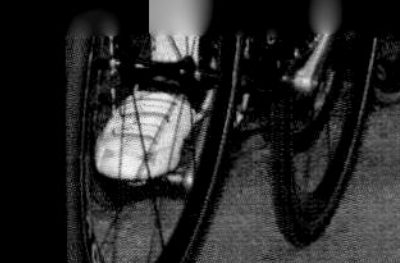

A SOLO FROM FINO

Run the day after the Grand Prix Ouest France in Plouay, the Boucles de l'Aulne de Chateaulin in the Finistere region smiled on Frederic Finot who permits his RAGT Semences team, out of the limelight till now, to take its first Coupe de France race.

For Frederic Finot and for his team, the season ends much better than it began.

In days gone by, a reputable criterium run the day after the World Championship (when they were run at the end of August),The Boucles de l'Aulne have become a road race on a course that is favourable to movement.

As often happens on such a course, a good attack comes very early on. Too soon perhaps for the interest of the race. There's no question however of blaming the riders of the thirteen teams involved in the attack. The gap between the breakaway group and the peloton soon becomes larger and it's obvious the winner will come from their number.

Among them, Frederic Finot notes that several others are much stronger than he on the multiple climbs at Stang ar Garront. He decides to try his chances 60 kilometers from the line. Behind, the others in the group are unable to work together so it's in small groups that they set up the chase; Alexandre Naulleau (La Boulangere) and Serhij Krushevskij (Oktos) almost make the grade but Frederic Finot is fuelled with the idea of winning a seventh event in his five year career.

Going to the very bottom of his reserves, the RAGT Semences rider keeps a lead of 27 seconds to take a hundred times merited win. ■

106 Competitors

No.	Rider	Place	Result
	Brioches LA BOULANGÈRE		
1.	BENETEAU Walter (Fra)		*Abandon*
2.	CHARTEAU Anthony (Fra)		*Abandon*
3.	LEFÈVRE Laurent (Fra)		*Abandon*
4.	NAULLEAU Alexandre (Fra)	**2nd**	+ 27"
5.	PINEAU Jérôme (Fra)		*Abandon*
6.	RENIER Franck (Fra)		*Abandon*
7.	ROUS Didier (Fra)		*Abandon*
8.	SPRICK Mathieu (Fra)		*Abandon*
	FDJEUX.COM		
11.	GILBERT Philippe (Bel)		*Abandon*
12.	CASAR Sandy (Fra)		*Abandon*
13.	DEREPAS David (Fra)	17th	+ 9'35"
14.	RENSHAW Mark (Aus)		*Abandon*
15.	MENGIN Christophe (Fra)	25th	+ 9'44"
16.	MOUREY Francis (Fra)	15th	+ 9'02"
17.	VAUGRENARD Benoît (Fra)		*Abandon*
18.	VOGONDY Nicolas (Fra)		*Abandon*
	COFIDIS		
21.	BESSY Frédéric (Fra)		*Abandon*
22.	CASPER Jimmy (Fra)		*Abandon*
23.	COYOT Arnaud (Fra)	**9th**	+ 3'02"
24.	EDALEINE Christophe (Fra)		*Abandon*
25.	ENGOULVENT Jimmy (Fra)		*Abandon*
26.	MONIER Damien (Fra)		*Abandon*
27.	FOFONOV Dmitriy (Kaz)		*Abandon*
	CRÉDIT AGRICOLE		
31.	AUGÉ Stéphane (Fra)		*Abandon*
32.	FEDRIGO Pierrick (Fra)		*Abandon*
33.	HALGAND Patrice (Fra)	11st	+ 7'29"
34.	HINAULT Sébastien (Fra)		*Abandon*
35.	JOLY Sébastien (Fra)	26th	+ 9'44"
36.	POILVET Benoît (Fra)		*Abandon*
37.	MURAVYEV Dmitriy (Kaz)		*Abandon*
38.	SALMON Benoît (Fra)		*Abandon*
	RAGT Semences - MG ROVER		
41.	LUHOVYY Roman (Ukr)		*Abandon*
42.	BERTHOU Eric (Fra)		*Abandon*
43.	REYNAUD Nicolas (Fra)		*Abandon*
44.	BUFFAZ Mickaël (Fra)		*Abandon*
46.	FINOT Frédéric (Fra)	**1st**	**4h19'47"**
47.	RINERO Christophe (Fra)		*Abandon*
	AG2R Prévoyance		
51.	AGNOLUTTO Christophe (Fra)		*Abandon*
52.	INAUDI Nicolas (Fra)		*Abandon*
53.	KRIVTSOV Yuriy (Ukr)		*Abandon*
54.	PORTAL Nicolas (Fra)		*Abandon*
55.	ORIOL Christophe (Fra)	**10th**	+ 3'04"
	Chocolade JACQUES - WINCOR NIXDORF		
61.	ARANAGA Andoni (Esp)	14th	+ 8'58"
62.	ARDILA Mauricio (Col)		*Abandon*
63.	BRARD Florent (Fra)	13rd	+ 8'47"
64.	GADRET John (Fra)		*Abandon*
65.	KOSTYUK Denis (Ukr)		*Abandon*
66.	RUDENKO Maxim (Ukr)		*Abandon*
67.	PIATEK Zbigniew (Pol)		*Abandon*
68.	VERHEYEN Geert (Bel)	23rd	+ 9'44"
	Mr BOOKMAKER - PALMANS		
71.	CASTRESANA Angel (Esp)	**6th**	+ 51"
72.	COENEN Johan (Bel)		*Abandon*
73.	GABRIEL Frédéric (Fra)	27th	+ 9'44"
76.	RENDERS Jens (Bel)		*Abandon*
77.	VAN DE WOUWER Kurt (Bel)		*Abandon*
	L.A - PECOL		
81.	BRU Jon (Esp)		*Abandon*
82.	OARBEASKOA Ruben (Esp)		*Abandon*
83.	ARROYO David (Esp)		*Abandon*
84.	ANDRADE OLIVEIRA Pedro (Por)		*Abandon*
85.	GARCIA da PEÑA David (Esp)	**7th**	+ 51"
86.	RIBEIRO Nuno (Por)		*Abandon*
87.	PINHEIRO Luis (Por)		*Abandon*
88.	BARBOSA Candido (Por)	21st	+ 9'44"
	LOKOMOTIV		
91.	KLIMOV Serguei (Rus)		*Abandon*
92.	BRUTT Pavel (Rus)		*Abandon*
93.	SEROV Alexandre (Rus)		*Abandon*
94.	ESKOV Nikita (Rus)		*Abandon*
95.	TROUSSOV Nikolai (Rus)		*Abandon*
96.	IGNATIEV Mikhail (Rus)		*Abandon*
97.	MINDLIN Anton (Rus)	18th	+ 9'35"
98.	AVERIN Maxim (Rus)		*Abandon*
	AUBER 93		
101.	AUGER Ludovic (Fra)	**8th**	+ 53"
102.	BRÉARD David (Fra)		*Abandon*
103.	BROUZES Niels (Fra)		*Abandon*
104.	TALABARDON Yannick (Fra)		*Abandon*
105.	NILSSON John (Swe)		*Abandon*
106.	OLIVIER Lénaïc (Fra)		*Abandon*
107.	PAUMIER Laurent (Fra)		*Abandon*
	OKTOS		
111.	BARTHE Stéphane (Fra)		*Abandon*
113.	LEVECOT Benjamin (Fra)		*Abandon*
115.	KRUSHEVSKIY Sergey (Uzb)	**3rd**	+ 27"
116.	LEMBO Eddy (Fra)		*Abandon*
117.	MIZOUROV Andrey (Kaz)	22nd	+ 9'44"
118.	RUSKYS Saulius (Ltu)		*Abandon*
	AMORE & VITA - BERETTA		
121.	CARLSTRÖM Kjell (Fin)		*Abandon*
122.	POMIETLO Michal (Pol)		*Abandon*
123.	KRZESZOWIEC Artur (Pol)	20th	+ 9'44"
124.	GRÖNQVIST Anders (Swe)		*Abandon*
125.	LJUNGBLAD Jonas (Swe)	**4th**	+ 51"
126.	MROZ Mateusz (Pol)		*Abandon*
127.	PASSUELLO Domenico (Ita)	19th	+ 9'43"
128.	SOUTHAM Tom (Gbr)	12nd	+ 7'29"
	CAPEC		
131.	IGLINSKIY Maxim (Kaz)	**5th**	+ 51"
132.	BAZAYEV Assan (Kaz)		*Abandon*
133.	MAMYROV Bakhtyiar (Kaz)	24th	+ 9'44"
134.	DYMOVSHIKH Alexandr (Kaz)		*Abandon*
135.	MEDYANNIKOV Andrey (Kaz)		*Abandon*
136.	BAIGUDINOV Kairat (Kaz)		*Abandon*
	Russian team		
141.	KARPACHEV Maxim (Rus)	29th	+ 9'47"
142.	TERENIN Ivan (Rus)	16th	+ 9'02"
143.	PTCHELKIN Andrei (Rus)		*Abandon*
144.	KHATUNTSEV Vasily (Rus)		*Abandon*
145.	SOKOLOV Evgueni (Rus)		*Abandon*
146.	KUZOVKIN Alexey (Rus)		*Abandon*
147.	VORGANOV Eduard (Rus)		*Abandon*
148.	POLUKHIN Sergey (Rus)	28th	+ 9'44"

LUDOVIC CAPELLE AS FINISHER

Frederic Guesdon must once again settle for second best in the GP d'Isbergues, this industrial town between Bethune and Hazebrouck.

Already placed three times in the top five of the race, the rider from Brittany pulled away from an attacking group two kilometers from the line. But when he saw the reaction of Wallon rider Ludovic Capelle, the fastest rider of the group, his morale took a dive.

Out of a group of fifteen riders, who, as well as the afore mentioned duo, comprised, JP Simon(Landbouwkrediet), S. Joly (Credit Agricole), S. Krushevskij (Oktos), Y. Gene and R. Martias, the two riders from La Boulangere, V. Van der Kooij (Bankgiroloterij),C. Zamana (Chocolat Jaques), Y. Talabardon (Auber 93), N. Roche (Cofidis), T. Eltink (Rabobank), J. Renders (Mr Bookmaker), J. Valach (Ed'System) and P. Mertens (Vlaanderen- T Interim), the two last attackers of the day could take the two first places. Their ex companions tried the same operation but failed, as did Rony Martias, victim of a crash on a bend just as he looked like making his mark.
As is often the case, the GP d'Isbergues smiles on the rider who isn't afraid to take the initiative from the start. After almost being caught by the peloton (coming back to less than ten seconds at the 35th kilometre) the fifteen attackers open up a lead (eight minutes at the mid way point) insufficient though to discourage the chasers. They had reduced the lead by two thirds by the time they arrived at the circuit of eight kilometers to be completed twice. Always efficient despite the rigors of the day, the leading group ensured the essentials... before tearing itself apart when victory was sure to come to its number. But not yet the man! ■

125 Competitors

Chocolade JACQUES - WINCOR NIXDORF

No.	Rider	Place	Time
1.	KOERTS Jans (Ned)		*Abandon*
2.	HIEMSTRA Bert (Ned)	58th	+ 1'15"
3.	BRARD Florent (Fra)	44th	+ 1'15"
4.	GADRET John (Fra)	45th	+ 1'15"
5.	LÖWIK Gerben (Ned)	52nd	+ 1'15"
6.	REINERINK Rik (Ned)	70th	+ 1'28"
7.	ZAMANA Cezary (Pol)	**3rd**	s.t
8.	VERHEYEN Geert (Bel)	64th	+ 1'15"

AG2R Prévoyance

No.	Rider	Place	Time
11.	BROCHARD Laurent (Fra)	14th	+ 54"
12.	AGNOLUTTO Christophe (Fra)	40th	+ 1'15"
13.	GERRANS Simon (Aus)		*Abandon*
14.	KIRSIPUU Jaan (Est)	28th	+ 1'15"
15.	NAZON Jean-Patrick (Fra)		*Abandon*
16.	PAURIOL Rémy (Fra)		*Abandon*

BANKGIROLOTERIJ

No.	Rider	Place	Time
23.	BAK Lars Ytting (Den)	51st	+ 1'15"
24.	PETERSEN Jørgen Bo (Den)		*Abandon*
25.	KEMNA Rudi (Ned)	25th	+ 1'15"
26.	VAN DER KOOIJ Vincent (Ned)		*Abandon*
27.	SMINK Julien (Ned)	57th	+ 1'15"
28.	VAN KATWIJK Alain (Ned)		*Abandon*

Brioches LA BOULANGÈRE

No.	Rider	Place	Time
31.	NAULLEAU Alexandre (Fra)		*Abandon*
33.	CHAVANEL Sébastien (Fra)		*Abandon*
34.	GENE Yohann (Fra)	12nd	+ 24"
35.	GESLIN Anthony (Fra)	30th	+ 1'15"
36.	PINEAU Jérôme (Fra)		*Abandon*
37.	MARTIAS Rony (Fra)	**5th**	s.t
38.	RENIER Franck (Fra)	16th	+ 38"

COFIDIS

No.	Rider	Place	Time
41.	MONCOUTIÉ David (Fra)	55th	+ 1'15"
42.	BESSY Frédéric (Fra)	72nd	+ 6'39"
43.	CABRERA Alexandre (Fra)	29th	+ 1'15"
44.	CASPER Jimmy (Fra)	38th	+ 1'15"
45.	ENGOULVENT Jimmy (Fra)	18th	+ 54"
47.	FARAZIJN Peter (Bel)	49th	+ 1'15"
48.	ROCHE Nicolas (Irl)	**10th**	s.t

CRÉDIT AGRICOLE

No.	Rider	Place	Time
51.	HUSHOVD Thor (Nor)		*Abandon*
52.	DEAN Julian (Nzl)		*Abandon*
53.	FEDRIGO Pierrick (Fra)		*Abandon*
54.	HINAULT Sébastien (Fra)		*Abandon*
55.	JOLY Sébastien (Fra)	11st	s.t
56.	KAGGESTAD Mads (Nor)		*Abandon*
57.	NAZON Damien (Fra)		*Abandon*
58.	POILVET Benoît (Fra)		*Abandon*

FDJEUX.COM

No.	Rider	Place	Time
61.	COOKE Baden (Aus)	24th	+ 1'15"
62.	EISEL Bernhard (Aut)		*Abandon*
63.	DA CRUZ Carlos (Fra)	15th	+ 54"
64.	GILBERT Philippe (Bel)	23rd	+ 1'15"
65.	GUESDON Frédéric (Fra)	**2nd**	s.t
66.	ROY Jérémy (Fra)	74th	+ 6'39"
67.	VAUGRENARD Benoît (Fra)	56th	+ 1'15"
68.	VOGONDY Nicolas (Fra)	61st	+ 1'15"

LANDBOUWKREDIET - COLNAGO

No.	Rider	Place	Time
71.	CAPELLE Ludovic (Bel)	**1st**	**4h45'36"**
72.	BRACKE Tony (Bel)	76th	+ 11'58"
73.	DE WAELE Bert (Bel)	50th	+ 1'15"
74.	SIMON Jean-Paul (Bel)	13rd	+ 42"
75.	VAN LOOCKE Jurgen (Bel)		*Abandon*
76.	SIJMENS Nico (Bel)		*Abandon*
77.	TIMOCHINE Mikhail (Rus)	31st	+ 1'15"
78.	VAN BONDT Geert (Bel)	26th	+ 1'15"

LOTTO - DOMO

No.	Rider	Place	Time
81.	VAN PETEGEM Peter (Bel)	69th	+ 1'25"
82.	BAGUET Serge (Bel)	68th	+ 1'25"
83.	DE CLERCQ Hans (Bel)	20th	+ 54"
84.	EECKHOUT Nico (Bel)		*Abandon*
85.	MARICHAL Thierry (Bel)		*Abandon*
86.	MOERENHOUT Koos (Ned)	47th	+ 1'15"

RAGT Semences - MG ROVER

No.	Rider	Place	Time
91.	CALZATI Sylvain (Fra)	19th	+ 54"
92.	BOURQUENOUD Pierre (Sui)	53rd	+ 1'15"
93.	DION Renaud (Fra)	34th	+ 1'15"
94.	DULAC Nicolas (Fra)		*Abandon*
95.	DUPONT Hubert (Fra)		*Abandon*
98.	RINERO Christophe (Fra)	62nd	+ 1'15"

Mr BOOKMAKER - PALMANS

No.	Rider	Place	Time
111.	HAMMOND Roger (Gbr)	59th	+ 1'15"
112.	COENEN Johan (Bel)	60th	+ 1'15"
113.	RENDERS Jens (Bel)	**7th**	s.t
114.	GABRIEL Frédéric (Fra)	36th	+ 1'15"
115.	HUNT Jeremy (Gbr)	22nd	+ 54"
116.	VANDENBROUCKE Frank (Bel)	65th	+ 1'15"
117.	HABEAUX Grégory (Bel)	75th	+ 6'44"
118.	WUYTS Peter (Bel)	54th	+ 1'15"

VLAANDEREN - T INTERIM

No.	Rider	Place	Time
121.	DEMEYERE Geoffrey (Bel)	71st	+ 1'34"
122.	PEETERS Jef (Bel)	66th	+ 1'15"
123.	DE SCHROODER Benny (Bel)		*Abandon*
124.	KLEYNEN Steven (Bel)	42nd	+ 1'15"
125.	VEUCHELEN Frederik (Bel)	46th	+ 1'15"
126.	MERTENS Pieter (Bel)	**6th**	s.t
127.	WILLEMS Frederik (Bel)		*Abandon*
128.	VAN HUFFEL Wim (Bel)	67th	+ 1'15"

AUBER 93

No.	Rider	Place	Time
131.	AUGER Ludovic (Fra)		*Abandon*
132.	BRÉARD David (Fra)	48th	+ 1'15"
133.	BROUZES Niels (Fra)		*Abandon*
134.	LAMOULLER Loïc (Fra)		*Abandon*
135.	NILSSON John (Swe)	41st	+ 1'15"
136.	OLIVIER Lénaïc (Fra)	33rd	+ 1'15"
137.	PAUMIER Laurent (Fra)		*Abandon*
138.	TALABARDON Yannick (Fra)	**8th**	s.t

FLANDERS - AFIN.COM

No.	Rider	Place	Time
141.	LEPRON Jérôme (Fra)		*Abandon*
142.	CORNELISSEN Björn (Ned)	77th	+ 11'58"
143.	COUTTS Alex (Gbr)		*Abandon*
144.	LANDRIE Jurgen (Bel)		*Abandon*
145.	LLOYD Daniel (Gbr)		*Abandon*
146.	MASSCHELEIN Thierry (Bel)		*Abandon*
147.	GERMER Gregg (Usa)		*Abandon*
148.	SCHEIRLINCKX Bert (Bel)	21st	+ 54"

OKTOS

No.	Rider	Place	Time
151.	BARTHE Stéphane (Fra)	63rd	+ 1'15"
152.	BOUCHER David (Fra)	43rd	+ 1'15"
153.	RUSKYS Saulius (Ltu)	27th	+ 1'15"
154.	GUROV Maxim (Kaz)		*Abandon*
155.	KRUSHEVSKIY Serhiy (Uzb)	**4th**	s.t
156.	LEMBO Eddy (Fra)		*Abandon*
157.	LEVECOT Benjamin (Fra)		*Abandon*
158.	MIZOUROV Andrei (Kaz)	17th	+ 54"

RABOBANK Espoirs

No.	Rider	Place	Time
161.	BOOM Lars (Ned)		*Abandon*
162.	DE MAAR Mark (Ned)	37th	+ 1'15"
163.	ELTINK Theo (Ned)		*Abandon*
164.	GILING Bastiaan (Ned)	32nd	+ 1'15"
165.	KOHL Bernhard (Aut)	39th	+ 1'15"
166.	PAUWELS Serge (Bel)	35th	+ 1'15"
167.	STAMSNIJDER Tom (Ned)		*Abandon*
168.	VASTARANTA Jukka (Fin)	73rd	+ 6'39"

eD' SYSTEM - ZVVZ

No.	Rider	Place	Time
171.	BRONIS Roman (Svk)		*Abandon*
172.	KUPKA David (Cze)		*Abandon*
174.	PRECECHTEL Michal (Cze)		*Abandon*
175.	TESAR Lubos (Cze)		*Abandon*
176.	VALACH Jan (Svk)	**9th**	s.t
177.	VANA Jindrich (Cze)		*Abandon*
178.	ZERZAN Pavel (Cze)		*Abandon*

PHOTO FINISH FOR THE END

Only a few millimetres prevented a Swiss rider from taking for the second time the Paris -(Gien) - Bourges, the final round of the Coupe de France. Beaten by Jerome Pineau, Martin Elmiger was unable to imitate his compatriot Niki Rutimann, winner 19 years earlier!

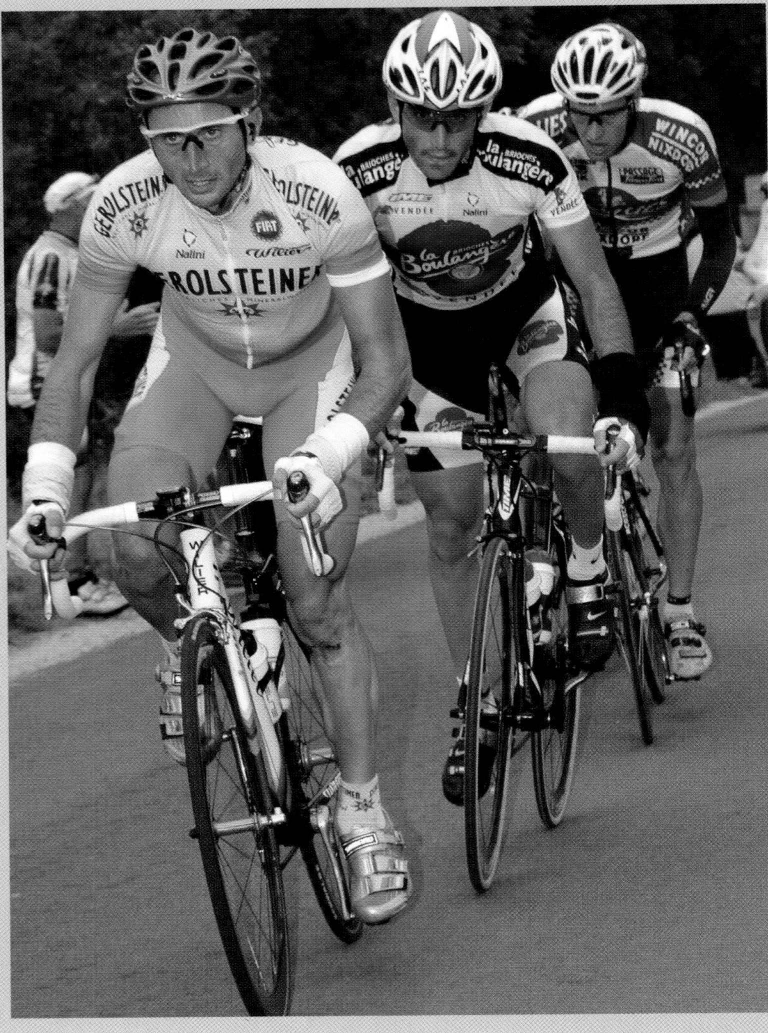

Jerome Pineau, cloely watching Davide Rebellin, on the climb at Chavignol, a strategic point in the race.

After crossing the line, Jerome Pineau complains about his tyres: "Impossible to win a sprint on these tyres designed for dry weather" he shouted. It's a few seconds before the voice of the commentator informs him that he has won the race after the judges had studied the photo. His bitterness then changes to an explosion of joy. The rider from Nantes declared "Of course, it was only a Coupe de France race, I'd really prefer a podium on the Paris – Tours next week. But to win ahead of riders like Rebellin, Jaksche and company somehow reassures me"

Despite sliding down the calendar in recent years, the event took place the week before the World Championship- the list of starters contained a few well known names. Davide Rebellin, Jorg Jaksche and also Cedric Vasseur, Leon van Bonand Jerome Pineau. These were the favourites whose names would come up in all the conversations. Beginning in clement weather, the race gets underway briskly. An attack by no less than 22 riders (among them Davide Rebellin, accompanied by three team mates) holds out for about fifteen kilometers before being caught. 48 kilometers are covered in the first hour! And the pace will not drop throughout the afternoon, despite the Sancerre hills in the second part of the race. It's one of these hills, (at Jars situated at km101) which will see the start of the breakaway from which will come the eventual winner in Bourges two hours later. An attack from Jerome Pineau initiates the breakaway. Seven men (his team mate M. Hary, D.Rebellin, C. Vasseur, M. Elmiger, N. Fritsch, J. Jaksche and J. Van de Walle) follow him and take off. The damage is done. For a long time trailing at 1 min 30 sec, the counter attack led by one time winner, Florent Brard burns itself out and the leading group enters Bourges with a comfortable lead of four minutes. The circuit through the town does not encourage the riders to try for a sprint: except for the Belgian Jurgen van de Walle. A too timid effort which only serves to leave Nicolas fritsch behind. Reputedly the two quickest men in the group, the Swiss Martin Elmiger and Jerome Pineau launch hostilities in the final 300 metres on a road surface soaked by the rain which has fallen since the Cote de Chavignol (km 138). For a long time dominated by the Phonak rider, the daggers drawn sprint turns in the favour of Jerome Pineau at the line. All this was too close to judge with the naked eye. This victory by the rider from Brioches la Boulangere, made leader of the French team at the recent World Championship, permits him to take third place in the Coupe de France, won as predicted by Thor Hushovd who was not present in the centre of France... ■

After the questions, the relief. Jerome Pineau gets the good news, he's declared winner of the 54th Paris- Bourges.

157.	DAY Ben (Aus)	53rd	+ 8'21"
158.	WUYTS Peter (Bel)		*Abandon*

EX WINNERS TAKING THE START — 4

JOHANSEN Allan (Den)	2002
BRARD Florent (Fra)	2001
HOFFMAN Tristan (Ned)	1996
MICHAELSEN Lars (Den)	1994

3 OLDEST

PIATEK Zbigniew	38 years (1966/05/01)
KEMNA Rudi	37 years (1967/10/05)
ZAMANA Cezary	36 years (1967/11/14)

3 YOUNGEST

AVERIN Maxim	18 years (1985/11/28)
MINDLIN Anton	19 years (1985/07/09)
TROUSSOV Nikolai	19 years (1985/07/02)

NATIONALITIES REPRESENTED — 23

France	48
Belgium	12
Netherlands	11
Russia	10
Denmark	6
Germany, Switzerland	5
Australia	3
Austria, Colombia, Estonia, Italy, Kazakstan and Poland	2
Belarus, Spain, Great Britain, Lithuania, Luxembourg, Slovenia, Sweden, Ukraine et Ouzbekistan	1

CLASSIFICATION

1.	**Jérôme Pineau (Fra) (moy ne: 46,7 km/h)**	**BLB**	**196,5 km**	**4h 12'28"**
2.	Martin Elmiger (Sui)	PHO		s.t
3.	Davide Rebellin (Ita)	GST		s.t
4.	Cédric Vasseur (Fra)	COF		s.t
5.	Jörg Jaksche (Ger)	CSC		+ 2"
6.	Jurgen van de Walle (Bel)	CHO		s.t
7.	Nicolas Fritsch (Fra)	FDJ		+ 5"
8.	Vladimir Goussev (Rus)	CSC		+ 5'01"
9.	Michael Albasini (Sui)	PHO		s.t
10.	Alexandre Botcharov (Rus)	C.A		s.t

121 Competitors

CRÉDIT AGRICOLE

1.	HERVÉ Cédric (Fra)		*Abandon*
2.	HALGAND Patrice (Fra)		*Abandon*
3.	BOTCHAROV Alexandre (Rus)	**10th**	+ 5'01"
4.	HINAULT Sébastien (Fra)		*Abandon*
5.	LE MEVEL Christophe (Fra)		*Abandon*
6.	JOLY Sébastien (Fra)		*Abandon*
7.	LEQUATRE Geoffroy (Fra)		*Abandon*
8.	LEBLACHER Eric (Fra)		*Abandon*

Brioches LA BOULANGÈRE

11.	BENETEAU Walter (Fra)		*Abandon*
12.	MARTIAS Rony (Fra)		*Abandon*
13.	SPRICK Mathieu (Fra)	68th	+ 8'21"
14.	GESLIN Anthony (Fra)	56th	+ 8'21"
15.	HARY Maryan (Fra)	15th	+ 5'16"
16.	KERN Christophe (Fra)	57th	+ 8'21"
17.	PINEAU Jérôme (Fra)	**1st**	**4h 12'18"**
18.	RENIER Franck (Fra)		*Abandon*

FDJEUX.COM

21.	BICHOT Freddy (Fra)		*Abandon*
22.	COOKE Baden (Aus)	48th	+ 8'21"
23.	DA CRUZ Carlos (Fra)	25th	+ 8'02"
24.	MENGIN Christophe (Fra)		*Abandon*
25.	FRITSCH Nicolas (Fra)	**7th**	+ 5"
26.	GILBERT Philippe (Bel)	28th	+ 8'02"
27.	GUESDON Frédéric (Fra)	45th	+ 8'21"
28.	VOGONDY Nicolas (Fra)	46th	+ 8'21"

COFIDIS

31.	CASPER Jimmy (Fra)		*Abandon*
32.	BESSY Frédéric (Fra)	66th	+ 8'21"
33.	FERNANDEZ BUSTINZA Bingen (Esp)	71st	+ 8'21"
34.	EDALEINE Christophe (Fra)	72nd	+ 8'21"
35.	ENGOULVENT Jimmy (Fra)		*Abandon*
36.	FARAZIJN Peter (Bel)	14th	+ 5'16"
37.	MONCOUTIÉ David (Fra)		Abandon
38.	VASSEUR Cédric (Fra)	**4th**	s.t

AG2R Prévoyance

41.	KIRSIPUU Jaan (Est)	51st	+ 8'21"
42.	NAZON Jean-Patrick (Fra)		*Abandon*
43.	ORIOL Christophe (Fra)		*Abandon*
44.	PORTAL Nicolas (Fra)		*Abandon*
45.	PÜTSEP Erki (Est)	73rd	+ 8'33"
46.	GERRANS Simon (Aus)	33rd	+ 8'02"
47.	PAURIOL Rémy (Fra)	31st	+ 8'02"

RAGT Semences - MG ROVER

51.	DION Renaud (Fra)		*Abandon*
52.	AUGER Guillaume (Fra)		*Abandon*
53.	BERTHOU Eric (Fra)	36th	+ 8'02"
55.	DULAC Nicolas (Fra)		*Abandon*
56.	FINOT Frédéric (Fra)		*Abandon*
57.	RINERO Christophe (Fra)	26th	+ 8'02"
58.	SEIGNEUR Eddy (Fra)		*Abandon*

OKTOS

61.	BARTHE Stéphane (Fra)		*Abandon*
62.	BOUCHER David (Fra)	27th	+ 8'02"
63.	GUROV Maxim (Kaz)	38th	+ 8'02"
64.	KRUSHEVSKIY Sergey (Uzb)	44th	+ 8'21"
66.	LEVECOT Benjamin (Fra)	HD	
67.	MIZOUROV Andrei (Kaz)	40th	+ 8'21"
68.	RUSKYS Saulius (Ltu)	HD	

AUBER 93

72.	BRÉARD David (Fra)	42nd	+ 8'21"
73.	BROUZES Niels (Fra)		*Abandon*
75.	NILSSON John (Swe)	21st	+ 8'02"
77.	PAUMIER Laurent (Fra)	32nd	+ 8'02"
78.	TALABARDON Yannick (Fra)	55th	+ 8'21"

GEROLSTEINER

81.	FÖRSTER Robert (Ger)	24th	+ 8'02"
82.	FOTHEN Markus (Ger)	39th	+ 8'02"
83.	HARDTER Uwe (Ger)	41st	+ 8'21"
84.	HASELBACHER René (Aut)		*Abandon*
85.	SERPELLINI Marco (Ita)	67th	+ 8'21"
86.	REBELLIN Davide (Ita)	**3rd**	s.t
87.	ZIEGLER Thomas (Ger)	59th	+ 8'21"
88.	WROLICH Peter (Aut)		*Abandon*

PHONAK

91.	ALBASINI Michael (Sui)	**9th**	+ 5'01"
92.	DESSEL Cyril (Fra)	60th	+8'21"
93.	ELMIGER Martin (Sui)	**2nd**	s.t
94.	AEBERSOLD Niki (Sui)		*Abandon*
95.	MURN Uros (Slo)	12nd	+ 5'16"
96.	RAST Gregory (Sui)	70th	+ 8'21"
97.	URWEIDER Sascha (Sui)	52nd	+ 8'21"
98.	USOV Alexandre (Blr)	61st	+ 8'21"

Chocolade JACQUES - WINCOR NIXDORF

101.	ARDILA Mauricio (Col)	50th	+ 8'21"
102.	BRARD Florent (Fra)	11st	+ 5'04"
103.	PIATEK Zbigniew (Pol)	22nd	+ 8'02"
104.	LÖWIK Gerben (Ned)		*Abandon*
105.	ZAMANA Cezary (Pol)	23rd	+ 8'02"
106.	VAN DE WALLE Jurgen (Bel)	**6th**	+ 2"
107.	KOSTYUK Denis (Ukr)	30th	+ 8'02"
108.	DUQUE Leonardo (Col)	54th	+ 8'21"

CSC

111.	VANDBØRG Brian (Den)	62nd	+ 8'21"
112.	HØJ Frank (Den)	65th	+ 8'21"
113.	MICHAELSEN Lars (Den)	17th	+ 8'02"
114.	BRUUN ERIKSEN Thomas (Den)		*Abandon*
115.	HOFFMAN Tristan (Ned)	64th	+ 8'21"
116.	GOUSSEV Vladimir (Rus)	**8th**	+ 5'01"
117.	SCHLECK Andy (Lux)	63rd	+ 8'21"
118.	JAKSCHE Jörg (Ger)	**5th**	+ 2"

LOTTO - DOMO

121.	BRANDT Christophe (Bel)	13rd	+ 5'16"
122.	VAN BON Leon (Ned)	69th	+ 8'21"
124.	GARDEYN Gorik (Bel)		*Abandon*
125.	STEEGMANS Geert (Bel)	20th	+ 8'02"
126.	VAN DIJK Stefan (Ned)	16th	+ 8'02"
127.	VAN IMPE Kevin (Bel)	58th	+ 8'21"
128.	VIERHOUTEN Aart (Ned)	18th	+ 8'02"

BANKGIROLOTERIJ

131.	BAK Lars Ytting (Den)		*Abandon*
132.	BOS Marco (Ned)		*Abandon*
133.	TEN DAM Laurens (Ned)		*Abandon*
134.	VAN DULMEN Frank (Ned)		*Abandon*
135.	JOHANSEN Allan (Den)		*Abandon*
136.	KEMNA Rudi (Ned)		*Abandon*
137.	PRONK Matthé (Ned)	49th	+ 8'21"
138.	VAN DER VEN Remco (Ned)	34th	+ 8'02"

LOKOMOTIV

141.	KLIMOV Serguei (Rus)	35th	+ 8'02"
142.	BRUTT Pavel (Rus)	29th	+ 8'02"
143.	AVERIN Maxim (Rus)		*Abandon*
144.	TROUSSOV Nikolai (Rus)		*Abandon*
145.	IGNATIEV Mikhail (Rus)		*Abandon*
146.	MINDLIN Anton (Rus)		*Abandon*
147.	SEROV Alexandre (Rus)		*Abandon*
148.	RODIONOV Oleg (Rus)		*Abandon*

Mr BOOKMAKER - PALMANS

151.	GABRIEL Frédéric (Fra)	43rd	+ 8'21"
152.	RENDERS Jens (Bel)	37th	+ 8'02"
153.	HUNT Jeremy (Gbr)		*Abandon*
154.	THIJS Erwin (Bel)	47th	+ 8'21"
155.	DUYCK Pieter (Bel)		*Abandon*
156.	DE SMET Andy (Bel)	19th	+ 8'02"

Jorg Jaksche (followed here by Rebellin and Van de Walle) also took part in the vital breakaway.

From the unknown to... Tom Steels

From France to Spain, from Italy to Switzerland, in Germany or in Holland, the title of National Champion in road racing went to a rider, until now, unknown to the podium. The exception to the rule was Belgium on this rather special day: for the fourth time it was Tom Steels who took the crown, at the same time beating the record held until now by a certain Rik van Steenbergen...

Tom Steels has always had the habit of celebrating success by shouting with joy, whether it be in the Tour de France or elsewhere. As he crossed the line to take the win in Tessenderlo, his shout was louder than ever, perhaps as a way of evacuating once and for all, the injuries, moral and physical, accumulated over recent seasons. "This title has come as deliverance for me, and I'm touching wood as I say that" said Steels after the race as he tapped the desk in the school room used by the press on the occasion. Once again, the Belgian Championship had the strange atmosphere of a half race, half parade, perhaps due to the flat course, but its length helped ,just the same, to bring the class riders to the fore. All but one. The hot favourite Tom Boonen, missed his chance when he let an attacking group of twenty riders led by Tom Steels get away from him on the 8th lap.
All the top teams from Belgium were present in the group and the race was soon sewn up. But the fourth title for Steels came with little real opposition: it was he who made the decisive attack, 25 kilometers from the line, in the company of last year's champion Geert Omloop and Geert Verheyen. From then on he could think seriously of a fourth title.

Fourth national Title for Tom Steels, the Belgian goes into the record books!

"LES BRIOCHES" KEEP THEIR HAND IN

On the magnificent course around Pont de Fossé, in the valley of Champsaur (Hautes – Alpes), Benoit Salmon could have thought history was about to repeat itself. This was the same place he had won the junior French Championship back in July 1992. Unfortunately for him, his route would cross that of a man from the East of France, by the name of Thomas Voeckler. The rather timid attacks from Salmon and also those from Cyril Dessel, the rider from St Etienne who had learnt days before of his exclusion from the Phonak team in the Tour de France, were to come to nothing. All that was left to do was to wind up the race with a decisive sprint. A sprint won by Thomas Voeckler despite stiff resistance from Cyril Dessel. A third title in four years for the team of Jean René Bernaudeau...
The course around Santander, where the Spanish championship took place was anything but ordinary. For a long time dominated by the solo attack from Haimar Zubeldia (Euskaltel), then by a shorter lived effort from the duo Pablo Lastras (Illes Baleares) and David Latasa (Kelme), the Spanish "National" seemed in the pocket of Alejandro Valverde, the fastest man in a group of 18 riders from which the victor was sure to come. But a sudden attack by "Paco" Mancebo at the 500 metre board pulled the rug from under Valverde, Sanchez, Martin Perdiguero and company, who were left to fight it out for the leftovers.
Thirty five rated riders out of a field of 164! The Italian Championship, run at Sante Croce sull'Arno in temperatures over 40° permitted Cristian Moreni to add this title to his stage win in the Vuelta in 1999, another in the Giro a year later, the Tour of Venetie in 2003, and also a stage win in the slightly less prestigious Route du

In Italy, Cristian Moreni explodes with joy. The national Championships are not a melancholy affair!

Sud just a week before. Moreni, a truly strong all round rider, would show himself to be the strongest in a group of ten which attacked early in the race (170kms from the line)! Danilo di Luca, rather fragile, launched the sprint prematurely, was passed by Paolo Valoti who was himself swept aside by Moreni, the young and promising Sergio Marinangeli and Mauro Gerosa, who jumped ahead of his ex team mate Paolo Bossoni to take the Bronze medal.

The German Championship this year were held in Freiburg am Brisgau, a locality which had several times been the scene of a stage in the Tour de France (the latest being in 2000 when Commesso won). A circuit of 21kms to be completed ten times was the terrain where a somewhat loose peloton would split on the only hill of the race. David Kopp (Lamonta), Stephan Schreck (T Mobile) and Thomas Ziegler (Gerolsteiner) were quick to make a move before finally giving up the ghost at the half way point. A group of strong men in which the T Mobile team counted six riders out of fifteen, soon took things in hand and logically it was a member of T Mobile who would launch the victorious attack: Andreas Kloden. Rapidly taking a lead of more than a minute, the Bronze medal winner in the Sydney Olympics could even take the time to sing to himself the German national anthem in the final kilometers. For the eleventh time in a row, the title was to go to the team run by Walter Godefroot, whether it be called Team Telekom or T Mobile, the result speaks for itself. ■

When in Holland, Erik Dekker has fun with one of his younger colleagues, Arthur Farenhout...

The Podiums for the principal National Championships

ITALY

Road Race

1.	Cristian Moreni	ALB
2.	Sergio Marinangeli	DVE
3.	Mauro Gerosa	VIN

Chrono

1.	Dario Cioni	FAS
2.	Andrea Peron	CSC
3.	Marco Pinotti	LAM

SPAIN

Road Race

1.	Francisco Mancebo	IBB
2.	Alejandro Valverde	KEL
3.	Francisco Lara	ALM

Chrono

1.	J.Ivan Gutierrez Palacios	IBB
2.	Luis Leon Sanchez Gil	LST
3.	Igor Gonzalez de Galdeano	LST

GERMANY

Road Race

1.	Andreas Klöden	TMO
2.	Stefan Schumacher	TLM
3.	Fabian Wegmann	GST

Chrono

1.	Michael Rich	GST
2.	Sebastian Lang	GST
3.	Jens Voigt	CSC

FRANCE

Road Race

1.	Thomas Voeckler	BLB
2.	Cyril Dessel	PHO
3.	Benoît Salmon	C.A

Chrono

1.	Eddy Seigneur	RAG
2.	Christophe Moreau	C.A
3.	Frédéric Finot	RAG

BELGIUM

Road Race

1.	Tom Steels	LAN
2.	Geert Omloop	MRB
3.	Geert Verheyen	CHO

Chrono

1.	Bert Roesems	REB
2.	Marc Wauters	RAB
3.	Leif Hoste	LOT

NETHERLANDS

Road Race

1.	Erik Dekker	RAB
2.	Koos Moerenhout	LOT
3.	Arthur Farenhout	AXA

Chrono

1.	Thomas Dekker	RB3
2.	Joost Posthuma	RAB
3.	Bart Voskamp	CHO

AUSTRALIA

Road Race

1.	Matthew Wilson	FDJ
2.	Robert McLachlan	EI2
3.	David McKenzie	NIC

Chrono

1.	Nathan O'Neill	COB
2.	Peter Milostic	EI2
3.	Luke Roberts	COM

UNITED STATES OF AMERICA

Road Race

1.	Fred Rodriguez	A&S
2.	Kirk O'Bee	NIC
3.	Russell Hamby	SIE

Chrono

1.	David Zabriskie	USP
2.	John Lieswyn	HNC
3.	Kenny Williams	EI2

SWITZERLAND

Road Race

1.	Gregory Rast	PHO
2.	Sascha Urweider	SRW
3.	Oscar Camenzind	PHO

Chrono

1.	Fabian Cancellara	FAS
2.	Fabian Jeker	SDV
3.	Jean Nuttli	VOL

DENMARK

Road Race

1.	Michael Blaudzun	CSC
2.	Stig Dam	EI2
3.	Matti Breschel	TPH

Chrono

1.	Michael Sandstød	CSC
2.	Frank Høj	CSC
3.	Brian Vandbørg	CSC

RUSSIA

Road Race

1.	Alexandr Kolobnev	DVE
2.	Mikhaïl Timochine	LAN
3.	Andrei Ptchelkin	EI2

Chrono

1.	Alexandr Bespalov	MIE
2.	Oleg Zhukov	NIP
3.	Dmitri Semov	MIE

UKRAINE

Road Race

1.	Oleg Ruban	EI2
2.	Vladimir Duma	LAN
3.	Denis Kostyuk	CHO

Chrono

1.	Yuriy Krivtsov	A2R
2.	Serhiy Matveyev	PAN
3.	Volodymir Starchyk	EI2

RESULTS OF OTHER EVENTS

A hectic finish to the 2nd stage of the Eneco Tour of the Netherlands at Nijverdal.

STAGE RACES

NO CATEGORY

5 - 9 April
Tour of Pays-Basque (Esp)

Final overall standings

1.	**Denis Menchov (Rus)**	**IBB**
2.	Iban Mayo (Esp)	EUS
3.	David Etxebarria (Esp)	EUS
4.	Bobby Julich (Usa)	CSC
5.	Levi Leipheimer (Usa)	RAB
6.	Alejandro Valverde (Esp)	KEL
7.	Floyd Landis (Usa)	USP
8.	Samuel Sanchez (Esp)	EUS
9.	Koldo Gil (Esp)	LST
10.	Jorge Ferrio (Esp)	ALM

Winners of stages:
AUT. Valverde (Esp) KEL, B. Zberg (Sui) GST, C. Zarate (Esp) KEL, D. Menchov (Rus) IBB, J. Voigt (Ger) CSC, B. Julich (Usa) CSC.

14 - 20 June
Tour of Catalunya (Esp)

Final overall standings

1.	**M.Artin Perdiguero (Esp)**	**SDV**
2.	Vladimir Karpets (Rus)	IBB
3.	Roberto Laiseka (Esp)	EUS
4.	David Latasa (Esp)	KEL
5.	Eladio Jimenez (Esp)	KEL
6.	Ivan Parra (Col)	KEL
7.	Alberto Lopez de Munain (Esp)	EUS
8.	Josep Jufre (Esp)	REB
9.	Pablo Lastras (Esp)	IBB
10.	Daniel Atienza (Esp)	COF

Winners of stages:
Iles Balears-Banesto IBB, M.AUT Martin Perdiguero (Esp) SDV x 3, D. Hondo (Ger) GST, M. van Heeswijk (Ned) USP, I. Galvez (Esp) IBB.

CATEGORY 1

22 - 26 March
Week of Catalunya (Esp)

Final overall standings

1.	**Joaquin Rodriguez Oliver (Esp**	**SDV**
2.	M.AUT Martin Perdiguero (Esp)	SDV
3.	Josep Jufre (Esp)	REB
4.	Stefano Garzelli (Ita)	VIN
5.	Alberto Contador (Esp)	LST
6.	Koldo Gil (Esp)	LST
7.	Iban Mayo (Esp)	EUS
8.	Frank Vandenbroucke (Bel)	FAS
9.	Aitor Osa (Esp)	IBB
10.	Leonardo Piepoli (Ita)	SDV

Winners of stages:
F. Cancellara (Sui) FAS, B. Zberg (Sui) GST, I. Galvez (Esp) IBB, L. Leipheimer (Usa) RAB, AUT. Edo (Esp) MIL.

27 - 28 March
Critérium International (Fra)

Final overall standings

1.	**Jens Voigt (Ger)**	**CSC**
2.	J. Ivan Gutierrez Palacios (Esp)	IBB
3.	Lance Armstrong (Usa)	USP
4.	Bobby Julich (Usa)	CSC
5.	Thor Hushovd (Nor)	C.AUT
6.	Ronny Scholz (Ger)	GST
7.	Marcus Zberg (Sui)	GST
8.	Floyd Landis (Usa)	USP
9.	Alexandre Vinokourov (Kaz)	TMO
10.	Sylvain Chavanel (Fra)	BLB

Winners of stages:
J.P Nazon (Fra) A2R, J. Voigt (Ger) CSC x 2.

5 - 9 May
4 Jours de Dunkerque (Fra)

Final overall standings

1.	**Sylvain Chavanel (Fra)**	**BLB**
2.	Laurent Brochard (Fra)	A2R
3.	Didier Rous (Fra)	BLB
4.	Pierrick Fedrigo (Fra)	C.AUT
5.	Danilo Hondo (Ger)	GST
6.	Max van Heeswijk (Ned)	USP
7.	Bert Roesems (Bel)	REB
8.	Sébastien Rosseler (Bel)	REB
9.	Nick Nuyens (Bel)	QSD
10.	Jurgen van Goolen (Bel)	QSD

Winners of stages:
J. Casper (Fra) COF, M. Streel (Bel) LAN, D. Rous (Fra) BLB, S. Devolder (Bel) USP, D. Hondo (Ger) GST, M. van Heeswijk (Ned) USP.

2 - 6 June
Euskal Bizikleta (Esp)

Final overall standings

1.	**Roberto Heras (Esp)**	**LST**
2.	Roberto Laiseka (Esp)	EUS
3.	Samuel Sanchez (Esp)	EUS
4.	Koldo Gil (Esp) LST	
5.	Haimar Zubeldia (Esp)	EUS
6.	Txema Del Olmo (Esp)	MIL
7.	Luis Perez Rodriguez (Esp)	COF
8.	M.AUT Martin Perdiguero (Esp)	SDV
9.	Angel Vicioso (Esp)	LST
10.	Leonardo Piepoli (Ita)	SDV

Winners of stages:
M.AUT Martin Perdiguero (Esp) SDV x 2, AUT. Vicioso (Esp) LST x 2, D. Konyshev (Rus) LPR, R. Laiseka (Esp) EUS.

2 - 5 August
Tour of Burgos (Esp)

Final overall standings

1.	**Alejandro Valverde (Esp)**	**KEL**
2.	Denis Menchov (Rus)	IBB
3.	Leonardo Piepoli (Ita)	SDV
4.	Marcos Serrano (Esp)	LST
5.	Jonathan Gonzalez Rios (Esp)	ALM
6.	Juan Carlos Dominguez (Esp)	SDV
7.	Vladimir Karpets (Rus)	IBB
8.	Mauricio Ardila (Col)	CHO
9.	J. Alberto Martinez Trinidad (Esp)	REB
10.	Ondrej Sosenka (Cze)	AUT&S

Winners of stages:
AUT. Valverde (Esp) KEL x 3, AUT. Clerc (Sui) QSD.

24 - 28 August
ENECO
Tour of Netherland (Ned)

Final overall standings

1.	**Erik Dekker (Ned)**	**RAB**
2.	Viatcheslav Ekimov (Rus)	USP
3.	Marc Wauters (Bel)	RAB
4.	Bart Voskamp (Ned)	CHO
5.	Bobby Julich (Usa)	CSC
6.	Frank Høj (Den)	CSC
7.	Rolf Aldag (Ger)	TMO
8.	Cyril Dessel (Fra)	PHO
9.	Laszlo Bodrogi (Hun)	QSD
10.	Marco Pinotti (Ita)	LAM

Winners of stages:
M. van Heeswijk (Ned) USP x 2, AUT. Petacchi (Ita) FAS, V. Ekimov (Rus) USP, L. van Bon (Ned) LOT, E. Dekker (Ned) RAB.

CATEGORY 2

22 - 26 March
Tour of Langkawi (Mas)

Final overall standings

1.	**Freddy Gonzalez Martinez (Col)**	**CLM**
2.	Ryan Cox (Rsa)	TBL
3.	Dave Bruylandts (Bel)	CHO
4.	Tiaan Kannemeyer (Rsa)	TBL
5.	Nicholas White (Rsa)	HSB

Winners of stages:
M. Perez Arango (Col) CLM, B. Lancaster (Aus) PAN, S. Sullivan (Aus) TBL, E. Wohlberg (Can) SIE, I. Quaranta (Ita) FPF, L. Pagliarini (Bra) LAM x 2, R. AUT Marin (Col) CLM, R. Bongiorno (Ra) PAN.

30 March - 1st April
3 Jours de La Panne (Bel)

Final overall standings

1.	**George Hincapie (Usa)**	**USP**
2.	Danilo Hondo (Ger)	GST
3.	Gerben Löwik (Ned)	CHO
4.	Fabian Cancellara (Sui)	FAS
5.	Marc Wauters (Bel)	RAB

Winners of stages:
D. Hondo (Ger) GST, B. Cooke (Aus) FDJ, M. Zanotti (Ita) VIN, L. Bodrogi (Hun) QSD.

12 - 18 April
Tour of Aragón (Esp)

Final overall standings

1. **Stefano Garzelli (Ita)** **VIN**
2. Denis Menchov (Rus) IBB
3. Leonardo Piepoli (Ita) SDV
4. Koldo Gil (Esp) LST
5. Francisco Mancebo (Esp) IBB

Winners of stages:
D. Menchov (Rus) IBB, AUT. Petacchi (Ita) FAS x 2, C. Zaballa (Esp) SDV, O. Laguna (Esp) REB.

20 - 23 April
Tour of Trentin (Ita)

Final overall standings

1. **Damiano Cunego (Ita)** **SAE**
2. Jure Golcer (Slo) FPF
3. Gilberto Simoni (Ita) SAE
4. Giuliano Figueras (Ita) PAN
5. Pavel Tonkov (Rus) VIN

Winners of stages:
D. Cunego (Ita) SAE x 2, J.M Mercado (Esp) QSD, J. Svorada (Cze) LAM.

8 - 16 May
Course de la Paix (Bel/Ger/Cze)

Final overall standings

1. **Michele Scarponi (Ita)** **DVE**
2. Slawomir Kohut (Pol) HOP
3. Roger Beuchat (Sui) VIN
4. Massimo Giunti (Ita) DVE
5. Christian Werner (Ger) TMO

Winners of stages:
L. Wackernagel (Ger) WIE, D. Bertolini (Ita) AUT&S, S. Siedler (Ger) WIE, M. Scarponi (Ita) DVE, M. Hvastija (Slo) ALB, Sl. Kohut (Pol) HOP, E. Zabel (Ger) TMO x 2, D. Loosli (Sui) SAE.

12 - 16 May
Tour of Asturies (Esp)

Final overall standings

1. **Iban Mayo (Esp)** **EUS**
2. Félix Cardenas (Col) BAQ
3. Haimar Zubeldia (Esp) EUS
4. Leonardo Piepoli (Ita) SDV
5. J. Angel Gomez Marchante (Esp) ALM

Winners of stages:
L.L Sanchez Gil (Esp) LST, D. Herrero Llorente (Esp) ALM, C. Barredo (Esp) LST, J. Gonzalez Rios (Esp) ALM, M.AUT Martin Perdiguero (Esp) SDV.

14 - 16 May
Tour de Picardie (Fra)

Final overall standings

1. **Tom Boonen (Bel)** **QSD**
2. Jimmy Casper (Fra) COF
3. Stefan van Dijk (Ned) LOT
4. Sébastien Chavanel (Fra) BLB
5. Ludovic Auger (Fra) AUB

Winners of stages:
T. Boonen (Bel) QSD x 2, S. van Dijk (Ned) LOT, J. Casper (Fra) COF.

19 - 23 May
Tour of Belgium (Bel)

Final overall standings

1. **Sylvain Chavanel (Fra)** **BLB**
2. Bart Voskamp (Ned) CHO
3. Max van Heeswijk (Ned) USP
4. Victor Hugo Peña (Col) USP
5. Rik Verbrugghe (Bel) LOT

Winners of stages:
G. Bortolami (Ita) LAM, T. Boonen (Bel) QSD, M. van Heeswijk (Ned) USP, B. Roesems (Bel) REB, B. Leukemans (Bel) MRB.

27 - 30 May
Tour of Luxembourg (Lux)

Final overall standings

1. **Maxime Monfort (Bel)** **LAN**
2. Torsten Hiekmann (Ger) TMO
3. Jörg Jaksche (Ger) CSC
4. Koos Moerenhout (Ned) LOT
5. Juan Antonio Flecha (Esp) FAS

Winners of stages:
L.Y Bak (Den) BGL, T. Steels (Bel) LAN, M. Monfort (Bel) LAN, F. Cancellara (Sui) FAS, K. Kirchen (Lux) FAS.

31 May - 6 June
Tour of Germany (Ger)

Final overall standings

1. **Patrik Sinkewitz (Ger)** **QSD**
2. Jens Voigt (Ger) CSC
3. Jan Hruska (Cze) LST
4. Igor Gonzalez de Galdeano (Esp) LST
5. Francisco Mancebo (Esp) IBB

Winners of stages:
M. Rich (Ger) GST, T. Boonen (Bel) QSD x 2, P. Sinkewitz (Ger) QSD, S. Hinault (Fra) C.AUT, AUT. Davis (Aus) LST, F. Mancebo (Esp) IBB.

7 - 13 June
Tour of Austria (Aut)

Final overall standings

1. **Cadel Evans (Aus)** **TMO**
2. Michele Scarponi (Ita) DVE
3. Maurizio Vandelli (Ita) RAD
4. Tomas Konecny (Cze) TMO
5. Jure Golcer (Slo) FPF

Winners of stages:
T. Steels (Bel) LAN x 2, C. Evans (Aus) TMO, G. Glomser (AUT) SAE, F. Simeoni (Ita) DVE, J. Kuyckx (Bel) VLA, L. Dierckxsens (Bel) LAN.

29 July - 8 August
Tour of Portugal (Por)

Final overall standings

1. **David Bernabeu (Esp)** **MIL**
2. David Arroyo (Esp) LAP
3. Nuno Ribeiro (Por) LAP
4. Txema Del Olmo (Esp) MIL
5. Rui Lavarinhas (Por) MIL

Winners of stages:
J.M Elias (Esp) REB, C. Barbosa (Por) LAP, J.C Julia (Esp) KEL, D. Arroyo (Esp) LAP x 2, AUT. Garcia Quesada (Esp) KEL, F. Sacchi (Ita) FAS, S. Paulinho (Por) LAP x 2, AUT. Ongarato (Ita) FAS

4 - 8 August
Tour of Denmark (Den)

Final overall standings

1. **Kurt-Asle Arvesen (Nor)** **CSC**
2. Jens Voigt (Ger) CSC
3. Stuart O'Grady (Aus) COF
4. Brian Vandborg (Den) CSC
5. Max van Heeswijk (Ned) USP

Winners of stages:
S. O'Grady (Aus) COF, F. Guidi (Ita) CSC, J. Tombak (Est) COF, J. Voigt (Ger) CSC, T. Vaitkus (Ltu) LAN, J. Casper (Fra) COF

6 - 12 September
Tour of Poland (Pol)

Final overall standings

1. **Ondrej Sosenka (Cze)** **AUT&S**
2. Hugo Sabido (Por) MIL
3. Francesco Pellizotti (Ita) ALB
4. Marek Rutkiewicz (Pol) ATI
5. Allan Davis (Aus) LST

Winners of stages:
F. Baldato (Ita) ALB x 2, M. Sapa (Pol) MIK, AUT. Davis (Aus) LST, R. Nocentini (Ita) AUT&S, M. Rutkiewicz (Pol) ATI, H. Sabido (Por) MIL, O. Sosenka (Cze) AUT&S.

Category 3

20 - 25 January
Jacob's Creek
Tour Down Under (Aus)

Final overall standings

1. **Patrick Jonker (Aus)** **EI2**
2. Robbie McEwen (Aus) LOT
3. Baden Cooke (Aus) FDJ
4. Philippe Gilbert (Bel) FDJ
5. Massimo Giunti (Ita) DVE

Winners of stages:
R. McEwen (Aus) LOT x 2, D. McPartland (Aus) TEN, P. Gilbert (Bel) FDJ, B. Day (Aus) MRB, B. Cooke (Aus) FDJ

2 - 6 February
Tour of Qatar (Qat)

Final overall standings

1. **Robert Hunter (Rsa)** **RAB**
2. Robbie McEwen (Aus) LOT
3. Tom Boonen (Bel) QSD
4. Jean-Patrick Nazon (Fra) A2R
5. Frank Høj (Den) CSC

Winners of stages:
F. Ventoso (Esp) SDV, T. Boonen (Bel) QSD, R. Hunter (Rsa) RAB x 2, F. Cancellara (Sui) FAS.

4 - 8 February
Etoile de Bessèges (Fra)

Final overall standings

1. **Laurent Brochard (Fra)** **A2R**
2. Sylvain Calzati (Fra) OKT
3. Joseba Zubeldia (Esp) EUS
4. Staf Scheirlinckx (Bel) COF
5. Pierrick Fedrigo (Fra) C.AUT

Winners of stages:
T. Steels (Bel) LAN, J. Kirsipuu (Est) A2R x 2, T. Hushovd (Nor) C.AUT, L. Brochard (Fra) A2R.

8 - 10 February
GP CTT Correios (Por)

Final overall standings

1. **Candido Barbosa (Por)** **LAP**
2. Angel Edo (Esp) MIL
3. Alberto Benito (Esp) ANT
4. Ricardo Serrano Gonzalez (Esp) BAQ
5. Nuno Marta (Por) WBP

Winners of stages:
C. Barbosa (Por) LAP x 2, J.AUT Gomez Marchante (Esp) ALM

11 - 15 February
Tour Méditerranéen (Fra)

Final overall standings

1. **Jörg Jaksche (Ger)** **CSC**
2. Ivan Basso (Ita) CSC
3. Jens Voigt (Ger) CSC
4. Michael Boogerd (Ned) RAB
5. David Moncoutié (Fra) COF

Winners of stages:
B. Cooke (Aus) FDJ x 2, P. Bettini (Ita) QSD, M. Cipollini (Ita) DVE, J. Jaksche (Ger) CSC.

15 - 19 February
Tour of Andalousia «Ruta del Sol» (Esp)

Final overall standings

1. **Juan Carlos Dominguez (Esp)** **SDV**
2. Carlos Garcia Quesada (Esp) KEL
3. Samuel Sanchez (Esp) EUS
4. J. Angel Gomez Marchante (Esp) ALM
5. Aitor Osa (Esp) IBB

Winners of stages:
T. Boonen (Bel) QSD, M. van Heeswijk (Ned) USP x 2, J.C Dominguez (Esp) SDV, E. Zabel (Ger) TMO.

18 - 22 February
Tour of Algarve (Por)

Final overall standings

1. **Floyd Landis (Usa)** **USP**
2. Victor Hugo Peña (Col) USP
3. Candido Barbosa (Por) LAP
4. Thomas Dekker (Ned) RB3
5. Lance Armstrong (Usa) USP

Winners of stages:
AUT. Benito (Esp) ANT, C. Barbosa (Por) LAP, M. Garrido (Ra) BAR, L. Armstrong (Usa) USP, F. Landis (Usa) USP.

24 - 27 February
Tour della Provincia de Lucca (Ita)

Final overall standings

1. **Alessandro Bertolini (Ita)** **ALB**
2. Thomas Ziegler (Ger) GST
3. Matteo Tosatto (Ita) FAS
4. Vladimir Miholjevic (Cro) ALB
5. Nicki Sørensen (Den) CSC

Winners of stages:
AUT. Petacchi (Ita) FAS x 2, AUT. Bertolini (Ita) ALB, F. Brard (Fra) CHO

24 - 28 February
Tour of Valencia (Esp)

Final overall standings

1. **Alejandro Valverde (Esp)** **KEL**
2. Antonio Colom (Esp) IBB
3. David Blanco Rodriguez (Esp) KEL
4. Leonardo Piepoli (Ita) SDV
5. Alex Zülle (Sui) PHO

Winners of stages:
AUT. Colom (Esp) IBB, AUT. Valverde (Esp) KEL x 2, J. Garcia Marin (Esp) BAQ, AUT. Usov (Blr) PHO.

3 - 7 March
Tour of Murcie (Esp)

Final overall standings

1. **Alejandro Valverde (Esp)** **KEL**
2. José Ivan Gutierrez Palacios (Esp) IBB
3. Cadel Evans (Aus) TMO
4. Ruben Plaza Molina (Esp) KEL
5. Evgeni Petrov (Rus) SAE

Winners of stages:
M. van Heeswijk (Ned) USP x 2, J.I Gutierrez Palacios (Esp) BAN, D. Di Luca (Ita) SAE, L. Pagliarini (Bra) LAM

5 - 7 March
3 Jours de Flandre Occidentale (Bel)

Final overall standings

1. **Robert Bartko (Ger)** **RAB**
2. Jaan Kirsipuu (Est) A2R
3. Kurt-Asle Arvesen (Nor) CSC
4. Servais Knaven (Ned) QSD
5. Frank Høj (Den) CSC

Winners of stages:
R. Bartko (Ger) RAB, J. Kirsipuu (Est) A2R x 2.

24 au 28 March
International week "Coppi/Bartali" (Ita)

Final overall standings

1. **Giuliano Figueras (Ita)** **PAN**
2. Mirko Celestino (Ita) SAE
3. Michele Scarponi (Ita) DVE
4. Ruggero Marzoli (Ita) AUT&S
5. Leonardo Bertagnolli (Ita) SAE

Winners of stages:
G. Gasparre (Ita) DEN, Fassa Bortolo FAS, M. Celestino (Ita) SAE, C. D'Amore (Ita) AUT&S, M. Scarponi (Ita) DVE, R. Marzoli (Ita) AUT&S.

6 - 9 April
Circuit de la Sarthe et des Pays de Loire (Fra)

Final overall standings

1. **Thomas Lövkvist (Swe)** **FDJ**
2. Franck Bouyer (Fra) BLB
3. Ronny Scholz (Ger) GST
4. Robbie McEwen (Aus) LOT
5. Laurent Brochard (Fra) A2R

Winners of stages:
F. Bouyer (Fra) BLB, L. Turpin (Fra) A2R, L. Brochard (Fra) A2R, T. Lövkvist (Swe) FDJ.

13 - 18 April
Tour of Rio de Janeiro (Bra)

Final overall standings

1. **Marcio May (Bra)** **EI2**
2. Luiz Amorim (Bra) EI2
3. Breno Sidoti (Bra) EI2
4. Federico Moreira (Uru) EI2
5. Soelito Goehr (Bra) EI2

Winners of stages:
M. Novello (Bra) EI2, J. Giacinti (Ra) EI2, M. May (Bra) EI2, M. Mugerli (Slo) EI2 x 2, G. Cordoves (Cub) EI2

20 - 25 April
Tour of Georgia (Usa)

Final overall standings

1. **Lance Armstrong (Usa)** **USP**
2. Jens Voigt (Ger) CSC
3. Chris Horner (Usa) WEB
4. Bobby Julich (Usa) CSC
5. Viatcheslav Ekimov (Rus) USP

Winners of stages:
G. Fraser (Can) HNC x 2, M. Cipollini (Ita) DVE, L. Armstrong (Usa) USP x 2, J. McCartney (Usa) HNC, C. Grajales (Col) JIT

21 - 25 April
Tour of Basse-Saxe (Ger)

Final overall standings

1. **Bert Roesems (Bel)** **REB**
2. Stefan Kupfernagel (Ger) TLM
3. Stephan Schreck (Ger) TMO
4. Corey Sweet (Aus) COM
5. Jan Boven (Ned) RAB

Winners of stages:
D. Hondo (Ger) GST x 4, B. Roesems (Bel) REB

22 - 25 April
GP Mitsubishi (Por)

Final overall standings

1. **Angel Edo (Esp)** **MIL**
2. Pedro Lopes (Por) LAP
3. Pedro Cardoso (Por) MIL
4. Carlos Torrent (Esp) ALM
5. Francisco Lara (Esp) ALM

Winners of stages:
AUT. Edo (Esp) MIL, C. Torrent (Esp) ALM, P. Cardoso (Por) MIL x 2

23 - 25 April
Tour of the Rioja (Esp)

Final overall standings

1. **Vladimir Karpets (Rus)** **IBB**
2. J. Angel Gomez Marchante (Esp) ALM
3. Josep Jufre (Esp) REB
4. David Navas (Esp) IBB
5. Dionisio Galparsoro (Esp) EUS

Winners of stages:
J. Kuyckx (Bel) VLA x 2, J. Gonzalez Rios (Esp) ALM.

RESULTS OF OTHER EVENTS

28 April - 2 May
Tour of Castille & Leon (Esp)

Final overall standings

1.	**Koldo Gil (Esp)**	**LST**
2.	David Navas (Esp)	IBB
3.	J. Ivan Gutierrez Palacios (Esp)	IBB
4.	Alejandro Valverde (Esp)	KEL
5.	Dionisio Galparsoro (Esp)	EUS

Winners of stages:
J.I Gutierrez Palacios (Esp) IBB, Illes Balears-Banesto IBB, AUT. Valverde (Esp) KEL x 3.

8 - 9 May
Clasica Alcobendas (Esp)

Final overall standings

1.	**Iban Mayo (Esp)**	**EUS**
2.	Eladio Jimenez (Esp)	KEL
3.	David Moncoutié (Fra)	COF
4.	J. Ivan Gutierrez Palacios (Esp)	IBB
5.	Roberto Heras (Esp)	LST

Winners of stages:
I. Mayo (Esp) EUS x 2, L.L Sanchez Gil (Esp) LST.

19 - 23 May
Tour of Bavière (Ger)

Final overall standings

1.	**Jens Voigt (Ger)**	**CSC**
2.	Andreas Klöden (Ger)	TMO
3.	Tomasz Brozyna (Pol)	ATI
4.	Massimiliano Gentili (Ita)	DVE
5.	René Weissinger (Ger)	VOL

Winners of stages:
AUT. Bucciero (Ita) SAE, E. Zabel (Ger) TMO x 2, M. Rich (Ger) GST, M. Gentili (Ita) DVE, S. Schumacher (Ger) TLM.

26 - 30 May
Tour of Alentejo (Por)

Final overall standings

1.	**Daniel Petrov Andonov (Bul)**	**CAB**
2.	Joaquim Andrade (Por)	WBP
3.	Joaquim Sampaio (Por)	CAB
4.	Nelson Vitorino (Por)	WBP
5.	Hernani Broco (Por)	LAP

Winners of stages:
AUT. Benito (Esp) ANT, H. Sabido (Por) MIL, D. Petrov Andonov (Bul) CAB, K. Vassilev (Bul) WBP, J. Sampaio (Por) CAB.

15 - 20 June
GP de Beauce (Can)

Final overall standings

1.	**Tomasz Brozyna (Pol)**	**ATI**
2.	Nathan O'Neill (Aus)	COB
3.	Scott Moninger (Usa)	HNC
4.	Radoslaw Romanik (Pol)	HOP
5.	Viktor Rapinski (Blr)	NIC

Winners of stages:
I. Dominguez (Cub) COB, T. Brozyna (Pol) ATI, C. Dionne (Can) WEB, R. Romanik (Pol) HOP, N. O'Neill (Aus) COB, C. Power (Irl) NIC, AUT. Olson (Usa) COB

16 - 20 June
Ster Elektrotoer (Ned)

Final overall standings

1.	**Nick Nuyens (Bel)**	**QSD**
2.	Paul van Hyfte (Bel)	VLA
3.	Philippe Gilbert (Bel)	FDJ
4.	Maxime Monfort (Bel)	LAN
5.	Michael Boogerd (Ned)	RAB

Winners of stages:
T. Boonen (Bel) QSD x 2, P. van Hecke (Bel) REB, N. Nuyens (Bel) QSD, N. Eeckhout (Bel) LOT.

19 - 22 June
Route du Sud (Fra)

Final overall standings

1.	**Bradley McGee (Aus)**	**FDJ**
2.	Sandy Casar (Fra)	FDJ
3.	Torsten Hiekmann (Ger)	TMO
4.	Cristian Moreni (Ita)	ALB
5.	Patrice Halgand (Fra)	C.AUT

Winners of stages:
C. Moreni (Ita) ALB, F. Mourey (Fra) FDJ, B. McGee (Aus) FDJ, T. Voeckler (Fra) BLB.

30 June - 4 July
Race of the Olympic solidarity (Pol)

Final overall standings

1.	**Bogdan Bondariev (Ukr)**	**ATI**
2.	Slawomir Kohut (Pol)	HOP
3.	Piotr Mazur (Pol)	MAH
4.	Tomasz Brozyna (Pol)	ATI
5.	Piotr Przydzial (Pol)	HOP

Winners of stages:
D. Rudnicki (Pol) LEG, R. Radosz (Pol) PSB, B. Bondariev (Ukr) ATI, K. Jezowski (Pol) MIK, J. Holmkvist (Swe) TBN, M. Gebka (Pol) DHL.

7 - 10 July
UNIQA Classic (AUT)

Final overall standings

1.	**Kjell Carlström (Fin)**	**AMO**
2.	Mikhaïl Timochine (Rus)	LAN
3.	Matej Jurco (Svk)	DEN
4.	Murilo Fischer (Bra)	DVE
5.	Danilo Di Luca (Ita)	SAE

Winners of stages:
R. Hunter (Rsa) RAB x 2, K. Carlström (Fin) AMO, P. Horrillo (Esp) QSD.

7 - 11 July
Trophée Joaquim Agostinho (Por)

Final overall standings

1.	**David Bernabeu (Esp)**	**MIL**
2.	Nelson Vitorino (Por)	WBP
3.	Daniel Petrov Andonov (Bul)	CAB
4.	Radoslaw Romanik (Pol)	HOP
5.	Rui Lavarinhas (Por)	MIL

Winners of stages:
D. Petrov Andonov (Bul) CAB, AUT. Edo (Esp) MIL, AUT. Rodriguez Hernandez (Esp) BEP, AUT. Benito (Esp) ANT, R. Plaza Molina (Esp) KEL.

17 - 25 July
Tour de Qinghai Lake (Chn)

Final overall standings

***1.**	**Phil Zajicek (Usa)**	**NIC**
2.	Ryan Cox (Rsa)	TBL
3.	Ghader Mizbani Iranagh (Iri)	GNT
4.	Jeff Louder (Usa)	NIC
5.	Andrei Mizourov (Kaz)	OKT

Winners of stages:
V. Rapinski (Blr) NIC x 3, J. Louder (Usa) NIC, S. Cadamuro (Ita) DEN, J. Maartens (Rsa) El2, M. Fertonani (Ita) PHO, AUT. Mizourov (Kaz) OKT, AUT. Schulze (Ger) VCF.
*Phil Zajicek a été déclassé quelques mois plus ta^rd

21 - 25 July
Tour of Saxe (Ger)

Final overall standings

1.	**Andrey Kashechkin (Kaz)**	**C.AUT**
2.	Tomas Konecny (Cze)	TMO
3.	Christian Pfannberger (AUT)	ZVZ
4.	Stephan Schreck (Ger)	TMO
5.	Matthé Pronk (Ned)	BGL

Winners of stages:
S. Schreck (Ger) TMO, O. Pollack (Ger) GST, D. Rebellin (Ita) GST x 2, R. Hunter (Rsa) RAB, B. Schröder (Ger) WIE.

23 - 25 July
Brixia Tour (Ita)

Final overall standings

1.	**Danilo Di Luca (Ita)**	**SAE**
2.	Paolo Tiralongo (Ita)	PAN
3.	Massimiliano Gentili (Ita)	DVE
4.	Raffaele Illiano (Ita)	CLM
5.	Przemyslaw Niemec (Pol)	MIE

Winners of stages:
I. Astarloa (Esp) LAM, J.AUT Perez Cuapio (Mex) PAN, Y. Mitlushenko (Ukr) LAN, E. Degano (Ita) TBL.

26 - 30 July
Tour of Wallonne (Bel)

Final overall standings

1.	**Gerben Löwik (Ned)**	**CHO**
2.	Bert de Waele (Bel)	LAN
3.	Christophe Agnolutto (Fra)	A2R
4.	Sven Vanthourenthout (Bel)	QSD
5.	Paul van Hyfte (Bel)	VLA

Winners of stages:
H. Roulston (Nzl) COF, F. Guidi (Ita) CSC, N. Reynaud (Fra) RAG, J. Kirsipuu (Est) A2R, Séb. Chavanel (Fra) BLB.

4 - 8 August
Rothaus Regio Tour (Ger)

Final overall standings

1.	**Alexandre Vinokourov (Kaz)**	**TMO**
2.	Stephan Schreck (Ger)	TMO
3.	Andrey Kashechkin (Kaz)	C.AUT
4.	Markus Fothen (Ger)	GST
5.	Cadel Evans (Aus)	TMO

Winners of stages:
S. Schreck (Ger) TMO, AUT. Vinokourov (Kaz) TMO x 2, S. Caethoven (Bel) VLA, N. Vogondy (Fra) FDJ.

10 - 13 August
Tour de l'Ain (Fra)

Final overall standings

1.	**Jérôme Pineau (Fra)**	**BLB**
2.	Leif Hoste (Bel)	LOT
3.	Jurgen van Goolen (Bel)	QSD
4.	Franck Renier (Fra)	BLB
5.	Thomas Dekker (Ned)	RB3

Winners of stages:
J. Pineau (Fra) BLB, AUT. Cruz (Usa) USP, J.P Nazon (Fra) A2R, C. Vasseur (Fra) COF.

17 - 20 August
Tour of Limousin (Fra)

Final overall standings

1.	**Pierrick Fedrigo (Fra)**	**C.AUT**
2.	Patrick Calcagni (Sui)	VIN
3.	Franck Renier (Fra)	BLB
4.	Luis Perez Rodriguez (Esp)	COF
5.	Gustavo Dominguez Lemos (Esp)	REB

Winners of stages:
S. Ruskys (Ltu) OKT, P. Fedrigo (Fra) C.AUT, D. Rous (Fra) BLB, C. Vasseur (Fra) COF.

24 - 27 August
Tour of Poitou Charentes (Fra)

Final overall standings

1.	**Stéphane Barthe (Fra)**	**OKT**
2.	Ronald Mutsaars (Ned)	RAB
3.	Jimmy Engoulvent (Fra)	COF
4.	Christophe Agnolutto (Fra)	A2R
5.	Peter Wrolich (AUT)	GST

Winners of stages:
D. Hondo (Ger) GST, S. Casar (Fra) FDJ, Sy. Chavanel (Fra) BLB x 2, L. Capelle (Bel) LAN

1 - 5 September
Tour of Hesse (Ger)

Final overall standings

1.	**Sebastian Lang (Ger)**	**GST**
2.	Stefan Schumacher (Ger)	TLM
3.	Jérôme Pineau (Fra)	BLB
4.	Jörg Ludewig (Ger)	SAE
5.	Ronny Scholz (Ger)	GST

Winners of stages:
U. Yus (Esp) BLB, R. Lochowski (Ger) WIE, S. Lang (Ger) GST, M. Rich (Ger) GST, S. Siedler (Ger) WIE.

1 - 5 September
Tour of Great Britain (Gbr)

Final overall standings

1.	**Mauricio Ardila (Col)**	**CHO**
2.	Julian Dean (Nzl)	C.AUT
3.	Nick Nuyens (Bel)	QSD
4.	Eric Leblacher (Fra)	C.AUT
5.	Daniel Moreno Fernandez (Esp) REB (s)	

Winners of stages:
S. Zanini (Ita) QSD, M. Ardila (Col) CHO x 2, T. Boonen (Bel) QSD, E. Degano (Ita) TBL.

9 - 10 September
Tour of Bohême (Cze)

Final overall standings

1.	**Lubor Tesar (Cze)**	**ZVZ**
2.	Jan Faltynek (Cze)	PSK
3.	Milan Kadlec (Cze)	VIN
4.	Christian Pfannberger (AUT)	ZVZ
5.	Martin Prazdnovsky (Svk)	El2

Winners of stages:
L. Tesar (Cze) ZVZ, T. Buchacek (Cze) FVT.

15 - 19 September
Tour of Rhénanie-Palatinat (Ger)

Final overall standings

1.	**Björn Glasner (Ger)**	**TLM**
2.	Mauricio Ardila (Col)	CHO
3.	Ronny Scholz (Ger)	GST
4.	Christian Werner (Ger)	TMO
5.	Marc Wauters (Bel)	RAB

Winners of stages:
L. Roberts (Aus) COM, T. Dekker (Ned) RAB (s), R. Aldag (Ger) TMO, T. Schmidt (Ger) GST, AUT. Korff (Ger) TMO.

23 - 26 September
Circuit Franco-Belge (Bel/Fra)

Final overall standings

1.	**Jimmy Casper (Fra)**	**COF**
2.	Steven de Jongh (Ned)	RAB
3.	Nico Mattan (Bel)	REB
4.	Frédéric Guesdon (Fra)	FDJ
5.	Allan Johansen (Den)	BGL

Winners of stages:
P. Bettini (Ita) QSD, J. Casper (Fra) COF, T. Boonen (Bel) QSD x 2.

24 - 26 September
Paris-Corrèze (Fra)

Final overall standings

1.	**Philippe Gilbert (Bel)**	**FDJ**
2.	Simon Gerrans (Aus)	A2R (s)
3.	Koen de Kort (Ned)	RB3
4.	Dmitriy Fofonov (Kaz)	COF
5.	Christophe Brandt (Bel)	LOT

Winners of stages:
J. Kirsipuu (Est) A2R, F. Brard (Fra) CHO, E. Berthou (Fra) RAG.

14 - 24 October
Herald Sun Tour (Fra)

Final overall standings

1.	**Jonas Ljungblad (Swe)**	**AMO**
2.	David McKenzie (Aus)	NIC
3.	Ben Brooks (Aus)	JEL
4.	Benoît Poilvet (Fra)	C.AUT
5.	Karl Menzies (Aus)	El2

Winners of stages:
K. Menzies (Aus) El2, B. Cooke (Aus) FDJ x 3, R. McLachlan (Aus) El2 x 3, D. Perras (Can) OFO, J. Ljungblad (Swe) AMO, M. Rex (Aus) El2, S. Gerrans (Aus) El2, M. Lloyd (Aus) El2, W. Walker (Aus) El2.

CATEGORY 5

10 - 23 January
Tour of Tachira (Ven)

Final overall standings

1.	**José Rujano (Ven)**	**CLM**
2.	Freddy Gonzalez Martinez (Col)	CLM
3.	Carlos Maya (Ven)	El2

Winners of stages:
M. Perez Arango (Col) CLM x 3, M. Ubeto (Ven) El2, H. Machado (Ven) El2, J. Rujano (Ven) CLM x 2, M. Medina (Ven) El2, R. Gomez (Col) El2, F. Gonzalez Martinez (Col) CLM x 2, J. Chacon (Ven) El2, C. Salazar Herrera (Col) El2 x 2.

11 - 18 January
Tour of Sao Paolo county (Bra)

Final overall standings

1.	**Antonio Nascimento (Bra)**	**El2**
2.	Tim Larkin (Usa)	OFO
3.	Breno Sidoti (Bra)	El2

Winners of stages:
AUT. Grizante (Bra) El2 x 3, M. May (Bra) El2 x 2, B. Sidoti (Bra) El2, D. Soeiro (Bra) El2, L. Amorim (Bra) El2, P. Azevedo (Bra) El2.

28 January - 1 February
Tour of Wellington (Nzl)

Final overall standings

1.	**Eric Wohlberg (Can)**	**SIE**
2.	Robin Reid (Nzl)	MPC
3.	Karl Menzies (Aus)	El2

Winners of stages:
E. Wohlberg (Can) SIE, C. Dionne (Can) WEB, R. Reid (Nzl) MPC x 2, J. Yates (Nzl) El2

10 - 20 February
Tour of Cuba (Cub)

Final overall standings

1.	**Pedro Pablo Perez (Cub)**	**El2**
2.	José Chacon (Ven)	El2
3.	Damier Martinez (Cub)	El2

Winners of stages:
P.P Perez (Cub) El2 x 3, J. Mariño (Cub) El2 x 4, K. Wamsley (Usa) El2, I. Ramirez (Ven) El2, J. van Pelt (Ned) El2 x 3, T. Gil (Ven) El2, L. Benitez (Cub) El2.

18 - 24 February
Tour of Arabic Emirates (Uae)

Final overall standings

1.	**Jeremy Yates (Nzl)**	**El2**
2.	Heath Blackgrove (Nzl)	El2
3.	Martin Velits (Svk)	DUK

Winners of stages:
H. Blackgrove (Nzl) El2, J. Winn (Gbr) El2 x 4, J. Yates (Nzl) El2, R. Reid (Nzl) MPC.

21 - 22 February
Critérium des Espoirs/Essor Basque (Fra)

Final overall standings

1.	**Carl Naibo (Fra)**	**El2**
2.	Dominique Rault (Fra)	El2

3. Thomas Lövkvist (Swe) FDJ

Winners of stages:
C. Naibo (Fra) El2 x 2, B. Eisel (AUT) FDJ.

5 - 11 March
Tour of Egypt (Egy)
Final overall standings
1. **Maros Kovac (Svk) DUK**
2. Serguey Tretyakov (Kaz) El2
3. Pavel Nevdakh (Kaz) El2

Winners of stages:
M. Kovac (Svk) DUK x 4, AUT. Ben Hassine (Tun) El2,
S. Tretyakov (Kaz) El2, M. Abdel Aziz (Egy) El2.

9 - 13 March
Giro del Capo (Rsa)
Final overall standings
1. **David George (Rsa) TBL**
2. Tiaan Kannemeyer (Rsa) TBL
3. Nicholas White (Rsa) HSB

Winners of stages:
T. Kannemeyer (Rsa) TBL, D. Kopp (Ger) TLM, L. Tesar (Cze) ZVZ,
R. Cox (Rsa) TBL, D. Impey (Rsa) El2.

11 - 14 March
Jadranska Magistrala (Cro)
Final overall standings
1. **Jure Zrimsek (Slo) El2**
2. Stefan Schumacher (Ger) TLM
3. Borut Bozic (Slo) PER

Winners of stages:
Z. Klemencic (Slo) TEN x 2, J. Zrimsek (Slo) El2, B. Bozic (Slo) PER.

11 - 13 March
GP Estremadura / RTP (Por)
Final overall standings
1. **Carlos Garcia Quesada (Esp) KEL**
2. Candido Barbosa (Por) LAP
3. José Adrian Bonilla (Crc) KEL

Winners of stages:
J.AUT Bonilla (Crc) KEL, C. Barbosa (Por) LAP,
C. Garcia Quesada (Esp) KEL, J. Andrade (Por) WBP.

11 - 21 March
Tour of Chile (Chi)
Final overall standings
1. **Marco Arriagada (Chi) El2**
2. José Medina (Chi) El2
3. Marcelo Arriagada (Chi) El2

Winners of stages:
AUT. Corvalán (Chi) El2 x 3, E. Cesario (Chi) El2, E. Simón (Ra) El2 x 3,
R. López (Uru) El2, AUT. Sartassov (Rus) El2, L. Sepúlveda (Chi) El2,
Marco Arriagada (Chi) El2, G. Miranda (Chi) El2.

16 - 20 March
Tour de Paraná (Bra)
Final overall standings
1. **Soelito Goehr (Bra) El2**
2. José Aparecido dos Santos (Bra) El2
3. Miguel Sattler (Uru) El2

Winners of stages:
V. Silva (Bra) El2, S. Goehr (Bra) El2 x 2, M. Sattler (Uru) El2, R. Silva (Bra) El2.

17 - 21 March
Road of King Nikola (Scg)
Final overall standings
1. **Massimo Demarin (Cro) PER**
2. Tomislav Danculovic (Cro) PER
3. Sebastian Skiba (Pol) LEG

Winners of stages:
J. Welniak (Pol) LEG, M. Demarin (Cro) PER, K. Fukushima (Jpn) BGT,
M. Wiesiak (Pol) NIP, L. Garamszegi (Hun) El2.

22 - 28 March
Tour of Normandie (Fra)
Final overall standings
1. **Thomas Dekker (Ned) RB3**
2. Joost Posthuma (Ned) RB3
3. Arkadiusz Wojtas (Pol) HOP

Winners of stages:
Y. Talabardon (Fra) AUB, AUT. Markov (Rus) HOP x 2, F. Lecrosnier (Fra) El2,
C. Thébault (Fra) El2, Rabobank Espoirs RB3, L. Roberts (Aus) COM,
R. Hayles (Gbr) El2.

2 - 11 April
Tour of Uruguay (Uru)
Final overall standings
1. **Jorge Giacinti (Ra) El2**
2. Daniel Fuentes (Uru) El2
3. Miguel Sattler (Uru) El2

Winners of stages:
C. Silva (Uru) El2, N. Pias (Uru) El2, R. Mascarañas (Uru) El2 ,
M. Medici (Ra) El2 x 2, W. Miraballes (Uru) El2 x 2, AUT. Colla (Ra) El2,
Luis AUT. Martinez (Uru) El2.

9 - 12 April
Week of Lombardie (Ita)
Final overall standings
1. **Michele Scarponi (Ita) DVE**
2. Timothy Jones (Zim) DVE
3. Radoslaw Romanik (Pol) HOP

Winners of stages:
M. Scarponi (Ita) DVE x 2,
I. Quaranta (Ita) FPF, Sl. Kohut (Pol) HOP.

15 - 18 April
Tour of Abruzzes (Ita)
Final overall standings
1. **Aleksandr Kuchynski (Blr) AMO**
2. Valter Bonca (Slo) PER
3. Domenico Quagliarello (Ita) El2

Winners of stages:
I. Fanelli (Ita) AMO, R. Marzoli (Ita) AUT&S,
R. Sutherland (Aus) RB3, P. Loretone (Ita) El2

15 - 17 April
Sea Otter Classic (Usa)
Final overall standings
1. **Chris Horner (Usa) WEB**
2. Michael Jones (Usa) HNC
3. Charles Dionne (Can) WEB

Winners of stages:
H. Godfrey (Nzl) HNC, T. Klasna (Usa) SIE, C. Horner (Usa) WEB.

23 - 25 April
Szlakiem Grodòw Piastowskich (Pol)
Final overall standings
1. **Piotr Przydzial (Pol) HOP**
2. Dawid Krupa (Pol) LEG
3. Tomasz Kiendys (Pol) MIK

Winners of stages:
J. Zarebski (Pol) HOP, M. Wiesiak (Pol) NIP, P. Przydzial (Pol) HOP.

25 April - 1st May
Circuit des Mines (Fra)
Final overall standings
1. **Joost Posthuma (Ned) RB3**
2. Jukka Vastaranta (Fin) RB3
3. Lars Boom (Ned) RB3

Winners of stages:
Rabobank Espoirs RB3, D. Bertolini (Ita) AUT&S x 2, J. Vastaranta (Fin) RB3,
R. Downing (Gbr) El2, I. Gabrovski (Bul) OKT, B. Mervar (Slo) FPF,
J. Posthuma (Ned) RB3, W. van Mechelen (Bel) VLA.

25 April - 1st May
Tour of Turkey (Tur)
Final overall standings
1. **Ahad Kazemi Sarai (Iri) El2**
2. Hossein Asgari (Iri) El2
3. Svetoslav Tchanliev (Bul) El2

Winners of stages:
Y. Sobal (Blr) El2 x 2, N. Kiral (Tur) El2, S. Tchanliev (Bul) El2,
S. Tretyakov (Kaz) El2, V. Rapinski (Blr) NIC, S. Lavrenenko (Kaz) El2.

27 April - 2 May
Tour of Greece (Gre)
Final overall standings
1. **Assan Bazayev (Kaz) CAP**
2. André Schulze (Ger) VCF
3. Maxim Iglinskiy (Kaz) CAP

Winners of stages:
M. Iglinskiy (Kaz) CAP, AUT. Schulze (Ger) VCF x 3, P. Lazar (Cze) El2.

4 - 9 May
Tour of Slovenia (Slo)
Final overall standings
1. **Mitja Mahoric (Slo) PER**
2. Aleksandr Kuchynski (Blr) AMO
3. Matic Strgar (Slo) El2

Winners of stages:
AUT. Kuchynski (Blr) AMO, B. Bozic (Slo) PER x 2, J. Ljungblad (Swe) AMO,
M. Mahoric (Slo) PER, T. Nose (Slo) El2, P. Möhlmann (Ned) AXA.

6 - 9 May
Prize of Slantchev Brjag (Bul)
Final overall standings
1. **Ivaïlo Gabrovski (Bul) OKT**
2. Andrey Yatsenko (Bul) El2
3. Vytautas Kaupas (Ltu) El2

Winners of stages:
I. Gabrovski (Bul) OKT x 4.

15 - 23 May
Olympia's Tour (Ned)
Final overall standings
1. **Thomas Dekker (Ned) RB3**
2. Rory Sutherland (Aus) RB3
3. Bas Giling (Ned) RB3

Winners of stages:
T. Dekker (Ned) RB3 x 2, M. van der Pluijm (Ned) VHE,
D. Kozontchouk (Rus) El2, J. Vastaranta (Fin) RB3,
AUT. Wallaard (Ned) AXA, AUT.I Ilesic (Slo) PER,
P. Möhlmann (Ned) AXA x 2, R. Sutherland (Aus) RB3.

23 - 30 May
FDB Milk Ras (Irl)
Final overall standings
1. **David McCann (Irl) El2**
2. Valter Bonca (Slo) PER
3. David O'Loughlin (Irl) El2

Winners of stages:
V. Bonca (Slo) PER, S. Cohnen (Ned) COM, D. Nally (Irl) ALM,
D. McCann (Irl) El2 x 2, M. Elliott (Gbr) El2 x 2, D. O'Loughlin (Irl) El2.

23 - 30 May
Tour of Japan (Jpn)
Final overall standings
1. **Shinichi Fukushima (Jpn) BGT**
2. Roberto Lozano (Esp) El2
3. Christian Heule (Sui) MKV

Winners of stages:
M. Wiesiak (Pol) NIP, T. Beppu (Jpn) El2,
R. Lozano (Esp) El2 x 2, AUT. Schulze (Ger) VCF, S. Guerrini (Ita) NIP.

25 - 30 May
Tour of Navarre (Esp)
Final overall standings
1. **Alexey Bougrov (Rus) El2**
2. Antonio Berasategui (Esp) El2
3. Jorge Nogaledo (Esp) El2

Winners of stages:
AUT. Berasategui (Esp) El2, AUT. Bougrov (Rus) El2, P. Urtasun (Esp) El2,
AUT. Perez de Lezaun (Esp) El2, H. Duclos-Lassalle (Fra) CAE,
J. Almagro (Esp) El2, I. Erviti (Esp) El2.

8 - 13 June
Baltyk-Karkonosze Tour (Pol)
Final overall standings
1. **Slawomir Kohut (Pol) HOP**
2. Jamie Burrow (Gbr) AMO
3. Aleksandr Klimenko (Ukr) ATI

Winners of stages:
M. Lewandowski (Pol) ATI, M. Gebka (Pol) DHL x 2,
L. Balciunas (Ltu) El2, Sl. Kohut (Pol) HOP, J. Rebiewski (Pol) MIK,
R. Radosz (Pol) PSB.

9 - 13 June
Ringerike GP (Nor)
Final overall standings
1. **Kimmo Kananen (Fin) TBN**
2. Simon Gerrans (Aus) El2
3. Gabriel Rasch (Nor) El2

Winners of stages:
M. Christensen (Den) TPH, M. Breschel (Den) TPH,
J.M Rasmussen (Den) TPH, K. Kananen (Fin) TBN,
J. Lucassen (Ned) AXA.

11 - 20 June
Tour of Tunisia (Tun)
Final overall standings
1. **Jeremy Maartens (Rsa) El2**
2. Alfonso Falzarano (Ita) El2
3. Simone Biasci (Ita) El2

Winners of stages:
AUT. Schulze (Ger) VCF x 2, M. Lange (Rsa) El2 x 3, AUT. Falzarano (Ita) El2,
P. Köhler (Ger) VCF, J. Maartens (Rsa) El2, G. Moureu (Ra) El2,
S. Biasci (Ita) El2

12 - 18 June
Tour of Korea (Kor)
Final overall standings
1. **Corey Lange (Can) MPC**
2. Shinri Suzuki (Jpn) SHI
3. Karl Menzies (Aus) El2

Winners of stages:
AUT. Acton (Ra) El2 x 3, D. McCann (Irl) GNT x 2,
Jae Jang Sun (Kor) El2, AUT. Taradguila (Uru) El2.

15 au 20 June
Tour of Serbia (Scg)
Final overall standings
1. **Koji Fukushima (Jpn) BGT**
2. Matej Marin (Slo) PER
3. Nebosja Jovanovic (Scg) El2

Winners of stages:
K. Fukushima (Jpn) BGT, S. Fukushima (Jpn) BGT, P. Nevdakh (Kaz) El2,
T. Schüler (Ger) TBH, S. Tchanliev (Bul) El2, B. Bozic (Slo) PER.

16 - 22 June
Circuit Montañes (Esp)
Final overall standings
1. **Fernando Serrano Sanchez (Esp) El2**
2. Antonio Lopez Villalgordo (Esp) El2
3. Alexis Rodriguez Hernandez (Esp) El2

Winners of stages:
AUT. Galdos (Esp) NIP, P. Brutt (Rus) LOK, O. Ruban (Ukr) El2,
I. Gutierrez Cataluña (Esp) El2, W. van der Linden (Bel) VLA,
J. Agirrezabala (Esp) El2, S. Dominguez (Esp) El2,
L. Tymchenko (Ukr) El2.

27 - 31 July
Dookola Mazowska (Pol)
Final overall standings
1. **Adam Wadecki (Pol) ATI**
2. Piotr Zaradny (Pol) MIK
3. Krzysztof Jezowski (Pol) MIK

Winners of stages:
P. Zaradny (Pol) MIK x 3,
J. Welniak (Pol) LEG, AUT. Wadecki (Pol) ATI.

5 - 7 August
Tour of Malopolska (Pol)
Final overall standings
1. **Ondrej Fadrny (Cze) PSK**
2. Sebastian Skiba (Pol) LEG
3. Robert Radosz (Pol) PSB

Winners of stages:
0. Fadrny (Cze) PSK, K. Jezowski (Pol) MIK x 2

25 - 29 August
Tour of Slovakia (Svk)
Final overall standings
1. **Piotr Chmielewski (Pol) ATI**
2. Dawid Krupa (Pol) LEG
3. Kamil Vrana (Cze) PSK

Winners of stages:
D. Skoczylas (Pol) PSB, J. van Groezen (Ned) VHE, M. Riska (Cze) PSK,
AUT. Wadecki (Pol) ATI, S. Skiba (Pol) LEG, F. Rabon (Cze) PSK.

28 August - 7 September
Tour of Santa Catarina (Bra)
Final overall standings
1. **Matias Médici (Ra) El2**
2. Antonio Nascimento (Bra) El2
3. Pedro Autran (Bra) El2

Winners of stages:
M. Medici (Ra) El2 x 2, M. Pinto (Bra) El2 x 3,
N. Aparecido Santos (Bra) El2, V. Justino (Bra) El2,
P. Azevedo (Bra) El2 x 2, AUT. Nascimento (Bra) El2,
AUT. Sartassov (Rus) El2, R. Ruiz (Bra) El2.

30 August - 12 September
Tour of Venezuela (Ven)
Final overall standings
1. **Federico Muñoz (Col) El2**
2. Franklin Chacón (Ven) El2
3. José Rujano (Ven) CLM

Winners of stages:
G. Cordovès (Cub) El2 x 7, M. Chacón (Ven) El2, J. Chacón (Ven) El2,
F. Gonzalez Martinez (Col) CLM, F. Muñoz (Col) El2,
Arthur Garcia (Ven) El2 x 2, G. Báez (Col) El2.

2 - 11 September
Tour de l'Avenir (Fra)
Final overall standings
1. **Sylvain Calzati (Fra) RAG**
2. Thomas Lövkvist (Swe) FDJ
3. Christophe Le Mével (Fra) C.AUT

Winners of stages:
T. Dekker (Ned) RB3, Séb. Chavanel (Fra) BLB x 3,
S. Caethoven (Bel) VLA, C. Kern (Fra) BLB, T. Farrar (Usa) HNC,
M. Mares (Cze) PSK, T. Eltink (Ned) RB3, T. Lövkvist (Swe) FDJ.

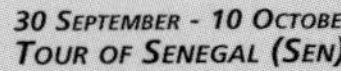

12 - 21 September
Tour of Bulgaria (Bul)

Final overall standings

1.	**Tomasz Kloczko (Pol)**	**CHL**
2.	Are Andresen (Nor)	SPA
3.	Nelson Vitorino (Por)	WBP

Winners of stages:
T. Kloczko (Pol) CHL, AUT. Baranauskas (Ltu) El2, G. Zajc (Slo) El2, N .Vitorino (Por) WBP, I. Gabrovski (Bul) OKT x 2, V. Kaupas (Ltu) El2, J. Volungevicius (Ltu) El2, R. Konstantinov (Bul) NES, E. Balev (Bul) El2, E. Poldmä (Est) KCT.

15 - 20 September
Tour of Hokkaido (Jpn)

Final overall standings

1.	**Kam Po Wong (Hkg)**	**El2**
2.	Giuseppe Ribolzi (Ita)	NIP
3.	Eddy Hilger (Usa)	MPC

Winners of stages:
T. Nishitani (Jpn) El2 x 3, Kam Po Wong (Hkg) El2, Sung Baek Park (Kor) El2 x 2.

17 - 18 September
Tour de la Somme (Fra)

Final overall standings

1.	**Serhiy Krushevskiy (Uzb)**	**OKT**
2.	Andrei Ptchelkin (Rus)	El2
3.	Frédéric Mille (Fra)	El2

Winners of stages:
AUT. Ptchelkin (Rus) El2, D. Boucher (Fra) OKT, W. van Mechelen (Bel) VLA.

30 September - 10 October
Tour of Senegal (Sen)

Final overall standings

1.	**Mariano Giallorenzo (Ita)**	**CLM (s)**
2.	Philippe Schnyder (Sui)	CLM
3.	Stéphane Botherel (Fra)	El2

Winners of stages:
R. Illiano (Ita) CLM x 3, P. van Agtmaal (Ned) AXA, D. Sosnovchenko (Rus) CLM (s) x 3, N. Verots (Fra) El2, S. Botherel (Fra) El2.

One day races

No category

29 August
GP Ouest France in Plouay (Fra) — 198 km

1.	**Didier Rous (Fra)**	**BLB**
2.	Sergue Baguet (Bel)	LOT
3.	Guido Trentin (Ita)	COF
4.	Danilo Hondo (Ger)	GST
5.	Giulio Tomi (Ita)	VIN
6.	Vladimir Duma (Ukr)	LAN
7.	Patrick Calcagni (Sui)	VIN
8.	Cédric Vasseur (Fra)	COF
9.	Sergio Barbero (Ita)	LAM
10.	Fabian Wegmann (Ger)	GST

18 September
Tour of Latium (Ita) — Rieti/Nettuno - 196 km

1.	**J. Antonio Flecha (Esp)**	**FAS**
2.	Gilberto Simoni (Ita)	SAE
3.	Jan Ullrich (Ger)	TMO
4.	Marco Serpellini (Ita)	GST
5.	Rinaldo Nocentini (Ita)	AUT&S
6.	Massimo Giunti (Ita)	DVE
7.	Gabriele Missaglia (Ita)	TBL
8.	Dario Frigo (Ita)	FAS
9.	Andrea Noe' (Ita)	ALB
10.	Luca Mazzanti (Ita)	PAN

Category 1

27 March
GP E3 in Harelbeke (Bel) — 195 km

1.	**Tom Boonen (Bel)**	**QSD**
2.	Jaan Kirsipuu (Est)	A2R
3.	Andris Nauduzs (Lat)	DVE
4.	Steven de Jongh (Ned)	RAB
5.	Marcus Ljunqvist (Swe)	ALB
6.	Gabriele Balducci (Ita)	SAE
7.	Andreas Klier (Ger)	TMO
8.	Roger Hammond (Gbr)	MRB
9.	Leon van Bon (Ned)	LOT
10.	Fabio Baldato (Ita)	ALB

14 April
GP of Escaut (Bel) — Schoten -200 km

1.	**Tom Boonen (Bel)**	**QSD**
2.	Robbie McEwen (Aus)	LOT
3.	Simone Cadamuro (Ita)	DEN
4.	Enrico Poitschke (Ger)	WIE
5.	Bernhard Eisel (AUT)	FDJ
6.	Alexandre Usov (Blr)	PHO
7.	Ludovic Capelle (Bel)	LAN
8.	Enrico Degano (Ita)	TBL
9.	Jeremy Hunt (Gbr)	MRB
10.	Roy Sentjens (Ned)	RAB

1st May
GP of Francfort (Henniger Turm) (Ger) — 205 km

1.	**Karsten Kroon (Ned)**	**RAB**
2.	Danilo Hondo (Ger)	GST
3.	Johan Coenen (Bel)	MRB
4.	Gregory Rast (Sui)	PHO
5.	Torsten Schmidt (Ger)	GST
6.	Björn Leukemans (Bel)	MRB
7.	Erik Zabel (Ger)	TMO
8.	Marcus Zberg (Sui)	GST
9.	Eddy Mazzoleni (Ita)	SAE
10.	Sergio Marinangeli (Ita)	DVE

17 August
3 Vallées Varésines (Ita) — 197,9 km

1.	**Fabian Wegmann (Ger)**	**GST**
2.	Danilo Di Luca (Ita)	SAE
3.	Vladimir Duma (Ukr)	LAN
4.	Filippo Simeoni (Ita)	DVE
5.	Roberto Petito (Ita)	FAS
6.	Davide Rebellin (Ita)	GST
7.	Paolo Tiralongo (Ita)	PAN
8.	Leonardo Bertagnolli (Ita)	SAE
9.	Dario Frigo (Ita)	FAS
10.	Paolo Savoldelli (Ita)	TMO

21 August
Tour of Venetia (Ita) — 206 km

1.	**Gilberto Simoni (Ita)**	**SAE**
2.	Matteo Tosatto (Ita)	FAS
3.	Massimo Giunti (Ita)	DVE
4.	Damiano Cunego (Ita)	SAE
5.	Franco Pellizotti (Ita)	ALB
6.	Rinaldo Nocentini (Ita)	AUT&S
7.	Luca Mazzanti (Ita)	PAN
8.	Paolo Tiralongo (Ita)	PAN
9.	Leonardo Bertagnolli (Ita)	SAE
10.	Andrea Noe' (Ita)	ALB

29 August
Tour of the Argovia (Sui) — Gippingen - 196 km

1.	**Matteo Tosatto (Ita)**	**FAS**
2.	Markus Zberg (Sui)	GST
3.	Martin Elmiger (Sui)	PHO
4.	Massimiliano Mori (Ita)	DVE
5.	Frank Schleck (Lux)	CSC
6.	Mauro Gerosa (Ita)	VIN
7.	Wesley van der Linden (Bel)	VLA
8.	Pieter Mertens (Bel)	VLA
9.	Roger Beuchat (Sui)	VIN
10.	Andrej Hauptman (Slo)	LAM

4 September
Coppa Placci (Ita) — 200 km

1.	**Leonardo Bertagnolli (Ita)**	**SAE**
2.	Davide Rebellin (Ita)	GST
3.	Filippo Simeoni (Ita)	DVE
4.	Luca Mazzanti (Ita)	PAN
5.	Przemyslaw Niemec (Pol)	MIE
6.	Marco Fertonani (Ita)	PHO
7.	Romans Vainsteins (Lat)	LAM
8.	Fabian Wegmann (Ger)	GST
9.	Mirko Celestino (Ita)	SAE
10.	Massimo Giunti (Ita)	DVE

11 September
Paris-Bruxelles (Fra/Bel) — Soissons/Anderlecht - 226 km

1.	**Nick Nuyens (Bel)**	**QSD**
2.	Philippe Gilbert (Bel)	FDJ
3.	Allan Johansen (Den)	BGL
4.	Jeremy Hunt (Gbr)	MRB
5.	Paolo Bettini (Ita)	QSD
6.	Marc Wauters (Bel)	RAB
7.	Rik Reinerink (Ned)	CHO
8.	Matthé Pronk (Ned)	BGL
9.	Manuele Mori (Ita)	SDV
10.	Nico Eeckhout (Bel)	LOT

12 September
GP «La Voix du Nord» in Fourmies (Fra) — 202 km

1.	**Andrey Kashechkin (Kaz)**	**C.AUT**
2.	Dmitriy Fofonov (Kaz)	COF
3.	Thor Hushovd (Nor)	C.AUT
4.	Stefan Adamsson (Swe)	TBL
5.	Romans Vainsteins (Lat)	LAM
6.	Sylvain Chavanel (Fra)	BLB
7.	Grischa Niermann (Ger)	RAB
8.	Nicolas Vogondy (Fra)	FDJ
9.	Marcus Zberg (Sui)	GST
10.	Ludo Dierckxsens (Bel)	LAN

19 September
GP des Nations (Fra) — a Elbeuf - 54 km (c.l.m)

1.	**Michael Rich (Ger)**	**GST**
2.	Uwe Peschel (Ger)	GST
3.	J. Ivan Gutierrez Palacios (Esp)	IBB
4.	Michael Rogers (Aus)	QSD
5.	Eddy Seigneur (Fra)	RAG
6.	Jens Voigt (Ger)	C.AUT
7.	Yuriy Krivtsov (Ukr)	A2R
8.	Bradley McGee (Aus)	FDJ
9.	Jean Nuttli (Sui)	VOL
10.	Frédéric Finot (Fra)	RAG

25 September
Tour of Emilie (Ita) — 196 km

1.	**Ivan Basso (Ita)**	**CSC**

2. Francesco Casagrande (Ita) VIN
3. Rinaldo Nocentini (Ita) AUT&S
4. Leonardo Bertagnolli (Ita) SAE
5. Jan Ullrich (Ger) TMO
6. Franco Pellizotti (Ita) ALB
7. Dario Frigo (Ita) FAS
8. Marcel Strauss (Sui) GST
9. Luca Mazzanti (Ita) PAN
10. Igor Pugaci (Mda) DEN

13 October
Milan-Turin (Ita) 198,5 km
1. **Marcos Serrano (Esp) LST**
2. Eddy Mazzoleni (Ita) SAE
3. Francesco Casagrande (Ita) VIN
4. Cadel Evans (Aus) TMO
5. Danilo Hondo (Ger) GST
6. Allan Davis (Aus) LST
7. Matthias Kessler (Ger) TMO
8. Dmitriy Fofonov (Kaz) COF
9. Cédric Vasseur (Fra) COF
10. Ondrej Sosenka (Cze) AUT&S

14 October
Tour of Piemont (Ita) 198,5 km
1. **Allan Davis (Aus) LST**
2. Alberto Ongarato (Ita) FAS
3. Francesco Chicchi (Ita) FAS
4. Steven de Jongh (Ned) RAB
5. Roger Beuchat (Sui) VIN
6. Andreas Klier (Ger) TMO
7. René Haselbacher (AUT) GST
8. Manuel Quinziato (Ita) LAM
9. Uros Murn (Slo) PHO
10. Patrick Calcagni (Sui) VIN

CATEGORY 2

17 February
Trophy of Laigueglia (Ita) 183,3 km
1. **Filippo Pozzato (Ita) FAS**
2. Lorenzo Bernucci (Ita) LAN
3. Romans Vainsteins (Lat) LAM
4. Serhiy Honchar (Ukr) DEN
5. Luca Paolini (Ita) QSD

22 February
Trophy of Luis Puig (Esp) Valencia/Benidorm - 197,3 km
1. **Oscar Freire (Esp) RAB**
2. Alejandro Valverde (Esp) KEL
3. Josu Silloniz (Esp) EUS
4. Erik Zabel (Ger) TMO
5. Luis Pasamontes (Esp) REB

29 February
Kuurne-Brussel-Kuurne (Bel) 188 km
1. **Steven de Jongh (Ned) RAB**
2. Paolo Bettini (Ita) QSD
3. Gerben Löwik (Ned) CHO
4. Stuart O'Grady (Aus) COF
5. Geert Omloop (Bel) MRB

24 March
A Travers la Flandre (Bel) à Waregem - 204 km
1. **Ludovic Capelle (Bel) LAN**
2. Jaan Kirsipuu (Est) A2R
3. Roger Hammond (Gbr) MRB
4. Dave Bruylandts (Bel) CHO
5. Franck Pencolé (Fra) OKT

28 March
Flèche Brabançonne (Bel)
1. **Luca Paolini (Ita) QSD**
2. Michael Boogerd (Ned) RAB
3. Nico Sijmens (Bel) LAN
4. Didier Rous (Fra) BLB
5. Axel Merckx (Bel) LOT

28 March
GP Miguel Indurain Estella - 189 km
1. **Matthias Kessler (Ger) TMO**
2. M.AUT Martin Perdiguero (Esp) SDV
3. Daniele Righi (Ita) LAM
4. Angel Vicioso (Esp) LST
5. J. Ivan Gutierrez Palacios (Esp) IBB

12 April
Tour of Cologne (Ger) 201,2 km
1. **Erik Zabel (Ger) TMO**
2. Danilo Hondo (Ger) GST
3. Kirk O'Bee (Usa) NIC
4. Björn Leukemans (Bel) MRB
5. Stefan Schumacher (Ger) TLM

12 April
Veenendaal-Veenendaal (Ned) 207 km
1. **Simone Cadamuro (Ita) DEN**
2. Robbie McEwen (Aus) LOT
3. Jo Planckaert (Bel) MRB
4. Jans Koerts (Ned) CHO
5. Serhiy Honchar (Ukr) DEN

25 April
Tour of Appenins (Ita) 195 km
1. **Damiano Cunego (Ita) SAE**
2. Giuliano Figueras (Ita) PAN
3. Rinaldo Nocentini (Ita) AUT&S
4. Luis Felipe Laverde (Col) FPF
5. Gilberto Simoni (Ita) SAE

1st May
GP de Larciano (Ita) 200 km
1. **Damiano Cunego (Ita) SAE**
2. Igor Astarloa (Esp) LAM
3. Ruggero Borghi (Ita) DEN
4. Rinaldo Nocentini (Ita) AUT&S
5. Michele Scotto d'Abusco (Ita) LAM

2 May
CSC Classic in Aarhus (Den)
1. **Kurt-Asle Arvesen (Nor) CSC**
2. Magnus Bäckstedt (Swe) ALB
3. Allan Johansen (Den) BGL
4. Michael Sandstød (Den) CSC
5. Marcin Lewandowski (Pol) ATI

6 June
Wachovia USPRO Championship (Usa) 250 km
1. **Francisco Ventoso (Esp) SDV**
2. Antonio Bucciero (Ita) SAE
3. Gordon Fraser (Can) HNC
4. Fred Rodriguez (Usa) AUT&S
5. Plamen Stoianov (Bul) HOP

4 July
Trophy Matteotti (Ita) Pescara - 188,5 km
1. **Danilo Di Luca (Ita) SAE**
2. Paolo Bossoni (Ita) LAM
3. Oscar Camenzind (Sui) PHO
4. Pasquale Muto (Ita) MIE
5. Matteo Carrara (Ita) LAM

25 July
GP Villafranca in Ordizia (Esp)
1. **David Herrero Llorente (Esp) ALM**
2. Gustavo Dominguez Lemos (Esp) REB
3. David Latasa (Esp) KEL
4. Jon Del Rio (Esp) ALM
5. Luis Perez Romero (Esp) REB

31 July
LUK Cup in Bühl (Ger) 82,2 km (c.l.m in duo)
1. **Bobby Julich (Usa)/Jens Voigt (Ger) CSC**
2. Uwe Peschel (Ger)/Michael Rich (Ger) GST
3. M. Fothen (Ger)/S. Lang (Ger) GST
4. L. Armstrong (Usa)/G. Hincapie (Usa) USP
5. K-AUT. Arvesen (Nor)/AUT. Peron (Ita) CSC

4 August
GP of Camaiore (Ita) 193,7 km
1. **Paolo Bettini (Ita) QSD**
2. Danilo Di Luca (Ita) SAE
3. Luca Paolini (Ita) QSD
4. Frank Schleck (Lux) CSC
5. Antonio D'Aniello (Ita) MIE

18 August
Coppa Agostoni (Ita) 196,8 km
1. **Leonardo Bertagnolli (Ita) SAE**
2. Dario Frigo (Ita) FAS
3. Gonzalo Bayarri (Esp) PHO
4. Roberto Sgambelluri (Ita) VIN
5. Patxi Vila (Esp) LAM

29 August
GP E.Merckx à Bruxelles (Bel) 43,9 km (c.l.m en duo)
1. **Thomas Dekker (Ned)/Koen de Kort (Ned) RB3**
2. Bobby Julich (Usa)/Jens Voigt (Ger) CSC
3. Uwe Peschel (Ger)/Michael Rich (Ger) GST
4. Erik Dekker (Ned)/Marc Wauters (Bel) RAB
5. V. Ekimov (Rus)/G. Hincapie (Usa) USP

2 September
Trophy Melinda in Clès (Ita) 194 km
1. **Davide Rebellin (Ita) GST**
2. Paolo Tiralongo (Ita) PAN
3. Dario Frigo (Ita) FAS
4. Leonardo Bertagnolli (Ita) SAE
5. Luca Mazzanti (Ita) PAN

4 September
Midden-Zeeland Delta Tour (Ned) 199 km
1. **Nico Eeckhout (Bel) LOT**
2. Robbie McEwen (Aus) LOT
3. Stefan van Dijk (Ned) LOT
4. Jans Koerts (Ned) CHO
5. Wouter van Mechelen (Bel) VLA

5 September
Tour of Romagne (Ita) 190,2 km
1. **Gianluca Bortolami (Ita) LAM**
2. Matteo Tosatto (Ita) FAS
3. Fabian Wegmann (Ger) GST
4. Francesco Failli (Ita) DVE
5. Massimo Giunti (Ita) DVE

8 September
GP van Steenbergen (Bel) Aartselaar - 201 km
1. **Tom Boonen (Bel) QSD**
2. Nico Eeckhout (Bel) LOT
3. Ralf Grabsch (Ger) WIE
4. Gerben Löwik (Ned) CHO
5. Oscar Laguna (Esp) REB

15 September
GP of Wallonie (Bel) Chaudfontaine/Namur - 193,1 km
1. **Nick Nuyens (Bel) QSD**
2. Philippe Gilbert (Bel) FDJ
3. Jérôme Pineau (Fra) BLB
4. Bert de Waele (Bel) LAN
5. Dmitriy Fofonov (Kaz) COF

19 September
GP of Prato (Ita) 177,4 km
1. **Nick Nuyens (Bel) QSD**
2. Francesco Bellotti (Ita) TBL
3. Mirko Celestino (Ita) SAE
4. Daniele Nardello (Ita) TMO
5. Bo Hamburger (Den) AUT&S

23 September
Coppa Sabatini (Ita) 197,7 km
1. **Jan Ullrich (Ger) TMO**
2. Franco Pellizotti (Ita) ALB
3. Michael Boogerd (Ned) RAB
4. Uros Murn (Slo) PHO
5. Fabian Wegmann (Ger) GST

26 September
GP Beghelli (Ita) 199 km
1. **Danilo Hondo (Ger) GST**
2. Fabio Baldato (Ita) ALB
3. Karsten Kroon (Ned) RAB
4. Filippo Pozzato (Ita) FAS
5. Lars Michaelsen (Den) CSC

CATEGORY 3

31 January
Doha International GP (Qat) 117 km
1. **Simone Cadamuro (Ita) DEN**
2. Tom Boonen (Bel) QSD
3. Francesco Chicchi (Ita) FAS
4. Giosue' Bonomi (Ita) SAE
5. Lars Michaelsen (Den) CSC

1st February
Challenge Majorque #1 (Esp) Palma/Palma - 82,5 km
1. **Allan Davis (Aus) LST**
2. Oscar Freire (Esp) RAB
3. Erik Zabel (Ger) TMO
4. Danilo Hondo (Ger) GST
5. Paolo Bettini (Ita) QSD

2 February
Challenge Majorque #2 (Esp) Alcudia/Port d'Alcudia - 159 km
1. **Oscar Freire (Esp) RAB**
2. Erik Zabel (Ger) TMO
3. Allan Davis (Aus) LST
4. Sebastian Siedler (Ger) WIE
5. Paolo Bettini (Ita) QSD

3 February
Challenge Majorque #3 (Esp) Soller/Port de Soller - 150,6 km
1. **Alejandro Valverde (Esp) KEL**
2. David Blanco Rodriguez (Esp) KEL
3. Ruben Plaza Molina (Esp) KEL
4. Antonio Colom (Esp) IBB
5. Koldo Gil (Esp) LST

3 February
GP de "La Marseillaise" (Fra) Gardanne/Aubagne - 150 km
1. **Baden Cooke (Aus) FDJ**
2. Jo Planckaert (Bel) MRB
3. Fabio Baldato (Ita) ALB
4. Stefan van Dijk (Ned) LOT
5. Gerben Löwik (Ned) CHO

4 February
Challenge Majorque #4 (Esp) Calabona-Manacor - 159,8 km
1. **Allan Davis (Aus) LST**
2. Erik Zabel (Ger) TMO
3. Danilo Hondo (Ger) GST
4. Steven de Jongh (Ned) RAB
5. Carlos Garcia Quesada (Esp) KEL

5 February
Challenge Majorque #5 (Esp) Magaluf-Palmanova - 149,3 km
1. **Unai Etxebarria (Ven) EUS**
2. Oscar Freire (Esp) RAB
3. Erik Zabel (Ger) TMO
4. Danilo Hondo (Ger) GST
5. Paolo Bettini (Ita) QSD

Final overall standings
1. **Antonio Colom (Esp) IBB**
2. Carlos Garcia Quesada (Esp) KEL
3. David Blanco Rodriguez (Esp) KEL

8 February
GP of Côte des Etrusques (Ita) San Vicenzo / Donoratico - 197,3 km
1. **Yuriy Mitlushenko (Ukr) LAN**
2. Andrus Aug (Est) DVE
3. Crescenzo D'Amore (Ita) AUT&S
4. Elio Aggiano (Ita) LPR
5. Andrea Ferrigato (Ita) AUT&S

15 February
Tour of Ligurie (Ita) Mignanego/Arenzano - 133,8 km
1. **Filippo Pozzato (Ita) FAS**
2. Crescenzo D'Amore (Ita) AUT&S
3. Fred Rodriguez (Usa) AUT&S
4. Paolo Bossoni (Ita) LAM
5. Aart Vierhouten (Ned) LOT

28 February
GP of Chiasso (Sui) 165,7 km
1. **Franco Pellizotti (Ita) ALB**
2. Leonardo Bertagnolli (Ita) SAE
3. Cédric Vasseur (Fra) COF
4. Fabian Wegmann (Ger) GST
5. Ivan Fanelli (Ita) AMO

29 February
Clasica of Almeria (Esp) 165,7 km
1. **Jérôme Pineau (Fra) BLB**
2. Thomas Voeckler (Fra) BLB
3. Benjamin Noval (Esp) USP
4. Julio Lopez de la Torre (Esp) REB
5. Björn Leukemans (Bel) MRB

29 February
GP of Lugano (Sui) 160 km
1. **Frédéric Bessy (Fra) COF**
2. David Moncoutié (Fra) COF
3. Vladimir Miholjevic (Cro) ALB
4. Marcus Zberg (Sui) GST
5. Ruben Lobato (Esp) SDV

3 March
Memorial J.Samyn à Fayt-le-Franc (Bel) 184 km
1. **Robbie McEwen (Aus) LOT**

2.	Ludovic Capelle (Bel)	LAN
3.	Jans Koerts (Ned)	CHO
4.	Saulius Ruskys (Ltu)	OKT
5.	Michel van Haecke (Bel)	MRB

6 March

Tour of Reggio de Calabre (Ita)		184 km
1.	**Andris Nauduzs (Lat)**	**DVE**
2.	Mauro Zinetti (Ita)	VIN
3.	Dmitri Konyshev (Rus)	LPR
4.	Angelo Furlan (Ita)	ALB
5.	Giosue' Bonomi (Ita)	SAE

8 March

Tour of Etna (Ita)		184 km
1.	**Leonardo Bertagnolli (Ita)**	**SAE**
2.	Kyrylo Pospeev (Ukr)	AUT&S
3.	Marlon Perez Arango (Col)	CLM
4.	Vladimir Duma (Ukr)	LAN
5.	Luca Mazzanti (Ita)	PAN

17 March

Nokere koerse (Bel)		184 km
1.	**Max van Heeswijk (Ned)**	**USP**
2.	Rudi Kemna (Ned)	BGL
3.	Jo Planckaert (Bel)	MRB
4.	Gerben Löwik (Ned)	CHO
5.	James Vanlandschoot (Bel)	REB

21 March

GP Rudy Dhaenens (Bel)		191 km
1.	**Geert Omloop (Bel)**	**MRB**
2.	Rudi Kemna (Ned)	BGL
3.	Roger Hammond (Gbr)	MRB
4.	Nico Mattan (Bel)	REB
5.	Roy Sentjens (Ned)	RAB

21 March

Tour of the Lake of Stau (Sui)		Klingnau - 190 km
1.	**Andris Nauduzs (Lat)**	**DVE**
2.	Sergio Marinangeli (Ita)	DVE
3.	Antonio Salomone (Ita)	TBL
4.	Sebastien Siedler (Ger)	WIE
5.	Mauro Santambrogio (Ita)	LPR

8 April

GP Pino Cerami (Bel)		Hornu - 193,1 km
1.	**Nico Sijmens (Bel)**	**LAN**
2.	Martin Elmiger (Sui)	PHO
3.	Thomas Dekker (Ned)	RB3
4.	Dave Bruylandts (Bel)	CHO
5.	Jan Kuyckx (Bel)	VLA

10 April

Tour of Drenthe (Ned)		202,1 km
1.	**Erik Dekker (Ned)**	**RAB**
2.	David McKenzie (Aus)	NIC
3.	Simone Cadamuro (Ita)	DEN
4.	Rudi Kemna (Ned)	BGL
5.	Joost Posthuma (Ned)	RB3

11 April

Klasika Primavera in Amorebieta (Esp)		182 km
1.	**Alejandro Valverde (Esp)**	**KEL**
2.	Eddy Mazzoleni (Ita)	SAE
3.	Jens Voigt (Ger)	CSC
4.	Unai Etxebarria (Ven)	EUS
5.	Ryder Hesjedal (Can)	USP

17 April

Circuit des bords de l'Escaut (Bel)		Temse/Bazel Kruibeke - 189 km
1.	**Stefan van Dijk (Ned)**	**LOT**
2.	Dennis Kraft (Ger)	ATI
3.	Borut Bozic (Slo)	PER
4.	Kevin van der Slagmolen (Bel)	VLA
5.	Anthony Geslin (Fra)	BLB

17 April

Groningen/Münster (Ned/Ger)		201,5 km
1.	**Robert Förster (Ger)**	**GST**
2.	Sebastian Siedler (Ger)	WIE
3.	David Kopp (Ger)	TLM
4.	René Weissinger (Ger)	VOL
5.	Michal Precechtel (Cze)	ZVZ

25 April

Tour of Noord-Holland (Ned)		200 km
1.	**Stefan van Dijk (Ned)**	**LOT**
2.	Allan Bo Andresen (Den)	BGL
3.	Jans Koerts (Ned)	CHO
4.	Rudi Kemna (Ned)	BGL
5.	Ronald Schür (Ned)	APA

1st May

GP S.AUT.T.S in Herning (Den)		199 km
1.	**Frank Høj (Den)**	**CSC**
2.	Michele Bartoli (Ita)	CSC
3.	Stefan Kupfernagel (Ger)	TLM
4.	Michael Sandstød (Den)	CSC
5.	Martin Hvastija (Slo)	ALB

2 May

Tour of Tuscany (Ita)		170 km
1.	**Matteo Tosatto (Ita)**	**FAS**
2.	Alberto Ongarato (Ita)	FAS
3.	Dmitri Konyshev (Rus)	LPR
4.	Matteo Carrara (Ita)	LAM
5.	Oscar Mason (Ita)	VIN

2 May

GP KRKA (Slo)		162 km
1.	**Uros Murn (Slo)**	**PHO**
2.	Borut Bozic (Slo)	PER
3.	Jure Zrimsek (Slo)	EI2
4.	Martin Prazdnovsky (Svk)	EI2
5.	Christian Heule (Sui)	MKV

11 May

Subida al Naranco (Esp)		162 km
1.	**Iban Mayo (Esp)**	**EUS**
2.	M.AUT Martin Perdiguero (Esp)	SDV
3.	Leonardo Piepoli (Ita)	SDV
4.	Samuel Sanchez (Esp)	EUS
5.	David Arroyo (Esp)	LAP

16 May

Köln-Bonn Airport Cup (Ger)		205 km
1.	**Pascal Hungerbühler (Sui)**	**VOL**
2.	Jef Peeters (Bel)	VLA
3.	Harald Morscher (AUT)	VOL
4.	Wim van Huffel (Bel)	VLA
5.	Stefan Kupfernagel (Ger)	TLM

28 May

E.O.S Tallinn GP (Est)		180 km
1.	**Mark Scanlon (Irl)**	**A2R**
2.	Nicolas Inaudi (Fra)	A2R
3.	Arnaud Coyot (Fra)	COF
4.	Mikhaïl Timochine (Rus)	LAN
5.	Jaan Kirsipuu (Est)	A2R

29 May

Ühispanga Tartu Tänavasõit (Est)		188 km
1.	**Mark Scanlon (Irl)**	**A2R**
2.	Slawomir Kohut (Pol)	HOP
3.	Jimmy Engoulvent (Fra)	COF
4.	Kjell Carlström (Fin)	AMO
5.	Allan Oras (Est)	EI2

29 May

TEAG Tour of Hainleite (Ger)		184 km
1.	**Peter Wrolich (AUT)**	**GST**
2.	Francisco Mancebo (Esp)	IBB
3.	Marius Sabaliauskas (Ltu)	SAE
4.	Gabriele Missaglia (Ita)	TBL
5.	Jan Ullrich (Ger)	TMO

30 May

GP of Llodio (Esp)		175,5 km
1.	**Unai Etxebarria (Ven)**	**EUS**
2.	M.AUT Martin Perdiguero (Esp)	SDV
3.	Matteo Carrara (Ita)	LAM
4.	Angel Vicioso (Esp)	LST
5.	Ion Del Rio (Esp)	ALM

1st June

Wachovia Invitational (Usa)		Lancaster - 147 km
1.	**Max van Heeswijk (Ned)**	**USP**
2.	Francisco Ventoso (Esp)	SDV
3.	Fred Rodriguez (Usa)	AUT&S
4.	Lars Michaelsen (Den)	CSC
5.	Ciaran Power (Irl)	NIC

3 June

Wachovia Classic (Usa)		Trenton - 147 km
1.	**Fred Rodriguez (Usa)**	**AUT&S**
2.	Gordon Fraser (Can)	HNC
3.	Lars Michaelsen (Den)	CSC
4.	Alberto Loddo (Ita)	SDV
5.	Ben Brooks (Aus)	JEL

23 June

Noord Nederland Tour (Ned)

Because of the extreme weather conditions (!) 22 runners were classified first equal at the finish!

3 July

Critérium of Abruzzes (Ita)		Alba Adriatica - 171,8 km
1.	**Enrico Degano (Ita)**	**TBL**
2.	Matteo Carrara (Ita)	LAM
3.	Paolo Bossoni (Ita)	LAM
4.	Uros Murn (Slo)	PHO
5.	Ruggero Marzoli (Ita)	AUT&S

4 July

Tour of Doubs (Fra)		Morteau/Pontarlier - 190,5 km
1.	**Mathieu Sprick (Fra)**	**BLB**
2.	Hayden Roulston (Nzl)	COF
3.	Bert de Waele (Bel)	LAN
4.	Frédéric Gabriel (Fra)	MRB
5.	Nicolas Reynaud (Fra)	RAG

17 July

GP of Rio Saliceto e Correggio (Ita)		169 km
1.	**Przemyslaw Niemec (Pol)**	**MIE**
2.	Paolo Tiralongo (Ita)	PAN
3.	Eddy Ratti (Ita)	FLA
4.	Paul Crake (Aus)	CAA
5.	Pasquale Muto (Ita)	MIE

31 July

Memorial R. Otxoa in Getxo (Esp)		185,3 km
1.	**Gert Vanderaerden (Bel)**	**MRB**
2.	Constantino Zaballa (Esp)	SDV
3.	Javier Pascual Rodriguez (Esp)	KEL
4.	Maxim Rudenko (Ukr)	CHO
5.	Luis Leon Sanchez Gil (Esp)	LST

8 August

Subida in Urkiola (Esp)		160 km
1.	**Leonardo Piepoli (Ita)**	**SDV**
2.	Francesco Casagrande (Ita)	LAM
3.	Carlos Garcia Quesada (Esp)	KEL
4.	Marcos Serrano (Esp)	LST
5.	Mauricio Ardila (Col)	CHO

8 August

Tour of Bochum (Ger)		175,2 km
1.	**David Kopp (Ger)**	**TLM**
2.	Lubor Tesar (Cze)	ZVZ
3.	Corey Sweet (Aus)	COM
4.	Stefan Kupfernagel (Ger)	TLM
5.	Enrico Poitschke (Ger)	WIE

10 August

GP Fred Mengoni (Ita)		204 km
1.	**Damiano Cunego (Ita)**	**SAE**
2.	Daniele Nardello (Ita)	TMO
3.	Cristian Moreni (Ita)	ALB
4.	Michele Gobbi (Ita)	DEN
5.	Massimo Giunti (Ita)	DVE

11 August

Trofeo of Castelfidardo (Ita)		179 km
1.	**Emanuele Sella (Ita)**	**PAN**
2.	Bostjan Mervar (Slo)	FPF
3.	Gerrit Glomser (AUT)	SAE
4.	Cristian Murro (Ita)	MIE
5.	Giancarlo Ginestri (Ita)	TEN

14 August

Memorial Henryk Lasaka (Pol)		165 km
1.	**Robert Radosz (Pol)**	**PSB**
2.	Petr Bencik (Cze)	ZVZ
3.	Tomasz Lisowicz (Pol)	MIK
4.	Linus Gerdemann (Ger)	WIN
5.	Marcin Sapa (Pol)	MIK

17 August

GP Tistaert in Zottegem (Bel)		178 km
1.	**David Kopp (Ger)**	**TLM**
2.	Kevin van Impe (Bel)	LOT
3.	Björn Leukemans (Bel)	MRB
4.	Gerben Löwik (Ned)	CHO
5.	Jeroen Boelen (Ned)	VHE

19 August

Coppa Bernocchi (Ita)		199,8 km
1.	**Angelo Furlan (Ita)**	**AUT&S**
2.	Fred Rodriguez (Usa)	ALB
3.	Giosue' Bonomi (Ita)	SAE
4.	Matteo Tosatto (Ita)	FAS
5.	Stefano Zanini (Ita)	QSD

21 August

Tour of Rijke (Ned)		198,2 km
1.	**Jans Koerts (Ned)**	**CHO**
2.	Gorik Gardeyn (Bel)	LOT
3.	Wilco Zuyderwijk (Ned)	VEA
4.	Mathew Hayman (Aus)	RAB
5.	Stefan van Dijk (Ned)	LOT

22 August

Châteauroux Classic of Indre (Fra)		181,5 km
1.	**Aleksandr Kuchynski (Blr)**	**AMO**
2.	José Luis Rubiera (Esp)	USP
3.	Cédric Hervé (Fra)	C.AUT
4.	Lénaïc Olivier (Fra)	AUB
5.	Luca Celli (Ita)	VIN

22 August

Clasica los Puertos (Esp)		Guadarrama - 148 km
1.	**Jorge Ferrio (Esp)**	**ALM**
2.	Carlos Golbano (Esp)	ALM
3.	Gustavo César Veloso (Esp)	REB
4.	David Fernandez Domingo (Esp)	ALM
5.	Vicente Reynes (Esp)	IBB

22 August

GP of the Black Forrest (Ger)		162,4 km
1.	**Markus Fothen (Ger)**	**GST**
2.	Sylvester Szmyd (Pol)	SAE
3.	Tomislav Danculovic (Cro)	PER
4.	Stefan Schumacher (Ger)	TLM
5.	Serguey Yakovlev (Kaz)	TMO

22 August

A Travers Gendringen (Ned)		197,4 km
1.	**Stefan van Dijk (Ned)**	**LOT**
2.	Fulco van Gulik (Ned)	BSP
3.	Stefan Kupfernagel (Ger)	TLM
4.	Wouter van Mechelen (Bel)	VLA
5.	Christoph Roodhooft (Bel)	MRB

22 August

USPRO Criterium Championship (Usa)		Chicago
1.	**Jonas Carney (Usa)**	**JEL**
2.	Tyler Farrar (Usa)	HNC
3.	Gordon Fraser (Can)	HNC
4.	David McCook (Usa)	MCG
5.	Alex Candelario (Usa)	JEL

24 August

Race of Raisin in Overijse (Bel)		195,6 km
1.	**Stefan Schumacher (Ger)**	**TLM**
2.	Geoffrey Demeyere (Bel)	VLA
3.	Bert Scheirlinckx (Bel)	FLA
4.	Steven Caethoven (Bel)	VLA
5.	Wim van Huffel (Bel)	VLA

25 August

GP Nobili Rubinetterie (Ita)		Borgomanero - 184,6 km
1.	**Damiano Cunego (Ita)**	**SAE**
2.	Alexandr Kolobnev (Rus)	DVE
3.	Paolo Valoti (Ita)	DVE
4.	Andrea Masciarelli (Ita)	VIN
5.	Ruggero Borghi (Ita)	DEN

28 August

Tour of Frioul (Ita)		Manzano/Gorizia - 198 km
1.	**Michele Gobbi (Ita)**	**DEN**
2.	Franco Pellizotti (Ita)	ALB
3.	Andrea Moletta (Ita)	TBL
4.	Mikhaylo Khalilov (Ukr)	ICT
5.	Francesco Failli (Ita)	DVE

31 August

Coupe Sels in Merksem (Bel)		195,9 km
1.	**Geoffrey Demeyere (Bel)**	**VLA**
2.	Peter Wuyts (Bel)	MRB
3.	Peter van Agtmaal (Ned)	AXA

4. Stefan van Dijk (Ned) LOT
5. Jans Koerts (Ned) CHO

5 September
GP Jef Scherens — *Leuven - 183 km*

1. **Allan Johansen (Den)** **BGL**
2. Karsten Kroon (Ned) RAB
3. Wouter van Mechelen (Bel) VLA
4. Remco van der Ven (Ned) BGL
5. Gert Steegmans (Bel) LOT

11 September
Tour of the hill of Chianti (Ita) — *191,6 km*

1. **Krzysztof Szczawinski (Pol)** **ICT**
2. Bo Hamburger (Den) AUT&S
3. Dario Frigo (Ita) FAS
4. Luca Mazzanti (Ita) PAN
5. Konstantin Klyuev (Rus) TEN (s)

12 September
Tour of Nüremberg (Ger) — *191,6 km*

1. **Sebastian Siedler (Ger)** **WIE**
2. David Kopp (Ger) TLM
3. André Korff (Ger) TMO
4. Sven Bauer (Ger) VCF
5. Luke Roberts (Aus) COM

12 September
T. Mobile International GP (Usa) — *San Francisco - 186 km*

1. **Charles Dionne (Can)** **WEB**
2. Fred Rodriguez (Usa) AUT&S
3. George Hincapie (Usa) USP
4. Ben Brooks (Aus) JEL
5. Kirk O'Bee (Usa) NIC

17 September
Championship of Flandres (Bel) — *Koolskamp - 182,6 km*

1. **Jimmy Casper (Fra)** **COF**
2. Nico Mattan (Bel) REB
3. Ludovic Capelle (Bel) LAN
4. Geert van Bondt (Bel) LAN
5. Lars Ytting Bak (Den) BGL

3 October
Memorial M. Galera (Esp) — *Armilla - 146 km*

1. **Luis Pasamontes (Esp)** **REB**
2. J. Antonio Lopez Gil (Esp) IBB
3. Koldo Fernandez de Larrea (Esp) EUS
4. Antonio Olmo (Esp) KEL
5. M.AUT Martin Perdiguero (Esp) SDV

12 October
Prize of clôture in Putte-Kappelen (Bel) — *177,2 km*

1. **Max van Heeswijk (Ned)** **USP**
2. Steven de Jongh (Ned) RAB
3. Hans Dekkers (Ned) RAB
4. Benny de Schrooder (Bel) VLA
5. Tommy van de Gehuchte (Bel) JVL

17 October
Chrono of Herbiers (Fra) — *48,150 km (c.l.m)*

1. **Bert Roesems (Bel)** **REB**
2. Vladimir Goussev (Rus) CSC
3. Sebastian Lang (Ger) GST
4. Yuriy Krivtsov (Ukr) A2R
5. Raivis Belohvosciks (Lat) CHO

23 October
Firenze/Pistoia (Ita) — *33 km (c.l.m)*

1. **Serhiy Matveyev (Ukr)** **PAN**
2. Michael Rogers (Aus) QSD
3. Ondrej Sosenka (Cze) AUT&S
4. Fabian Cancellara (Sui) FAS
5. Dario Cioni (Ita) FAS

24 October
Japan Cup (Jpn) — *Utsunomiya - 151,3 km*

1. **Patrik Sinkewitz (Ger)** **QSD**
2. Damiano Cunego (Ita) SAE
3. Manuel Quinziato (Ita) LAM
4. Sylvester Szmyd (Pol) SAE
5. Leonardo Bertagnolli (Ita) SAE

CATEGORY 5

10 January
Copa América (Bra) — *Interlagos - 34 km*

1. **Alem Rayes (Uru)** **EI2**
2. Edy Cisneros (Ra) EI2
3. Armando Camargo (Bra) EI2

6 March
Trophy Porec (Cro) — *132 km*

1. **Matej Stare (Slo)** **PER**
2. Gabor Arany (Hun) EI2
3. Stefan Schumacher (Ger) TLM

7 March
GP of Lillers (Fra) — *175 km*

1. **Benny de Schrooder (Bel)** **VLA**
2. Franck Perque (Fra) EI2
3. Kevin van der Slagmolen (Bel) VLA

7 March
Tour of the Lake Majeur (Sui) — *à Brissago - 163 km*

1. **Aitor Galdos (Esp)** **NIP**
2. Mykhaylo Khalilov (Ukr) ICT
3. Sascha Urweider (Sui) SRW

14 March
Circuit of Pays de Waes (Bel) — *à Kemzeke - 182 km*

1. **Christoph Roodhooft (Bel)** **MRB**
2. Gorik Gardeyn (Bel) LOT
3. Tomas Vaitkus (Ltu) LAN

19 March
Classic Loire-Atlantique (Fra) — *in Basse Goulaine - 181 km*

1. **Erki Pütsep (Est)** **A2R**
2. Denis Robin (Fra) EI2
3. Franck Pencolé (Fra) OKT

20 March
Paris-Barentin-Yvetot (Fra) — *197 km*

1. **Petter Renäng (Swe)** **TBN**
2. Piergiorgio Camussa (Ita) EI2
3. David Martinez (Fra) EI2

25 March
Sacrifice Cup (Gre)

1. **Evgueni Gerganov (Bul)** **EI2**
2. Svetoslav Tchanliev (Bul) EI2
3. Petko Atanasov (Bul) EI2

27 March
Prize of 6 Monts à Harelbeke (Bel) — *161 km*

1. **Kevin Ista (Bel)** **EI2**
2. Benjamin Vanherzeele (Bel) EI2
3. Wouter Weylandt (Bel) EI2

3 April
Enfer of Mergelland (Ned) — *181,9 km*

1. **Allan Johansen (Den)** **BGL**
2. David Kopp (Ger) TLM
3. Jens Heppner (Ger) WIE

4 April
Tour of Lac Leman (Sui) — *180 km*

1. **Dmitri Konyshev (Rus)** **LPR**
2. Mauro Santambrogio (Ita) LPR
3. Dmitri Gaynitdinov (Rus) ICT

4 April
Archer GP (Gbr) — *185 km*

1. **Julian Winn (Gbr)** **EI2**
2. John Tanner (Gbr) EI2
3. Heath Blackgrove (Nzl) EI2

18 April
Zellik-Galmaarden (Bel) — *185 km*

1. **Jurgen Vermeersch (Bel)** **EI2**
2. Koen Das (Bel) EI2
3. Kor Steenbergen (Ned) EI2

18 April
Tour of Düren (Ger) — *159,8 km*

1. **David Kopp (Ger)** **TLM**
2. Stefan Cohnen (Ned) COM
3. Phillip Thuaux (Aus) TDU

25 April
Tour of Berne (Sui)

1. **Alexandre Usov (Blr)** **PHO**
2. Roman Peter (Sui) EI2
3. Sascha Urweider (Sui) SRW

25 April
Shay Elliot Memorial Race (Irl)

1. **David O'Loughlin (Irl)** **EI2**
2. Malcolm Elliott (Gbr) EI2
3. Mark Lovatt (Gbr) EI2

1st May
Prize Victor of Bruyne in Hoboken (Bel) — *172 km*

1. **Jurgen van Loocke (Bel)** **EI2**
2. Ward Bogaerts (Bel) EI2
3. Kevin van der Slagmolen (Bel) VLA

1st May
Tour of Overijssel (Ned) — *149,9 km*

1. **Jens Mouris (Ned)** **AXA**
2. Piet Rooijakkers (Ned) LMT
3. Ruud Aerts (Ned) VHE

2 May
Memorial Andrzej Trochnowski (Pol) — *202 km*

1. **Mariusz Witecki (Pol)** **DHL**
2. Sebastian Jezierski (Pol) LEG
3. Dariusz Skoczylas (Pol) PSB

3 May
Miedzynarodowy 3-Majow (Pol) — *à Lublin*

1. **Piotr Przydzial (Pol)** **ATI**
2. Wojciech Pawlak (Pol) MIK
3. Lukasz Podolski (Pol) PSB

9 May
Circuit of Campine (Ned) — *200 km*

1. **Marvin van der Pluijm (Ned)** **VHE**
2. Wouter van Mechelen (Bel) VLA
3. Joost van Leijen (Ned) VEA

9 May
Lincoln GP (Gbr) — *165 km*

1. **David O'Loughlin (Irl)** **EI2**
2. Robin Sharman (Gbr) EI2
3. Malcolm Elliott (Gbr) EI2

20 May
Hasselt-Spa-Hasselt (Bel) — *166 km*

1. **Marc de Maar (Ned)** **RB3**
2. Huub Duijn (Ned) EI2
3. Thomas Ongena (Bel) EI2

22 May
Klasyk im. Wincentego Witosa (Pol) — *215 km*

1. **Marcin Sapa (Pol)** **MIK**
2. Kazimierz Stafiej (Pol) ATI
3. Pawel Bentkowski (Pol) CHL

29 May
GP Kooperativa (Svk) — *188,7 km*

1. **Laszlo Garamszegi (Hun)** **EI2**
2. Martin Prazdnovsky (Svk) EI2
3. Stanislav Kozubek (Cze) EI2

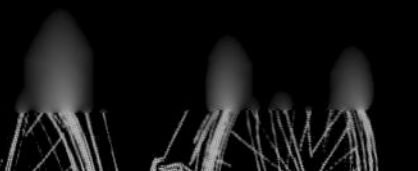

Results of Other Events

30 May
Tour du Finistᵉ (Fra) — 166,9 km

1.	**Daniele Balestri (Ita)**	**ICT**
2.	Mickaël Buffaz (Fra)	RAG
3.	Bert Scheirlinckx (Bel)	FLA

30 May
GP Palma (Svk) — 171 km

1.	**Krzysztof Jezowski (Pol)**	**MIK**
2.	Dawid Krupa (Pol)	LEG
3.	Martin Cerepan (Svk)	EI2

31 May
Flèche Hesbignonne in Cras Avernas (Bel)

1.	**Rory Sutherland (Aus)**	**RB3**
2.	Geert van Bondt (Bel)	LAN
3.	Ludovic Capelle (Bel)	LAN

6 June
Mémorial Philippe van Coningsloo (Bel)

1.	**Bart Heirewegh (Bel)**	**EI2**
2.	Davy Daniels (Bel)	JAR
3.	Maxim Iglinskiy (Kaz)	CAP

19 June
GP of Carnago (Ita) — 170 km

1.	**Cristian Murro (Ita)**	**MIE**
2.	Tiaan Kannemeyer (Rsa)	TBL
3.	Paul Crake (Aus)	CAA

20 June
Giro of Oro (Ita) — Storo/Ponte Arche - 169 km

1.	**Jure Golcer (Slo)**	**FPF**
2.	Eddy Ratti (Ita)	FLA
3.	Gianpaolo Cheula (Ita)	VIN

23 June
Brussel-Ingooigem (Bel) — 185,6 km

1.	**Steven Caethoven (Bel)**	**VLA**
2.	Bert de Waele (Bel)	LAN
3.	Gorik Gardeyn (Bel)	LOT

26 June
Circuit «Het Volk» Espoirs (Bel)

1.	**Stijn Vandenbergh (Bel)**	**EI2**
2.	Sven Renders (Bel)	JVL
3.	Jean-Paul Simon (Bel)	EI2

3 July
Tour of Jura (Sui) — 185,6 km

1.	**Yannick Talabardon (Fra)**	**AUB**
2.	Laurent Paumier (Fra)	AUB
3.	Florian Ludi (Sui)	EI2

3 July
Reith-Alpbach Classic (AUT) — 144 km

1.	**Paul Crake (Aus)**	**CAA**
2.	Björn Schröder (Ger)	WIE
3.	René Weissinger (Ger)	VOL

11 July
GP of Judendorf (AUT) — 175 km

1.	**Andreas Matzbacher (AUT)**	**SAE**
2.	Christian Pfannberger (AUT)	ZVZ
3.	Stefan Rucker (AUT)	ELK

11 July
Giro del Medio Brenta (Ita) — 172 km

1.	**Ruslan Pidgornyy (Ukr)**	**EI2**
2.	Andrea Moletta (Ita)	TBL
3.	Maurizio Carta (Ita)	MIE

18 July
GP Bradla in Bratislava (Svk) — 172 km

1.	**Raffaele Illiano (Ita)**	**CLM**
2.	Sebastian Skiba (Pol)	LEG
3.	Martin Prazdnovsky (Svk)	EI2

4 August
Mi-Août Bretonne #1 (Fra) — à Plougasnou - 164 km

1.	**Yann Pivois (Fra)**	**EI2**
2.	Stéphane Conan (Fra)	EI2
3.	Mickaël Leveau (Fra)	EI2

5 August
Mi-Août Bretonne #2 (Fra) — à Hénon - 141 km

1.	**Yannick Talabardon (Fra)**	**AUB**
2.	Sébastien Duret (Fra)	EI2
3.	Nicolas Moncomble (Fra)	EI2

6 August
Mi-Août Bretonne #3 (Fra) — à Plérin - 156 km

1.	**Stéphane Conan (Fra)**	**EI2**
2.	Stéphane Petilleau (Fra)	EI2
3.	Laurent Paumier (Fra)	AUB

7 August
Mi-Août Bretonne #4 (Fra) — à Guilliers - 172 km

1.	**Nicholas White (Rsa)**	**HSB**
2.	Niels Brouzes (Fra)	AUB
3.	Nicolas Moncomble (Fra)	EI2

8 August
Havant GP (Gbr) — 173 km

1.	**Russell Downing (Gbr)**	**EI2**
2.	Dean Downing (Gbr)	EI2
3.	Tilo Schüler (Ger)	TBH

8 August
Scandinavian Open (Swe) — 197,2 km

1.	**Marcus Ljungqvist (Swe)**	**ALB**
2.	Frederik Mödin (Swe)	EI2
3.	Jonas Ljungblad (Swe)	AMO

13 August
Coupe of Carpathes (Pol) — 213 km

1.	**Arkadiusz Wojtas (Pol)**	**HOP**
2.	Marek Rutkiewicz (Pol)	ATI
3.	Aleksandr Klimenko (Ukr)	ATI

15 August
Puchar Ministra Obrony Narodowej (Pol) — 196 km

1.	**Adam Wadecki (Pol)**	**ATI**
2.	Grzegorz Zoledziowski (Pol)	LEG
3.	Marcin Lewandowski (Pol)	ATI

21 August
Szl.Walk Majora Hubala (Pol) — 190 km

1.	**Kazimierz Stafiej (Pol)**	**ATI**
2.	Grzegorz Zoledziowski (Pol)	LEG
3.	Wojciech Pawlak (Pol)	MIK

21 August
GP of Vigo (Esp) — 128 km

1.	**Jorge Nogaledo (Esp)**	**EI2**
2.	Claudio Estevão (Por)	EI2
3.	Ramon Troncoso (Esp)	ILI

22 August
Flèche Portuaire Flamande (Bel) — Zeebrugge / Antwerp - 181,8 km

1.	**Peter Ronsse (Bel)**	**JAR**
2.	Vadim Vdovinov (Kaz)	CAP
3.	Robby Meul (Bel)	JAR

28 August
Tour of Sachsenring (Ger) — 142,8 km

1.	**Björn Papstein (Ger)**	**TLM**
2.	Udo Müller (Ger)	RSH
3.	Jan Pokrandt (Ger)	RSH

12 September
Volta ABC Paulista (Bra) — 117 km

1.	**Renato Ruiz (Bra)**	**EI2**
2.	Rogerio Silva (Bra)	EI2
3.	Armando Filho (Bra)	EI2

30 September
Circuit of Houtland à Lichtervelde (Bel) — 175 km

1.	**Bert de Waele (Bel)**	**LAM**
2.	Dennis Haueisen (Ger)	RSH
3.	Jurgen Roelandts (Bel)	JVL

9 October
Melbourne-Warrnambool (Aus) — 306 km

1.	**William Walker (Aus)**	**EI2**
2.	Jonathan Clarke (Aus)	EI2
3.	David Pell (Aus)	EI2

N.B: (s) signifies junior. The status of some Elite 2 riders employed at the end of the year by professional teams.

THE MOST PROLIFIC MEN OF THE YEAR

Alessandro Petacchi (Ita)

Fassa Bortolo — **21 victories**

- 1st and 2nd stages Tour of Province de Lucca
- 1st, 2nd and 7e stages Tirreno-Adriatico
- 2nd and 5e stages Tour of Aragon
- 1st, 4e, 6e, 8e, 10th, 12nd, 14th, 15th and 20th stages TOUR of ITALY
- 3rd stage Eneco Tour of Netherland
- 2nd, 4th, 7th and 13rd stages TOUR of SPAIN

Alessandro Petacchi

Tom Boonen (Bel)

Quick Step-Davitamon — **19 victories**

- 2nd stage Tour of Qatar
- 1st stage Tour of Andalousia
- GP E3 in Harelbeke
- GAND-WEVELGEM
- GP of l'Escaut
- Tour of Picardie (+ 1st and 2nd stages)
- 2nd stage Tour of Belgium
- 2nd and 7th stages Tour of Germany
- Prologue and 1st stage Ster Elektrotoer
- 6th and 20th stages TOUR de FRANCE
- 3rd stage Tour of Britain
- GP van Steenbergen
- 3rd and 4th stages Circuit Franco-Belge

Alejandro Valverde (Esp)

Kelme-Communidad Valenciana — **15 victories**

- 3rd épreuve Challenge de Majorque
- Tour of Valence (+ 2nd and 3rd stages)
- Tour of Murcie
- 1st stage Tour du Pays Basque
- Klasika Primavera (Amorebieta)
- 3rd, 4th and 5th stages Tour de Castille and Leon
- Tour de Burgos (+ 1st, 2nd and 3rd stages)
- 3rd stage TOUR of SPAIN

Damiano Cunego (Ita)

Saeco — **13 victories**

- Tour of Trentin (+ 1st and 2nd stages)
- Tour of the Appenins
- GP of Larciano
- TOUR of ITALY (+ 2nd, 7th, 16th and 18th stages)
- GP Fred Mengoni
- GP Nobili Rubinetterie (Borgomanero)
- TOUR of LOMBARDIE

Max van Heeswijk (Ned)

US Postal-Berry Floor — **12 victories**

- 2nd and 4th stages Tour of Andalousia
- 1st and 3rd stages Tour of Murcie
- Nokere koerse
- 6th stage 4 Jours de Dunkerque
- 3rd stage Tour of Belgium
- Wachovia Invitational (Lancaster)
- 6th stage Tour of Catalunya
- 1st and 2nd stages Tour of Netherland
- Prix de clôture à Putte-Kappelen

Lance Armstrong (Usa)

US Postal-Berry Floor — **11 victories**

- 4th stage Tour of the Algarve
- Tour of Georgia (+ 3rd and 4th stages)
- 5th stage Tour du Languedoc-Roussillon
- TOUR de FRANCE (+13rd, 15th, 16th, 17th and 19th stages)

Thor Hushovd (Nor)

Crédit Agricole — **10 victories**

- 3rd stage Etoile de Bessèges
- Classic Haribo
- GP de Denain
- Tour de Vendée
- 1st and 2nd stages Tour du Languedoc-Roussillon
- 1st stage Critérium du Dauphiné Libéré
- Championship of Norway chrono
- Championship de Norvège (on ligne race)
- 8th stage TOUR de FRANCE

Danilo Hondo (Ger)

Gerolsteiner — **9 victories**

- 1st stage 3 Jours de La Panne
- 1st, 2nd, 4th and 5th stages Tour de Basse Saxe
- 5th stage 4 Jours de Dunkerque
- 5th stage Tour of Catalogna
- 1st stage Tour de Poitou-Charentes
- GP Beghelli

N.B: Only those events on the UCI calendar are taken into consideration

Top 100 UCI

The UCI classification therefore survived. With the imminent arrival of the Pro Tour, this classification was originally called «Classement FICP-Velo Magazine» and in 1984 is honoured the greatest champions of the last twenty years. From Sean Kelly, its first leader, to Damiano Cunego, who appeared in first place after the Tour of Lombardie, or a few days before this often criticised and denigrated challenge, which still more or less faithfully represented the pecking order in the world pack, simply disappeared. Nevertheless, the crowning of Damiano Cunego (at the age of 23 years and a few weeks, he was one of the youngest) may well signal the real career start for one of the riders with the greatest potential for the future decade.

Dario Cioni (on left) and Alessandro Petacchi, two key elements of the Fassa Bortolo squad.

Ranking	*Name/Given name Nationality*	*Team*	*UCI Points*
1.	**Damiano Cunego (Ita)**	**SAE**	**2260,4**
2.	Paolo Bettini (Ita)	QSD	2239
3.	Erik Zabel (Ger)	TMO	2011
4.	Oscar Freire (Esp)	RAB	1993
5.	Alejandro Valverde (Esp)	KEL	1892
6.	Davide Rebellin (Ita)	GST	1883
7.	Lance Armstrong (Usa)	USP	1726
8.	Stuart O'Grady (Aus)	COF	1701
9.	Alessandro Petacchi (Ita)	FAS	1464
10.	Tom Boonen (Bel)	QSD	1449
11.	Ivan Basso (Ita)	CSC	1415,5
12.	Danilo Hondo (Ger)	GST	1374,75
13.	M.Angel Martin Perdiguero (Esp)	SDV	1351
14.	Francisco Mancebo (Esp)	IBB	1322
15.	Jan Ullrich (Ger)	TMO	1318
16.	Robbie McEwen (Aus)	LOT	1305
17.	Roberto Heras (Esp)	LST	1303,6
18.	Erik Dekker (Ned)	RAB	1303,45
19.	Jens Voigt (Ger)	CSC	1276
20.	Thor Hushovd (Nor)	C.A	1084
21.	Tyler Hamilton (Usa)	PHO	1070
22.	Gilberto Simoni (Ita)	SAE	1034
23.	Iban Mayo (Esp)	EUS	1033,6
24.	Andreas Klöden (Ger)	TMO	990
25.	Juan Antonio Flecha (Esp)	FAS	961
26.	Michael Boogerd (Ned)	RAB	946
27.	Denis Menchov (Rus)	BAN	937
28.	Allan Davis (Aus)	LST	904,25
29.	Santiago Perez Fernandez (Esp)	PHO	872
30.	Bobby Julich (Usa)	CSC	860
31.	Max van Heeswijk (Ned)	USP	860
32.	Bradley McGee (Aus)	FDJ	856,5
33.	Danilo Di Luca (Ita)	SAE	843,4
34.	Leonardo Piepoli (Ita)	SDV	842
35.	Jérôme Pineau (Fra)	BLB	819
36.	Sylvain Chavanel (Fra)	BLB	818
37.	J. Ivan Gutierrez Palacios (Esp)	IBB	810
38.	Alexandre Vinokourov (Kaz)	TMO	803
39.	Stefano Garzelli (Ita)	VIN	792
40.	Dario Cioni (Ita)	FAS	757
41.	Laurent Brochard (Fra)	A2R	748
42.	Jaan Kirsipuu (Est)	A2R	746
43.	Thomas Voeckler (Fra)	BLB	741
44.	Franco Pellizotti (Ita)	ALB	727
44.	Michael Rogers (Aus)	QSD	727
46.	Serhiy Honchar (Ukr)	DEN	724
47.	Nick Nuyens (Bel)	QSD	716
48.	Philippe Gilbert (Bel)	FDJ	710
49.	George Hincapie (Usa)	USP	706
50.	Samuel Sanchez (Esp)	EUS	704
51.	Jörg Jaksche (Ger)	CSC	652
52.	Vladimir Karpets (Rus)	IBB	651,75
53.	Leonardo Bertagnolli (Ita)	SAE	643
54.	Fabian Jeker (Sui)	SDV	642
54.	Georg Totschnig (Aut)	GST	642
56.	Michael Rich (Ger)	GST	637
56.	Fabian Wegmann (Ger)	GST	637
58.	Michele Scarponi (Ita)	DVE	634
59.	Carlos Sastre (Esp)	CSC	633
60.	Fabian Cancellara (Sui)	FAS	629
61.	Marcos Serrano (Esp)	LST	627,6
62.	Igor Astarloa (Esp)	LAM	614
63.	Roger Hammond (Gbr)	MRB	610
64.	Floyd Landis (Usa)	USP	608
65.	Yaroslav Popovych (Ukr)	LAN	584
66.	Matthias Kessler (Ger)	TMO	583
67.	Kurt-Asle Arvesen (Nor)	CSC	582
68.	Markus Zberg (Sui)	GST	581
69.	Frank Høj (Den)	CSC	564
70.	Viatcheslav Ekimov (Rus)	USP	556
71.	Cristian Moreni (Ita)	ALB	553
72.	Stefan van Dijk (Ned)	LOT	551
73.	Luca Mazzanti (Ita)	PAN	547
74.	Steffen Wesemann (Ger)	TMO	546
75.	Eddy Mazzoleni (Ita)	SAE	535,4
76.	Gerben Löwik (Ned)	CHO	532,45
77.	Eladio Jimenez (Esp)	KEL	528
78.	Christophe Moreau (Fra)	C.A	524,5
79.	Sandy Casar (Fra)	FDJ	514
79.	J. Enrique Gutierrez Cataluña (Esp)	PHO	514
81.	Tadej Valjavec (Slo)	PHO	512
82.	Marc Wauters (Bel)	RAB	511
83.	Kim Kirchen (Lux)	FAS	508
84.	Dmitriy Fofonov (Kaz)	COF	507
85.	Matteo Tosatto (Ita)	FAS	506
86.	Cadel Evans (Aus)	TMO	503
86.	Levy Leipheimer (Usa)	RAB	503
88.	Jimmy Casper (Fra)	COF	502
89.	Koldo Gil (Esp)	LST	501,6
90.	Massimo Giunti (Ita)	DVE	498
91.	Oscar Pereiro (Esp)	PHO	491
92.	Pierrick Fedrigo (Fra)	C.A	488
93.	David Moncoutié (Fra)	COF	484
94.	Mirko Celestino (Ita)	SAE	480
95.	Angel Gomez Marchante (Esp)	ALM	479
95.	Olaf Pollack (Ger)	GST	479
97.	Carlos Garcia Quesada (Esp)	KEL	473
98.	José Azevedo (Por)	USP	472
99.	Magnus Bäckstedt (Swe)	ALB	471
100.	Luca Paolini (Ita)	QSD	466

Alejandro Valverde (Comunidad Valenciana-Kelme)

- Spain and Italy, with 19 riders each, are the best represented countries, followed by Germany (11) and France (9.)
- With 7 riders in the top 100, the CSC, Gerolsteiner & T Mobile teams, head Fassa Bortolo, Saeco & US Postal (6 riders each.)
- 7 riders come from 2nd division teams (including 3 Kelme) in this UCL top 100.

Top 20 Neo-Pros

This classification takes into account the UCI points scored during the year, by ridfers in their first season with a GS1 (1st division) or GS2 (2nd division,) whether they come from the Elite 2 or the 3rd division (in this case the rider's name is preceded with an asterisk.)

Ranking	Name/Given name	Nationality	Team	UCI Points
1.	**J. Angel Gomez Marchante (Esp)**	**ALM**		**479**
2.	Emanuele Sella (Ita)	PAN		370
3.	Maxime Monfort (Bel)	LAN		359
4.	*Thomas Lövkvist (Swe)	FDJ		339
5.	Vladimir Goussev (Rus)	CSC		288
6.	Maxim Iglinskiy (Kaz)	CAP		223
7.	Sebastian Siedler (Ger)	WIE		205
8.	Markus Fothen (Ger)	GST		188
9.	Paul Crake (Aus)	CAA		184
10.	Francisco Ventoso (Esp)	SDV		175
11.	Brian Vandborg (Den)	CSC		172
12.	Luis Leon Sanchez Gil (Esp)	SDV		171
13.	Murilo Fischer (Bra)	DVE		166
14.	Christian Knees (Ger)	WIE		160
15.	Jon Del Rio (Esp)	ALM		156
16.	Francesco Failli (Ita)	DVE		131
17.	Pieter Mertens (Bel)	VLA		129
18.	*Viktor Rapinski (Blr)	NIC		119
19.	*Johan van Summeren (Bel)	REB		115
20.	*Preben van Hecke (Bel)	REB		111

The neo-pro Thomas Dekker proved on countless occasions that he is the right type to win at the very highest level !

Top 30 Women

Ranking	Name/Given name	Nationality	Team	UCI Points
1.	**Judith Arndt (Ger)**	**28**		**813,1**
2.	Mirjam Melchers (Ned)	29		710,5
3.	Oenone Wood (Aus)	24		699,66
4.	Trixi Worrack (Ger)	23		485,5
5.	Edita Pucinskaite (Ltu)	29		477
6.	Anita Valen (Nor)	36		389
7.	Zoulfia Zabirova (Rsu)	31		375,33
8.	Petra Rossner (Ger)	38		332,5
9.	Angela Brodtka (Ger)	23		319
10.	Joane Somarriba (Esp)	32		307
11.	Karin Thürig (Sui)	32		281
12.	Nicole Cooke (Gbr)	21		279,66
13.	Sara Carrigan (Aus)	24		277
14.	Priska Doppmann (Sui)	33		267,33
15.	Deirdre Demet-Barry (Usa)	32		265
16.	Olga Slyusareva (Rus)	35		242,33
17.	Tatiana Guderzo (Ita)	20		218
18.	Lyne Bessette (Can)	29		201
19.	Leontien Zijlaard-van Moorsel (Ned)	34		187
20.	Olivia Gollan (Aus)	31		178,66
21.	Sissy van Alebeek (Ned)	28		178,5
22.	Modesta Vzesniauskaite (Ltu)	21		176,66
23.	Christine Thorburn (Usa)	35		174
24.	Nicole Brändli (Sui)	25		173
25.	Regina Schleicher (Ger)	30		167
26.	Kristin Armstrong (Usa)	31		166
27.	Fabiana Luperini (Ita)	30		162,33
28.	Allison Wright (Aus)	24		161
29.	Katia Longhin (Ita)	31		155
30.	Annette Beutler (Sui)	28		149

Top 30 Espoirs

Ranking	Name/Given name	Nationality	Team	UCI Points
1.	**Thomas Dekker (Ned)**	**20**		**313**
2.	Janez Brajkovic (Slo)	21		228
3.	Dominique Cornu (Bel)	19		162
4.	Bas Giling (Ned)	22		144
5.	Tomas Nose (Slo)	22		131
6.	Konstantin Siutsou (Blr)	22		126
7.	Domenico Pozzovivo (Ita)	22		107
8.	Giovanni Visconti (Ita)	21		102
9.	Vincenzo Nibali (Ita)	20		100
9.	Rory Sutherland (Aus)	22		100
11.	Mads Christensen (Den)	20		99
12.	Blazej Janiaczyk (Pol)	21		98
13.	Phillip Deignan (Irl)	21		97
14.	Andriy Grivko (Ukr)	21		92
15.	Daniele Colli (Ita)	22		90
16.	Tom Veelers (Ned)	20		87
17.	Ivan Terenin (Rus)	22		80
18.	Marc de Maar (Ned)	20		76
19.	Maxim Belkov (Rus)	19		73
20.	Jeremy Yates (Nz)l	22		71
21.	Wouter Weylandt (Bel)	20		70
22.	Ivan Seledkov (Rus)	21		67
23.	Kai Reus (Ned)	19		62
24.	Andreas Dietziker (Sui)	22		58
25.	Elia Rigotto (Ita)	22		57
26.	Francesco Rivera (Ita)	21		53
26.	Matic Strgar (Slo)	22		53
26.	Jukka Vastaranta (Fin)	20		53
29.	Branislau Samoilau (Blr)	19		51
30.	William Bonnet (Fra)	22		50

Top 30 Juniors

Ranking	Name/Given name	Nationality	Team	UCI Points
1.	**Roman Kreuziger (Cze)**	**J2**		**330**
2.	Simon Spilak (Slo)	J2		300
3.	Blel Kadri (Fra)	J2		140
4.	Patrick Grestch (Sui)	J1		114
5.	Robert Gesink (Ned)	J2		105
6.	Rob Ruijgh (Ned)	J2		94
7.	Lukasz Modzelewski (Pol)	J2		92
8.	Eros Capecchi (Ita)	J2		88
9.	Anders Berandt Hansen (Den)	J2		87
10.	Rafâa Chtioui (Tun)	J2		84
11.	Stefan Denifl (Aut)	J1		80
12.	Ben Hermans (Bel)	J2		72
13.	Janar Jermakov (Est)	J2		70
13.	Timofei Kritskiy (Rus)	J1		70
13.	Pawel Mikulicz (Pol)	J1		70
13.	Chris Stockburger (Usa)	J1		70
17.	Stefan Schäfer (Ger)	J2		62
18.	Sjoerd Commandeur (Ned)	J2		56
19.	Petr Novotny (Cze)	J2		55
20.	Mathias Belka (Ger)	J2		51
20.	Marcel Wyss (Sui)	J2		51
22.	Szymon Biesek (Pol)	J2		50
22.	Rafael Nick (Sui)	J2		50
24.	Cyril Gautier (Fra)	J1		47
24.	Alexandr Slivkin (Rus)	J1		47
26.	Cornelius van Ooijen (Ned)	J2		45
27.	Gasper Svab (Slo)	J2		44
28.	Michael Schär (Sui)	J2		40
28.	Michiel van Aelbroeck (Bel)	J2		40
28.	Michael Vanderaerden (Bel)	J2		40

While some of the big names in world cycling (Lance Armstrong, Jan Ullrich and a few others) were notable by their absence most of the season, others were amazing assiduous..

Grands Tours

Two riders lined up at the start of three of the Major National Tours : the Italians in the Fassa Bortolo team, Alessandro Petacchi and Marco Velo. The former only finished the Giro with no less than 9 stage wins to his name, the latter competed in the Giro and the Vuelta. 74 other riders took part in two of the three Grands Tours. Here is the list of finishers in each of them. During the year, 466 riders took part in at least one Grand Tour.
(G = Giro, T = Tour de France, V = Vuelta)

ANDRIOTTO Dario (Ita)	VIN / G (54) - V (103
BARANOWSKI Darius (Pol)	LST / V (33) - T (94)
BELTRAN Manuel (Esp)	USP / V (13) - T (46)
BRUSEGHIN Marzio (Ita)	FAS / G (58) - T (68)
CAÑADA David (Esp)	SDV / G (18) - V (47)
CIONI Dario (Ita)	FAS / G (4) - V (52)
CUNEGO Damiano (Ita)	SAE / G (1) - V (16)
FORNACIARI Paolo (Ita)	SAE / G (100) - V (117)
GARATE Juan Manuel (Esp)	LAM / G (10) - V (23)
GARCIA ACOSTA J. Vicente (Esp)	IBB / T (86) - V (106)
GARZELLI Stefano (Ita)	VIN / G (6) - V (11)
GEROSA Mauro (Ita)	VIN / G (62) - V (95)
GONZALEZ GALDEANO Igor (Esp)	LST / T (44) - V (96)
GRABSCH Bert (Ger)	PHO / T (81) - V (86)
GUSTOV Volodymir (Ukr)	FAS / V (97) - G (103)
GUTIERREZ J. Enrique (Esp)	PHO / T (28) - V (31)
HRUSKA Jan (Cze)	LST / V (99) - T (117)
LJUNGQVIST Marcus (Swe)	ALB / G (63) - T (132)
MANCEBO Francisco (Esp)	IBB / V (3) - T (6)
MAZZOLENI Eddy (Ita)	SAE / G (21) - V (70)
MIHOLJEVIC Vladimir (Cro)	ALB / G (24) - V (78)
MØLLER Claus Michael (Den)	ALB / T (70) - V (80)
NOE' Andrea (Ita)	ALB / G (17) - T (99)
NOZAL Isidro (Esp)	LST / V (7) - T (73)
PEREZ FERNANDEZ Santi (Esp)	PHO / V (2) - T (49)
PICCOLI Mariano (Ita)	LAM / G (59) - V (115)
RIGHI Daniele (Ita)	LAM / G (96) - V (107)
SABALIAUSKAS Marius (Ltu)	SAE / T (42) - V (87)
SASTRE Carlos (Esp)	CSC / V (6) - T (8)
SERRANO Marcos (Esp)	LST / V (12) - T (54)
SEVILLA Oscar (Esp)	PHO / V (22) - T (24)
SIMONI Gilberto (Ita)	SAE / G (3) - T (17)
SPEZIALETTI Alessandro (Ita)	SAE / G (66) - V (116)
SZMYD Sylvester (Pol)	SAE / G (43) - V (74)
TOSATTO Matteo (Ita)	FAS / G (107) - T (110)
VALJAVEC Tadej (Slo)	PHO / G (9) - V (26)
WILSON Matthew (Aus)	FDJ / G (132) - T (144)

Classics

Here is the list of riders seen the most at the start of the World Cup Classics. Switzerland's Gregory Rast was the only one at the start of all 10 legs. He was classified six times. 630 riders took part in this year's World Cup.

RAST Grégory (Sui)	FDJ	10
BAZHENOV Alexandr (Rus)	DVE	9
BETTINI Paolo (Ita)	QSD	9
CELESTINO Mirko (Ita)	SAE	9
DEKKER Erik (Ned)	RAB	9
ELMIGER Martin (Sui)	PHO	9
FLECHA Juan Antonio (Esp)	FAS	9
FREIRE Oscar (Esp)	RAB	9
NARDELLO Daniele (Ita)	TMO	9
SERPELLINI Marco (Ita)	GST	9
BARTOLI Michele (Ita)	CSC	8
BORTOLAMI Gianluca (Ita)	LAM	8
BOSSONI Paolo (Ita)	LAM	8
LASTRAS Pablo (Esp)	IBB	8
MARICHAL Thierry (Bel)	LOT	8
MURN Uros (Slo)	PHO	8
PAOLINI Luca (Ita)	QSD	8
PETITO Roberto (Ita)	FAS	8
REBELLIN Davide (Ita)	GST	8
WESEMANN Steffen (Ger)	TMO	8
ZBERG Marcus (Sui)	GST	8

TEAM STATISTICS

1st DIVISION

(classification as of 17/10)

1.	T.MOBILE	TMO	8718
2.	Team CSC	CSC	8269
3.	GEROLSTEINER	GST	7817
4.	SAECO	SAE	7144
5.	RABOBANK	RAB	7044
6.	US POSTAL-BERRY FLOOR	USP	6932
7.	QUICK STEP-DAVITAMON	QSD	6812
8.	PHONAK	PHO	6594
9.	FASSA BORTOLO	FAS	6371
10.	COFIDIS	COF	5528
11.	ILLES BALEARS-BANESTO	IBB	5325
12.	LIBERTY Seguros	LST	5288
13.	LOTTO-DOMO	LOT	5129
14.	SAUNIER DUVAL-PRODIR	SDV	4932
15.	EUSKALTEL-EUSKADI	EUS	4512
16.	Brioches LA BOULANGERE	BLB	4290
17.	FDJEUX.COM	FDJ	3863
18.	CREDIT AGRICOLE	C.A	3720
19.	LAMPRE	LAM	3612
20.	ALESSIO-BIANCHI	ALB	3609
21.	AG2R Prévoyance	A2R	3469
22.	LANDBOUWKREDIET-COLNAGO	LAN	3459
23.	Vini CALDIROLA-NOBILI	VIN	3420
24.	RELAX-BODYSOL	REB	2885
25.	Chocolade JACQUES	CHO	2793
26.	MrBOOKMAKER-PALMANS	MRB	2760
27.	DE NARDI	DEN	2113
28.	MILANEZA-MAIA	MIL	1819
29.	BANKGIROLOTERIJ	BGL	1118
30.	RAGT Semences-MG ROVER	RAG	765

THE VICTORIES

Only victories achieved in the UCI referenced events are taken into account.

1. QUICK STEP-DAVITAMON — QSD — 47

T. Boonen (20), P. Bettini (8), N. Nuyens (5), P. Sinkewitz (3), L. Bodrogi (2), P. Horrillo (2), J.M Mercado (2), A. Clerc (1), L. Paolini (1), M. Rogers (1), R. Virenque (1), S. Zanini (1).

2. FASSA BORTOLO — FAS — 41

A. Petacchi (21), F. Cancellara (5), F. Pozzato (3), J.A Flecha (2), K. Kirchen (2), M. Tosatto (2), D. Cioni (1), A. Gonzalez Jimenez (1),
A. Ongarato (1), R. Petito (1), F. Sacchi (1) +c.l.m par équipes Semaine Coppi/Bartali.

3. US POSTAL-BERRY FLOOR — USP — 34

M. van Heeswijk (12), L. Armstrong (11), F. Landis (2), D. Zabriskie (2), A. Cruz (1), S. Devolder (1), V. Ekimov (1), G. Hincapie (1), B. Joachim (1) +c.l.m par équipes Tour de France et Tour d'Espagne.

4. GEROLSTEINER — GST — 32

D. Hondo (9), D. Rebellin (6), M. Rich (5), S. Lang (2), G. Totschnig (2), B. Zberg (2), R. Förster (1), M. Fothen (1), O. Pollack (1), T. Schmidt (1), F. Wegmann (1), P. Wrolich (1).

5. RABOBANK — RAB — 27

R. Hunter (8), O. Freire (6), E. Dekker (5), R. Bartko (2), S. De Jongh (1), T. Dekker* (1), K. Kroon (1), L. Leipheimer (1), M. Lotz (1), M. Rasmussen (1).
* victoire obtenue en tant que stagiaire.

6. SAECO — SAE — 26

D. Cunego (13), L. Bertagnolli (3), D. Di Luca (3), G. Simoni (2), A. Bucciero (1), M. Celestino (1), G. Glomser (1), D. Loosli (1), A. Matzbacher (1).

7. Brioches LA BOULANGERE — BLB — 25

Syl. Chavanel (5), Séb. Chavanel (4), J. Pineau (4), D. Rous (3), T. Voeckler (3), F. Bouyer (2), A. Geslin (1), C. Kern (1), M. Sprick (1), U. Yus (1).

7. T.MOBILE — TMO — 25

E. Zabel (6), A. Vinokourov (6), M. Ullrich (4), C. Evans (2), S. Schreck (2), R. Aldag (1), M. Kessler (1), A. Klöden (1), A. Korff (1), S. Wesemann (1).

9. FDJEUX.COM — FDJ — 23

B. Cooke (8), T. Lövkvist (4), B. McGee (4), P. Gilbert (2), S. Casar (1), B. Eisel (1), F. Mourey (1), N. Vogondy (1), M. Wilson (1).

10. AG2R Prévoyance — A2R — 22

J. Kirsipuu (8), L. Brochard (3), J.P Nazon (3), E. Pütsep (2), M. Scanlon (2), S. Dumoulin (1), Y. Krivtsov (1), N. Portal (1), L. Turpin (1).

2nd DIVISION

(classification as of 17/10)

1.	Comunidad VALENCIANA-KELME	KEL	4143
2.	DOMINA VACANZE	DVE	3252
3.	ACQUA & SAPONE-MOKAMBO	A&S	2296
4.	PANARIA-MARGRES	PAN	2227
5.	Costa de ALMERIA-PATERNINA	ALM	1960
6.	VLAANDEREN-T INTERIM	VLA	1300
7.	L.A-PECOL	LAP	1287
8.	Cafés BAQUES	BAQ	1248
9.	BARLOWORLD	TBL	1125
10.	NAVIGATORS	NIC	865
11.	ACTION-ATI	ATI	821
12.	WIESENHOF	WIE	802
13.	Formaggi PINZOLO FIAVE'	FPF	733
14.	ED'SYSTEM-ZVVZ	ZVZ	672
15.	COLOMBIA-SELLE ITALIA	CLM	628
16.	MICHE	MIE	553
17.	TENAX	TEN	431
18.	Team LPR - PIACENZA	LPR	296
19.	LOKOMOTIV	LOK	142
20.	ELK Haus-SIMPLON	ELK	64

THE VICTORIES

1. Comunidad VALENCIANA-KELME — KEL — 25

A. Valverde (15), C. Garcia Quesada (2),
J.C Julia (2), J. A Bonilla (1), A. Garcia Quesada (1), E. Jimenez (1), J. Pascual Rodriguez (1),
R. Plaza Molina (1), C. Zarate (1).

2. COLOMBIA-SELLE ITALIA — CLM — 20

F. Gonzalez Martinez (4), R. Illiano (4), M. Perez Arango (4), J. Rujano (3), D. Sosnovchenko* (3), M. Giallorenzo* (1), R. A Marin (1)
*Stagiaire

3. DOMINA VACANZE — DVE — 14

M. Scarponi (6), M. Cipollini (2), A. Nauduzs (2), A. Aug (1), M. Gentili (1), A. Kolobnev (1), F. Simeoni (1).

4. ACQUA & SAPONE-MOKAMBO — A&S — 12

D. Bertolini (3), O. Sosenka (3), R. Marzoli (2), F. Rodriguez (2), C. D'Amore (1), R. Nocentini (1).

5. L.A - PECOL — LAP — 11

C. Barbosa (6), S. Paulinho (3), D. Arroyo (2).

5. VLAANDEREN- T.INTERIM — VLA — 11

S. Caethoven (3), J. Kuyckx (3), W. van Mechelen (2), B. de Schrooder (1), G. Demeyere (1), W. van der Linden (1).

3rd DIVISION

(Top 10 at 17/10)

1.	Team LAMONTA	TLM	1267
2.	HOOP CCC-POLSAT	HOP	934
3.	AMORE & VITA-BERETTA	AMO	797
4.	OKTOS	OKT	676
5.	KNAUF-MIKOMAX	MIK	591
6.	COMNET-SENGES	COM	581
7.	VOLKSBANK-IDEAL	VOL	576
8.	WÜRTH-BOM PETISCO	WBP	555
9.	HEALTH NET	HNC	546
10.	PERUTNINA PTUJ	PER	538

NATIONS STATISTICS

(TOP 20 AT 17/10)

1.	ITALIE	13545,30
2.	ESPAGNE	11957,20
3.	ALLEMAGNE	10077,75
4.	AUSTRALIE	7090,75
5.	ETATS-UNIS	6600,00
6.	FRANCE	6091,50
7.	PAYS-BAS	6057,50
8.	BELGIQUE	5914,00
9.	RUSSIE	4047,15
10.	SUISSE	3957,00
11.	UKRAINE	2744,00
12.	DANEMARK	2637,00
13.	KAZAKHSTAN	2546,00
14.	PORTUGAL	2534,00
15.	COLOMBIE	2339,00
16.	POLOGNE	2023,40
17.	SLOVENIE	1978,00
18.	AUTRICHE	1892,90
19.	NORVEGE	1878,00
20.	REPUBLIQUE TCHEQUE	1736,25

Above, Germany's Bjorn Glasner, one of lynchpins of the Lamonta team, who topped the 3rd division in 2004.

Opposite, by winning the 3rd stage of the Circuit Franco-Belge, Tom Boonen rounded up to 20 his number of wins this year!

TOP 10 BY NATION

ITALY

1.	Damiano Cunego	SAE	2260,4
2.	Paolo Bettini	QSD	2239
3.	Davide Rebellin	GST	1883
4.	Alessandro Petacchi	FAS	1464
5.	Ivan Basso	CSC	1415,5
6.	Gilberto Simoni	SAE	1034
7.	Danilo Di Luca	SAE	843,4
8.	Leonardo Piepoli	SDV	842
9.	Stefano Garzelli	VIN	792
10.	Dario Cioni	FAS	757

SPAIN

1.	Oscar Freire	RAB	1993
2.	Alejandro Valverde	KEL	1892
3.	M.Angel Martin Perdiguero	SDV	1351
4.	Francisco Mancebo	IBB	1322
5.	Roberto Heras	LST	1303,6
6.	Iban Mayo	EUS	1033,6
7.	Juan Antonio Flecha	FAS	961
8.	Santiago Perez Fernandez	PHO	872
9.	J. Ivan Gutierrez Palacios	IBB	810
10.	Samuel Sanchez	EUS	704

GERMANY

1.	Erik Zabel	TMO	2011
2.	Danilo Hondo	GST	1374,75
3.	Jan Ullrich	TMO	1318
4.	Jens Voigt	CSC	1276
5.	Andreas Klöden	TMO	990
6.	Jörg Jaksche	CSC	652
7.	Michael Rich	GST	637
7.	Fabian Wegmann	GST	637
9.	Matthias Kessler	TMO	583
10.	Steffen Wesemann	TMO	546

AUSTRALIA

1.	Stuart O'Grady	COF	1701
2.	Robbie McEwen	LOT	1305
3.	Allan Davis	LST	904,25
4.	Bradley McGee	FDJ	846,50
5.	Michael Rogers	QSD	727
6.	Cadel Evans	TMO	503
7.	Baden Cooke	FDJ	448
8.	Luke Roberts	COM	263
9.	Simon Gerrans	EI2	200
10.	David McKenzie	NIC	188

UNITED STATES OF AMERICA

1.	Lance Armstrong	USP	1726
2.	Tyler Hamilton	PHO	1070
3.	Bobby Julich	CSC	860
4.	George Hincapie	USP	706
5.	Floyd Landis	USP	608
6.	Levy Leipheimer	RAB	503
7.	Fred Rodriguez	A&S	425
8.	Chris Horner	WEB/SDV	317
9.	David Zabriskie	USP	231
10.	Kirk O'Bee	NIC	154

The Comunidad Valenciana-Kelme team was logically enough the strongest in the 2nd division.

FRANCE

1.	Jérôme Pineau	BLB	819
2.	Sylvain Chavanel	BLB	818
3.	Laurent Brochard	A2R	748
4.	Thomas Voeckler	BLB	741
5.	Christophe Moreau	C.A	524,50
6.	Sandy Casar	FDJ	514
7.	Jimmy Casper	COF	502
8.	Pierrick Fedrigo	C.A	488
9.	David Moncoutié	COF	484
10.	Didier Rous	BLB	453

Nick Nuyens (foreground) and Philippe Gilbert, two rising young stars of Belgian cycling!

NETHERLANDS

1.	Erik Dekker	RAB	1303,45
2.	Michael Boogerd	RAB	946
3.	Max van Heeswijk	USP	860
4.	Stefan van Dijk	LOT	551
5.	Gerben Löwik	CHO	532,45
6.	Steven de Jongh	RAB	411
7.	Leon van Bon	LOT	371
8.	Thomas Dekker	RB3	370,80
9.	Karsten Kroon	RAB	366
10.	Roy Sentjens	RAB	269,45

BELGIUM

1.	Tom Boonen	QSD	1449
2.	Nick Nuyens	QSD	716
3.	Philippe Gilbert	FDJ	710
4.	Marc Wauters	RAB	511
5.	Peter van Petegem	LOT	457
6.	Bert Roesems	REB	435
7.	Axel Merckx	LOT	427
8.	Leif Hoste	LOT	400
9.	Maxime Monfort	LAN	359
10.	Ludovic Capelle	LAN	329

RUSSIA

1.	Denis Menchov	IBB	930
2.	Vladimir Karpets	IBB	651,75
3.	Viatcheslav Ekimov	USP	556
4.	Alexandr Kolobnev	DVE	394
5.	Vladimir Goussev	CSC	323
6.	Pavel Tonkov	VIN	289
7.	Evgeni Petrov	SAE	274,40
8.	Alexandre Botcharov	C.A	239
9.	Mikhaïl Timochine	LAN	193
10.	Dmitri Konyshev	LPR	190

SWITZERLAND

1.	Fabian Jeker	SDV	642
2.	Fabian Cancellara	FAS	629
3.	Markus Zberg	GST	581
4.	Martin Elmiger	PHO	434
5.	Alexandre Moos	PHO	386
6.	Oscar Camenzind	PHO	306
7.	Steve Zampieri	VIN	283
8.	Roger Beuchat	VIN	258
9.	Patrick Calcagni	VIN	253
10.	Gregory Rast	PHO	227

THE BLACK LIST OF PROFESSIONAL CYCLING

The year in cycling is unfortunately also a year of problems...

13TH JANUARY

Returning from Warsaw, the polish rider Marek Rutkiewicz, ex Cofidis and newly RAGT Semences is arrested at Roissy Airport. Illegal substances are found in his baggage and at his home in Hyeres (France). The headquarters of his ex team are searched as is the surgery of Dr Menuet, the official doctor to the team. Nothing suspicious is found.

14TH JANUARY

The New Caledonian rider Robert Sassone, also an ex member of the Cofidis team, is visited by the police at his home in Hyeres. Several illegal substances are found: EPO, growth hormone, testosterone, etc.

16TH JANUARY

Bob Madejak, a Polish team worker for Cofidis, is arrested. He is suspected as being the organiser of a doping system for several or the team's riders.

18TH JANUARY

Philippe Gaumont and Cedric Vasseur are questioned by police at Roissy airport when they return from training camp in Spain.

23RD JANUARY

Philippe Gaumont (who ceases to be a pro cyclist a few days later) admits having used doping products. He is suspended by his team. The president of the team later announces it will continue to sponsor a cycling team in the future.

28TH JANUARY

Daniel Majewiski, a rider in Elite 2 living in Limoux, is arrested after several products which are illegal in France but legal in Spain and Eastern Europe are found in his flat.

14TH FEBRUARY

Francisco Perez Sanchez (Spanish), failing two tests for EPO in the Tour de Romandie 2003 is suspended for 18 months (until 17th April 2005).

2ND MARCH

It is learnt that Robert Sassone failed a test for betemethasone, a glucocorticosteroid in the 6 Days of Noumea at the end of 2003.

24TH MARCH

The ex Kelme rider, Jesus Manzano gives an interview to the Spanish newspaper AS. He claims there was a systematic doping system in the team which had sacked him after the Tour of Spain 2003.

25TH MARCH

The American rider, Adam Sbeih receives a 2 year suspension (till 25th August 2005) for using EPO at the American Track Championship in 2003.

28TH MARCH

The ex pro Oleg Kozlitine, sporting director for the third division Oktos team admits selling EPO to Philippe Gaumont. He is sacked from the team

2ND APRIL

Suspected of buying growth hormones from Oleg Kozlitine, Mederic Clain (Cofidis) is questioned by Judge Pallain, who is in charge of what has become known as the Cofidis case. Cedric Vasseur and Marek Rutkiewicz are also called to the court in Nanterre. Clain and Vasseur are suspended from the team until such a time as they are cleared.

9TH APRIL

The managers of the Cofidis team decide to suspend their activities to take stock of the situation.

30TH APRIL

Cofidis decide to return to competition for the 4 Jours de Dunkerque. The first stage is won by their team member Jimmy Casper. Mederic Clain and Cedric Vasseur remain suspended.

4TH MAY

The doctor Jean Jaques Menuet and the manager Alain Bondue quit the Cofidis team to calm the situation. Mederic Clain is fired.

31ST MAY

Jean Michel Tessier (France, Oktos) fails a test for Amphetamine in the GP de Villers-Cotterets. Days later he announces his retirement.

1ST JULY

Gorka Gonzalez Larranaga (Euskaltel) is tested with a level of hematocrite superior to 50%. He is thrown off the Tour de France

5TH JULY

The Euskaltel- Euskadi team ceases its collaboration with the doctor Jesus Losa. He was accused by David Millar of selling him EPO.

13TH JULY

Traces of methadone are found in the urine of Christophe Brandt (Belgium, Lotto- Domo) at the end of the 2nd stage of the Tour de France. His team pulls him out of the race. He is totally cleared a month later and came back to racing in September.

19TH JULY

Dave Bruylandts (Belgium, Chocolade Jaques) having failed a test for EPO in the GP Pino Cerami (8th April) starts a 2 year suspension.

20TH JULY

David Millar is fired from his Cofidis team after admitting taking EPO. His title of World Time Trial Champion 2003 is taken away from him.

29th July

World Mountain Bike Champion, Belgian Filip Meirhaeghe (Jonge Vlaanderen 2016) is found guilty of using EPO in two rounds of the Coupe de Monde VTT. He is suspended for 15 months and announces his retirement...

30th July

Two Portuguese riders of the LA- Pecol team, Hernani Broco and Jorge Torre are tested positive for corticosteroids in the GP Mitsubishi. They are suspended.

4th August

David Fuentes (USA, McGuire Cycling Team) was tested positive for oxymetholone in a national the 25th March. The American Federation is yet to announce its decision.

5th August

Massimiliano Lelli (Italy, Cofidis), arrested days earlier, is accused by the legal authorities in Nanterre of buying and selling doping products.

11th August

Colombian champion José Joaquin Castelblanco is tested positive for testosterone on his national tour (which he wins). The rider claims he is innocent.

17th August

South African David George (Barloworld) and the Italian Renzo Mazzolzni (Tenax) are rejected by the 3Vallées Varésines because of a hematocrite level of over 50%.

21st August

Same cause, same sanction for the Italian Rafaele Illiano (Colombia- Selle Italia) at the start of the Tour de Venetie.

28th August

Marco Gili (Italy, Vini Caldirola) is banned from competition for 15 days. At the start of the Tour du Frioul he is tested with a hematocrite level of more than 50%. His team sacks him on the spot.

3rd September

Francesco Casagrande (Italy, Lampre) and Carlos Golbano (Spain, Paternina) miss a blood test before the Tour of Spain and are suspended for 15 days. The Italian takes advantage of the situation to transfer to the Vini Caldirola team!

8th September

Ex World Champion Oscar Camenzind (Switzerland, Phonak) is declared positive for EPO after a random drug test on the 22nd June. He is suspended for 2 years but announces his retirement.

24th September

Tyler Hamilton (USA, Phonak) is found guilty of doping by blood transfusion in the Vuelta on a single sample analysed in Lausanne. Double samples came up with different results in the Tour of Spain where Hamilton won on the 11th September (40kms time trial), and for the Olympic Games. From his single positive result the rider risks a suspension of 2 years. A disciplinary procedure against the 33 year old rider is in the hands of the American authorities.
He is the first athlete to fail a doping test based on blood doping. He is also the first athlete to fail a test developed by Australian scientists and recognised by IOC. The rider will however keep his Olympic Gold medal as tests were not conclusive.

29th September

Crowned Portuguese champion at the end of June, Pedro Lopes (LA Pecol) is found guilty of using corticosteroids in the event. He is suspended for six months.

30th September

The Austrian, Christian Pfannberger (ED'Systems- ZVVZ), found guilty of using steroids in his national championship (in which he finished 2nd), is suspended for 2 years.

1st October

Picked for his national team for the World Championship, Dario Cioni (Italy, Fassa Bortolo), is sent home after an internal test shows a high hematocrite level.

8th October

The Ligue Velocipedique Belge suspends for 4 years (2 suspended) with a fine of 10000 Swiss Francs, Johan Museeuw (retired since April), Chris Peers (Chocolade Jaques) and Jo Planckaert (Mr.Bookmaker.com). The case is connected to the affair of vet José Landuyt and physical trainer Herman Versele, two men suspected of dealing in doping products.

14th October

The American rider Phil Zajicek (Navigators) received a warning from hid federation following a positive test for caffeine in his urine at the Tour of Qinghai Lake in China in July. His win in the event is cancelled.

30th October

The Spaniard Santiago Perez (Phonak), recently second in the Vuelta, is suspected of blood doping in the event. The Phonak team could be excluded from the future Pro Tour.

To be continued?

ABBREVIATIONS USED

TEAMS

A2R AG2R Prévoyance (Fra)
A&S ACQUA & SAPONE - MOKAMBO (Ita)
ALB ALESSIO - BIANCHI (Ita)
ALM PATERNINA - Costa de Almeria (Esp)
AMO AMORE & VITA BERETTA (Pol)
ANT ANTARTE / ROTA DOS MOVEIS (Por)
APA APAC Cycling Team (Ned)
ASC ASC - VILA DO CONDE (Por)
ASP AC SPARTA PRAHA (Cze)
ATI ACTION ATI (Pol)
AUB AUBER 93 (Fra)
AXA AXA-UBBINK (Ned)
BAQ Cafés BAQUE (Esp)
BAR BARBOT – GAIA (Por)
BEP BEPPI – OVARENSE(Por)
BGL BANKGIROLOTERIJ (Ned)
BGT Team BRIDGESTONE ANCHOR (Jpn)
BLB Brioches LA BOULANGERE (Fra)
BSP BERT STORY - PIEL'S (Ned)
C.A CREDIT AGRICOLE (Fra)
CAA CORRATEC-ARBOE (Aut)
CAB CARVALHELHOS - BOAVISTA (Por)
CAE CREDIT AGRICOLE ESPOIRS (Fra)
CAP CAPEC (Kaz)
CHL DOMINSCOUT - SNIEZKA - LODY (Pol)
CHO Chocolade JACQUES - WINCOR NIXDORF (Bel)
CKK CK KRONBORG PRO (Den)
CLM COLOMBIA - SELLE ITALIA (Col)
COB COLAVITA OLIVE OIL-BOLLA (Usa)
COF COFIDIS (Fra)
COM Team COMNET - SENGES (Ger)
CSC Team CSC (Den)
DEN DE NARDI (Ita)
DHL DHL - AUTHOR (Pol)
DUK DUKLA TRENCIN (Svk)
DVE DOMINA VACANZE (Ita)
ELK ELK HAUS - SIMPLON (Aut)
EUS EUSKALTEL - EUSKADI (Esp)
FDJ FDJEUX.COM (Fra)
FAS FASSA BORTOLO (Ita)
FLA FLANDERS - AFINCOM (Bel)
FPF Formaggi PINZOLO FIAVE' (Ita)
FVT FAVORIT (Cze)
GLU GLUD & MARSTRAND HORSENS (Den)
GNT GIANT ASIA Racing Team (Tpe)
GST GEROLSTEINER (Ger)
HNC HEALTH NET - MAXXIS (Usa)
HOP HOOP CCC – POLSAT (Pol)
HRS TEAM HARALDSHUS (Den)
HSB Team HSBC (Rsa)
HYG Team HYGIA – KOGA (Ger)
IBB ILLES BALEARS - BANESTO (Esp)
ICT Team ICET (Ita)
ILJ IMOHOLDING-LOULÉ Jardim Hotel (Por)
ITB ITALPASTA-TRANSPORT BELMIRE (Can)
JAR JARTAZI GRANVILLE TEAM (Bel)
JEL JELLY BELLY - ARAMARK (Usa)
JET JET FUEL COFFEE (Can)
JIT JITTERY JOE'S Cycling Team (Usa)
JVL JONG VLAANDEREN 2016 (Bel)
KCT KALEV CHOCOLATE-MERIDA (Est)
KEL KELME - Communidad Valenciana (Esp)
LAM LAMPRE (Ita)
LAN LANDBOUWKREDIET - COLNAGO (Bel)
LAP L.A - PECOL (Por)
LEG LEGIA BAZYLISZEK - SOPRO (Pol)
LMT LÖWIK MEUBELEN - TEGELTOKO (Ned)
LOK LOKOMOTIV (Rus)
LOT LOTTO - DOMO (Bel)
LPR Team LPR - PIACENZA (Ita)
LST LIBERTY Seguros (Esp)
MCG MCGUIRE Pro Cycling (Usa)
MIE Team MICHE (Ita)
MIK KNAUF – MIKOMAX (Pol)
MIL MILANEZA - MAIA (Por)
MKV MACANDINA Kewa Rad– VC Gippingen (Sui)
MPC MARCO POLO Cycling Team (Hkg)
MRB MrBOOKMAKER.COM - PALMANS (Bel)
NES KOLOEZDACHEN KLUB NESEBAR (Bul)
NIC NAVIGATORS Insurances (Usa)
NIP Team NIPPO (Jpn)
OFO OFOTO Cyling Team (Usa)
OKT OKTOS (Fra)
PAN PANARIA - MARGRES (Ita)
PCF PAGCOR CASINO FILIPINO (Phi)
PER PERUTNINA PTUJ (Slo)
PHO PHONAK Hearing Systems (Sui)
PSB Grupa PSB KREISEL (Pol)
PSK PSK WHIRLPOOL (Cze)
QSD QUICK STEP - DAVITAMON (Bel)
RAB RABOBANK (Ned)
RAD RESCH & FRISCH EYBL WELS (Aut)
RAG RAGT Semences-MG ROVER (Fra)
RB3 RABOBANK Espoirs (Ned)
RCB RC BIKEPALAST.COM SALZBURG (Aut)
REB RELAX - BODYSOL (Esp)
RSH Team RSH (Ger)
SAE SAECO (Ita)
SAK SAVA KRANJ (Slo)
SBX SUBWAY - EXPRESS (Usa)
SDS SAEY - DESCHACHT Sportgroep (Bel)
SDV SAUNIER DUVAL - PRODIR (Esp)
SEA Team SEASILVER (Usa)
SHI SHIMANO Racing (Jpn)
SIE SIERRA NEVADA (Usa)
SIM SHARPER IMAGE-MATHIS Bros. (Usa)
SPA Team SPAREBANKEN VEST (Nor)
SPR FIDEA CYCLING TEAM (Bel)
SRW SAECO - RÖMER'S - WETZIKON (Sui)
TBH Team BH - Dessau (Ger)
TBL BARLOWORLD- ANDRONI GIACCATOLI (Ita)
TBN Team BIANCHI NORDIC (Swe)
TDU Team cyclingnews.com- DOWN UNDER (Aus)
TEN TENAX (Ita)
TFB Team FUJI BIKES (Ned)
THC Team HERVIS APO SPORT (Aut)
TLM Team LAMONTA (Ger)
TMA Team MOSER - AH (Ned)
TMN Team MONEX (Usa)
TMO Team T.MOBILE (Ger)
TPH Team PH (Den)
USP US POSTAL Service-BERRY FLOOR (Usa)
VCF VC FRANKFURT- BRÜGELMANN (Ger)
VEA VAN VLIET - EBH ADVOCATEN (Ned)
VHE VAN HEMERT - EUROGIFTS (Ned)
VIN Vini CALDIROLA - NOBILI (Ita)
VLA VLAANDEREN - T INTERIM (Bel)
VOL VOLKSBANK IDEAL LEINGRUBER (Aut)
WBP WÜRTH - BOM PETISCO (Por)
WCT WISMILAK Cycling Team (Ina)
WEB WEBCOR Cycling Team (Usa)
WIE Team WIESENHOF (Ger)
WIN WINFIX ARNOLDS SICHERHEIT (Ger)
ZVZ ED'SYSTEMS - ZVVZ (Cze)

●●● **GS1 (1st Division)**
●●● **GS2 (2nd Division)**
●●● **GS3 (3rd Division)**

NATIONALITIES

ARG Argentina
AUS Australia
AUT Austria
BEL Belgium
BLR Belarus
BRA Brazil
BUL Bulgaria
CAN Canada
CHI Chile
CHN China
COL Colombia
CZE Czech Republic
DEN Denmark
ESP Spain
EST Estonia
FIN Finland
FRA France
GBR Great Britain
GER Germany
GRE Greece
HKG Hong-Kong
HUN Hungary
INA Indonesia
IRI Iran
JPN Japan
KAZ Kazakstan
LAT Latvia
LTU Lithuania
LUX Luxembourg
MAS Malaysia
MDA Moldavia
NED Netherlands
NOR Norway
NZL New Zealand
POL Poland
POR Portugal
RSA South Africa
RUS Russia
SLO Slovenia
SVK Slovakia
SUI Switzerland
SWE Sweden
UKR Ukraine
URU Uruguay
USA United States of America
UZB Ouzbzkistan
VEN Venezuela
ZIM Zimbabwe